Hunter-Gatherer
Childhoods

Hunter-Gatherer Childhoods

Evolutionary, Developmental & Cultural Perspectives

Edited by Barry S. Hewlett and Michael E. Lamb

ALDINETRANSACTION
A Division of Transaction Publishers
New Brunswick (U.S.A.) and London (U.K.)

Library of Congress Catalog Number: 2004007786
ISBN: 978-0-202-30749-7
Printed in the United States of America

Library of Congress Cataloging-in-Publication Data

Hunter-gatherer childhoods: evolutionary, developmental, and cultural
    perspectives / Barry S. Hewlett and Michael E. Lamb, editors.—1 st ed.
        p. cm;—(Evolutionary foundations of human behavior)
    Includes bibliographical references and index.
        ISBN 0-202-30748-4 (cloth: alk. paper)- ISBN 0-202-30749-2 (pbk. :
alk. paper) 1. Hunting and gathering societies—Cross-cultural studies. 2.
Children—Cross-cultural studies. 3. Child development—Cross-cultural
studies. I. Hewlett, Barry S., 1950-. II. Lamb,Michael E., 1953- III. Series.

GN388.H85 2004
306.3'64-dc22   2004007786

To our children,
Allison, Aya, Damon, Darryn, David, Erika, Forrest,
Jeanette, Jessica, Jordan, Lindsey and Philip
for bringing joy, energy and knowledge to our lives.

Contents

II   WHY DOES CHILDHOOD EXIST?

III   WHO CARES FOR HUNTER-GATHERER CHILDREN?

Acknowledgments

Several people and institutions made this volume possible. First and foremost, we would like to thank all the hunter-gatherer families and ethnic groups discussed in the volume for sharing their lives with the often strange ways of scholars. Second, we want to thank all the contributors to the volume for their energy and enthusiasm. The workshop and various formal and informal meetings were stimulating and enjoyable. It was particularly gratifying to see young and "older" scholars from quite different theoretical orientations share data and engage in lively debates. We sincerely appreciate the institutional support of the Section on Social and Emotional Development of the United States National Institute of Child Health and Human Development, Washington State University, Vancouver, and the Heriot-Watt University Conference Center in Edinburgh, Scotland. Finally, we want to thank Mai Shaikhanuar-Cota at Aldine and Laurence Mintz at Transaction for their support and expertise in publishing this volume.

Preface

This volume both results from and is part of a continuing effort to promote discussion and debate among researchers conducting field-based child-focused studies on active or recently sedentarized hunter-gatherers, regardless of theoretical orientation or academic discipline.

Participants were initially invited to a two-day workshop, sponsored by the U.S. National Institute of Child Health and Human Development, that took place just before the start of the Conference on Hunting and Gathering Societies (CHAGS) in Edinburgh, Scotland, in September 2002. Papers were circulated before the workshop, critically and informally discussed during the workshop, and later presented formally at the CHAGS meetings. The discussions focused on understanding the experiences and daily lives of hunter-gatherer children, children's views and feelings about culture change and about their natural and social environments, theoretical explanations for similarities and differences in the lives of forager children, and diverse aspects of child development, including weaning, responsiveness to crying, multiple care, and identity. In order to permit further discussion of the developing ideas, revisions were also presented at the American Anthropological Association Meetings in New Orleans in November 2002. The reports were further revised following these presentations for inclusion in this volume.

The process included young researchers who had not yet or had only recently completed their Ph.D.s, researchers who had worked with hunter-gatherer children for some time, and senior scholars who could elucidate broader theoretical issues and research conducted in other cultures and species. Sarah Hrdy was thus asked to provide a cross-species perspective on juveniles, Nurit Bird-David was asked to provide a "culturalist" view of hunter-gatherer children and to describe the South Asian hunter-gatherers she had studied, and Melvin Konner was invited to reflect broadly on changing views of hunter-gatherer childhood since he began his field research nearly 40 years ago. Bram Tucker, Vishvajit Pandya, and Larry Sugiyama had not conducted child-centered research, but had gathered relevant ethnographic or behavioral field data on hunter-gatherer children in regions of the world not represented by the other participants: Madagascar (Tucker), Andaman Islands (Pandya), and South America (Sugiyama). Of course, some of the invited scholars were not able to participate, so the book does not include chapters on hunter-gatherers from the arctic regions of North America and Russia, or from Southeast Asia. These absences notwithstanding, we hope that the publication of this book will serve to stimulate further research and scholarship on hunter-gatherer childhood, thereby advancing our understanding of the way of life that characterized most of human history and of the processes that may have shaped both human evolution and human development.

Contributors

Douglas W. Bird	Department of Anthropological Sciences, Stanford University, Stanford, California
Rebecca Bliege Bird	Department of Anthropological Sciences, Stanford University, Stanford, California
Nicholas Blurton Jones	Department of Education, Anthropology and Psychiatry, University of California, Los Angeles, California
John Bock	Department of Anthropology, California State University, Fullerton, California
Nurit Bird-David	Department of Anthropology, University of Haifa, Haifa, Israel
Patricia Draper	Department of Anthropology, and Geography, University of Nebraska, Lincoln, Nebraska
Hillary N. Fouts	National Institute of Child Health and Human Development, Bethesda, Maryland
Kristen Hawkes	Department of Anthropology, University of Utah, Salt Lake City, Utah
Paula Ivey Henry	Department of Anthropology, University of New Mexico, Albuquerque, New Mexico
Barry S. Hewlett	Department of Anthropology, Washington State University, Vancouver, Washington
Bonnie L. Hewlett	Department of Anthropology, Oregon State University, Corvallis, Oregon
Ayako Hirasawa	Graduate School of Asian and African Area Studies, Kyoto University, Kyoto, Japan
Nancy Howell	Department of Anthropology, University of Toronto, Canada
Sarah Blaffer Hrdy	Department of Anthropology, University of California, Davis, California

Nobutaka Kamei   Research Fellow of the Japan Society for the Promotion of
                      Science, Kyoto University, Kyoto, Japan

Melvin Konner   Department of Anthropology and Program in Neurosci-
                      ence and Behavioral Biology, Emory University, Atlanta,
                      Georgia

Michael E. Lamb   Department of Social and Developmental Psychology,
                      Cambridge University, Cambridge, England

Frank W. Marlowe   Department of Anthropology, Harvard University, Pea-
                      body Museum, Cambridge, Massachusetts

Gilda A. Morelli   Department of Psychology, Boston College, Chestnut Hill,
                      Massachusetts

James F. O'Connell   Department of Anthropology, University of Utah, Salt
                      Lake City, Utah

Vishvajit Pandya   Dhirubhai Ambani Institute of Information and Commu-
                      nication Technology, Gujarat, India

Lawrence S.   Department of Anthropology, University of Oregon, Eu-
   Sugiyama   gene, Oregon

Akira Takada   Graduate School of Asian and African Area Studies, Kyoto
                      University, Kyoto, Japan

Edward Z. Tronick   Child Development Unit, The Children's Hospital, Boston,
                      Massachusetts

Bram Tucker   Department of Anthropology, Ohio State University,
                      Columbus, Ohio

Alyson G. Young   Department of Anthropology, Ohio State University,
                      Columbus, Ohio

I

Theoretical and Conceptual Issues

Photo 1.   Hadza children playing. Courtesy of F. Marlowe

1

Emerging Issues in the Study of Hunter-Gatherer Children

Barry S. Hewlett and Michael E. Lamb

This book is designed to bridge critical gaps in our understanding of the daily lives, knowledge, and development of hunter-gatherer children. Children represent more than 40 percent of most hunter-gatherer populations but anthropologists working with these groups seldom describe their daily life, knowledge, and views, thereby ensuring, in essence, that about half the population is omitted from most hunter-gatherer ethnographies. Reflecting on this, Hirschfeld (2002) has pondered why anthropologists do not like children, and Bird-David (Chapter 4) identifies several reasons why child-focused research on hunter-gatherers has been so limited.

Although studies of hunter-gatherer children have been rare, child-focused anthropological research was relatively common from the 1930s to the 1960s, when Freudian theorists hypothesized about the links between early childhood experiences and adult personality and culture. Margaret Mead (1930, 1933) pioneered child-focused research, while John and Beatrice Whiting (1941, 1975) and their many students (e.g., Robert LeVine, Sara Harkness, Thomas Weisner, Lee and Ruth Munroe) refined and extended these "culture and personality" field studies into the 1970s. These studies led to the rejection of several psychoanalytically inspired ideas about child development and encouraged many social scientists to question some Western-centric notions about children, including the beliefs that identity conflict and mood swings are universal features of adolescence (Condon 1987; Mead 1933), that older siblings are infrequent and incompetent caregivers (Weisner and Gallimore 1977), and that infant sleep-wake patterns are universal (Super and Harkness 1982).

The Freudian and culture-and-personality approaches were still limited, however, by their concern with children primarily as it afforded better understanding of adults; children, their knowledge, and their activities

were not viewed as theoretically or ethnographically interesting in their
own right. And although hunter-gatherer cultures were included in the
Whitings' cross-cultural research on adolescents [see, for example, Burbank's (1989) account of Australian Aborigines and Condon's (1987) description of the Inuit], the groups selected for field study had not actively
engaged in hunting and gathering for at least a generation and so the research did not elucidate the daily lives of adolescents in hunting and gathering societies.

Like the studies by Mead, the Whitings, and their students, the majority of child-centered studies conducted by anthropologists based in the
United States (e.g., Schiefflein 1990) and Europe (e.g., Toren 1993) have involved farming cultures, in part because they represent the majority of the
small-scale or "traditional" cultures in the world. Consequently, most of
what contemporary anthropologists know about children (summarized in
the "socialization" chapters of introductory anthropology texts) reflects research on farming and pastoral cultures. Unfortunately, many scholars
and popular writers such as Judith Harris (1998) then use these generalizations to characterize child life in "preliterate" or "traditional" cultures
as compared with child life in urban industrial cultures. For example, Harris (1998:90-96) indicates that, in most traditional societies, weaning is
abrupt, sibling rivalries lead many older children to hit younger siblings,
physical punishment is widespread, infants are taught little because parents consider infants to be incapable of learning, and girls are preferred
babysitters. These generalizations are not true of most hunter-gatherer societies, however. Whereas most of Harris's characterizations of traditional
childcare apply to the Ngandu farmers who are neighbors of and regularly
trade with the Aka hunter-gatherers, for example, older Aka children
rarely, if ever, hit younger children, physical punishment of children is rare
(and is even grounds for divorce), weaning is both very gradual and child-
directed, both boys and girls are babysitters, and infants (six- to ten-
month-olds) are routinely given small digging sticks, axes, or spears by
parents, who instruct them in their use by moving their arms appropriately. Harris appropriately summarized the literature on children in "traditional" societies available to her, but her summary nicely exemplifies the
farmer bias in the literature and reflects critical gaps in our understanding
of children in hunter-gatherer cultures.

A specific interest in hunter-gatherer children emerged in the 1960s
shortly after the completion of the first in-depth studies of the Mbuti
(Turnbull 1965), the Hadza (Woodburn 19968b), the San (Lee 1979), and
the Siriono (Holmberg 1950), as well as the first international conference
on hunting and gathering societies (the "Man the Hunter Conference")
in 1966. Interest in foragers also coincided with growing acceptance of
Bowlby's (1958, 1969) proposition that the attachment-forming processes

of human infants evolved in a hunting and gathering context (which Bowlby called "the environment of evolutionary adaptedness"). Three of the authors in this volume—Melvin Konner, Patricia Draper, and Nick Blurton Jones—were among those first anthropologists to conduct child-focused research with hunter-gatherers in the late 1960s.

By contrast to anthropology, developmental psychologists have always conducted child-focused research. Libraries are filled with books and journals on child development, but most of the studies described involve very brief observations in artificial or laboratory settings, rather than in extended naturalistic settings, perhaps at home or with friends. Artificial methods allow researchers to control for a variety of factors in quantitative analyses, but they impede the holistic understanding of children. All of the contributors to this volume have conducted long-term naturalistic observations of children or juvenile primates.

In addition, most developmentalists have studied global economic cash economies with cultures characterized by complex levels of hierarchy, inequality, and global capitalism. Research by child developmentalists is increasingly "cross-cultural," but the cultures selected for comparison (e.g., Dutch, German, French, Japanese, Chinese) tend to be similar with respect to socioeconomic inequality, the material accumulation of wealth, and an emphasis on formal education. Most class-stratified societies are also governed by strong nation-states that make parental and alloparental roles as protectors and educators less important because the state provides a police/military force as well as some amount of formal education. Stratified cultures differ in some important ways (e.g., some are much more sociocentric than others) but they are all characterized by everyday inequalities dramatically different from the relatively egalitarian lifestyles and worldviews of hunter-gatherers. In the latter cultures, sharing is extensive (e.g., 80 percent of the game meat captured by Aka families is shared with others) and individuals are discouraged from drawing attention to themselves. The hunter-gatherers described in this volume live in nation-states and may be affected by their laws and government policies (e.g., settlement programs), but, in general, they receive little daily protection or formal education from the nation-state (Pandya, in Chapter 18, and Kamei, in Chapter 16, describe some exceptions to this pattern). Studies of contemporary stratified cultures do help us understand child development, of course, but it is important to keep the limitations of context in mind, especially when proposing universal or general features of childhood and child development.

It is also valuable to understand how childhood unfolds in the contexts that characterized most of human history. Global capitalism has been around for about two hundred years, class stratification (chiefdoms and states) about five thousand years, simple farming and pastoralism about ten thousand years, and hunting-gathering hundreds of thousands of years (at least 90 percent of human history). The importance of understanding children and childhood in hunting and gathering cultures notwithstanding, Bird-David (Chapter 4) and Lee (1979) suggest caution when interpreting the results of such research:

> Contemporary hunter-gatherers have much to teach us, but we must proceed with extreme caution to avoid misreading the lessons they offer. The hunters are not living fossils. They are human like ourselves with a history as long as the history of any other human group. It is their very humanity that makes them so important to science. (Lee 1979:1)

As mentioned earlier, in any event, children have largely disappeared from anthropology textbooks and ethnographies, appearing occasionally in discussions of childhood in farming societies. This book on hunter-gatherer children begins to bridge these dramatic gaps by placing children in the foreground. Scholars from around the world describe provocative theoretical frameworks and ethnographic details about the few remaining contemporary hunter-gatherer societies in Asia, Africa, and South America.

TERMINOLOGY AND GENERALIZATIONS ABOUT HUNTER-GATHERER CULTURES

Hunter-Gatherers

Hunter-gatherers are a very diverse group of peoples living in a wide range of ecological, social, and political conditions. This diversity is, in part, why childhood is plural in the title of this book. The hunter-gatherer lifestyle they share is defined as "subsistence based on hunting of wild animals, gathering of wild plant foods, and fishing, with no domestication of plants, and no domesticated animals except the dog" (Lee and Daly 1999:3). The terms "hunter-gatherer" and "forager" are used interchangeably in this book to refer to mobile hunter-gatherers. We do not discuss sedentary hunter-gatherers (also called "collectors" by Binford 1980), such as Native Americans of the Northwest Coast, who often store food (mobile hunter-gatherers often know how to store food but seldom do so), such as acorns or salmon, accumulate material wealth, and are socially stratified. As a result, social life in sedentary hunter-gatherer cultures and simple farming cultures can be quite similar.

Woodburn (1982b) described foragers or mobile hunter-gatherers as "immediate-return" cultures, and all others as "delayed-return" cultures. Delayed-return cultures are characterized by cultural ideologies and subsistence systems in which individuals wait for a return on their investment (they plant crops today and wait six months to harvest, for example, or save money for college) whereas immediate-return cultures have ideologies and subsistence systems that emphasize rapid return on individual investment (eating an entire elephant in a few days, for example, without storing any for future consumption). Woodburn focused on the cultural ideology (values and attitudes about resources) rather than on the modes of production, in part, because it is difficult to make any generalizations about "hunter-gatherers," particularly when both mobile and sedentary hunter-gatherers are considered. Similarly, Barnard (2002) has proposed a shift from analyzing "modes of production" to analyzing "modes of thought" (such as the emphases on extensive giving/sharing or maintaining egalitarian social relations) because the modes of thought persist beyond the mode of production. Many peoples who used to hunt and gather actively are now sedentary, farming, or raising cattle, but they continue to share extensively and their modes of thought resemble those of active mobile hunter-gatherers. Bird-David (1992) and Hewlett et al. (2000) have also suggested that egalitarian and trusting social relations are linked to patterns of childcare and may be more distinctive than modes of production, especially when a group of foragers becomes sedentary.

These issues are introduced here because some of the contributors examine forager children whose parents may not hunt and gather very much any more (i.e., they may have moved to settlements) but their "modes of thought" and many elements of forager child life persist after sedentarization and farming (see Hirasawa, Chapter 17) have started. Studies of forager groups undergoing extensive cultural change cannot tell us much about the daily life of forager children, of course, but they can tell us about the styles of caregiver-child interaction and about the strength, skill, and knowledge needed to engage in those foraging activities that persist. All forager groups described in this book are experiencing cultural change and are affected by their nonforaging neighbors and other international events (e.g., logging, game preserves), but the extent to which they are affected varies. Table 1.1 summarizes variations among the cultures described in this volume with respect to how often they hunt and gather. Adults in most of the cultures studied continue to hunt and gather actively and all have forager "modes of thought." The contributors all describe the historical and ethnographic background of the cultures they studied so that readers can judge how much cultural change may have affected their hypotheses or findings.

Although debate about how to characterize mobile hunter-gatherers continues, most scholars agree that mobile hunter-gatherers, foragers, or immediate-return cultures live in small and flexible social groups of 25–35 individuals who move camp several times a year; seldom store food; do

Table 1.1   Ethnic Groups, Ages of Focal Children, and Impact of Culture Change

Chapter and Author	Age Focus	Ethnic Group	Foraging[a]
2 Konner	Infancy and early childhood	!Kung/Ju/'hoansi and comparisons	High at time of study
3 Hrdy	Infancy and early childhood	Cross-species and cross-cultural	Not applicable
4 Bird-David	Childhood (3–18 years)	Nyaka and comparisons	Intermediate
5 Bock	3–18 years	Five ethnic groups in Okavango Delta	Intermediate
6 Bird and Bliege Bird	4–14 years	Martu	Low to intermediate
7 Tucker and Young	3–18 years	Mikea	Intermediate
8 Marlowe	0–8 years	Hadza	High
9 Ivey Henry et al.	12–15 months	Efe	High
10 Blurton Jones et al.	0–18 years	Hadza	High
11 Sugiyama and Chacon	0–20 years	Yora	Low to intermediate
12 Draper and Howell	2–20 years	!Kung/Ju/'hoansi	High at time of study
13 Takada	2–4 months	!Xun	Low to intermediate
14 Fouts and Lamb	18–59 months	Bofi	High
15 Hewlett	10–20 years	Aka (comparison with Ngandu farmers)	High
16 Kamei	4–15 years	Baka	Intermediate
17 Hirasawa	1–13 months	Baka (comparison with Bombong farmers)	Intermediate
18 Pandya	5–13 years	Ongee	Low to intermediate

[a] High: frequent movement, no or small farms, no outside provisioning (e.g., by governments or churches), no or limited access to formal education, limited links to market economy.

Intermediate: hunt and gather for 40 to 60% of subsistence, sedentary most of year near a road, frequent access to formal education, some market trading with outsiders.

Low: continue to hunt and gather, but most subsistence comes from farming, pastoralism, or outside provisioning; frequent access to formal education, and some access to piped water.

not have centralized authorities (i.e., strong chiefs); share extensively (i.e., daily, with many different individuals); have egalitarian social relations; and practice shamanism (Lee and Daly 1999).

Childhood/Children

Discussing the term "children" in Chapter 4, Bird-David observes that most forager cultures distinguish babies and toddlers from "children" and that children become "adults" as soon as they marry. Interestingly, the categories used by foragers are similar to those identified in life history theory: All of the groups studied recognize distinctive periods before weaning and between weaning and first mating (and adulthood) but none subdivide childhood into early childhood, late childhood, and adolescence. Bird-David further notes that foragers frequently talk about children, but that academics studying foragers do not; she suggests it is like two ships passing in the night.

As shown in Table 1.1, the contributors have studied children ranging in age from birth to around 20 years, reflecting the extraordinary length of time that human children are economically dependent on adults. We use the term "childhood" in the book's title because most contributors focus on what others do for and with juveniles. Most of the contributors focus on middle childhood, but five pay considerable attention to infancy. Although only one contributor emphasizes adolescence, several others consider adolescents in their analyses and discussion.

WHAT'S NEW?

The chapters in the volume contribute both ethnographically and theoretically to our understanding of forager children. Ethnographically, several of the chapters provide unprecedented insights into forager child life. For example:

1. In the first systematic study of forager children's hunting (as opposed to collecting), Bird and Bliege Bird (Chapter 6) found that Martu five-year-olds were just as efficient at large lizard hunting as 14-year-olds and that Martu children learned to hunt on their own in the absence of adults.
2. In the first systematic study of children as caregivers in a foraging culture, Ivey Henry and her colleagues (Chapter 9) reported that Efe boys and girls were equally involved in the care of one-year-old infants (whereas girls dominate infant care in farming groups) and that a variety of demographic and ecological factors, such as group size, explained the extent to which children provided care.
3. In the first systematic comparative study of forager grandparents, Blurton Jones and his colleagues report in Chapter 10 that Hadza grandfathers were less likely than grandmothers to be living in camps with their grandchildren.
4. In the first systematic study of play by foragers, Kamei (Chapter 16) reported that Baka children engaged in very little physical play. Play provided a forum for learning how to negotiate social

interaction with other children rather than to practice adult activities and roles.

5. In the first systematic study of forager weaning, Fouts and Lamb (Chapter 14) found that Bofi children decided when to wean, that weaning was not a traumatic event, and that other care providers were less likely to answer infant cries when mothers were absent than when they were present.

6. In the first systematic study of forager children's (10- to 20-year-olds) grief, Hewlett (Chapter 15) found that Aka children remembered many deaths. Unlike the neighboring farmers, Aka children and adolescents remembered just as many female deaths as male deaths and were comforted by physical soothing (e.g., being held) more than by acts of material provisioning.

7. In the first systematic study of forager children with only one biological parent, Sugiyama and Chacon (Chapter 11) indicated that single parents lived in larger households with more allocaregivers than did children who had two living parents.

8. Mikea children forage simply because it is interesting and fun and there is not much else to do (Tucker and Young, Chapter 7).

9. Nyaka parents do not feel the need to "socialize" their children and do not believe that parents' activities greatly affect their children's development (Bird-David, Chapter 4).

10. Both !Kung and !Xun caregivers use "gymnastic" activities to stimulate their infants, but for different reasons. !Kung mothers believe that it promotes motor development whereas !Xun mothers think that it quiets infants or helps them fall asleep (Takada, Chapter 13).

11. When Baka foragers became more sedentary, frequent holding, rapid responses to fussing and crying, and frequent breastfeeding remained characteristic, but sibling care became more common and weaning began to take place earlier and more abruptly (Hirasawa, Chapter 17).

12. Hadza fathers provide substantial amounts of care during infancy and early childhood when they live with the mothers, but grandmothers became the major sources of nonmaternal care when biological fathers are not present, perhaps because many single mothers live with their mothers (Marlowe, Chapter 8).

13. The health and activity levels of Ju/'hoan children are not related to the numbers of living parents or grandparents they have, perhaps because extensive sharing makes these relatives less crucial than they are in other cultures (Draper and Howell, Chapter 12).

This list selectively references some of the ethnographic contributions made by this collection of chapters, but the list shortchanges the theoretical context and contributions by the authors. Often the ethnographic data would not have been collected if it were not for the provocative theoretical issues that generated the research questions. Evolutionary, developmental and cultural theoretical questions and issues are outlined below and detailed in each chapter.

ORGANIZATION AND THEORETICAL INTEGRATION

Three general but complementary theoretical approaches guide the research conducted by the contributors to this volume: evolutionary, developmental, and cultural. The evolutionary approach emphasizes the ways in which individuals (adults or children) try to enhance their reproductive fitness (i.e., adaptation) in particular social, ecological, and demographic settings. For instance, forager children hunt and gather in natural environments where it is relatively safe and easy (Tucker and Young, Chapter 7), but do not do so in dangerous environments (Ivey Henry et al., Chapter 9). The developmental approach includes a broad range of theories, linked by the assumption that age is a key factor in explaining much of the observed variability in children's abilities (e.g., motor, social, emotional, or social). Consequently, developmental researchers tend to focus on specific age ranges (Ivey Henry et al. focus on 12- to 15-month-olds for example, and Fouts and Lamb focus on 18- to 59-month-olds). The cultural approach uses the concept of culture (minimally defined by reference to shared knowledge and practices that are transmitted nonbiologically from generation to generation) to explain what happens during childhood. Culture is symbolic, historic, and integrated; it influences how individuals perceive and feel about the world around them. A "culturalist" approach to children emphasizes local views of children and how these views influence children's and adult's behavior. For instance, Pandya (Chapter 18) reports that the colonial culture and views of children dramatically affected the colonists' treatment of Andaman hunter-gatherer children. Chapters in Parts II and III emphasize evolutionary approaches, most chapters in Part IV are developmental in focus, whereas Chapters 13, 16, 17, and 18 use culture as an important explanatory factor.

An integrated approach is essential to understand the nature of child life. Evolutionists are interested in how reproductive interests influence human behavior but it is necessary to understand how these behaviors develop during childhood and how cultural ideology and identity influence children's reproductive choices. Developmental trajectories and patterns are influenced by cultural ideas about children as well as the children's reproductive interests. Cultural schema and knowledge are manipulated by children's reproductive interests and culture may change dramatically as the child ages (e.g., "cultures of childhood").

While each chapter tends to emphasize one of the three approaches, the contributors integrate the three approaches in a variety of ways. Each chapter provides cultural and historical contexts of childhood (i.e., history of the people, physical and social settings, caregiving practices, ideologies regarding children). Each chapter is also developmental in that children's abilities or activities at specific ages are identified and examined. The researchers who examined gymnastic behaviors (Chapter 13), weaning (Chapter 14), grief (Chapter 15), and play (Chapter 16) all use developmental theory and hypotheses to guide their research. In addition, the authors of the chapters on weaning and grief use evolutionary approaches to interpret their results, whereas those who studied gymnastics and play consider cultural influences on developmental patterns. Evolutionary theory guided the research described in Chapters 5 to 12, but the questions and results are also of great interest to developmental psychologists: At what ages do children learn particular skills? Why do they learn these skills? Who cares for forager children of different ages? How do different caregivers affect children's development? What can be more basic to developmental psychology than the question, Why does childhood exist?

ORGANIZATION OF THE BOOK

The book is divided into five parts. In addition to this introduction, Part I includes three chapters that provide the historical, theoretical, and conceptual background for the other chapters. Parts II to V include their own brief introductions and contain chapters exploring a range of hypotheses using data gathered in the field.

Part I introduces provocative theoretical and conceptual issues that are revisited later in the book. Konner (Chapter 2) begins with an excellent overview of research on foragers in which he integrates evolutionary and developmental approaches while asking whether forager childcare patterns might have been affected by phylogenetic history (i.e., the history of juvenile care in primates) and whether foragers have an infinite ability to adapt their patterns of childcare to changing social ecologies. In the course of this analysis, Konner reexamines his own classic research on !Kung infants and children, carefully summarizing and evaluating major studies of forager children conducted in the intervening 25 years, including research on the !Kung, Hadza, Efe, and Aka discussed elsewhere in this book. Konner also raises questions about allocare and infant-parent attachment that are addressed in Parts III and IV.

Hrdy, too (Chapter 3), raises issues that are revisited throughout the book: Why does childhood exist? (Part II), Who cares for children? (Part

III), and What psychological features characterize mother-infant attachment? (Part IV). Like Konner, Hrdy integrates evolutionary and developmental approaches, but whereas Konner emphasizes phylogenetic history and maternal primacy among foragers, Hrdy emphasizes facultative adaptation and allocare.

In the final chapter in this introductory section, Bird-David asks from a culturalist perspective why there has been so little research on forager children and why it is important to understand how foragers themselves view children and their development. Although all the contributors deal with culture (providing cultural and historical backgrounds, for example), the chapters in Parts IV and V place special emphasis on culture as a factor shaping childhood among foragers. By contrast, the evolutionary researchers contributing to Parts II and III seldom, if ever, mention "culture" in their chapters. Culture is, in fact, an integral part of the evolutionary approach to childhood (Hewlett and Lamb 2002), although few proponents of the evolutionary approach pay explicit attention to this concept.

Part II contains three chapters in which scholars describe empirical data bearing on the question raised by Hrdy (Chapter 3) and articulated more thoroughly by Blurton Jones in his introduction to Part II: Why do humans have longer childhoods than other primates and mammals? Is the extraordinary length of human childhood an artifact of human life history (e.g., low adult mortality), as suggested by data in Chapters 6 and 7, or, as suggested by Bock in Chapter 5, an adaptation to the complexities of human lifestyles? Do children, for example, need a long period of dependent apprenticeship to learn the complex subsistence and social skills needed to be successful adults as many anthropologists and psychologists have long assumed? Additional data on this debate are also provided in Chapter 9 by Ivey Henry et al. and Chapter 11 by Sugiyama and Chacon.

Part III includes five chapters in which contributors examine the distribution of childcare responsibilities, a topic introduced by Konner (Chapter 2) and Hrdy (Chapter 3) when discussing the importance of maternal and allomaternal care, respectively. Although most chapters in Part III provide data that support Hrdy's cooperative breeding hypothesis, some of the data reported in these and other chapters (e.g., Hirasawa, Chapter 17) are also consistent with Konner's emphasis on maternal primacy. In addition, as Hrdy (Chapter 3) and Blurton Jones (Introduction to Part II) point out, the questions Who cares for children? and Why childhood? are related. The "grandmother hypothesis" (Hawkes et al. 1998) proposes that the long human lifespan is the product of selection favoring the provisioning of benefits by older women to their descendents rather than that long childhoods are necessary for the acquisition of life skills. Hrdy (Chapter 3) suggests that extended childhoods and cooperative breeding co-evolved whereas brain size increased later in the course of evolution.

Are fathers or grandmothers more important to the survival of forager children? Paternal provisioning, especially postweaning, used to be viewed as central to child survival (Lancaster and Lancaster 1983), with fathers expected to go hunting and return with game to share with their families. Hawkes (1991) pointed out, however, that forager men shared most of the meat with other adults in camp and that the hunters' families actually received relatively small portions of the meat. Men also bypassed small game, which could be captured on a daily basis, to go after larger game, which was often captured irregularly. Among the Hadza at least, by contrast, grandmothers and other older adult women provided food for postweaning children on a regular, dependable basis in the form of tubers and other high-caloric food items. With these data in mind, Hrdy (Chapter 3) suggests that fathers are important but unreliable caregivers or providers whereas Hewlett (1991b) and Marlowe (1999a) describe them as central secondary providers, especially when they are present in infancy and early childhood. Three chapters (8, 10, 11) in Part III and two in later sections of the book (Chapters 14 and 17) contain field data relevant to the father-grandmother comparison.

Part IV comprises four chapters in which contributors examine developmental issues in light of the debates and issues raised in Parts I, II, and III. For example, Konner and Hrdy clearly integrated developmental and evolutionary theory, with Hrdy describing the ways in which maternal and child psychology influence the level and nature of allocare and attachment formation. Fouts and Lamb (Chapter 14) and Hewlett (Chapter 15) examine attachment in young children and adolescents. Takada (Chapter 13) and Kamei (Chapter 13) discuss the physical stimulation of infants and play among children, respectively, using the "culturalist" perspective introduced by Bird-David in Chapter 4 to interpret their results. In addition, Kamei returns to another issue discussed in Chapters 4 (Bird-David) and 6 (Bird and Bliege Bird): are there cultures of childhood, that is, bodies of knowledge or practices that relate to living and interacting with other children rather than adults?

Part V, the final section of the book, includes three chapters, two of which examine the impact of culture change on the experiences of infants and children in forager communities. As noted earlier in this chapter, all the foraging societies discussed in this book have experienced some degree of culture change: The Yora (Chapter 11) have undergone dramatic population loss, Martu adults (Chapter 6) drive trucks when hunting, and the !Kung and !Xun now live in settlements. The authors of Chapters 17 (Hirasawa) and 18 (Pandya) make culture change central to their reports, however. Hirasawa examines the impact of sedentarization on Baka infant care and Pandya examines the impact of history, politics, and formal schooling on Ongee children and childhood.

DISCUSSION

Infancy and Early Childhood

Most theoretical and empirical studies of hunter-gatherer children involve infants and, to a lesser extent, children who have not yet been weaned. It is not clear why the focus has been so narrow (the impact of Bowlby's attachment theory, and Western scholarly emphases on early sensitive periods of development are possible explanations), but we can now draw on systematic and detailed studies of infancy and toddlerhood among the !Kung, Ache, Baka, Aka, Bofi, !Xun, Hadza, and Efe. This database enables scholars like Konner (Chapter 2) to develop and evaluate characterizations about the care of infants and young children in hunter-gatherer cultures. Konner's excellent summary and data provided by other contributors suggest that, in comparison with the patterns of care that characterize farming and urban-industrial cultures, young children in foraging cultures are nursed frequently; held, touched, or kept near others almost constantly; frequently cared for by individuals other than their mothers (fathers and grandmothers, in particular) though seldom by older siblings; experience prompt responses to their fusses and cries; and enjoy multiage play groups in early childhood.

Other features appear to be characteristic of some rather than all forager groups. Reflecting the emphasis of many foragers on the development of autonomy, for example, some forager care providers do not intervene when infants or young children use or touch items that caregivers in many other cultures may perceive as dangerous (knives, machetes, spear points, axes, sharp digging sticks, hot pots). Thus, several participants at the conference reported observing the kind of behavior Marlowe describes in Chapter 8: "Children grasp knives and suck on them." Similarly, weaning in some groups, although not among !Kung, is gradual and often child-directed (see Chapter 14) and infants often initiate breastfeeding on their own. Breastfeeding by women other than the child's mother is common among the Ongee, Efe, Aka, and Agta but not among the Hadza or !Kung. Reflecting a commitment to gender egalitarianism, older boys and girls provide equivalent amounts of infant care.

As noted earlier, the data reported in this book support both the cooperative breeding and maternal primacy hypotheses. The cooperative breeding hypothesis is supported by data reported in Chapters 2 (Konner), 8 (Marlowe), 9 (Ivey Henry et al.), and 12 (Draper and Howell), whereas support for the maternal primacy hypothesis can be found in Chapters 8 (Marlowe), 11 (Sugiyama and Chacon), and 13 (Hirasawa). At the conference, several participants pointed out that babies in foraging cultures typically die when their mothers die, but not when their fathers, aunts, or grandmothers die. In addition, even in the cultures characterized by particularly high levels of allocare (Efe and Bofi), mothers are more likely than other available caregivers to respond to their children's crying and fussing.

It is important to remember that forager infants receive much more direct care, holding in particular, than do their peers in farming communities. Forager infants and young children are held almost continually by a variety of individuals, including fathers, grandmothers, and other children. A restricted focus on either grandmothers or fathers misses the fact that almost everyone provides more infant care in foraging cultures than in other cultures and that variations in the ecological, demographic, and cultural context affect which "others" help out. Aka men, women, and children net hunt so fathers are more available to their infants than foragers whose hunting techniques involve men leaving camp alone. Aka men are also more likely to provide for children because they contribute half the calories to the diet and hunt small- and medium-sized game. By contrast, Hadza women forage for more predictable fruit and tubers with other women while Hadza men tend to forage alone, travel further, and are gone longer in search of less predictable foods so it is not surprising that grandmothers become secondary providers (Marlowe 2003). Individuals can enhance their own reproductive fitness by attending to genetically related children or by trying to attract new spouses by helping care for their existing offspring.

These data and theories raise several questions for future research. Why do foragers have this distinctive pattern of intensive care in infancy and early childhood? Konner emphasizes the need to understand phylogenetic origins, but the analysis needs to be taken further. Why are forager caregivers so indulgent? Why do foragers always hold their infants? Hrdy concludes that cooperative breeding existed in humans before brain capacity increased, but why did it emerge? Finally, does the quality of care (e.g., responsiveness, ability to soothe) vary among care providers? Allocare is extensive and common, but we do not know if child caregivers, fathers, grandmothers, and others afford similar or different types of experiences for the children in their care, and what significance this may have.

Older Children (4- to 20-Year-Olds)

Few researchers have studied forager children between the ages of weaning and first marriage. Draper (1976) pioneered child-focused research with older (4- to 14-year-old) !Kung children in the late 1960s and early 1970s, while Blurton Jones, who studied !Kung infants with Konner in the early 1970s, turned his focus to older Hadza children in the 1980s. Blurton Jones and his colleagues encouraged a new generation of child-focused researchers, many of whom have contributed to this book, and we now have a clearer picture of what forager children in many cultures contribute to subsistence, what they do during the day, and how skilled they are in subsistence tasks. Despite these efforts, so many questions remain unanswered that we cannot yet offer broad generalizations like those that can be made about infancy and early childhood, although Konner (Chapter 2) suggests two: that premarital sex is common and that childhood is carefree (i.e., children are generally not expected to provide food or care for siblings as they would be in farming cultures). Qualitative ethnographic accounts suggest that premarital sex is indeed common, although no systematic studies on this topic have been conducted. By contrast, Blurton Jones et al. (1989) and several contributors to this book provide data about the responsibilities and activities of forager children, suggesting that, under certain social-ecological conditions—for instance, where foraging areas are close to camp, free of predators, and children cannot easily get lost—children spend a considerable amount of time in subsistence activity and provide up to 50 percent of the calories they consume (Bird and Bliege Bird, Chapter 6; Tucker and Young, Chapter 7). This suggests that childhood may not be carefree as suggested by Draper (1976) and Konner (Chapter 2), but the ethnographic accounts that accompany the behavioral observations suggests that children frequently "work" by choice. Forager children are often not expected to contribute to subsistence or childcare until first marriage, although they may be praised for hunting or collecting. By contrast, older children in most farmer groups expect older female siblings, in particular, to care for their younger brothers or sisters.

Other data suggest that, in at least some forager cultures, "cultures of childhood" exist (Bird-David, Chapter 4; Bird and Bliege Bird, Chapter 6; and Kamei, Chapter 16); children learn complex subsistence skills very quickly and easily at a relatively early age (Bird and Bliege Bird, Chapter 6; Tucker and Young, Chapter 7; Blurton Jones, Introduction to Part II); children up to the age of about seven are usually in the proximity of adults, although this is not the case among the Martu; grandparents are important sources of care and food during middle childhood because many children live with grandparents at these ages; and foragers do not feel strongly about socializing their children.

Unfortunately, research on 4- to 20-year-olds is only now beginning, so many questions remain to be addressed in the future. Among the most important might be the following:

1. How is forager culture transmitted? What is the impact of group living? What are the costs and benefits of the different types of transmission and acquisition?
2. When do children acquire the knowledge to make the tools needed to take advantage of complex technology? Children may be very

good at using the tools at an early age, but most of these tools (e.g., nets, spears, mortar and pestle) are made or provided by parents.

3. What is the impact of frequent practice on skill acquisition? Physical maturation is emphasized in Chapters 6 and 7 while skill is emphasized in Chapters 5 and 11 but it is crucial to understand whether and how experience and body size affect the acquisition of specific skills.

4. When, how, and why do forager children acquire the social skills needed to survive in highly egalitarian societies? What are the interactions between experience and cognitive development?

5. We know the least about forager adolescence. How is it different or similar to childhood?

6. A "culture of childhood" exists, but we know almost nothing about forager children's views, ideologies, or explanations of their own lives.

7. Like many developmental psychologists, Bogin (1999) suggests that early childhood (from weaning or eruption of the first permanent molars until ages of five to seven) should be distinguished from late childhood ages (five to seven until puberty) and adolescence. Several chapters in this book distinguish childhood from adolescence, but as Blurton Jones points out (Introduction to Part II), we know very little about these distinctions and their recognition in hunter-gatherer societies.

We hope that this book will encourage researchers to seek answers to questions such as these in the years ahead.

2

Hunter-Gatherer Infancy and Childhood

The !Kung and Others

Melvin Konner

In the 1970s, based on research among the !Kung San, then hunter-gatherers of northwestern Botswana, and on reviews of the ethnographic literature, some generalizations about hunter-gatherer childhood were put forward. Some features of !Kung infancy and childhood appeared to be representative of hunter-gatherers as described by ethnographers, a set of generalizations that may be called the hunter-gatherer childhood (HGC) model. These descriptions, along with more quantitative studies of !Kung infancy and childhood, suggested that present-day child care methods are discordant with those in the human environments of evolutionary adaptedness (EEAs), a discordance that could have developmental implications. Viewed against the phylogenetic background of the parental care patterns of higher primates, it also seemed possible that the HGC model was a species-specific instance of a general pattern characteristic of catarrhines. In addition, some specific theories of development were addressed. For example, the intensity of the mother-infant relationship among the !Kung and some other hunter-gatherers was viewed as supporting John Bowlby's model of the role of attachment in infancy.

However, excellent new research on hunter-gatherer infancy and childhood on the Agta, Efe, Hadza, Aka, and Ache called some of these generalizations into question. As much as or more than the !Kung research, these studies were methodologically sophisticated and focused on infancy and childhood. At the same time, new theory in life history evolution strongly suggested that hunter-gatherer childhood should not follow a single pattern but should adjust itself to widely varying ecological conditions (Belsky 1997; Chisholm 1993, 1999; Hrdy 1997, 1999); infant and child care should be facultative, not obligatory, adaptations. This may be called the childhood as facultative adaptation or CFA model. It challenged the HGC model and the discordance hypothesis, questioning whether there is anything distinctive about hunter-gatherer childhood as a general adaptation. If correct, it could also undermine the claim that hunter-gatherer childhood supports the validity of specific theories of development, for example Bowlby's theory.

The CFA model is highly consistent with recent advances in natural selection (neo-Darwinian) theory applied to life histories. All life involves compromises and trade-offs, some that appear abhorrent to modern observers. Mothers in all species have many competing demands on their energy that mitigate their investment in individual offspring, notably the demands of other offspring and the mother's own prospect for future reproduction (Hrdy 1999). Infanticide at or near the time of birth has long been known as a choice sometimes exercised by mothers in traditional societies, including hunter-gatherers. Among the !Kung, for example, it was reported in about 1 percent of births (Nancy Howell 1979), with the stated goal of enhancing the quality of care and survival of existing children and to avoid caring for seriously defective children, almost certain to fail. Some hunter-gatherers may have used it to bias the sex ratio in favor of males, a practice strongly correlated with the percentage contribution of males to the calorie content of the diet (Hewlett 1991a). Birth spacing and children's contribution to subsistence are other features of hunter-gatherer childhood now clearly in the realm of partly facultative adaptations (Blurton Jones 1993; Hill and Hurtado 1996).

Nevertheless, as pointed out by Tinbergen, there are two kinds of evolutionary causes of any character (Tinbergen 1963): (1) adaptation through natural selection in the environment of evolutionary adaptedness, and (2) constraints on the organism's solutions to adaptive challenges due to its phylogenetic history (Maynard Smith et al. 1985). If the monkey and ape background to hominid evolution entailed a consistent pattern of care of infants and juveniles, one would expect it to have coevolved with aspects of normal or optimal development that might have become dependent on it. If so, this would presumably limit the range of facultative adaptations easily achieved in human evolution, or at least the range achieved without developmental consequences.

This chapter has three purposes. First, it reviews what was actually claimed in the 1970s and 1980s based on the !Kung research and surveys of the older literature, against the background of well-studied higher primates, with some reference to more recent analyses of !Kung data. Second, it reviews the newer hunter-gatherer studies and the challenges presented to the HGC model by this research. Third, it considers whether the HGC model has any remaining validity.

!KUNG INFANCY AND CHILDHOOD

By the 1950s, ethnographers described !Kung infants as having extremely close physical relationships with their mothers and being highly indulged in every way. !Kung childhood and adolescence were said to be relatively carefree and the child group played a key role in socialization after infancy. Physical punishment was rare. Extensive observational research on infancy and childhood supported these generalizations. The results, described in papers published in the 1970s and 1980s, may be summarized as follows.

Nursing Pattern. !Kung infants were breast-fed whenever they fretted and often at other times. In dawn-to-dusk observations, nursing occurred for a few minutes at a time, several times an hour, throughout the waking hours (Konner and Worthman 1980). A sample of 45 infants observed with a higher-resolution procedure—15-minute observations divided into 5-second time blocks—confirmed the pattern. The percentage of 15-minute periods without nursing was less than 25 percent throughout the first 80 weeks of life, even though the observations were never begun during nursing.

In a separate set of observations, 17 mother-infant pairs with infants aged 12–139 weeks (mean = 63.9, s.e. = 9.9) were studied for 6 hours in three 2-hour sessions on separate days, from 0830 to 1030, 1230 to 1430, and 1630 to 1830 hours, with nursing bouts recorded to the nearest 30 seconds (Konner and Worthman 1980). Overall mean values were: nursing bouts per hour, mean = 4.06, s.e. = 0.41; total nursing per hour, mean = 7.83 minutes, s.e. = 1.27; bout length, mean = 1.92 minutes, s.e. = 0.18; average time between bouts, mean = 13.9 minutes, s.e. = 1.28; and longest time between bouts, mean = 55.16 minutes, s.e. = 3.79. Bout length and total nursing time were independent of infant's age, but age strongly predicted the interval between nursing bouts ($r = .71$, two-tail $p < .005$).

Weaning and Birth Spacing. Traditionally the modal weaning age was during the fourth year (Konner 1977). This was observed prospectively and confirmed by cross-sectional data on the number of infants and children at each age who had not yet been weaned at the time they were first contacted. Weaning was gradual and generally took place some time during the mother's next pregnancy, usually being completed well before the birth. If there was no next sibling, nursing could continue until after age five, in one case (at very low frequency) as late as age eight. Supplementary feeding, including premasticated food, began around six months. Weaning did not involve punishment or abrupt cessation of nursing, but weaning conflict could be severe, involving protest and depressed behavior for weeks to months. Retrospective interviews of adult women showed that memories of weaning and the attendant sibling rivalry could be a lifelong psychological theme (Shostak 1981). Still, some children were weaned easily.

Sleeping Arrangements and Night Nursing.   No quantitative observations were done at night, but qualitative observation and interviews showed that it was apparently universal for !Kung infants to sleep with their mothers on the same skin mat at least until weaning. Of 21 mothers nursing infants as old as three years, 20 reported waking to nurse at least once each night, and all stated that their infants nursed without waking them up from two to "many" times or "all night." It was shown that this pattern of highly frequent nursing during the day supplemented by nursing several times a night could explain hormonal changes reducing fertility (Konner and Worthman 1980; Stern et al. 1986). It was suggested that this pattern and departures from it might influence lactation success or failure, infant digestive distress, sleeping pattern, blood glucose dynamics, milk composition, and maternal mood and attitude toward nursing.

Physical Contact.   The !Kung were described as having very high levels of skin-to-skin physical contact in infancy, the great majority with the mother: "[!Kung] newborns . . . are carried in a sling which keeps them upright and pressed against the mother's side. No clothing separates the infant's skin from his mother's" (p. 290). Quantitative data based on spot observations showed "a gradual decline in passive physical contact with the mother from a high of about 70 percent in the first months to about 30 percent in the middle of the second year" (Konner 1976a:224) with a peak at about 15 weeks. A second graph of passive physical contact with *anyone* in the same spot observations showed a peak of about 90 percent between 10 and 20 weeks, declining to about 42 percent in the mid-second year. A third paper (Konner 1976b) analyzed passive physical contact within the 15-minute observations, finding patterns quite similar to the results from the spot observations. It also broke down the overall physical contact into maternal, nonmaternal, and child components, as discussed below.

Nonphysical Interactions.   While traditional societies use more physical contact and more indulgent nursing practices, industrial societies might compensate with distal communication. For example, in a comparison of mother-infant interaction in Boston with that in a Guatemalan Indian village, the total number of interactions was roughly equal, but in Guatemala about 80 percent of the interactions were physical while in Boston about 80 percent were vocal (Klein et al. 1977; Sellars 1973). But this is not a generally applicable pattern of difference between modernized and traditional societies. The Guatemalan data were compared with data on interaction among the !Kung collected by a very similar method (Konner 1977). The Boston data, also obtained by the same method, showed that professional-class infants had somewhat more verbal interaction than did working-class infants (Tulkin 1977), but the cross-cultural comparison showed that the Guatemalan infants received much less verbal stimulation than even the Boston working class (4 as opposed to 10 percent of observed five-second blocks contained a caregiver vocalization). !Kung observations, however, showed levels of infant vocalization, caretaker vocalization, and reciprocal vocalization equal to those of the Boston working class (Konner 1977).

Overall Indulgence.   Ethnographers had described the !Kung as exceptionally indulgent in infant and child care. Cross-cultural comparison confirmed this; punishment, especially physical punishment, was rare in infancy and early childhood and uncommon in later childhood. Parents were described as generous and undemanding in almost all aspects of child life and behavior.

One aspect of !Kung indulgence, responsiveness to crying, has been carefully studied. Early papers emphasized the prompt and reliable response to crying in !Kung infants (Konner 1972), with a level of response to spontaneous fret/cry of 78 percent during the 8- to 12-month period (Konner 1977). More detailed analyses of !Kung infant crying showed that while !Kung infants displayed the "normal crying curve" with a peak in the first three months, and also had the same number of crying bouts as infants in a Dutch sample, they had shorter crying bouts and their total crying duration was about half that of Dutch infants (Barr et al. 1991). These analyses confirmed that responsiveness is very high, and the investigators explained the difference in cry/fret duration by reference to differences in caregiving, including physical contact and responsiveness to crying. (Further analysis of response to crying is presented in the next section.)

Nonmaternal Care.   This section reviews what was said about care given by !Kung women other than the mother. The role of the father and relations with other children are reviewed separately below. These observations are of interest because the !Kung have often been misrepresented as having almost exclusive maternal care. The first paper (Konner 1972), in a section titled "The Milieu of Development in the First Year," said of !Kung infants,

> From their position on the mother's hip they have available to them her entire social world. . . . When the mother is standing, the infant's face is just at the eye-level of desperately maternal 10-to-12-year-old girls who frequently approach and initiate brief, intense, face-to-face interactions,

including mutual smiling and vocalization. When not in the sling they are
passed from hand to hand around a fire for similar interactions with one
adult or child after another. They are kissed on their faces, bellies, genitals,
sung to, bounced, entertained, encouraged, even addressed at length in conversational tones long before they can understand words. Throughout the
first year there is rarely any dearth of such attention and love. (p. 292)

A subsequent paper (Konner 1976b) attempted to quantify nonmaternal
care, and Figures 2.1 and 2.2 are drawn from that paper. Figure 2.1a shows
the total time in physical contact with anyone. Figure 2.1b stratifies this contact by percentage contribution of mothers, nonmothers, and children as a
subset of nonmothers. Both graphs also plot the corresponding results of

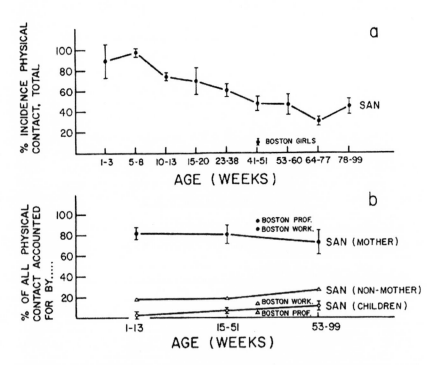

Figure 2.1.   a) Percentage of 5-second time blocks during continuous time-
     sequence observations in which infoant and caretaker were observed to be
     in physical contact, mean and standard error. For San each dot represents
     6 infants, for Boston girls, 60. b) Percentage of physical contact time blocks
     accounted for by various categories of individuals, mean and standard
     error. For San each dot or triangle represents 18, for each Boston socioec-
     nomic class, 30. From Konner, M., "Infants and Juveniles in Comparative
     Perspective," in Lewis, M. and Rosenblum, L.A., eds., *Friendship and Peer
     Relations,* New York: John Wiley and Sons, 1975.

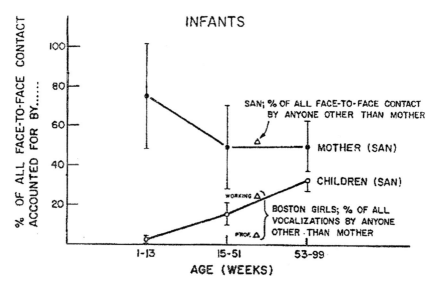

Figure 2.2. Distribution of face-to-face interaction between !Kung San infants and different categories of individuals. Mean and standard error. From Konner, M., "Infants and Juveniles in Comparative Perspective," in Lewis, M. and Rosenblum, L.A., eds., *Friendship and Peer Relations*, New York: John Wiley and Sons, 1975.

Steven Tulkin's study of ten-month-old girls in Boston, using very similar methods (Tulkin and Kagan 1972; Tulkin 1977). !Kung mothers accounted for 75-80 percent of all physical contact infants received, with no significant change over the first 20 months. However, it was emphasized that

> the percentage of all physical contacts with anyone *other* than the mother (20 to 25%) is higher than that of either class in Boston. This means that in spite of the extremely close relation to the mother, the infant also has a closer relation to others, getting proportionately more contact with others than do Boston infants. (p. 113)

Figure 2.2 shows the distribution of face-to-face contact, which suggests a much higher level of nonmaternal involvement, although the standard errors are large. For the first three months, mothers accounted for about 75 percent of face-to-face contact, but this declined to 50 percent thereafter and remained at that level well into the second year.

The same paper from which these figures were taken also reported data on !Kung two- to five-year-olds and a comparison sample in London, originally reported separately and more extensively (Blurton Jones and Konner 1973). !Kung children, especially boys ($p < .01$; girls $p < .10$), ranged a greater maximum distance from their mothers even though the London children were observed in safe, familiar outdoor spaces in good weather. !Kung children were face-to-face with mothers less and nurtured less by mothers or anyone else than London children (all significant for both sexes at $p < .02$ or better), suggesting that strong maternal dependency did not persist into childhood. A subsequent paper (Konner 1977) proposed an explanation in terms of the density of social context, citing comparative experimental data on nonhuman primates:

> The dense social context, by providing ample alternative stimulation for both mothers and infants, improves the likelihood that mothers will accept the dependent demands of infants. Paradoxically, this results in decreased proximity seeking and other dependent demands at later ages. (p. 318)

Although the last inference may not be justified, it emphasized the importance of a highly social context for the !Kung mother-infant relationship. A new analysis of responsiveness to crying in !Kung infants' crying bouts in the original data set shows clearly that nonmothers, especially other adult women, play a prominent role (Kruger and Konner, 2002). !Kung babies cried, at the most, for about one minute per hour, mainly in bouts of ten seconds or less. Eighty-eight percent of all cry bouts received a response, and almost all the others resolved within ten seconds. Responses occurred at the rate of one for every three seconds of crying, the most typical being oral or tactile comforting.

This analysis supports the claim that the caregiving environment of !Kung infants is sensitive and indulgent, but it also offers a nuanced picture of nonmaternal care. !Kung mothers provided significantly more frequent comforting responses (excluding nursing) than did all others combined. Only mothers used nursing as a response, and it was most likely at the younger ages. Finally, the mother always responded to long crying bouts (≥30 seconds), and for half of these she was the sole responder. Still, the !Kung mother was almost never alone with a crying baby. On her own, she accounted for only about half of the bout-based responsiveness rate: 46 percent of bouts were responded to by mother alone, while 88 percent of the total received some response. Thus for nearly half the bouts other caregivers either were the sole responders or joined the mother in responding. Even when others did not respond to the cry bout, they were nearly always present and offering care to the baby, sometimes as the primary attendant, at some point during a 90 minute observation set. In summary, the mother was by far the most frequent individual responder to crying and was most responsible for soothing an upset baby, but others made major contributions to the degree, timeliness, and consistency of the response.

Father Care and Involvement.   An early paper stated, "Fathers account for a greater proportion of vocalizations to infants during the first 3 months (10%) than do American fathers" (Konner 1976:114)). The comparison was with a study in Boston (Rebelsky and Hanks 1971) that kept a microphone in cribs around the clock and estimated the average amount of vocalization by fathers to three-month-olds to be 37 seconds per 24-hour period. Thus !Kung fathers were described as both less involved than mothers and more involved than Western fathers. A chapter focused on !Kung paternal care in two editions of the same book (Katz and Konner 1981; West and Konner 1976) said,

> Since fathers . . . are often available . . . their potential contact with in-
> fants and children is high. They often hold and fondle even the youngest in-
> fants, though they return them to the mother whenever they cry and for all
> forms of routine care. Young children frequently go to them, touch them, talk
> to them and request food from them, and such approaches are almost never
> rebuffed. Boys are not expected to become involved in hunting activity until
> early adolescence at the soonest and then follow their fathers and uncles on
> hunts for years before being able to conduct hunts themselves. Information
> transfer on such hunts has an "observational learning" rather than a "teach-
> ing" character. . . . Traditional male initiation rites involve making boys
> dance in the cold for a few days, frightening them in the dark, and making
> small cuts on their foreheads to signify their accession to manhood. (Katz
> and Konner, 1981, p. 167)

This sketch was one of five drawn to show the range of father involvement in nonindustrial societies in the ethnographic record. The paper noted
that "the !Kung are classified by Barry and Paxson as 'high' on closeness of
fathers to infants and young children in the sample of non-industrial societies surveyed. They thus represent the upper end of the range of direct
male care of offspring seen in the ethnographic record." (n = 80 societies,
Barry and Paxson 1971; Katz and Konner, 1981, p. 177).

The data on infants came from 15-minute observations marked in continuous five-second time blocks, as described above. Forty-three infants
were observed six times at from one to four age points, throughout the
daylight hours and throughout the year. Criteria for observation onset
were that the infant was awake, not in the sling, not nursing, and within
fifteen feet of the mother. Father availability was not a criterion. Data on
the number and percentage of observations of boys and girls in two age
groups in which fathers interacted with the infant at all were analyzed.
Overall father participation for the sexes and ages combined was 13.7 percent. Fathers were more likely to interact with boys than girls at the older
age only ($\chi^2 = 4.61$, $p < .05$).

Since observation onset was contingent on the mother's presence, the comparison was biased against fathers, but it showed that randomly distributed 15-minute time samples would have about a 90 percent chance of finding interaction between mother and infant, compared with 13.7 percent for fathers. However, the density of interaction within the 15 minutes is also much greater for mothers than for fathers. Table 2.1 shows the amount of interaction and its breakdown by type of proximity, with boys and girls combined. Shown are the average number of five-second time blocks in which father or mother were the primary caregivers, and whether they were face-to-face, in physical contact, within two feet, and more than two feet away from the infant. For the father, figures for all observations and for only those in which he is present are shown separately.

Father participation, defined as father score divided by combined parental score, was 2.3 percent for younger and 6.3 percent for older infants. Although the differences in total participation are very large, the distribution of caregiving among the four proximity types was remarkably similar, including a parallel decrease with age in the proportion of physical contact, even though only mothers nursed or cleaned infants. In a different data set, the father was present in 30 percent of observations on !Kung two- to six-year-olds, as opposed to 19 percent in parallel observations made in London (Blurton Jones and Konner 1973).

To place these findings in cross-cultural perspective, a study of 3- to 11-year-olds in six cultures including the United States showed father presence ranging from 3 to 14 percent, with 9 percent in the United States (Whiting and Whiting 1975). While these data are not really comparable due to the larger age range, !Kung fathers did seem to be closer than fathers in other subsistence types. This was underscored by several other comparisons, discussed below.

Table 2.1 Mean Number of 5-Second Blocks Parent Was Primary Caregiver, by Proximity

	Father (all observations)	Father (when present)	Mother (always present)
Age: 0–26 weeks			
Physical contact	3.80	43.27	123.46
Face-to-face	0.74	8.46	11.56
Within 2 feet	0.09	1.07	10.54
2 to 15 feet	0.00	0.00	11.00
Age: 27–99 weeks			
Physical contact	3.85	32.13	58.41
Face-to-face	0.25	1.43	3.69
Within 2 feet	2.26	13.00	32.91
2 to 15 feet	0.77	4.41	8.38

Relations with Children.   During the second half of the second year, toddlers began to play with other, mainly older, children, and an early paper was devoted to these relationships (Konner 1976). It was emphasized that given the modal group size of around 30, peer groups in the strict sense—groups of children the same age and sex—were very unlikely and indeed were not observed. Play groups almost always consisted of both sexes and a range of ages. Among the adaptive functions suggested for these play groups were facilitating relationships in two- to five-year-olds (bypassing the commonly observed Western developmental pattern of parallel play), socialization of younger children, practice of caregiving by older children, and lightening the mother's burden of child care.

Carefree Childhood.   There were also extensive studies of older children by Draper and others (Draper 1972, 1976; Marshall 1976). Children were not assigned tasks of any economic importance nor were they expected to feed themselves by foraging, although they often did. They played in mixed-age, mixed-sex groups that meandered around the village-camp or the surrounding bush. Draper studied the assignment of responsibility to children as it relates to subsistence ecology, and she showed that children in more !Kung groups were given more tasks, while traditional !Kung children were among the most responsibility-free in the cross-cultural range. Nevertheless, descriptions of child groups noted that although

> the principal concern of the group is always play. . . . This may and typically does include . . . play at subsistence, which however playful, may produce food. . . . It invariably includes also, though incidentally, protection and care and teaching of infants and children by older children. (Konner 1976)

Thus the relatively carefree life of !Kung children included a limited amount of useful work.

Adolescent Sexuality.   Adolescence was treated in a chapter that emphasized the reproductive experience of girls (Konner and Shostak 1986), but the relevant demographic facts had already been established (Howell 1979). Prospective study of menarche (marked by a dramatic ritual) gave a mean age of 16.6 and a median of 17.1 years, with the majority passing this milestone between 16 and 18 (p. 178), by which time about half were married. Careful retrospective study of women who were 45 years old or older in 1968 estimated the age at first birth at a mean of 18.8 and a median of 19.2 years, with all but a handful of mothers having had their first births between ages 17 and 22 (p. 128). (Completed fertility determined retrospectively was 4.7 live births, with a mean age of last birth in the middle thirties.)

Playful experimentation with sex began in early childhood and continued through middle childhood (Konner and Shostak 1986; Shostak 1981).
Since children did not assume responsibility for subsistence until the late
teens and their play groups were frequently out of sight of adults, sexual
curiosity flourished. Adults did not approve of sexual play and when it became obvious they discouraged it, usually by verbal chastisement with no
real consequences. Interviews with adults revealed that they considered
sexual experimentation in childhood and adolescence to be inevitable and
normal. For adults, sexual activity was considered essential for mental
health, and !Kung sometimes referred to mentally ill people (for example,
a woman who ate grass) as deranged because of sexual deprivation.

Despite childhood sexual experimentation, the transition from the sexual play of childhood to the real sex of adulthood could be difficult, especially for girls. Half were married before menarche (16.5 years), typically
to men about ten years older. Thus a teenage girl was confronted with the
sexual advances of an adult man after having had prior experience only
with boys her own age. These advances were supposed to be delayed
until menarche, but the transition from sex play with age-mates to adult
sex could be stressful (Shostak 1981). The years from age 16.5, when first
menstruation occurred, to age 19, the mean age at first birth—a delay due
mainly to adolescent subfertility—were important ones. The young
woman was sexually mature but did not have to care for a family and
made little contribution to subsistence. She could gradually adopt adult
roles and adult sexuality without having to deal with the consequences of
early pregnancy.

THE GENERALIZED HGC MODEL AND
THE EVIDENCE FOR DISCORDANCE

A review attempted to set the !Kung findings in phylogenetic context
among the primates, to evaluate evidence in the older literature for similar
patterns in other hunter-gatherers (i.e., other EEAs) and to assess possible
changes since the hunter-gatherer era that might be viewed as discordant
(Konner 1981). The review stressed that there were many gaps in the
data, and that changes from the higher primate background to the hunter-
gatherer pattern were likely to be largely genetic, while subsequent
changes would be overwhelmingly cultural.

Hunting-gathering was defined to exclude equestrian hunting as a recent historical development and greater emphasis was placed on warm-
climate hunter-gatherers as more representative of the EEAs. No cases were
excluded for other reasons, such as a history of contact with non-hunter-
gatherers. There were at that time no other systematic studies of hunter-

gatherer infancy and childhood besides that of the !Kung. Nevertheless there were fairly detailed accounts of infancy and childhood that accorded with the !Kung findings (e.g., Turnbull 1965; Holmberg 1969; Balikci 1970). In addition to these isolated supporting instances, there was cross-cultural survey research on child training practices, much of this research organized and summarized up to the 1960s (Textor 1967). Random perusal of Textor's summary is methodologically unsound (it is essentially a compendium of all significant relationships among variables derived from all previous quantitative cross-cultural research), but deliberate hypothesis testing carries less risk of improper rejection of the null hypothesis.

The hypothesis that hunting-gathering societies resembled the !Kung in infant and child care more than did other nonindustrial societies was supported by this examination. The variables assessed in older studies were not always the most relevant in current terms. Still, the data compiled by Textor showed a consistent tendency for societies relying on food gathering to have more indulgent infant and child training practices than other nonindustrial societies.

Specifically, "pain inflicted on infant" was lower ($p < .05$), while "overall indulgence of infant" ($p < .05$) and the ease and lateness of toilet training ("anal satisfaction potential"; $p < .01$) were rated as higher in societies subsisting primarily by food gathering ($19 \leq n \leq 40$) than in those subsisting by other means ($22 \leq n \leq 34$). In childhood, "anxiety over responsible behavior" ($p < .01$), "anxiety over obedient behavior" ($p < .01$), and "anxiety over self-reliant behavior" ($p < .05$) were rated as lower in food gathering ($30 \leq n \leq 35$) than in other societies ($37 \leq n \leq 42$). Only at adolescence, when "female initiation rites" ($p < .01$) were found to be more severe in foraging societies ($n = 38$) than in nonforaging ones ($n = 27$), was the pattern of indulgence reversed. Also, adolescent peer groups were less common ($p < .05$) in foraging ($n = 23$) than in nonforaging societies ($n = 14$), consistent with other findings and demographic predictions indicating the unlikelihood of same-age peer groups at any time during childhood in hunting-gathering societies. (For citations of the specific cross-cultural studies relied on by Textor, see his volume or Konner 1981, note 6.)

Another study, focused on infancy (Lozoff and Brittenham 1978), compared ten warm-climate hunting-gathering societies with 176 other nonindustrial societies on infant care practices rated by Barry and Paxson (1971) The ten (!Kung San, Hadza, Mbuti, Semang, Vedda, Tiwi, Siriono, Botocudo, Shavante, and Chenchu) were all those that met the criteria of living between the latitudes of 22°30' N and 22°30' S, and having less than 10 percent dependence on agriculture, animal husbandry, and fishing for their subsistence, as coded by Murdock and Morrow (1970). Very close mother-infant contact, late weaning, and indulgent responsiveness to infant crying were highly characteristic of the hunting-gathering groups. Late weaning was also found in other nonindustrial societies, and the mother was always the principal caregiver in infancy, but other aspects of the mother-infant bond were closer and more indulgent in hunter-gatherers.

In addition, whether measured by body contact, sleeping distance, response to crying, or weaning age, mother-infant contact and maternal indulgence of infants were lower in the United States than in the 176 nonindustrial cultures. This supported a previous finding (Whiting and Child 1953) that patterns of infant and child training in Chicago during the 1940s were substantially below the median in indulgence for a large representative sample of nonindustrial societies (including hunter-gatherers), except in the area of aggressiveness training, where Chicago was more indulgent. In "oral socialization," "anal socialization," sex and modesty training, and independence training, parents in Chicago were considered very strict or at least more strict than the average nonindustrial society.

The range of variability in intermediate-level societies (those relying primarily on horticulture, agriculture, animal husbandry, and/or fishing) was much greater than that for hunting-gathering societies or industrial societies, and they constitute the great majority of the empirical base on which cultural anthropology rests. Variation in child-care practices is not random with respect to basic mode of subsistence and ecological situation. For example, Textor compared cultures that were large or small states with those in which the highest level of political integration is the minimal state, autonomous community, or family (Textor 1967).

Like the earlier-mentioned comparison (foraging vs. nonforaging societies), this one suggested a trend in the cultural evolution of child care. The hypothesis of decreasing indulgence with increasing political complexity was confirmed on six measures of infant and child care comparable to the ones mentioned in the foraging-nonforaging comparison. In addition, three other variables relating to child life showed significant differences. Punishment of premarital sex was more severe in 89 more complex than in 90 less complex societies ($p < .001$). Exclusive mother-child households (father sleeps elsewhere, no extended family) were more likely in more complex societies ($p < .001$). Paradoxically, desire for children was higher in more complex societies,[1] where indulgence of children was lower.

This appeared to be consistent with what was thought to be the higher birth rate of agricultural societies, but an excellent cross-cultural study by Hewlett (1991a) called this difference into question. Although in the expected direction, the higher fertility and lower infant mortality in agricultural and pastoral societies are not statistically significant. Even small differences could account for Neolithic population expansion, but not substantial differences in infant and child care. However, Hewlett found that hunter-gatherers were more likely to have multiple caregiving than horticultural and pastoral cultures, due to the greater population density (compactness) of the immediate settlement. He confirmed that hunter-gatherer group size makes them more likely to have multiage child play groups and cited other cross-cultural research showing that fathers are more involved with infants and children among hunter-gatherers and on islands, apparently because male-male competition is low (Alcorta 1982; Hewlett 1991a).

PHYLOGENETIC RECONSTRUCTION OF SELECTED CHILD-CARE VARIABLES

Based on the then available literature, an attempt was made to reconstruct the higher primate and human cultural background to infant and child-care practices (Konner 1981). Hypothetical sketches characterized the evolution of parental care based on studies of higher primates (monkeys and apes), human hunter-gatherers, intermediate-level (nonindustrial, nonforaging) societies, and industrial societies. Data on contemporaneous patterns led to inferences about sequences, with all the usual reservations about that strategy. The higher primate picture was confirmed in reviews by others (Martin 1995; McKenna 1981, 1987; Pereira and Fairbanks 1993).

1. Physical Contact with Mother and Others

Mammals vary in mother-infant physical contact (Blurton Jones 1972). "Cache" vs. "carry" alludes to two of the options, distinguishing mammals that hide their infants while mothers forage (e.g., some ungulates, rabbits, and tree shrews) from those in which infants cling to their mothers or are carried (marsupials, bats, and most primates). A third category, following, involves low direct physical contact but high proximity. Nonhuman higher primates without exception (whether or not tarsiers are included) maintain continuous physical contact with infants in the first weeks of life; except in marmosets, the mother accounts for most of this contact. There is a gradual decline in physical contact over the course of the first weeks to months, depending on the pace of development in a given species.

Although the !Kung data reported above come mainly from out-of-the-sling observations (underestimating total physical contact), carrying devices afford an approach to assessing physical contact cross-culturally that can be used with older ethnographies (Whiting 1971). Variations include (1) almost constant carrying in a sling at the mother's side, back, or front, with or without direct skin contact; (2) some carrying alternating with time in a crib, cradle, or hammock, or on a blanket on the ground or floor; and (3) very little or no carrying, with infant tied in a cradleboard or swaddled tightly. (Cradleboard-bound or swaddled infants can also be carried, without skin-to-skin contact.) These variations were related to ecological conditions, especially climate. Forty out of 48 cultures in the tropics (between latitude 20° N and 20° S) had close and frequent physical contact, usually with carrying devices, whereas 29 out of 37 societies outside those latitudes used heavy swaddling or cradleboards, regardless of continental location.

Based on these data, Whiting argued that hunting-and-gathering is neither necessary nor sufficient for carrying in close physical contact. However, the two exceptions to the rule about cold-climate societies are the Eskimo and the Yahgan of Patagonia, both nonmounted, "classical" hunter-gatherers with close contact. Hunting-gathering may thus be a sufficient condition for close contact but not a necessary one. In any case, since the great majority of human evolution took place in tropical regions, the inference that early humans had close physical contact, probably using a sling for carrying, remains sound, while intermediate-level societies cover the range from close contact in a sling to little or no contact in a tightly tied cradleboard. It is likely that the two variables of level of subsistence organization and, perhaps more important, ambient temperature together explain much of the variation in carrying method. Perhaps leaving behind the hunting-gathering mode of subsistence permitted, but did not cause, a decrease in direct contact using a sling as the main carrying method.

Until the recent reintroduction of the baby carrier, the Western infant was kept horizontal in a baby carriage or pram or reclining in a stroller, and experienced fewer motor challenges, less tactile and vestibular stimulation, less direct maternal contact, and less vertical posture compared to young infants in hunter-gatherer societies (Konner 1977). The widespread use of baby carriers, including sling- or pouchlike devices, beginning in the late 20th century may be a partial return to ancestral patterns, although without the high levels of skin-to-skin contact characteristic of hunter-gatherers.

2. Nursing Frequency

Mammals may be divided by feeding type into two groups, "continual" vs. "spaced" feeders (Ben Shaul 1962; Blurton Jones 1972; Ewer 1968). Continual feeders' infants cling to their mothers (most primates, bats, and marsupials) or follow them (the most precocial ungulates). Spaced feeders leave their infants in nests (tree-shrews and rabbits) or in movable caches (eland and certain other ungulates). Milk composition (Ben Shaul 1962) and sucking rate (Wolff 1968) are correlated with spacing of feeds; continual feeders have more dilute milk, with lower fat and protein content, and suck slowly. Spaced feeders have more concentrated milk and suck faster. Lipid and protein composition and sucking rates of higher primates, including humans, is consistent with their classification as continual feeders. This was shown to be true for most monkeys (Horwich 1974), chimpanzees (Clark 1977), and human hunter-gatherers. All of the latter for whom observations were available were reported to nurse at least twice an hour.

In intermediate-level societies, the range of variation is great. While feeding frequency following the !Kung pattern occurs in some cultures, in others this is precluded by the organization of subsistence activities, notably mother's work load (Nerlove 1974; B. Whiting 1963, 1972; Whiting and Edwards 1988; Whiting and Whiting 1975). In many intermediate-level societies the organization of work necessarily results in daily mother-infant separations of several hours, precluding very frequent nursing. For example, among the Kikuyu of Kenya the mother might work in the garden part of the day, leaving her infant with a girl or young woman (often an older sibling of the infant), in the home village compound (Leiderman and Leiderman 1977).

Mothers in the industrialized West have long been spaced feeders. Differences between "demand" and "scheduled" (three- or four-hourly) feeding bouts are of minor interest in this context, since in American homes "demand" feeding sorted itself out to about six 4-hourly feeds a day in the mid-20th century (Aldrich and Hewitt 1947) and about three hours in more recent decades—far from the meaning of demand feeding among hunter-gatherers. Even if there are no long-term psychological effects of the change from frequent to spaced feeding, it would be useful to know the effects on infant feeding difficulty, colic, sleep-activity cycles, and blood glucose dynamics, as well as on maternal mood, sustained milk production, and likelihood of conception, all largely unknown (but see Stern 1986). In view of the marked suppression of gonadal hormone secretion in !Kung nursing women, with the degree of suppression a function of time between nursing bouts (Konner and Worthman 1980), there may be a prolactin-mediated, timing-dependent suppression of gonadal function by nipple stimulation (Stern et al. 1986). This would help to account for frequent conception during breast-feeding in modern populations.

3. Age at Weaning

In most higher primates, weaning follows the onset of pregnancy. In many Old World monkeys this occurs at about a year of age, although in baboons (larger and slower developing) it is usually two years (DeVore 1965). In chimpanzees (Clark 1977; Goodall 1986) and in at least some human hunter-gatherers (Konner 1972, 1977) it occurs at about four years. In most monkey species the age at weaning is one-fourth to one-third the age at sexual maturity for females (Martin 1990; Schultz 1963, 1969; Tanner 1962). However, the great apes have significantly later weaning ages and longer birth spacing than human hunter-gatherers, a difference probably due to the unique (among primates) human trait of provisioning juveniles with food after weaning (Lancaster and Lancaster 1983, 1987). It has been suggested that earlier weaning in early humans became possible when bone marrow was discovered to be a suitable weaning food (Binford 1983). In many traditional cultures, "kiss-feeding" or offering premasticated food ensures that infants have the mother's germs in any case, and some antibodies, particularly IgAs, are delivered with the food, probably specific to microbes to which mother and infant have been jointly exposed. The advantage of such softened food in the weaning process, partly predigested by the mother's saliva, is probably significant, and the behavior is widely seen in intermediate-level as well as in hunting-gathering societies (Eibl-Eibesfeldt 1983, 1988).

Age at weaning in intermediate-level societies reportedly ranges from immediately after birth in the Marquesas Islands (Linton 1939) to a number of cultures that wean as late as do the !Kung. As with direct-contact carrying, leaving the hunting-gathering subsistence mode behind appears to permit rather than constrain societies to wean earlier. The relative acceptability to infants of cow's milk and cereal gruels may mediate the effect of subsistence mode on weaning age. The decline of weaning age in !Kung hunter-gatherers as they became more settled and gained access to cow's milk exemplifies this. Still, 83 percent of 176 societies in the Barry and Paxson (1971) sample that were *not* hunter-gatherers had weaning ages of two years or older. Thus weaning is late in intermediate-level societies, though perhaps not as late as in hunter-gatherers. Most of the world's settled agricultural populations have in recent times had a birth interval of two to three years, with weaning in the second year (Morley 1973:306).

In the United States in the 1970s about 10 percent of infants were breast-fed at three months of age, and about 5 percent at six months (Fomon 1974:9), as opposed to 58 percent breast-fed at a year of age during the period 1911-16 (p. 2). Similar declines and similarly low current levels were observed in Britain, Sweden, Poland, and other modern industrial countries. The developing world has seen a similar decline in breast-feeding (Fomon 1974:1-16; Morley 1973), although rates appear to have stabilized (UNICEF, 2000). The American Academy of Pediatrics (1997) has officially recommended breast-feeding for over a quarter of a century, and this has increased breast-feeding in the United States, but it has not affected the worldwide decline, especially among the poor (Corbett 2000; Guttman and Zimmerman 2000; Sellen 1998), which is almost a hallmark of modernization.

4. Sleeping Distance and Night Nursing

Mother-infant sleeping distance remains a neglected feature of the human infant's caregiving environment from the viewpoint of research, even though bedtime protest and night waking are very common (Bernal 1973; Goodlin-Jones et al. 2001; Spock and Parker 1998). In all higher primates and among hunter-gatherers for whom - ethnographic information is available, mother and infant slept in immediate proximity, if not direct physical contact. As noted above, almost all !Kung mothers reported that their infants woke up repeatedly during the night to nurse, and some additional nighttime nursing bouts usually took place while the mother slept, and it has also been shown in cosleeping American mother-infant pairs in the laboratory (McKenna et al. 1999).

However, variation in mother-infant sleeping distance is restricted in nonindustrial societies. Of 90 cultures in the Barry and Paxson (1971) sample for which information was available, mother and infant slept in the same bed in 41, in the same room with bed unspecified in 30, and in the same room in separate beds in 19. In none of the 90 did mother and infant sleep in separate rooms, a feature of the mother-infant bond that probably did not precede the industrial state.

Current Western culture derives from that of the agricultural people of northern Europe, who used cradles and swaddling extensively. Departing from the universal pattern for nonindustrial societies, Americans often have infants sleeping in separate rooms from their parents. The syndromes of bedtime protest (Spock 1976; Spock and Parker 1998) and night-waking (Bernal 1973) may be artifacts of Western sleeping arrangements (Konner and Super 1987; McKenna et al. 1993, 1999).

In any case, American middle-class sleeping arrangements are often honored in the breach as well as the observance (Rosenfeld et al. 1982). A well-known pediatrician wrote a column in the 1970s for a mass circulation national women's magazine explaining how to get infants to sleep in a separate room. Deluged with letters from women who sleep with their babies, he wrote a second column saying that this was alright too (T. B. Brazelton, personal communication). It is clear that some mothers in Western cultures have returned to the practice of cosleeping (Brazelton 1990; Hanks and Rebelsky 1977; Schacter et al. 1989; Sears and White 1999), with consequences for reproductive endocrinology as well as subsequent night-waking (Elias et al. 1986; Elias et al. 1986; Stern et al. 1986).

5. Paternal Care

Judging from the distribution of male parental behavior in monkeys and apes, it seems clear that in the ancestral parenting adaptation of higher primates, male involvement was minimal (Martin 1990). Prominent exceptions are the marmoset family (*Callitrichidae*) and the gibbon family (*Hylobatidae*), both of which independently evolved pair bonding with high levels of direct paternal care (Mitchell and Brandt 1972; Taub and Mehlman 1991; Wright 1990). In addition, there are modest but notable levels of interaction between adult males and infants in Japanese macaques (*M. fuscata*), Barbary macaques (*M. sylvanus*), olive baboons (*P. anubis*), and

Hamadryas baboons (*P. hamadryas*), although it is not clear that the inter-action is always beneficial to the infant (Hrdy 1974).

Humans have both pair bonding and relatively high father involvement for higher primates generally, but there is great cross-cultural variation. Barry and Paxson used "regular close relationship" to describe the highest level of father involvement in their cross-cultural sample (the !Kung, for ex-ample), and their criteria suggest that this was comparable to "half or less of time" on the maternal scale. Since there were few cultures with fathers in this highest category, and few with mothers in this or the next lowest cat-egory, paternal and maternal care distributions were almost nonoverlap-ping. For early childhood the overlap increased considerably. The rankings are shown in Table 2.2. If this equivalency of rankings is approximately cor-rect, then 4 percent of fathers are close to infants, compared with 98 percent of mothers. (If "mother provides half or less of care" is omitted, the respec-tive figures for mothers are 90 and 27 percent. But it is highly likely that most infants in the "half or less" category had "regular close relationships" with mothers.) In early childhood 9 percent of fathers are close, compared with 66 percent of mothers. In this spectrum !Kung fathers are close. It was also possible to stratify the closeness of father-infant relationships by sub-sistence ecology, as shown in Table 2.3.

The closeness of fathers in horticultural societies suggests that the divi-sion of labor is important; where women provide the most subsistence fa-thers are called into play. There appears to be a divergence among foraging societies, with gathering strongly predisposing fathers toward closeness,

Table 2.2 Percentage of Cultures by Ranked Level of Parent-Child Proximity

%		Role of Father	%		Role of Mother
Infancy					
5	1	no close proximity			(No rough equivalent)
15	2	rare proximity	0	7	Practically all care is by others
37	3	occasional proximity	0	6	Most care except nursing by others
39	4	frequent proximity	2	5	Mother's role is significant but . . .
4	5	regular close relationship	8	4	Mother provides half or less of care
			44	3	Principally mother, others imp't roles
			43	2	Principally mother, others minor roles
			3	1	Almost exclusively the mother
Early Childhood					
1	1	no close proximity			(No rough equivalent)
11	2	rare proximity			(No rough equivalent)
19	3	occasional proximity	2	5	Practically all time away from mother
60	4	frequent proximity	33	4	Majority of time away from mother
9	5	regular close relationship	39	3	Half or less time with mother
			27	2	Principally mother, others imp't
			0	1	Almost exclusively mother

Source: Data from Barry and Paxson (1971).

Table 2.3   Father-Infant Proximity and Primary Mode of Subsistence

	Father-Infant Proximity	
Primary Mode of Subsistence	*Distant*	*Close*
Gathering	1	7
Hunting	3	0
Fishing	6	4
Herding	4	1
Simple agriculture	12	6
Horticulture	3	10
Advanced agriculture	16	6

hunting predisposing toward distance (although $n = 3$), and fishing about equally divided. Lozoff and Brittenham (1978), using a smaller sample of hunting-gathering societies, found them to have closer father-infant and father-child contact than other nonindustrial societies. The discrepancy may be due to the type of hunting prevailing in cultures that depend predominantly on this subsistence mode.

MODELS OF HIGHER PRIMATE AND HUNTER-GATHERER CHILDHOOD

The Catarrhine Mother-Infant Complex.   It appeared that old world monkeys and apes had certain features of the maternal relationship in common. These features are listed in Table 2.4. It gradually became apparent that there were important species differences in some of these measures. For example, even within the macaque genus (*Macaca* spp.) the response to separation varied from severe (rhesus, *M. rhesus*, and pigtails, *M. nemestrina*) to relatively mild (bonnets, *M. radiata*) depending on the extent of nonmaternal care (alloparenting). This feature in turn varies among the

Table 2.4   The Catarrhine Mother-Infant Complex

1. Hemochorial placenta
2. Singleton birth
3. Twenty-four-hour physical contact in first weeks
4. Twenty-four-hour proximity until weaning
5. Nursing more than three times per hour while awake
6. Night nursing until weaning
7. Weaning at around 30% of the age of first ovarian cycles
8. Separation from mother → protest
9. Isolation rearing → dysfunctional behavior

old world monkeys and apes; in some species mothers allow no allopar-enting while in others it is substantial (Hrdy 1974). Alloparenting affords the possibility of earlier weaning, shorter birth spacing, and higher repro-ductive rates (Ross and MacLarnon 2000).

Male (not necessarily paternal) involvement also varies dramatically. Barbary macaques (*M. sylvanus*) and Japanese macaques (*M. fuscata*) have a significant amount of male interaction with infants and juveniles and gib-bons (Hylobatidae) have very extensive male-infant contact and carrying. Orangutan (*Pongo pygmaeus*) infants and juveniles, in contrast, rarely en-counter adult males except for the occasional sexual tryst with their moth-ers. Most monkey and ape infants have males around most of the time, sometimes affording protection, but without significant direct interaction.

Overall, however, the model withstands scrutiny in the light of current data. Old world monkeys and apes have an exceptionally intimate pla-cental juxtaposition of maternal and fetal circulations (hemochorial pla-centa), singleton births, continuous physical contact for the first weeks or months (possibly important to the formation of the relationship; Maestrip-ieri 2001), and continuous proximity until weaning. Nursing is frequent (at least three times per hour) to continual and night nursing universal. Wean-ing occurs at one-fourth to one-third of the age at first ovarian cycling, with variation due in part to the presence or absence of alloparental care. Separation leads to protest of varying degrees of severity in many but not all species and isolation rearing produces seriously dysfunctional behav-ior in all species in which it has been studied.

The HGC Model. Humans, like Old World monkeys and apes, are ca-tarrhines, but can only be included in the complex if the M-I relationship in the human EEAs conforms to it, since departures are very evident in other ecological settings. The question of whether the M-I relationship in the EEAs can be subsumed under the general catarrhine model hinges in turn on the validity of the HGC model already discussed. This model includes, but goes substantially beyond, infancy. Table 2.5 lists the main features of the HGC model as it was proposed in the 1970s and 1980s in sources already cited.

Each feature of the model was derived from observations of the !Kung, supported by descriptive accounts of other hunter-gatherers in the older ethnographic literature. The generalizations were presented as hypotheses for further study, in the hope that others would do serious research on hunter-gatherer childhood. This hope was realized, and the recent studies have been excellent. Features 5, 8, and 11 have two asterisks, signifying an important challenge coming from this new research. Feature 6 has one as-terisk, signifying too little information in other studies to generalize. Some results of those studies will now be considered.

Table 2.5   Features of !Kung Infancy and Childhood: The Original HGC Model

1. Prolonged close physical contact with mother
2. High indulgence of dependent needs and demands
3. Frequent nursing (four times/hour) throughout waking hours
4. Mother and infant sleep on same bed or mat; night nursing
5. Weaning after age three and four-year birth spacing**
6. Strong separation and stranger protest until late ages*
7. Dense social context that seems to reduce pressure on mother
8. Nonmaternal care much less than maternal care until second year**
9. Paternal care much less than maternal care but more than most cultures
10. Transition to multiaged, mixed-gender child play group
11. Minimal childhood responsibility for subsistence or baby care**
12. Minimal restrictions on childhood or adolescent sexuality

*Too little information in other studies to generalize.
**Signifies an important challenge coming from the new research.

HUNTER-GATHERER CHILDHOOD: RECENT SCIENTIFIC STUDIES

Hadza.   The Hadza of northern Tanzania live among rocky hills near Lake Eyasi, and were about 95 percent dependent on hunting and gathering at the time of scientific study (Blurton Jones 1993; Kaare and Woodburn 1999; Woodburn 1968a). Compared to the !Kung, the Hadza environment is climatically milder and more productive of game and plant foods. Their nutrition was adequate and their population growing slowly but steadily. Researchers agree that Hadza infancy and childhood conform in some ways to the HGC model (Blurton Jones 1990, 1993; Blurton Jones et al. 1989; Marlowe, Chapter 8 in this volume):

> The Hadza child's first year of life appears not to differ greatly from that of the !Kung infant. The mother is the principal caretaker. The baby spends most of its time riding on the mother's side or back. Suckling is frequent, and often, but by no means always, "on demand." . . . The baby is likely to be surrounded by relatives, old, adult, and young, and receives attention from them and is carried by them. . . . Face-to-face interactions described in Western cultures (and in !Kung) can be seen between the Hadza mother and infant and other people and the infant. (Blurton Jones 1993:316)

Quantitative studies have confirmed these descriptions (Marlowe, Chapter 8 in this volume, Table 8.1). Mothers account for by far the largest percentage of time in interactions with infants during their first year of life, and continue to predominate over other individuals through the third year. During 30-minute focal follow observations of infants, mothers interacted with them in 78 percent of minutes, fathers and older sisters in 18 percent each, older brothers in 8 percent, maternal grandmothers in 9 percent, and others in 29 percent. (Since any number or combination of people could interact with the infant during a given minute, the percentages do not add up to 100.) During the first four years, using the same observational method, mothers interacted in 43 percent of minutes, fathers and older sisters in 17 percent, older brothers in 9 percent, maternal grandmothers in 10 percent, and others in 41 percent.

These findings resemble those of the recent analysis of !Kung response to infant crying (Kruger and Konner 2002). Since caregiver response was nonexclusive, several different people could and often did respond to a crying bout, but the mother predominated and was involved in the great majority of bouts. Similarly, the Hadza data show maternal primacy in the context of multiple caregiving. Looking at a different, more exclusive Hadza measure—who if anyone was holding the child during instantaneous hourly scan observations—only "about 30 percent of all holding of children (≤4 years old) is by someone other than mother" (Marlowe, Chapter 8 in this volume, p. 185).

Given the theoretical emphasis on grandmothers (e.g., Hawkes et al. 1998), it is surprising to find fathers interacting with infants substantially more of the time. This disparity is heightened when fathers are genetically related rather than being stepfathers, a relatively common role among the Hadza due to a substantial divorce rate (Marlowe, Chapter 8 in this volume). Where there is no genetic father, the maternal grandmother plays a larger role. Other analyses showed that fathers communicated with, played with, and nurtured their genetic children more than they did their stepchildren, and that paternal care was inversely correlated with the mating opportunities available to the father, as measured by the number of fertile or single younger women in the camp (Marlowe 1999a, 1999b).

Later childhood also shows significant parallels to the !Kung:

> Hadza children lack none of the charm and imagination of !Kung children. They have a robust humor and a pride in life that we find attractive and impressive. . . . Between the ages of 3 and 8, Hadza children seldom accompany their mothers on gathering excursions. Children over 8 may accompany their mothers, but do not always do so. . . . The children, usually in sizable mixed-age groups, may spend some hours out of camp. Sometimes they are at a favorite play site or at the water hole. (Blurton Jones 1993:316)

Sexual play is permitted in childhood and has often been observed. In adolescence, premarital sex is "routine and expected" (Frank Marlowe, personal communication, 2004), with marriage occurring around age 17 for girls and 20 for boys.

However, there are also departures from the !Kung case and the HGC model:

> Hadza are weaned a good deal younger than !Kung, at around 2.5 years old. Soon after they are 2 years old, Hadza children begin to be left behind when the mother gathers, although they may be suckled before the mother leaves camp and as soon as she returns. (p. 316)

After infancy, the most striking difference is the amount of subsistence work that Hadza children do (Blurton Jones et al. 1989, 1994b, 1997). Children play a lot, but "more often they are gathering food, independently of the women. . . . Returns . . . are substantial. . . . In the foraging groups, even 3-year-olds try their hand at digging or picking up baobab pods and processing them" (Blurton Jones 1993:316) In addition,

> unlike !Kung children, Hadza children appear to be given many errands and to perform useful tasks, bidden and unbidden. Such tasks cost the children time and energy, and sometimes expose them to the hazards of the bush. Children of either sex may be asked to hold a protesting toddler when the mother leaves camp to forage. . . . Children commonly are sent to fetch water and sometimes firewood. . . . Even toddlers are sent to carry things from one house to another. (pp. 316–317)

Finally, regarding the degree of indulgence of infants and children, Hadza researchers are of two opinions. According to Blurton Jones, "the Hadza are strikingly different" from the !Kung in the amount of punitive, prohibitive, and directive parenting. For example, "[M]others break off suckling bouts, evoking protest from the infant. One also often hears crying and observes parents ignoring a crying infant" (p. 316). Also,

> We see Hadza parents use physical punishment, and we see and hear them shout prohibitions and commands at children. . . . This bleak picture should not be exaggerated, and quantitative analysis may also redress the balance. Hadza children are active and cheerful most of the time and are welcomed in their home. Even among these people, who seldom publicly show affection or warmth, parents can be heard to speak warmly of and to their child. But the overall picture is certainly not the developmental psychologist's dream presented by the !Kung. (pp. 317–318)

However, describing more recent research, Marlowe writes, "Hadza children are allowed to do as they like most of the time. . . . Children throw tantrums and pick up sticks and hit adults, who do little more than fend off the blows and laugh" (Marlowe, Chapter 8 in this volume, p. 179). He quotes two early ethnographers as saying that parents are doting and punishment absent and adds, "I too found children received considerable affection and were rarely punished. I only saw one spanking during a year of observation of men and children," a spanking delivered by a stepfather.

A strong focus on adaptive explanations in subsequent publications has produced debate about the reasons for the differences in ultimate cause terms (Blurton Jones et al. 1994b, 1997). While these debates are interesting and may ultimately be resolved, with the exception of Marlowe's work they have taken priority over the projected quantitative analysis of infant and child behavior itself, making it difficult to assess the Hadza's conformity to some aspects of the HGC model. Still, it is possible to estimate the degree of conformity; with the exception of weaning age and interbirth interval, the correspondences are quite good.

Efe.   The Efe are small-stature (Pygmy) hunter-gatherers of the Ituri tropical rain forest of the northeastern Democratic Republic of the Congo, formerly Zaire (Bailey 1991a; Peacock 1991). They spend a great deal of time in the forest, but "the majority of their caloric intake comes from cultivated foods acquired from the Balese" (Tronick et al. 1987:97), for which they trade hunted game. They are seminomadic, living in small camps of 6 to 50 people comprising several extended families.

Excellent research on Efe infancy began in the 1980s. An initial publication was conceptualized as a direct contrast between the Efe and the !Kung and as a challenge to what the authors called the CCC or continuous care and contact model, which they proposed to replace with the "caretaker-child strategy model" (Tronick et al. 1987). The contrast was striking and began with birth, ideally solitary in the !Kung in the higher parities but a group affair among Efe. Mothers may not be the first to hold the newborn, and as the newborn is passed among the women present, several attempt to nurse it whether or not they are lactating. One of them, or even a woman from another camp, is recruited to nurse the infant until the mother's milk comes in.

However, the mother also nurses the infant in this period, despite the belief that colostrum is valueless. Her contact with the infant begins a few hours after the birth:

> For the first few days of life the newborn is kept in or around the hut and is almost always in physical contact with the mother or another person. A mother does not resume her normal work schedule until four to five days postpartum. When regular tasks are resumed, the infant may accompany her mother on long out-of-camp trips. If this occurs, child-care responsibilities are generally shared by individuals at the work site. When the mother's work requires a short out-of-camp trip, she often leaves the infant in the care of another. Almost all females attempt to comfort a distressed or fussy infant. Comfort includes allowing the infant to suckle and often occurs in the

mother's presence. But if unsuccessful the infant is returned to her mother. (p. 99)

Multiple caregiving continues, with individuals other than the mother accounting for 39 percent of physical contact at three weeks, increasing to 60 percent at 18 weeks. Infants passed from hand to hand 3.7, 5.6, and 8.3 times per hour at 3, 7, and 18 weeks, respectively. Each infant was cared for by from 5 to 24 different people (mean = 14.2), and eight out of ten infants were sometimes nursed by women other than their mothers (5 of 7, 2 of 8, and 6 of 9 at 3, 7, and 18 weeks). This multiple care is highly indulgent: "Most interactions with infants appear positive and playful. But if infants do fuss or cry, they are responded to quickly" (p. 100). Attempts to comfort an infant within ten seconds of fussing occurred 85 percent of the time in the first seven weeks and 75 percent at 18 weeks. Multiple caregiving, although high, is very variable; the proportion of time with someone other than the mother ranges from 0 to about 65 percent at three weeks and about 20 to 80 percent at the later ages.

Since the oldest infants in this initial report had not entered the main phase of attachment development, a subsequent report, also presented as undermining the CCC model, is of interest (Tronick et al. 1992). It focused on "social contact"—time that the infant was not engaged in a solitary activity. (Social contact estimates include overlapping contact, as when both the mother and others were in contact simultaneously.) Mothers were in social contact with infants about 50 percent of the time at five months (range = 36-70 percent) and about 21 percent at 36 months (14-40 percent), characterized in the text as a decline with a significant linear trend. However, the peak of maternal contact shown in the accompanying figure is 63 percent, occurring at age eight months. (The data were not tested for a curvilinear trend.)

More important is the difference between their Figures 1 and 2, reprinted here as Figures 2.3a and 2.3b. The first shows the total time in social contact with mothers, children, adults, and fathers, and with the exception of fathers, nonmaternal contact is high at all ages. The second compares mother and father contact with the *average* child and the *average* adult. The average adult never spends more than a small fraction of the mother's time in social contact, and is in contact less than the father is at all ages except eight months.

The average child begins to rival the mother for contact time only at three years. All three nonmother categories show their lowest ratio to mother contact at eight months of age, when the mother is in social contact over an order of magnitude more than the average child, average adult, or father.

The authors conclude that "the developmental course of the Efe infants' and toddlers' social relationships does not conform to the patterning of

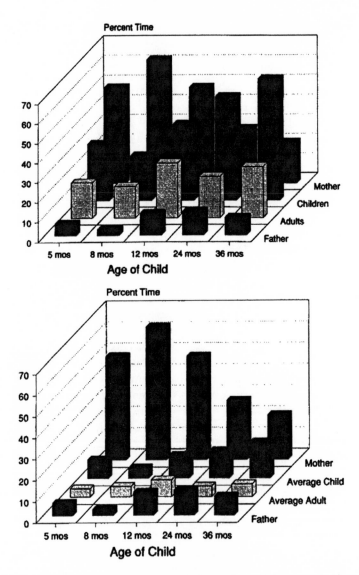

Figure 2.3. Percentage of time mother, father, other adults, and children are in social contact with Efe infants and toddlers. (a) Mother and father compared to sums of all other adults and all children. (b) Mother and father compared to averages of all other adults and all children. Maternal primacy is very striking in Figure 3b. From Tronick: Dev Psychol, Volume 28(4): 568–577, 1992, Figures 1 and 2.

relationships predicted by CCC models" (p. 573) without discussing these comparisons. However, they appropriately emphasize the density of social contact these infants experience:

> Efe infants and toddlers spend almost all of their time in social contact with other individuals, and although the amount of social contact declines with age, 3-year-olds still spend most of their time in physical and social contact with other people. . . . Efe infants and toddlers are almost never alone in the sense of being out of sight or hearing of other people. (pp. 573–4)

Such descriptions are qualitatively reminiscent of published accounts of social context among the !Kung, although Efe maternal contact is certainly lower.

Fathers contributed much less than all other adults or all children, but more than the average other adult at most ages. The distribution of care across individuals other than parents was not reported, but this could mean that the father is the second most important caregiver (although certainly not a close second).

Another study filled this gap (Morelli and Tronick 1992), focusing on ages one, two, and three years. Unfortunately, the comparison was only with other men and boys, not with all other adults and children, but the results are still instructive. The *average* time the child spent in social activity with all other men was more than half of that with the father at all ages, and this appeared to be mainly one man at each age. The average time with boys was greater than the time with father at one year and the disparity increased markedly thereafter. The authors conclude that "the role Efe fathers played in the lives of their children relative to other males did not appear to be particularly special or unique" (p. 49).

Infants' social contact with children tripled over the first three years, reaching 29 percent at 5 months and 62 percent at 3 years, whereas contact with adults did not change significantly (Tronick et al. 1992). At the earlier age, contact with the average child was about 9 percent, declining to 5 percent at eight months and then rising to 18 percent at three years-at which point contact with the average child was twice that with the father and almost equal to that with the mother. In an average hour, five-month-olds encountered from 0 to 4 children, three-year-olds from 1 to 6. Although the paper used the terms "child" and "peer" interchangeably, the demographics make same-age peers even less likely than for the !Kung, and it appears from the context that infants and toddlers interact with children of all ages.

A subsequent report on the same data set focused on testing kin selection hypotheses (Ivey 2000). This analysis confirmed the major role played by nonmaternal care, referring to the Efe as "the most extreme example of alloparenting in a foraging population," (pp. 857-858) and demonstrates that women predominate very markedly among caregivers except in childhood, when there is no significant sex difference. The analysis strongly confirmed kin selection theory, showing a very large predominance of relatives in every category compared with unrelated controls matched for age, sex, and availability. The report also underscored the indulgence of care, stating that "Efe one-year-olds are in close proximity to a caregiver 100% of observed time and spend an average of 85% of time in direct care" (p. 859).

Most interesting, perhaps, is the stratification of female nonmaternal caregivers by reproductive status (Figure 4, p. 861). About 11 percent of the female allocare is provided by reproductive women, 22 percent by prereproductive females (girls), 29 percent by postreproductive women, and the largest portion, 38 percent, by nonreproductive women. This is significant because the Efe have an average completed fertility of 2.6, the lowest ever measured for a natural population (Ellison et al. 1986). But the distribution of births per woman is bimodal, with a high proportion of women infertile due to pelvic inflammatory disease. Given the high proportion of allocare by nonreproductive female relatives, it is reasonable to hypothesize that very low fertility makes the exceptionally high level of allocare advantageous (Hewlett 1991a). The multiple breast-feeding observed may also be an adaptation by kin groups to high infertility, since the women who are effective reproducers would by this cultural adaptation reduce the likelihood of suppressing fertility with highly frequent nursing.

Efe girls were expected to help their mothers in food-gathering and in tasks within the camp (Peacock 1985). If the patterns described for Ituri culture generally (Turnbull 1962, 1965) apply to the Efe, children were subject to occasional physical punishment but left to play most of the time. Boys were circumcised at age 11 or 12, a painful and sometimes traumatic experience, but girls at first menstruation are subject to a lengthy and positive celebration. Attempts to restrict sexual activity in adolescence are not very serious unless they involve liaisons with Bantu men in nearby villages, and sexual activity is not unusual (Peacock 1985).

Aka. The Aka are small-stature (Pygmy) hunter-gatherers of the tropical forest of the southwestern Central African Republic and northern People's Republic of the Congo (Bahuchet 1999). Their environment, the tropical rain forest of the western Congo basin, is varied but rich, and at the time of the infancy study they were predominantly foraging for a living, spending 56 percent of their time hunting, 27 percent gathering, and 17 percent in village work for nearby agriculturalists. However, their diet was mainly farm-produced food, for which they traded hunted game.

Infertility was infrequent and the total completed fertility (mean number of live births reported by postmenopausal women) was 5.5, compared with 4.7 for the !Kung. The birth interval was about 3.6 years, compared with about 4 for the !Kung. Infant mortality was the same as the !Kung, about 20 percent in the first year. Camps consisted of 20 to 35 people (half younger than 15) in one to 15 nuclear families, and people moved, aggregated, and dispersed according to food availability. Women played an important role in net hunting, a crucial subsistence method (Noss and Hewlett 2000).The general character of infancy and childhood is familiar, and the classic monograph describes it in detail:

> Aka infancy is indulgent: Infants are held almost constantly, they have skin-to-skin contact most of the day . . . and they are nursed on demand and attended to immediately if they fuss or cry. Aka parents interact with and stimulate their infants throughout the day. They talk to, play with, show affection to, and transmit subsistence skills to their infants. . . . I was rather surprised to find parents teaching their eight- to-twelve-month-old infants how to use small pointed digging sticks, throw small spears, use miniature axes with sharp metal blades, and carry small baskets. . . . Unlike their village neighbors, Aka infants are carried in a sling on the side rather than on the back, which allow for more face-to-face interaction with the caregiver. (Hewlett 1991b:32–33)

There are also divergences from the !Kung and the HGC model. Because women, including nursing mothers, participate actively in net hunting, a baby may be set down on the forest floor and left crying while the mother completes the kill. (This contrasts with the Ache, who rarely set their infants down on the forest floor for any reason.)

Nonmaternal caregivers play a major role.

> While in the camp setting, Aka one- to-four-month-olds are held by their mothers less than 40 percent of the time, are transferred to other caregivers an average of 7.3 times per hour, and have seven different caregivers on average that hold the infant during the day. (p. 34)

Outside the camp, however, the mother holds the infant nearly 90 percent of the time and the transfers occur only twice an hour:

> Besides being indulgent and intimate, Aka infancy also lacks negation and violence. . . . Seldom does one hear a parent tell an infant not to touch this or that or not to do something. . . . Violence or corporal punishment for an infant that misbehaves seldom occurs." (p. 35)

Indeed, hitting an infant by either parent is said by the Aka to be potential grounds for divorce.

What is most distinctive about Aka infancy is the involvement and intimacy of fathers (Hewlett 1988, 1991b). "Aka fathers do more infant caregiving than fathers in any other known society" (p. 169) is the conclusion, cited approvingly in a policy report on fathers for the Society for Research in Child Development (Engle and Breaux 1998), which calls Aka men "the most nurturant fathers yet observed" (p. 5). However, the highest number reported for Aka father involvement is 22 percent, which is the percentage of all infant holding done by the father during the first four months—a time when the mother accounts for 51 percent and others account for 27 percent (Hewlett 1991b:79, Table 15).

Nevertheless, since "others" are numerous, the father has an excellent opportunity to take a strong second place in the infant's heart. On the net hunt in the same age range, fathers hold infants 6.5 percent of the time, compared with mothers' 87.3 percent. Expressed differently, on trips to the bush over the first 18 months and discounting the contributions of others, fathers held infants only 8 percent, declining to 3 percent, as much as mothers did. But in camp, fathers held the infant 43 percent as much as mothers in the first 4 months, 25 percent as much in the 8-12 month period, and 45 percent as much between 13 and 18 months. Neither any other single nonmaternal caregiver nor even all nonmaternal caregivers put together rival the father as a secondary attendant.

Still, these data also show the mother to be the overwhelmingly important caregiver during infancy, accounting for 87-96 percent of holding during net hunts and, in the forest camps while not hunting, doing 51 percent of the holding in the first four months, 87.5 percent in the 8- to 12-month period, and 57.3 percent between 13 and 18 months. As with the Efe, it is of theoretical interest that the mother's role jumps so markedly during the period of infancy when attachments are known to become very strong (Ainsworth et al. 1974; Belsky 1999; van IJzendoorn and Sagi 1999). It is thus not surprising that infants exhibit far fewer attachment behaviors toward fathers than toward mothers during this age period. Fathers receive 15.5 percent of such behaviors, others (in total) 22.2 percent, and mothers 58.8 percent. Fathers, then, receive about a fourth as many attachment behaviors as mothers at this age, although this rises to 58.4 percent of the mother's amount in the second year. Providing further support for attachment theory is the fact that over the whole age range the behavior "fuss for" was coded for mothers almost eight times as often as for fathers, even though less than a fifth of the instances of fussing for mother ended in nursing.

Weaning is a crucial transition, and "usually begins at age three or four when the mother becomes pregnant again":

> The child . . . is not able to walk fast enough to keep up with the net hunt . . . so the four to five year old frequently stays behind in camp with one or two other children and an adult. . . . The children play, explore and

practice subsistence skills and seldom venture more than fifty meters from camp. . . . In camp the majority of a child's time is spent within a multiage play group, but always in the company of adults. (pp. 36–37)

The transition from the intimate parent-infant bond to the play group is very gradual (Hewlett 2004, personal communication). Unlike the !Kung, the Aka multiage play group may be same-sex. When they can keep up, children follow their parents on net hunts. They may or may not help in the hunt, at their own discretion. "Instruction is still primarily by observation and imitation, but verbal instructions are also given."

Beginning around age 11 or 12, the sexes segregate, as in the great majority of all cultures (Schlegel and Barry 1991). Girls collect water, nuts, or fruit together, while boys hunt small game. Adolescents may sleep and eat with their parents but often do not, traveling to visit relatives and explore the region. Initiation includes circumcision for boys and filing the incisor teeth to a point in both sexes. There is not a great deal of ritual attached to these events, but they are painful, require courage and fortitude, and give the successful initiate a sense of having left childhood behind. Premarital sexual freedom exists, but apparently is not acted on to the same extent as it is among the !Kung (Barry Hewlett, personal communication, 2004).

Ache.   The Ache (Guayaki) of Eastern Paraguay foraged for a living in a dense, subtropical, broadleaf, evergreen forest (Hill and Hurtado 1999). Although settled on a Catholic mission, they were full-time hunters until the 1970s, and in the 1980s were studied by a team of scientists interested in demography, subsistence ecology, life history, and child development. At this time they obtained 20–25 percent of their food from foraging in the nearby forest, and their patterns of life before settlement were reconstructed. According to a report focused on infant development, "women alternate between walking and carrying their young children, brief periods of vegetable, fruit, and larval food collection, and resting on the ground. Women spend very little time in direct food acquisition and in activities incompatible with infant care. Instead, they focus their attention on child supervision when not walking from one campsite to another. . . . Children younger than three years of age rarely venture more than a meter from their mother and spend some 80-100 percent of the time in tactile contact with them" (Kaplan and Dove 1987).

Ache are more nomadic than other well-studied hunter-gatherers, and when in the forest men provide 87 percent of subsistence (by energy intake) and spend twice as much time as women in the food quest. They thus approximate the popular notion of women deferring subsistence activities in favor of infant care, which is not true of most hunter-gatherers. As for indulgence, "Ache children of less than 4 years of age are spoiled by

American standards (they are almost never chastised and win most conflicts with parents simply by crying and whining)" (Kaplan and Dove
1987:197). Still they are helpful and obedient when older.

These characterizations were confirmed by subsequent research (Hill
and Hurtado 1996). This quantitative ethnography contained explicit descriptions of Ache infancy and childhood reminiscent of the !Kung:

> Traditionally Ache infants spent the first year of their life in close proximity
> to their mother, suckling at will and sleeping in their mother's lap at night.
> Indeed, scan sampling and focal infant follows suggest that in the forest, in-
> fants under one year of age spend about 93% of daylight time in tactile con-
> tact with their mother or father, and they are never set down on the ground
> or left alone for more than a few seconds. (p. 219)

This closeness seems related to the difficulty of keeping infants alive in
a hostile environment, and this research confirmed earlier reports that
"high-quality child care overrides other competing needs" (p. 220). Consequently mothers collect less food than other women, even though mothers have more dependents to feed.

> After about one year of age Ache children still spend 40% of their daylight
> time in their mother's arms or lap, but they sit or stand on the ground next
> to their mothers 48% of the day. It is not until about three years of age that
> Ache children begin to spend significant amounts of time more than one
> meter from their mother. Even still, Ache children between three and four
> years of age spend 76% of their daylight time less than one meter away from
> their mother and are monitored almost constantly. (p. 220)

The pattern of breast-feeding partly conforms to the HGC model in
nursing frequency, but not in weaning age or birth spacing:

> Ache children generally continue nursing on demand until their mother is
> pregnant with her next child . . . although they may begin eating some
> solid foods such as armadillo fat or insect larvae . . . as early as 6–12
> months. . . . Because Ache mothers wear little clothing and carry or sleep
> with children resting on their bare chest, nursing is frequent throughout the
> day and night. Weaning is an extremely unpleasant experience . . . with
> children screaming, hitting, and throwing tantrums for several weeks. . . .
> Some mothers who became pregnant very soon after the birth of a child sim-
> ply continued to breast-feed all the way through their next pregnancy, and
> then, if the interbirth interval was too short (i.e., less than two years), would
> simply kill the newborn child and continue nursing the first. (pp. 220–221)

The median age at weaning was calculated as 25 months, but this may
be shorter than it had been: "Unfortunately we have no way at present to
determine the age at weaning in the precontact situation" (p. 221).

Although nursing is described as frequent, it was measured as less frequent than that of the !Kung. The mean interval between nursing bouts was about 30 minutes, with an average bout length declining from more than ten to about two minutes over the first 18 months (pp. 310, 338). This pattern, which may have developed after reservation settlement, could help explain a possible shortening of birth spacing. However, within the small sample studied there was no relationship between nursing measures and birth interval. Furthermore, birth spacing even in the precontact period was shorter than that of the !Kung, and the investigators believe that Ache demographic history was characterized by rapid growth followed by sudden declines, in contrast to the very slow, steady growth of the !Kung population.

After infancy, younger children tend to stay in camp playing with objects, pets, and each other, and seeking maternal attention. Transportation in the forest depends on a sling that keeps infants in contact with their mothers, their heads resting on her chest. Around 18 months they begin to ride on top of the mother's carrying basket, clinging to her head and ducking to avoid branches and vines. Between three and five they may ride "piggyback" on their fathers, grandparents, or other adults. After age five they are weaned from the back and encouraged or made to walk on forest trips, a crisis in their lives as it was for the !Kung.

> Children scream, cry, hit their parents, and try everything they can think of to get adults to continue carrying them. Often, they simply sit and refuse to walk, prompting older band members to leave them behind. This tactic leads to a dangerous game of "chicken" in which parents and children both hope the other will give in before the child is too far behind and may become lost. We observed one small boy to be lost for about half an hour during a parent-child transportation conflict. When the boy was finally located it was unclear whether he or his parents were more frightened. A small child cannot survive long in the Paraguayan forest, and if not found within one day is unlikely to survive. In any case, the boy's tactic paid off temporarily, since he was carried for the remainder of the day. (p. 222)

Learning about the forest and about subsistence has already begun by this time, but it intensifies in middle childhood. Children acquire knowledge of edible fruits, stinging plants and animals, and vines with thorns, and as they accumulate time foraging with women, both boys and girls become skilled foragers for fruit, insect larvae, and small animals. By age eight they learn the crucial, difficult, and subtle art of tracking adults in the forest. They spend considerable time in the trees, "collecting fruits for themselves or knocking down fruits for the adult women to collect below. There is no segregation of play or foraging parties by sex, and children spend most of their time within 50 m of the adult women in mixed age-sex groups" (p. 223).

At around age ten boys and girls begin to be independent, sometimes sleeping at a relative's fire or traveling with another band for a time. God-parentlike relationships become important at this time. Boys carry bows and arrows, although they do not learn to make them, and girls baby-sit, run errands, and draw water. Girls may produce as much food as adult women by age 12, but do not carry a burden-basket until they are married; boys exceed girls in food production by age 16, but do not reach adult male levels until their mid-20s. Still, the pubertal transformation is often dramatic, with girls preceding boys as in most human populations.

When a girl has her first menstruation, at an average age of 15.3 years, she experiences an initiation and purification ritual, along with "all men who have had sex with her. . . . Every woman we interviewed who had reached menarche before contact reported that she had engaged in sexual intercourse with at least one adult man prior to menarche. . . . 85% of the women . . . had also been married before menarche" (pp. 224–225). Still, the teen years are a time of playfulness, especially for boys:

> Both boys and girls begin experimenting with sex around twelve years of age . . . in a manner very similar to that described for the !Kung (Shostak 1981). Boys . . . spend most of their teen years visiting other camps and trying to form friendships and alliances with their same-sex age mates and older men. It is quite common to see these boys intimately joking, tickling, and touching each other or the adult men who have chosen to befriend them. (p. 224)

As in many higher primates, including most human hunter-gatherers, such "play" forms coalitions vital to survival and reproduction.

As for girls, "despite their precocious sexual activity . . . girls are generally reluctant and sexually reserved with most males most of the time. Indeed the best description of their behavior would be aggressively flirtatious but sexually coy to the point of causing frustration." Boys accuse girls of being "stingy with their genitals," and "the major activity of girls at this time is walking around in small groups laughing and giggling and carrying on in any manner that will attract attention. They frequently spend much of the day visiting from hearth to hearth and are fed abundantly wherever they go" (p. 225).

Agta.   The Agta dwell in diverse habitats widely distributed over the rugged Sierra Madre mountain range that parallels the eastern coast of the main island of the northern Philippines (Griffin and Griffin 1999; Griffin and Estioko-Griffin 1985). The main habitat is a semiseasonal tropical rain forest crossed by many streams, rivers, and waterfalls. The Agta, like the Aka and Efe, depend on neighboring agricultural people for the bulk of their plant foods as well as for other consumer goods, which they get in trade for hunted game. They are seminomadic, widely distributed in small camp groups. Agta men are full-time hunters and fishermen, but the unique feature of the Agta adaptation is that women hunt to a degree unknown in any other hunter-gatherer group, killing up to half of the hunted game (Estioko-Griffin 1985; Estioko-Griffin and Griffin 1981; Griffin et al. 1992). Since hunting has been viewed by many theorists as incompatible with infant and child care, the Agta are an important test of the HGC model.

Their population was found to be declining due to a high death rate, especially in infancy and childhood (Headland 1989). Crude birth rate was slightly higher than the that of the !Kung; Agta birth spacing (determined retrospectively for women over 45), when the last child lived until the birth of the next sibling, was slightly over three years (Goodman et al. 1985). An overall summary of infant and child care was as follows:

> The baby remains against the body of the mother nearly constantly in its first weeks, but is also in contact with the father, siblings if any, and other kin that may drop in to visit, nap, or play. . . . Babies sleep by mothers' breasts, between mother and father. . . . Grandparents may take in toddlers and older children on a "drop-in" basis or in the case of the parents overnight departure for hunting and fishing. During the first 12 months an infant is usually carried in a sling at the mother's back, side, or front. . . . Nursed on demand, it is returned to the back for sleeping after suckling. Women are quite comfortable thus engaged in collection of forest materials, and *some sporadically hunt and kill game while transporting the baby.* As the baby grows in its first year, it is increasingly handled by others, albeit in brief episodes. . . . An infant under 1 year may be passed among several adults and youths, being returned to its mother if it becomes fussy. (Griffin and Griffin 1992:301)

The italics are added to emphasize the remarkable fact that even some hunting by mothers does not interrupt continuous physical contact. Data on carrying, based on spot observations throughout the day, underscored this: "Infants are carried in a cloth sling much of the time before exploratory crawling and first walking begins. Carrying does not cease then; usually a toddler is carried frequently by the mother" (p. 305). Except for the women's hunting, this could be a description of !Kung infant care. The same can be said about the growth of independence:

> Children are left in camp by mothers at increasingly frequent and lengthy intervals. Late in the first year an infant may be left for an hour or two; sisters or mother's mother or father are acceptable caregivers. . . . One sister sporadically nursed her sister's infant as well as her own, permitting the young mother time outside the camp. More frequently, however, babies are carried by mothers until the age of two or slightly more. (p. 302)

Weaning is gradual, but weaning age can be roughly estimated from the following information (T. Headland 2004, personal communication): "Sometime when the child is roughly between age 20 to 28 months, it nurses less and less. . . . This gradual decrease in nursing seems to run about 3 to 6 months." Since the criterion for the !Kung in the early studies was complete weaning, it is appropriate to estimate the earliest *completed* weaning age for Agta at 23 months. Also, "small children are almost never nursed after 28 to 30 months." From this description a reasonable estimate of weaning age would be midway between 23 and 29 months, or 26 months, but this is lower than an earlier published estimate of Agta weaning age: "With the appearance of the child's molar at about two and a quarter years, the nursing often continues but with less intensity (Early and Headland 1998:92–93)."

Multiple caregiving, as observed by descriptive ethnographers, was substantial:

> The infant is eagerly passed from person to person until all in attendance have had an opportunity to snuggle, nuzzle, sniff, and admire the newborn. . . . A child's first experience, then, involves a community of relatives and friends. Thereafter he enjoys constant cuddling, carrying, loving sniffing, and affectionate genital stimulation. (Peterson 1978:16, cited by Hewlett (1991a:13)

However, quantitative data, based on spot observations of children under eight years old, were quite consistent with maternal primacy:

> Within the residential cluster, mothers of children from age [0] to 8 years are caregivers slightly more than 50% of the time. Grandmothers and elder sisters come in at a modest 7.5 and 10.4%, and fathers follow with only 4.4%. (p. 303)

Fathers do not often carry infants while in camp, but "are most often seen carrying toddlers and older children on subsistence trips and on residential moves" (p. 306). Fathers, in contrast to mothers, were "never observed" in pacification play with a fussing or crying baby (p. 307). There is considerable individual variation, however. Of seven fathers of infants under two years of age, the ratio of observations of maternal to paternal caregiving ("baby-sitting") was two-thirds in one case, more than half in another, and zero in two others. However, all four who had infants under *one* year of age had father-to-mother ratios between about one-sixth and zero. Overall, "The Agta fathers are not particularly active with children when compared with the !Kung, the Aka, and even the Ache" (p. 317). The muted role for fathers is made more remarkable by the fact that Agta women do so much hunting.

The transition to a multiage child group is familiar: "Play groups are not age or gender segregated, but made up of most children in [the] local group. . . . Teen-aged girls bring toddlers on their hips to observe or join play" (p. 302). As in the !Kung, this play includes care of younger children by older ones, but it also includes a contribution to subsistence. All Agta fish beginning in early childhood and are adept at it by adolescence. Both sexes begin hunting after puberty (Estioko-Griffin and Griffin 1981). Regarding premarital sex,

> Premarital female chastity is not an ideal of much currency. . . . Although some data are difficult to collect concerning sex, almost certainly girls are able to engage in sexual activity with relative ease; promiscuity is not favored in any circumstance. Males may have as little or great difficulty in engaging in sex as females. (Estioko-Griffin and Griffin 1981:138)

SUMMARY OF THE NEWER EVIDENCE

New quantitative studies have focused on infancy and childhood in at least five hunter-gatherer cultures: the Hadza, the Efe, the Aka, the Ache, and the Agta. Each of these groups has been described as departing from the HGC model as originally presented based on studies of the !Kung and reviews of older literature on other hunter-gatherers. We can now place these departures in context with a systematic comparison.

Table 2.6 shows the findings of recent studies regarding key features of the HGC model. It suggests a high level of support for most of the original

Table 2.6 The Hunter-Gatherer Childhood (HGC) Model in Five Cultures[a]

	Frequent nursing	Weaning age/IBI (months)	Sleeping with mother	Physical contact, all	Overall indulgence	Nonmaternal care	Father involvement	Maternal primacy	Multiage child group	Carefree childhood	Premarital sex
!Kung	+++	42/48	+++	+++	+++	++	++	+++	+++	+++	+++
Hadza	+++	30/38	+++	+++	+	++	++	++	+++	+	+++
Efe	+++	30/38	++	+++	+++	+++	+	++	++	++	++
Aka	+++	42/48	+++	+++	+++	+++	+++	++	+++	++	++
Ache	+++	25/37	+++	+++	++	+	++	+++	+++	+++	+++
Agta	+++	27/36	+++	+++	+++	++	+	+++	+++	+	+++

[a]The !Kung compared with five other recently studied hunter-gatherers on 11 aspects of infant and child care included in the HGC model. From published data and descriptions supplemented by personal communications. For explanation and references, see text.

generalizations. Hunter-gatherers have frequent nursing, mother-infant cosleeping, high physical contact, high overall indulgence (possibly excepting the Hadza), substantial to high nonmaternal care and father involvement, maternal primacy, transition to a multiage child group, a relatively carefree childhood (except the Hadza), low restriction of premarital sex, and strong adolescent initiation rites. Only the Aka match the !Kung in age at weaning and interbirth interval, but the other three cultures have weaning ages over two years and interbirth intervals over three years. This is at the upper end of the range for preindustrial cultures and sustains the generalization that hunter-gatherers have relatively late weaning and long birth spacing.

To place these generalizations in a broader phylogenetic context, the care of infants and juveniles in Old World monkeys and apes is characterized by (proportionately) somewhat later weaning age and interbirth interval, variable and species-specific importance of nonmaternal care, minimal father involvement except in gibbons, the absence of postweaning provisioning (the basis of a relatively carefree childhood), mixed-sex play groups that may be same-age groups in strongly seasonal breeders, and the absence of initiation rites. Other features of HGC are present in most higher primates, including frequent nursing, late weaning, mother-infant cosleeping, high overall indulgence, maternal primacy, and adolescent sexuality. The wide distribution of these features in monkeys and apes suggests that they are common features of the catarrhines and may have been present in the common ancestor, which lived between 30 and 40 million years ago (Martin 1990:692).

DISCUSSION: MEETING THE CHALLENGES

It remains for us to consider the theoretical implications of the divergences observed in four main areas: weaning and birth spacing; maternal primacy; overall indulgence; and responsibility in childhood. Finally, we will discuss the relative importance of the discordance hypothesis in relation to the HGC model and the childhood as facultative adaptation hypothesis in relation to the CFA model.

Weaning and Birth Spacing. Perhaps the strongest challenge to the !Kung-based HGC model is provided by data on weaning and birth spacing in the Hadza, the Efe, the Ache, and the Agta. Respectively, they have weaning ages of 30, 30, 25, and 27 months, and interbirth intervals of 38 (Frank Marlowe, personal communication, 2004), 38, 37, and 36 months. Among the Aka the process is essentially superimposable on that of the !Kung, with about 42 months of nursing and 48 months between births. The

Hadza and the Ache clearly have shorter interbirth intervals, higher completed fertilities (TFR) per female reproductive life, and faster-growing populations than the !Kung. The Agta would be faster-growing but for high mortality. The !Kung model for Paleolithic population growth, that of mainly stable and gradual growth of about half a percent a year (Howell 1979), may have applied to some populations but is unlikely to have applied to all or even most. Indeed, the Ache life tables have suggested a model of Paleolithic demography that entails rapid increases alternating with crashes (Hill and Hurtado 1996). This, if true, presents a serious challenge not only to current ideas about hunter-gatherer demography, but also to life history theory, which predicts greater population stability in long-lived, slowly developing species (Charnov 1993; Pianka 1970, 1988; Stearns 1992).

However, it may be significant that prospective measures of Ache weaning were made during the reservation period, and the possibility that weaning was later and birth intervals longer in the forest period is acknowledged (Hill and Hurtado 1996). Given the forest-period birth spacing of just over three years, and the fact that "Ache children generally continue nursing on demand until their mother is pregnant with her next child" (p. 221) as among the !Kung, it is likely that traditional Ache weaning age was around 30 months, or 2.5 years. Indeed, the observation that Ache mothers, "if the interbirth interval was too short (i.e., less than two years), would simply kill the newborn child and continue nursing the first" (pp. 220–221) strongly suggests a traditional desired weaning age of substantially more than two years.

The Hadza have a weaning age of 30 months in a setting that is far closer to their traditional way of life, and this is less likely to be an artifact of cultural change. So far, however, it appears to be a lower limit of hunter-gatherer weaning age. The Efe interbirth interval of 38 months occurs against a background of exceptionally high infertility in the population. This could explain shorter interbirth intervals in the fertile women, achieved in part through multiple caregiving, including nursing by other women.

Overall, however, these six populations have a lower limit of weaning age that is high by developing-world standards and extremely high by Western standards. Even if most hunter-gatherers were more like the Hadza, the Efe, the Ache, and the Agta than like the !Kung and the Aka, Paleolithic weaning would still have been relatively late and interbirth interval relatively long. Against the background of ape patterns, however, this would represent a significant evolutionary shortening, and a departure from the catarrhine mother-infant complex. It has long been known that a key difference between parenting in human and other primates is the fact that only humans provision young with food after weaning (Lancaster and

Lancaster 1983). Provisioning evidently shortened nursing and birth spacing, but less so in the EEAs than in subsequent human adaptations.

Maternal Primacy.   One of the most contested claims that came out of
the !Kung literature has been the argument that hunter-gatherer maternal
care supports the Bowlby approach to the development of attachment,
which includes a hypothesis of monotropy—attachment behaviors focused on a single caregiver (Belsky 1999; Bowlby 1970–1980; Bretherton
1992; Sroufe et al. 1999; Sroufe and Waters 1977). Both the Efe and Aka
studies have been cited as undermining this claim, but the challenge is
now easily met. First, the claim of maternal primacy in the !Kung literature
was never as strong as it was made out to be. Second, to the (substantial)
extent that maternal primacy was emphasized, there is little in the new
hunter-gatherer infancy research to undermine it.

The first of these statements is supported by the review on pp. 23–29
above, so let us focus here on the second, with an emphasis on maternal
primacy, deferring discussion of the more abstract concept of attachment
monotropy to the end of the section. With the exception of weaning age,
still very late by Western standards, the Ache experience is virtually superimposable on that of the !Kung. The Hadza represent more of a departure, since they wean earlier and separate more frequently than the !Kung,
but there is nothing in the Hadza literature inconsistent with a hypothesis
of maternal primacy. Indeed, quantitative analysis strongly supports the
hypothesis (Marlowe, Chapter 8 in this volume, Table 8.1).

The Aka seem at first glance to represent more of a challenge. They have
the highest level of father involvement and intimacy not only among
hunter-gatherers but throughout the cross-cultural range, and this observation represents a very important addition to our understanding of social
development, because of both the quantity and quality of the care. Still,
even in forest camps where their involvement was highest, fathers held infants less than half as much as mothers at all ages, with a decline to 25 percent during the 8- to 12-month period when attachment is developing.
Nonparental involvement in care was very high by hunter-gatherer standards, yet mothers held their infants 87 percent of the time on net hunts
and more than half the time in the forest camps, rising to 87 percent during the 8- to 12-month period. Because there were numerous nonparental
caregivers, the average nonparent did not approach the father in involvement, suggesting that only the father had an opportunity to become a significant additional attachment object, and his involvement was a distant
second to the mother's. The nature of the attachment to the father should
be studied, and will no doubt be interesting, since secondary attachments
certainly exist, but the Aka father's role does not challenge the claim of
maternal primacy.

The Efe studies have been cited as strongly undermining both the !Kung model and the maternal primacy hypothesis. There is good evidence of multiple caregiving among the Efe—substantially more than among the !Kung—but no evidence that any individual could rival the mother's primacy. Mothers accounted for about half the social contact with infants during the first half-year, rising to 63 percent at eight months. More important, there was no time in infancy when the father, the average nonparent adult, or the average child accounted for more than a fraction of the mother's social contact. Efe multiple caregiving is impressive, but does not represent a challenge to maternal primacy.

Finally, all the above comparisons rely on observations during the day. Proximity, nursing, and other aspects of parenting during the night have been repeatedly emphasized as important aspects of hunter-gatherer and other traditional infant care (Konner 1977, 1981; Konner and Super 1987; McKenna et al. 1993). Ache, Hadza, Aka, and Agta mothers slept with their infants, with ample opportunity for night nursing. Efe infants are reported to sleep with others at times, but quantitative data are not presented on this question, and descriptions suggest maternal cosleeping and night nursing on the great majority of nights throughout infancy. The data on cosleeping therefore also support maternal primacy.

The theoretical question of attachment monotropy is far more difficult. Bowlby's claim was that the infant will tend to focus on one primary caregiver, usually but not necessarily the mother, even in the context of multiple caregiving and beyond what would be predicted by the distribution of contact time and care across caregivers (Cassidy 1999). Despite the fact that this focus could be on an adoptive mother, a father, a grandparent, an aunt, or an orphanage attendant, the monotropy claim was viewed as an attempt to tie mothers to home, and was strongly and repeatedly challenged. In addition, the monotropy idea challenged prevailing psychological models such as learning theory and social cognition, which predicted a distribution of attachment proportional to contact and care.

However, many studies show that multiple caregiving does not prevent the development of attachment to the mother or other primary caregiver. This has been found repeatedly for high-quality day care (Caldwell et al. 1970; Kagan et al. 1978; McKim et al. 1999; NICHD 1997), general cross-cultural settings (van IJzendoorn and Sagi 1999), African multiple care settings (Ainsworth 1967; Leiderman and Leiderman 1977), and, most strikingly, in the Israeli kibbutz, where the amount of nonmaternal care is very high in both amount and continuity (Sagi et al. 1995). The quality of the attachment may be affected (Russell 1999; Sagi et al. 1994), but the focus on the mother is not prevented.

Monotropy in infant attachment would require special nervous system adaptations that may seem implausible. But we have ample evidence from romantic attachments that an unreasonable focus on one individual, independent of objective behavioral input, is well within the capability of the human nervous system. Brain research is gradually taking the mystery out of monotropic attachments, in the realm of imprinting in birds (Bock and Braun 1999; Horn 1991), pair-bonding in mammals (Insel 1997, 2000), mother-infant separation in primates (Rilling et al. 2002), and romantic attachment in humans (Bartels and Zeki 2000; Marazziti et al. 1999). In due course brain imaging may take the mystery out of putative monotropy in human infant attachment as well, but for the time being it remains an open question.

As for maternal primacy in hunter-gatherers, it is strongly supported by the !Kung studies and consistently evident in older ethnographies, and it is also found in recent scientific studies, including those presented as exceptions to this rule. Most notably, perhaps, it is very evident in the Agta, the only hunter-gatherer culture on record where women do half the hunting. If maternal primacy were facultative, it seems likely that the Agta would depart from it. They do not, nor do any other hunter-gatherers studied so far. Exclusive maternal care is nonexistent, and was never claimed, but maternal primacy is a general feature of hunter-gatherer childhood. It may be that maternal primacy affords an opportunity for attachment that gives the mother a unique place in the hierarchy of infant attachments.

Responsibility in Childhood.   Here the Hadza present their strongest challenge. Hadza children forage for themselves very extensively, and the contrast with the !Kung case has been explicitly addressed (Blurton Jones et al. 1994b). While !Kung children do make a contribution to subsistence, it is very small compared with the Hadza. Since the Hadza live overwhelmingly by hunting and gathering in a rich environment that is if anything closer to our EEAs than that of the !Kung, they raise a clear possibility that in many such past environments children were expected to contribute substantially to subsistence. Investigators familiar with both cultures suggest that it is less safe for !Kung children to forage, because they can be more frequently out of the line of sight to their parents or the village-camp, and !Kung parents are anxious about this risk. The Hadza environment of relatively bare rocky hillsides makes it more difficult to get lost. There is also a difference in the amount of baby care assigned to older children in the two cultures. The !Kung multiaged child group occupies and supervises young children and even toddlers, but there is little or no formal assignment of baby care to older children. Agta children of both sexes fish during childhood. It seems likely that the level of responsibility assigned to children is a facultative adaptation among hunter-gatherers although it is always compatible with play.

CONCLUSION

The CFA model has merit—most human behavioral adaptations are facultative—but the demise of the HGC model has been greatly exaggerated. Facultative adaptation is always an option for natural selection, and it would be expected to apply to infant and child care in the human EEAs. But natural selection operating in any species must contend with constraints derived from phylogenetic history, and in the case of the HGC model there are deep homologies with parallel patterns in Old World monkeys and apes, suggesting the possibility that the common ancestor had already evolved these patterns between 30 and 40 million years ago.

Excellent recent studies have challenged some aspects of the model. The Ache keep their infants and toddlers off the forest floor and wean them at age two, but otherwise bear a strong resemblance to the !Kung in their patterns of care. The Efe have more multiple caregiving and the Aka have more paternal care, but the difference between them and the !Kung is less than has been suggested. Multiple caregiving and father involvement were always described as greater in the !Kung than in most cultures, and both were part of the HGC model as originally proposed. Moreover, maternal primacy is high in both the Efe and the Aka, making them only weak challenges to models of infant emotional development that center on attachment to a primary caregiver.

The Hadza comprise the greatest challenge to the model. They not only have earlier weaning than the !Kung, as do the Ache, but they were reported have significantly lower indulgence in infancy. Recently, however, more detailed studies of parent-infant interaction have suggested that this difference too has been overemphasized (Marlowe, chapter 8 this volume). The data on task assignment and specifically on foraging in childhood are excellent, and they clearly show a marked contrast to the !Kung. Although !Kung children do forage to some extent, it is not strongly expected of them and their productivity is much lower. This difference is of great interest, and it is clear that child foraging is a facultative human adaptation. It is also likely that weaning age is partly facultative, varying between two and four years of age, probably in response to the quality and predictability of the foraging environment, the availability of suitable weaning foods, and the presence of infertile women who aid in infant care.

Although of much poorer quality, the descriptive data in older ethnographies should not be discounted. There is no reason to believe that anthropologists who studied hunter-gatherers had a bias that would lead them to find conformity to features of the later HGC model. Their accounts support most aspects of the model.

But even without them, the high-quality recent studies allow some generalizations. Hunter-gatherer childhood was characterized by close physical contact, maternal primacy in a dense social context, indulgent and responsive infant care, frequent nursing, weaning between two and four years of age, high overall indulgence, multiaged child groups, variable responsibility in childhood, and relatively weak control of adolescent sexuality. These appear to be durable features of the model. Departures from them since the end of the hunting-gathering era constitute a discordance and may have psychological and biological consequences that merit further study.

NOTES

1. In making these comparisons Textor relied on the following previous studies: Whiting and Child (1953) for pain, overall indulgence and toilet training; Barry, Bacon, and Child (1967) for anxiety in childhood; Brown (1963) for initiation rites; and Harley (1963) for peer groups.

2. In addition to sources mentioned in note 1, Textor relied on Westbrook (1963) for attitudes toward premarital sex and on Ayres (1954) for desire for children.

3

Comes the Child before Man

How Cooperative Breeding and Prolonged Postweaning Dependence Shaped Human Potential

Sarah Blaffer Hrdy

The causal chain of adaptive evolution . . . begins with development.

Mary Jane West-Eberhard,
Developmental Plasticity and Evolution

INTRODUCTION: A NEW PARADIGM EXPANDS

Back in my mother's day, educated women were under the impression that if a baby cried and his mother rushed to pick him up, she would spoil him, conditioning the baby to cry more. According to psychological wisdom of the day, babies were born "blank slates" ready to be molded and shaped by caretakers. It was the second half of the 20th century, before baby books influenced by British evolutionary psychiatrist John Bowlby began to tell a different story. Bowlby (1969) argued that baby primates are born powerfully motivated by the "set goal" of remaining in contact with their mother, and that infants need a "warm, intimate and continuous" relationship, an "attachment," in order to develop normally.

At the time Bowlby was developing attachment theory, not much was known about childrearing among hunter-gatherers (Konner, Chapter 2 in this volume). Bowlby relied heavily on clinical observations of children along with field observations of nonhuman primates, particularly wild chimpanzees, gorillas, and baboons and mother-infant studies of captive rhesus macaques. As it happened, infant care in these species is exclusively by the mother, who carries her baby everywhere. Extrapolating from these sources, Bowlby emphasized cases where human infants as well were exclusively with their mothers. If babies find it comforting to be held and carried by their mothers, this he reasoned is because in humankind's "environment of evolutionary adaptedness," this is where babies would be safest from predators. Bowlby envisioned this mother-infant dyad nested within a nuclear family composed of husband and wife plus baby.

Influenced by Mary Ainsworth and her observations of infant care in Ugandan households, Bowlby somewhat qualified this mother-focused model. He noted that the term "mother" was meant as a literary convenience to signify "the person who mothers the child and to whom he becomes attached" (1969:221, footnote 2). In time Bowlby also acknowledged the role of the father and other secondary attachment figures. But scratch him hard, and at his core Bowlby retained a chimp- or rhesuslike template for human infants' environment of evolutionary adaptedness, a world where the mother carried her baby everywhere. Indeed, the reason Bowlby gave for selecting chimps and baboons as models was that he assumed their lifeways resembled that of early man (Bowlby 1969:229).[1] "Only in more economically developed societies, and especially in Western ones," Bowlby argued, "are infants commonly out of contact with their mothers for many hours of the day" (p. 246).

Bowlby's profound insight concerning the human infant's need for a "secure base" has become widely accepted, and remains one of the greatest contributions to human well-being ever made by an evolutionary theorist. In the last two decades, however, evolutionary anthropologists like Pat Draper, Henry Harpending, Barry Hewlett, and Jim Chisholm, along with anthropologically oriented psychologists like Michael Lamb, have started to rethink Bowlby's assumptions about the exclusivity of the mother-infant relationship and the insularity of the mother-father unit. They questioned the simple dichotomy that infants were either securely and adaptively attached to their mothers or else not (Lamb et al. 1985; Ahnert and Lamb, in press; Chisholm 1996, 1999, and references therein). At the same time, the evolutionary paradigm was expanding to consider the role of *alloparents*, group members other than the parents, who might also care for infants (especially older infants) and help provision both children and their mothers. Mothers were embedded in a wider social network, and family compositions were less stable, more variable, and dynamic than previously assumed. Within such flexible arrangements it is not always possible to identify the genetic father so it may be more precise to refer to helpers other than the mother, or *allomothers*. In this chapter, both terms are used. Allomothers may include a child's siblings, uncles, aunts, and grandmothers as well as its father or because of a sexual relationship with the mother, men who *might* be fathers, as well as nonkin like foster children living in the group. Instead of one track (infant is or is not securely attached to mother) developmental trajectories varied with the availability and willingness of such caretakers.

Bowlby correctly observed that infant survival in nomadic, foraging context required close physical contact with *someone*. But as anthropologists like Paula Ivey Henry, Gilda Morelli, Ed Tronick (Chapter 9), and Barry Hewlett have shown, in such cases as the Efe or the Aka, that "someone" was not necessarily the mother. Furthermore, new information (reviewed here) suggests that in environments with high levels of child mortality, alloparental care and provisioning is more than helpful; it is *essential* for child survival.

Most social scientists continue to favor "mother-as-caretaker-within-the-nuclear-family" models. However, I believe that human family patterns were more flexible, and assistance from group members other than genetic parents ("alloparents") were essential for successful childrearing. Hence, in this chapter I will stress allomaternal contributions in addition to those of the lactating mother. For comparisons, I will also draw on the extensive literature on "cooperative breeding" in other animals to explore the ways that cooperative child childrearing might have transformed the social and ecological context in which early hominid infants developed. Because cooperative breeding allows slower maturation without compromising survival, allomaternal assistance would have facilitated the evolution of prolonged periods of nutritional dependence—the life phase we know as "childhood." Such allomaternal care and provisioning is heavily dependent on inducements from immatures themselves, so I will also examine how this need to elicit and maintain succor affected the evolution of specific human cognitive and emotional capacities. I argue that a cooperative breeding model provides a more compelling explanation for distinctive human emotional and mental aptitudes than do competing hypotheses.

THE "SEX CONTRACT" MODEL UNDER FIRE

Even as this shift to a cooperative breeding paradigm was under way, human behavioral ecologists were beginning to dismantle support for the main alternative "sex contract" hypothesis, and with it the presumption that prolonged childhood evolved in the context of mated pair with a labor clearly divided between nurturing mothers and provisioning by hunter-fathers (Blurton Jones et al., Chapter 10 in this volume; Hawkes 1991; Hawkes et al. 1998). Ever since Darwin, anthropologists had taken for granted that increasingly efficient hunting by genetic fathers subsidized the slow maturation of human progeny. According to this conventional wisdom, long childhoods were required for extended development of large brains and for the prolonged socialization and learning of language, cultural traditions, and tool-based subsistence technologies that characterized our species. Supposedly, survival and reproductive benefits from uniquely human capacities like symbolic thought and language more than offset the costs of large brains and slow growth (with the attendant risk of dying before maturity and any chance at all to reproduce). If long childhoods required paternal investment to subsidize full maturation into a fully sapient adult, it was argued, human mothers would just need to choose mates accordingly. A "sex contract" between the mother and her mate evolved: in exchange for exclusive sexual access, the male provided for the female and her young, subsidizing much longer periods of dependency than are found in other apes and providing the economic underpinning of the nuclear family.[2]

But there has been growing unease with this model. Improved brain capacity would not pay off in evolutionary terms unless smarter individuals outbred dumber but faster maturing apes. Could being smarter possibly pay off enough to offset several years' delay in the time when a young female breeds? How could an organ so costly as the human brain, together with such a long delay in maturation, be selected for? Worse, evidence emerging from still extant foragers was not always consistent with other assumptions of the sex contract model.

Based on ethnographic data from contemporary hunter-gatherers like the Hadza, Blurton Jones et al. (Chapter 10 in this volume) and Hawkes (1991) proposed that obtaining meat had more to do with "showing off" so as to increase sexual access to women (i.e., mating effort) than provisioning progeny (parental effort). Pursuing the logic that sociobiologists use to explain the evolution of nuptial gifts in animals (e.g., Weddell 1993) Hawkes hypothesized that males used meat to advertise their worth and to compete for access to mates.

Unquestionably, animal protein and fat provided by hunters increased the fecundity of women as well as the survival of their children [Marlowe (2001); see also O'Connell et al. (2002) for extension of this argument back in time to include our Pleistocene ancestors], and unquestionably this desirable commodity was exchanged for sex, often with the father of a woman's children. But Hawkes argued that the *primary* payoff to men was *more* sex, not necessarily the increased survival of children men had already fathered. "Father-as-hunter-and-sole-provider" might have characterized Paleolithic hunters from northern latitudes as well as bourgeois patriarchal families, the type of Victorian society most familiar to Darwin, but Hawkes, O'Connell, and Blurton Jones were starting to question whether such sex contracts constituted the fundamental economic unit for provisioning children among hunting-gathering ancestors in the African tropics hundreds of thousands of years ago.

Using comparative data from foraging societies, Hillard Kaplan (1994) calculated that it takes some 13 million calories to rear immatures to a point where they produce as much as they consume. Because it takes more calories than a mother by herself could produce (over and above her own needs) to get to this point, offspring would have needed nutritional subsidies from allomothers until they were 18 years of age, or older. In contrast to all other apes, human mothers produce a new baby before her previous, weaned infant is nutritionally independent (Kaplan et al. 2000; Lancaster and Lancaster 1983). How could natural selection have favored an ape female who produced offspring so far beyond her means to rear? Such mothers must have had help. In hunting and gathering societies, help from fathers was important, sometimes critically so, but what about when due to death, defection, or inadequacy, a deficit remained? Then who helped? It is not that contributions by husbands or hunters are unimportant, but that a mother who relied exclusively on a sex contract with the father to provision their children, risked failure. What were her alternatives?

THE COOPERATIVE BREEDING HYPOTHESIS

The cooperative breeding hypothesis presumes that mothers evolved in groups where a broader range of individuals—not just the genetic father—assisted the genetic mother in protecting, carrying, or provisioning offspring, thereby permitting her to produce and rear costlier, slower-maturing offspring than otherwise would survive. Divisions of labor between breeders and nonbreeding helpers would have permitted mothers to reproduce faster. Concomitant sharing and cooperation also permitted reliance on a wider range of resources and with it the option to move into new habitats. This is one reason why cooperative breeding has independently evolved in a small but diverse array of arthropod, avian, and mammalian species (Emlen 1991; Solomon and French 1997a; Stacey and Koenig 1990). Somewhere between 8 and 17 percent of birds (Heinsohn and Double 2004) and perhaps 3% of mammals breed cooperatively. In the case of humans, I believe it was cooperative breeding that originally allowed them to spread out of Africa and expand into diverse habitats around the globe as also occurred in other geographically successful cooperative breeders like canids, lions, elephants, and various corvids.

Alloparental assistance by genetic relatives is well explained by Hamilton's rule. Individuals help when the cost of caring is less than the benefits to their charges calibrated by degree of relatedness. But high degrees of relatedness between an allomother and his or her charges are not the only motivations for helping. Ways in which helpers benefit include obtaining a safe refuge while buying time to mature, acquire subsistence skills, practice parenting skills, or awaiting opportunities to breed; acquiring improved social status or opportunities to signal quality to prospective mates; obtaining occasional mating opportunities; enhancing the territory or cooperating community in ways that improve future breeding opportunities or increase the helper's chance of inheriting access to these resources (for review, see Cockburn 1998). Ecological constraints may facilitate the evolution of cooperative breeding if breeding territories or other inherited resources critical for reproduction are in short supply (Emlen 1991; Pen and Weissing 2000:2417ff.).

Individuals who lack help, access to resources, or relevant skills have little chance of breeding successfully anyway. This reduces the fitness costs of helping. Furthermore, when helpers have the option to strategically schedule assistance, they can limit helping to phases when they are well nourished or can spare the time. When helping does interfere with their own reproduction, however, allomothers may decline to help (Russell et al. 2003). Finally, allomothers at or near the end of their reproductive careers have little if anything to lose by helping, which may explain selflessness in defense of infants sometimes exhibited by old female primates (Hrdy and Hrdy 1976).

REQUIREMENTS AND HALLMARKS OF COOPERATIVE BREEDING: COMPARATIVE EVIDENCE

Philopatry and a high degree of sociality are essential for shared caretaking to evolve in the first place. To set the stage for the evolution of cooperation, one sex or the other has to remain in its natal group in order to be susceptible to infant solicitations (Emlen 1995; Solomon and French 1997a). Another requirement is sufficient phenotypic flexibility so individuals can shift between nonreproductive and reproductive caretaking roles.

Flexibility and opportunism are hallmarks of cooperatively breeding species. Wild dogs provide a classic example. Typically, wild dog packs have a single breeding pair attended by allomothers who provision the alpha female while she gestates and lactates; bring predigested meat back to her pups; guard them while the alpha female hunts; and also allow her pups once weaned and past the age of receiving predigested "baby food" to eat first at kills. Nevertheless, when feasible, subordinate female "helpers" ovulate and breed themselves. Genetic analyses reveal that most pups are produced by the alpha female, but as many as 8 percent are borne to subordinates. Even when the alpha female has a dominant mate, 10 percent or more of pups may be sired by subordinates (cited in Creel and Creel 2002). Typically pups are suckled by their mother, but they may also be suckled by an allomother who undergoes pseudopregnancy and lactates without giving birth. The Creels even observed one subordinate nullipara begin to lactate ten days after the litter was born. Thereafter, she ended up spending more time with the pups than the mother and did most of the suckling.

Following Sherman et al. (1995), cooperative breeding occurs along a continuum ranging from modest assistance (like carrying or protecting infants while mothers forage) to extensive assistance that includes prolonged babysitting, provisioning, or even suckling. Helping behavior ranges from facultative to obligate assistance, depending on how feasible it is for mothers to rear offspring on their own, but food sharing and allomaternal provisioning of young are probably essential for the prolonged periods of nutritional dependency I focus on here.

The key feature of cooperative breeding is that when available, allomaternal assistance alters basic quantity-versus-quality life-history trade-offs underlying maternal decision-making. In a paradoxical departure from the usual trade-offs, mothers in a cooperative breeding system can produce more, larger, or more closely spaced offspring even as total cost of rearing each offspring to independence increases. They can invest less per offspring and give birth again sooner, without sacrificing child survival. Divisions of labor between reproductive and nonreproductive group members lower the costs of mothering as allomothers in addition to mothers respond to signals of infant and juvenile needs by providing protection, care, and/or provisioning. Allomaternal provisioning also permits offspring to remain dependent longer, because they can afford to take longer to grow up without risking starvation. Buffered by allomaternal assistance, mothers in cooperatively breeding species also tend to survive longer presumably because they are healthier, better provisioned, and remain in safer locales (in a hive, in a den, near camp; e.g., Rowley and Russell 1990; Keller and Genoud 1997).

Whether we are talking about dunnocks or acorn woodpeckers, wild dogs, mongooses, or elephants, mating arrangements in cooperative breeders are very flexible. Breeding associations range from reproductively "single" mothers or monogamous pairs surrounded by nonbreeding helpers (some social mongooses or marmosets), to socially bonded pairs who are also facultatively polyandrous or polygynous where alloparental male help is very important (e.g., other marmosets; many birds). Helpers may be either close relatives or hopeful immigrants waiting to inherit a territory. Helpers may be totally excluded from breeding opportunities or have occasional opportunities to breed. This flexible style of family life varies with local ecologies (or economics) and depending on which sex currently has the most leverage, a not uncommon pattern in traditional human societies (Emlen 1995; Hrdy 2002).

If humans evolved as cooperative breeders, there would be no need to invoke the development of sapient brains or other uniquely human rationales as the original selection pressures favoring longer childhoods. Improved child survival, and with it slower maturation (Hamilton 1966) along with prolonged periods of postweaning dependence, would have evolved as routine corollaries of cooperative breeding. So far the strongest evidence in support of this proposition comes from birds.

COOPERATIVE BREEDING AND LONG "CHILDHOODS"

The link between cooperative breeding and prolonged dependence was first demonstrated by behavioral ecologist Tom Langen in a comparative study of birds. Of 261 passerine birds, 217 species did not ever breed cooperatively, 10 did so occasionally, while 34 species were frequent cooperative breeders. Average duration of postfledgling nutritional dependence was twice as long (just over 50 days) for birds that frequently bred cooperatively compared to birds who never bred cooperatively (just over 20 days). Species that occasionally bred cooperatively fell in between, at just over 30 days (Langen 2000:Figure 1) Cooperating and noncooperating species do not differ in duration of incubation or nesting periods, but they differed significantly in duration of nutritional dependence postfledging.

Langen (2000) argues that prolonged postfledging dependence is made possible because additional care from alloparents reduces the cost of parenting, and offspring have less incentive to become independent. A new sort of division of labor develops as nonbreeders feed fledglings, freeing breeders to initiate the next nesting attempt (p. 367). Langen's terminology is aviocentric, but his logic applies more generally. In theory, the same arguments should apply to social mammals. Unfortunately though, mammals have not been as intensively studied as birds have, and it is also harder to pinpoint the timing of independence. As yet, no comparable analysis across mammals has been done, Hence we cannot extend Langen's arguments to mammals with the same conviction with which we apply them to birds. That said, the greater prenatal and postnatal costs of rearing young documented in the best studied species of cooperatively breeding mammals (especially perhaps those with suppressed ovulation) are consistent (see Creel and Creel 1991:Table 2). Consider also the case of Callitrichids, who according to Harvey et al. (1987:Figure 16-4) appear to mature almost as slowly as humans do provided that their much lower birth weights are taken into account and controlled for. Allomaternal provisioning means that offspring can take their time maturing without risking starvation, even though their mothers wean them, conceive again and produce new offspring. This is the case with wolves and wild dogs, where alloparents provide regurgitated meat to pups. Premasticated "baby food" means that even in mammals (where only lactating females provide the earliest food) males can provision older immatures, just as both sexes are able to do in birds and humans. Even after pups outgrow the milk and "formula" phase, parental and alloparental forbearance buffers less-than-self-sufficient, still inexperienced, hunters over long apprenticeships during which they become proficient hunters. Experienced grown-ups tolerate youngsters at kills and may even allow them feeding priority. Although scramble competition at kills would normally mean that smallest group members feed last, least, or not-at-all, this is not what happens among cooperatively breeding carnivores like wild dogs, where preferential access to food by pups and cubs is typical (e.g., see Creel and Creel 2002:165; Malcolm and Marten 1982).

I hypothesize that dependents were similarly buffered among our ancestors and that cooperative breeding thus helps to explain prolonged and delayed childhood and adolescence in humans (compared to other apes), a developmental process that may have begun with *Homo erectus* (Tardieu 1998:173–174), although this proposition remains controversial. The hypothesis that allomaternal buffering provided the initial condition permitting delayed growth spurts does not rule out the possibility that once started, delayed maturation and greater brain growth coevolved.

ALLOMATERNAL ASSISTANCE AMONG NONHUMAN PRIMATES

The central assumption of the cooperative breeding hypothesis is that allomothers increase the reproductive success of mothers. Do they? After all, allomothers might have their own reasons for "helping," like obtaining practice by babysitting. It is now well documented for some species of cooperatively breeding birds and mammals that alloparental assistance permits mothers to breed more rapidly and/or increases offspring survival (e.g., Emlen 1991; Langen and Vehrencamp 1999; Solomon and French 1997a; Stacey and Koenig 1990), but such evidence has been slow in coming for primates. The main problem in demonstrating alloparental effects has been the difficulty of obtaining information on lifetime reproductive success for long-lived primates. In addition, the mother-centered models for our own species—reinforced by data from the other apes—were so compelling that many anthropologists and psychologists tended to overlook the role of other caretakers even though primatologists had been reporting on rudimentary cooperative breeding (allomaternal care without provisioning) in primates for many years (e.g., Hrdy 1976).

Across primates, allomaternal assistance ranges from simple protection or occasional interventions during disputes, to carrying babies, to cases where allomothers (often males likely to be the father) spend *more* time holding infants than mothers do (see continuum of primate allomaternal care in Figure 3.1). If we include paternal care, on the order of half or more of all 175 or so species of primates are characterized by some degree of shared caretaking. Allomaternal attention to infants is a far more important feature of primate behavior than has been generally realized (Hrdy 1999).

Mothers in species with "infant-sharing" depend on allomothers less than full-fledged cooperative breeders where allomothers provision as well as care for youngsters. Nevertheless, in infant-sharing Hanuman langurs, infants are carried by females other than the mother up to 50 percent of daylight hours from the first day of life (Hrdy 1977). Energetic savings to the mother mean the mother can conceive again sooner, and breed at a faster rate without impairing her own or her offspring's survival Mitani and Watts 1997; Ross and MacLarnon 2000). Without allomaternal provisioning weaned youngsters are under pressure to provision themselves, ruling out leisurely development as an option.

Currently the only primates counted among full-fledged cooperative breeders—where allomothers provision as well as carry their charges—are at the extreme end of the primate continuum of shared care, among marmosets and tamarins. Adult males—typically former sexual partners of the mother—are so eager to carry the babies (usually twins) that by the second week after birth, males carry them as much as 60 percent of the time. Unlike cooperative breeding birds where allomothers feed immatures right from hatching, or those carnivores where subordinate females serve as wet nurses, only the lactating mother has ever been observed to suckle Callitrichid babies. Nevertheless, by one week, an adult male is doing most of the carrying, and by three weeks—with weaning still more than two months away—marmoset allomothers supplement the mother's milk with "finger food" in the form of crickets and other small-prey items. The more males in the group, the higher the mother's reproductive success (Bales et al. 2002; Snowdon 1996). Such help is costly to males, who spend less time foraging and fail to gain weight until after their charges are mobile.

Cottontop tamarin mothers are so dependent on this assistance, that regardless of how old or experienced the mother is, if adult or sibling caretakers are not available, mothers short on assistance abandon their young at high rates (Bardi et al. 2001; Johnson et al. 1991). Humans are the only other primates with such high rates of abandonment. (Detailed evidence

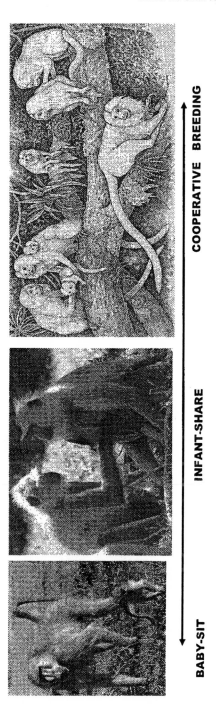

BABY-SIT   **INFANT-SHARE**   **COOPERATIVE BREEDING**

Figure 3.1. At one end of the primate continuum of caretaking, visualize the adult male baboon who remains near infants born to females with whom he has previously mated. As experiments with playback tapes demonstrate, he watches out for them and should the need arise, positions himself to protect them not just from predators, but also from attacks by other baboons, especially strange males (Palombit 1999). This helpful male is often the genetic father (Buchan et al. 2003), but given the polyandrous mating habits of baboon mothers, he will typically have a less than certain probability of paternity. This implies a relatively low cost for males offering such nonexclusive care. Langurs and other "infant-sharing" langurs monkeys fall further along this continuum. Babysitting by female group members (often prereproductives) frees mothers to forage more efficiently. At the extreme right edge of the continuum, there is extensive investment by a tamarin male who carries heavy twins most of the time, but who also has a high probability of being their genetic father. Other males also help by catching small prey items to feed infants approaching the age of weaning. Images courtesy of R. Palombit; S. Hrdy; S. Landry.

for unusually situation-dependent and contingent maternal commitment
is summarized in Hrdy (1999:Chapters 8, 12, 14); the main exception to the
pattern is in inexperienced first-time or "primiparous" mothers, which
may have trouble rearing infants in other primates as well as in humans
without social support) (see Figure 3.2).

HUMAN EVIDENCE THAT ALLOMOTHERS HELP

Anthropologists have long been aware that older siblings, cousins, and
other family members play important roles as child-minders (Hames 1988;
Konner, Chapter 2 in this volume; LeVine et al. 1996: Tronick et al. 1987;
Weisner and Gallimore, 1977). The more attention one pays to the original
field studies and the less attention is paid to categorical statements from the
secondary literature, the less monotropic maternal caretaking seems (discussed in Konner, Chapter 2 in this volume). Yet it was the end of the 1980s
before sociobiologists began to consider the evolutionary implications and
to collect the data showing that allomaternal assistance actually affected reproductive success. In a pioneering 1988 paper, Paul Turke at the University of Michigan linked the availability of allomaternal assistance to
increased maternal reproductive success among islanders living on Ifaluk

Figure 3.2.   Aka camp in the Central Africa Republic where infants are cared
       for by a range of caretakers, mostly relatives of various ages and both
       sexes. Courtesy of B. Hewlett.

in Micronesia. In this matrilineal and matrilocally living population, women who bore a daughter first had higher reproductive success than those women whose first two children were sons. Similarly in a study of a Trinidadian village in the Caribbean, nine mothers who lived in households with nonreproductive helpers on hand—usually daughters—had significantly higher reproductive success than 29 mothers without (Flinn 1989). In a study of Mandinka horticulturalists in the Gambia of West Africa, children had better survival than did same-age children without older sisters (Sear et al. 2002:58). As in the Ifaluk case, daughters helped more than brothers, but Truk was the only place where birth-order (having a daughter first) seemed to matter.

All of these studies documented beneficial effects from having a big sister. Elsewhere though, benefits from having older siblings did not show until later in life, when younger siblings themselves reproduced (e.g., see demographic data analyzed for !Kung hunter-gatherers in Botswana by Hames and Draper 2001). Mechanisms responsible for this correlation are not known, but it seems possible that adult siblings may provide shelter or food in times of crisis, contributing that way to the survival of nieces and nephews. Although most research in this area has focused on prereproductive helpers, it is worth keeping in mind that collateral kin can help at any point in their life cycle.

Ever since Hawkes and coworkers (1989) became intrigued by how hard and efficiently postreproductive women were working at food gathering among Hadza foragers in East Africa, evidence has been accumulating that the presence of older matrilineal kin (both grandmothers and great-aunts) enhances the growth and survival of immature relatives. Such data are all the more remarkable because the correlation is found over a broad socioecological spectrum. The best documented cases come from East and Central African hunters and gatherers (Hawkes et al. 2001b; Ivey 2000; Ivey Henry, Chapter 9), West African horticulturalists in the Gambia (Sear et al. 2000), 18th-century German peasants (Voland and Beise 2002), and rice-growing peasants in Tokugawa, Japan (Jamison et al. 2002). Among South Asian swidden agriculturalists (Leonetti et al. 2002). Grandmothers also contribute to shorter birth intervals, although exactly how is not known.

For both 18th-century Germany (Voland and Beise 2002) and the Gambia (Sear et al. 2002), the survival advantage of having a maternal grandmother nearby showed up around the age of weaning—a very vulnerable life phase attended by emotional stress and the introduction of new foods. The timing of the effect suggests provisioning is at issue. However, mothers in the Gambia population were primarily Muslim, living patrilocally in their husband's home. At first glance, then, it seems odd that it would be the *maternal* grandmother's presence that mattered so much. But Sear et al. (2002:59) note how common it is for West African mothers to foster babies out around weaning in order to help their babies "forget the breast." Hence the most solicitous available caretaker not already a household member would be—were she still alive, and nearby—the maternal grand-mother.

THE VERY VARIABLE ROLE OF FATHERS

The most surprising finding from this West African horticultural society in the Gambia was not that maternal grandmothers mattered so much. Rather it was how little difference the presence of the father or older brothers made. Even when the father was absent altogether, alloparents were able to compensate (e.g., Blurton Jones et al., Chapter 10 in this volume; Sear et al. 2002). Yet where game is more important, as among Ache foragers of Paraguay, the death of a child's father undermined his survival chances (Hill and Hurtado 1996). Perhaps not surprisingly, mothers under such conditions cover their bets by lining up several possible "fathers." Whereas in some societies, a wife suspected of adultery puts herself in peril, in oth-ers, her options for manipulating information about paternity are en-hanced by customary beliefs about how long pregnancy lasts, or about how many men contribute to the formation of a fetus.

Across vast areas of South America, there is a prevailing belief that a fetus is built up from contributions of semen from all the men a woman has sex with in the ten months preceding birth. This presumably quite an-cient belief encompasses multiple language groups, from the Ache and Kaingang people in Paraguay, all the way north as far as the Yanamami and Bari in Venezuela, eastward to the Canela, Mehinaku, and Arawete peoples in Brazil, westward to the Matis of Peru. Over a vast region, moth-ers rely on the convenient biological fiction that it takes contributions of semen from more than one man to "make" a baby to reduce male sexual jealousy and facilitate sexual sharing of a woman by possible "fathers" who will jointly help provision both the mothers and their children (Beck-erman and Valentine 2002). Among the Bari and the Ache, the only two groups for which we have data on child survival rates, children with two "fathers" survived better than those with only one. However, children as-cribed to too many "fathers" survived less well, presumably because men may balk at provisioning them (Beckerman et al. 1998; Hill and Hurtado 1996).

Many cooperatively breeding mammals *do* routinely bear litters with more than one genetic father (e.g., wild dogs, wolves, dwarf mongooses, lions). But humans do not. Nevertheless, a belief in partible paternity pre-sumably persists because in a part of the world where provisioning by males is unpredictable, and where mothers need more help than one man by himself can provide, the willingness of several men to provision mothers and their children is critical for the survival of patrilineal as well as matrilineal lines. Generation after generation having multiple "fathers" (along with any "memes" that facilitated it) paid off. As soon as a Bari woman misses a period she may attempt to seduce one of the better fishermen or hunters in her group. This may be the flip side to the observation that the best hunters and the best fisherman have the most lovers (e.g., Hill and Hurtado 1996).

Such a belief system makes it is easier for mothers to draw several men into a web of possible paternity. The custom may also facilitate cooperation and alliances among men (often kin) belonging to the same community. Ritual reinforces these beliefs. Among the Canela of Brazil, for example, sex with multiple partners takes place during public ceremonies, in full view of everyone, and with the approval of the community. Subsequently, all the men a woman had intercourse with are publicly acknowledged as cofathers to the next infant she bears. Within limits, traditional beliefs about shared paternity function to diminish, not necessarily eliminate, sexual jealousy. In large areas of Central Africa, as well as in parts of Western Asia, there is customary sharing of wives within fraternal clans and among both genetic and fictional "brothers" (Hrdy 2001c). We are still in the early days of the study of the reproductive consequences of "polyandrous motherhood" (Guyer 1994). Already though it is clear that we need to reexamine the reflexive assumption that children develop best reared in nuclear families and cared for exclusively by mothers, for whether or not these presumptions pertain depends on economic and social circumstances.

If our ancestors lived among groups of relatives, as is true among most hunter-gatherers, generalized tendencies to behave altruistically toward needy group members would be adaptive (Wiessner 2002). Wiessner argues persuasively that among the !Kung San, successful hunters are not just provisioning other group members, who are more likely than not kin. They are also providing incentives for capable, willing allomothers to remain in their group. Meat becomes a reward hunters can use to produce long-term residential and political configurations favorable to rearing their children, as well as increasing the resource-holding potential of the group as a whole (Wiessner 2002:427, Tables 3 and 4).[3]

It is now clear for many species that degree of relatedness affects whom individuals help and how much (Emlen 1995). Once again, cooperatively breeding birds provide the best-documented examples. For example, among dunnocks, provisioning by alpha and beta males is calibrated to each male's probability of paternity (Davies 1992). The calculus for caring can be especially complex in the case of possible progenitors [see Westneat and Sargent (1996) for an excellent overview]. Whereas in some species or situations, males respond to decreased certainty of paternity by withholding care or even by destroying offspring, in others, even males who are less than certain of paternity help [e.g., see Osorio-Beristain and Drummond (2001) for birds; Palombit (1999), Buchan et al. (2003) for baboons]. In this respect, humans exhibit marked intraspecific variation, depending on circumstances. In some situations a father is essential for child survival, while in others the effects of his presence are hard to even document. Among the Ache, a child whose father dies may be killed by a stepfather, or preemptively eliminated by the mother herself (Hill and Hurtado 1996). Similarly, among modern Canadians there is a significant increase in the risk of abusive treatment if a stepfather (or boyfriend) rather than the baby's father is living with the mother(Daly and Wilson 1988). Yet in modern Sweden, where extensive social welfare allotments defray costs to unrelated "fathers", no such effect was found (Temrin et al. 2000). Consider also the Mandinkan case from the Gambia, West Africa. There allomothers play an important role in subsidizing the costs of childrearing and death of the father made no detectable difference unless the mother remarried and thereby placed her child at risk from a stepfather (Sear et al. 2002). It is not my intent here to downplay the importance of fathers, but only to call attention to how variable is the role they play, depending on what other sources of support, alloparental or otherwise, are available.

THE IMPORTANCE OF REAL AND
PERCEIVED ALLOMATERNAL SUPPORT

For all mammals, the best single predictor of infant survival is maternal commitment. But in humans, this commitment—at least initially—is influenced by the mother's own perception of social support. Mothers register social signals given off by those around them, and translate this information into how much material support is likely to be forthcoming. Thus, even when the mother is *initially* the main caretaker (almost always the case in lactating mammals), availability of allomaternal support matters. The ethnographic and historical record for societies in which child survival is far more uncertain than in our own provides ample evidence that mothers short on allomaternal support are more likely to abandon infants at birth (Hrdy 1999:372 ff.).

Even small increases in level of social support make a difference. Adolescent U.S. mothers (even those where the father remains with them) are more sensitive to their infants' needs and have more securely attached infants if a supportive grandmother is also on hand (Spieker and Bensley 1994). Women visited in their homes during their pregnancy by trained nurses and during the first two years after birth had a lower incidence of child abuse (Olds et al. 1986). Follow-up studies confirmed the long-term benefits (in terms of these allomaternal interventions (Olds et al. 2002).

Social workers and medical personnel have long been aware that children benefit from living in extended, multigenerational families. Even when socioeconomic conditions are controlled, rates of morbidity and mortality continue to rise among children in single-parent homes (Weitoft et al. 2003). Nor does this effect appear to be due to the absence of the father per se (e.g., Golombok et al. 1997). Rather the evidence suggests that it is the various forms of support provided by multiple caretakers that matters. Furthermore, if maternal competence is compromised by immaturity, by inexperience, by father absence, or by resource scarcity, the presence of alloparents turns out to be more important still. For example, babies born to unmarried, low-income U.S. teenagers tested better on cognitive development at age four if a grandmother was present (Furstenberg 1976). By three years of age, children are able to interpret the feelings and intentions of others, and can even imagine what it is like to be someone altogether different (Harris 2000:54-55). Infants who have older siblings develop this "theory of mind" sooner, and with greater sophistication (Ruffman et al. 1998; Perner et al. 1994). For children at risk, the guidance, emotional support, protection, and material support of grandmothers have a positive effect at all ages (reviewed in Werner 1984).

The most obvious explanation for faster growth rates among the Gambian children with maternal grandmothers nearby (Sear et al. 2000) is that these postmenopausal women, unencumbered by dependent offspring of their own, provided their grandchildren with extra food. However we cannot yet rule out alternative possibilities. Years ago Widdowson (1951) reported that institutionalized children in the charge of an emotionally warm and nurturing matron grew faster. So too, the faster-growing Gambia children may have responded to emotional support from an affectionate grandmother by thriving. Indeed, the cooperative breeding hypothesis specifically predicts that children should be responsive to emotional cues from caretakers since in human environments of evolutionary relevance signals of emotional commitment would have been correlated with prospects of continued provisioning. That is, we should expect human immatures to possess psychological devices for monitoring signals of commitment from both mothers *and* allomothers. Continued rapid growth should be expected when infants perceive these cues, but detection of indifference or neglect should slow growth down so as to conserve resources and increase chances of surviving future anticipated neglect. This may be why even with adequate nutrition available, some children nevertheless "fail to thrive" (Pollitt and Leibel 1980).

A vast historical and sociological literature now documents emotional, cognitive, physiological, as well as material benefits for children growing up in extended families with older siblings, grandmothers, kin, or as-if kin in attendance (e.g., El Hassan Al Awad and Sonuga-Barke 1992; Stack 1974; Spieker and Bensley 1994). Until recently though, few researchers thought of such advantages in *evolutionary* terms, primarily I suspect because most sociological and psychological studies were done in populations with low rates of infant and child mortality. Not until the sociobiologically oriented field studies of the late 1980s did the actual *survival* advantages from allomaternal assistance in humans become apparent.

SUMMARY, CAVEATS, AND AN ASIDE ON GENETIC RELATEDNESS

Old paradigms are in flux. As we replace old models based on "sex contracts" with new ones based on cooperative breeding, there is all the more reason to proceed with caution lest the pendulum swing unchecked. As old biases are corrected, and kin-selected altruism moves to center stage, it is time to worry lest a new set of biases replace the old ones.

After years of neglecting the role of alloparents, it may now be time to worry about overemphasizing collateral kin. For example, we should be careful not to cast grandmothers as universally more useful than they really are. This is why it is important to pay attention to outliers, to the odd findings that do not readily conform to the model in hand, and why it is important for journal editors and reviewers to urge publications of "negative results." Consider Draper and Howell's (Chapter 12, in this volume) reexamination of !Kung demography as it relates to the body mass index (BMI) of children. These authors detected no advantage from having grandparents. This could be because the cooperative breeding hypothesis is wrong or, as Draper suggests, because we need to take social context into account. Perhaps it is the band rather than kin group per se that provides critical assistance under these particular demographic and ecological conditions. For genetic relatedness is not the *only* determiner of nurturing. If the cost of caring is low enough and benefits to recipients are high enough, individuals who are only distantly related should still help (Hamilton 1964). This generalization applies in spades to humans, where payoffs from generosity and kindness come in many currencies, and where other group members may react negatively to those who fail to help a child.

HAMILTON'S RULE AND THE PROXIMATE CAUSES OF HELPING

Ultimately, individuals in species with a history of cooperative breeding would be predisposed to help mothers rear their young because their own inclusive fitness (that is, individual fitness plus the fitness effects upon close kin) was enhanced by aiding relatives rear offspring. Helping also provides valuable practice, increases group acceptance, or paves the way to later breeding opportunities for experienced individuals who inherit mates or territories. But what are the mechanisms? At a proximate level, there must be selection pressure on nonmothers to find infants appealing in the first place. Helpers have to assess and respond to infant needs depending on the urgency of need and the caretaker's own condition. In the case of older females approaching the end of their reproductive careers, "donative intent" goes up (apparently a fairly general rule in primates) but postreproductives nevertheless should prioritize their service depending on degree of relatedness and especially *level of need* (Blurton Jones et al., Chapter 10 in this volume; Hrdy 1999:Chapter 11). That said, many primates (perhaps especially females?) exhibit a bias toward helping, as if their internalized version of Hamilton's rule more nearly read: *Find infants appealing and help them if you can, so long as the cost is not prohibitive and so long as it does not interfere with caring for your own new baby.* This may be because the female primates I am most familiar with (humans and langurs) evolved in kin groups.

In many primates, males and females respond differently to solicitations from infants. In infant-sharing species belonging to the subfamily Colobinae, for example, newborn infants exercise a magnetic appeal on females (and this may be why they are born with flamboyantly colored natal coats to advertise their neonativity), but such signals may be less attractive to males (Hrdy 1976). Male nonchalance in species like langur monkeys contrasts with the fanatically nurturing behavior and the prioritizing of infant care by adult males seen in species with *obligate* male care. For example, among titi monkeys, fathers are actually more responsive to infant signals, and more eager to carry infants than their mothers are.

In humans, however, both sexes respond to attractive behaviors (like smiling or babbling), and both sexes respond to "cuteness" and/or vulnerability (round heads, small face, big eyes, immature body form), but there are nevertheless significant differences in how the sexes respond to them. In one of the few studies of this, Thomas Alley (1983) asked 120 childless undergraduates to examine drawings that only differed in size and how babylike or immature the body proportions were. For both sexes the "mean cuddliness ratings" decreased with perceived age, and for both sexes, having a younger sibling increased responsiveness. However, on average women were significantly more protective than men (i.e., they would intervene if someone struck the infant). Compared to most women, men probably have a higher threshold for responding to infants (e.g., see Babchuk et al. 1985; Silk 2002). Nevertheless, what stands out here is just how responsive men are to prolonged exposure.

The most revealing research in this area has been done on prolactin-mediated systems. The first hint that there was a connection between prolactin levels and "paternal" behavior came from a study of marmosets (Dixson and George 1982). The discovery was initially met with skepticism, in part because prolactin was viewed as a lactation-related hormone linked to *maternal* rather than paternal behavior. Critics protested that prolactin must be a response to stress in these males rather than a corollary of nurturing tendencies. Subsequently, the introduction of improved, noninvasive techniques permitted robust replications of Dixson and George's discovery (Schradin and Anzenberger 1999 for review), and higher prolactin levels were also correlated with male helping behavior in other cooperative breeders, such as provisioning by male scrub jays (Schoesch 1998). Interestingly, prior experience is a factor in primate male responsiveness as it also is in females, and the rise in prolactin levels is even more pronounced among males with prior caretaking experience (Snowdon 1996).

It took two decades and a paradigm shift in how biologists conceptualized sex roles before anyone studied the hormone profiles of men in proximity with infants. As soon as they did, it became clear that endocrinological shifts in men spending time in proximity to pregnant women and new infants are surprisingly similar to those found among cooperatively breeding male marmosets (Gubernick et al., no date; Hewlett and Aster, no date; Storey et al. 2000; Wynne-Edwards and Reburn 2000). Prolactin levels in cohabiting men gradually rose over the course of their companion's pregnancy. In addition, men exposed to pregnant women and new babies experience a drop in testosterone after birth (Fleming et al. in prep; Grey et al. 2002; Storey et al. 2000)—something no one would have expected to find in parents with a strict division of labor between nurturing mothers and protective male hunters. However, male flexibility in this respect is compatible with the hypothesis that humans evolved in cooperative breeding systems where if no other allomother was available, a male might pinch-hit.

Without question, hormonal changes during pregnancy and lactation are more pronounced in mothers than in their male partners. With some important exceptions, female primates tend to be more sensitive to infant signals and solicitations than males are. No one is suggesting that fathers are equivalent to mothers. So different are the physiological and sensory thresholds of the two sexes that experimenters use different scales to measure them. But the point remains, whether caretakers are mice, marmosets, or humans, that *both sexes can potentially be primed to be more nurturing by innate physiological responses to infant stimuli.* The neurological framework is in place. Just being near infants or pregnant mothers renders males or virgin females more nurturing, so that giving birth is not a prerequisite for nurturing.

If humans evolved as cooperative breeders, an obvious prediction would be that some potential for nurturing response to prolonged contact with infants should be found among males generally, not just in husbands or genetic fathers—something that remains to be seen.

SPECULATIONS ON COOPERATIVE BREEDING, AND CHILDHOOD MILESTONES SUCH AS MIND-READING, MILK TEETH, AND BABBLING

Once allomothers become important for child survival, selection would have acted on any number of life history traits that made allomothers more available (e.g., delayed dispersal, delayed maturity, longer lifespans). In particular, Hawkes et al. (1998 and elsewhere) have explored the implications of assistance by older matrilineal kin for lifespans that last long past menopause. Selection should also favor emotional traits that make allomothers more helpful and more responsive to signals of need (e.g., increased empathy in particular age-sex classes). One outcome would be that natural selection should have favored humans whose neuronal systems registered the act of helping others (even those they are not related to) as pleasurable. This is precisely what studies show that use magnetic resonance imaging to track the effects of altruistic behavior on pleasure centers in the brain (Rilling et al. 2002). Experiments using "ultimatum games" and other experiments to determine internalized rules used when sharing reveal humans to be far more altruistic than anticipated. Whether in modern or traditional societies, humans appear to employ innate rules about what is fair (Henrich et al. 2001). The discovery that rational self-interest often takes a backseat to internalized rules of sharing and fair play is revolutionizing traditional economic theories (Fehr and Fischbacher, 2003). Remarkable as all this seems, even more momentous selection pressures appear to have been at work on human infants.

Assuming that our ancestors were cooperative breeders among whom maternal commitment was unusually contingent on social support, human offspring would have needed to monitor and interpret the moods and intentions of others more than other apes do. Infants who could engage their mothers right from birth would have an advantage over those who could not. Beyond the discomfort and separation cries characteristic of all infant apes, human infants would have been under greater selection pressure to appeal to both mothers and allomothers. Perhaps not surprisingly then, right from birth human infants seek out human faces, and initiate contact with others. Remarkably early in development, babies imitate faces, smile, and laugh in ways that apes reared exclusively by their mothers have not been observed to do (Meltzoff and Prinz 2002; Papousek et al. 1991). Early learning biases persist, and are refined and reinforced through experience (see esp. Tomasello 1999), as babies become more discriminating. Eyes play a key role in the attendant social engagements (Baron-Cohen [1995] 2001). Human infants seek out and fixate on eyes, and preferentially respond to a direct gaze. By three to four months, infants smile less at adults who avert their gaze, and resume smiling when the adult looks straight at them (Farroni et al. 2002). The sociocognitive tools for monitoring others and reading their intentions by seeking out their eyes, following their gaze, etc., are more developed in humans than in other apes (Baron-Cohen [1995] 2001). Emerging evidence for chimpanzees reveals that other apes are capable of observational learning and imitation (Whitten et al. 2003), but humans appear to be unusually eager to do so, and are unusually adept at it. Just how different chimps and humans are in respect to reading intentions (Tomasello 1999) remains a matter of debate. But by and large, humans are more able to understand what someone else is trying to do and why, and from an early age they are more interested in sharing the experiences of others. Understanding how someone else is thinking about a task, along with shared interest in their goals, improves our ability to learn through observation, and makes humans especially prone to accumulate and transmit new knowledge. Indeed, Simon Baron-Cohen ([1995] 2001) and James Chisholm (2003) have argued that mental aptitudes for reading what is in the minds of others evolved *because* they proved valuable for identifying and interpreting the intentions of others. I agree. But why should humans and chimps differ in this respect? Why (to use Tomasello's excellent descriptor) are humans so "hyper-social"?

According to proponents of the "Machiavellian intelligence" hypothesis, reading the minds of others was a strategic advantage in competitive worlds characterized by shifting alliances—as is typical of many primate societies (Byrne and Whitten 1985). But since many primates, and certainly other apes, live in complexly competitive social worlds, the Machiavellian intelligence hypothesis still does not explain why humans are so much better at imagining the intentions of others, even unseen others, than other apes seem to be. Chimpanzees, after all are at least as dominance-oriented and competitive as humans are, probably more so. So we are still left with the question of why capacities for formulating "theories of mind" and especially for shared engagement are so much better developed in humans (Tomasello 1999).

I suggest that what really distinguishes humans from other apes is not so much our competitive heritage as our more cooperative one, and that cooperative breeding left offspring who grew up in such systems with neuronal underpinnings for shared engagement. Infants born into cooperative breeding systems are desperately seeking caretakers, and even their own mother's commitment (far and away the most important factor in their survival) is going to be contingent not just on the cues she receives from her infant, but on her perception of how much support from allomothers she is likely to have. To be so dependent and still prosper, infants have to be adept at reading their mother's intentions and soliciting other caretakers if needed. As Chisholm (2003) stresses, "theory of mind" reduces the uncertainties such youngsters would face, helping them to predict how others (both mothers and allomothers) are going to respond. In other words, it was the discriminative solicitude of mothers themselves that imposed the necessity that was the mother to this inventiveness. Through practice and conditional rewards, infants get incrementally better at reading the intentions of their caretakers, learning to engage them, and eliciting solicitude.

In the case of creatures as intelligent and manipulative as all apes are, such precociously expressed abilities to read and interpret the intentions of others continues to develop throughout the first years of life. There is a racheting effect as early attempts to monitor mother (and perhaps others) develop into sophisticated mind-reading and experience-sharing abilities (Tomasello 1999:67; Baron-Cohen [1995] 2001). Being able to intuit and care about what others are thinking, to cognitively and emotionally put oneself in someone else's shoes, and to think about what they are thinking (and learn from it) has in turn had spectacular repercussions in the evolution of our peculiarly "hypersocial," information-sharing, and culture-transmitting species (Tomasello 1999), a species preadapted for all manner of cooperation. Sociocognitive development right from birth plays an important role in the development of the neural underpinnings for such talents. Indeed, it is intriguing to note that chimp infants raised from birth in experimental situations with both their mother and human allomothers, also engage their caretakers more, gazing into their faces and smiling far more than has ever been observed among wild or exclusively mother-reared, chimps (Bard in press; Matsuzawa 2001). Such observations may help us to imagine the first steps in the transition to human sociocognitive aptitudes. The point I stress here then is that increased reliance on allomaternal care and provisioning, and with it prolonged maturation, *preceded* the emergence of peculiarly human talents, and facilitated (even permitted) their evolution since natural selection cannot favor traits at the genetic level before they are already useful at the phenotypic level West-Eberhard 2003).

Continuing in this speculative vein, I am struck by some of the unusual traits that humans share with other cooperative breeders, talents that in chimpanzees and other apes are either poorly developed, or else only present in individuals raised in close association with humans. In most cases, the capacity to extract information from human signals such as finger-pointing and looking at something while tapping on it is better developed in dogs than among highly intelligent fellow apes (Hare et al. 2003). (The only known exceptions involve chimpanzee infants reared in intimate contact with human allomothers, Matsuzawa 2001). Domestic dogs, however, not only descend from cooperatively breeding wolves—who presumably would have benefited from being neurologically equipped to read intentions—but also have a 15 thousand year history of coevolving with—and depending on handouts from—humans. In this sense, domestic dogs share an evolutionary heritage similar to that of children—depending on handouts from other humans. Similarly, like humans, cooperatively breeding tamarins turn out to be remarkably astute at assessing the "character" of individuals with whom they share food. In experimental situations where one individual has to help another before it can get access to a food treat, tamarins were more likely to assist an unrelated individual who had a past history or "reputation" for sharing and reciprocation, than to help individuals known not to reciprocate (Hauser et al. in press).

Babbling—the repetitive, rhythmical vocalizations long assumed to be uniquely human—represents the strangest of all these convergences. Babbling spontaneously emerges around seven months, about the time babies begin to accept preweaning foods. This is also roughly the same time that babies begin to grow their "milk" teeth, beginning with two tiny incisors at the bottom, then four more on top, eventually twenty in all, sharp little teeth to help chew their first foods, mostly solids mashed or premasticated by someone else. Far from unique, babbling is also found in Callitrichids, the only primates (unless we count humans) known to have full-fledged cooperative breeding. In pygmy marmosets, babbling emerges between the first and third weeks, just about the time allomothers take over most of the care (Elowson et al. 1998). My guess is that babbling in human babies, like smiling, originated for the same reason that babbling developed in Callitrichids. As Snowdon points out, babbling is an alluring behavior that attracts the attention of caregivers and elicits interest, solicitude, and edible tidbits.

It has long been assumed that infants babble because the practice helps them learn to talk. No doubt it does. But I suspect that babbling evolved before language, and for a different reason. Our ancestors were born clever apes who babbled at caretakers because they needed to engage them. Best babblers were best fed, and also learned to talk, thus entering into a whole new world of possibilities.

CONCLUSION: LONG CHILDHOODS
IN COMPARATIVE PERSPECTIVE

To the extent that anthropologists thought about childhood at all, most viewed it as a prolonged developmental phase between weaning and the end of brain development that was a "unique stage in the life history of human beings" evolving around two million years ago to provide extra time for large brains to develop and for children to learn necessary skills (see extensive reviews in Bogin 1996; 1998). According to this view, "Much of human evolution, especially the evolution of childhood and adolescence, the human capacity for symbolic language, and culture are the result of the introduction of new life stages into the general pattern of growth and development" (1999, p. 171–72). Taking a broad sociobiological perspective however, prolonged developmental phases between weaning and maturity are not unusual. Long periods of offspring dependence are routine corollaries of cooperative breeding. From this perspective, we do not need to invoke peculiarly costly brains, tool use, or uniquely human cognitive, symbolic, or linguistic skills—the uniquely human traits that long childhoods supposedly evolved to accommodate—in order to explain the origin of long childhoods in the hominid line. Other cooperative breeders from crested magpie jays to wolves had long "childhoods" nutritionally subsidized by allomothers.

So why did such extraordinary gifts evolve in humans but not in other apes? After all, chimpanzees living in the Tai forest obtain massive amounts of calories from nuts that they laboriously crack open, using skills acquired through their mothers. Surely chimps would also benefit from improved subsistence skills and learning capacities (Boesch and Boesch-Achermann 2000). Enhanced learning capacities should be useful for any creature as social and manipulative as a chimp is. Yet chimps never evolved human-sized brains: Why not? Brains are energetically extremely costly, and delayed maturity extremely risky (Aiello and Wells 2002). How could a chimp marginally better at nutcracking garner sufficient reproductive rewards to make delayed maturation and a little bit bigger brain worthwhile? The slightly dumber nutcracker would still be more likely to outbreed him or her. But this constraint would be far less of an obstacle if we assume that the line of apes leading to humans had already embarked on cooperative breeding, and hence already matured slowly. Under those conditions, the costs of large brains would evolve at a discount (Hrdy 1999:86–87). I believe it was the ecological release that cooperative breeding generates along with the special sociocognitive aptitudes that contingent care demands from infants if they are to survive, that unleashed the coevolutionary processes resulting in sapient brains.[4]

This explanation for sapient intelligence is not incompatible with other coevolutionary models based on the proposition that prolonged childhoods and big brains are useful (Bock, Chapter 5 in this volume; Kaplan et al. 2000b). But the cooperative breeding hypothesis specifically predicts that shared care and provisioning along with longer childhoods among *Pan*-like ancestors came first.[5] That is, longer childhoods *preceded* and set the stage for the coevolutionary processes that selected for bigger brains and other trademarks of the hypersocial human species (cf. Bird and Bliege Bird, Chapter 6 in this volume). Costly brains and the spectacular linguistic, symbolic, and technological capacities they permit evolved at a discount because among our cooperatively breeding ancestors, maturation was already delayed. Small reproductive payoffs from being smarter would be sufficient to select for sapient brains in worlds where building blocks (e.g., a rudimentary theory of mind) were already in place. Small survival and reproductive advantages from slightly greater intelligence did not have to compensate completely for the enormous costs of delayed maturation (Hrdy 1999:287).

As it happens, delayed maturation is particularly well suited to finance energy-costly brains since both children and their providers can take advantage of food availability to "pay as they go" (Langen 2000; Ricklefs 1984). This argument is similar to that employed by Bird and Bliege Bird (Chapter 6 in this volume), but the perspective used here is broadly comparative across taxa and the focus is on developmental context. The emphasis here is not just on postreproductive kinswomen, but on the ecological release provided by allomothers generally, that is grandmothers, siblings, aunts, uncles, fathers, possible or "would be" fathers, as well as helpful but unrelated opportunists. Which class of allomother mattered most, and at exactly which stage of the child's development, would have varied with circumstances.

Obviously, every human being's childhood is unique, a rich and formative experiences that shapes and educates the person each of us long-lived and clever apes becomes. But if we stand back and examine "childhood" in broad comparative perspective, that allomaternally buffered delay in maturation ceases to look quite so unusual.

ACKNOWLEDGMENTS

I am indebted to Jim Chisholm, Pat Draper, Barry Hewlett, and Michael Lamb for opening new ways of thinking about infant development, and to Hugh Drummond, Kristen Hawkes, Mel Konner, Michael Lamb, Sasha Hrdy, and Bill Zimmerman for valuable criticisms and discussion. Thanks also to Tom Alley for discussions of what adults find "cute," to Elena Berg for guiding me through the bird literature, to Paul Harris and Mary Main for calling my attention to the relation between "gaze" and theory of mind, and to Chuck Snowdon for his ideas on marmoset "babbling."

NOTES

1. Note that by the late 1960s, field studies from titi monkeys, vervets, patas monkeys, and langurs were already available, species where infants spent some or much of each day being carried by allomothers.

2. The following passage is typical of the literature: "The latest studies of ancient human family structure report that monogamous pair-bonding and nuclear families were dominant throughout human history in hunter-gatherer societies. . . . The most straightforward explanation of the trend toward monogamy is that smart female hominids went to work on chimpanzee hominid-like males and—step by step, mate-selection by mate-selection—shaped them up into loving husbands and fathers with true family values" (Lawrence and Nohria 2002:182). Echoing longstanding patriarchal presumptions about husbands guaranteed paternity by "coy" and monandrous mates, the authors remind us that women would choose the husband most able to support them. No mention is made of help from any quarter besides this "loving husband."

3. Wiessner hypothesizes that men hunt not just for prized meat, but because meat in camp encourages helpful kin and affines to stick around. This would make hunting a form of parenting effort rather than mating effort (cf. Hawkes 1991). Instead of provisioning mothers and young with meat, these hunter-politicians would be providing their children with helpful alloparental networks. The two hypotheses generate competing predictions that should ultimately be testable.

4. For an interesting parallel consider conditions under which spectacular problem-solving abilities have evolved outside the ape lineage, in an avian line. New Caledonian crows stand out for intelligence among "bird brains" (e.g., Chappell and Kacelnik 2002) almost as much as humans do among apes. As hypothesized here for humans, these geniuses emerged from a lineage of clever crows with a legacy of cooperative breeding.

5. For my money, this creature would have been more bonobo- than chimplike, a creature with female-female bonding; male-mother-infant intimacy; and frequent social exchanges that include food-sharing between allomothers and the infants of friends (Parish 1998 and pers. Com.).

4

Studying Children in "Hunter-Gatherer" Societies

Reflections from a Nayaka Perspective

Nurit Bird-David

When at the beginning of the century, the common wisdom was that animistic people think like children, the young Margaret Mead asked very logically, How then do children in these societies think (Mead 1932)? Mead was exceptional in giving children a central place in her ethnographic and theoretical work. With few exceptions, notably within the school of Culture and Personality of which she was a proponent, "children" have not been studied much as a social group, not to mention as a variable cultural concept. "[I]t would be fair to say," wrote Tim Ingold in the *Companion Encyclopedia of Anthropology* (1994), "that in the majority of anthropological accounts, children are conspicuous by their absence" (Ingold 1994:745). What research does exist "has been fitful rather than systematic," posited Christina Toren, in an encyclopedic essay on children (1996:92). While children have been studied more often than such programmatic generalizations suggest (largely, from an adult-skewed "socialization" perspective, on which see more below), it is fair to say that child-focused research has remained marginal and undertheorized. It is rarely represented in major anthropological publications, in undergraduate textbooks, or in overviews of state-of-the-art trends in anthropology. As Hirschfeld has recently summed it up, "A substantial, coherent, and—most critically—theoretically influential program of child-focused research did not emerge" (2002:625).

The "hunter-gatherers" field of study has been no exception, as is evident for example in the 1999 *Cambridge Encyclopedia of Hunters and Gatherers* (Lee and Daly 1999). Photographs of children abound in this authoritative reference book, but scholarly references to them are scarce. Children are rarely mentioned in the ethnographic profiles, let alone in the topical essays. Students working within the ecological-evolutionary tradition, the work of many of whom is represented in this volume, have to date given the most systematic attention to children. Their attention has largely been directed—narrowly in terms of cultural anthropology—to questions of mortality, child rearing, and work. *The Foraging Spectrum* (Kelly 1995), for example, in reviewing this body of literature, indexes only "child mortality" and "child rearing." While generalizations necessarily smooth over important exceptions, it is fair to say here, too, that children are surprisingly understudied in hunter-gatherer research.

The neglect of children is enigmatic. Why have so few studies focused on children, when, given even a conservative estimate of two children per family, children constitute a significant part of any studied population? Why are children so invisible when, in fact, in the field, ethnographers commonly spend a great deal of time with them? Children are often more accessible than the adults. Curious about the ethnographer's ways of doing things, they often accompany her. They are good interlocutors when she takes the first steps in studying their native language. Often, she is regarded as a child herself because, initially at least, she is incompetent in the local ways of living. On various occasions and during certain tasks she may be assigned a place with the children and may sleep with them as a solution to her irregular lone existence within the studied community. Why, moreover, have theoretical developments in the field not stimulated child-focused research? Hirschfeld (2002) raises the point that given the contemporary sense that culture is learned, serious attention should have been given to children. A great deal of learning, after all, occurs during childhood; children are experts at learning (Hirschfeld 2002). Interest in subaltern cultures and minority groups has largely bypassed children, who clearly are one of the more consequential groups (Hirschfeld 2002).

The neglect of children is even more enigmatic in hunter-gatherer studies. Ethnographers have rarely addressed them, even when "children" is a key notion in these peoples' own cultures. For example, both adult and child tropical-forest hunter-gatherers see themselves as "children" of the forest. The South Indian Nayaka, with whom I worked, use the word *makalo* (children) to describe themselves vis-à-vis the forest and vis-à-vis all invisible and previous dwellers in their area, whom they call respectively "big parents," or in some cases "grandparents." "Children" is a concept that is central to their sense of themselves, their place in the world, and their relations with their surroundings; it recurs in their moral and ritual discourse. The concept of "children" appears to enjoy a wide currency in the cultures of other hunter-gatherers, of course, with the expected variations that we need to explore.

The object of this chapter is to reflect on, first, *why* have children been so understudied in hunter-gatherer research, and second, *how* this lacuna can be addressed. Even if we simply maintain that "hunter-gatherers" developed their own cultural ideas and worldviews over a very long period of time, without entering into the tenuous area of whether, what, and how we can learn from them about human evolution, the study of children in these societies holds a very rich potential. One obvious direction to explore is how do children become adults who master these long-developed worldviews? Vishvajit Pandya's chapter in this book touches on this question from a historical perspective, as he looks at Andamanese schooling. An equally important direction to pursue is, How do the children themselves view what happens around them? Bonnie Hewlett addresses this aspect in this book, as she examines Aka adolescents' responses to loss and bereavement. Since "children" appears to be a cardinal concept in hunter-gatherers' cultures, yet a third question to ask is, How is this concept constructed and understood in these cultures? What are its symbolic uses and meanings? This last question is given more attention in this chapter than the first two, drawing on Nayaka ethnography with which I am personally familiar.

WHY HAVE CHILDREN BEEN ANALYTICALLY INVISIBLE?

The above is a complex question. Scholars' own modern perceptions and worldviews provide some answers, and before we turn to the observed ethnographic reality, we must pay due attention to them. Social scientists have tended to project onto all children, everywhere, an idea of childhood that is peculiarly modern (Toren 1993). Modern thought sees the child as in a natural state, a sort of "natural human material" waiting to be shaped by adults into a member of their specific culture. The child is "half-baked," so to speak, if not outright "raw." She is a person not yet fully developed; someone in a liminal situation who has not yet reached the human end-product, adulthood (see Hirschfeld 2002). Universalizing this view leads at best to investigating the *process* through which the child is made an adult, namely, "socialization," turning the naturally given object into a social subject. At worst, such universalizing leads to projecting the "natural" child itself as a human universal, i.e., assuming that the child is the same everywhere. In the second case, there is little impetus for ethnographic comparisons of children and their own cultures. In the first case, the resultant inquiry is heavily adult-centered, "focusing on the adult end-state and adult influence on 'achieving' it" (Hirschfeld 2002:615). It is assumed that the child is passive and starts from a position outside or on the margins of society, from whence adults "work" to enculturate him (see Poole 1994).

When it comes to "hunter-gatherers," other modern perceptions play a critical role as well. In modern scholarship, reflecting *its* concerns, "hunter-gatherers" have been cast as representatives of *our* past. Early 20th-century students regarded peoples later to be classified as "hunter-gatherers" as "survivors," or even as "living fossils" of a distant human past. Midcentury, this temporal absurdity was tempered by claiming only a logical relation between peoples, past and present, who hunt and gather for subsistence, namely, only a membership in the *same society-type* ("hunter-gatherers"). However, the original sentiment persisted, outlasting fierce controversies in the 1980s and early 1990s. To date the category "hunter-gatherers" still frames continued research into evolutionary questions, as well as an ethnographic context for culturalist research. Within an evolutionary perspective—however sophisticated it is, and now it *is* compared with a century ago—these peoples are framed en masse as developmentally behind "us," and in a metaphoric sense, at least, as children of a sort. This characterization creates a blind spot for researchers.

For cultural anthropologists, talking about "children" and "hunter-gatherers" in the same breath is sensitive, given the intellectual historical baggage of the field. The founding "fathers" of cultural anthropology, such as Edward Tylor ([1871] 1958) and Lucien Levi-Bruhl (1979), treated "primitive thought" and Western children's thought as if they were alike. The comparison is still sometimes, albeit rarely, made today (see Hallpike 1979), embarrassing anthropologists. Colonial regimes and modern states have been increasingly critiqued for their paternalistic attitudes toward natives as children. An extreme example of this attitude was the appointment of a state bureaucrat as the general guardian of the natives in Australia in the 1930s. This mind-set creates a cloud of uneasiness around the issue of "children," in dealing with "hunter-gatherers."

Finally, we need to bear in mind the politics and economics of academic careers in anthropology. Many ethnographies draw on fieldwork carried out by young ethnographers in the course of doctoral and postdoctoral studies. These researchers are young people, commonly without children of their own, and they are less observant of child-focused practices.

Along with observers' modern conceptions, some reasons for the neglect of children in hunter-gatherer studies are attributable to the subjects of the studies themselves and their daily reality. First, in these societies, children do not constitute a visible separate social group. In these very small communities, they live in close proximity with everybody else. The magic number of the band's size is 25 (Lee 1968:8), fewer than half of whom, perhaps only 10, would be children, and they would be of all ages. Thus, in any given age bracket there are very few children. The children, of course, play with each other or go together to collect fruits or fish in the surrounding areas (see more below). However, they spend equal amounts of time with adults. In my experience, at least, they often share sleeping mats with adults, sit with them around the campfires, go with them on foraging trips, etc. It is more common to see a mixed-age grouping of adults and children than groups of children and adults each by themselves (but see Bird and Bird 2000).

Second, as shown by other chapters in this volume, caring for children *as* children in our sense of the term, ends at a very young age, around three or four years old. Until this age, the children are with caregivers most of the time, but thereafter they are relatively independent. At a time where in modern societies children begin schooling, say at age six, Nayaka children independently go hunting small game, visiting and staying with other families, free from supervision by their own specific parents, though not necessarily from adults. Descriptions of the independence of children abound in the ethnographic literature.

Teaching, additionally, is done in a very subtle way. No formal instruction and memorizing here, no classes, no exams, no cultural sites in which packages of knowledge, abstracted from their context, are transmitted from one person to another. Knowledge is inseparable from social life. As I have elaborated elsewhere, I believe knowledge in this context has to do with learning how to behave within relations, in order to keep these relations going, rather than with knowing things for their own sake, as a known detached from the knower (Bird-David 1999). Young people learn their skills from direct experience, in the company of other children or other adults, in the course of everyday life. If by "children" we have in mind dependents in need of food and custodial care, here we do not see them as such. Babies and toddlers clearly fall into this category, but not the ages above them.

The analytical invisibility of children in hunter-gatherer studies is all the more striking given, as mentioned, that "children" is a key cultural notion in their own cultural discourse and imagery. Thus, we seem to have here a classic case of ships that pass in the night: hunter-gatherers elaborate on the category "children," while their anthropologists rarely give children any attention. Let me suggest a way in which we can create a connection, even if it is only a starting point, between the scholarly and the indigenous views.

"CHILDREN" IN "HUNTER-GATHERER" ANALYSIS

First of all, we should perhaps disaggregate the category "children" into, on the one hand, babies and toddlers and, on the other hand, all other minors. In our own legal and economic sphere, the distinction is not critical. Certainly, caring parents of babies and toddlers know the difference; they sleep less, are tied down more, they worry more, and so on. However, from the state's point of view—the parents' legal responsibility, the economic burden, statistical surveys of all sorts, welfare benefits, and so on—

a distinction is not made. "Children" covers all persons from birth until they reach their age of legal majority.

The kind of hard data provided in this book, and I think hunter-gatherers' own notions, support the idea of distinguishing between babies and toddlers and other youngsters. By children, Nayaka—and perhaps also other hunter-gatherers—do not mean very young babies. Young babies, they say, do not have names, because they cannot respond to them. Burial procedures are much simpler for babies than for other people. Woodburn, for instance, describes a case of an infant (a two-day-old) who was buried unceremoniously by a man at dawn in the hut of its parents (Woodburn 1982a:198). According to Bonnie Hewlett (Chapter 15 in this volume), the Aka believe that dead young babies come back again reborn as other babies. The death of a very young baby, perhaps, registers with the community as a failed birth, rather than as the death of a person. We see how permeable the boundary is in Western attitudes toward stillborns and infant deaths. Indeed, this ambivalence is reflected in the debates about abortion as to whether the embryo is a person or not. Perhaps hunter-gatherers, who are plagued by high mortality rates, and value social interactions as a key social activity, do not regard young babies as distinguished "selves." Young babies are, to some extent, an extension of the mother's self, until they start to communicate and interact with others, independently.

What age, then, is the lower boundary of childhood? In the modern state, it should be remembered, the end of childhood is variable, often determined by the state in relation to specific domains or purposes (e.g., vis-à-vis schools, parents' legal responsibility, parents' rights regarding their children's welfare, the age for acquiring a driver's license, drinking alcohol, getting married, and so on). If in the modern state only the upper boundary of "childhood" is variable, in the case of hunter-gatherers both the upper and lower boundaries are. Basically, a person becomes a child when he or she starts socially engaging with others, independently, responsively, and responsibly. Other parameters are influential, such as, when he or she is weaned, starts walking, is no longer carried by adults all the time, engages with other persons independently of his or her parents, and so on. Based on these criteria, along with much of the material discussed in this book, childhood seems to begin at three to four years of age.

The upper boundary of childhood is variable as well. In the Nayaka case, initiation rites are not elaborate. When they are performed at all, they are performed for girls only, at the onset of their menstruation. Athletic prowess is important for boys, for example, to be able to climb high trees and collect honey and *sikai* (*Sapindus trifoliatus*), because these skills have economic implications. Above all, however, having children of one's own is critical. In English, a "child" means both the counterpart of the parent in a parent-child relation, and a young rather than an old person. In general use, however, "children" generally denotes the latter sense of the term. "The children go to school," emphasizes not that they have parents, but that they are young persons. A teenage mother, similarly, while a parent herself, is still regarded as a child because she is young. "Children," in other words, is commonly understood in the sense of the dichotomy between child/ adult rather than child/parent. Among the Nayaka, too, *makalo* means both offspring and young ones. However, the former sense predominates. "Child" is commonly perceived as a "child of" within a child/parent or a child/caregiver *relation*. Becoming a parent, namely switching one's position from one side of the dichotomy (child) to the other (parent), is therefore a critical index of adulthood among the Nayaka, and I think also, among other immediate-return hunter-gatherers. Roughly estimated (in such very small communities, statistical generalizations are untenable) the Nayaka become parents, and hence adults, at a relatively old age (compared with the stereotypical "traditional society"): over 18 years of age for women, and 22 for men.

The children's society is more visible when analytic attention is restricted to persons between these age limits, excluding the baby/toddler stage. While they spend a great deal of time with adults, children also group occasionally among themselves. They play together (a common Nayaka game, for example, is sliding on a plantain leaf down a muddy slope, one child after another, or in a row embracing each other); fish in a nearby stream; pick fruit in the hamlet's surroundings, and so on. The groupings are age and gender mixed. Additionally, the older they get, the more likely it is that they will share sleeping mats at night with each other, or when the need arises—the Nayaka rarely sleep alone—with single people who are as yet unmarried or may be divorced or widowed (see Bird-David 1983, 1987). Among some hunter-gatherers, an exclusive juvenile foraging takes place, systemically separate from adult foraging, on a regular, daily basis (see, for example, Bird and Bliege Bird 2000, and Chapter 6 in this volume).

More commonly than recognized hitherto, children in hunter-gatherer societies seem to play a role in the sharing of large game. A much-stressed characteristic of many hunter-gatherer societies, the sharing of large game is of central importance in the operation of these societies (Woodburn 1998). That ethnographers who often refer to this central activity do not mention the children is a good illustration in itself of the systemic blindness to them in anthropology in general and in hunter-gatherer studies in particular (see above). When the Nayaka hunters come back to the hamlet with the game, it is the children who run toward them. The parents remain at their respective hearths, seemingly indifferent to the commotion. The children bring a metal pot, a plate, or just a large plantain leaf from each hearth, in which the family's share is placed. Excitedly, they take an active part in the butchering, holding the torches for light or manipulating the limbs of the animal to ease its cutting and commenting on the equality of the meat's distribution among their families. When the distribution ends, they carry the portions to the respective hearths. Other ethnographers have reported on children's involvement in the sharing of a large game animal, for instance, among the Batek (Lye Tuck-Po, personal communication 2001), and among the Inuit (Barbara Bodernhorn, personal communication 2001). In the case of Cree, the meat itself is handled as if it were a child: the hunters pass the carcass to the women; the carcass is shown great care; nothing is thrown away or wasted; the feast in which the meat is distributed is similar to the feast held after the birth of a baby (Tanner 1979:153, 163). This brings us to the symbolic sense of "children" as a key notion in hunter-gatherers' cultures.

CHILDREN AS A KEY CONCEPT IN HUNTER-GATHERERS' CULTURES

Appreciating the symbolic sense of "children" in these cultures, I think, is only possible if we destabilize some of our own taken-for-granted senses of this term. First, "children" in this context are understood largely as "children of," namely, children of parents (i.e., within a child/parent relation), as opposed to just *young persons,* in and for themselves, as we might intuitively read the term. This is certainly clear in the case of the Nayaka *makalo,* and I would hypothesize that it applies to other hunter-gatherer cases as well, of course with different nuances, all of which are worthy of research. Second, "children (of)" connotes mutual care, sharing, and growing old together, more than reproduction and descent as we might read into the term. Third, "children" do not connote a *separate* autonomous section of society. The Nayaka *makalo,* for instance, cannot be considered a distinct minority group or a subaltern culture, as Hirshfeld (2002, see above), speaking from a Western perspective would have it.

In modern imagery, "parent" and "child" are generalized respectively as separate and autonomous categories: "children" and "parents." This distinction is maintained despite the fact that in reality the child and parent in a child-parent pair are normally with each other more than each is with others of its group. "Children" and "parents" often stand for subsequent generations, following one another. The concept of "generation" is such that, as Ingold put it, "with each new generation, those preceding it regress ever further into the past" (Ingold 2000:136). One generation goes and the other comes, each *replacing* the other. This image, of course, ignores the commonplace concrete situation of parents and children whose lives overlap, and who share life for a significant period of time.

Compared with this modern imagery, in the Nayaka imagery the "parent-child" relatedness as such is generalized. "Children" is used as synonym for a closely shared living, mutual attentiveness and concern, belonging, and a sense of shared identity. "Children" is not conceived separately from "children-parents" relations. "Children" connotes a horizontal section of society that is not separate and autonomous from the "parents" but, to the contrary, is inherently inseparable from and overlapping with it.

This point is clearly evident in the Nayaka ritual discourse, wherein the notion of *makalo* recurs. The celebrants refer to themselves as *makalo* and address the forefathers and animistic beings as *dodappanu* ("big" parents). By doing so, they do not portray themselves as the replacement generation for the parents but, to the contrary, emphasize the interconnections between the "children" and the "big parents," and the expectation for mutual caring and sharing between them. In terms of the local imagery, framing the living Nayaka as "children" evokes a sense of the forefathers as not "dead and gone," but present and available to be engaged with. They are evoked in this way as beings to whom one can turn for help. The notion of "children" carries similar associations in some modern contexts, alongside its use in the sense of "the replacement generation."

Within the local symbolic framing, then, "childhood" is a condition of those living. The child phase ends at death. Although death is generally handled very simply (as it is as well among African hunter-gatherers; see Hewlett, Chapter 15 in this volume; Woodburn 1982a), the ritual of death resembles a rite of initiation. The dead person is removed from the living. He is at a liminal stage where he is dangerous to anybody who may come upon him. Ultimately, he returns as a "big" father and joins all the other "big parents."

What additional meaning does the notion of "children" carry with it? Or, rather, to put it more correctly, what does the pair of categories "children" and "parents" mean, because these terms are often used together, and each gets its meaning from its relation with the other. I speak for the Nayaka, but I think it holds true to one degree or another also for other hunter-gatherers. Children are not first and foremost perceived as persons in need of physical care (note the restriction of the term to those above the baby toddler stage, above). They *can* obtain food for themselves and are relatively independent, as mentioned. The simple conditions of life preempt a great deal of the physical care that we need to provide our children—buying clothes, dressing, getting a reluctant child to sleep in a separate room away from everybody else, taking him or her outside to play, and so on. Instead, children are perceived as persons whose social skills are not developed yet. Nayaka say that a baby has no *budi* (sense), is not aware of others, does not know yet how to respond to them, is socially clumsy. Fred Myers describes a similar situation for the Pintupi (Myers 1986:197), while Jean Briggs (1998) perceptively portrays how children are helped to learn to deal socially with other persons. In the local view, children require looking after and engaging with, as they lack social skills and must be taught how to care for fellow-beings and share with them. The learning does not end as one grows up; it is an art and a skill that one continues learning and perfecting. Compared to the early people, Nayaka see themselves still as children, in this sense of the term. If illness strikes, they ask the early people whether they have unknowingly done something to offend the big-parents and plead their innocence.

When Nayaka describe themselves as "children of the forest," they do not simply imply that the forest feeds them, as may be inferred by someone with a modern viewpoint who sees children primarily as dependents in need of feeding. The child/parent relation as it is generalized—even cosmologically—connotes an emotional sort of caring. It projects people as belonging to each other, as "of the same family." "Children of the forest" connotes an emotional attachment, a shared living, a shared sense of identity and mutual responsibility.

CONCLUSIONS

We end up with a paradox: a familiar anthropological dissonance between our analytical categories and the local sense of things. The growing trend within anthropology has been to study children as a separate "class," "minority," or "subaltern culture" (e.g., see Hirschfeld 2002; Ingold 1994; Toren 1996) instead of as simply initiates or "raw material" in the process of becoming full members of society. In the local sense of things, "children" are not a separate, distinct class. To the contrary, child-parent *relations* are the focus of the Nayaka because the notion of "children" stands for a shared living experience.

II

Why Does Childhood Exist?

Photo 2. Efe children playing in subsistence activity. Courtesy of P. Ivey Henry

II

Introduction

Nick Blurton Jones

Compared to their closest relatives, people have an elongated juvenile period, beginning to reproduce at a greater age than other great apes (hominoids). The difference has been noted, and explanations offered since before the beginning of anthropology. Most prominent, and oldest among these explanations has been the observation that forager subsistence involves many learned skills and extensive knowledge, and the idea that the juvenile period must be extended to allow these skills to be acquired before adulthood. Other ideas about extended juvenile periods have been offered in recent years, for example, that juveniles can avoid risks by growing more slowly (and thus perhaps for longer; Janson and van Schaik 1993), that a new phase, "childhood," has been inserted into the life history, thus elongating the time to first reproduction (Bogin 1988, 1999), and so on. (Several of these alternatives are outlined and discussed in relation to the comparative and fossil evidence in Paine and Hawkes, in preparation.)

Meanwhile, biologists who study life histories have established a very general relationship between the length of the juvenile period (weaning to first reproduction) and the length of the adult lifespan (e.g., Charnov 1993). Within major taxa these bear a constant relationship to each other. This arises because age at first reproduction is a result of a compromise between the benefits of growing to a larger size (which takes longer) and the costs of a shorter time in which to recoup these benefits (more time spent growing means less time reproducing). The governing factor appears to be external influences on adult mortality rates. If mortality increases, there will be less time to recoup the benefits of growing for longer and it will pay to begin reproducing earlier. If mortality decreases, there will be more time to reproduce and it will pay to take a little more time and grow larger. Alvarez (2000) has shown that humans fit closely with the relationship between juvenile period and adult mortality (and several associated measures).

Thus there is now an alternative view of the length of the human juvenile period: that there is nothing to explain about the juvenile period, so long as we can account for the longer adult lifespan. In an ecology where highly productive foods exist but are too difficult for juveniles to acquire, then juveniles must be provisioned. This opens an opportunity for older helpers to enhance their fitness by acquiring food that they transfer to younger relatives. This could select for prolonged vigor in the older individuals. While, in this context, Hawkes et al. (1989, 1998) have attended primarily to women (grandmothers), others such as Marlowe (2000a) and Kaplan et al. (2000b) have emphasized the role of men. Chapters on older men and women as helpers of mothers and children are presented in Part III.

The studies represented in the current section address the contrasting ideas about the role of learning in the evolution of a longer juvenile period by examining details of the behavior of children, especially their subsistence behavior.

Bock supports a view close to that outlined by Kaplan et al. (2000b). These authors do not espouse the early idea that everything must be learned before maturity. They suggest that theories such as Charnov's should consider not merely physical growth, but any investment in "embodied capital" such as skill and knowledge that will affect later reproductive success, and in the body's maintenance mechanisms that affect mortality. They suggest that where skill and knowledge play a large role in subsistence, selection will favor a longer juvenile period (it will pay to spend more time learning, even if individuals continue to learn after maturity) together with greater investment in brain and in the body's maintenance functions. They propose that long life, encephalization, and a later age at maturity should evolve together. They suggest that hunting is the part of human subsistence that most strongly favored these changes. It becomes important to show the dependence of subsistence skills, and especially hunting or its component skills, upon experience. Bock has documented the age changes in various important subsistence skills among children on the Okavango Delta, and investigates the extent to which increases with age reflect skill, or merely strength. He took a variety of measures of strength. Seeking to understand the interaction of strength and experience has led to his proposal of a "punctuated development model" to encompass the interaction of strength and skill in shaping the sequence and age patterning of skills and learning.

Bird and Bliege Bird are also involved in trying to discriminate effects of size and strength from learning. They ask whether Mardu children are really such inept foragers and slow learners, and find that they actually forage in the best patch for individuals who are short and walk more slowly than adults. This finding resembles their earlier reports on Merriam children (Bird and Bliege Bird 2000, 2002; Bliege Bird and Bird 2002b), who select an optimal set of prey for people of their walking speed, they are optimal foragers on littoral fauna. Tucker looks at foraging by Mikea children and points out that we often underestimate the efficiency of child foragers because they have other things on their minds—playing, staying out of the sun, watching passers by, and so on. These studies add to recent evidence that the traditional "needing to learn it all before you can reproduce" idea is inadequate. Children learn many things but learn them very rapidly. In some foraging skills they match adults from an early age [Bird and Bliege Bird (2002) found that Merriam children were better spear-fishers than most adults]. Losing "bush experience" in boarding school did not impair foraging skills among Hadza children (Blurton Jones and Marlowe 2002). !Kung do not begin to learn to hunt until they are 20 or so (Nancy Howell, personal communication, 2002), and Walker et al. (2002) show that Ache hunting success increases during the adult years, as it also does among Hadza (Marlowe 2000a; Blurton Jones and Marlowe 2002). These findings contradict the earliest ideas about subsistence learning and the juvenile period, that learning is not all accomplished before adulthood. Most Ache and Hadza men are married with children long before they reach their peak hunting efficiency. Foraging must be learned but it is learned as a juvenile and as an adult and seems to have little direct relationship to the age at which reproduction begins. While researchers in this field currently think of themselves as supporting opposed theories about evolution of the juvenile period, they all agree that more data collection and more modeling are needed. We might also do well to bear in mind that the differences between humans and our closest relatives might not have all arisen together in a single evolutionary step.

So far I have only discussed the length of the juvenile period, using the biologists' definition: weaning to first reproduction. The chapters in this section use childhood and juvenile interchangeably, for anyone who is no longer an infant (weaned) and not yet an adult (bearing children). But other authors have divided this period into varying numbers of pieces. Among these authors Bogin (1988, 1999) has made the most effort to relate his concepts to the primate and animal literature. Paine and Hawkes (in preparation) report a seminar on evolution of human life history in which, among other things, it became clear that Bogin's concept of childhood was valuable, not in its concept of "insertion" elongating the juvenile period but in its pointing to a disconnection between weaning and other measures such as eruption of the first permanent molar tooth (M1). While these tend to coincide in other primates, weaning is very early in humans (even foragers) when compared to other hominoids and long precedes events such as eruption of M1. Bogin's concept of childhood covers the period from weaning to eruption of M1 and he notes that the end of this period coincides with the "5-7 year old shift" often written about by developmental psychologists. These concepts have played no part in recent studies of young hunter-gatherers (such as the detailed studies of parent-child interaction reported in Parts III and IV). But perhaps they should.

Tucker's discussion of the playful nature of Mikea children's foraging raises another issue, which receives more attention in Chapter 16 by Kamei. Play is probably a way in which children make a start on learning many things. Bock (1995, 2002a) has shown how parents trade off the value of children's productive work against the imputed future value of their play. Bock suggests a way in which theory might be used to predict how much time children (and/or parents) allocate to different activities. So far, his suggestions have not been followed up by other researchers.

In closely knit forager societies it is also possible that both children's play and their productive work affect the attitudes others have toward them: they begin to gain reputations for being lazy or hard-working, skillful or clumsy, helpful or uncooperative, domineering or a pushover, and so on. An individual's reputation may affect how others treat him or her and this may have important and lasting effects on their adult lives. This may be true in any society but in a species that has such good recognition of individuals and such good ways of communicating attitudes, and in societies that have few members and tend to live with a limited subset of those members throughout their lives, such early formed reputations may be especially powerful.

5

What Makes a Competent Adult Forager?

John Bock

INTRODUCTION

In this chapter I examine the ways in which experience-based embodied capital, operationalized as skill, and growth-based embodied capital, operationalized as strength, interact to produce age-specific competency at different foraging activities among children in a multiethnic community in the Okavango Delta of Botswana. The chapter begins with a presentation of alternative theories of the evolution of childhood, and proceeds to a brief review of several recent studies that have tested hypotheses derived from these alternative theories through examining children's activities in traditional societies. Next I introduce the study community and describe the data collection and analysis methods. I then present the results of the study, which are followed by a discussion of these results including their implications for our understanding of the effects of growth- and experience-based embodied capital on the development of foraging competency in this community and broader implications for theoretical development and future research.

MODELS OF THE EVOLUTION OF CHILDHOOD

The lifeway of hunting and gathering characterizes the context of human evolution. The initial foray into alternative subsistence ecologies involving the production of food, such as farming, occurred only about ten thousand years ago, at least 90 thousand years after anatomically modern humans emerged (Binford 1968; Lancaster and Lancaster 1987; Lee and Devore 1968; Washburn and Lancaster 1968). Since that time, most human populations have shifted their dependence from hunting and gathering to agricultural food production (Bender 1975). For many populations the transition has occurred within the last millennium and is not yet complete (Johnson and Earle 1987). This means that the human life history pattern-the timing of and allocation of resources to critical life events such as growth, maturation, reproduction, and mortality-likely evolved in the context of a hunting and gathering lifestyle (Hawkes et al. 1998; Hill and Hurtado 1996; Kaplan et al. 2000a). Childhood is an aspect of human life history that differs from that of the other apes in the duration and the degree to which offspring are dependent on parents or others for provisioning. Recent theoretical debate has centered on whether these differences are due to features of the hunter-gatherer subsistence ecology in which humans evolved (Bock 1995; Bock 2002a; Bock and Sellen 2002a; Bogin 1999; Kaplan et al. 2000a) or are due to other selective forces such as the low rate of extrinsic mortality of primates in general (Charnov and Berrigan 1993; Blurton Jones et al. 1999; Blurton Jones and Marlowe 2002; Bird and Bliege Bird 2002; Bliege Bird and Bird 2002; Bird and Bliege Bird, Chapter 6 in this volume).

Three life history models have been recently used to understand the slow growth and extended juvenility of humans (Leigh 2001): the brain growth model (Bogin 1999); the adult mortality model (Charnov and Berrigan 1993); and the embodied capital model (Kaplan 1996; Kaplan and Bock 2001; Kaplan et al. 1995, 2000a). The brain growth and embodied capital models both focus on learning as a powerful selective force on the juvenile period in humans and see the large human brain and the long juvenile period as a response to the great amount of learning-based knowledge necessary to be a competent forager. In these models, slow growth provides the time needed to fully program the brain with the environmental knowledge, requisite technical skills, and social aptitude to effectively extract resources from the environment. The models differ, however, in that the embodied capital model provides a framework in which the costs of slow growth are distributed across generations. This leads to different predictions between these two models regarding growth rates through the life course. The brain growth model predicts rapid early growth but does not address continued growth of the rest of the body after the brain has stopped growing, while the embodied capital model predicts both early growth and variation in later growth (Leigh 2001).

The adult mortality model developed by Charnov (1993) and extended to humans by Blurton Jones, Hawkes, and colleagues (1999) argues that organisms shift investment at some point from their own growth into producing offspring. According to this model, the human juvenile period is not different from the other apes adjusted for lifespan. We have a long juvenile period simply because we are unusually long-lived (Alvarez 2000). In this case, natural selection is not directly acting to extend juvenility but is rather a consequence of slow growth. Knowledge and skills acquired during the juvenile period are beneficial according to this model, but those benefits are not sufficient selective pressure to have extended the juvenile period. Leigh (2001) states that the adult mortality model accurately predicts extension of ontogenetic phases but does not generate predictions consistent with the variation in growth rates seen in humans.

EMPIRICAL STUDIES

These models place differing emphasis on the selective impact of learning on the evolution of childhood. Recent empirical studies have focused on the effect of skills acquired through experiences, such as social learning, on children's competence in tasks related to food procurement (Bock and Sellen 2002b). Bliege Bird and Bird (2002a, 2002b) found that Meriam children in Australia were far more constrained in their marine foraging returns by body size than by experience-based skill. In this study, however, the technology needed to forage was not a factor in variation in costs associated with differences between adult and children foraging. In a review of ethnographic data from twelve traditional societies, Shennan and Steele (1999) conclude that the acquisition of craft-making skills occurs largely through vertical transmission from same-sex parent to child and requires most or all of childhood to acquire. In addition, they argue that this transmission of craft-making skills is a form of parental investment. In their study of Aka foragers, Hewlett and Cavalli-Sforza (1986) also show that the acquisition of most food procurement skills is the result of vertical transmission, and that most skills are acquired by age ten. Clearly, in situations where there is reliance on technology for food procurement, inclusion of the costs of producing that technology makes it unlikely that children will be net producers of food resources. Moreover, recognition of the costs of technology production indicate that provisioning of technology to offspring by parents is a form of parental investment that increases either the rate of energy capture or skill acquisition by offspring, or both. Several studies have found that among nomadic hunter-gatherers, parents spend far less time with their children after sedentization and the initiation of farming (Ju/'hoansi: Draper and Cashden 1988; Ache: Hill and Hurtado 1996), suggesting that the benefits of vertical transmission, and therefore parental time investment, may be less in non-hunter-gatherer subsistence ecologies. Overall, the results have not been conclusive, and appear to be strongly related to the complexity of tasks intrinsic to a given local subsistence ecology as well as to the nature of precursor and sequential tasks.

One potential confound is the tasks examined. In their study of Hadza adolescent skill development, Blurton Jones and Marlowe (2002) argue that both school attendees and non-school attendees have similar skill levels. They found, for instance, that there was no difference in bow and arrow shooting accuracy. This is only one component of a complex task in the actual process of food procurement that includes technology production, locating and tracking prey, stealthy lying in wait or stealthy pursuit of prey, and accurately delivering a projectile to a potentially moving target. [See Liebenberg (1990) for a thorough description of the component tasks involved in hunting with traditional weaponry on the African savanna.] Even if there is no difference in bow and arrow shooting accuracy between school attendees and nonattendees, this does not mean that they are equally able to accomplish all of the tasks that are precursors to actually shooting an arrow at an animal, or turning a wounded animal into food.

Other studies have found that experience has strong effects on task performance related to food procurement. Ohtsuka (1989) found that age had a significant effect on the hunting ability of Gidra Papuan men, controlling for strength and body size. Walker et al. (2002) found strong age-effects among Ache foragers in male ability to locate potential prey. Controlling for measures of strength and body size, older men had significantly higher encounter rates. This is corroborated to some extent by several studies in conservation biology that demonstrate significantly higher encounter rates by indigenous foragers compared to professional biologists (Hill et al. 1997; Stander et al. 1997). Bock (1995, 2002a) showed that among the Okavango Delta peoples of Botswana, there was a significant effect of age on mongongo nut processing returns among women. These studies, however, focus on complex and difficult tasks, often depending on the production and use of technology as well as the successful sequential performance of many subcomponents. It is clear from these studies that a more holistic approach that analyzes the relationship between growth and experience in a given ecological context is critical before we can completely distinguish the effects of experience and growth on performance in foraging-related tasks.

THE PUNCTUATED DEVELOPMENT MODEL

Kaplan and associates (Kaplan 1996; Kaplan and Bock 2001; Kaplan et al. 1995; Kaplan et al. 2000a) have proposed a theory of human life history evolution based on returns to investment in embodied capital. This theory integrates human capital theory in economics with life history theory from evolutionary biology by treating the processes of growth, development, and maintenance as somatic investments. Investment in embodied capital has two aspects, the physical and functional. The physical payoff to investment in embodied capital is the actual tissue involved. The functional payoff to investment in embodied capital is manifested in qualities such as strength, immune function, coordination, skill, knowledge, and other abilities, which are based in organized somatic tissue (for a complete treatment, see Kaplan et al. 2000a). The total of both the physical and functional aspects of embodied capital can be viewed in relation to the capacity to be a competent adult. Building on the embodied capital model, the punctuated development model was created as a theoretical framework to understand the effects of experience and growth on task performance within the context of a local ecology (Bock 2002a).

GROWTH-BASED AND EXPERIENCE-BASED EMBODIED CAPITAL

We can further distinguish embodied capital into growth-based forms and experience-based forms (Bock 2002a). Growth-based forms of embodied capital are attributes like body size, strength, balance, and general coordination. Experience-based forms of embodied capital are attributes such as cognitive function, memory function, task-specific skills, learned knowledge, endurance, and specific coordination. Growth-based forms tend to be more related to general competency, while experience-based forms tend to be more related to specific competency. The ability to perform any task is comprised of a suite of both growth-based and experience-based embodied capital. Depending on the physical demands and complexity of the task, we can imagine the gamut from those heavily weighted toward growth-based embodied capital to those nearly entirely dependent on experience-based embodied capital, with many tasks requiring hefty portions of both.

This model assumes that complex tasks involve thresholds of ability that must be reached before we can consider someone able to perform a given task. It is possible for a person to have one or two of the necessary forms of embodied capital but still be unable to perform a task. One must achieve a certain level at each of these components before the threshold of ability is crossed. Even after one is able to perform the task at a rudimentary level, depending on the difficulty of the task there may be considerable opportunity for improvement.

PARENTAL INVESTMENT AND LEARNING

This model can be used to frame the effects of paternal investment of time and resources on child outcome in terms of different forms of embodied capital. In different subsistence ecologies and for different tasks, the investment in growth needed to bring a return in learning varies (Bock 2002a; Bock and Johnson 2002b). As growth-based embodied capital constrains the payoff to investment in experience-based embodied capital there will be diminishing returns to investment in learning. The degree to which growth constrains learning will vary as a function not only of subsistence ecology but also of the economics of production (Bock and Johnson 2002b). It may also be strongly influenced by the value of labor and the opportunity cost to alternative activities (Bock 2002b). In foraging economies as in all others, the variety of tasks performed can be expected to reflect a number of different levels of growth constraints on payoffs to learning. Investment of resources and time by parents in their offspring can be used to build growth-based embodied capital or it can be used to develop experience-based embodied capital. The optimal solution is expected to ultimately depend on the reproductive interests of parents, which is also subject to the societal based gender- and age-patterning of production, and on the specific labor needs of the household.

When a parent is faced with these allocation decisions across a number of offspring determining the optimal solution quickly becomes a complicated endeavor. In one-child families, assessing the costs and benefits of investment in different forms of embodied capital is relatively clear-cut from a theoretical standpoint. With each additional child, this assessment becomes more complex with the addition of opportunity costs and multiple time frames. A parent's reproductive interests are unlikely to coincide with those of any one of their children (Blurton Jones 1993; Bock 1995, 1999, 2002a, 2002b; Worthman 1999). Rather an evolutionary perspective leads us to believe that parents should be concerned that their reproductive interests are manifest in all of their children. They should even be willing to act to the detriment of a child if doing so benefits the parents themselves. Such conflicts are rife when investment in one child affects investment in others (Trivers 1972a).

THE STUDY COMMUNITY

These issues are examined using data collected in a multiethnic community of approximately four hundred people in the Okavango Delta of northwestern Botswana (Bock 1995, 1998; Bock and Johnson 2002a, 2002b). Five ethnic groups are represented, including two San-speaking groups, the Bugakhwe and the ǁAnikhwe, and three Bantu groups, the Hambukushu, the Dxeriku, and the Wayeyi. ǁAnikhwe and Bugakhwe people inhabit the Okavango drainage in Namibia and Botswana, with ǁAnikhwe historically having a riverine orientation in their foraging, while Bugakhwe have been savanna foragers. The ||Anikhwe living in the study community currently practice a mixed economy, but farm at a much less intensive level than the Bantu groups in the area. All ||Anikhwe families acquire the bulk of their resources from foraged foods. Among 50 ||Anikhwe there were only four head of cattle, compared to a typical Bantu homestead of 20 people with 12 head. Bugakhwe in this community are largely oriented toward fishing, hunting, and the collection of wild plant foods. None own cattle, and a few have small gardens where they grow tobacco and specialty foods such as vegetables.

Hambukushu, Dxeriku, and Wayeyi people inhabit the Okavango River drainage from Angola through the Caprivi Strip of Namibia into northern Botswana. Historically, they have participated in mixed economies of farming, foraging, and pastoralism.

People from all of the ethnic groups live in extended family homesteads based on patrilocal organization. Among the Bantus, polygyny is common, with 45 percent of the men over 35 participating in polygynous relationships at any one time. Polygyny is rare among the San speakers but marriage and reproductive unions are fluid among all the ethnic groups. Multipartnered sexuality is commonplace, and disputes over paternity and child support are common in the tribal court. For all the ethnic groups most men marry and become fathers in their thirties.

At the time of the study, this community was fairly isolated. There was very little cash economy in the study community, so most men of all ethnic groups over the age of 35 had worked in migratory labor, usually in the mines of South Africa, for an average of five years. Many of the ||Anikhwe and Bugakhwe men over the age of 25 had been soldiers in the South African Defence Force during the bush wars of the 1970s and 1980s. Few women, however, had ventured beyond the next community, 30 kilometers away. There was no school or clinic, or borehole, so water was drawn from a river source. The nearest primary school was in the next community, and children attending that school needed to board while attending school. While there are no school fees in Botswana, the cost of boarding, uniforms, and books as well as the lost labor made school costly to parents. At any one time, approximately 25 percent of the children in the community attended primary or secondary school. Those attending secondary school boarded at communities at least one hundred kilometers away. Due to the lack of vehicles and roads, children attending school returned home only sporadically.

Historically, the Bantus represented in this community have all had some degree of matrilineality in their social organization with a tradition of the avunculate (Larson 1970). In earlier times a boy's strongest male influence would not be from his father but from his mother's eldest brother. Both ||Anikhwe and Bugakhwe were strongly influenced by Bantus over

at least the last one hundred years and also have some degree of matrilin-
eality and the avunculate. The situation is not clear-cut, however, since all
ethnic groups in the study community have been under strong political
and social influence of Tswana-speaking tribes for at least two hundred
years. The Tswana have a strong tradition of patrilineality in their social
organization and customs regarding marriage, the family, and childrearing, which have been codified as Botswana's Customary Law. All disputes
are settled using this legal code regardless of the ethnic origin of the liti-
gants, and this has had a profound impact on the maintenance of social organization and tradition by non-Tswana groups.

Fieldwork in this community began in 1992 as part of a dissertation
project focusing on the determinants of children's activities. There was an
additional field session in this community covering most of 1994, and
there have been frequent subsequent visits, with the latest in 2001. A second community composed mostly of ǁAnikhwe and Wayeyi families that
was far more market incorporated was included in the study beginning in
1996, with two years of data collection ending in 1997.

METHODS

In this analysis, two types of data are used: strength measurements and
tests of performance ability.

The "Field Days"

Anthropometric measurements and tests of general performance ability
were collected from 54 girls and 74 boys on August 28, August 29, and October 8, 1994. The first two dates comprised a weekend and both children
who attend school away from the community and those who do not were
included. The third date was a "makeup" date that allowed us to measure
any child not previously tested. The tests of general performance ability included throwing for distance, running, and a test of arm strength using a
25 kilogram spring balance. Each test was set up as a station, and the children were rotated through the stations in the same order. These test days
were organized along the lines of a field day. The community was divided
into three parts. Shortly after dawn, three researchers equipped with a list
of children three to 18 years old from each homestead ventured into a different part of the community, visiting homesteads and meeting with the
most senior person available. Researchers asked permission to test the children in that homestead in a series of throwing, running, and carrying tests
as well as permission to measure the height and weight of the children. Permission was invariably granted. The children were then called together and

told to proceed to the researchers' house at a certain time indicated by the position of the sun. These times were staggered to facilitate data collection.

At the end of the first two days, we noted which children were absent. The following test day, special effort was made to impress upon those children and responsible adult caretakers that the participation of all children would be of great help to the researchers. At the completion of testing children were provided with soft drinks, popcorn, and other snacks, and as always, were allowed to use any recreational equipment they desired such as soccer balls, frisbees, and ball and bat.

Measuring Growth-Based Embodied Capital

Arm pull strength was obtained in order to estimate the effect of strength on task performance. A 25 or 50 kilogram Homs hanging spring balance was attached to a tree trunk. Each participant would then sit cross-legged in the sand at such a distance from the tree that the person's arm was fully extended when grabbing the hook on the balance, but not so that he or she needed to lean forward. A researcher sat or squatted behind the person so that his or her back remained perpendicular to the ground during the test. The participant was instructed to grab the hook with whichever arm was stronger and to pull the hook toward him or her using only the arm, not the back, shoulders, or legs. If a person was using these other body parts, the test was begun again after further instruction. A researcher watched the scale on the spring balance to determine the maximum value that the individual could sustain, rather than a peak value resulting from a quick pull or jerk on the hook. This value was recorded to the nearest kilogram.

Measuring Skill in Mongongo Nut Processing

Mongongo nut processing return rate experiments were conducted with children and adults of both sexes between January and November 1994. For these experiments, a sack of mongongo nuts was bartered in return for transporting a group to a mongongo tree patch. A woman was then enlisted to perform the first stage of processing, leaving the nuts with their outer shell exposed ready to process. For the processing rate experiment, an individual was given five hundred grams of whole nuts in the outer shell. These were also counted. The individual was instructed to process them as if he or she were at home, and the digital timer started. After fifteen minutes the individual was told to stop and the number of nuts processed was counted. The remaining nuts were weighed, as were the product. In addition, the number of intact inner-shelled nuts was counted, and it is this quantity that is used in the analysis.

Measures of Fishing Skill for Both Males and Females

Fishing return rates were collected throughout both planned and op-portunistic observation of children between 3 and 18 years old during the period from January to November 1994. Focal follows of individuals were undertaken twelve times a week. Homesteads were sampled on a rotating basis, as were children within homesteads. The follows lasted two hours, and consisted of point samples every ten minutes. At the point sample, the activity in which the child was engaged, the location, and identity of co-participants was recorded. In addition, the time of any resource acquisi-tion was noted, as well as the type, amount of resource, and method of acquisition. Weights were obtained using Homs hanging spring balances. A second type of data collection regarding the fishing return rates was op-portunistic in nature. Most fishing activity either took place or originated at a beach on the central lagoon. In addition, fishing had a periodicity with respect to the time of day. Most fishing took place from midmorning to midafternoon. On selected days this area was visited prior to the usual start of fishing. All children were offered a hook and a length of line, in-cluding children who would usually be considered too young to fish. The start and stop times of fishing, the location of the fishing, the time of any resource acquisition, and the weight of each fish caught were recorded for each child until all children had ceased fishing.

Four types of fishing by children were observed: hook and line from shore, hook and line from a dugout canoe, basin, and basket. There is a gender difference with respect to these methods. Hook and line fishing from a boat is nearly exclusively a male activity. Very young boys, some girls, and some older boys who cannot find a boat at the time they wish to fish will do hook and line fishing from shore. Basin and basket fishing are exclusively female activities with basin fishing being done by extremely young girls.

Operationalization of the Variables and Data Analysis

Because experience- and growth-based embodied capital both encom-pass a number of individual characteristics, they can be operationalized in a number of ways. Arm strength as collected in this study is a measure of growth-based embodied capital and is an indicator of body size, muscu-loskeletal maturation, and—to a lesser extent—general coordination. Arm strength is a particularly appropriate measure of growth-based embodied capital in this analysis since both mongongo nut processing and fishing rely on movement and manipulation of technology via the arms. The ex-tent to which this usage affects competence in resource acquisition will be reflected in the contribution of arm strength to variation in return rates for a given resource as determined by regression analysis.

Age covaries with many measures of growth and maturation. For instance, In this population age accounted for 92 percent of the variation in height and 94 percent of the variation in weight (Bock 1995). We can also expect that if there are benefits to skill gained from experiences such as social learning, the more experiences one has the greater the skill level embodied within that individual. Since experiences accumulate with age, we should also expect age to covary strongly with experience-based embodied capital. To isolate the component of experience-based embodied capital related to age, multiple regression was used. In this way, growth-based embodied capital measured as strength can be controlled for and the partial effects of experience-based embodied capital on competence can be assessed.

For the three tasks, mongongo nut processing by females, basket fishing by females, and canoe fishing by males, multiple regressions of return rate on age and arm strength for all tasks are presented in Tables 5.1 through 5.5, showing the partial influence of experience- and growth-based embodied capital on competency. In addition, the bivariate relationship between significant predictors and returns are presented as OLS regressions. These graphical formats help to visualize the relationships, but do not isolate the partial effects of experience- and growth-based embodied capital on task performance.

RESULTS

The results begin with an examination of the effects of growth- and experience-based embodied capital on mongongo nut processing. They continue with an analysis of girls' fishing using baskets from shore, and conclude with an examination of boys' fishing using hook and line from canoes.

Mongongo Nut Processing

Multiple regression analysis shows both that age has a significant positive effect and that age-squared has a significant negative effect on mongongo nut processing competence, consistent with the bivariate model (see Table 5.1). The multiple regression also shows, however, that strength as a measure of growth-based embodied capital does not have a significant effect on mongongo nut processing ability when age is controlled for.

Mongongo nut processing has a distinctive inverted U-shaped relationship of age and processing ability (see Figure 5.1). Ability increases through the teens and twenties and peaks in the mid-thirties to mid-forties, then begins a steady decline. This is similar in shape to age-specific return rates for

Table 5.1 Multiple Regression of Mongongo Processing Returns on Age and
        Arm Strength for Females of All Ages[a]

Model	Unstandardized Coefficients B	Std. Error	Standardized Coefficients Beta	t	Sig.
Full (constant)	−17.960	10.303		−1.743	.012
Age	3.212	0.639	4.621	5.022	.001
Age squared	−0.037	0.007	−4.542	−4.936	.001
Arm strength	−0.248	0.298	−0.305	−0.830	.431

[a] $n = 20$. Age has a significant positive effect while age squared has a significant negative effect while controlling for arm strength.

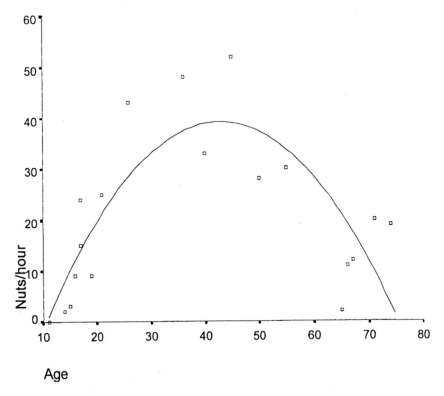

Age

Figure 5.1. Age-specific mongongo nut processing returns for females of all
        ages. Each point represents the number of nuts successfully processed in
        15 minutes. A polynomial regression fit to these data shows a significant
        effect of age that is positive at earlier ages and negative at later ages.
        $n = 20$, $R^2 = 0.6119$.

other foraging activities such as hunting (Kaplan et al. 2000a). The continued increases to the return rate after growth stops in the early twenties suggests that growth-based embodied capital is not the primary influence on mongongo nut processing competence.

Basket Fishing by Girls

Multiple regression analysis of the effects of age and arm strength on girls' basket fishing returns shows that when controlling for age, the influence of arm strength becomes nonsignificant (see Table 5.2). This indicates that there is no additional significant effect of arm strength and that variation in girls' basket fishing returns is due to the effects of age alone.

This can be seen graphically in the univariate regression analysis of return rate on age (see Figure 5.2) among girls.

While experience-based embodied capital is a major influence on girls' basket fishing return rates measured as kilocalories/hour, a different relationship emerges when examining the mean weight of fish caught. Multiple regression of return rates on age and arm strength shows that arm strength is a significant predictor of mean weight while age is not (see Table 5.3). This indicates that different attributes are important in the development of competence in locating fish and in landing larger fish. Experience may be important in knowing where to find fish, but to catch larger fish requires a larger basket and the strength to move the basket through deep water.

Canoe Fishing by Boys

Multiple regression analysis shows that age does not significantly affect return rate for boys' fishing, but that arm strength has significant positive effects (see Table 5.4). This indicates that for boys' fishing, in contrast to girls' fishing, growth-based embodied capital is a major determinant of competence.

Table 5.2 Multiple Regression of Mean Return Rate for Basket Fishing on Age and Arm Strength for Girls 3–18 Years Old[a]

Model	Unstandardized Coefficients		Standardized Coefficients		
	B	Std. Error	Beta	t	Sig.
Full (constant)	291.165	23.687		12.292	.007
Age	18.270	1.793	1.000	10.189	.009
Arm strength	0.582	0.818	0.070	0.711	.551

[a] $n = 16$. Age has a significant positive effect while arm strength has no significant effect.

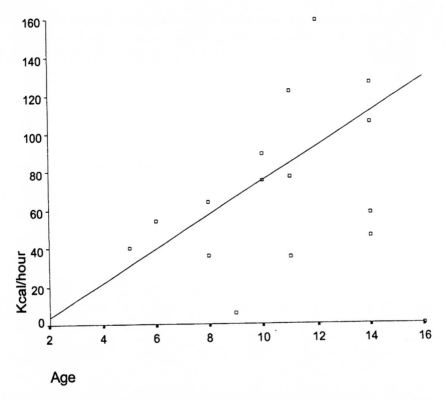

Figure 5.2. Fishing returns by age for girls. Each point represents the average return rate for a girl over the study period. n = 16, R^2 = 0.5468.

Table 5.3 Multiple Regression of Mean Weight of Fish for Basket Fishing on Age and Arm Strength for Girls 3–18 Years Old[a]

Model	Unstandardized Coefficients B	Std. Error	Standardized Coefficients Beta	t	Sig.
Full (constant)	–21.936	23.983		–0.915	.384
Age	–4.125	3.702	–0.331	–1.114	.294
Arm strength	8.730	2.319	1.119	3.765	.004

[a] n = 16. Arm strength has a significant positive effect while has age no significant effect.

Again, univariate OLS regression shows significant effects of arm strength (see Figure 5.3) on boys' return rates to fishing from a canoe. This may be due to the benefits to being able to pole the canoe into water close to the reed beds, a long distance through deeper water.

Table 5.4   Multiple regression of mean return rate for canoe fishing on age and arm strength for boys 3–18 years old[a]

Model	Unstandardized Coefficients B	Std. Error	Standardized Coefficients Beta	t	Sig.
Full (constant)	−8.896	32.438		−0.274	.787
Age	−6.358	5.291	−0.339	−1.202	.247
Arm strength	8.843	2.457	1.016	3.599	.002

[a] $n = 20$. Arm strength has a significant positive effect while age has no significant effect.

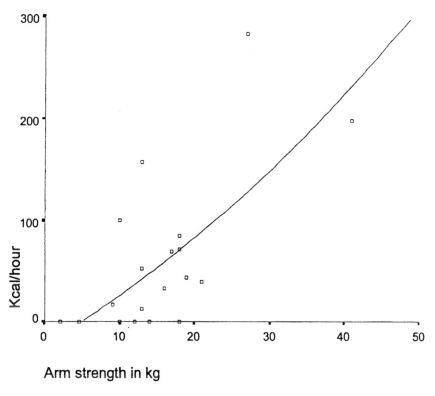

Arm strength in kg

Figure 5.3.   Fishing returns by arm strength for boys. Each point represents the average return rate for a boy over the study period. n = 20, R^2 = 0.5971.

The benefits of arm strength do not extend to catching larger fish, however. Multiple regression of return rates on age and arm strength shows that age is a significant predictor of mean weight while arm strength is not (see Table 5.5). Again, this is the opposite result of that found for girls' basket fishing and seems to be due to the differing demands of technology in

Table 5.5 Multiple Regression of Mean Weight of Fish for Canoe Fishing on Age and Arm Strength for Boys 3–18 Years Old[a]

Model	Unstandardized Coefficients		Standardized Coefficients		
	B	Std. Error	Beta	t	Sig.
Full (constant)	−201.703	87.421		−2.307	.035
Age	27.135	11.843	.607	2.291	.036
Arm strength	2.385	4.962	.127	.481	.637

[a] $n = 20$. Age has a significant positive effect while has arm strength no significant effect.

the acquisition of fish by girls and boys. Although stronger boys can move the boats close to the reeds, more experienced boys may have higher skill levels in knowing exactly where to encounter larger fish or in using the hook and line technology, or both.

Other forms of fishing

There are two other forms of fishing observed in this community, basin fishing by young girls and hook and line fishing from shore by both boys and girls. Basin fishing is performed by girls who are too young and small to use a basket. This form of fishing has very low success and there is no significant effect of age or arm strength on return rate. Hook and line fishing from shore is performed by girls when they are able to obtain hook and line and by boys who are unable to use a canoe due to their young age or missed opportunity. This form of fishing also has very low success and there are no significant effects of age or arm strength on return rate for either boys or girls engaging in this activity.

DISCUSSION

Overall, the results show that the nature of the task at hand and the type of technology employed are the major influences on the relative effects of growth- and experience-based embodied capital on task performance. In mongongo nut processing, strength only brings benefits when employed in a highly skilled way and there was no significant effect of strength independent of age. The varied effects of age and arm strength on return rate and mean fish size illustrate the importance of attempting to isolate subcomponents of tasks and to understand how each of these subcomponents independently and sequentially contributes to competency in a task. For any specific component, as the skill requirement decreases, competence appears to be based on the strength needed to move and manipulate the technology in an effective manner. At the same time, however, it is clear that there may be benefits of experience and skill accruing simultaneously in another component of a task. While continued practice may improve performance at a task, the benefits of practice are contingent upon an individual having sufficient baseline strength, coordination, and muscle memory.

This chapter uses the punctuated development model (Bock 2002a) to examine the relative contribution of growth-based and experience-based embodied capital in the development of competency in foraging tasks. The model predicts that growth and experience will interact to affect return rates in productive tasks. In particular, the type of technology employed is expected to be a major influence on the skill and/or strength requirements for a given task. Two aspects of technology come into play: the strength needed to move and/or manipulate the technology and the skills needed to apply technology to a specific resource. For some tasks, both of these elements are present, while others are weighted toward one or the other. The effects of growth-based embodied capital, operationalized as arm strength, and experience-based embodied capital, operationalized as age, were examined in relation to competence, measured as return rate and package size, at three foraging tasks: mongongo nut processing, girls' basket fishing, and boys' canoe fishing. The study found that:

- Competence in mongongo nut processing is significantly predicted by age; arm strength is not a significant factor.
- Girls' return rates at basket fishing are significantly predicted by age; arm strength is not a significant factor.
- The mean size of fish caught by girls basket fishing is a function of arm strength; age is not a significant factor.
- Boys' return rates at canoe fishing are significantly predicted by arm strength; age is not a significant factor.
- The mean size of fish caught by boys canoe fishing is a function of age; arm strength is not a significant factor.

Mongongo nut processing is a task heavily dependent on the application of technology directly to a product. While the strength required is not great, the misapplication of the technology employed can result in serious injury, spoilage of the product, or both. Both types of fishing are also dependent on the application of technology directly to the product, but differ in that fish are mobile prey that must be located and the technology must be brought to them. The differences between girls' and boys' return rates is due to the different ways in which the fish are encountered and the differences in the way in which technology is used to actually capture the prey.

Girls have a limited range when basket fishing. They need to stay close to shore, due to the presence of large numbers of crocodiles and hippos, as well as occasional elephants and buffalo. Girls who know where fish are more likely to be present have a distinct advantage, and this knowledge is based in experience. The basket is relatively light when moving from one place to another so strength is less important for girls when locating fish. Boys face a different limitation in encountering prey when canoe fishing. The fish are plentiful along the reed beds, yet to pole a heavy dugout through the deep water to the reeds takes arm strength. Weaker boys are less likely to travel to where the fish are. Girls with restricted mobility can carry their lightweight technology to the microhabitat within their range that has the highest likelihood of encountering fish. Boys have heavy technology that has a wide range and can be brought to a larger habitat with high likelihood of encounter.

While in terms of mobility, girls have less heavy technology requiring less strength to move, in terms of prey capture girls have heavier technology requiring more strength to apply directly to the fish. While conical baskets move relatively easily through the water when they are being transported, when used to catch fish they must be moved at a much quicker pace and pushed through much deeper water. In order to pick up a large fish, a considerable amount of strength is required. Boys using hook and line, however, are not limited by strength but rather by the ability to set the hook by maintaining an appropriately light touch on the line.

These results illustrate how growth-based and experience-based embodied capital interact to produce competence. To process mongongo nuts, one has to have reached a threshold of strength. Further increases in strength, however, are unimportant compared to the development of skills in applying that strength to cracking open the nut. For fishing by both girls and boys, strength and skill have complementary and additive effects across intrinsic elements in the task. The skill and strength requirements of these subcomponent tasks are in turn heavily dependent on the technology involved. And as we have seen, the same technology can rely on skill and strength alternately in different task subcomponents. In the production of the same resource, skill and strength can contribute to food procurement through alternate and potentially simultaneous pathways.

In light of these results, we can think back across human evolutionary time and consider whether growth or learning was the primary selective force on human childhood. Or we can consider that both growth and learning are endogenously and simultaneously produced, and that the form of human childhood is the outcome of the selective advantages of the interaction between growth and learning (Bock 2002a). During our evolutionary history, benefits to children's activities could accrue to the parents or to the child in the form of immediate resource acquisition used to defray the cost of parental provisioning of the child in question and siblings, as well as to future benefits to the child in the development of skills (Bock 2002a). In any subsistence ecology, the kinds of tasks and the technology available will determine the relative contribution of growth-based and experience-based embodied capital to competence in resource acquisition. The age profile of these relative contributions will be determined by the interaction of growth and experience summed across each task.

In considering this interaction we should also be cognizant of the costs of technology. Intensive tool use, although with a very small tool kit, began with early *Homo*. Although Shennan and Steele (1999) argue that Oldowan tools are simple enough to be produced by children, by the time anatomically modern humans were exploiting highly extractive niches it is likely that the more complex technology involved was not being manufactured by any children who may have employed it. Rather, parents or other parties provisioned children with technology used to acquire resources. This provisioning is a way for parents to manipulate children's time allocation and the benefits of their activities. Prior research in this same community has demonstrated that parents manipulate children's time into different activities to realize both short- and long-term gain (Bock 2002a). In addition, technology in this community is provided by parents to offspring. The canoes used by boys and the fishing baskets used by girls were manufactured or provided by parents. Girls, in fact, are provided with baskets of various sizes as they age. Taking this into account, it is clear that when children forage using technology they may not be providing net benefits in terms of their provisioning if the cost of providing the technology outweigh the benefits of the child's foraging returns. The costs of technology production are as much a form of parental provisioning as direct supplementation.

This study helps to highlight the importance of careful assessment and measurement of features of subsistence ecology when evaluating individual resource acquisition. In particular, understanding competency requires that we reverse engineer tasks such as fishing or hunting that seem simple when viewed only as an outcome. By focusing on the details of the process of food procurement, the elements of competency can begin to come into view. This study also draws attention to the importance of integrating multiple temporal and spatial frames of reference into the analysis of any task, as well as the use of multiple currencies to understand trade-offs and opportunity costs. Future research incorporating these perspectives will help us to understand not only the lives of children in the context of local adaptation, but also how the evolved childhood provides the framework for children's developmental trajectories and their development into competent adults.

ACKNOWLEDGMENTS

The author would like to thank the Office of the President of Botswana for permission to conduct this research as well as the people of the study community for so graciously welcoming us into their lives for the last 14 years. Sara Johnson's collaboration on all aspects of this research was invaluable. Indispensable research assistance was provided by Prince K. S. Ndjarakana. Funding was provided by two LSB Leakey Foundation General Grants, the Department of Anthropology and Graduate School of the University of New Mexico, the Andrew W. Mellon Foundation, and the James A. Swan Fund of the Pitt Rivers Museum of the University of Oxford, as well as a National Science Foundation grant to Henry Harpending and Jeffrey Kurland. I thank Nick Blurton Jones, Pat Draper, Barry Hewlett, Sara Johnson, Steve Josephson, and Michael Lamb for their insightful suggestions and comments and immensely helpful feedback.

6

Martu Children's Hunting Strategies in the Western Desert, Australia

Douglas W. Bird and Rebecca Bliege Bird

Mothers and fathers gone out hunting and leave us kids in camp. When we got hungry we go hunting for little lizard, get him and cook it and eat him up. Me little bit big now, I go hunting myself, tracking goanna and kill him. . . . Soon as mother leave him, little ones go hunting, kill animals, blue tongue, mountain devil, take them home before mother and father come back, cook and eat it. Mothers, they bring him goannas and blue tongue and father one still long way. Mother come back and feed all them kids. . . . After lunch mother and father go hunting for supper, all the little kids walk and kill little lizard, take him home, cook and eat him. . . . Morning again, father one he go hunting. All little kids go hunting self. . . . Mother go out separate from father and come back with big mob of animals. Me big enough to hunt around self. . . . Morningtime, father one bin for hunting long way way. He bin get and kill an emu, bring and cook him. Everyone happy, they bin say he good hunter. Mother and father sometime bin come back late from hunting. They bin go long way. (Yuka Napanankga, Mardu woman from Kukatja Community, Western Australia; Napanankga 1995:143)

The contributions to this book make it abundantly clear that human juvenility is unusual in the extreme. Human juvenile periods not only last a long time, they are time *consuming*. Once weaned, children in all societies rely on their elders for well over a decade (Kaplan et al. 2001, 2003). In this volume John Bock, Nicholas Blurton Jones, Sarah Hrdy, and Bram Tucker focus our attention on the important implications of understanding this prolonged juvenility: aspects of our unique fertility profiles, our long life spans, our low mortality, our patterns of social and local organization, and our highly complex systems of cooperation are probably all linked to our peculiar juvenility.

What is responsible for this strange life history pattern? Is childhood designed as a period to gain experience, skills, and knowledge? Or do we learn a lot because we have a long childhood? Maybe both, but hunter-gather studies are especially important in addressing such issues: many researchers have argued that the evolution of a unique human foraging niche involving intergenerational resource flows corresponds with the evolution of our long juvenile period (Isaac 1978; Kaplan and Robson 2002; Kaplan et al. 2003; O'Connell et al. 2002). Until recently there has been little research on the lives of hunter-gatherer children, especially relative to their role in a subsistence economy. Many scholars have assumed that children are primarily the recipients of adult labor, and that, especially among foragers, they contribute little to their own maintenance (e.g., Bogin 1988; Tooby and Cosmides 1992; Quiatt and Kelso 1985). This may reflect a general notion about childhood as a period primarily of practice for the complexities of adulthood. Implicit in the concept of "growing up" is the idea that children's lives are all about gaining the skills to become successful adults.

This view of juvenility has been challenged by some recent studies of contemporary hunter-gatherers. For example, Blurton Jones and colleagues (Blurton Jones and Marlow 2002; Blurton Jones et al. 1994a, 1997, 1999) have shown that Hadza children in Tanzania are effective foragers and children's subsistence efforts are constrained primarily by size and strength rather than the difficulty of learning adult skills. Some developments in life history theory also suggest that delayed human maturity is principally a product of decreased extrinsic mortality, where selection favors longer juvenile periods with decreasing extrinsic *adult* mortality because of the advantages of growing longer (and thus larger) (Charnov 1993; Charnov and Berrigan 1993). For primates, the age of maturity and extrinsic adult mortality vary widely, but their product is approximately invariant: humans fall well within the confidence interval for all primates in which these variables have been measured (Alvarez 2000).

Nevertheless, even in societies where children are very productive from a young age, they remain critically dependent on others for over a decade after they are weaned, and it often takes many years to reach peak efficiency (Bock 2002a; Kaplan and Bock 2001; Kaplan et al. 2003). In a recent comparison across a broad range of foraging societies, youngster's consumption of resources exceeds what they produce for themselves so that offspring continue to depend on nutritional subsidies from others up to age 18 or older (Kaplan and Robson 2002). This is not the case with other hominoids: mother-child food sharing occurs in most ape societies, but only human mothers provide a substantial fraction of their weaned children's diets.

Some researchers have suggested that a such a foraging niche (focused on widely shared resources that are difficult for juveniles to acquire) is the key to understanding unique aspects of the evolution of our genus, in particular specialized foraging by men and women, which increased the benefits of widespread food sharing and central place foraging (e.g., Isaac 1978; Washburn and Lancaster 1968). Kaplan and colleagues (2000a, 2001, 2003) have argued that the costs and benefits of caring for a highly dependent young primate, along with changes in the opportunities for access to game animals, made certain foraging activities unattractive to women. In response, men began to focus on skill-intensive foraging that (once learned) is highly efficient for provisioning high-cost offspring through intergenerational resource flows. This in turn favored more direct maternal care and fed back to decrease extrinsic mortality and increase the benefits of growing longer to maturity (i.e., getting larger gives more to invest in production for maintenance and reproduction).

> It is this partnership of men and women that allows long-term juvenile dependence and learning and high rates of survival. . . . Human pair bonding and male parental investment is the result of complementarity between males and females. The commitment to caring for and carrying vulnerable young . . . together with the long period required to learn human hunting strategies, renders hunting unprofitable for women. (Kaplan et al. 2000a:173)

Others, including ourselves, have argued that human social organization may have less to do with male-female pair bonding to provision costly children than the above model would predict (e.g., Bliege Bird 1999; Hawkes 1991, 1996, in press; Hawkes and Bliege Bird 2002; Hrdy 1999). We have suggested that among the Meriam of Australia's Torres Strait Islands, highly skilled male hunting is designed more as a public display than as a means to efficiently provision offspring (Bliege Bird and Bird 1997; Bliege Bird et al. 2001, 2002; Smith and Bliege Bird 2000; Smith et al. 2003). Moreover, like the Hadza, foraging efforts among Meriam children are primarily constrained by size, not the complexity of learning how to forage like an adult (Bird and Bliege Bird 2000, 2002; Bliege Bird and Bird 2002; Bliege Bird et al. 1995). If size allows, Meriam children learn even the most complex fishing activities very quickly.

But what about hunting? Researchers have rarely recorded independent hunting by children. Most of children's foraging seems focused on activities like fishing and gathering fruits and vegetables. While in many cases boys begin to practice hunting skills at very young ages, peak efficiency in acquiring large game is not usually reached until well into adulthood (Hill and Hurtado 1996). And in some cases peak energy production from many skill-based activities (like hunting) is not reached for more than a decade after puberty (e.g., Kaplan et al. 2000b; Ohtsuka 1989). Whether or not this results from changes in the intensity of effort or the cognitive complexity of hunting, it is hard to imagine that children could possibly hunt large game that are often the specialty of men. However, this says nothing about whether from a child's perspective large game hunting would be an efficient option no matter how practiced or large they were. And as Mrs. Napanangka states in the introductory quote, children of Australia's Western Desert *do* hunt. Among the Martu at Parnngurr Out-station, children above the age of five often search for and pursue game animals. But they focus their efforts in different resource patches than adults. Are these differences the result of the time it takes to learn adult hunting strategies, or are they the result of differences in the payoffs to be gained for small-sized foragers? By choosing different types of prey are children practicing hunting skills that they will use later in life, or are they simply making the best of a small situation?

BACKGROUND AND METHODS

The term Martu (or *Mardu* in many previous orthographies) convention-ally refers to foraging groups whose traditional estates surround Lake Disappointment, the Rudall River, and the Percival Lakes in the northwest section of Australia's Western Desert (Figure 6.1). For the people that com-monly call themselves *Martu*, the term is not necessarily exclusive: in some situations they use it to refer to traditional speakers of the core dialect groups of the area, especially Manyjilyjarra, Kartujarra, Warnman, Puti-jarra, and Nyangajarra. In other circumstances *Martu* may designate hu-mans in general. Today, people sometimes use *Martu* to distinguish indigenous people around the world, as opposed to people who "don't be-long." While there are many speakers of Manyjilyjarra and Kartujarra, there are very few people who still speak Warnman, Putijarra, and Nyan-gajarra. All Martu (numbering about eight hundred to one thousand peo-ple) now use a lingua franca referred to as *Martu Wangka*, with components of numerous Western Desert dialects.

The linguistic situation reflects the enormous changes that have oc-curred among the Martu over the last century. Limited contact with white explorers and settlers began in the early twentiethth century with pastoral efforts on the western and southern fringe of Mardu territory. In the 1930s some Martu began a process of migration westward from their desert es-tates, visiting and eventually settling in Jigalong (a maintenance depot, and later protestant mission) and surrounding cattle stations (for detailed his-tory, see Tonkinson 1974). However, many families, especially those from the easternmost part of Martu territory, remained in the heart of the desert until the mid-1960s, when prolonged drought and depopulation drove them into Jigalong and pastoral stations such as Balfour Downs. While

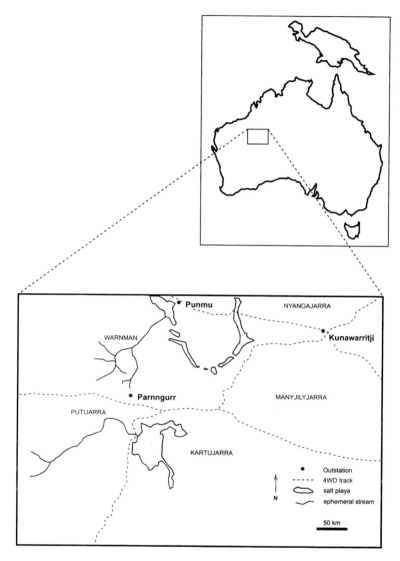

Figure 6.1. Martu territory and dialect groups.

many Martu stayed in Jigalong, many also left soon after their arrival, either for employment in towns and stations, or back to the desert proper. In the mid-1980s numerous families (mostly those that were the last to leave the desert) returned permanently to Martu homelands. By 1986 they had established two "outstation" camps (Punmu and Parnngurr) in the

newly designated Rudall River National Park (another outstation at Kunawarritji, Well 33 on the Canning Stock Route, soon followed). The re-
occupation of Martu estates was initiated primarily to resist mining
expansion near sacred sites, but it was also a response to the increasing influence of alcohol and "Western" culture, especially among Martu youth.
Many Martu felt that their ability to keep sacred Law and practice their religion depended on moving back to their homelands (Tonkinson 1991:
174–178).

Especially for the families at Parnngurr (comprising a core population
of about one hundred people), their return to the desert meant a return to
a foraging economy. Government rations were trucked out when possible,
but often vehicle access to the camp was cut off for months at a time.
Throughout the mid- to late 1980s and early 1990s, much of the daily subsistence at Parnngurr came from hunting and gathering. Walsh (1990; Veth
and Walsh 1988) conducted critical research on foraging activities in and
around Parnngurr during this period, focusing on Martu ethnobotany,
seasonal variability, and gathering ecology.

Today, the importance of foraging has declined relative to what it was
at Parnngurr's establishment. The supply route to the community is more
reliable (although still precarious, especially with occasional summer
storms), and regular government funds (e.g., social security and Community Development Employment Program, CDEP) along with a small store
(usually stocked with basic food and household items) have increased reliance on a cash/welfare economy. Hunting is usually poor near the permanent settlement; foragers often require vehicles to visit more distant
hunting and gathering grounds on day trips, and there are few working
four-wheel-drive trucks in the community. Introduced fauna, especially
camels, may also be depressing certain game populations. Martu also face
changing demands on their time: with sedentism, clothing, and vehicles
came the need to allocate more time to cleaning, washing, and maintenance; men and women are often involved in ritual activity, with some
men spending months at a time away from the community; time is also
taken up with various government meetings and functions; and obtaining
CDEP wages means at least some time working during the week on various community projects.

Nevertheless, Mardu at Parnngurr continue to hunt and gather on a
regular basis, their foraging frequency limited primarily by vehicles and
fuel to access more distant hunting and gathering locales. Although most
people at Parnngurr would prefer to hunt every day, the majority forage
about two to four days out of the week. Vehicle trips to foraging locations
within fifty kilometers of the community occur nearly every day, and extended camps to more distant locales are common, especially during the
cool/dry season (*Wantajarra*, May–August).

CHILDREN

An ethos of self-sufficiency surrounds Martu children. Desert-born adults recall a childhood spent foraging with other children to keep themselves fed while the women hunted burrowed game (especially *parnaparnti*-sand goanna, *Veranus gouldii*) and men hunted mobile game (kangaroo, bustard, and emu). Children would remain behind, usually with teenagers or a young adult. If camped in sandhill areas near rocky outcrops they would spend their day hunting medium-sized lizards (*winyjikiti*-ridge-tail go-anna *Veranus acanthurus*, and *lungkuta*-blue tongue skink *Tiliqua scincoides*), picking fruit (especially *kumpulpaja-Solanum diversiflorum* and *jinyjawirri-Solanum ellipticum*), hunting small birds, digging grubs (*lunki-Cossid* spp. larvae), or collecting bird eggs. If near the margins of ephemeral water-courses, they would dig wild onion (*minyarra-Cyperus bulbosus*) or pencil yams (*kanjamarra-Vigna lanceolata*) during *Wantajarra*. Early in *Wantajarra* children would also collect and process woollybutt grass (*kunaruntu-Eragrostis eriopoda*.[1] Much of what children acquired was for their own immediate consumption and they often cooked their own meals on small fires. Children were actively discouraged from accompanying men or women on their separate hunting trips, but encouraged (and relied upon) to assist adults in collecting fruit, roots and corms, or grubs. By the age of first marriage (for girls, just after the time of first menstruation) and at the beginning of initial stages of initiation (for boys), between 13 and 16 years, youths were expected to begin to take on adult responsibilities and adult foraging strategies. Boys began to hunt with men, and girls to hunt with women.

Parnngurr children today always accompany adults on foraging and camping trips away from the community, but are left in temporary resi-dential or day camps unless women are gathering (fruit, roots, or grubs) or men are hunting using the vehicle. Women spend much of their time hunt-ing for *parnaparnti* goanna in the sandhills and flats, and rarely take chil-dren with them (although nursing mothers occasionally carry infants). Women hunt on foot with a digging stick, and they often remark that chil-dren are too slow to keep pace while they are searching and tracking. While in the past men would never take children on foot hunts, now chil-dren often accompany them when hunting in a vehicle, particularly for bustard (*kipara-Ardeotis australis*), so that their wives can walk long dis-tances in search of *parnaparnti*. During men's vehicle hunts, children are expected to help spot animals and to assist in burning patches of grass if needed. While children can sometimes be a disturbance, they are usually silent while men are tracking and pursing an animal. (For further details on men's and women's hunting, see Bird et al. 2003, in press; Bliege Bird and Bird, in press).

When children are left behind, depending upon camp location and season, they often decide to pick *kumpulpaja* and *jinyjawirri* or hunt lizards. Generally all children in camp, boys and girls, will forage together in the same group. Their efforts are highly praised by young and old alike, but their decisions about whether or not to forage and what to look for are not directly influenced by adults. When hunting, children occasionally search for *lungkuta* and *parnaparnti* around camp in the sandhills and flats, but when rocky outcrops are nearby, they almost always prefer to hunt for *winyjikiti* goanna. Capturing *winyjikiti* is difficult. Children fan out and search the sands between the rocks for recent tracks, and carefully follow signs of the lizards to a likely den. They then use a *wana* (a long metal crowbar or specialized wooden digging stick) to turn over rocks and pry apart friable crevices. When one child locates a promising den, others may come to assist, just as adult women do when cooperating on *parnaparnti* goanna hunts. And as women do, when children capture the *winyjikiti*, they pull it from the nest by the tail, swiftly crack its head on the *wana*, and break the legs. After hunting, children sometimes cook and eat their lizards before adults return to camp.

DATA COLLECTION

All Martu participants, including the children, spent most of their lives in the desert, and the formative years of those aged 35 and older were spent as full-time foragers. In the following analysis, unless we indicate specific age categories, individuals referred to as "children" are age 4–14, and "adults" are 15 years or older. Ages of youngsters are known from birth records, but for adults born in the desert there are no birth records. For these individuals we estimated ages within five-year age categories relative to each other (older or younger) and the timing of known events (World War II and the date of first contact with government welfare patrols and anthropologist Robert Tonkinson in 1963).

Foraging is defined as time spent searching, pursuing (including tracking and extracting an individual prey), collecting, and processing wild foods. Travel is defined as time spent on foot or in the vehicle en route to foraging locations. Each of these activities is mutually exclusive. We define hunting (as opposed to gathering) as foraging activities that primarily involve searching for *mobile* animals, whether they burrow, run, or fly to escape capture. Most of the data we analyze here were collected during *Wantajarra* (cool/dry season) by four researchers (ourselves and two postgraduate students, Christopher Parker and Bonnie Bass) on twelve extended camping trips (some lasting for a month) away from Parnngurr. Data from these extended camps are available from three field seasons

2000–2002. For the children's analysis, we also included five focal follows from five separate day trips out of Parnngurr in 2002.

Martu participants traveled by car to field camps of their choosing, and from those camps walked or drove to foraging locations. During foraging trips we conducted detailed focal individual foraging follows: each researcher accompanied a single individual and noted all time allocated to travel, search, pursuit, collecting, and processing, along with the weight of each item (if game) or parcel (if fruit, vegetable, or insects) captured at the end of foraging. A total of 157 focal individual foraging follows (131 adults: 95 female and 36 male; 26 children: 14 female and 12 male) are used in the analysis of hunting presented below. In addition to the focal follows, during the extended camping trips we recorded the duration of all foraging episodes and the weight (by item or type) of all food captured by all camp or trip participants. For this analysis a total of 156,084 foraging hours were recorded over 307 individual foraging trips by 32 *different* Martu (20 adults and 12 children). Energy values were taken from published sources analyzing the composition of aboriginal foods (Brand-Miller et al. 1993). Edible weights for animals were calculated in the field by weighing uncooked individuals and asking foragers to discard the waste material from those same individual animals into a receptacle (n=88, including samples from all game animals reported here). On extended camps, individuals averaged 1702 ± 210 (SE) kilocalories per forager per day, not including those in camp who did no foraging (only the smallest children and the researchers). We supplied an average of five hundred kilocalories per day per participant, primarily in the form of flour and sugar.

We also recorded walking speeds while some foragers *searched* for game on foot during hunting activities. This was accomplished using hand-held differentially corrected GPS while the primary author walked along with a hunter. Speeds were recorded in spot observations at two-minute intervals during search, but only when recording accuracy was ±6 meters or less. This provided a dataset of 150 spot observations during thirteen focal follows of *different* foragers (6 adults: 3 women and 3 men; 7 children: 4 girls and 3 boys; the number of spot observations ranged between 9 and 13 per follow). To control for the effects of variable landform and activity type, we only recorded walking speeds while foragers were walking in the sandhill flats (for children, this was usually en route to rocky outcrops). To measure the effects of body size on walking speed, we also recorded the height of the child foragers.

RESULTS

If we concern ourselves with hunting activities that both adults and children choose *independently*, only two hunting "patches" (*sensu*, Smith

1991) are available on foot from most *Wantajarra* camps: the sandhill patch where hunters search primarily for *parnaparnti* (sand goanna), and rocky outcrops where hunters search for *winyjikiti* (ridge-tail goanna). Where rocky outcrops are within walking distance from camp, accessing them requires at least some travel through sandhills. The focal follow data from hunting demonstrate clear differences in the decisions of adults and children. In 131 hunting follows where search took place on foot, adult foragers never chose to search in rocky outcrops. Children on the other hand, hunted for *winyjikiti* in rocky outcrops on all (26) focal hunting follows, and on only two of these follows did children spend time searching in the sandhills while traveling to the outcrops. On average, children earned 402.4 ± 67.9 (SE) kilocalories/hour foraging in the rocky outcrops. Adults earned 1102.1 ± 276.5 kilocalories/hour foraging in the sandhills. Here we investigate two hypotheses concerning these differences:

H1: The difference is caused by the difficulty of learning how to hunt *parnaparnti* (sandhill patch) relative to *winyjikiti* (rocky outcrops). If so, we would expect a clear increase in overall return rates (kilocalories/hour foraging) with age (assuming age correlates with experience). As experience increases with age, children should switch from *winyjikiti* to *parnaparnti* hunting when the overall return rate in rocky outcrops is exceeded by the expected payoff from the sandhill patch.

H2: If children focus on *winyjikiti* primarily due to the constraints of being small foragers, we would expect stronger effects on return rates with size (i.e., height) than experience (i.e., age). Height may affect return rates in the form of influencing average walking speeds in the sandhill patch: children are shorter, thus may walk slower and encounter prey less frequently. If prey in the rocky outcrops is found at higher density than prey in the sandhills, shorter and slower foragers may encounter less prey in the sandhills than they would encounter walking for the same length of time in the rocky outcrops.

H1

Figure 6.2 demonstrates that age alone is a very poor predictor of hunting efficiency among children in the *winyjikiti* rocky outcrop patch (linear regression, $r^2 = .025$, $f = .62$, $p = .44$, $n = 26$ follows for which we have corresponding return rates and forager age). Nor is there a general tendency toward increasing efficiency with age subgroups: foragers age five to seven on average earn 467.1 ± 114.3 kilocalories/hour foraging ($n = 8$), those age 8–11 earn 237.7 ± 89.3 kilocalories/hour foraging (n = 12), and those age 12–14 earn 652.9 ± 112.9 kilocalories/hour foraging (n = 6).

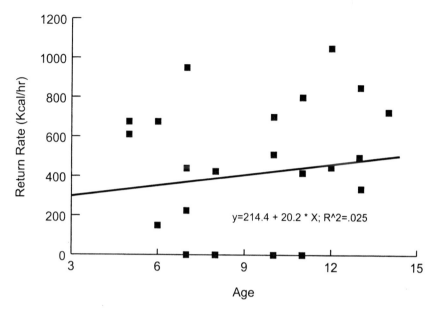

Figure 6.2. The relationship between children's age and hunting return rates.

While sample sizes for subgroups are small, the return rates for children age 5–7 are not significantly different from those age 12–14 (df = 12, $t = -1.13, p = .28$).

H2

Figure 6.3 shows that unlike age, standing height has a significant effect on children's foraging efficiency in the *winyjikiti* rocky outcrop patch ($r^2 = .25$, $f = 4.94$, $p = .04$, $n = 17$ follows for which we have corresponding return rates and forager height). Regardless of age, taller children gain higher foraging returns than shorter children. Part of this increase is due to the smaller sample size (i.e., there are two foragers with low return rates for which we are lacking height measures). If we assume an average height by age category (ages 5–7; 8–11; 12–14) of children for which we lack height ($n = 9$), the effect of height on efficiency is less ($r^2 = .17$), but still significant ($p = .04$).

Can this height effect account for the fact that given the choice, children choose to hunt *winyjikiti* in the rocky outcrops rather than *parnaparnti* in the sandhills? Accessing rocky outcrops inevitably involves some travel *through* the sandhill patch: adults choose the sandhills, children choose the

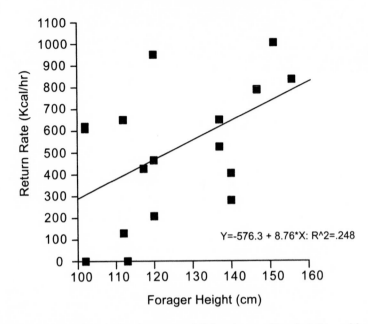

Figure 6.3. The relationship between children's standing height and hunting return rates.

outcrops. It might be that because height and walking speed are closely correlated (partial correlation, $R = .70, p = .01$), these, not age per se, determine the rate at which foragers encounter prey, especially if children were to hunt in the sandhills where encounters with prey are less frequent (see below).

To account for the independent effects of height, walking speed, and age on efficiency, we perform a number of tests. First, we model children's *winyjikiti* hunting efficiency with both age and height in a multiple regression. As Table 6.1 shows, the combined effect of age and height is a stronger predictor of efficiency than either is alone ($r^2 = .52$ vs. $.025$ and $.25$, respectively). However, since age, height, and walking speed are closely correlated, their differential effects on efficiency are difficult to interpret in a multiple regression. As such, we first examine a regression of age on height to obtain the residual variation in height after accounting for differences due to age. We then do the same with a regression of height on age to obtain the residual variation in age after accounting for differences in walking speed due to height. Finally, we use the residual from each of these regression models as independent variables in two simple linear regression models predicting walking speed. By itself, age is significantly correlated with walking speed (partial correlation $R = .57, p = .04$), but

Table 6.1   *Winyjikiti* Hunting in Rocky Outcrops: Multiple Regression
Coefficients for Children's kcal/hr Foraging vs. Age and Height

Summary			Coefficient	Std. Error	t-Value	p-Value
n	17	Intercept	−2162.02	692.33	−3.12	.001
r^2	.52	Age	−167.07	58.73	−2.85	.013
Adj. r^2	.46	Height	32.95	9.10	3.62	.003

height alone is a better predictor ($R = .96, p < .001$). If we control for the interaction between age and height using residual analysis, we find that residual height is a far better predictor of walking speed than residual age (linear regression of residual height versus walking speed, $R = .78$, $p < .002$; regression of residual age, controlling for height, on walking speed, $R = .14, p = .65$). In other words, the effects of age on walking speed are due to the correlation between age and height, and once we remove that effect, height remains the most significant predictor of walking speed *and* efficiency.

EFFECTS OF WALKING SPEED ON ENCOUNTER RATES AND PATCH CHOICE

While in the sandhill patch, children (all below 160 centimeters in height) walk at an average speed of 2.86 ± .01 kilometers/hour, and adults (all above 150 centimeters) walk at 3.77 ± .08 kilometers/hour (df = 148, t = (7.20, $p < .001$). Because the density of prey in rocky outcrops and sandhills differs, walking speed has differential effects in the two patches: children in rocky outcrops encounter prey (averaging 350 grams/item) at 1.56 ± .27 items/hour *searching* ($n = 24$), while adults encounter prey (averaging 450 grams/item) at a rate of .90 ± .12 items/hour searching in the sandhill patch ($n = 131$) (means are significantly different, df = 153, $t = -2.14$, $p = .03$). At children's average walking speed, *if they chose to search for prey only in the sandhill patch*, their encounter rate would be .68 items/hour search, yielding 307 grams/hour search, or an overall foraging return rate of 442 kilocalories/hour. This compares favorably to the 402 kilocalories/hour children acquire in rocky outcrops. If we examine only the benefits of foraging in terms of energetic return, children should be equally likely to choose sandhills as rocky outcrops for their hunting trips. However, because they walk slower, smaller children would be even less successful in the sandhills than in the rocky outcrops. If smaller hunters (101–130 centimeters in height, mean walking speed = 2.25 ± .12 kilometers/hour, $n = 36$ spot observations) chose to forage in the sandhill patch, they would

gain 268 grams/hour search, yielding roughly 385 kilocalories/hour foraging. In rocky outcrops children this height earn 448.7 ± 86.7 kilocalo-
ries/hour foraging for *winyjikiti* ($n = 7$).

While on average the return rates for all children might be similar in the
two patches, additional *costs* of acquiring prey in the sandhills may preclude smaller hunters from hunting there. The average length of time children spend hunting in the rocky outcrops is only 48 ± 7 minutes, while
adults average 193 ± 9 minutes hunting in the sandhills. In order to acquire one prey item (450 grams) in the sandhills, children must forage for
88 minutes on average and walk at least four kilometers. In order to acquire one prey item of 350 grams in the rocky outcrops, children need only
forage for 38 minutes and walk 1.8 kilometers. Although the gross foraging return rates are the same, foraging in sandhills as compared to rocky
outcrops requires 2.3 times greater time investment and 2.2 times more
walking as does rocky outcrop foraging for only 1.3 times as many calories
per hour.

DISCUSSION

Our data suggest that height and walking speed are more important constraints on hunting success than age. Once Martu children systematically
begin to hunt for goanna lizards, they are already well practiced: in our
sample the youngest hunters can be nearly as efficient as the older children. Beyond about five years, age alone has little effect on children's
hunting success in rocky outcrops. However, standing height and walking
speed do predict increases in children's success. Moreover, the data indicate that walking speed (which is more closely correlated with height than
age) has an important effect on children's decisions to avoid the sandhills
and focus on hunting in rocky outcrops. Children who are smaller walk
more slowly and take longer to cover enough ground to acquire at least
one sandhill goanna. Such slow walkers find the costs of sandhill foraging
higher relative to the increase in benefits received compared to hunting in
rocky outcrops. On average, children who choose to hunt in rocky outcrops find more prey more quickly and with less walking. Foragers might
begin to increase their return rates by switching from hunting in rocky outcrops to the sandhills when their height (roughly 150 centimeters) permits
higher-speed walking over long distances, or perhaps when body size allows them to tolerate higher-cost foraging strategies.

One of the problems with our analysis here is that we lack height measurements for adult foragers: some of the larger children and some of the
smaller adults would walk and search at similar rates, and yet *they still
choose different hunting patches*. Why this is so will require specific investi-

gation of the effects of height, walking speed, body weight, and age in the sandhill patch. It may be the case that exogenous factors not measured here may play an important role in influencing children's time allocation to different activities (Bock 2002a, Chapter 5 in this volume). For example, camping within reasonable walking distance of both sandhill and rocky outcrop patches may provide opportunities for adults to leave older children to care for youngsters in locales where smaller children can be especially productive. Thus, it may be that larger children, when accompanied by smaller children, would have to walk more slowly in the sandhills: they choose rocky outcrops to increase their efficiency when caring for and foraging with small children. Hawkes et al. (1995a) have shown similar effects of children on a mother's patch choice among the Hadza. Testing this among Martu would require experimental foraging in the sandhills by children of different ages and in different group compositions.

Another possibility is that the costs of walking longer distances in the hot sun may be lower for individuals of higher body mass than for those with lower body mass. Children are notorious for their intolerance of heat stress and thirst. This might explain why short but high-mass adults will still choose sandhills over rocky outcrops even though they are the same height as some of the thin but light children.

It should also be noted that our analysis does not *directly* control for learning experience: we have no quantitative measure of learning curves with age, which are likely to be different for different foraging activities. We only show that among children, size is a better predictor than age for both walking speed and foraging efficiency; we *assume* that age indicates the amount of experience and learning (and that increases in these would be roughly equivalent in the two hunting patches analyzed, see below). One way of addressing this issue would be to investigate differences in the percentage of time that foragers have spent in the desert as opposed to time in European settlements for individuals of all ages. But for experience to account for the increase in hunting success with forager height, this would mean that taller children (at any age) have spent more time foraging in the desert. We doubt that this is the case.

Another possible critique is that there are many other factors (than those investigated here) inherent in adult hunting activities that make them too difficult for children (see Bock 2002a). This may indeed be the case for large game hunting and the use of lethal weapons, but whether children avoid these as a result of size or learning constraints would require experimental data. Ohtsuka (1989) demonstrates that among Gidra hunters on the Papuan Oriomo Plateau, regardless of size or strength, men age 35–45 have four times the hunting efficiency as teenagers and young men. But we do not know from this how long it takes to learn such activities or how changes in motivation to learn how to hunt vary with age.

Does it take an entire childhood? Blurton Jones et al. (1999) and Blurton Jones and Marlowe (2002) provide data showing that among the Hadza, growth-based constraints are more important than experience in success at using hunting weapons. When size allows, foragers *can* gain experience related to hunting fairly quickly if so motivated.

If learning and experience account for Martu children's hunting decisions, this would suggest that it takes over ten years to learn to hunt like adults in the sandhill patch. But in comparing current options for Martu to hunt on foot, we would argue that the *learning* constraints are similar in both available patches (*winyjikiti* in rocky outcrops or *parnaparnti* in the sandhills). Hunting in the sandhills is cognitively difficult, but no more so than hunting in rocky outcrops. Foraging in both patches focuses on similar types of prey (goanna). Both require complex knowledge about where and when to hunt, and intricate strategies to search for, track, and extract the prey. Tracking prey in both patches requires hunters to synthesize complex information about goanna feeding and denning behaviors and their signatures across substrates that vary with location, season, and weather conditions. Foragers in both patches use identical tools (digging sticks), and both require roughly equal amounts of exertion to pursue and extract the prey once encountered. The primary difference is how far a forager must walk to encounter prey: while prey are smaller in rocky outcrops, they are more often encountered than in the sandhills. For children this means that choosing to focus their hunting in rocky outcrops is often a better option.

It may be that some of these cognitive costs are reduced for younger hunters by following the older children. More data on youngsters foraging independent of more experienced children will help to address this issue. Nevertheless, during the hunts reported here, children searched and tracked by themselves, and only while extracting goanna from the den did older children sometimes help youngsters.

There might be broader implications of these results for how we view the evolution of human childhood. If the extended juvenile period for humans evolved for more learning to occur, we would expect experience rather than size to be the primary constraint on foraging success. As Bock (2002a, Chapter 5 in this volume) has pointed out, growth-based constraints *alone* cannot account for the long time it takes for many foragers to reach peak efficiency. But some researchers investigating such constraints among young foragers have found that size differences have stronger effects than age and experience (Bird and Bliege Bird 2000, 2002; Bliege Bird and Bird 2002b; Blurton Jones, Chapter 10 in this volume; Blurton Jones et al. 1997, 1999; Blurton Jones and Marlowe 2002; Tucker, Chapter 7 in this volume). This is so even for Martu children who often hunt game. These results suggest to us that the constellation of modern human life history variables and physical characteristics (e.g., prolonged juvenility, large adult body size, large brains, and long and productive postreproductive lives) may result from benefits other than those strictly linked to learning complex foraging activities. It could be that our extensive learning is a product, rather than the cause, of extended juvenile periods (Blurton Jones and Marlowe 2002). Theorists have suggested that this constellation of human life history characteristics emerged as a result of decreased extrinsic *adult* mortality that came with the coevolution of productive postreproductive lives and "delayed" maturation, tapping into the benefits of growing longer with resources that require both strength and skill to extract (e.g., Alvarez 2000; Charnov 1993; Hawkes et al. 1998; Kaplan et al. 2003). If so, distinctive characteristics of anatomically modern humans (including our extensive learning) would be expected from any long-lived primate of our body size with low adult extrinsic mortality. If all of these characteristics coevolved, the social behavior linked to them (e.g., central place foraging, intergenerational food sharing, large game hunting) would have emerged relatively recently in human evolution, possibly only with the spread of anatomically modern human traits over the last glacial maximum of the Pleistocene (O'Connell et al. 1999, 2002).

CONCLUSION

Martu children are active and independent hunters. Their efforts are unsupervised without direct instruction by adults. Their skills and decisions, while praised by their elders, are more directly influenced by other children. So far our data show that for children's hunting in the Western Desert's rocky outcrops, forager size is a more important effect on hunting success than age. Moreover, children's decisions to hunt in rocky outcrops as opposed to the sandhills (that adults target) are not likely to be the result of learning constraints. By focusing their efforts in rocky outcrops, children (who walk slower than adults) can encounter prey at a higher rate. On average, this provides return rates for children that are equivalent to those they might expect if they hunted in the sandhills, while avoiding the long search distances involved in sandhill hunting. Only when walking speeds approach the adult average does hunting in sandhills consistently offer higher efficiency. These data may be consistent with the argument that prolonged human juvenility evolved for reasons other than to learn complex hunting strategies, but a great deal of further work will be required to evaluate how learning and size influence age-linked variability in extractive foraging activities.

ACKNOWLEDGMENTS

Primarily we wish to thank all of the Martu community from Parnngurr, Punmu, and Kunawarritji for their patience, good humor, expertise, and friendship. We owe a great deal to the Taylor and Biljabu families who have hosted us and organized much of our research. We thank Bob Tonkinson and Peter Veth for introducing us to the Martu and assisting us with our project, and especially Chris Parker, who participated in much of the data collection. Many thanks to Barry Hewlett for asking us to participate in the hunter-gatherer children workshop at CHAGS 2002. The ideas discussed here have developed from valuable discussions with John Bock, Nicholas Blurton Jones, Kristen Hawkes, Sarah Hrdy, Frank Marlowe, James O'Connell, Dan Sellen, Eric A. Smith, and Bram Tucker. The Martu ethnographic project is funded by the National Science Foundation and the L.S.B. Leakey Foundation.

NOTE

1. This is especially remarkable: numerous authors (e.g., Latz 1996:51–55, O'Connell and Hawkes 1981, Tonkinson 1991:45–46) and our own observations of woollybutt winnowing attest to the intricacy and skill needed to process these seeds—no doubt it takes years of practice to master the technique

7

Growing Up Mikea

Children's Time Allocation and Tuber Foraging in Southwestern Madagascar

Bram Tucker and Alyson G. Young

INTRODUCTION

Human childhood poses interrelated evolutionary, economic, and ecological puzzles. The evolutionary puzzle is that the human juvenile period is considerably longer than the premature developmental periods in other great apes, making long childhood a derived trait of potential significance (Bock and Sellen 2002b). Humans invest in growth and delay the start of reproduction for 15 to 20 years (Bogin 1999; Hill and Kaplan 1999). This seems contrary to Darwinian logic because a long childhood period has the potential to increase risk of mortality prior to reproductive maturation. Natural selection could favor prolonged investment in growth and delayed reproduction for several reasons. First, the costs of reduced fertility could be overridden by the mortality-reducing benefits of a long training period, such as a longer period to learn difficult foraging tasks (Kaplan et al. 2000). Second, long childhood could be a side effect of selection for a long lifespan more generally. Among mammals, body size, lifespan, and the length of the juvenile period are highly correlated (Charnov 1993, 2001; Charnov and Berrigan 1993).

The economic dimension of the puzzle has to do with the labor costs of supporting children. Children cannot meet all their resource needs from their own labor, so parents and alloparents must cooperate to provision children and take care of their needs, qualifying humans as "cooperative breeders" (Hrdy 1999). Children like all household members are simultaneously resource producers and consumers. They are both labor that benefits the household and hungry mouths that must be fed. Before the age of "positive net production," children consume more food than they produce

147

from their own labor; they are a net cost to the household. The rest of the household must work harder to support them (Chayanov [1925] 1986; Kaplan 1997; Lee and Kramer 2002). After the age of positive net production, young people can take on alloparental responsibilities and care for their younger siblings, easing the childcare responsibilities of adults (Kramer 2002).

The ecological dimension of this puzzle is that the costs of raising children vary with environmental conditions. Some environments favor children's active participation in the household economy more than others (Hawkes et al. 1995a). In some environments, children can dig their own tubers and pick their own fruit. In other environments, children foragers are endangered by the elements or frustrated by difficult or costly foraging tasks. When children can produce their own food, they reduce the physical and economic burdens on adults, potentially facilitating adults' future reproduction (Nag et al. 1978; Kramer and Boone 2002). Ecological variation in children's work roles may be one of the reasons that forager fertility rates are so variable (Kelly 1995:206-208; but see Early 1985).

Kaplan and colleagues (Kaplan 1997; Kaplan et al. 2000) argue that delayed reproduction and a lengthened juvenile period were favored by natural selection because of the mortality-reducing benefits of a long learning time, to learn how to forage for high-quality foods. They note that while other apes forage primarily for "collected" resources such as fruits and foliage that are easy to procure and low in food value, humans specialize on "extracted" resources such as tubers, roots, nuts, honey, and hunted game that are difficult to procure and high in food value. They argue that human foraging is so skill-intensive that it takes most of the lifetime to learn, so that children's foraging is more about learning than food procurement. Their model leads to two predictions. First, children and adolescents are dependent on adults' foraging success, and particularly men's large game hunting, to meet their food needs. Kaplan (1997) found that in three neotropical foraging societies, Machiguenga, Piro, and Ache, young people do not reach the age of positive net production until around the age of 20. Second, because age-related increases in foraging success are primarily the result of increased learned skill, foragers ought to continually improve even once they have stopped growing, achieving mastery at middle age. Kaplan et al. (2000) claim that Hiwi women of Venezuela master root digging at around ages 35 to 45, and Hiwi males master honey foraging at age 25. Hambukushu of the Kalahari master mongongo nut cracking at age 35. Ache women of Paraguay reach peak palm extraction rates during their early twenties. A more thorough study of Ache men (Walker et al. 2002) combining longitudinal hunting data with an archery contest showed that men almost always increase in foraging efficiency with age, and that archery skill peaks around age 40.

Other researchers have disagreed with parts of the theory advanced by Kaplan and his colleagues. Hawkes and her colleagues disagree that households depend on men for food and that male hunting is an efficient strategy for provisioning a household (Hawkes 1990, 1991, 1993, 2001; Hawkes et al. 1991, 2001a, 2001b). They argue that hunted meat is a poor resource choice for feeding children because daily hunting success is highly variable, and children need to eat every day. When hunters are successful, they are obliged to give most of their meat away and cannot control the distribution. Hawkes argues that men hunt and generously distribute meat because of fitness-enhancing benefits that may conflict with the cooperative goals of the household. Men may hunt as a form of social competition to win allies, mates, and deferential treatment for their families. Or they may hunt as a way to communicate to others the qualities they possess. Such communication is "honest" because men without the advertised qualities find hunting success too costly to mimic (Bliege Bird et al. 2001; Hawkes and Bliege Bird 2002; Smith and Bliege Bird 2000; Smith et al. 2003).

While Kaplan (1997) finds that the age of positive net production for Machiguenga, Piro, and Ache is around 20, there is good reason to suspect that this varies among foraging groups according to environmental circumstances. Ju/'hoansi San children near the Botswana/Namibia border rarely accompany adult *mongongo* nut foragers, while Hadza children of the Eastern Rift Valley of Tanzania are active foragers of baobab fruit and wild tubers and berries (Blurton Jones et al. 1989, 1994a, 1994b; Hawkes et al. 1995a). Even if it does take a lifetime to learn how to forage, one would expect Hadza to achieve positive net production at an earlier age than San.

While Kaplan et al. (2000) argue that juveniles forage less productively than adults because they have not yet learned to forage efficiently, others argue that children make optimal foraging decisions for foragers of their smaller size and lesser strength. Bird and Bliege Bird (2002) note that among intertidal collectors in the Torres Straits, Australia, children are less selective reef flat collectors than are adults. Children gather almost all edible species of shellfish, while adults target specific high-yielding *Hippopus* species. This difference is consistent with the predictions of the prey choice model from optimal foraging theory (MacArthur and Pianka 1966; Schoener 1971; Stephens and Krebs 1986). Because children are slower, their encounter rate for highly ranked resources such as *Hippopus* is effectively lower than that of adults, so they include more species in their diet breadth.

In another study of this population, Bliege Bird and Bird (2002b) contrast age-related trends in foraging efficiency for activities that are cognitively challenging but physically easy, such as fishing and spearfishing, versus activities that are cognitively easy but physically difficult, such as shellfish collecting. Their data reveal significantly stronger age-related trends in the latter, suggesting that strength is the more important determinant than learning for these marine exploitation tasks.

Our goal with this chapter is to examine children's foraging behavior in what is probably one of the best environments for young foragers. The Mikea Forest of southwestern Madagascar is a safe place for children. The dense dry tropical forest contains almost no predators and few poisonous plants and animals. Within this forest, Mikea forage for wild tubers, small game, and honey in addition to cultivating maize and manioc, herding livestock, and participating in market-oriented activities. Mikea children as young as four or five successfully unearth wild *Dioscorea* tubers for household consumption. Mikea children tuber foragers have exceptionally high net acquisition rates, averaging between 536 net kilocalories/hour for girls and 504 net kilocalories/hour for boys. As such, the Mikea example offers a potentially interesting test case for theories of juvenile dependency and foraging strategies.

We present scan-sampling time allocation data and foraging return rate data from the Mikea community of Behisatse. We find that while Mikea children experience over twice as much leisure time as do adolescents and adults, they allocate similar time to foraging, especially for the wild tuber called *ovy* (*Dioscorea acuminata*). Mikea children make a significant contribution to the household food procurement effort. Although they do not appear to achieve positive net production, it is possible that they are capable of doing so, at least during some seasons. Mikea children harvest *ovy* patches with strategies that are optimal for their lower strength and skill, as predicted by Charnov's marginal value theorem (Charnov 1976). We conclude by questioning whether "efficiency" is commensurate with children's foraging goals. Rather than children's foraging excursions being rigorous training sessions, children appear to forage as a leisure activity, an extension of play.

THE MIKEA OF MADAGASCAR

The southwest coast of Madagascar is a heterogeneous dry environment conducive to foraging (Figure 7.1). The landscape is a mosaic of dense, dry, deciduous forest covered in vines; anthropogenic clearings residual from agricultural and herding activities; thorny forests of octopus trees (*Didiera madagascariensis*) on sandy dunes; open savanna and savanna woodland; grassy lakebed pans; and dense coastal mangrove swamps. For the past four or more centuries, the Mikea Forest has provided refuge and sustenance to Malagasy escaping political, personal, or economic crises. During the 17th through 19th centuries, southern and western Madagascar was dominated by several cattle-herding kingdoms. Petty elites raided each

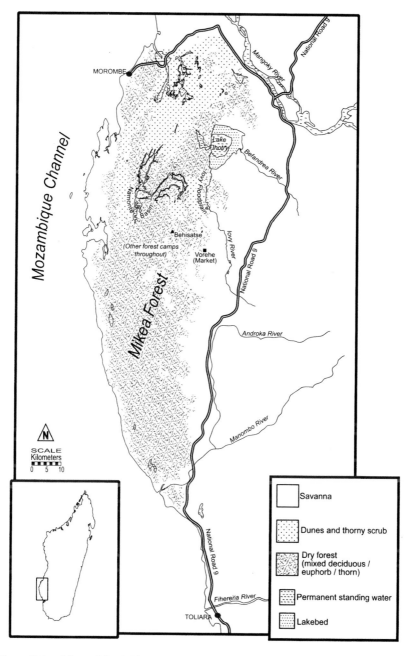

Figure 7.1. Map of the Mikea Forest, with placenames mentioned in text. Approximate forest extent based on 1994 Landsat imagery processed by James Yount.

other for booty of cattle and slaves within each polity, uniting periodically in warfare against neighboring polities (de Flacourt [1660] 1908; Drury [1729] 1826; Fagereng 1950). Cattle and slaves were sold to passing European ships in exchange for glass beads, silver coins, and firearms (Parker Pearson 1997). Today's Mikea are the descendants of neighboring Masikoro herders and Vezo fishermen who fled into the forest to resist tribute demands and threats of slavery and livestock loss, or in other cases, to avoid interpersonal disputes and accusations of witchcraft. Other Malagasy became Mikea during the twentieth century, when they adopted forest residence and foraging as an alternative to French colonial policies of forced relocation, taxation, and mandatory labor (Yount et al. 2001; Tucker 2003). Mikea are foragers of recent vintage.

For most Malagasy, the word "Mikea" connotes a forest-dwelling hunter-gatherer (Poyer and Kelly 2000; Yount et al. 2001). Mikea forage for a wide variety of tubers (*Dioscorea bemandry*, *Tacca pinnatifida*, others), but the *ovy* tuber *Dioscorea acuminata* is the most important foraged food source.[1] Other gathered foods include honey, wild cucurbits, baobab fruit (*Adasonia digitata*), and a few other wild fruits (*Flacourtia indica*, *Zizyphus vulgaris*). There are no large game animals in the Mikea Forest except for the exceedingly rare wild boar (*Potamocorus larvatus*). Small game include a variety of birds (*Numida meleagris*, *Lophotibis cristata*, *Coua coquereli*, others) and small mammals, including tenrecs (*Tenrec ecaudatus*, *Echinops telfairi*, *Setifer setosus*), feral cats (*Felis sylvestris*), and lemurs (*Chierogaleus medius*, *Microcebus murinus*, *Lepilemur ruficaudatus*). Mikea also forage in the intertidal zone for fish, crabs, octopus, and sea cucumbers (for more details, see Tucker 2001).

Despite their reputation as forest-dwelling foragers, all Mikea households rely to some extent on nonforaging activities. Their most significant agricultural ventures include slash-and-burn maize agriculture in the forest, and semi-intensive manioc cultivation in the savanna and lakebeds. Many households own cattle, goats, chickens, and guinea fowl, and more rarely, turkeys, ducks, and swine. Mikea are regular participants in the local market economy. They sell their production at weekly village markets such as the Wednesday market in Vorehe, where they purchase tobacco, soap, clothing, and other necessities. Many practice mobile retailing, purchasing goods in one place to resell at a markup elsewhere. Mikea also participate in the labor market. Mikea girls replant rice shoots, boys guard cattle, and men do agricultural or herding labor for neighboring villagers.

The data discussed in this chapter were collected in the Mikea hamlet of Behisatse,[2] a group of bark-thatched huts in the north-central part of the Mikea Forest. Mikea households are mobile, moving flexibly throughout the year to tend economic activities at multiple sites. During the study periods in 1996–99, eleven different households resided at Behisatse for a month or more. They used Behisatse as a home base when foraging for *ovy* and attending slash-and-burn maize fields and goat herds. Other locations in their yearly round included the villages of the Iovy Floodplain, where they tended manioc fields and performed wage labor; and the villages and hamlets of the Namonte Basin, where they attended family ceremonies, foraged in the lakes and dunes, tended livestock, and occasionally planted small gardens in the lakebeds. Many households also spent time in other forest hamlets and camps functionally similar to Behisatse, hosted by in-laws. Some practiced complete nomadic foraging for a week or two each year.

Our data sample across the four seasons recognized by the Mikea. Eighty-five to 95 percent of rainfall falls within the wet season, *litsake* (December–February). Rainfall varies stochastically from 100 to 1500 mm per year (Tucker 2001). The rest of the year is divided into an early dry season, *fararano* (March-May); a middle dry season, *asotre* (May-August); and a late dry season, *faosa* (August-December). The dry seasons differ significantly by temperature. Temperatures in *fararano* are similar to those of *litsake* (mean 33, minimum 21, maximum 41° C). *Asotre* is the southern winter and is the coolest season of the year (mean 26, minimum 7, maximum 36° C). *Faosa* is the hottest season (mean 33, minimum 18, maximum 42° C).[3]

METHODS, ANALYSES, AND RESULTS

A. Age Classification

Exact age of the study subjects is unknown. Instead, we use age rank order to explore age-related trends, and an age classification scheme in tests of significant differences. Our categories correspond roughly to those used by Mikea when describing people's age. These categories can be further distinguished by weaning status, degree of personal mobility, and marital status:

- Infant (*aja mena*): Babies that have not yet been weaned, and have no mobility beyond that supplied by caretakers. Infants do not forage or engage in any other work.
- Children (*olo kely*): Children who are weaned and prepubescent, are mobile enough to leave camp and travel/work with others in the environs of the camp, but are not old enough to travel alone.
- Adolescents (*olo be-be; kidabo lahy*): Young people nearing, experiencing, or just past puberty, unmarried, with complete independent personal mobility, who can travel to the well or to the market alone. They frequently talk about marriage and sex. Some are sexually active.
- Adults (*olo be*): Married people and parents.

B. Time Allocation

Scan-sampling time allocation data were collected in the Mikea hamlet of Behisatse during eight noncontiguous months between 1996 and 1999 (see Table 7.1). The procedure worked as follows. "Sampling months" consisted of 19- to 24-day blocks during which the research team resided at Behisatse. "Sampling events" were half-hour increments spanning daylight time, which was from 6:00 to 18:30 during summer months and 6:30 to 18:00 during winter months. A randomized schedule of sampling events was constructed at the beginning of each sampling month. All sampling events were scheduled twice during each month so that we sampled twice or three times per day, either 52 times (summer) or 48 times (winter) per month.

During each sampling event, we recorded the location and behavior of Behisatse residents and visitors of all ages. Our direct observation was limited to in-camp activities, which we categorize as leisure and housework. If people were absent from the camp at the time of the observation, their location was recorded as "not in camp" and the purpose of their absence was ascertained through subsequent observation and interview. People

Table 7.1 Summary of Time Allocation Sampling Strategy

Month & year	Dates	No. of days	No. of observation times	No. of data points	Average population	Season
Jul 1996	Jul 7–15, 19–Aug 3	24	48	672	23.19	*Asotre*, Middle dry
Nov 1997	1–10, 14–18, 20–28	24	52	1071	21.38	*Faosa*, Late dry
Jan–Feb 1998	Jan 8–15, 22–29; Feb 7, 8, 14	19	52	1136	23.54	*Litsake*, Wet season
Mar 1998	5–10, 12–16, 21–29	20	52	1139	36.30	*Fararano*, Early dry
July 1998	Jun 30–Jul 2, 8–14, 16–20, 24–28, 30–Aug 1	22	48	720	17.15	*Asotre*, Middle dry
Oct 1998	6–26	20	48	547	12.88	*Faosa*, Late dry
May 1999	9–17, 20–30	20	48	771	16.67	*Asotre*, Middle dry
July 1999	Jun 27–Jul 17	21	48	581	12.19	*Asotre*, Middle dry
TOTAL				6637		

were either absent for a few hours, usually on a food production chore near camp (foraging, farming, or herding). Or they were away for a few days, often with a specific objective in mind (tending fields in other locations, attending the market, attending a ceremony, etc). Visitors are excluded from the current analyses, for they likely behave differently than residents. Infants are also excluded, since by our definition they do no work. The resulting dataset includes 6637 observations of 46 individuals.[4] Figure 7.2 summarizes these data by age and sex. Data are expressed as percents of the total number of observations within each age/sex category. Figure 7.3 examines time allocation to food production activities in further detail. We make four observations from these data:

1. Children spend their time differently than people in older age categories, while there is little difference between adolescent and adult

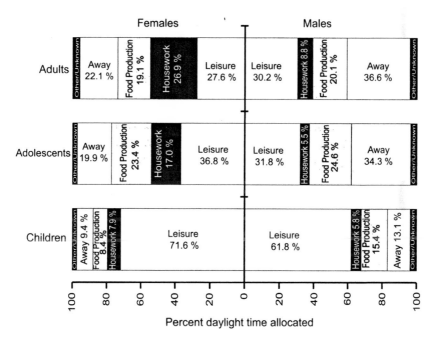

Figure 7.2. Percent daylight time allocation by age/sex group. "Leisure" includes resting, chatting, eating, sleeping, dancing, smoking, listening to cassette, playing games, grooming, etc. "Housework" includes meal preparation, food processing, direct childcare, manufacturing and repairing tools and structures, fetching firewood, fetching water, etc. "Food production" includes foraging, herding, agriculture (see Figure 7.3). People were "Away from camp" to attend ceremonies, markets, etc.

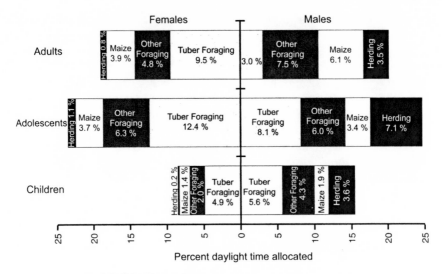

Figure 7.3. Percent of daylight time allocated to food production activities, by age and sex.

time allocation. This implies that Mikea adopt adult roles around the age of puberty, many years before marriage.

2. The most important activity for people in all age/sex groups is leisure, as is commonly found in time allocation studies (Johnson 1975; Hill et al. 1985; Hurtado et al. 1985; Hurtado and Hill 1987:179). Leisure includes individual and social non-work activities such as resting, eating, playing, chatting, listening to the cassette player, and playing dominoes.[5] Percent time spent in leisure is the main difference between children's time allocation and that of older people. Children enjoy roughly twice as much leisure time as adolescents or adults. Figure 7.4 displays the percent of leisure observations for each of the 46 individuals in the dataset by age rank. There is a clear, negative relationship between age and leisure time for both sexes. The trend is more linear for females ($R^2 = 0.82$) than males ($R^2 = 0.23$), for males appear to increase leisure time again as they reach middle age.

3. People in all age/sex categories make important contributions to household food production. Adults and adolescents of both sexes spend similar amounts of time on food production tasks, while children, especially girls, spend somewhat less time. The most significant food production task for all age/sex groups except adult males is foraging, and more specifically, tuber foraging. Figure 7.5 plots the percent of tuber foraging time for each of the 46 individuals in the

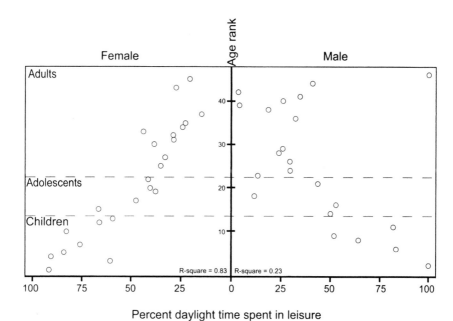

Figure 7.4. Percent of daylight time that each of the 46 individuals in the time allocation dataset were observed to be engaging in leisure activities, by age rank and sex.

dataset by age rank. While the five youngest children spend less time digging tubers than others, beyond this point there is little age-related tendency in time spent tuber foraging (females, $R^2 = 0.03$; males, $R^2 = 0.06$).

4. Males and females do many of the same activities. Differences in sexual division of labor are less important for children than for adolescents and adults. The main differences between female and male labor are time devoted to housework and herding. Housework, especially food processing and meal preparation, is primarily practiced by females, while males do most of the livestock care. Adult males spend less time foraging for tubers and more time foraging for honey and small mammals, although it should be noted that women do all the same foraging activities but less frequently.

C. Foraging Return Rates

Foraging returns were monitored during seven time allocation sampling months in 1997–99, and again during a nine-day period in October

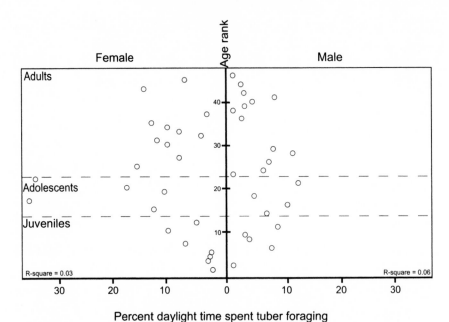

Figure 7.5.   Percent of daylight time that each of the 46 individuals in the time
    allocation dataset were observed to be foraging for wild tubers, by age
    rank and sex.

2003. Data were collected in a foraging log that recorded the time people
left camp to forage, the time they returned to camp, and the number and
weight of resources captured. Given the significance of wild tuber foraging in the time allocation data discussed above, we limit discussion to *ovy*
foraging.

People foraged for *ovy* in teams of 1 to 12 individuals, with an average
team size of 2.25 people. In some cases people returned to camp with bundles of tubers representing their individual effort, while in other cases they
pooled the tubers into team bundles before returning to camp. During the
1997–99 field seasons we observed 114 team foraging events; of the individuals within these teams, 128 were clearly carrying tubers they themselves had procured. In 2003 we sought to enlarge the individual return
rate data. Because our time was limited to only nine days, we offered a
small cash incentive (500 Malagasy francs, enough to purchase a cup of
coffee and a rice cake in the market) to foragers each time they allowed us
to weigh their tubers. We asked that individuals present only the tubers
they dug themselves. We recorded 124 individual return rates. Participants received the same cash gift regardless of how long they spent for-

aging or how many tubers they brought back, so these data ought to accurately reflect individuals' return rates. However, the cash incentive encouraged people to forage more frequently, and in teams of different composition than they would have normally.

"Foraging success" is quantified as net acquisition rate (NAR). Net acquisition rate is the number of kilocalories harvested minus the caloric costs of foraging, divided by the time spent foraging. We converted the weight of tubers harvested into gross caloric gain using the rate 119 kilocalories/100 grams, based on a nutritional analysis of an *ovy* sample conducted by Kelly and Poyer (1997). We estimate the costs of foraging at 4.3 kilocalories/minute (258 kilocalories/hour). We base this estimate on focal follow observations in which a minute-by-minute record was kept of tuber foragers' specific actions—walking, digging, etc. The number of minutes spent on each action was multiplied by the caloric expenditure per minute for that action using data from Passmore and Durnin (1955) and Durnin and Passmore (1967). This estimate is within the range that Durnin and Passmore (1967:47) classify as "moderate work." Tuber foraging is more costly than walking (2.1 to 3.1 kilocalories/minute) and less costly than digging (5.0 to 10.5 kilocalories/minute), the two main actions involved.[6]

First we explored the relationship between age and NAR, using the individual return rate data from both 1997-99 and 2003. The plots in Figures 7.6a and 7.6b explore age trends cross-sectionally in each dataset and Figure 7.7 examines longitudinal trends for eight individuals who shifted age categories between datasets. We offer the following observations:

1. Both cross-sectional and longitudinal analyses reveal that foraging efficiency increases with age, for both sexes. Figures 7.6a and 7.6b display the cross-sectional data from 1997–99 and 2003 respectively, by sex. Age rank accounted for 18 percent of the variance in NAR for females and 39 percent for males, in 1997–99; it accounted for 48 percent for females, and 33 percent for males in the 2003 dataset.

   Combining the two datasets ($N = 254$), we examine statistical differences in the means of the age categories with a series of independent t-tests on log-transformed data (an analysis of variance comparing all categories simultaneously was not possible due to significant differences in variances even when the data are logarithmically transformed). The data reveal significant differences in all pairwise comparisons. Children experienced significantly lower mean NAR than adolescents ($t = 5.923$, df $= 137$, $p = .000$), and than adults ($t = 11.372$, df $= 111$, $p = .000$). Adolescents averaged significantly lower NAR than adults ($t = 11.372$, df $= 111$, $p = .000$).

   Longitudinal trends, differences in eight individuals' mean NAR in 1997–99 versus 2003, are displayed in Figure 7.7. To control for

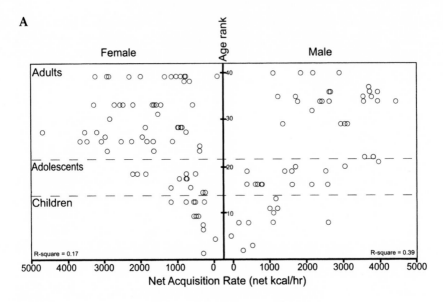

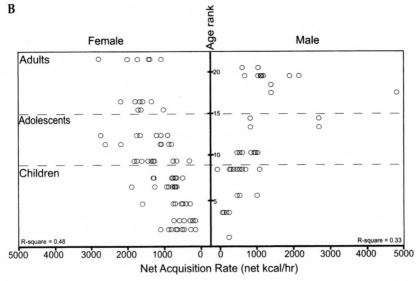

Figure 7.6. **A**: Individual foraging returns from 1997–1999, plotted by age rank and divided by sex (N=128). Each row of points represents observations of the individual of the corresponding age rank on the y-axis. Some rows have one point, indicating that the individual was only observed once. Others have multiple points representing multiple observations of the same individual. **B**: Individual foraging returns from 2003, plotted by age rank and divided by sex (N=124).

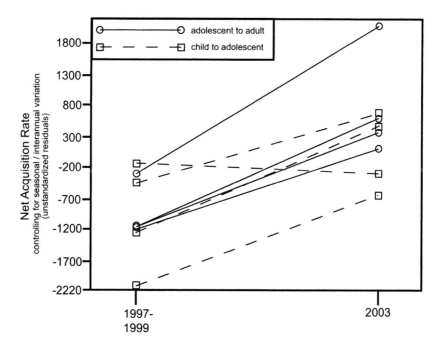

Figure 7.7. Longitudinal trends in NAR for the eight individuals present in both 1997–1999 and 2003. The circles and squares indicate the forager's mean NAR in both datasets. The y-axis variable controls for seasonal and interannual variation in NAR.

seasonal and interannual variation, NAR was first regressed by season and the unstandardized residuals used as the dependent variable. For seven of the eight individuals mean NAR increased as children became adolescents, and as adolescents became adults.

2. Within most age categories, males and females harvest tubers at statistically similar rates. Mean NAR for female children versus male children does not differ significantly ($t = .509$; df = 77; $p = .612$), nor does female versus male adolescents ($t = .268$; df = 58; $p = .789$). Adult males average significantly higher NAR than adult females ($t = 2.114$; df = 103; $p = .037$).

Next we explored foraging team composition, and the success rates of individuals when foraging in teams with differing numbers of children. These analyses are only performed using the 1997–99 data, since the teams observed in 2003 may not have been "natural" due to the cash incentive. We offer the following observations:

1. Children rarely forage alone. Children were involved in 41 of the 114 observed team events in 1997–99. Children foraged alone in two cases (5 percent); they foraged with other children in four cases (10 percent); with adolescents in 12 cases (29 percent); and with adolescents and adults in 23 cases (56 percent). Adult males rarely foraged with children.

2. Children experience the same success rates when they forage in the company of other children as when they forage with adolescents and adults ($t = 1.537$, df = 33, $p = .175$). Adolescents and adults forage at the same rates when accompanied by children as when not accompanied by children ($t = .369$, df = 47, $p = .714$).

D. Economic Dependency and Self-Sufficiency

Finally, we combine data from the analyses above to estimate the degree to which each age/sex group meets its own food needs through tuber foraging. The first column in Table 7.2 lists the mean tuber foraging net acquisition rate for each age/sex group. These values are multiplied by the average time spent tuber foraging from the time allocation data (converted to minutes) to arrive at an estimate of daily caloric production.

We do not know age- and sex-specific daily energy requirements for Mikea. Assuming a 1500–2000 kilocalories/day requirement for children and adolescents and a 2000–2500 kilocalories/day requirement for adults, then children do not meet their own caloric needs, while adolescents and adult females probably do. Mikea may achieve positive net production during adolescence, especially when the caloric contributions of their other productive activities are considered. Children only acquire a fraction of the energy they need to survive, but in doing so, they reduce adults'

Table 7.2   Average Daily Caloric Production from Tuber Foraging

	Average NAR (net kcal/hr)	Average time spent foraging (minutes/day)[a]	Average daily production (kcal)
Female children	537	35	313
Male children	505	41	345
Female adolescents	1196	89	1774
Male adolescents	1372	59	1349
Female adults	1851	68	2097
Male adults	2419	22	887

[a] Duration of activities was estimated as follows. The time allocation values for tuber foraging reported in Figure 7.3 are percent daylight time. Assuming 12 hours (720 minutes) of daylight time, 4.9 % observations = 35/720 minutes.

provisioning responsibilities. Children would be capable of positive net production if they increased their time allocation to three to four hours daily.

DISCUSSION

In the remainder of this chapter we consider how Mikea children achieve their high return rates, and also why they forage at lower rates than adolescents and adults. First we argue that the Mikea Forest is a safe environment for Mikea children. Then we discuss why *ovy* foraging is a feasible task for young foragers, in reference to the plant's ecology and age-specific foraging strategies. Finally, we question the degree to which children strive to forage "efficiently."

A. The Mikea Forest as a Foraging Environment for Children

In a series of papers, Blurton Jones et al. (1994a, 1994b) and Hawkes et al. (1995a) explore why San children of the Kalahari spend little time foraging while Hadza children of Tanzania forage avidly. Although the Kalahari Desert of Botswana and the dry savanna around Lake Eyasi in northern Tanzania are similar environments in many ways (and not unlike the Mikea Forest), these studies conclude that important ecological differences affect how young people best contribute to the household economy. For Ju/'hoansi San living along the Botswana/Namibia border, dry season residential sites are located along dry watercourses, while the most productive foraging microenvironments are mongongo nut groves on sand dunes located 13 to 18 kilometers away. While children are efficient nut gatherers within the patch, the high travel costs are prohibitive. Children cannot carry heavy loads of nuts. There is little shade or water along the way, so children are susceptible to dehydration and heat stress. Children who find it difficult to keep pace with adults could become lost, and could die of exposure or be preyed upon by wild animals. The extra load of nuts children could contribute is too small to offset these hazards. Once back in camp, the nuts must be boiled and cracked before they yield food value. Team rates are maximized if children stay at camp and process nuts while their mothers forage. By contrast, Hadza foragers have lower travel costs and fewer hazards. Hadza children dig //*ekwa* (*Vigna frutescens*) and *makalita* (*Eminia atenullifera*) tubers in the immediate environs of camp without adult supervision. They also accompany adults to *Cordia* and *Grewia* berry groves five to seven kilometers away. Loads of berries are considerably lighter than loads of mongongo nuts. The Hadza savanna woodland provides more shade and sources of water. Berry foragers consume berries as they pick, providing them with energy and water for the walk home. Hadza women could achieve higher return rates if they left their children at home and foraged for tubers, but the costs of foraging with children are offset by the children's own foraging successes. Team rates are maximized by foraging together.

In comparison to the Kalahari or Lake Eyasi, the Mikea Forest is both a safe and productive environment for children foragers. Children can forage alongside adolescents and adults without depressing their foraging rates, at least during the early dry season. *Ovy* grow within several kilometers of camp. Heat stress and dehydration are less of a threat than in the Kalahari, for temperatures are generally lower, the forest provides shade, and Mikea children know several sources of water including rainwater in tree bowls, wild watermelons, and water-engorged tubers such as *babo* (*Dioscorea bemandry*) and *ba* (scientific name unknown). Parties of children can forage in the forest and anthropogenic clearings with little fear of physical danger, for there are very few predators, poisonous snakes, stinging insects, or irritating plants. The only dangerous wildlife are scorpions and fossa (*Cryptoprocta ferox*), a rare predatory mongoose. Zoologists claim that there are no poisonous snakes in Madagascar (Preston-Mafham 1991:104) although Mikea believe a few species to be deadly.

Nevertheless, children sometimes expressed fear about wandering too far from their parents and caretakers. They feared encounters with *olo raty*, "bad people," including cattle thieves, evil sorcerers, brain stealers, and *vazaha*, a term referring collectively to foreigners, white people, policemen, military, gendarmes, and other representatives of authority. They also feared encounters with monsters, such as the evil one-horned ungulate *tsongaombe*, the undead wraith *tsiboko*, and the sinister *biby maseake* ("cruel animal").

Ovy is a more profitable tuber than Hadza's *//ekwa* and *makalita* tubers. *Ovy* grows deeper than *makalita* but perhaps at similar depths as *//ekwa*, both requiring on average a hole 75 to 125 cm deep. But *ovy* is easier to dig because it grows in sandy soil devoid of rock. Hadza foragers digging *//ekwa* face "a complex underground jigsaw puzzle and a large excavation, circumnavigating or removing large rocks and boulders" (Blurton Jones and Marlowe 2002:209). Mikea children can successfully dig *ovy* with just their bare hands, although a metal spade and wooden scoop are preferred tools. *Ovy* also has better food value. *Ovy* contains 119 kilocalories/100 grams (Kelly and Poyer 1997) whereas *makalita* has 73 kilocalories/100 grams and *//ekwa* has 85 kilocalories/100 grams (Hawkes et al. 1995a: 691). The entire *ovy* tuber is edible, whereas the flesh of *//ekwa* and *makalita* are chewed and a quid expectorated. While some tubers require drying, grinding, and leaching to remove toxins, *ovy* requires only roasting or boiling.

Mikea children are significantly better tuber foragers than Hadza children. The child and adolescent return rates for the Hadza are actually quite low. Rates reported in Hawkes et al. (1995a) are expressed in grams/hour. When converted into net kilocalories/hour, many of these rates become negative or near zero.[7] Hadza youths averaged 85 net kilocalories/hour, while Mikea children averaged 656 net kilocalories/hour. A *t*-test finds significant differences in the means of these two datasets ($t = -4.040$, df = 44, $p = .000$).

B. Children's Foraging Strategies

We suggest that young people have qualitatively different foraging strategies than older people. The costs and benefits of these strategies are explained in reference to the lifecycle and patch dynamics of the *ovy* tuber, and the logic of Charnov's (1976) marginal value theorem.

Mikea informants explained that the *ovy* plant begins life when a seed falls from a nearby vine and germinates during the wet season. A vine grows up from the seed and climbs the surrounding vegetation, while a small, carrot-sized tuber grows below the ground. When the dry season begins, the leaves dry up and fall, and the vine dies and breaks into small fragments. When the next wet season rolls around, the small tuber dies and turns to mush (*fatin'ovy*). The upper tip of the *ovy*, called the "*ovy* head" (*lohan'ovy*), regenerates a new, larger tuber in its place, and a new vine grows above the surface. This continues for many years. Each year, the *ovy* tuber is larger in size and deeper beneath the ground. After two years the ovy is the size of a zucchini and the head is 20 centimeters or more beneath the ground; after four years the ovy is the size of a person's arm and the head is 30 centimeters or more deep. So long as the *ovy* head remains in the ground, a new tuber will regenerate each year, even if the previous year's tuber has been harvested; thus *ovy* foraging is potentially sustainable.

Ovy grows wild throughout much of the forest and anthropogenic clearings. However, foragers rarely search for virgin patches. Rather, they identify a patch by finding a spot, often around the base of some bushes, where many holes have been dug in the ground. *Ovy* patches have complex, multiyear histories of partial exploitation and reexploitation that can be read in the ground by counting the number and size of holes dug by previous foragers. A single *ovy* patch contains plants of many different ages. Once the forager arrives at a patch, he or she begins a process called *mifaokovy*, which involves scanning through the leaf litter and sand for the white, underground portion of the vine called the *firambony*. The forager can tell by the thickness of the *firambony* how old the plant is, and thus the depth and size of the tubers. It appears that adults target mature *ovy* plants, which provide large tubers but with considerable digging effort. Children target young *ovy* plants, which provide small tubers with less digging (adolescents may have an intermediate strategy).

Charnov's (1976) marginal value theorem posits that the length of time a forager spends in a patch is determined by the rate of gain within the patch and the travel time to the next patch. Foragers remain in a patch until the gain rate, net of the cost of travel to the next patch, is maximized, which normally occurs long before the patch is depleted. Foragers who either travel or harvest at a more efficient pace ought to spend less time in one patch before moving to the next. Because adults are capable of excavating larger tubers, they maximize their in-patch return rates more rapidly than do children, and so exploit patches faster but less thoroughly. Children forage in patches that adults have already exhausted of large tubers.

Two analyses support this story. First, there are interesting seasonal differences in foraging return rates and team compositions. Adolescents and adult females often foraged alongside children during the early dry season *fararano*, and rarely during the other seasons (Figure 7.8). In *fararano*, the recent rains have led to the regeneration of the tuber patches. Tuber foraging is significantly more profitable during this time of year (mean *fararano* = 2116 kilocalories/hour; mean other seasons = 1299; $t = -4.167$, df = 126, $p = .000$). On 22 March 1998 over 120 kilograms of *ovy* were brought into camp! Children forage with older people during *fararano* because both are interested in the same patches, even though within the patches they choose different plants to harvest. By the middle and late dry seasons, adults have already exhausted the patches near camp of the large tubers they prefer, and are traveling increasing distances each day. Children continue to forage near camp for the smaller (younger, shallower) tubers that the elders do not consider worth their while.

In 2003 we counted the number of tubers harvested in addition to the weight of the tuber bundle. This allowed us to calculate the average weight of each tuber. The average tuber dug by children weighed 203 grams (carrot sized); by adolescents, 337 grams; and by an adults, 499 grams. An analysis of variance reveals that these means are significantly different ($F = 37.433$; df = 114; $p = .000$). There are no significant differences by sex ($t = .172$; df = 112; $p = .863$).

C. Children's Foraging Goals

The main characteristic of children's time allocation is prolonged leisure time. Most of this time is spent in play. Play activities include games of tag (especially at night during full moon), tug of war, gymnastics, dominoes, and *kiombiomby*. *Kiombiomby* is pretend oxcart; the team of

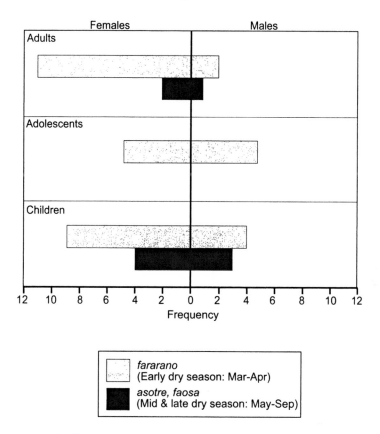

Figure 7.8. The frequency that individuals of different ages and sex foraged for tubers in teams that included children, by season.

"oxen" are either two children (holding forked sticks to simulate the oxen's horns), two blocks of wood, two wild watermelons, or two rats, tied together. These pairs are tethered to another stick, melon, or block of wood to simulate the cart. Another popular play activity for children is digging holes in the sand, perhaps practice for *ovy* excavation. For girls, grooming and coiffing are popular preoccupations. Everyone enjoys listening and dancing to music played on to the cassette player or by wandering bands of minstrels.

Despite enjoying twice as much leisure time as adolescents and adults, children spent almost as much time as older people foraging for tubers. Table 7.2 suggests that children could achieve positive net production if they made modest increases in their time allocation. So, why don't they?

Few studies have tried to predict time allocation to foraging. Hawkes et al. (1985) argue that foragers should increase their time allocation to foraging on days when foraging returns are high. Smith (1987) criticized this study for not fully appreciating the role of opportunity costs. Hawkes et al. state that because foraging has multiple fitness-enhancing benefits, including provisioning the household, generous transfer, and competitive display, more food acquisition per unit time (rate maximization) is always better. Smith counters that foragers may also be time-minimizers, when either the marginal utility of foraged products diminishes rapidly, or when activities alternative to foraging have high fitness-enhancing benefits. A mother with a young child may allocate less time to foraging on a high-returns day, so that she can return home earlier to nurse. A young man may return earlier from hunting when hunting is particularly profitable, so as to have more social interaction with potential mates.

We argue that Mikea children are not trying to be "efficient" at all. There is little reason for them to be either rate-maximizers or time-minimizers. Because parents provision children from their surplus, children are not energy-limited. Because they have few alternative uses for their time, and their alternatives are not likely to bestow fitness advantages, they are also not time-limited. The life of a child in a small foraging camp is often quite dull. Children forage for the physical and mental challenge, and because it is an enjoyable social activity. During one focal follow, the senior author witnessed a "food fight" between the boys and the girls. Several kilograms of edible tubers were destroyed in the ensuing volley. For children, foraging is an extension of play that occurs outside camp.

CONCLUSION

We have examined children's time allocation and foraging return rates in the Mikea Forest of southwestern Madagascar in order to contribute to current debates about the evolution, economy, and ecology of childhood in foraging societies.

To Kaplan and colleagues (Kaplan 1997; Kaplan et al. 2000) long childhood is the evolutionary result of a dietary shift to difficult-to-acquire but high-quality resources such as wild tubers and hunted game, tasks that require high intelligence and a long training period to master. In their theory, lesser learned skill accounts for why children target different resources than adults, and why children forage at lower rates. Consistent with their explanation, Mikea increase in foraging efficiency with increasing age, achieving their highest rates during adulthood. However, several aspects of age-specific foraging behavior among Mikea deviate from Kaplan et al.'s (2000) predictions.

First, Mikea children do not specialize on collected resources such as fruits and foliage, but rather, dedicate similar amounts of time to foraging for wild tubers, a high-quality "extracted" resource, as do older people.

Second, Mikea children do not appear to be actively trained by older people. Mikea children experience the same return rates when foraging with potential trainers (adolescents and adults) as when foraging with other children. Women only forage with children during the early dry season, when both children and adults are interested in the same patches.

Third, children may make rational, "educated" decisions for foragers of their smaller size and lesser strength. Children preferentially dig young *ovy* plants, whose tubers are small but shallow, while adults target deeper, larger tubers. Children exploit patches more thoroughly than adults.

Fourth, Mikea children are neither pressured to bring home a full load of tubers, for they know adults will provision them, nor are they pressed for time when foraging, for they have little else to do. So while they probably do learn while foraging, they learn at their own leisurely pace. Their objectives when foraging may be primarily social and recreational.

Fifth, despite the fact that Mikea children are probably not striving for efficiency, they approach the age of positive net production during adolescence, considerably earlier than Piro, Ache, Machiguenga, Ju/'hoansi San, and Hadza. Achievement of positive net production is more-or-less coincidental with the adoption of adult sexual division of labor and workload. Young people increase their foraging efficiency when opportunity costs increase.

If children's observed foraging return rates are not an accurate representation of their maximum foraging potential—of how efficiently they *could* forage if efficiency were their goal—then age of positive net production is a somewhat ambiguous concept, and so is juvenile dependency. The question may not be when children can feed themselves, but rather, when do children want to work hard enough to feed themselves? This makes it difficult to argue that juvenile dependency early in life permits one to be a provisioner later in life. The contrary is also possible: provisioning by older people may permit juvenile dependence.

Children's limited motivation to self-sufficiency may be part of an inherent parent-offspring conflict. To the degree that children can meet their own food needs, they free up parental resources for investment in future offspring. It may not be in children's best individual interest to do this, for new babies would increase children's competition for resources. Previous studies of the relationship between children's production and household reproduction implicitly assume that children's goals are necessarily cooperative (Chayanov [1925] 1986; Kaplan 1997; Lee and Kramer 2002).

The possibility that Mikea children foragers are not trying to be efficient illustrates a problem with using age- and sex-specific economic data to test theories about the profitability of children's foraging. Contests in which foragers compete for the best success rate may produce better data for evaluating absolute age-specific ability (see Blurton Jones and Marlowe 2002; Bock 2002a; Walker et al. 2002).

Mikea children foragers are more productive than children in other hunter-gatherer and forager-horticulturalist populations in large part because of the ecology of the Mikea Forest and the *ovy* plant. Ecological variation may be just as important as ethnographic generalization when constructing and testing theories about the evolution of childhood. We hope that the Mikea case will expand anthropological imagination as to the range of possibilities in children's foraging production.

ACKNOWLEDGEMENTS

We dedicate this chapter to Dadebo and Tekely, with hopes that they one day become great tuber foragers. We wish to thank Doug Bird, Frank Marlowe, Nick Blurton Jones, Pat Draper, and Barry Hewlett for stimulating discussions with the senior author at CHAGS9 in Edinburgh. Useful feedback was provided by Paul Sciulli, Nick Blurton Jones, Doug Crews, Jim Yount, Bob Kelly, Clark Larsen, Ivy Pike, Tsiazonera, Jaovola Tombo, Veve Tantely, Scott Young, and the editors of this volume. Tucker's research among the Mikea was funded by a Fulbright IIE grant, a National Science Foundation Dissertation Improvement Grant, a Sigma-Xi grant-in-aid of research, and travel grants from the University of North Carolina at Chapel Hill (1996) and the Ohio State University (2003).

NOTES

1. In the rest of Madagascar, the word *ovy* refers to any tuber, including the domestic potato *Solanum tuberosum*. Most Malagasy people refer to wild *Dioscorea* yams as *ovi'ala*, "forest potato." We conform to Mikea word choice. Mikea reserve the term *ovy* specifically for *Dioscorea acuminata*.

2. "Behisatse" is a pseudonym.

3. Temperatures were recorded at Behisatse as part of the scan sampling time allocation project, using a manual thermometer hung in the shade of the ethnographer's hut.

4. We also recorded absences of entire households during the sampling months. The inclusion of these observations allows a tracking of nine households throughout the entire study period. These observations will be useful for future studies of household mobility, but are not useful here because they reveal no differences in activity age or sex. The entire dataset includes 20,241 observations.

5. Actually, people enjoyed somewhat more leisure time than is measured here, for only leisure within camp was visible to the data collectors. Undoubtedly in some of the cases recorded as "food production" or "away," at the observation time

the subject was actually taking a break from foraging or farming to enjoy a rest, chat, cigarette, game of tag, romantic interlude, etc.

6. While this estimate is inexact, it is probably workable. If tuber foraging is more or less costly than we estimate, say 3 kilocalories/minute or 5 kilocalories/minute, then expenditure per hour is 180 or 300 kilocalories/hour rather than 258. This would make minor changes to our net acquisition values, and no changes in statistical results and interpretations.

7. We calculated Hadza net acquisition rates the same way as for Mikea, assuming that foraging costs 4.3 kilocalories/hour. *Makalita* may be slightly less difficult, and *//ekwa* slightly more difficult, due to the comparative depths and difficulties caused by rocks and roots.

III

Who Cares for
Hunter-Gatherer Children?

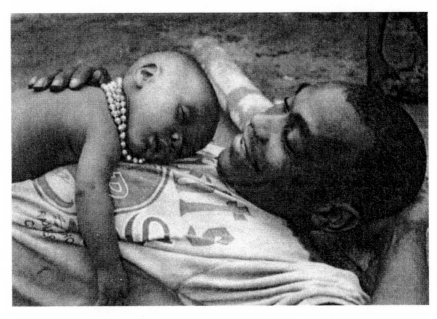

Photo 3. Aka infant sleeping on father's chest. Courtesy of B. Hewlett

III

Introduction

Barry S. Hewlett

This section is an extension of the first. The explanations for why childhood exists are linked to discussions of who cares for forager children (see Blurton Jones' introduction to Part II and Hrdy, Chapter 3). In explaining why childhood is so prolonged, the "grandmother hypothesis" (Hawkes et al. 2000) predicts grandmothers or older women should be especially important child caregivers. But as mentioned in Chapter 1, foragers provide much higher levels of direct care (e.g., holding and maintenance of proximity to children, frequency of breastfeeding) than adults in cultures characterized by other modes of production. Because overall levels of care are so high and childhood is relatively long among foragers, many individuals can contribute to care or provisioning.

Konner (Chapter 2) indicates that nonmaternal care and high father involvement are common, but variable, in hunter-gatherer infancy and early childhood, whereas Hrdy (Chapter 3) characterizes humans by their cooperative patterns of childcare. It is essential to read these two chapters in order to place the new research presented in this section in appropriate theoretical and ethnographic context. For instance, Ivey Henry et al. examine child caregiving among the Efe foragers in Chapter 9, but Ivey Henry and her colleagues have published extensively in the past 15 years on all types of nonmaternal caregivers. Child caregiving in Efe must be understood in the context of the earlier studies, most of which are reviewed by Konner in Chapter 2.

Chapters in this section also examine data on the extent to which forager fathers or grandmothers are more important to children's survival. As mentioned in Chapter 1, father's provisioning used to be viewed as central to forager child survival, but Hawkes et al. (2001a) point out that forager men actually share most of their meat with other adults in camp, while members of the hunter's family actually receive a relatively small portion of the meat. Men also bypass small game, which could be captured on a daily basis, to go after larger game, which is often captured irregularly. It is grandmothers or other older adult women, among the Hadza at least, who provide regular food and care to postweaning children because they collect tubers and other high-caloric food items for their grandchildren. With these data in mind, Hrdy (Chapter 3) suggests that fathers are generally not reliable caregivers or providers, whereas Hewlett (1991b) and Marlowe (1999a) identify them as important secondary providers, especially in particular contexts (e.g., when present in infancy and early childhood).

Chapters in this section extend our understanding of multiple or cooperative child care practices common to many forager groups. Chapters 8 and 10 use very different sets of data to understand who cares for Hadza children. Marlowe (Chapter 8) uses behavioral observations of children, whereas Blurton Jones et al. (Chapter 10) use data on residence patterns to determine the nature of care. In both, mothers are primary, but Blurton Jones et al. show that grandmothers are more likely than fathers to live in camps with related children who may need their assistance, whereas Marlowe identifies fathers as regular caregivers when they are in camp while grandmothers become important when fathers leave camp.

Ivey Henry et al.'s study of child care among the Efe is the first systematic study of children caring for infants in a foraging culture. Much has been written about the importance of sibling care, but all previous studies have been conducted with farmers or families in poverty in the developed world.

Sugiyama and Chacon's Chapter 11 could have been placed in either Part II or Part III of this book as these researchers provide new empirical data regarding allocare and children's skill acquisition. The Yora have been devastated by culture contact and many children have lost one or both biological parents to diseases of contact. Their data support aspects of Konner's HGC model, where mothers are primary and fathers are highly involved, as well as Hrdy's cooperative breeding hypothesis because children with one biological parent, especially those with single mothers, live in households with more potential allocaregivers than do children with living with both biological parents.

Draper and Howell's Chapter 12 is particularly important as it suggests that contrary to existing evolutionary hypotheses the number and type of potential allocaregivers may not be important to the health and development of hunter-gatherer children. !Kung children with many lineal relatives are not healthier or more active than !Kung children with a few lineal relatives. Draper and Howell hypothesize that egalitarian social relations and extensive sharing diminish the importance of lineal relatives to children's health and survival.

8

Who Tends Hadza Children?

Frank W. Marlowe

In many species of mammals virtually all care of the young is provided by mothers (Clutton-Brock 1991), as it is among red deer (Clutton-Brock 1982). In most species of bony fish (the teleosts), when care is provided at all, it is provided by the father (Krebs and Davies 1993). In other species, such as swans, both parents provide care equally (Black 1996). Among a number of species, including several birds (Emlen 1984), callitrichid primates (Garber 1997), and social carnivores such as wolves and wild dogs (Asa 1997), there is a more complex pattern of care provided by several members of a social group including siblings, more distantly related kin, or even unrelated individuals. Such species are called cooperative breeders.

In many cooperative breeders, caretakers are available because they are waiting for a breeding opportunity or territory to open up, which is true of the white-fronted bee eater (Emlen 1994). Sometimes, as in naked mole rats (Sherman, Jarvis et al. 1991) and some species of callitrichids (French 1997), the nonbreeding female's ovulation is inhibited by a dominant, breeding female. Human foragers would not be cooperative breeders by this criterion since females do not appear to be waiting for a reproductive opportunity to breed (unless one interprets our late age at maturity as just that). If the existence of multiple caretakers is the criterion of cooperative breeding, virtually all human societies qualify, and cooperative breeding was probably an important aspect of human evolution (Hrdy, Chapter 3 in this volume). The question is, How much allomaternal care is enough to qualify as cooperative breeding, and how much is there among foragers?

The care of young can be divided into direct and indirect care. Indirect care includes such things as foraging for provisioning foods, nest construction, and territory defense; direct care includes behaviors requiring physical proximity, such as holding, feeding, and grooming (Kleiman and Malcolm 1981). Some behaviors are difficult to classify. For example, protecting offspring from predators or conspecifics would seem to fall under direct care but might be difficult to distinguish from territory defense. Acquiring food is indirect care but giving food to young is direct care, and among most human foragers, there is extensive food sharing outside the household (Hawkes et al. 2001b; Kaplan and Hill 1985; Kitanishi 1998; Peterson 1993; Woodburn 1998). This food sharing amounts to provisioning of young other than one's own. If we consider provisioning then, contemporary foragers are extremely cooperative breeders.

Over the past decade, increasing attention has been paid to the benefits children might gain from having their grandmothers around compared to having their fathers around. Much of this attention has been focused on the Hadza (Hawkes et al. 1989, 1997, 1998). Previous analyses have dealt mainly with foraging returns (Blurton Jones et al., Chapter 10 in this volume; Hawkes et al. 2001a). Here, I analyze the amount of direct care children receive from their fathers vs. their grandmothers, and other categories of kin, to assess their relative importance.

THE HADZA

The Hadza are hunter-gatherers who live in a savanna-woodland habitat near Lake Eyasi in northern Tanzania. They number about one thousand altogether (Blurton Jones et al. 1992a), three to four hundred of whom are still full-time foragers, or were when this research was conducted in 1995–96. Women usually forage everyday in groups of three to ten women and children, digging wild tubers, collecting baobab fruit, and gathering berries. Men usually go foraging alone, collecting honey, berries, and baobab, and using bows and arrows to hunt a variety of birds and mammals from very small to very large (see Marlowe 2003 for amounts of different foods taken).

Hadza women take nurslings with them when they go foraging but leave toddlers in camp. Even though women can dig tubers with an infant on their back, it does lower their foraging returns (Marlowe 2003). This means someone else needs to compensate. Postmenopausal women bring many kilocalories back to camp and are clearly one important source of provisioning for nursing mothers and their families (Hawkes et al. 1989). It appears fathers may also be an important source (Marlowe 2003). Men in general are certainly an important source of food, since they account for about half of all food brought into camp and big game is widely shared across households (Hawkes et al. 2001b; Marlowe, in press a). By three or four years of age, children begin to do some foraging while playing, and by ten years of age they obtain about half their own caloric requirements (Blurton Jones et al. 1989). No one ever reaches an age where they stop receiving food from others but by 18 most can acquire at least as many calories as they consume (Marlowe, in press a).

The Hadza live in camps that average 29 people. They frequently move in and out of camps so that camp membership changes more often than camp location, which moves about six or seven times a year. There is a bias toward living with wife's kin over husband's kin. Since men are older than their wives by an average of seven years, some residential bias is due to the greater likelihood that the husband's parents are already dead, but there are other reasons why Hadza couples more often coreside with the wife's mother (Marlowe 2004). Among Hadza couples where the husband and wife have living mothers, 68 percent live in the same camp with the wife's mother (Woodburn 1964, 1968b; for a more thorough analysis, see Blurton Jones et al., Chapter 10 in this volume). The median age at first birth is 19 years, the total fertility rate is 6.2, infant mortality ($\leq$1 year old) is 21 percent, and juvenile mortality ($\leq$15 years) is 46 percent (Blurton Jones et al. 1992a).

I found the median age at first marriage to be about 17 for females and 20 for males. Marriages are not arranged and there is usually no wedding ceremony. Marriage typically follows a brief sexual relationship and is evident when a couple begins living together. Polygyny is rare; only about 4 percent of men have two wives at any given time and these marriages are not very stable. Serial monogamy is the best way to describe the mating system since divorce is fairly common (Blurton Jones et al. 2000). This results in about one-third of all children eight years old or younger living with stepfathers (Marlowe 1999b).

Fathers do more playing with children than mothers (Marlowe 1999b). All caretakers whether mother, father, grandparent, sibling, or others appear to be equally sensitive to fussing and crying (something I recorded but have not analyzed), but mothers seem to be far more effective at soothing the child. Fathers will sometimes hold a crying infant in the middle of the night and sing to get the infant to go to sleep. Both girls and boys appear to be closer to their mother and spend more time with her, though once boys are about six or seven years old, the time they spend with their father increases.

Hadza children are allowed to do as they like most of the time. Young infants will often grasp sharp knives and be allowed to suck on them. During their "terrible twos" children throw tantrums and pick up sticks and hit adults, who do little more than fend off the blows and laugh. One early German observer described Hadza mothers and fathers as doting (Obst 1912), while another said children were not punished (Kohl-Larsen 1958). I too found children received considerable affection and were rarely punished. I only saw one spanking during a year of observation of men and children. This was by the one and only stepfather who had a stepchild younger than his own child, since his wife had conceived a child with a non-Hadza man during a period of separation. When adults want a child to stop doing something they usually only make a loud grunt of disapproval. The parenting style then could be described as affectionate and lenient but not extremely indulgent, or at least less indulgent and attentive apparently than the Ju/'hoansi (N. Blurton Jones, personal communication, 2002; Konner, Chapter 2 in this volume).

METHODS

I collected data in six Hadza camps during 1995 and 1996 (for more details see Marlowe 1999a). The sample includes 218 different people but seven of these appeared in two camps, and thus for some analyses $n = 225$. I conducted instantaneous scan observations hourly in camp from sunrise to sunset, a total of 34,312 person scans. I also conducted 30-minute focal individual observations of men with children eight years old or younger (139,590 person-minutes), using the "One-Zero Recording Rule" (Martin and Bateson 1986). Within each minute, behaviors were scored as having occurred or not, with a maximum possible score of 30 per 30-minute focal follow.

I conducted follows of children as well, and it is mainly these follows that are analyzed here. The day was broken into three equal parts of four hours each with each part sampled randomly. I conducted a total of 5,280 minutes of focal observations of children eight years old or younger years old. There were 68 such children but follows were conducted on only 59 (40 males and 19 females), which is an average of 90 minutes each. Of these 59 children, 53 had a male head of household present, whether a genetic father (33), a stepfather (11), a grandfather (5), or an uncle (1); 50 had mothers present; 20 had maternal grandmothers present; and 9 had paternal grandmothers present. All 68 children are included in scans (43 male, 25 female). Only children four years old or younger were held (Table 8.1) and there were 41 such children in the focal follows (30 male, 11 female).

The variables used to measure direct care were: nursed, held, nurtured (which includes holding, carrying, cleaning, feeding, and pacifying), and proximity (within three meters). From these, I also created a variable "all interaction," with a score of one and only one if, within any minute any variable such as "held" or "talked to" or simply "near" (within three meters) occurred, and zero if none occurred. All interaction therefore reflects any behavior directed at the child, or at least proximity to within three meters. It should therefore reflect all proximity within about ten meters. Scans and follows of children were conducted during daytime hours only. All variables are calculated as percentage of the daylight hours by dividing absolute frequencies by the number of scans the child appears in, or the number of minutes observed in focal follows.

Table 8.1 Percentage of Time Children ≤8 Years Old Were in Camp, Were Nursing, Were Held by Anyone, and Were Interacting with Mother, Father, Older Sister, Older Brother, Maternal Grandmother, and Others

Age category (n)	% Time in camp (scans) (n)	% Time held (scans) (n)	% Time nursing (follows) (n)	% Time interacting (in follows) with:					
				Mother	Father	Older sister	Older brother	Mat. grand-mother	Others.
<1 yr	62.82	52.84	16.64	78.43	17.78	18.33	7.78	9.44	29.07
(11)	(11)	(11)	(11)	(11)	(9)	(2)	(5)	(6)	(11)
1–1.9	71.47	25.19	8.30	43.76	21.81	0.00	30.00	3.89	39.79
(11)	(11)	(11)	(10)	(10)	(8)	(0)	(2)	(2)	(10)
2–2.9	83.64	15.69	2.25	30.06	21.11	18.19	3.89	9.44	39.52
(8)	(8)	(11)	(8)	(7)	(5)	(4)	(4)	(3)	(8)
3–4	73.12	0.93	0.08	7.59	5.78	9.63	7.22	21.11	49.70
(12)	(12)	(12)	(12)	(9)	(5)	(3)	(8)	(4)	(11)
TOTAL ≤4 (42)	72.00	23.69	7.68	42.68	17.37	17.2	8.62	9.74	40.68
	(42)	(42)	(41)	(37)	(27)	(7)	(19)	(15)	(40)
4.1–5	79.94	0.00	0.00	21.67	0.00	1.11	0.00	0.00	49.70
(4)	(4)	(4)	(4)	(2)	(1)	(1)	(0)	(1)	(4)
5.1–6	71.40	0.00	0.00	14.44	13.33	18.89	30.00	0.00	80.00
(4)	(4)	(4)	(4)	(1)	(2)	(1)	(1)	(0)	(2)
6.1–7	65.54	0.00	0.00	3.33	1.11	0.00	0.00	10.00	59.44
(7)	(7)	(7)	(7)	(2)	(2)	(1)	(0)	(1)	(6)
7.1–8	55.30	0.00	0.00	6.39	6.67	14.07	8.056	0.00	83.33
(11)	(11)	(11)	(5)	(4)	(1)	(3)	(4)	(0)	(5)
TOTAL ≤8 (68)	69.06	14.65	4.86	36.29	15.52	13.37	9.77	9.18	52.74
	(68)	(68)	(59)	(46)	(33)	(15)	(24)	(17)	(57)

Interaction is measured as a percentage of time (in follows) with the child as the unit of analysis, but only for those children where persons in the particular category are present in camp. Holding (in scans) is reported in two ways: (a) as percentage of time all children were held, whether a particular category of caretaker was present or not, and (b) as percentage of time only those children with a particular category of caretaker present in camp were held. Measuring caretaking for all children illustrates just how important or frequently certain categories of people provided care, whereas using only the subset of children with a particular category of caretaker present controls for the availability of caretakers. Even if they are only rarely available, certain categories of people may have high levels of caretaking when they are present. Holding by different caretakers is compared in pie charts showing the percentage of all the time children were held. In all analyses of differences in nurturing between fathers and stepfathers the child's age is controlled since stepchildren tend to be older than genetic children.

These data were collected only in camp, which means people who are more often out of camp are less likely to be providing or receiving care. I therefore present how much time people of different ages are out of camp. Since mothers usually take their young infants with them when they forage, the percentage of time mothers care for their infants on forays should be slightly higher than the percentage shown here. The total time in a 24-hour period that parents care for their children is also higher, since children sleep against their parents all throughout the nighttime hours.

RESULTS

Among those 18 years old and older, women were out of camp 4.1 hours and men 5.7 hours per day (Figure 8.1a). The time gone from camp was lowest for those between ages two and four years old (Figure 8.1b). This is because it is difficult to take toddlers foraging since they are too young to walk very far and too old and heavy to carry. This fact is the main reason babysitters are needed and may be one of the main reasons most human foragers take food back to a central place.

The amount of time children nurse varied from about 20 percent soon after birth to 5 percent by age two and most were completely weaned by three years of age. This coincides with the age at which children were left in camp as shown in Figure 8.1b. Males nursed about twice as much as females in the first six months but after that the difference vanishes. There was only one instance of a child nursing any woman other than its mother and this was its maternal grandmother who was postmenopausal and used her breast as a pacifier.

The percentage of time in camp that children were in close proximity (less than three meters) to adults fell from close to 100 percent after birth to 15 percent by age eight. Among all children eight years old or younger most interaction was with mother, father, sisters, brothers, and maternal grandmother. By age three, interaction with all others exceeded that with mother and father because by this time children played with other children most of the time (Table 8.1).

Other than nursing, holding is perhaps the most important form of direct care, at least of those under two years old. The percentage of time that children were held by everyone combined while in camp fell from about 85 percent soon after birth to close to 0 percent by age four (Table 8.1). For this reason, in analyses of holding, I use only children four years old or younger. Those who held fell into the categories shown in Table 8.2.

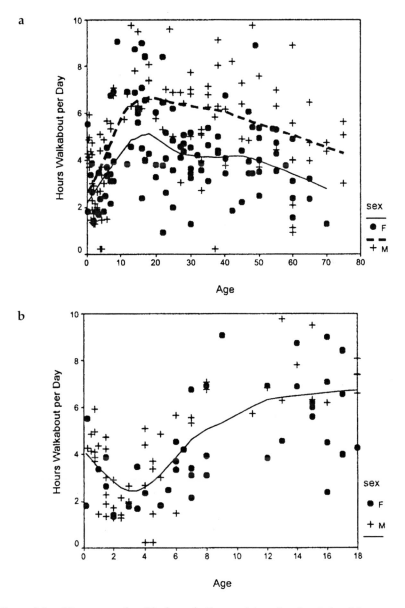

Figure 8.1. Hours per day Hadza of all ages (**a**) and sub-adults (**b**) were out of camp by age and sex, used as a proxy for foraging time (n = 225). Crosses and a dotted line denote males; closed circles and a solid line denote females. Regression lines are Lowess best fit. Note that toddlers age 2–4 are in camp most, and when they are gone it is often in a playgroup just outside camp.

Table 8.2   Categories of caretakers who held children 4 years old or younger

In-laws	Paternal kin	Maternal kin	Other kin	Others
aunt-in-law	father	mother	sister	female
step-grandfather	paternal grand-father	maternal aunt	female cousin	male
	paternal grand-mother	maternal grand-father	female kin	female visitor
	paternal uncle	maternal grand-mother	male kin	male visitor
	stepfather/pat. uncle	maternal uncle		mother's cowife
				stepfather
				other child

Of all 42 children four years old or younger, 27 had a genetic father present in the household, five had a stepfather present, and ten had no father present in the household (though one of these had a genetic father in the same camp). Among all 42 children, mothers accounted for a far larger share of holding than anyone else (72 percent of all holding). After mother, maternal grandmother held most (6.7 percent), followed by father (6.1 percent). Females who were not close kin held 7.5 percent, and all other people combined held 8.2 percent (Figure 8.2a). Maternal kin held much more (83 percent) than paternal kin (17 percent). Much of this difference is the result of a residential bias toward living with maternal kin more often than paternal kin.

If we look at only those 27 children (four years old or younger) who have a genetic father present, we get a different picture. Fathers did the most holding, 25.6 percent of all holding, excluding mothers, which is twice as much holding as maternal grandmothers did (Figure 8.2b). Among the 15 children (four years old or younger) with no genetic father present in the household, maternal grandmothers increased their involvement and accounted for 70 percent of all holding, excluding mothers (Figure 8.2c). Their involvement increased even more when a stepfather was present in the household. They did 83 percent of all holding, excluding mothers, of the five children (four years old or younger) with a stepfather. Maternal grandmothers did 83 percent of all holding (excluding mothers) of the five children (four years old or younger) with a stepfather in the household. In a multiple linear regression controlling for age and sex of child, maternal grandmothers did significantly more holding of children with a stepfather than those with a genetic father present ($\beta = -.421$, $p = .014$, df = 28)

For the 27 children with a genetic father present, holding by fathers and maternal grandmothers was inversely related. In a multiple linear regression controlling for age and sex of child and amount mother held, the more maternal grandmother held, the less time father held ($\beta = -.483$, $p = .050$,

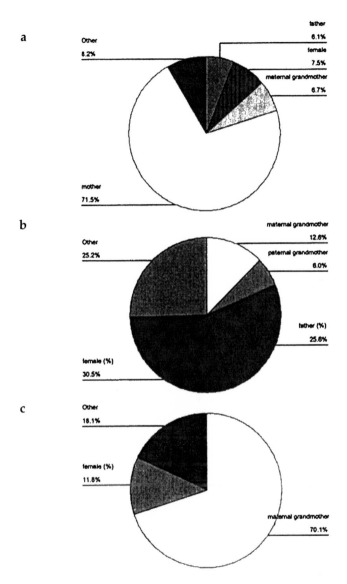

Figure 8.2. The percent of all holding (in scans) by (**a**) all catagories of people, with slices collapsed into "Other" for those <4% (n = 42 children ≤ 4 years old, mean age = 1.94), and (**b**) excluding mother where genetic father was present (n = 27 children ≤ 4 years old, mean age = 1.57), and (**c**) excluding mother where no genetic father was present (n = 15 children ≤ 4 years old, mean age = 2.6).

df = 22). There is no difference in the total amount a child is held when a child's genetic father or stepfather is present, since maternal grandmothers appear to compensate. Mothers do much more holding when no father is present, and maternal grandmothers do much more holding when a stepfather is present, which explains the lack of difference in the total amount children are held, controlled for child's age (Figure 8.3).

Men provided more nurturing to their putative genetic children eight years old or younger than to their stepchildren, and the one stepfather who provided the most nurturing was actually the child's paternal uncle since this child's father had died and his brother had taken on his widow (Figure 8.4). The degree of putative genetic relatedness of a man to a child predicted the amount of nurturing the child received from him; with those more closely related receiving more nurturing (β = .270, p = .020, df = 49, n = 53 children eight years old or younger with a male head of household present, controlled for child's age and sex).

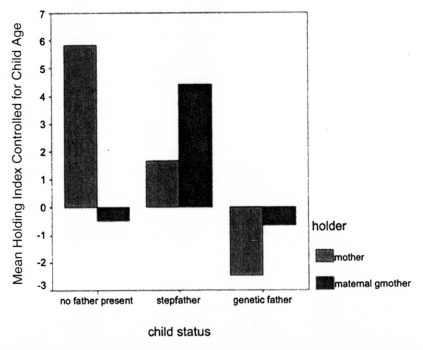

Figure 8.3. An index of the percent of time (in scans) a child was held by its mother and maternal grandmother, controlled for the child's age, according to whether a child had a genetic father present, a stepfather present, or neither present (n = 42 children 4 years old and under).

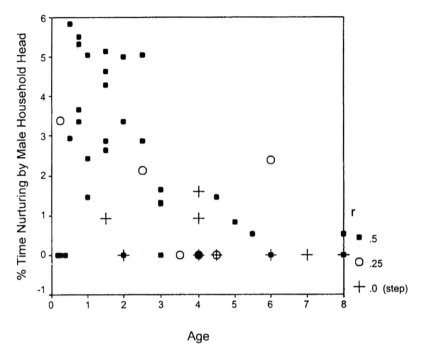

Figure 8.4. The percent of time (in follows of men) children were nurtured by the male head of household by child's age and relationship to the man (Effect of degree of genetic relatedness; β = .270, p = .020, df = 49, n = 53 children ≤ 8 years old with a male head of household present, controlled for child's age and sex).

Men showed a sex bias in their nurturing, whether we look at all children or only those with fathers present. In a multiple linear regression controlling for age of the child and its degree of putative genetic relatedness to the man, male head of household provided significantly less nurturing to girls than to boys (β = −.331, *p* = .002, df = 49, *n* = 53 children eight years old or younger with a male head of household present). Mothers showed no such sex bias. Girls were held more by maternal grandmothers than boys (β = .338, *p* = .027, df = 39, *n* = 42 children four years old or younger, controlled for child's age), although this is partly a function of residential bias, since among only those children where maternal grandmothers were present in camp, sex was not a significant predictor of maternal grandmother's holding (β = .374, *p* = .143, df = 14, *n* = 17 children four years older or younger, controlled for child's age). Overall, girls did not receive any less direct care than boys.

In these data, older sisters hold very little, only about 0.1 percent of the time a child was held. This would suggest that older siblings do very little childcare, or at least very little holding. However, this is an artifact of the number of children four years older or younger who happened to have an older sister in the age range to provide direct care. Of the 42 children four years old or younger, only ten had an older sister or half-sister. In some cases, the older sisters were too young or too old. For example, two children had an older sister who was already married with children of her own. Among the ten children with an older sister, she is the one who holds more than any other category besides mother, father, and grandmother. Excluding those categories, older sister accounts for 14 percent of all the time a child is held.

DISCUSSION AND CONCLUSION

Hadza children require considerable direct care only during their first two or three years of life. By age three or four, they are usually in playgroups with other children in or near camp, a pattern comparable to that among several other foraging societies (Hirasawa, Chapter 17 in this volume; Kamei, Chapter 16 in this volume; Konner, Chapter 2 in this volume). Hadza children over three or four are looked after by the older children they are playing with, though it is still necessary that some adult be in camp within earshot, otherwise lions, leopards, and hyenas would eventually lose their fear of camps during the day and these children would become easy prey. Toddlers are never left in camp without an adult there but this can be almost anyone. More than once, all adults slipped out of camp to forage and left me to baby-sit.

Hadza mothers are quite willing to hand their children off to anyone willing to take them. The child is not always so willing, however, and if he or she starts crying, the mother will usually retrieve the child. Despite a willingness to leave children with others, Hadza women provide the bulk of direct care. Nevertheless, about 30 percent of all holding of children (four years old or younger) is by someone other than mother.

Hadza grandmothers, especially maternal grandmothers, provide considerable direct care and provisioning (Hawkes et al. 1989, 1997, 1998). However, they provide less direct care, whether holding or interaction, than do fathers, at least when there is a genetic father in the household. When there is no genetic father present, it is the maternal grandmother who provides the bulk of allomaternal direct care. This is partly because single women and women who had recently remarried are more likely to live with their mothers than women who are still married to the genetic father of their youngest child (Blurton Jones et al., Chapter 10 in this volume). Both fathers and maternal grandmothers are important in terms of direct care and it appears they are often alternative sources of help since a woman depends more on one when the other is not living with her.

The Hadza say they have no preference for one sex over the other in children and this is reflected in the behavior of mothers if not the behavior of fathers. Since mothers provide the bulk of direct care and do not provide more care to sons than daughters, female children do not get significantly less care overall than male children. The Hadza also say that a stepfather should fill the role of father and that there should be no difference between them, but stepfathers clearly provide less care than genetic fathers.

Siblings appear to do less holding than is typical of many foraging and farming societies (Hewlett 1991a) and certainly less than some Pygmy foragers (Fouts and Lamb, Chapter 14 in this volume; Ivey Henry et al., Chapter 9 in this volume). However, in a recent unanalyzed study in one camp, I observed older sisters doing considerable holding of infants, so much of the difference may simply be an artifact of the particular age-sex distribution in my 1995/1996 sample. If they do indeed provide less care than among many other foragers, this might be because they begin foraging at an earlier age. One often sees Hadza girls three or four years old already digging for tubers in camp. And by three or four years old, boys are engaged in target practice with their bows much of the time. However, early foraging also occurs in some other foraging societies, such as the Mardu and Mikea (Bird and Bliege Bird, Chapter 6 in this volume; Tucker and Young, Chapter 7 in this volume).

My data on direct care among the Hadza lend support to the view promoted by Mel Konner with regard to the !Kung and other foragers (Konner, Chapter 2 in this volume). That is, mothers do the bulk of direct care of infants. Fathers and grandmothers come in a distant second, unless no father is present, in which case maternal grandmother does considerable direct care. By the time of weaning during the second year of a child's life, fathers, grandmothers, and older sisters begin to do an appreciable amount of care, especially babysitting. By age three or four years old, children begin to spend much of their time playing and foraging with age-mates and slightly older children. It is within these playgroups where most learning takes place. Children continue to be with both parents and siblings throughout the night however, although stepchildren may often sleep with their maternal grandmothers.

Humans are surely cooperative breeders if by this we mean simply that individuals other than parents provide care. Even without allomaternal direct care, the food sharing among most foraging societies would qualify them as cooperative breeders. Among the Hadza there is considerable allomaternal direct care as well, especially in the form of babysitting, which usually entails little cost but provides potentially great benefits. This underappreciated form of care was not specifically analyzed here but will be in the future.

ACKNOWLEDGMENTS

This research was supported by Leakey grant #SL952012 and NSF grant #9529278. I thank Nicholas Blurton Jones for mentoring, David Bygott and Jeannette Hanby for hospitality, COSTECH for research permission, and the Hadza for tolerance and companionship. I also thank Hillary Fouts, Barry Hewlett, and Michael Lamb for comments.

9

Child Caretakers Among Efe Foragers of the Ituri Forest

Paula Ivey Henry, Gilda A. Morelli, and Edward Z. Tronick

INTRODUCTION

Researchers of human biological and behavioral ecology are testing, and in many cases revising, our understanding of human parenting behavior with tools developed from evolutionary theory (Ellison 2001; Hrdy 1999; Small 1999). The finding of the occurrence and facultative nature of shared childcare, or alloparenting, among hunter-gatherers (Blurton Jones 1993; Hewlett 1988; Tronick et al. 1987), runs contrary to long-standing Western characterizations of optimal parenting and child development (Hrdy 1999). It also veers from earlier quantitative descriptions of parenting and child behavior among foraging peoples (Draper 1976; Draper and Cashdan 1988; Konner 1976, and this volume). Allocare has significant theoretical implications when viewed from an evolutionary and developmental perspective and its occurrence among foragers suggests that humans may, in fact, be obligate cooperative breeders, dependent on nonparental resources for the successful rearing of young (Hrdy 2001b, Chapter 3 in this volume; Ivey 2000).

Several unique aspects of the human life history pattern that distinguish humans from nonhuman primates appear to be related to the distribution of parenting effort across group members: food-sharing between mates and direct paternal investment in young; post-reproductive intergenerational investment (i.e., grandparenting); and, the extended nutritional dependency of multiple young. The dependency characteristic of human development and reproduction sets the stage not only for adult investment in children's care, but for children's investment in the care of other children, especially siblings. This investment implies consequences for parental reproduction and the development of child caregivers and their wards.

The Efe foragers of the Ituri Forest of northeastern Democratic Republic of Congo exhibit one of the more extreme examples of shared infant care reported in traditional cultures (Tronick et al. 1987). Research on Efe child rearing has shown that infant interactions—even that of neonates—are not monopolized by the mother, and that Efe infants experience a rich physical and social exchange with other group members. Alloparenting is extensive, involving an average of 14 nonmaternal caregivers at four months of age and 11 nonmaternal caregivers at one year (Morelli et al. 1999; Tronick et al. 1992). It is also intensive, occurring from birth through early childhood, and includes the fostering of children by families in non-natal camps in later childhood. Children account for a significant core of caregiving interactions, comprising an average of 29 percent of care of five-month-old infants, and 39 percent of the care received by infants at one year (Tronick et al. 1992). Efe infants may benefit from such care, as the number of allocaregivers at one year has been associated with survivorship to three years of life (Ivey 2000).

This chapter examines the distribution of care of one-year-old infants by Efe children in relation to theoretical predictions suggested by evolutionary ecological theory (Bogin 1999; Clutton-Brock 1991; Hrdy 1999; Small 1999). Rather than childcare as a maternal monopoly; sibling care as an artifact of labor, fertility, and settlement patterns in traditional farming societies; or care by children as a task of only girls; the data presented in this chapter lend support to the hypothesis that a key aspect of the human evolutionary pattern of reproduction and development involves the contribution of dependent children to alloparent younger kin.

HYPOTHESES

Central to the development of life history theory in human evolutionary ecology are the trade-offs that individuals face between the diversion of energy to competing tasks that affect survival and reproduction. Cross-cultural analyses of allocare, for example, emphasize its role in maternal time allocation, including the nature of maternal labor and the access and trade-offs of labor substitution, especially in traditional farming economies (McKenna 1987; Whiting and Edwards 1988). Less attention is paid to children's time allocation to care and the trade-offs their care efforts may involve among foraging peoples. We know that investment in physical growth and skill development during childhood and adolescence is expected to enhance success in future reproduction (Bogin 1998; Kaplan 1996). We also know that effective care within a specific ecological setting requires a suite of unique skills that include physical strength, vigilance, and sensitivity to infant behavior. Though the skill demands for a child caregiver may be high, children are observed to provide infant care under diverse ecological conditions (Barry and Paxton 1971; Weisner and Gallimore 1977).

The following hypotheses address theoretical expectations concerning the distribution of Efe children's effort to infant care across caregiver demographics, infant care behavior, and the influence of child caregiving on parental behavior:

H_1: Efe children are expected to perform more infant care in middle childhood than in early childhood or adolescence.

A cross-cultural survey of apprenticeships in childcare by Whiting and Edwards (1988) found that the preferred age for child nurses is between six and ten years of age. As children gain skills or strength to care for infants, they are expected to be increasingly trusted as caregivers. However, as they age, they also are expected to face additional trade-offs in the diversion of effort toward the development of economic and social skills for future reproduction. In early childhood, the costs of performing infant care to the infant and to the caregiver may be high, whereas in adolescence, decreased availability due to the pursuit of alternative economic, social, and prereproductive activities is expected to result in lower time investment in infant care.

H_2: Female children are expected to perform more infant care than males throughout childhood.

Sex is an important predictor of the differential trade-offs of parental investment for adults (Lancaster 1994; Trivers 1972b), and while the payoffs of allocating time to alternative activities are expected to diverge at different ages under varying ecological conditions, the sexual division of adult labor suggests that children will increasingly perform activities appropriate to their prospective adult reproductive and productive roles (Barry et al. 1957; Rogoff and Morelli 1989). Sex is predicted to affect alloparental investment by Efe children primarily for two reasons: (1) for females, childcare is a skill that they will employ almost continuously through the reproductive stage of their lifespan, and is one that has crucial association with their success in parenting; and (2) for males, economic, social, and reproductive development is expected to diverge from that of female peers, as boys decrease their time available to infants as they increase their involvement with tasks less compatible with the care of children, such as increased travel, toolmaking, hunting, and coalition and mating effort (MacDonald and Hewlett 1999). This segregation of activities is likely to be more pronounced during adolescence.

H_3: More skill- and strength-based forms of childcare (defined for our purposes as skilled care), including direct care tasks such as cleaning, bathing, feeding, carrying, and comforting infants, are expected to be performed by older children more than younger children because of greater competence, and by older girls more than older boys due to experience, motivation, and attention to infant behaviors.

The quality of care that infants receive has a significant impact on their survival (McKenna 1987; Scheper-Hughes 1987), and the altricial aspects of human development demand an intense degree of protection, vigilance, and sensitivity (Bogin 1999; Ellison 2001). Young infants require nearly continuous contact and special attention to assess state and condition and to provide nutritional, physical, and psychosocial support. Older infants who have gained some mobility and independence from caregivers face an increased risk of injury and encounters with environmental hazards. Mobile infants require special attention and intervention in order to interrupt behaviors that put them at risk. In addition, the heavier weight and high activity levels of older infants will increase the energetic demand of carrying and other forms of skilled care.

H_4: The amount of time that children spend engaged in infant care and the amount of skilled care that they provide are expected to be positively associated with their estimated genetic relatedness to the infant.

Consistent with evidence that genetic relatedness is a significant predictor of many forms of investment behavior (Essock-Vitale and McGuire 1980; Hawkes 1983; Trivers 1972b), siblings are observed to be the most common child caregivers across cultures (Weisner and Gallimore 1977). While the obvious basis is kin selection (Hamilton 1964), the human life history pattern implies additional dimensions. Dependency during childhood on adult provisioning increases parental ability to recruit offspring to perform activities, such as infant care, that enhance parental productive and reproductive efficiency (Alexander 1979). And the altriciality and long duration of human infancy demands intensive and extended investment efforts to tasks such as carrying and comforting that are costly in terms of caregiver economic and reproductive efficiency (Blurton Jones 1972; Hinde 1984). In addition, children in the same family are expected to spend more time in close proximity to one another, making it more likely that they have the opportunity to participate in childcare. As a result, siblings and other related children are expected to perform more infant care than unrelated children, and to spend more time engaged in care activities that require additional strength and/or skill.

H$_5$: The contribution of children to infant care is negatively associated with the time devoted by parents and other allocaregivers to infant care, and is positively associated with the time that mothers engage in economic activities independent of direct infant care tasks.

Infant care is an important constraint on the time allocation and economic productivity of foraging mothers (Blurton Jones and Sibly 1978; Estioko-Griffin 1985; Hill and Hurtado 1996; Hurtado et al. 1992; Ivey 2000; Peacock 1985). While children impact a parent's productive demands by increasing the need to acquire and process adequate calories to support offspring, they also may offset parental time and energetic constraints by assisting with infant care or economic tasks. Children's assistance in infant care is expected to negatively affect parental time allocation to childcare tasks and positively affect time allocation to productive tasks. The contributions of other allocaregivers are also expected to be influenced by children's participation in care.

THE EFE

The Efe are a subgroup of Mbuti peoples who live in the northeastern region of the Ituri Forest of Democratic Republic of the Congo (formerly Zaire). A number of studies report on the ecology and time allocation of Efe men and women (Bailey and Peacock 1988; Bailey 1991a; Ivey 2000; Peacock 1985); hunting and land use practices (Wilkie 1988; Wilkie and Curran 1993); reproductive endocrinology (Ellison et al. 1986; Ellison 2001); and neonatal (Tronick and Winn 1992) and child development Morelli 1997; Morelli and Tronick 1991; Morelli et al. 1999, 2003; (Tronick et al. 1987).

The Efe live in temporary camps of broad-leaf woven huts, moving an average of every six weeks, and comprising an average of 21 individuals, with a range of about six to 45. They practice a mixed subsistence strategy of foraging, bow-hunting, and exchange of labor and forest goods for garden produce and material goods with their horticultural neighbors, the Lese. Efe men predominantly hunt in groups with bow-and-arrow technology, employing dogs and beaters to flush game to awaiting bowmen. They also hunt solitarily by stealth, and collect honey and small amounts of forest plants. Efe women typically forage in groups of women and children for forest fruits, nuts, and other vegetation, fish in the streams that meander through the Ituri, and collect food from abandoned Lese gardens. The Efe also provide seasonal garden labor in exchange for horticultural carbohydrates, with women spending more time in garden work than men (Bailey and Peacock 1988). Previous time allocation studies found that Efe women spend a modest amount of time laboring in gardens (Peacock 1985), and this time appears to have decreased considerably by the time this study was conducted, nearly a decade later. By 1988, many Lese gardens had contracted to subsistence level due to continued deterioration of the road and the collapse of the cash market in the 1980s, significantly reducing exchange labor opportunities for the Efe.

A small number of Efe, usually older individuals, engage in farming, but gardens are small and communal, with low and seasonal yield (Wilkie 1989). Only one family in the present study had a small, shared plot of cassava (manioc).

METHODS

This chapter reports on focal observations conducted on 20 Efe infants 12 to 15 months of age and their mothers over a two-day period from 1988 through 1989. All of the infant subjects were walking by 12 months, and a majority was mobile by nine months. It is important to note that while these data are derived from one sample and a specific behavioral observation method described below, the general analyses replicate findings from at least two other samples of same-age Efe, employing two independent observation sampling methods (Ivey 2000: notes; Morelli 1987; Tronick et al. 1987).

We focus on the care of one-year-olds because this is an age when their weight and high activity levels present new demands to caregivers, especially children. Infants in the sample were known to the observer from birth or soon thereafter, as this project was undertaken as part of a longitudinal study on Efe children's development (Tronick et al. 1992). There was a systematic habituation of the subjects to the observers, including extended visits in camp from five months to one year prior to the data collection period. The demographic record-keeping efforts of Ituri project researchers and local assistants since 1985 facilitated the accuracy of age estimates of children in a population without birth records, and the estimation of potential genetic affiliation of community members (Bailey and DeVore 1989). Age ranking and consanguineal relationships were cross-verified from independent sources during repeated visits to the camps.

The focal follow sampling technique was employed, with infants as focal subjects (Borgerhoff Mulder and Caro 1985). Observations were recorded wherever infants were located, including camps, forest, villages, gardens, or trails. The location and activity of the focal infant's mother were also noted throughout the observation session. When mothers were out of sight (about 8 percent of the time), the observer collected information from camp members on maternal location and activity, which was verified upon her return. Observations were rescheduled only if infants were reported ill by their caregivers or moved to a camp not located in our study area (approximately 36 kilometer radius), and therefore not familiar to the observer.

Data on infant behavior, caregiver behavior, and maternal activity were collected on a laptop computer that recorded the absolute duration of behavioral events, in eight 15-minute continuous coding sessions sampled across a two-day period. The presence of people at the start of the focal coding, as well as the departures and approaches of all individuals during the focal coding were recorded as they occurred in order to calculate the total proportion of time that individuals were in *proximity* (eyeshot or close hearing range) to the infant. Interobserver reliability was established in the field, yielding a mean (Cohen's) kappa coefficient of .90 (range .85–.96) for all behaviors reported in this study.

For several of the analyses we group child caregivers into one of three age categories: early childhood (four- to seven-year-olds), middle childhood (eight- to twelve-year-olds), and adolescence (thirteen- to seventeen-year-olds).[1] We also identify children fostered by kin. Foster children are children whose parents were deceased or not living in the camp, and whose caregivers (the person or people identified as primarily responsible for the child's biological and psychological needs) are someone other than the child's biological parents. Some foster children are orphans, while others are children whose parents are not able to care for them (but expect to do so sometime in the future (e.g., single parents)).

We distinguish between two types of caregivers. A *potential caregiver* is defined as a person in proximity to the infant, that is, within sight or close hearing range of the infant. *Proximity* to an infant is a proxy measure for children's availability to care, and we reasoned that these individuals within proximal distance may be expected to recognize and respond to infant distress. As the comings and goings of people in proximity to the infant were noted as they occurred throughout the observation session, we were able to calculate time estimates for this measure.

A *caregiver* is defined as a person in contact with the infant; contact includes all forms of physical contact (for example, carrying, playing, nursing) and verbal contact (e.g., addressing the infant or being addressed by the infant). This definition assumes that caregivers are to some increased degree responsible for the immediate physical and social well-being of the infant.

RESULTS

In this study, the proportion of time potential caregivers were in proximity to the focal child and the proportion of time caregivers spent in different types of care were calculated for each infant. As background, infants were observed in eighteen different camps, with camp membership averaging 21. There were 157 children between the ages of 4 and 17 years in proximity to infants during observations: 69 girls and 88 boys.

Does Child Age and Gender Relate to Children's Role as Potential Caregivers and as Caregivers?

Potential Caregivers.   Children were significantly less likely to spend time in proximity to infants as they got older. Four-year-olds were observed in proximity to one-year-olds 80 percent of the time, seventeen-year-olds in proximity 50 percent of the time. This trend was repeated when children were grouped by age category. Adolescent boys and girls spent about 56 percent of their time in proximity to infants, and this was significantly less than the time children in early childhood spent in proximity—about 72 percent of their time. Children in middle childhood were intermediate between the two age ranges.[2]

Time in proximity to the infant did not vary according to child gender, and this was true even when boys and girls were compared separately for each of the three age ranges.

Caregivers.   The amount of time that actual child caregivers spent in care did not vary significantly with child age: about 27 minutes for children in early ($n = 32$) and middle ($n = 36$) childhood, and 58 minutes for adolescents ($n = 24$)); or with gender: about 41 minutes for girl caregivers ($n = 38$) and 30 minutes for boy caregivers ($n = 54$) over a twelve-hour day, based on estimates from sampled data. These findings are at odds with our predictions. However, there was a trend for older girls to spend more time in care than younger girls, and for girls to spend more time in care than boys starting at middle childhood (Figure 9.1).

To assess whether the population of boys and girls participating in care differed from one another, and across ages, we also examined if the *percentage* of boys and girls caring for infants was similar to the *percentage* of boys and girls who did not. We found that as many girls were likely to care for infants as were not; but the percentage of boys caring for infants was consistently less than the percentage of boys not caring for infants.

When we did an age comparison,[3] we found that boys in early ($n = 22$) and middle ($n = 18$) childhood were significantly more likely to care for children than were adolescent boys ($n = 14$). This was not observed for girls. Girls in early childhood ($n= 10$), middle childhood ($n = 18$), and adolescence ($n = 10$) did not differ significantly in the percentage of children who cared and who did not.

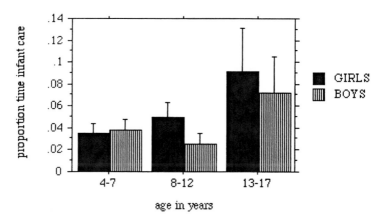

Figure 9.1. The proportion of observed time that Efe child caregivers 4- to 17-years of age spend in care of infants by age group.

What Factors Are Associated with the Care of Infants by Boys and Girls?

It appears that a number of factors relate to the likelihood of girls and boys participating in childcare based on the results of logistic regression analyses (Table 9.1). Models included demographic variables that characterize group composition, such as dependency ratio, number of relatives available, and number of women in camp without dependent offspring; and variables that characterize the potential child caregiver, such as age, relatedness to the infant, number of dependents in the family, and family composition. In a best-fit logistic regression analysis, care by girls was positively associated with relatedness but negatively associated with group size (the number of people living in camp) and the presence of a female sibling of the infant.[4] Care by boys was positively associated with relatedness, but negatively associated with group size and the age of the potential caregiver. Surprisingly, there was no effect of the number of dependents in the infant's or the child's family on the probability that girls or boys engaged in infant care.

Does Skilled Care Vary by Child Age and Gender?

Efe boys and girls overlap to a remarkable degree in the types of infant care activities they perform, contrary to predictions. For example, there

Table 9.1 Multiple Logistic Regression Model of the Probability of Infant Care by Efe Children 4- to 17 Years of Age in Proximity of Infants[a]

Variable	Parameter	p	Odds Ratio
Girls			
Proportion time in proximity to infant		*controlled*	
Age	1.127	.0259	3.085
Z-score of relatedness	−.099	.0164	.906
Group size	−1.666	.0193	.189
Model log likelihood = −30.242, r^2 = .363, n = 69			
Boys			
Proportion time in proximity to infant		*controlled*	
Age	−0.260	.0019	0.771
Z-score of relatedness	2.438	.0023	11.455
Group size	−0.066	.0295	0.936
Model log likelihood = −38.117, r^2 = .351, n = 88			

[a] These analyses were conducted controlling for proximity, with a binary dependent variable of infant care or no infant care.

were no significant sex differences in the probability that girl and boy caregivers would engage in several general categories of childcare, including social play, feeding, grooming, and holding the young. However, when childcare activities that were skill-based or required strength—including bathing, feeding, carrying and comforting an infant—were grouped into the category *skilled care*, age differences were observed. As predicted, older children were more likely to engage in skilled forms of care than were younger children, but girls were no more likely than boys to participate in skilled care.[5] About half of child caregivers performed some kind of skilled care (53 percent of girls and 52 percent of boys), but girls spent on average twice as much time engaged in a skilled-care activity.[6]

Two activities that make up the skilled-care category deserve attention: carrying and comforting. Twenty-four percent of child caregivers were responsible for all of the carrying that infants received from children. While girl caregivers carried infants for longer periods of time than did boy caregivers, the difference was not significant (0.3 compared to 0.1 percent of the time).[7] Age was also not significantly related to carrying, although older girls did most of the carrying.

Infants in distress are often difficult to manage. As a result, older children (compared to younger children) and girls (compared to boys) may invest more time comforting a fussing infant. Similar to the distribution of carrying by children, 30 percent of child caregivers were responsible for all of the comforting that infants received from children. There was a positive trend of comfort time by age for girl (but not boy) caregivers, although this increase did not reach significance. Girls did spend more time caring for a fussing or crying infant than did boys[8]—0.5 percent compared to 0.2 percent of the time. Age was also not significantly related to time spent comforting infants.

Efe parents commonly recruit children to perform caregiving tasks or children may initiate contact with infants on their own (Morelli 1987). In this sample, observed directives from mothers of infants to children to watch or tend an infant did not predict variation in children's contributions to allocare. There was also no significant effect of sex or age of child on the probability that a child would initiate interaction with an infant.

How Is Relatedness Associated with the Children's Care of Infants?

Relatedness strongly predicted time in proximity to an infant for boys[9] but not for girls. It also predicted the probability that children would engage in infant care (as noted above), but among children who did perform care, the effects of kinship were mediated by child caregiver sex and age. Older related adolescent girl caregivers spent significantly more time engaged in skilled care, carrying, and comforting fussing infants than older unrelated girl caregivers;[10] whereas relatedness was not predictive of infant care activities by younger girls.

While relatedness predicted the probability of boys' participation in care, surprisingly it did not predict the total amount of observed time that boy caregivers engaged in care, nor participation in any type of care behavior measured. Similar results were obtained when relatedness was measured as a continuous variable, a categorical variable, or as a z-score comparing relatedness of individuals in proximity to the infant.

Siblings four to 17 years of age who performed infant care ($n = 32$) provided an average of 28 percent of the allocare that one-year-olds received, and these caregivers contributed an estimated average of 54 minutes of infant care per twelve-hour day. Caregiving sisters ($n = 13$) spent a mean of 72 minutes in care, whereas, brothers ($n = 19$) averaged 42 minutes with an infant per day. Interestingly, nonsibling related child caregivers ($n = 12$), many of whom were foster children, spent a mean of 66 minutes a day in infant care. Unrelated child caregivers[11] ($n = 48$) provided a mean of 14 minutes of care.

The time that foster children spent in infant care raises the possibility that they may be providing reciprocal services for the protection and provisioning they receive from foster parents. Twenty-seven percent of children living in the 18 sampled camps had no parents living in camp—they were orphans, children of separated parents, or children living temporarily away from natal camps. Ten of these foster children were living with a focal infant's nuclear family, and they spent significantly more time providing care to infants than did other nonsibling child caregivers; this finding holds when relatedness to the infant was controlled for in the analyses.[12] The proportion of time that foster children engaged in care, however, did not differ significantly from siblings, even though siblings had more opportunity to provide care by spending significantly more time in proximity to infants than did foster children.[13]

Foster children, siblings, and other children, however, may be expected to differ in the type of care behaviors they perform. Foster children who were cared for by a focal infant's family were like sibling caregivers in that they spent similar amounts of time playing with, feeding, comforting, and grooming infants. Neither foster children nor siblings significantly differed from other children ($n = 51$) in these behaviors. Foster children and siblings were also alike in the time they spent carrying infants and in skilled care, but in this regard they were unlike other children, who spent significantly less time in these types of care. (The difference between time spent carrying infants neared significance for siblings over other child caregivers).[14] When foster children are removed from analyses of skilled-care behaviors, girl caregivers were found to perform more carrying than did boy caregivers.[15]

It is important to note that most foster children living in focal families were boys (nine out of ten), and foster caregivers tended to be older than the average child caregiver (about 12 years of age compared to about eight years of age for siblings and ten years of age for other caregivers).

Does Child Contribution to Infant Care Relate to Parental Activities?

Children's assistance in infant care appears to influence maternal and paternal time allocation to caregiving. The proportion of time that mothers spent in infant care was negatively related to the number of four- to seventeen-year-olds participating in care. And the proportion of time fathers spent in infant care was negatively related to the presence of siblings to the infant over five years of age.[16]

The contribution of children to infant care is also associated with maternal economic efforts. Efe children increase a mother's workload: the number of dependents (i.e., dependent offspring and fostered children) a mother provisioned significantly predicted the amount of time she devoted to food preparation and other work.[17] But children also help to offset the cost of their own care by reducing the maternal burden of coordinating economic and infant care activities. The number of child caregivers who assisted a mother was positively related to the time that mothers spent acquiring food away from camp without the concomitant demand of direct infant care.[18] Neither the age nor the sex of the child caregiver was associated with variation in maternal work demands or the physical location of children's care.

Another means of assessing the significance to the family of care by dependent children is to evaluate their influence on the behavior of other potential allocaregivers in the group. Efe children's assistance appears important enough to warrant the participation of alternative caregivers in the absence of care by offspring. An absence of siblings in the infant's family was associated with care by reproductive-age women without children,[19] and their contribution helps explain the lack of differences in the mean amount of allocare received by one-year-old infants with and without siblings. The proportion of time that nonsibling children provided care was significantly related to the infant care time of sisters over five years of age,[20] but not to that of brothers. The proportion of time that siblings engaged in infant care was negatively associated with the number of dependents in the family, for both sisters and brothers.[21]

SUMMARY

The involvement of Efe children as potential or actual caregivers lends partial support for hypotheses of the relation of child age and gender to the care of one-year-olds. Time in proximity to an infant was negatively related to child age, but it was not related to child gender. Time in actual care was not related to child age or gender. However, age trends noted for girls are in line with our predictions, and when data on foster children (mostly boys) are removed from the analysis, significant differences between care by boys and girls emerged.

Most types of care in which child caregivers were involved did not vary systematically with child age or gender. Older child caregivers were more likely to be involved in skilled forms of care than younger child caregivers, but gender did not predict participation in all skilled care. Girl caregivers did spend more time than boy caregivers carrying and comforting infants; and while comforting increased with the age of the girl caregiver, the trend was not significant.

The effect of relatedness on children's care was generally in line with predictions; however, its effects were tempered by age and sex. While relatedness predicted time in proximity for boys, it did not predict availability for girls. Relatedness strongly predicted the probability that children of both sexes would participate in care, but did not predict the amount of infant care boy caregivers would provide, nor their involvement in any specific type of care activity. Age modified the effect of relatedness on girls' participation in care. Older related girls engaged in skilled care, including carrying and comforting infants, more than older unrelated girls, but there were no relatedness effects among younger girls. Nevertheless, siblings and foster children living in a focal infant's family performed considerably more care than other children.

Assistance in infant care by Efe children influences parental caregiving and productive behaviors. While dependent children increase a mother's workload, their assistance reduces maternal time in direct infant care, and frees her to forage independently. Fathers, too, appear to benefit from children's infant care efforts. The importance of care by dependent young among the Efe is underscored by the increased participation of other allocaregivers in their absence.

DISCUSSION

Care of infants by Efe children was similar for girls and boys on most of the measures looked at in this study, but it was related in modest ways to child age and relatedness to infant. The findings contribute to the theoretical development of the evolutionary ecology of humans by directing attention to the role of children's caretaking behavior as an element of their developmental experience and a factor in parental time allocation among a foraging people.

Efe children's routines are characterized by the parental and alloparental investment that they receive; the helping behaviors that they perform; their efforts to acquire food and other resources; and their social engagement with others. As the allocare of infants is constrained by the tether of nursing demands, child caregivers of infants must maintain close proximity to the women who nurse the infant (most often mothers). This means being in the same settings mothers frequent, including out-of-camp settings. The likelihood that a child will be available to care and will perform care is influenced by the sex, age, and kinship distribution of children's activities and responsibilities.

Childcare by Boys and Girls from Early Childhood into Adulthood

Care by Boys and Girls in Early and Middle Childhood. Young Efe children experience a significant decrease in maternal attention postweaning, and as this difficult transition (including being encouraged to walk rather than be carried, and to stay behind in camp rather than accompany their mothers) wanes, they appear to be comfortably situated in a mixed-age and -sex play group of peers within their camp. In early childhood their responsibilities are few, and consist of running errands within camp and intermittent childcare duties (Morelli et al. 2003). While specific play behaviors, such as play nursing or bow-hunting, may diverge for girls and boys around four and five years of age, their responsibilities and time with their parents and peers appear fairly consonant.

Consistent with results obtained for various infant care activities, girls' and boys' routines in middle childhood begin to diverge somewhat. Efe girls older than six or seven years often travel with women in the forest to search for food, and when capable, carry and care for infants while the mother gathers food, fishes, or carries acquired resources back to camp. Young boys may accompany women on foraging trips, but later in childhood they also may accompany their fathers or uncles on hunts as early as eight years old. Still, the frequency of boys' participation in hunts varies with age, the hunting activity of the group, and individual motivation, and it is usually not with any consistency until late adolescence. Within the camp setting, children continue to play with mixed-age and -sex peers with intermittent childcare and errand-running responsibilities.

While there is emerging variation in their participation in adult economic activities, boys continue to join women's foraging treks (especially when ripe fruit is being gathered) and to tend younger children. They appear less likely, however, to perform other adult female activities, such as food processing, firewood gathering, hut-building, and basket or mat weaving than girls. Some gender differences in child caregivers' infant care behaviors also emerge, as boy caregivers spend less time tending a fussing infant or carrying them than do girl caregivers.

Care by Boys and Girls in Adolescence and into Adulthood. Across cultures, adolescence is characterized by increasing divergence of sex roles toward the economic and social activities of adults (Schlegel and Barry 1991). Adolescent Efe girls and boys are less likely to be in close proximity to infants than are younger children, and the reduction in availability to provide care may be attributed to sex differences in routines. While girls continue to assist their mothers in food acquisition and household tasks, this assistance in late childhood appears to be of much greater significance to maternal time allocation and economic efficiency. Peacock (1985) found that the labor contributions of girls over fourteen years of age so lessened workloads for their mothers that women with older girl helpers had similar activity budgets to women without dependent children. Greater economic demands on adolescent girls' time may constrain their ability to assist in allocare, especially for children in other families, accounting for the kinship pattern of infant care by older girls. Boys at this age, too, are less available to care, at least in part due to their increased involvement in adult male economic and social activities. Adolescent boys spend less time in camp and more time in travel between camps or villages, and on cooperative hunts with adult men, as observed in other foraging populations (MacDonald and Hewlett 1999).

Just as Efe children's economic and social participation increases in adolescence, new caregiving responsibilities emerge with age. Older children increasingly are engaged in types of infant care behaviors that require additional skill and strength, such as carrying and comforting a fussing child. Younger children will pass an inconsolable infant to an older child caregiver if the baby's mother is unavailable, and older children are more often observed to participate in the bathing, grooming, and carrying of infants. When younger children carry infants, it is for short periods, usually in camp or after mothers reach a patch within the forest in which they will extract food or other resources. Adolescent girls are the typical caregiver other than the mother to carry infants on forest trails some distance from camp.

It is difficult to know exactly why there was an apparent sex bias in foster children toward boys. Inherent demographic variation in access to foster children for families in need of infant care assistance is one factor; however, it also appears that the residence patterns of girls are more constrained than they are for boys. This may relate to the Efe mating system, whereby adolescent girls are often promised as marriage exchange partners for male relatives. Girls rarely live with their future mates until some time after menarche, and their residence is usually restricted to their native camp, or to that of close relatives. Orphaned girls, therefore, have less flexibility to move to a camp where their services may be needed. Also, boys may in fact benefit in future access to mates from their service in other camps. In addition, while the economic assistance of adolescent girls has measured value to adults, the economic productivity of boys during adolescence appears to be low. Therefore, fostered boys may be especially vulnerable to the beneficence of adult caregivers, and their infant care service may help to offset the costs of their own provisioning. These aspects of Efe socioecology may explain why many of the boys who assisted in infant care were fostered children, and fostered boys provided much more care than did nonfostered boys.

The diverging developmental trajectories of Efe children in adolescence foreshadow the differential role of childcare in adult lives. Parenting is an important aspect of daily life for both men and women (Tronick et al. 1992). Efe men have ample opportunity to care for young children. There is little physical separation by sex in the camp setting, and their in-camp activities are not usually incompatible with care of children. And while Efe men are commonly in the company of other men, adult males with a cohabiting mate are significantly more often in the presence of their mates (Bailey and Aunger 1989). Moreover, men often accompany their wives to forage or trade in villages, at times carrying infants while mothers are encumbered with other burdens.

Still, women (mothers and nonmothers) spend more time caring for young children than do men, and childcare plays a pivotal role in most women's lives. The need to learn to parent is common among primates

(Altmann 1980; Hrdy 1981), and primiparous mothers without such experience appear to be at a disadvantage in terms of the quality of care they provide (Lancaster 1986; Weisner 1987). Children develop competency from practice holding, carrying, feeding, grooming, protecting, playing with, and comforting young of varying developmental status and temperament, and these competencies have fundamental developmental and survival consequences for children and their wards (Bogin 1999). When older girls assume more strength- and skill-based infant care responsibilities, these responsibilities occur as part of a continuum of caregiving experience that is expected to extend through the majority of their adult lives. And while the average child caregiver spends only a few minutes per day in skilled care, some children are responsible for much more. The maximum amount of time a child caregiver spent in skilled care was 53 minutes in a twelve-hour day. Overall, children's allocare experience is expected to be a key component of their developing capacities, much as socializing with others, acquiring and processing resources, sharing and competing become part of the suite of competencies they master.

Efe Children's Care in Socioecological Perspective

The Association of Children's Assistance to Parental Behavior. Children's developmental status affects their participation in care; however, their contributions are also significantly influenced by the social and ecological environment. The suggested impact of children's care on parental behavior implies that parents face trade-offs in the time they have available for infant care and for economic activities. Anthropometric, time allocation, and diet studies report that adult Efe are nutritionally stressed and experience considerable constraints in their ability to acquire food (Bailey and Peacock 1988; Dietz et al. 1989; Jenike 2001), and Efe mothers appear especially time-stressed by economic demands (Ivey 1993; Peacock 1985). Mothers of the one-year-olds in this sample spent 21 percent of observed time foraging in the forest, and another 12 percent of their time processing the food they acquired. They often manage the demands of economic activities and childcare by doing both at the same time (23 percent of the time observed). Children's help with economic activities or childcare appears to reduce maternal workload, as noted and, in part, serves to offset the costs of their dependency (Blurton Jones 1993).

Care by Children May Help Them Secure Food Resources in Unpredictable or Risky Environments. Efe children are nutritionally stressed (Bailey 1991b), and often complain of hunger, but they do not appear time-limited in their access to food. Even though they could and do forage, they are significantly constrained in their ability to acquire food for themselves. In part, this is because forest resources are highly limited, unpredictable, and dispersed in time and space. They require travel, knowledge, and often strength and skill to extract. Successful acquisition of protein foods requires well-developed hunting skills, and carbohydrate sources are often difficult to find and procure, and entail the identification of nontoxic from toxic varieties. Variability in flowering and fruiting results in wide fluctuations in food availability from year to year, and the high diversity of tropical forests means that the density of foods is typically low or very patchy in distribution. As a result, foraging typically requires long search times, and in years with poor seed set can be both literally and figuratively fruitless (Sunderland et al. 1999). Garden labor opportunities are highly limited, are seasonal, and involve systems of exchange between adults; and in this sample, Efe women spent little time engaged in garden work.

Young Efe children are able to harvest feral sweet potatoes (*Ipomoea batata*) in fallow fields, pull down *Gnetum africanum* vines to collect the leaves, and gather mushrooms and small *Canarium schweinfurthii*, *Ricinodendron heudelottii*, and *Panda oleosa* fruits when they encounter them. But these resources are limited in availability, and children are only rarely observed to extract foods beyond the periphery of a women's foraging group. Other forest foods collected by women often entail considerable strength and/or skill to extract, such as *Irvingia* sp. fruits, which must be split for their edible kernels, and the large deeply buried and thorn-root-encircled *Dioscorea* sp. yams. While children's return rates will vary with the resource exploited and children's age, strength, and skill, the highly intermittent access and low expected return rate of food resources for Efe children implies that they remain highly dependent on adult economic efficiency.

Observations and formal interviews with mothers also suggest that Efe children, like some other hunter-gatherer children (Blurton Jones et al. 1994b), are unlikely to forage by themselves because of significant hazards in the environment; and therefore, are additionally dependent on adult travel patterns. The Ituri rain forest presents a number of risks to travel, including the ability to become lost, dangerous plants and animals, and treacherous trails that can cause serious injury. When children play on the periphery of camps, or wander around while women work to gather resources, they are rarely out of sight of adults. The exceptions are illustrative: when camps are located very close to Lese villages, children then may travel in groups on the trails between camp, village, and garden. While women's foraging groups may travel significant distances from camp, individual women seldom travel alone in the forest. Bailey (1988) suggests that protection from approaches by men may in part account for this pattern, but inherent risks in the rain forest environment suggest additional factors. Only adult men are regularly observed traveling through the forest alone, and sometimes adolescent boys, although this is uncommon.

The risky aspects of forest travel, along with the knowledge, strength, and skill often needed to forage, limits Efe children's ability to procure food on their own. The suggested lack of opportunities for children to acquire foods alone is expected to enhance the payoff of assistance to time-stressed food acquirers, and infant care may be one important constraint on adult productivity that children can affect. And, because allocare is dispersed over a number of caregivers, few children are substantially burdened by the task of infant care. The cost of infant care to individual children is expected to shift with children's sex, age, and relatedness, accounting in part for the similarities and differences observed in Efe children's care.

Children's Relationships and Their Access to Social Resources. Demographic characteristics of the Efe population also influence the significance of children's participation in allocare, their access to kin, and opportunities for reciprocation. Efe group size is variable, but often small. Virilocality and sororal marriage exchange between clans increases access to both paternal and maternal relatives in natal and neighboring camps, but due to high mortality, camp members may have few living close relatives. Efe alloparenting occurs in the context of high mortality throughout the lifespan due to disease brought on by periodic nutritional stress and ubiquitously high parasite loads (Bailey 1991a, 1991b; Mann et al. 1962). Infant mortality to one year of age is around 23 percent and many families had also lost older children. It is of interest that the only demographic characteristic measured associated with survivorship from one to three years of age in this study is the number of allocaregivers an infant experienced at one-year.[22] Children's assistance in infant care may not only have important consequences for parental economic efficiency, but potentially influences the health and survivorship of their wards, who may be future social partners.

Adult mortality is also high; in fact, the fathers of two of the 20 subject infants died during the study period: one before the child was born and another when the child was two years old. Only four of the infants in this sample had a grandmother available to them. Only two infants had a living grandfather. While families are the central source of provisioning and protection for children, high adult mortality underscores the precarious nature of individual access to kin. Across the lifespan Efe are often dependent on the economic, investment, and social behavior of other members of their group, and small group size, high mortality, and unpredictable access to resources experienced by the Efe may be offset by the extended web of caretaking associations and reciprocation that include not only infant care, but the care of older children as well.

The common presence of foster children illustrates the significance of mortality experienced by the community, and the contingency of extended kinship ties and reciprocation. As foster children tend to live in families with other children, they are often subject to increased competition over familial resources. Because of the value of adolescent females to male relatives in marriage exchange, and the disproportionate number of single males among the Efe (Bailey 1988), fostered boys may be especially vulnerable to neglect by stressed adult food acquirers. Their extraordinary contributions, when compared to other children, may be an accentuated strategy of access to investment by allocare. Direct assistance in infant care is one means by which foster children can reduce conflict over scarce food resources within their adopted family.

Children's Care as a Developmental and Evolutionary Strategy. The patterning of children's care among the Efe is, in part, a product of specific factors that enhance the benefits of caregiving assistance; but its suggested uniqueness may lie in a lack of data on the developmental and parenting behaviors of other foraging groups. Hewlett (1991a) conducted a review of quantitative information on allocare among foragers, finding widespread use of alternative caregivers with variation in subsistence behavior to be a main determinant of caregiver availability. Socioecological factors that vary across hunter-gatherer peoples may limit children's opportunities to participate in care or increase the risks involved in their doing so (Hames and Draper, in press). Some women's economic activities, such as long-distance foraging treks and hunting [e.g., !Kung (Konner 1976; Blurton Jones and Sibly 1978), Aka (Hewlett 1988), Agta (Estioko-Griffin, 1985)], may preclude children's common assistance in infant care. Other environments may present physical hazards that result in unacceptable risks to infants in the care of unskilled child caregivers (e.g., !Kung (Draper and Cashdan 1988; Konner 1976), Ache (Kaplan and Dove 1987; Hill and Hurtado 1996)). However, even within these groups, qualitative ethnographic data suggests that care by children occurs intermittently, within safer contexts (Konner, Chapter 2 in this volume). Moreover, the ubiquitous mixed-age and -sex play group of children among foragers (Konner, Chapter 2 in this volume) is a significant setting in which children's care occurs. As toddlers enter this realm of peers, it appears to occur as a continuum of interaction with and care by children, rather than as an abrupt departure from maternal care. Even where direct recruitment of children to perform caretaking tasks is low, there may be positive lifespan outcomes associated with the presence of older siblings, as observed among the Ju/'Hoansi (!Kung) (Draper and Hames 2000).

We suggest that the participation of children in care is emergent from an evolved developmental and reproductive pattern expected to be widely evident among foragers. In this context, the emphasis on sibling care among farming peoples (e.g., Nag et al. 1978; Whiting and Edwards 1988; Weisner 1987) may be seen as an elaboration of a preexisting adaptation, influenced by the artifacts of enhanced labor demands, household density, and settlement patterns. Observations of newly sedentary foraging peoples have reported an increase in children's care of infants (Draper and Cashdan 1988; Hirasawa, Chapter 17 in this volume); but unfortunately, the marginal nature of extant forager environments (and resulting risks to children) limits our ability to extrapolate to foragers in general. A review of ethnographic reports (rather than summaries that commonly overlook details on caregiving practices or child behavior) of forager children's behavior will be necessary to yield more evidence with which to test our thesis. Childhood commonly fails to capture the attention of anthropological research (Benthall 1992), hence the importance of this volume on hunter-gatherer children. Such information expands not only our perceptions of child behavior, but of evolved patterns of child development and human life history (Chisholm 1988; Hewlett and Lamb, Chapter 1 in this volume; Kaplan et al. 2001).

The developmental experience of learning to parent is expected to be key to the evolutionary success of the human pattern of reproduction, in part, through its effects on developmental plasticity (Lancaster and Lancaster 1983; Bogin 1999). Cultural variation in views on children's capabilities at different ages, expectations of children's work behavior, and sibling interactions, along with prevailing ecological and environmental factors, are likely to play a role in children's and adolescents' opportunities to care for children. For example, while the Ju/'Hoansi (!Kung) of the Kalahari ask little caregiving work of their children (Draper and Hames 2000), Efe mothers commonly place their children in the care of other children. The savanna setting of the Kalahari affords some distance between in-camp adult activities and children's play groups—thereby limiting children's opportunities to care—while the dense Ituri forest precludes children's play groups from being far from the presence of adults. When an Efe mother places her infant in the arms of an older child, there are always the watchful eyes of adults nearby to assist if needed. To the extent that hunter-gatherer life can be characterized by proximal contact between adults and older dependent young (as expected due to predator defense and other environmental hazards (Blurton Jones et al. 1994b), intermittent care by children may be expected to be a feature of human evolutionary experience.

Comparative data on the evolution of parental care across species implies that offspring retained in the natal group play an important role in the development of kin and reproduction of adults; and across species, allocare is associated with intensive parental investment and cooperative group structures (Clutton-Brock 1991; McKenna 1987; Reidman 1982). A review of primate studies suggests that alloparenting is a common feature among nonhuman primate species as well (Hrdy, Chapter 3 in this volume). Sibling investment behaviors imply significant developmental and life history consequences (e.g., Blurton Jones and Marlowe 2002; Bock and Sellen 2002a; Chisholm 1988; Flinn 1999; Kramer 2002; Lancaster and Lancaster 1987; Low 1989; Weisner 1987), and we welcome more attention to this aspect of forager children's behavior and development.

ACKNOWLEDGMENTS

This research was supported by grants from the National Science Foundation (BNS-8609013), the National Institute of Child Health and Development (I-RO1-HD22431), and the Spencer Foundation. The authors would like to acknowledge the generosity and kindness of the Efe families and their community, and to thank Dr. David Wilkie and Bryan Curran for critical assistance with this research, and reviewers for their comments.

NOTES

1. Recognizing variation inherent in developmental timing and temporal age between the sexes, and within populations (on discussion of developmental plasticity, see Bogin 1999), age groups were based on a number of factors. The age of four years was included as the lower boundary as Efe children in this sample were weaned and observed performing infant care tasks. The early childhood upper boundary of seven years reflects the widely recognized and cross-culturally verified five- to seven-year-olds' shift in cognitive abilities that mark the transition into middle childhood (Rogoff et al. 1975; Weisner 1996). The middle childhood age range eight to 12 years approximately corresponds to the juvenile period, and the 13- to 17-year age group reflects the developmental shift into adolescence (Bogin 1999; Worthman 1999). Adolescent females in the sample were unmarried, nulliparous, and, with few exceptions, living in natal camps.

2. For all analyses, findings are referred to as statistically significant if $p < .05$. For analyses in this section $r^2 = .067$ for age differences, and $F = 4.724$ for girls and $F = 4.256$ for boys for comparisons within gender.

3. For this analysis, log likelihood = -53.631.

4. Estimated degree of consanguineal relatedness to the infant was converted into z-scores; z-scores of relatedness standardize variation in the infant's access to consanguineal kin within a group.

5. For this analysis, $r^2 = .039$.

6. Mean skilled care for girls = 1 percent of observed time, compared to 0.5 percent of observed time for boys.

7. For this analysis, $F = 5.184$.

8. For this analysis, $F = 5.597$.

9. For this analysis, $r^2 = .189$

10. For these analyses, $F = 10.908, 6.779$, and 8.012 for skilled care, carrying, and comforting, respectively.

11. Due to the reduced accuracy of estimating genetic relatedness more distal than .0625 (second cousins) in this sample, and the inherent level of relatedness across group members in low-density endogamous populations, children whose consanguineal kinship could not be reliably assessed within this range were considered "unrelated" to the infant.

12. Foster caregivers are related on average .097, and other caregivers are related on average .017, to focal infants in the sample. For this analysis, Mann Whitney $U = 134.500$.

13. For this analysis, Mann Whitney $U = 91.00$.

14. For these analyses, comparison of foster children and other children in time spent carrying infants and in skilled care, Mann Whitney $U = 123.500$ and 126.000 respectively; comparison of siblings and other children in time spent carrying and skilled care, $F = 6.779$ and $F = 3.450, p = .06$ respectively.

15. For this analysis, Mann Whitney $U = 658.500$.

16. For these analyses, $r^2 = .35$ for findings reported on maternal time allocation; and Mann Whitney $U = 15.000$ for findings reported on paternal time allocation.

17. For these analyses, $r^2 = .202$ and $r^2 = .189$ for data reported on food preparation and maintenance, respectively.

18. For this analysis, $r^2 = .19$.

19. For this analysis, $\chi^2 = 4.615$.

20. For this analysis, $r^2 = .20$.

21. For these analyses, $r^2 = .23$ and $r^2 = .16$, for sisters and brothers, respectively.

22. For this analysis, log likelihood $= 8.410$.

10

Older Hadza Men and Women as Helpers

Residence Data

Nick Blurton Jones, Kristen Hawkes, and James F. O'Connell

Much of our research among the Hadza has attended to two questions about childcare. Is hunting primarily a form of paternal investment, or does it affect men's fitness by other routes? How effective is the help that grandmothers appear to be giving to their younger kin? In other words, do grandmothers have a significant effect on their adult children's reproductive success? We have reported our observations made during the 1980s on hunting and on sharing meat (Hawkes et al. 1991, 2001a, 2001b), food acquisition by women (Hawkes et al. 1989, 1997), and food acquisition by children (Blurton Jones et al. 1989, 1997; Hawkes et al. 1995a). Frank Marlowe has collected similar data in the 1990s and has concentrated primarily on Hadza fathers and children (1999a, 1999b, Chapter 8 in this volume).

Here we report a preliminary effort to use data gathered for demographic study to tackle some of our questions about childcare. Between 1985 and 2000 NBJ conducted eight censuses of eastern Hadza (Hadza speakers living south and east of Lake Eyasi). We have started to look at whether older adults live where we would expect, if selection had acted on their behavior via their help in raising grandchildren. By "older adults" we mean men and women aged 40 and older who have children aged 18 and older, who are thus grandparents or soon to be grandparents.

Humans help each other a great deal, much more than is observed among other mammals. The help takes many forms but among hunter-gatherers, transfers of food are extensive, and probably very important. When help is abundant it may obscure other important features of reproductive strategies (Hill and Hurtado 1996). For example, if a woman gave birth to more children than she could handle, we might expect her to lose a bigger proportion of them than a more prudent woman would lose. But we might not observe a difference in their children's survivorship if help is diverted from the prudent woman and given to the woman in trouble. Then not only would we see a reduced difference between the prudent and the imprudent women but we would also see a reduced difference between women with helpers and women without helpers. So before seeking any effect of a helper, we need to know more about how helpers distribute their help.

Employing our evolutionary ecology perspective we can offer some expectations about how help might be distributed. Kin selection is one of the processes by which evolution could favor helping. Kin selection theory (Hamilton 1964), well described for a more general audience by Wilson (1975:117–119) and Krebs and Davies (1981:18–21), leads us to expect help to be most often directed to close kin, if the benefit to the fitness of the kin, discounted by the degree of genetic relatedness between helper and recipient, exceeds the cost to the fitness of the helper. We expect help to be given most readily to those whose receipt of the help will most enhance the fitness of the helper. This will include giving the help where it will have most effect. Kin selection is believed to underlie parental behavior and in this chapter we proceed on the assumption that it is likely to underlie grandparental behavior. We do not attempt to work in this chapter with other evolutionary mechanisms that can produce helpful behavior such as reciprocal altruism or costly signaling (Bliege Bird et al. 2001).

We have started to look at whether older adults behave as we would expect, if selection had acted on them via their help to their adult children (as opposed to, in the case of men, via other components of fitness such as competing for mates). Much help consists of giving food, some consists of direct care and attention to children. Both are most easily done between individuals who live in the same camp or the same household. So we have started to look at who lives with whom. Do parents of adult children most often stay where their help will be most effective? Before we summarize some of our previous work on grandmothers, and describe the background to our hypotheses, we must introduce the Hadza and the database used in this study.

THE HADZA

Since the peoples with whom members of the Conference on Hunting and Gathering Societies concern themselves range so widely, from those who some generations ago may have depended primarily on hunted and gathered foods, among them modern Americans, Canadians, and Russians, through many populations struggling to preserve aspects of their traditional life in a land-hungry world, to "newly discovered" forest-living South Americans, we need to set the scene for the Hadza. The Hadza are best known from James Woodburn's fieldwork beginning in 1959, initially reported at the "Man the Hunter" meeting and published in 1968 (1968a, 1968b). His 1970 work remains the best description of Hadza material culture and his many subsequent publications seem to us always close to the mark. The earliest ethnographic reports come from Baumann ([1894] 1968), and especially Obst (1912), and Kohl-Larsen (1958) (based on fieldwork in 1930s). Many Hadza today live in ways that appear to differ little from those described by these authors. But much has changed around them and much has been done to them, especially the series of failed settlement attempts imposed upon them by outsiders. We attempt to summarize the current Hadza situation on variables that may be compared with other populations.

In 1985–86 farm food comprised only 5 percent of the calories in the diet of the people with whom Hawkes and O'Connell stayed. In 1995, Marlowe worked in a greater variety of locations, including some very near villages. The average proportion of farm food was very similar (F. Marlowe, personal communication, 1997).

We know no Hadza who owns a gun, a horse, a donkey, or a motorcycle or car. Hunting is by bow and poisoned arrows and is conducted on foot. A couple of bicycles now belong to two Hadza "villages." The only livestock we have seen with Hadza are a few chickens, which seldom last long.

We know only one Hadza who has access to piped water, and he works for a European-owned fish farm. The great majority of Hadza live in houses that closely resemble those illustrated in Obst (1912) or Woodburn (1970). These are rapidly constructed out of branches and subsequently covered in grass over the next few days. Camps move frequently; even some of those that nowadays await tourists move often. Distances over which people move are very varied. In our series of censuses, the average person is 16 kilometers from where seen in the previous census. The three regions (perhaps four) described by Woodburn are still comparably recognizable.

Some six Hadza receive a regular salary, most as community development officers, but we include in this category one man who worked for NBJ on all of his field visits.

All Hadza are now familiar with researchers, and believe that Europeans are interested in them because of their skills and ability to live in the bush. Since about 1995, tourists have begun to visit some Hadza camps. This is perhaps the biggest "outside" influence on Hadza life. In complete contrast to former times, when Hadza went to great efforts to avoid strangers, some Hadza make sure that they camp where they can be found, and in locations that are quite accessible by four-wheel-drive vehicle. In the 1980s many of their camps were very inaccessible even by off-road vehicle. Some still are. Tourists leave cash, which Hadza usually refused to take from us until tourism began. Hadza who camp near villages spend a large portion of this cash immediately on alcohol. Hadza who camp far from villages use a much greater portion on clothes, knives, and axes, for which they have to walk at least a day to one of the traveling rural markets that have so invigorated the Tanzanian countryside since the early 1990s.

All one thousand or so Hadza, by definition, speak their mother tongue. Despite its including click consonants morphologically close to those of the Khoisan languages (Maddieson et al. 1992), linguists have been unable to convincingly link Hadzane to any other African language family (Sands 1998). A consensus seems to be emerging that it should be called an "isolate," perhaps in its own language family. Most Hadza men speak the national language KiSwahili, and the language of one of their neighbors (who represent Bantu, Cushitic, and Nilotic languages). Many women have the same repertoire, and some speak no Swahili. Many children have some Swahili.

There have been periods when some dozens of Hadza children attended school: at Yaeda in the late 1960s, at Munguli in the early to mid-1970s, and since 1990 children have been collected in the bush and taken to boarding school at Endamagha. Many children do not go, and among those who go, many run away home and complete few terms of school. In 1999–2000, under guidance and funding by the aid organization Canadian Universities Service Overseas (CUSO), about ten young men and women were attending secondary schools outside Hadza country. In the 1960s a group of about ten had also attended secondary school. Very few Hadza outside these last two groups know how to read or write. These read and write KiSwahili, which is used in school. Orthographies for Hadza were developed by Lutheran missionary Helen Erickson in the late 1950s and by Bonny Sands and Gudo Mahiya in 1991.

In every generation a few Hadza girls marry a "Swahili" as they often call any non-Hadza (despite having names for each of the neighboring tribes, as listed by Dempwolff 1915–1916). About half, maybe more, of these young women return later, sometimes bringing their children with them to grow up as Hadza. We know three Hadza men with "Swahili" wives.

Around 1992 (with help from CUSO, and a little from us) Hadza obtained limited rights to a small part of their traditional lands by establishing a "village": an administrative entity with surveyed boundaries. Land use bylaws are being developed by local personnel funded by one of the local tour companies. Most of the area that we can document as being occupied predominantly or exclusively by Hadza since the late 1800s has now been occupied and administratively "given away" to immigrants from neighboring farming tribes. Neither Hadza nor Hadza researchers were consulted during this process, despite frequent Hadza letters of protest, and the ease with which the researchers can be found on the web. Thus Hadza now share their land with the large Datoga herder population who may have been in the area for up to a one hundred years, and an increasing and destructive population of pioneer farmers, who fell trees and clear land in an area with insufficient rainfall to support agriculture with any consistency.

Despite this relatively tumultuous recent history, the daily lives of probably more than 90 percent of Hadza comprise the kind of daily routine described by Obst (1912), Woodburn (1968a, 1968b), and Blurton Jones et al. (2000). Between 7:00 and 9:00 a.m. people arise, wait for the cold to wear off, women sharpen and harden their digging sticks (sometimes helped by their children) and muster to prepare to go out to forage. Men leave, individually, for an early morning "walk about" (hunt) and move to "the men's place," on the edge or just outside camp where those in camp spend the day. Small children face the question, Will mother take me with her or leave me in the care of older brother? Young teenage girls decide whether to go with the women or stay home and play with the toddlers. Teenage boys decide whether to go as "guards" for the women or stay home, often to leave later with a few friends. Between 9:00 and 11:00 the children in camp usually do some foraging. Between 11:00 and 1:00 they might forage more, or eat and play. The temperature reaches its daily high by 1:00 p.m. At about this time, women who are in the bush digging tubers gather to cook and eat some of the tubers. They then often spread out and continue digging. Between 1:00 and 3:00 everyone who is in camp tends to be resting in the shade. Between 3:00 and 5:00 the women come home, and children rush to get a share of the food they brought. Between 5:00 and 7:00 the temperature has fallen to pleasant levels and most people are at home. Women and children go to fetch water. Children play vigorous games, forage some more, and if there are several teenage girls in camp singing and dancing will begin and last until 9:30 or 10:00 at night. In late dry season men will be organizing and preparing themselves for a cold night in a hunting blind at a nearby water hole or game trail. By 7:00 all but the men who left for the night are in their houses and around the fire. People eat an evening meal, and then visit and chat in each other's houses and fireplaces. On moonless nights an epeme dance may be held, in which all participate. Silence, but for coughs, the occasional crying child, once in a while a noisy domestic dispute, closely investigating hyenas, and distant comforting lions, lasts from late evening until next morning. Thus, while a couple shares a house, in which man and wife sleep, along with their younger children, eat much of the food that they both acquire, and eat an evening meal together, their daytime lives are, as Woodburn reported (1968a, 1968b), noticeably separate.

METHODS OF DATA COLLECTION

The observations reported in this chapter come primarily from a series of censuses, the first conducted in 1985 by Lars Smith and NBJ (Blurton-Jones et al. 1992) and the subsequent ones by NBJ, helped in 1995 and 1997 by Frank Marlowe and in 1997 in collaboration with linguist Bonny Sands.

In each census, accompanied by a Hadza field assistant, usually Gudo Mahiya, we tried to visit as many Hadza camps as possible, write down the households and the names of all the people in them including children, with a note about rough age status and parentage. We also weighed and measured as many people as would agree for a small payment. We asked the whereabouts of all the people recorded in previous censuses, noting whether they were alive or dead, and where they were thought to live. We found camps by asking people in the first camp where there was another, and so on. From 1991 onward we recorded the location of camps by GPS, before that by map and compass. Depending on time, funding, and current conditions we covered more, or less, ground. The censuses cannot be regarded as complete, and the number of people seen in each varies quite a lot (Table 10.1).

In addition, from 1992 to 2000 we conducted reproductive history interviews with as many women aged 18 to 50 or more as we could. The data from these are not used in this chapter, although they did contribute greatly to ascertaining identity and parentage of people, and were the major source of relative age data used to calculate birth dates. Many historical markers were used. Especially important was a very large earthquake that every

Table 10.1   The Series of Censuses[a]

Year	Funding	N camps visited	N individuals in household lists	N individuals measured	Average camp size
1985	NSF/UCLA	37	735	0	19.8
1986	NSF	6	257	400	42.8
1989	NSF	4	131	131	32.7
1990	NSF	16	633	411	39.5
1991	Ladefoged NSF	24	579	421	24.1
1992	NSF	16	412	403	25.7
1995	NSF	23	495	543	21.5
1997	NSF/UCLA	26	504	479	19.4
1999	NSF	28	674	710	24.1
2000	Wagner, SWR.	33	499	378	15.1

[a] Average camp sizes are from N of individuals in household lists divided by N of camps visited. The high average camp size in 1986 is due to the brief settlement at Yaeda in October, and in 1990 is due to the concentration of people at Mongo wa Mono. Average of the averages is 26.5.

adult remembers and that seismologists date to May 1964, and a set of photographs taken by Kohl-Larsen and brought to the Hadza (along with his films) by Annette Wagner while making her films *Hadzabe heisst wir Menschen* and *Tindiga die da laufen* . . . for SWR's Lander-Menschen-Abenteuer series.

Similar data were collected in just one region of eastern Hadza country during 1986 and 1989. Data used here come from the household lists, supplemented by the anthropometry—if someone was measured but not listed in a house, they have been entered as residing in the camp where they were measured (excluding two occasions when people walked from another camp specially to be measured). Each census covered as many camps as we could locate in the time available (usually two to three months).

Two settlement efforts interrupted the series. In 1990 Hadza had been encouraged quite aggressively to assemble at Mongo wa Mono. Only when government officials visited them with the news that they were under no compulsion to stay at the settlement were they confident enough to disappear back to the bush. But many stayed, and Mono continues to be an atypically large and stable aggregation of people, now mostly people who had traditional ties to the Siponga region in which Mono lies. In October 1986 a brief effort was made by a missionary to have Hadza settle at Yaeda chini, site of an extensive settlement scheme in the 1960s. About three hundred people stayed in Yaeda for about a month before returning to the bush. This settlement engendered a measles epidemic in which many children died. The Yaeda gathering is omitted from our analyses; camp lists from after the settlement broke up were available for 1986 and are used. Lists at Mongo wa Mono are used and in some years were recorded under the separate "subvillages" into which people assembled themselves. The same was done when a much less formal assemblage gathered at Sanola in the mid-1990s. Hadza were under the impression that the Mono and Yaeda settlements were forced upon them by the government and they had frightening memories of the 1964 roundup mentioned by Woodburn (1968a). The Sanola gathering was much less formal, though centering around missionary activity, and by this time Hadza had learned that the government does not these days force people to change their way of life. At each settlement agricultural food was provided and comprised a temporary attraction to many people. Such settlements attract non-Hadza, especially poachers.

GRANDMOTHERS AND GRANDFATHERS, BACKGROUND TO THE IDEAS

Primates are long-lived mammals and humans are long-lived primates. Theories to account for the evolution of human longevity are numerous but some recent authors attribute the evolution of the long and active human lifespan to a peculiarity of human child care: the provisioning of juveniles. This costly habit is thought to have arisen from the nature of foods available in savanna habitats. Since mother has to feed simultaneously not only her current infant but also her previous several offspring, help from other individuals becomes especially effective.

At first, like other primate infants, human infants receive frequent suckling and almost continuous contact (except among a few mainly urban cultures). But after weaning, human and nonhuman primate juveniles face very different situations. Primate juveniles, weaned but not reproductively mature, obtain most of their own food by their own efforts. Human juveniles ("children"), in contrast, are given large amounts of food by adults, parents, and others. Tucker (Chapter 7 in this volume), Blurton Jones et al. (1989, 1997), Bird and Bliege Bird 2000, 2002, and Bliege Bird and Bird (2002a, 2002b, and Bird and Bliege Bird, Chapter 6 in this volume) report and discuss some of the variation in how much food forager children can and do get for themselves. Kaplan et al. (2000a), and Hawkes et al. (1995a) have suggested that this provisioning of juveniles arises because the hunter-gatherer economy targets foods that come in large and rich packages but that are difficult for juveniles to find and process. Like others before them, these authors suggested that the savanna habitat is rich in such resources and poor (or seasonally poor) in resources that are easy for juveniles to obtain, whereas the forested habitats of most other higher primates are rich in foods that juveniles can obtain. These authors linked the origin of provisioning of juveniles to the colonization of the savanna early in human history. If they are right, the extended "dependency" of human juveniles has its primary origin in nothing more mysterious than ecology.

One consequence of this ecology is that while primates raise one baby after another, humans face a cumulative task: new babies arrive long before the previous ones are nutritionally independent, and the faster babies arrive (high fertility, short interbirth intervals) the greater the burden on parents. This ecology, in which adults can obtain large packets of highly nutritious foods but in which juveniles can at best get only a portion of their requirements, creates an opportunity for helpers. Food given to juveniles will have a large effect on their growth and survivorship. If individuals other than mother provide some of this food, mother will be able to divert more resources toward other forms of childcare and to gestating and bearing more offspring. Natural selection would favor donors who gave to close kin, and who gave to those among the kin who would give the greatest fitness returns to that help, which would depend in part on the effectiveness of the help in increasing the reproductive success of the recipients. Thus in addition to mothers, there will be a potential selective advantage to fathers, grandparents, siblings, aunts, and uncles in providing food for juveniles. Selection is expected to have weighed the advantage to these potential helpers that is derived from helping younger kin against the advantage that is derived from directing their time and effort elsewhere. Local and temporal differences in payoff are expected to lead to local and temporal differences in behavior.

If older individuals can enhance their fitness by helping to care for younger kin (grandchildren), selection may be able to prolong the vigor and lifespan of the older helpers. Recent accounts of evolution of human life history (Hawkes et al. 1998; Kaplan et al. 2000a) attend to this possibility but disagree about whether the evolutionarily significant helpers are men, women, or both. The theories share the same account of why human children are in need of so much care—the nature of the savanna foraging niche invaded at some early point in human evolution.

Among the authors who have suggested that the dependency of juveniles on provisioning would favor the continued vigor of older kin, Kaplan et al. (2000a) show that in several populations young adults raising children are unable to acquire enough calories to feed themselves and their children. Many resources flow down to them from older adults. Young adults and their children are net receivers of food, only older adults are net producers. Kaplan et al. link the evolution of a longer lifespan to the increased payoff from investment in "embodied capital" (growth and especially skills; see Bock, Chapter 5 in this volume), which allows a longer lifespan in which to recoup the benefits of the accumulated "embodied capital." It seems to follow clearly from their observations that adults who survive into and beyond middle age should leave many more descendants than those who die young. Kaplan et al. tend to emphasize the role of men, pointing to the increase in hunting success in middle age, and the large proportion of hunter-gatherer diets provided by meat obtained by men. They suggest that we should also expect that older males are important providers and their contribution may have led to selection for longer adult life in males as well as females. The contribution of men to their older children and to their grandchildren might be much diluted if they remarried and raised a second family in midlife. The size of the dilution would depend on local conditions. In some societies second wives live with the first wife and resources may be less diverted from the first family (there may even be benefits from cooperation between the wives). In others (including the Hadza) the man must leave his first wife and children to live with a new wife, and it would be difficult for him to direct resources to the first wife.

Hawkes et al. (1998) have emphasized the opportunity for selection to prolong the life of postreproductive females, and pointed out how several predictions about life history follow and are supported by the data. While following Hadza women on their foraging excursions, Hawkes (Hawkes et al. 1989) was impressed with the vigor and hard work of older Hadza women, some of whom looked as if they were well into their sixties. Later age estimates based on relative ages and historical markers showed that these eyeball estimates were realistic. Quantitative data showed that the older women, past childbearing age, worked longer hours, and at least as efficiently as women of childbearing age. Thus the older women acquired more food than younger women. These data also showed that older women who worked longer hours had grandchildren who gained more weight, during periods when the young mother had a suckling child (Hawkes et al. 1997). Hawkes suggests that the older woman might especially influence the health and survival of the small, weaned children.

The demographic data show that even in this growing population, there are many middle-aged and old people and that a woman aged 45 can on average expect 21 more years (Blurton Jones et al. 2002a), close to figures for !Kung—20 years (Howell 1979), and for Ache—22 years (Hill and Hurtado 1996). We have few systematic measures of strength and vigor but the older women appear strong and active until very late in their lives. Marlowe and NBJ's experimental tuber digging sessions (Blurton Jones and Marlowe 2002) showed only a small decline in kilograms dug per hour among the oldest women. Most of these older women walk farther and faster than many of us would care to. Figure 10.1 shows the probability that a Hadza female aged 0 to 70 has a living mother.

These observations provoked what we refer to as the grandmother hypothesis (GMH), that the opportunity for helpers provided by the savanna ecology, where juveniles must be given food, led to selection for survival and vigor after the end of the ovulatory lifespan. The elongation of adult lifespan (lower adult mortality) led in turn (as predicted from Charnov's 1993 models of evolution of mammal life histories) to other characteristics of the human life history: a later age at onset of reproduction, resulting in larger size, when compared to our nearest relatives. But whereas larger size would be expected to go with lower fertility, we observe greater fertility among humans. This could be accounted for if two females were pooling their resources. But because selection generally acts more weakly on older individuals, and the chances of having adult offspring to help are sometimes not great (Hill and Hurtado 1991), GMH requires a substantial demographic effect of the postovulatory females upon fitness of children and grandchildren and offspring of other close kin.

While Hawkes and colleagues have written extensively on Hadza grandmothers, and on men's fitness-enhancing strategies (Hawkes et al. 1991, 2001a; Blurton Jones et al. 2000; O'Connell et al. 2002), grandfathers as potential helpers have so far received little attention from this research group. We would expect older females to be much more significant helpers than older males. Not only do the references cited above imply that men's

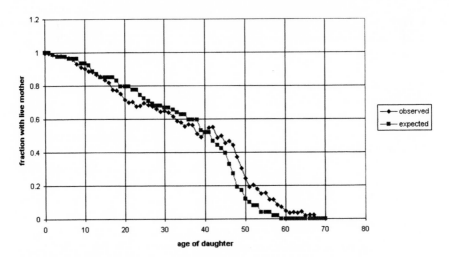

Figure 10.1.   Proportion of females of any age who have a living mother. Diamonds—observed. Squares—calculated from mother's average age at birth (28 years), and survivorship curve for Hadza females.

hunting does not have much influence on the fitness of their offspring, but we know that males remain fertile much longer than females. So we should expect males to continue to direct effort toward matings and production of new offspring, balancing the potential fitness benefits of this effort against the potential fitness costs of not directing resources toward existing offspring. Although many Hadza marriages last a very long time (several couples in Lars Smith's 1977 census were still together 23 years later in 2000), divorce is frequent and among the over forties there are many single women. Men quite often marry a younger woman in midlife and few men are single in their fifties and sixties. Thus there is opportunity in the data for different patterns of male and female residence to emerge. That men over 40 can marry a young woman and produce a second crop of children should affect our predictions about where men over 40 will be living. We would be surprised if Hadza men could gain more fitness by their help to adult children than by fathering several more children of their own.

HYPOTHESES

We present some hypotheses concerning with which people we would expect older men and women to live. We only consider cases in which the particular older and the specified younger kin are both alive and recorded in a census. When we say "older woman" or "grandmother" we mean any woman aged 40 and over who is alive and whose location was recorded in a census. Our usage is the same for "older man" and "grandfather." When we say "live with" we mean living in the same camp. The older generation does not normally share a house with their adult children but if they are in the same camp they may have their house nearby [Woodburn (1968b) shows an example]. When Hadza move they may at first simply clear an area under a bush to sleep on and only later take the hour or so needed to construct a house. Camps move, and because people may move individually or as a family, camps change composition quite frequently, at least several times a year, and often every few weeks.

We will be taking a crude, empirical approach to residence, simply who is seen in the same camp during a census. This may or may not coincide with what informants tell us is the prescribed pattern of residence. It may or may not coincide with what the literature reports. We might categorize the Hadza as matrilocal: Hadza men say they have to leave home to find a wife because women like to stay in their home region. But as shown in Figure 10.2, this does not necessarily mean that the wife lives with her mother.

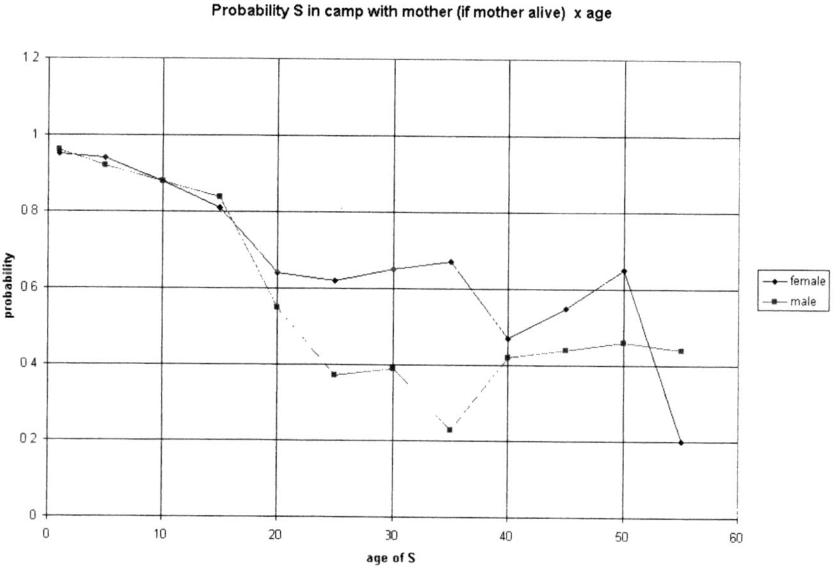

Probability S in camp with mother (if mother alive) x age

Figure 10.2. Shows proportion of the observations in which mother and daughter (diamonds), or mother and son (squares) are in the same camp as each other, if mother is alive and in a census, and daughter or son is alive and in a census.

Woodburn (1968b) reports that both husband and wife value coresidence with their mothers but while 43 percent of a sample of 28 married men were in camp with their mother, 68 percent of a sample of 34 women whose mothers were alive were in the same camp as their mother. Alvarez (2003) has shown that original ethnographers have described much variation, flexibility, and opportunism in residence patterns, particularly if the patterns were observed rather than reported by informants. Woodburn's account is a good illustration. Alvarez further showed that these subtleties were lost in the widely used codings of residence. The literature generally reports that most hunter-gatherer populations are patrilocal (e.g., Ember 1975). Despite this, Ember showed that hunter-gatherer residence patterns were quite varied. Larger economic contributions by women favored bilocality and matrilocality. Warfare was also a significant predictor of patrilocality when combined with the economic contribution of the sexes. Alvarez indicates that bilocality was more numerous in the data than usually claimed. Alvarez's and Ember's papers encourage us to expect observed residence to vary within and between populations depending on economic/ecological factors, and especially on the extent to which an older man or woman can actually provide significant help.

Do the older Hadza men and women go where we would expect them to go if they were increasing their fitness by helping their descendants? Three aspects are important in making our predictions:

1. Who will be helped most, who will show the largest increase in fitness as a result of receiving the help? In general we expect small children to be more affected by help than older children, and we expect help to small children also to allow their mother to divert resources to the next baby and thus enhance her fertility.

2. Who are the closest kin, and how reliably can the degree of relatedness be assessed by the helper? We are expecting the old people to behave in ways that increase their own inclusive fitness and not necessarily in ways that give most help to the most needy. Women can be certain that the babies they bear are their genetic descendants. Men cannot. This concept of "paternity confidence" has been much debated. It might lead us to predict that the value to men from helping kin should always be discounted by some small amount. In the present instance, while the older man may not be able to be certain that his daughter is his biological descendant, he can be more confident about her children than about his son's children.

3. What are the alternative routes by which the older adults could increase their fitness? Among the Hadza, women are able to acquire and process quite large supplies of food each day, particularly from tubers and Baobab fruit (Hawkes et al. 1989, 1995a, 1997; Blurton

Jones et al. 1989, 1997). In a setting where women acquire little or depend upon men for their economic opportunities, the older women might not be expected to follow our predictions. But the most obvious issue is the physiological difference in fertility of older men and women. Whatever the origins of this difference, it must be expected to affect the fitness payoff to behavior. Older men continue to face a trade-off between pursuit of matings with fertile women, and distributing help to their younger kin. But no matter what new husband the older women sought out, it would not increase her fertility, although one can imagine ecologies in which marrying the right older man might be an excellent way to enhance the fitness of her younger kin. Among the Hadza, older men are quite often able to marry young women and start a new family. This is especially true of older men with reputations for being a good hunter. This makes us suspect that marrying an older man whose influence could help her young kin is not a widely available option for older Hadza women. Thus we assume that alternatives are available for older men but not for older women. We expect older women to go where their help may be effective. Since we cannot at present assess where the alternatives available to men are most readily gained, we cannot make firm predictions about with whom we expect the older men to live.

If the behavior of older adults were shaped by its effects on their fitness via the fitness of their children and grandchildren we would expect:

1. Grandmothers would more often live in a camp with their daughters than their sons, because their genetic representation in the grandchildren can be more reliably assessed for the daughter's children (improving daughter-in-law's reproductive success may not increase grandmother's own fitness).
2. Grandmother would more often stay with daughters who have more small children. Small children are more vulnerable to undernutrition so we can expect the help to be more effective.
3. This may be less true, and grandmothers might even avoid daughters who already have a teenage daughter of their own who can help them. Girls aged ten and over can forage and supervise toddlers quite well; by 15 girls acquire and bring home more food than they could eat (Blurton Jones et al. 1997). Marlowe (Chapter 8, Figure 8.2) shows that teenage girls are out of camp for several hours a day (probably foraging), although they do not figure as frequent holders of babies. If a teenage daughter is an effective helper, then additional help from grandparents may make little difference.

4. There would be no effect of teenage boys: they help a little but also go off on their own a lot (as also shown in Marlowe, Chaper 8 in this volume, Figure 8.2), and do much less digging than when they were younger. Hawkes et al. (1995a) and Blurton Jones et al. (1997) show that teenage boys bring home very little food. Grandparental help may be as important for mothers of teenage boys who also have younger children as it is for any mother.

5. Grandmothers would be expected to especially frequently live in camp with daughters who have a child still suckling (see above discussion of Hawkes et al. 1997).

6. Older women might be more likely to stay with their son and his wife if his wife had no mother of her own. This young woman, producing probable grandchildren for the older woman, is lacking the help others are expected to get from their mother. The older woman's help would be especially effective, which might, in the long run, compensate for the less than total probability that all the grandchildren are her genetic kin.

7. If a woman has a grown daughter who appears to be infertile, we would expect the older woman to live less with her than with her fertile daughters. We would expect that help would have zero effect on the fitness of an infertile woman. Her mother would not enhance her own fitness by living with this daughter. Primary sterility is very low among Hadza and we have records of only seven women who have reached our rather arbitrary criterion age of 27 without a birth.

8. We have no strong expectation that older men will conform to the predictions we made above for older women. If older men were not pursuing fitness by other means but were behaving as if their help were effective and contributed to their own inclusive fitness, we would expect older men to fit with the above predictions. But because (a) they have other ways to enhance their fitness, (b) we have argued on several grounds that Hadza men's hunting cannot be accounted for by the effect of the food transferred to their offspring (Hawkes et al. 1991, 2001a), and (c) the rates of divorce do not restrict the older parents to living in the same camp, we do not expect the older men to show the same residence pattern as the older women.

RESULTS

First, to fill in some of the basic "natural history" Table 10.1 shows the censuses, total numbers of individuals recorded and/or measured, and the average camp size in each census (26.5, including adults and children). Figure 10.1 shows the proportion of females 70 years or less observed in the censuses whose mother was known to be alive at the time, and the "theoretical" value. The theoretical value is calculated from Hadza female mortality and the average age at birth (calculated from age-specific fertility smoothed by polynomial regression). Thus mother is on average 28 years older than the subject, and her probability of having survived from 28 to the subject's age x is found from the Hadza female l_x curve as $l_x/l28$ (a preliminary life table for the Hadza, sexes combined, is available in Blurton Jones et al. 2002a). The observations are not wildly different from the theoretical value. Since the life table is derived partly from the same body of data this shows us mainly that no gross errors were made in scoring the observations.

Figure 10.2 shows, for males and females, the proportion of times a person who was in a census, and whose mother was known to be alive and her location recorded in a census, was in the same camp as the mother, across the lifespan. The reader can see that about 60 percent of women aged 20–35 were in camp with their mother if she was alive and her location recorded in a census. About 40 percent of men aged 20–35 were in camp with their mother. These percentages closely resemble those cited above from Woodburn (1968b) based on data gathered between 1959 and 1961, roughly 30 years before the data in Figure 10.2 were gathered.

For the tests of the hypotheses, we examined locations of men and women aged 40 and over with at least one daughter aged 18 or over (or son aged 18 or over if required by the hypothesis) recorded in the same censuses. It is important to note that our comparisons do not reflect dead grandmothers or absent daughters. While older "daughters" are less likely to have a living mother (Figure 10.1), our analyses report on only those who do have a living mother, and Figure 10.2 suggests that residence with mother shows a plateau during the childbearing years, so results are relatively unlikely to be merely results of daughter's age. We scored the number of times mother and daughter (or father and daughter) were in the same camp as each other, and the number of times they were in different camps.

Table 10.2 shows results for older women of simple 2×2 tables testing the first six predictions made above. Each pair of rows represents a comparison between two categories of adult children, drawn from the entire record of people seen in census, and with no regard to whether a record was used in any other comparison. Thus, in the first comparison, the database contains 339 plus 225 = 564 records of an older woman in the census who also had at that time a daughter aged 18 or more in the census. Mother was in camp with the daughter on 339 of these 564 records. The database contains 243 plus 293 = 536 records of an older woman in the census who also had at that time a son in the census (regardless of whether she also had a daughter). All the comparisons produced a significant

Table 10.2   Residence Data for Women Aged 40 and Over

	Mother in camp with	Mother apart from	χ^2
Daughter over 18	339	225	
Son over 18	243	293	24.55, $p < .001$
Daughter > 18 with under 7s	199	110	
Daughter > 18 with no under 7s	140	115	5.14, $p < .025$
Daughter > 18 suckling C < 2	154	74	
Daughter > 18 has no < 2	185	151	8.87, $p < .005$
Daughter has teenage daughter	56	52	
Daughter has no teenage daughter	283	173	3.86, $p = .05$
Daughter has teenage boy	59	43	
Daughter has no teenage boy	280	182	0.18, $p > .70$
Son's wife has no mother alive	49	145	
Son's wife has living mother	47	234	5.4, $p < .025$

chi-squared, except, as predicted, for the comparison of mother staying with a daughter who has a teenaged boy compared with a daughter who has no teenaged boy. All the significant results were in the direction predicted. Older women were more often in camp with their adult daughters than with their adult sons. Older women were more often in camp with their adult daughter if she had children under seven years old. We chose seven as a cutoff because children over seven obtain significant amounts of food for themselves, and can run a variety of errands such as getting water. The same result is obtained with a cutoff of five years. Older women were more often in camp with their adult daughter if the daughter had a child under two (and therefore still suckling). Older women were less often in camp with their adult daughter if she had a teenage daughter but not if she had a teenage son. Older women were more often in camp with their adult son if his wife's mother was dead than if she was alive.

The seventh prediction can only be tested for our tiny sample of seven infertile women. Mothers of five of the seven childless women stayed more with another daughter than with the childless daughter. One of the two exceptions was a mother who lived with a childless adult daughter who was raising the children of her sister who had died during the study period. Thus grandmother was in camp with her grandchildren by the dead daughter.

The quantitative data on older women confirm all of the expectations. Grandmothers behave as if their help makes a difference, and as if selection has acted upon them through their effect on their grandchildren's number and survival. These results also imply that it may be difficult to test whether grandmother affects the fertility of her daughter and survival of her grandchildren. She places her help where it is needed; we will find few data points to make fair comparisons of fertility or mortality in presence and absence of grandmother. The picture is further complicated by the observation that sometimes grandmother has some grandchildren come to live with her, away from their mother. We have yet to examine this practice quantitatively.

The results for men (Table 10.3) did not follow the predictions for helpers very closely. One prediction had a significant result: older men who have a daughter aged 18 or over are more likely to be in camp with her than with a son. But the effect was much weaker than for women (above, in discussing paternity confidence we had pointed out that confidence will lower for men but even for men will be higher for daughter's children than for son's children). There was a nonsignificant tendency for a man to be in camp with his son if the son's wife had no mother. There was a nonsignificant tendency for men to be seen in camp more often with a daughter who had no teenage boy than with daughters who did have a teenage boy. We did not predict this and have no post hoc offering beyond the occasional statement by informants to the effect that women need a male to "carry meat" for them. This statement is contradicted by our abundant observations of women going to a kill site and carrying meat home. But overall, the data on older men do not support the view that they live where their fitness would be most enhanced by help to younger kin.

Table 10.3 Residence Data for Men Aged 40 and Over

	Father in camp with	Father apart from	χ^2
Daughter over 18	188	268	
Son over 18	134	260	$4.52\ p < .05$
Daughter > 18 with under 7s	101	134	
Daughter > 18 no under 7s	88	134	$0.58\ p > .30$
Daughter > 18 suckling, $C < 2$	83	97	
Daughter > 18 has no < 2	106	171	$2.78\ p > .10$
Daughter has teenage daughter	28	38	
Daughter has no teenage daughter	161	230	$0.04\ p > .50$
Daughter has teenage boy	20	44	
Daughter has no teenage boy	169	224	$3.16\ p > .05$
Son's wife has no mother alive	20	92	
Son's wife has living mother	23	191	$3.21\ p > .05$

DISCUSSION

Our analysis of who lives with whom among the Hadza is very preliminary. While we use the data from 15 years of fieldwork the analysis of this
aspect of the data is only a few months old.

Data Analysis

Hadza move so frequently, and camp compositions are so flexible that we
did not hesitate to treat the data as if each census was independent of the
other censuses. But the data confound individuals and occasions, and in
principle, results could be biased by the behavior of a few individuals who
were greatly overrepresented in the data. But in these data no individual can
appear in more than eight censuses, in a sample of some hundreds of individuals (age range 85 or less), observed in censuses. A further complication
is that some older people have two or more daughters, and could appear as
a data point with respect to each daughter (but only if each daughter was
seen in the census, and people are frequently missing from a census). Others
have only one daughter. People with no daughter were not included in
the analysis. So sometimes an older woman has chosen between two daughters who may live apart, sometimes she faces no choice because both
daughters live in the same camp, and sometimes she can choose between
living in camp with her only daughter, or elsewhere. We should remember
that camp composition and location are extremely changeable. Camps
move every two to four weeks, and at each move, some people go to a different camp, while others come to join the remaining movers. Nor can we
think of one camp as the older woman's "home" and another as the daughter's "home." Given continuous observation we would be able to see
whether mother or daughter packed up and moved but we have no such
data. The reader should not picture a stereotype derived from residence ty-
pologies, nor from our own highly sedentary pattern.

It might be worth developing alternative methods of data analysis. We
could for instance use only one observation per older woman, taken from
a random selection of the censuses in which she appears. We might do better to generate yearly hazard records that allow us to employ the analyses
commonly used in demography. We could use these to investigate what
factors affect the probability of mother and daughter being seen together.
The independent variables could then include measures like number of
daughters, number of censuses in which each individual was seen, the
predicted factors such as degree of relatedness, age, and number of grandchildren, and so on.

Despite these reservations we can justifiably claim that the data on
the older women conformed to the predictions and the data on the older

men mostly did not. We should perhaps not be too concerned about the strength or weakness of the results. Weakness in the results would however imply that there is plenty of variance in the data with which to examine effects of grandmother after controlling for the way she distributes her help. We have presented data on just one aspect of the older women's residence, living in camp with adult children. Sometimes children are sent away from their mother's house or camp to live with someone else. This is quite often a grandmother. We have yet to look at whether similar predictions can be made and tested about which children stay most often with which grandmother or grandfather.

Women

The data on older women all conformed to our hypotheses, which were based on the assumption that help by older women is effective and is distributed in a way that enhances the older woman's inclusive fitness. The data are thus compatible with a key part of the grandmother hypothesis, that the help given by older women to younger kin can increase the older woman's fitness. The results conform with expectations from the grandmother hypothesis. But the observations are also compatible with a competing view of the evolutionary history of postreproductive life. Postreproductive life may have arisen as a by-product of some process unrelated to female provisioning of descendants. Then, given that females live into old age, those who help their descendants may leave a few more descendants than those who do not. Of course, this competing view relies on taking the increased lifespan as a given, or accounting for it by unclear theories such as that if selection for low mortality up to around age 40 was sufficiently vigorous to produce maintenance and repair mechanisms sufficient to produce low mortality, then we would expect these mechanisms to leave a sizeable sample of individuals who live even longer. This view appears incompatible with evolutionary analyses of aging and mortality (e.g., Ricklefs 1998). Meanwhile GMH has successfully accounted for work patterns of older women, increased age at maturity, increased size, higher than expected fertility, and residence patterns of older women. Data on the distribution of the food acquired by older women remain to be analyzed. Data on the time allocation of younger women with and without a coresident mother might also be useful. It is hard work to raise children, even in a society such as the Hadza. Just how do women manage with and without helpers, and how do they make use of their helpers? We are reminded of the observation that Navajo women spent more time interacting with their children if they lived in an extended family group than if they lived as a nuclear family (Chisholm 1983). GMH is also more compatible with an array of archaeological data summarized by O'Connell et al. (1999) than are some of its competitors. But the size of the effect of grandmothers upon their descendants remains an important missing piece of evidence.

If we are to argue, as in GMH that help to younger kin is the selective force behind longevity (ovulatory span being a conserved character), we must be able to show roughly how strong this force is. The observations on how efficiently help is distributed suggest that it will be difficult to measure the strength of the effect of help. But the weakness of some of the effects reported here suggests that it may be possible. It could be that the effect of grandparents is most easily tested in populations where the grandparents have fewest opportunities to distribute their help efficiently. For instance, in a more sedentary population, neither grandmother nor daughter may find it at all easy to move. Then we may see a daughter who happened to live close to her mother doing much better than her sister who happened to have settled far away. Sear et al. (2000) may be such a case.

There is another difficulty to be addressed when we try to measure the effect of older women as helpers. It is not only grandmothers who help. There are also aunts, greataunts, and older sisters. We would expect their behavior to be determined by the number of their adult daughters and grandchildren, and by the availability of the grandmother. But in the camps in which Hawkes and O'Connell gathered data between 1985 and 1986 (the source of the data used in Hawkes et al. 1997) there were no women of childbearing age without an elderly female helper. The same was true of the camps in which NBJ collected similar data in fall 1986 and winter 1989. But not all these helpers were grandmothers. The census data do not allow us to observe which women have no helper in the way that we could see, while living in a camp for extended periods, who foraged with whom and who gave food to whom. But we must examine the frequency with which young women are in camp with aunts and older sisters before we conclude that young women separated from their mother are without helpers.

Men

As we expected, the results for men did not follow the predictions for helpers very closely. Only one prediction had a significant result: older men who have a daughter over 18 are more likely to be in camp with the daughter than with a son. But the effect was much weaker than for women. Overall, older men did not behave as we expected helpers to behave.

For many readers, familiar with the literature proposing the importance of hunting as provisioning, these results for men might be unexpected. But we must remember that helping kin is just one route to fitness and that men have more alternative routes available to them than older women do.

One of these routes, a new marriage to a younger woman, might itself be a result of the importance of hunting, either as provisioning, or from its effects as an advertisement of "quality": vigor, health, value as a neighbor, and so forth (Bliege Bird et al. 2001). Blurton Jones et al. (1997) and Marlowe (2000a) report from different datasets that men who had reputations as more successful hunters were more likely to have younger wives. We might propose for future study the idea that the men who have been the least successful hunters would be the most likely to distribute their help among kin in the way that older women do.

These results on older men can be added to our previous arguments about the route by which Hadza big game hunting may enhance men's fitness. Data on success rates at hunting or trapping small game, which provide a daily supply of protein, suggests that this would be an effective way to promote the health and development of a man's children. Yet Hadza men almost never trap, and often pass up small game. Pursuit of big game leaves many meatless days and unpredictable spans of meatless days, even given that meat is widely shared among camp members (Hawkes et al. 1991). Data on the shares of meat given and received show no advantage to the successful hunter's household. Unsuccessful hunters, who have given out little or no meat, receive as much as successful hunters receive (Hawkes et al. 2001a). A kin selection (paternal investment in younger kin) account of Hadza big game hunting seems to fail whenever we examine it. Our data on residence of older men add to our view that economic support of young kin is not a major route by which Hadza men enhance their fitness.

Residence Patterns

We have many other questions to ask the data. What about uncles and aunts? Where do divorced men go? With whom do orphans live? Do men try to marry into a large family of cooperating women? Do women with many helpers get husbands with a higher reputation as a hunter or trader? We have yet to look at children who leave their mother to stay with their grandmother. We have just started also looking at how far people move, and whether, as Hadza tell us, men often have to change the region they live in, to accommodate their wife's preference for staying in her natal region. First indications are that in each census, people are on average only 16 kilometers from where we last saw them, and that more men than we expected are living in the same region as their mother.

There are many other interesting features of residence patterns that we have yet to examine fully. We should for instance show how well or poorly the data conform to any proposed general rule of residence. It should be clear from the data we present that any fit will be poor. Under a matrilocal prescription we might expect that when mother and daughter are both alive, they should be living in the same camp as each other. Line 1 of Table 10.2 shows that this is the case only 339 times out of 564. Hadza women aged over 18 and whose mothers were alive were living matrilocally only about 60 percent of the time. Line 2 gives 45 percent for men. These figures are startlingly close to those reported by Woodburn from observations made some 30 years previously. Not only are Hadza still "bilocal" but they are so in close to the same quantities.

We could think about whether assuming a matrilocal prescription could lead us to the same predictions, to other predictions, or, most likely, to not very many predictions without inventing additional prescription rules. The observations reported by Sear et al. (2000) show that maternal grandmother can influence grandchild fitness even in a patrilineal, patrilocal society. It would be interesting to know how older women behave when the cultural prescription is not matrilocal. Young women's mothers may be quite frequent "visitors" to the daughter's camp but still report themselves as "really resident" elsewhere. Their visits may be more frequent or lengthy when daughter has a bigger child-rearing burden, and fewer alternative helpers, and even more so if daughter's husband has left or died (the literature gives the impression that the daughter often returns to her mother's or father's house if this occurs). It would be even more valuable if we knew about the economic contributions of men and women at the same time, and about the fitness-enhancing alternatives to help that are available to them. Studying such things may not be easy. For example, if Hadza women like to stay in their own country, where they know all the plants and localities, this need not imply staying with their mother. Since camps move so frequently any adult woman will know most of her natal region and women's preference limits them only to a region, not to the same camp as their mother. In some other society it could be that men negotiate economic opportunities with neighboring farmers or herders. Men may then be arranging work opportunities for women as well as trade opportunities for themselves. In such a case the economic contribution of women may actually depend on the negotiation skills of their husbands. Divorce rates could influence conformity to residence prescriptions. If the prescription is for men to stay with their fathers, and couples rarely divorce, the options for an older woman to stay with her married daughters may be restricted. If, as among the Hadza, divorce is quite frequent, women have more options about where to live, and there is an opportunity for the difference between men and women that we observed. Residence behavior would be a productive arena in which to explore the interplay between evolutionary ecology prediction, and cultural prescriptions. How widely can we generate observed residence from evolutionary ecology cost-benefit thinking? Can we also generate residence prescriptions?

11

Juvenile Responses to Household Ecology Among the Yora of Peruvian Amazonia

Lawrence S. Sugiyama and Richard Chacon

INTRODUCTION

We explore predictions regarding trade-offs in juvenile time allocation in response to different ecologies of parental and alloparental investment among the Yora of the Peruvian Amazon. The Yora remained relatively isolated until 1984, when they experienced their first peaceful contacts with outsiders. Within two years, approximately half the population died from contact-related diseases (Hill and Kaplan 1989). Although this tragic situation is all too common in the history of first contacts with indigenous groups, the omnipresence of endemic health risks (e.g., Gurven et al. 2000; Sugiyama 2004; Sugiyama and Chacon 2000; Sugiyama and Scalise Sugiyama 2003) means that high parental mortality may be common in such groups even in the absence of contact-initiated epidemics (e.g., Chagnon 1997; Hill and Hurtado 1996). In either case, high postcontact Yora mortality provides an opportunity to analyze juveniles' responses to different parental circumstances.

Other studies have looked at households with one biological parent and one stepparent. Although our sample is small, the study village included a large proportion of juveniles living in households with one biological parent and no stepparent. Single biological parents without a coresident mate do not have to "negotiate" resource allocation to their offspring with a stepparent, who may exert pressure on the biological parent to invest more in their mutual offspring and less in the biological parent's offspring by a previous mate. Examining single-biological-parent households is thus important because it focuses attention on parental investment and the al-loparental investment of nonmates.

Our discussion addresses longstanding issues in hunter-gatherer stud-ies: are there recurrent features of hunter-gatherer childhood that reflect evolved features of human life history, and within that, to what degree do individuals facultatively respond to their particular circumstances? Spe-cifically, we ask whether (1) Yora household composition and feeding patterns indicate that they are cooperative breeders in which mothers en-hance alloparental investment to their offspring via recruitment of multi-ple caregivers; (2) there is facultative variation in juvenile work strategies in response to household parental ecology; and (3) juvenile work and for-aging patterns are primarily practice or productive.

STUDY POPULATION BACKGROUND

The Yora are a small group of Panoan-speaking people inhabiting the upper Manu and Mishagua rivers in southeastern Peru, first contacted in 1984. Within two years of contact, epidemics reduced the population from 300 to 150 people (Kim Fowler, personal communication 1990; Hill and Ka-plan 1989). Initial reports were that Yora were highly mobile foragers who traveled by canoe, hunted and fished with bow and arrow, and gathered feral plantains and wild resources (Hill and Kaplan 1989). By 1990, there was a Yora horticultural village, Putaya, located in the Mishagua river headwaters near the Putaya confluence. Past village, fishing, and garden sites were located along these rivers. Intermittent periods of riverine mo-bility and horticultural production may therefore characterize precontact Yora settlement. As of 2003, some Yora continue to be highly mobile, trav-eling as far south as the Bolivian border (M. Gurven, personal communi-cation, 2003).

In Putaya, eleven open-sided thatched houses with raised palm wood floors were located along both sides of the forty-meter-wide Mishagua river. Houses ranged from 50 to several hundred meters from their nearest neighbors and, with one exception, were within sight of at least one other. Gardens were adjacent to most houses, with houses linked via trails roughly parallel to the river. One could thereby walk a circuit past each vil-lage house in just over one half hour. During the dry season, when one could easily walk across the river, walking from one end of the village to the other took half the time it took to make a circuit of the village.

During our study, hunting and fishing continued to occupy half of all time allocated to subsistence; the rest was allocated to horticulture (Sugi-yama and Chacon 2000; Walker et al. 1998). Similarly, about half of ob-served food consumption came from hunting and fishing, and half came from gardening. Hunters stalked game with bow and arrow or pursued it with hunting dogs (Sugiyama and Chacon 2000; Walker et al. 1998). Large game was butchered near the kill site, and packaged for distribution before returning to the village. A variety of fish were taken with bow and arrow, cast net, or hook and line. Turtle and lizard eggs were also collected, along with wild fruits and nuts. Game and fish were usually consumed the day they were acquired. Members of several households sometimes cooperated in foraging, the catch distributed between participants and members of other households. Once food entered a household, all members present shared the food. The main cultigen, sweet manioc, was served boiled, roasted, or as manioc beer. Plantains, sugar cane, maize, sweet potatoes, achote, tobacco, and cotton were also cultivated (Sugiyama and Chacon 2000; Walker et al. 1998). Because households were the primary economic unit, we use them as a significant unit of analysis in this study.

People living in small, face-to-face, kin-based groups who are dependent on foraging for a livelihood mirror critical aspects of the environment of human life history evolution (e.g., Hagen 1999; Howell 1979; Hrdy 1999; Lee and DeVore 1976; Sugiyama 1996, 2004; Tooby and DeVore 1987). Ethnographic studies of these societies are useful for testing hypotheses about general and facultative human life history features (e.g., Hill and Hurtado 1996). The Yora provide a venue for such study: although they practice horticulture, they depend on subsistence foraging and continue to live in small kin-based groups with little access to Western medicine, contraception, or mechanized technology (Sugiyama 2004; Sugiyama and Chacon 2000; Walker et al. 1998).

LIFE HISTORY THEORY

One goal of hunter-gatherer research has been to identify, document, and explain life history patterns of foragers to gain insight into the evolution of human life history (e.g., Bird and Bliege Bird 2002; Blurton Jones et al. 1994a, 1994b; Blurton Jones and Marlowe 2002; Bock 2002a, Chapter 5 in this volume; Hawkes et al. 1998; Hewlett 1991a, 1991b, 1992a; Hill and Hurtado 1996; Kaplan et al. 2000a; Konner 1981, Chapter 2 in this volume; Walker et al. 2002). Evolutionary environments vary in their ecological and social particulars; thus, within a species' general life-history pattern, selection produces suites of reproductive, decision-making, and other motivational adaptations that elicit adaptively strategic trade-offs in life effort in response to recurrent environmental variables (e.g., Chisholm 1996; Clutton-Brock 1991; Daly and Wilson 1984; Hagen et al. 2001; Hill and Hurtado 1996; Hrdy 1992; Stearns 1992; Tooby and Cosmides 1992; Trivers 1972b, 1974; Trivers and Willard 1973). Understanding how individuals use local environmental cues to adjust their allocation of life resources is a main goal of human life history research (e.g., Belsky 1997; Betzig et al.

1988; Chisholm 1993; Blurton Jones et al. 1989; Blurton Jones et al. 1994a, 1994b; Blurton Jones and Marlowe 2002; Bock 2002a, Chapter 5 in this volume; Draper and Cashdan 1988; Draper and Harpending 1982; Hagen et al. 2001; Hill and Hurtado 1996).

General Features of Human Life History

In general, successful reproduction entails high maternal investment (e.g., Ellison 2001; Hrdy 1999; Konner 1977; Stern et al. 1986). Humans are altricial: at birth and for years afterward, offspring are helpless and dependent on adult care (e.g., Bogin 1999). Human juvenile success suffers with loss of this investment (e.g., Hill and Hurtado 1996; Hurtado and Hill 1992; Hagen et al. 2001; Marlowe 2003), which is often supplemented by alloparents (individuals other than the biological parents; e.g., Draper and Hames 2000; Hawkes et al. 1998; Hrdy 2001b, 2002, Chapter 3 in this volume; Hill and Kaplan 1999; Kaplan and Hill 1985; Kaplan et al. 1990; Turke 1988). Human life history is also characterized by delayed maturity, long lifespan, and exceptional intelligence and learning capabilities. We focus on one explanation of these characteristics, skills or knowledge acquisition, and on one model of that explanation (see, e.g., Blurton Jones and Marlowe 2002; Bock, Chapter 5 in this volume; Leigh 1999; Pagel and Harvey 1993; Sugiyama 2004).

Kaplan et al. (2000a) propose that as evolution of hominid dietary reliance on high-quality, difficult-to-acquire resources (e.g., game animals) progressed, fitness benefits were realized from a longer prereproductive period of foraging skill and/or knowledge acquisition. This led to coevolution of increased resource flow from older individuals to juveniles to support this period of growth and learning. The higher mortality risk accompanying extended juvenility and lifespan was countered by increased food sharing and provisioning of sick/injured individuals (Kaplan et al. 2000a). This theory prompted tests of juvenile foraging efficiency to see whether efficient adult foraging requires an extended period of knowledge-based skill acquisition (Part II of this volume; Bird and Bliege Bird 2002; Bliege Bird and Bird 2002b; Blurton-Jones and Marlowe 2002; Bock 2002a; Walker et al. 2002). While currently debated, it is clear that juvenile foragers' contributions to their own subsistence varies based on local ecology, technology, and type of foraging practiced (Bird and Bliege Bird 2002; Bliege Bird and Bird 2002b; Blurton Jones et al. 1994a, 1994b; Blurton Jones et al. 1989, 1997; Blurton-Jones and Marlowe 2002; Bock 2002a, Chapter 5 in this volume; Tucker and Young, Chapter 7 in this volume; Walker et al. 2002). We ask whether Yora juvenile foraging patterns support the skills-acquisition hypothesis, are focused on achieving immediate returns, or both (e.g., Bock, Chapter 5 in this volume).

Parental Investment Theory and Facultative
Responses to Parental Condition

Parental investment (PI) theory focuses on how individuals allocate resources between existing offspring, current versus future offspring, and quantity versus quality of offspring (e.g., Alexander 1974; Bateman 1948; Lessells 1991; Stearns 1992; Trivers 1972b, 1974, 1985; Trivers and Willard 1973). Hamilton's (1964) theory of kin selection posits that individuals who are genetically related to a juvenile can further their fitness by aiding him/her. By combining kin selection with PI theory, we can extend the study of parental allocation of resources to include alloparental investment. Specifically, we expect adults to invest differentially in juveniles depending on (a) the juvenile's probable relatedness to the adult, (b) the probability that the juvenile will be able to translate investment into future reproductive success, and (c) the alternative potential uses of the resources (Clutton-Brock 1991; Daly and Wilson 1988; Hrdy 1999; Lancaster and Kaplan 2000; Trivers 1972b, 1974).

Conversely, selection is expected to have produced adaptations by which juveniles assess their own condition, their options within their environment, the condition of potential caregivers, and potential caregivers' available alternative avenues of investment, as well as a decision-making psychology that, ancestrally, generated behavioral choices that tended to enhance their ability to survive and reproduce (e.g., Belsky 1997; Chisholm 1993; Draper and Hames 2000; Hill and Hurtado 1996; Hrdy 1999, 2001b; Konner, Chapter 2 in this volume; Sulloway 1996). Juveniles could increase investment in themselves, reduce risks of losing available investment, or acquire more resources on their own. Loss of a biological parent is a significant change in the offspring's socioecological environment, to which strategic responses are expected. In turn, potential caregivers are expected to be sensitive to juveniles' ability to contribute to their own welfare, and to adjust their reproductive and investment strategies accordingly (e.g., Blurton Jones et al. 1994a, 1994b, 1996, 1997; Daly and Wilson 1987, 1988; Draper and Harpending 1982, 1987; Kramer 2002; Strassman 1997; Sulloway 1996; Trivers 1974). We ask whether there is facultative variation in parental and alloparental provisioning and in juvenile work strategies in response to household parental ecology.

HYPOTHESES

Hypothesis 1

All else equal, biological parents (BP) gain higher fitness by investing in their own offspring rather than those of others. Generally, mothers invest a lot in their offspring, but among foragers paternal investment is also generally high (e.g., Hewlett 1991a, 1992b, 1992a; Konner, Chapter 2 in this volume). Even among the Hadza, who are cited as an exception (e.g., Hawkes and Bliege Bird, 2002; Konner, Chapter 2 in this volume), males preferentially invest in their own offspring: men living with biological offspring hunt more and bring in more game than those living with stepchildren. This may be particularly important when a man's mate is pregnant (Marlowe 1999a, 1999b, 2003). Further, stepchildren are at risk of neglect or abuse due to stepparental reluctance to invest in the offspring of others (e.g., Bugos and McCarthy 1984; Daly and Wilson 1984, 1988; Hausfater and Hrdy 1992; Hill and Hurtado 1996; Lancaster and Gelles 1987). We therefore predict:

Hypothesis 1: Juveniles are more likely than not to live with all surviving biological parents.

If biological father is alive, juveniles are more likely than not to live with him.

Hypothesis 2

Multiple caregivers can increase juvenile survival and reproductive prospects (e.g., Beckerman et al. 1998; Hawkes et al. 1998, 2001b; Hewlett 1989; Hill and Hurtado 1996; Hrdy 1999, 2001b, Chapter 3 in this volume; Marlowe 1999a, 1999b, 2001). Postreproductive females may support their daughters' reproduction (e.g., Hawkes and Bliege Bird 2002; Hawkes et al. 1997, 1998, 2000; Hrdy 1999, 2001b, Chapter 3 in this volume; Sear et al. 2000), while males often contribute resources to mates, other adults, and juveniles (Hewlett 1989, 1991a, 1992b, 1992a; Hill and Hurtado 1996; Ivey 2000; Kaplan et al. 2000a; Marlowe 1999a, 1999b, 2001; Winterhalder 1996). Hrdy (1999, 2001b, Chapter 3 in this volume) thus argues that humans are essentially cooperative breeders—a species in which rearing juveniles involves a number of adult and juvenile conspecifics (i.e., allomothers). If Yora follow a pattern of cooperative breeding, if household residence is highly associated with investment (see below), and if mothers facultatively recruit alloparents for their offspring, we predict that:

Hypothesis 2: (a) Juveniles are more likely to live in extended family than in nuclear family households.

(b) Juveniles will live in households with multiple potential alloparents.

(c) Juveniles living with 1BP (and no stepparent) will live in larger households and have more coresident potential alloparents than those living in 2BP households.

Hypothesis 3

The Yora household is assumed to be a primary venue for investment. Although age, local environment, technology, and foraging strategies affect the degree to which juveniles can provision themselves, cross-culturally, food provisioning is a recurrent form of benefit transfer from adults to juveniles (e.g., Blurton Jones et al. 1994a, 1994b, 1996; Bogin 1999; Draper and Hames 2000; Hawkes et al. 1997; Kaplan et al. 2000a). Energy intake and its correlates are useful proxies for fitness (e.g., Hagen et al. 2001; Kelly 1995; Kaplan and Hill 1995; Sellen 1999; Winterhalder 1996). Here we use observations of juveniles eating as an index of food provisioning by household, which we think justified because ethnographic observations indicate that the proximate distributors of food eaten in Yora households were household members, predominantly adults (except when juveniles independently acquired foraged items). Because unweaned juveniles' consumption is primarily nursing, and because they are limited in their mobility, we test hypotheses 4-7 with data from weaned juveniles only. We predict that:

Hypothesis 3: Weaned juveniles are more likely to eat at home than elsewhere.

Hypothesis 4

Alloparental care by close relatives can have positive fitness consequences for the provider (Daly and Wilson 1986; Flinn 1989; Hamilton 1964; Hrdy 1999, Chapter 3 in this volume; Hawkes et al. 1998, 2000). Thus, juveniles may seek investment from potential alloparents in households other than their own. All else equal, alloparental investment is best placed with those most in need. On average, we expect single parents to have fewer resources to give their offspring than two parents, such that:

Hypothesis 4: Weaned juveniles living with 1BP will eat at home relatively less often, and away from home more often, than those living with 2BP.

Hypothesis 5

Yora juveniles are free to move about the village. They may therefore increase opportunities to receive alloparental investment both directly (e.g., food provisioning) and indirectly (e.g., protection, precautionary warnings, behavioral models) by spending time in households other than their own. Weaned juveniles living with 1BP may therefore attempt to make up for missing parental investment by seeking investment from non-parent adults in other households. If so, we predict that:

Hypothesis 5: Weaned juveniles living with 1BP will spend relatively more time in other households than those living with 2BP.

Hypothesis 6

Juveniles living with 1BP could compensate for lost parental investment by increasing time spent foraging, by taking over a primary caregiver's work so that he/she can devote more effort to activities directly benefiting the juvenile, or both. When net proceeds from juvenile foraging are higher than net benefits from freeing up time for their adult caregivers, juveniles are expected to increase work effort in foraging or other subsistence tasks directly. Factors that bear on this trade-off include (1) juvenile foraging efficiency; (2) age- or sex-specific base rate of work effort by juveniles with both parents living; (3) efficacy of juvenile work in nonforaging household labor; (4) adult foraging return rate; and (5) degree to which juvenile household labor increases adult caregiver foraging. All else equal, we expect that:

Hypothesis 6: Juveniles living with 1BP will work more than those living with 2BP.

Hypothesis 7

Ethnographic observation and prior analysis (Sugiyama and Chacon 2000; Walker et al. 1998) show that Yora juveniles do engage in household, horticultural, and foraging work. In contrast to the Hadza (Blurton Jones et al. 1989, 1997), Mikea (Tucker and Young, Chapter 7 in this volume), and Mer (Bliege Bird and Bird 2002b) environments, where children can independently forage in relative safety, the neotropical forest environment of the Yora is potentially dangerous (Sugiyama and Chacon 2000; and see Hill and Hurtado 1996). Adolescent or adolescent/child groups do go on independent fishing trips away from the village, however, and all but the youngest juveniles were seen fishing in the river running through the village. If weaned juveniles can work and forage successfully and have free time available to increase foraging, then we expect that:

Hypothesis 7: Weaned juveniles living with 1BP will spend more time in subsistence work than those living with 2BP.

Hypothesis 8

Analysis of age-specific hunting success of Ache neotropical bow-hunters suggests that bow hunting takes a long time to master (Walker et al. 2002). This was our impression among the Yora as well. Conversely, we found hook and line, net, and bow fishing to be relatively easier (in that order of difficulty). As Bock (Chapter 5 in this volume) and others (e.g., Bird and Bliege Bird 2002; Bliege Bird and Bird 2002b; Blurton Jones and Marlowe 2002; Bock 2002a; Kaplan 1997; Kaplan et al. 2000a; Walker et al. 2002) have noted, strength, skill, and knowledge may all have effects on juvenile foraging success. Fishing from the bank requires little strength, but traveling by canoe does. If juvenile foraging is primarily practice and knowledge acquisition, and hunting is more knowledge-intensive than fishing, we expect weaned male Yora juveniles to engage in more hunting than fishing because hunting skills must be honed. However, if production is a primary foraging goal—as it appears among the Hadza (Blurton Jones et al. 1997), Mikea (Tucker and Young, Chapter 7 in this volume) and Mer (Bird and Bliege Bird 2002; Bliege Bird and Bird 2002b)—then fishing should predominate, with juvenile hunting seen primarily in association with adults from whom knowledge-based hunting skills can be acquired. Our experience among the Yora and among Shiwiar blowgun/shotgun hunters is that successful adult hunting of large game using traditional weapons requires expert knowledge and a certain amount of strength. And, our ethnographic observations suggest that production was a primary goal of Yora juvenile fishing. We therefore predict that:

Hypothesis 8: (a) Weaned juveniles will spend more time fishing than hunting.
(b) Time spent fishing will increase with age during the juvenile period (because long-distance canoe travel requires more size/strength)
(c) Time spent hunting will increase with age across the lifespan.
(d) Time allocated to fishing will peak earlier in life than time allocated to hunting.

METHODS

Data were gathered via scan sampling, residence survey, and genealogy. Focal person follows and departure/return records were used to collect ethnographic data on adult and juvenile foraging strategies. During the

59-day study period the population of Putaya varied between 56 and 71 people living in 11 households. From two to six instantaneous scan samples were run on each of 29 days, yielding one hundred scans and 6,448 individual behavioral observations (Hames 1992a, 1992b; Walker et al. 1998). Scans covered all daylight hours. During each scan one of us made a circuit of the village, visited each household, and sought each individual then living in Putaya. For each individual we recorded the time, location of observation, and activity observed. Once people became accustomed to the scans, they altered their behavior very little upon our approach. When someone was not in the village, we asked household members where he/she was, and later cross-checked this information either directly or by confirming the report when we encountered the person later in the day. People kept track of the comings and goings of others, and reports were generally accurate. If someone could not be found, and his/her activity not confirmed, we recorded no behavior for that individual for that scan.

Demographic Makeup of Sample

During data collection (1990) Yora were living in three locations: 66 persons in the study village of Putaya, 37 persons in Cashpajali (as of 1986; Hill and Kaplan 1989), and a third group in the mission town of Sepahua. The Putaya sample included 38 males and 32 females, of which 27 were adults and 43 were juveniles. Juveniles included 13 unweaned infant/toddlers, 17 children between weaning and puberty, and 13 adolescents between puberty and age of first reproduction. Of these 43 juveniles, 24 (55.8 percent) had two living parents, 17 (39.5 percent) had one living parent, and two (4.7 percent) had no living parents. One juvenile, a short-term visitor to Putaya, was excluded from analysis. The household marriage situation of the remaining 42 juveniles consisted of 18 (42.9 percent) living with both biological parents (2BP household), 12 (28.6 percent) living with one biological parent (1BP household), six (14.3 percent) living with a biological parent and a stepparent (stepparent household), and six (14.3 percent) living with alloparents only (alloparent household).

Overall, there was a significant relationship between juvenile lifestage (infant/toddler, child, or adolescent) and primary caregiver composition in the household (1BP, 2BP, alloparents, or biological mother and stepfather) (χ^2 = 14.432, df = 6, p = .028). Here we focus on those juveniles living in 1BP and 2BP households. From the perspective of individual juveniles, there were ten infants toddlers, three children, and five adolescents living in 2BP households, while there were two infants/toddlers, seven children, and three adolescents living in 1BP households. Clearly, the number of juveniles in the village is small, and carving the sample into multiple categories reduces the numbers in each. When we compare the chronological age of juveniles in 1BP and 2BP households, however, the Kruskal-Wallis test shows no significant association between juveniles' ages and household type ($\chi^2 = 1.82$, df = 1, $p = .177$).

Between two and 11 people lived in each Yora household. Among juveniles living with either 1BP or 2BP, household size ranged from four to 11 people. Two juveniles lived in 1BP households with seven members, three in households with nine members, and seven in households with 11 members. Three juveniles lived in 2BP households with four members, nine with seven members, three with nine members, and three with 11 members. The Kruskal-Wallis test indicates that juveniles living with 1BP live in larger households than those living with two biological parents ($\chi^2 = 1.82$, df = 1, $p = .177$), even though juveniles living with 1BP and 2BP do not differ in number of juvenile coresidents ($\chi^2 = 0.282$, df = 1, $p = .596$). The difference is that juveniles living with 1BP tend to live in households with more adults.

RESULTS

Household Composition

Hypothesis 1: Does household composition reflect biparental investment?

Of the 23 juveniles with two living biological parents, 18 (78.3 percent) lived with 2BP, two (4.9 percent) resided with their mother, and three (7 percent) with their mother and a stepfather. Of the 12 juveniles who resided primarily with one biological parent (1BP household), nine lived with the mother (78.6 percent) while three lived with the father (21.4 percent); in all but two of these cases, the other biological parent was deceased. All six children who lived with one biological parent and one stepparent lived with their biological mother and a stepfather; in three of these cases, the biological father was alive and living in the village (Table 11.1).

Table 11.1   Juveniles' Household Composition and Biological Parent Mortality

Parents living	2BP	1BP Mother | Father	Stepparent Mother | Father	Alloparents	Total
0	—	—	—	2	2
1	—	7 | 3	3 | 0	3	16
2	18	2 | 0	3 | 0	1	24
Total	18	12	6	6	42

In sum, 33 of 36 (91.6 percent) juveniles with biological mother living resided in a household with their biological mother, while only three (8.3 percent)—all of whom resided with alloparents—did not. Twenty of 27 (74 percent) juveniles with biological father living resided in a household with their father, while only seven (26 percent) did not. Again, when father was living, juveniles were more likely to live in a household with him than not ($\chi^2 = 6.26$, df = 1, $p = .012$). Twenty-nine of 40 (69 percent) juveniles with at least one biological parent lived with all surviving parents; juveniles were more likely to live with all remaining biological parents than not ($\chi^2 = 8.1$, df = 1, $p = .004$). Only six juveniles did not reside with one of their parents who were living, and all of these lived with their mother. Of the six juveniles living with alloparents only, three were living with a father's sister (and father's sister's husband), two were living with mother's sister, and one was living with his mother's father's brother (and mother's father's brother's wife).

Hypothesis 2: Is household composition indicative of cooperative breeding?

Of 11 households, only two included mother, father, and biological offspring. One household included only a married couple. Another included a nuclear family sharing the same roof (condominium style) with a three-generation extended family and two juveniles receiving allomaternal care. Of the seven extended family households (counting the two condo families as one household), two included a stepparental relationship, six included adult alloparental relationships in addition to a stepparent, and two included three generations of individuals. Only three juveniles resided in the same household as a grandparent: two with grandfather and one with grandmother. Overall, 39 juveniles lived in households with extended family members and/or alloparents under the same roof, while only three juveniles lived in nuclear family households.

From the standpoint of individual juveniles, their households had between zero and five potential adult alloparents, and between zero and five potential older juvenile alloparents. On average, juveniles resided with 1.83 potential adult alloparents ($M = 1.83$, SD = 1.45), and 2.19 potential older juvenile alloparents ($M = 2.19$, SD = 1.53). As noted above, juveniles living with 1BP lived in larger households than those living with 2BP ($\chi^2 = 1.82$, df = 1, $p = .177$), because the former tended to have more resident adults.

Juvenile Time Allocation

An overview of Yora time allocation provides the context for our comparison of juvenile time allocation in 1BP and 2BP households. Of the 6,448 individual scan-sampling observations, 3,626 were of individuals under twenty who had not reached the age of first reproduction, and 2,638 were of children and adolescents. There were 2,537 observations of weaned juveniles living with either 1BP or 2BP, and no difference between the relative number of observed and expected observations for weaned juveniles living in 1BP and 2BP households ($\chi^2 = 0.017$, df = 1, $p = .897$).

Figure 11.1 shows an overview of time allocation by lifestage for all ages. Overall, 41 percent of time is devoted to leisure, including relaxing/resting, playing, and socializing. Subsistence activities take up 39 percent of time, including gardening, hunting, fishing, and cooking (23.22 percent), consumption (14.56 percent), and distribution (1.6 percent). Household maintenance accounts for 6.65 percent of time allocation, while childcare accounts for 6.26 percent. Note, however, that childcare often co-occurs with other activities; data reported here include only childcare not performed concurrently with another activity. These figures therefore underrepresent time allocated to childcare.

A general comparison of daylight time allocation by lifestage including all infants/toddlers, children, adolescents and adults, indicates that time allocated to leisure is negatively correlated with lifestage ($R = 8.68$, $p = .000$). Among all weaned juveniles, there is a significant association be-

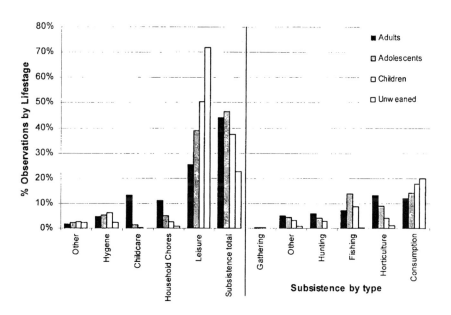

Figure 11.1   General time allocation by lifestage (100%=All observations for each lifestage)

tween lifestage and relative time allocated to work (χ^2 = 287.5, df = 1, p = .000). Nevertheless, weaned juveniles spent a significant amount of time working (see below). Overall, children spent relatively less time working than adolescents (χ^2 = 51.855, df = 1, p = .000), and adolescents relatively less time working than adults (χ^2 = 66.404, df = 1, p = .000). Of the work observed, there is a positive correlation between advancing lifestage and time allocated to household maintenance tasks (e.g., cleaning, hauling water, tending the fire, household repairs) (R = 0.593, p = .000). Similarly, children spend relatively less time doing subsistence work than do adolescents or adults (χ^2 = 62.946, df = 1, p < .000), whereas adolescents and adults do not differ in time allocated to subsistence work overall (χ^2 = .584, df = 1, p = .445), although this obscures important differences (see below).

Hypothesis 3: Is primary residence the main source of food for juveniles?

Hypothesis 1 was based on the assumption that the household was a primary venue for investment. Here we test this assumption with one data source, observations of where juveniles were eating. As predicted, overall, weaned juveniles were observed eating at home more often than elsewhere (χ^2 = 43.90, df = 1, p = .000).

Hypothesis 4: Do weaned juveniles living in 1BP households eat at home less often, and away from home more often, than those in 2BP households?

They do not. Weaned juveniles living with 1BP ate at home more often than away (χ^2 = 4.612, df = 1, p = .032), while those living with 2BPs did not differ in how often they ate at home vs. away (χ^2 = 49.7825, df = 1, p = .000). Weaned juveniles living with 1BP ate at home more often than expected compared with those living with 2BP (χ^2 = 6.249, df = 1, p = .012), but did not differ in the relative frequency with which they ate away from home (χ^2 = 1.632, df = 1, p = .201) (see Figure 11.2).

Hypothesis 5: Do weaned juveniles in 1BP households spend more time away from home than those in 2BP households?

In general, they do not. Weaned juveniles living with 1BP and 2BP did not differ in relative time spent away from home (χ^2 = 0.594, df = 1, p = .44). And, those living with 1BP spent relatively *more* time at home than those living with 2BPs (χ^2 = 9.795, df = 1, p = .002) (see Figure 11.3).

Hypotheses 6 and 7: Do weaned juveniles living with 1BP work more than those living with 2BP?

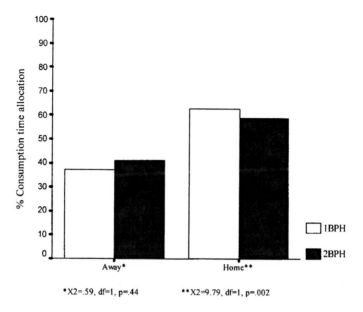

Figure 11.2.   Weaned juveniles' consumption at home vs. away (100% = all consumption for juveniles of a household type)

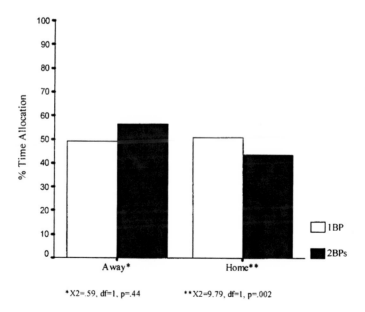

Figure 11.3.   Weaned juveniles' time spent at home vs. away (100% = all observations for juveniles of a household type)

They do not. Overall, weaned juveniles living with 1BP and 2BPs did not differ in the relative frequency they were observed working overall (χ^2 = 1.1, df = 1, p = .298), or in subsistence (χ^2 = .812, df = 1, p = .368). However, those living with 2BPs were observed relatively more often than juveniles living with 1BP doing household maintenance chores (e.g., cleaning, hauling water, washing) (χ^2 = 4.47, df = 1, p = .034) and hunting work (including processing game) (χ^2 = 7.647, df = 1, p = .006). No significant differences were found between 1BP and 2BP juveniles for fishing (χ^2 = .006, df = 1, p = .939) horticulture (χ^2 = .966, df = 1, p = .326) or gathering (χ^2 = 3.481, df = 1, p = .062) (see Figure 11.4).

Hypothesis 9. Is juvenile foraging oriented toward skill and knowledge acquisition, or production?

If juveniles forage primarily for knowledge/skill acquisition, then juveniles in 1BP might not be able to make up for investment losses by increasing time allocated to foraging. We can put juvenile foraging goals into perspective by examining them in relation to changes in foraging behavior across the lifespan. Linear regression of age across the entire juvenile period on percentage of time allocated to fishing is significant, with age accounting for 46 percent of the variance in juvenile time allocated to fishing (F = 34.02, p = .000, n = 43, R^2 = 46 percent). Across the lifespan, cubic re-

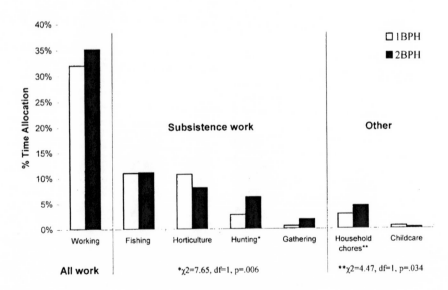

Figure 11.4. Weaned juveniles' time allocation to work

gression indicates a significant inverted-U-shaped relationship between age and percentage of time allocated to fishing: fishing increases with age through the juvenile period but decreases during adulthood until about age 50 ($F = 7.68, p = .000, n = 75, R^2 = 0.239$). The Kruskal-Wallis test shows that males allocate significantly more time to fishing than do females ($\chi^2 = 20.37$, df = 1, $p = .000$). Also, the relationship between age and fishing time allocation is primarily the product of male behavior: the cubic regression model accounts for 47.5 percent of the variance in male fishing behavior ($F = 10.25, p = .000, n = 39, R^2 = 47.5$ percent), but for females is not significant at conventional levels ($F = 2.64, p = .066, n = 37, R^2 = 19.9$ percent). Finally, female fishing time peaks at about age 17, while male time allocation to fishing peaks around age 23 (Figure 11.5).

The Kruskal-Wallis test shows that average male time allocated to hunting was far greater than that for females ($\chi^2 = 21.351$, df = 1, $p = .000$). While the increase in hunting time with age across the lifespan is generally

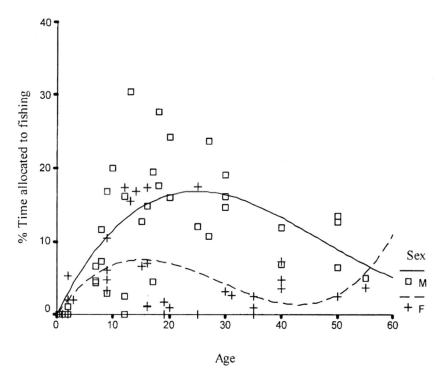

Figure 11.5. Percent male and female time allocation to fishing across the lifespan

linear for both males and females, cubic regression indicates that the increase in female hunting time with age appears to level off between about 20 and 40 years, and then accelerates ($F = 4.77$, $p = .001$, $n = 36$, $R^2 = 30.9$ percent). Quadratic regression shows male hunting time increasing to at least age 55 but at a slightly decelerating rate after about age 30 ($F = 12.75$, $p = .000$, $n = 38$, $R^2 = 42.9$ percent) (Figure 11.6).

Among juveniles, the regression model shows significant linear effects of age [$r = 0.555$ (42), $p = .000$] and sex [$r = 0.434$ (42), $p = .002$] on time allocated to hunting. Age accounts for 29.1 percent of the variance in time allotted to hunting by juveniles; sex accounts for an additional 11.6 percent. Neither BP status nor the number of coresident juveniles is significantly associated with time allocated to hunting, although they account for 5.6 and 2.7 percent of variance, respectively. Among adults, sex accounted for the greatest proportion of the variance in time spent hunting, 41.6 percent

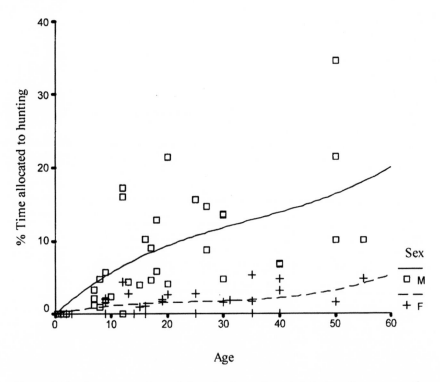

Figure 11.6. Percent male and female time allocated to hunting across the
lifespan

($r = 0.66, p = .000$). Age and number of household juveniles accounted for a small percentage of variance in time spent hunting (6.2 and 6.9 percent, respectively), although neither was significantly correlated with hunting time ($r = 0.316, p = .083$, and $r = .305, p = .095$, respectively).

Finally, juveniles of all ages spent significantly more time fishing than hunting ($\chi^2 = 80.49$, df $= 1, p = .000$). Although adolescents spent less time hunting ($\chi^2 = 3.868$, df $= 1, p = .049$), gardening ($\chi^2 = 6.96$, df $= 1, p = .008$), and gathering ($\chi^2 = 3.93$, df $= 1, p = .047$) than adults, adolescents spent more time fishing than adults ($\chi^2 = 41.154$, df $= 1, p = .000$). While juveniles were never observed hunting outside the village without adults, juveniles often went fishing alone or in groups. The Kruskal-Wallis test indicates that, in a sample of 60 person-days fishing, adolescents and adults do not differ in average kilograms of fish taken per hour ($\chi^2 = 0.65$, df $= 1$, $p = .42$) (see Figure 11.7).

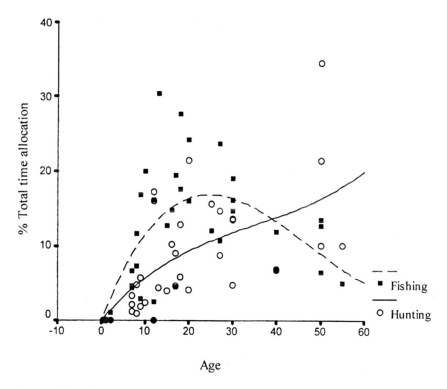

Figure 11.7. Percent male time allocated to fishing and hunting across the lifespan

DISCUSSION

As predicted by PI theory, the majority of juveniles (29 of 40) who had a living biological parent resided with all living biological parents, and 20 of 27 juveniles with father living resided in the same household as their father. Infants and toddlers, particularly, spend a large portion of their time at home. And primary residence is linked with at least one important source of investment: food. Overall, weaned juveniles ate at home significantly more often than elsewhere. However, weaned juveniles also received significant alloparental food transfers: approximately 40 percent of their time spent eating was in households other than their own. Hrdy's (1999, 2001b, Chapter 3 in this volume) view of humans as cooperative breeders is also supported by household composition patterns. Juveniles were more likely to live in extended and multiple family households than with nuclear family only, and they lived, on average, with several potential adult and juvenile alloparents. Juveniles living with 1BP lived in larger households, with more potential alloparents, than juveniles living with 2BPs. Only three juveniles had grandparents living in the village; all three lived in the same household as the grandparent. Older individuals may have suffered high mortality during postcontact epidemics; thus, that there were few juveniles with grandparents in the village may be a stochastic effect of these epidemics, although in small populations with high mortality such circumstances may be common from juveniles' perspectives (e.g., Chagnon 1997; Hill and Hurtado 1996).

Time allocation data did not support predictions about facultative juvenile responses to living with 1BP versus 2BP, or about differences in provisioning to juveniles living with 1BP and 2BP. Our assumption that living with 1BP would mean less investment at home was not supported. Weaned juveniles living with 1BP were observed eating at home more, rather than less, often than those living with 2BP. Weaned juveniles living with 1BP did not differ from those living with 2BP in how often they were observed eating away from home. We also see no evidence that 1BP juveniles seek alloparental support by spending more time in households other than their own. In fact, 1BP juveniles spent more time at home than their 2BP peers. Data on time allocation to work, subsistence, and foraging also showed few differences between 1BP and 2BP juveniles. However, weaned 2BP juveniles spent more time hunting than did 1BP juveniles. Most 1BP juveniles lived with mother; thus, one possible benefit of living in a 2BP household is that one has better access to an adult male model for observational learning of hunting strategies. Additionally, one may be called upon to help out in hunting more often.

Could it be that juveniles do not have adaptations to assess their circumstances and facultatively adjust behavior in response? It is possible, but other data indicate that this is unlikely to be the case (e.g., Belsky 1997; Betzig et al. 1988; Bliege Bird and Bird 2002b; Chisholm 1993; Blurton Jones et al. 1994a, 1994b; Blurton Jones et al. 1989, 1997; Bock 2002a, Chapter 5 in this volume; Draper and Harpending 1982; Flinn 1988; Konner, Chapter 2 in this volume; Sulloway 1996). It could be that our measures were not sensitive enough to observe strategic differences in behavior based on household ecology; however, we did find differences—in the opposite direction than predicted. We believe that what we failed to anticipate was that a significant amount of alloparental care in 1BP households is (apparently) arranged by parental-alloparental household coalitions: the greater number of potential adult alloparents within the households of 1BP juveniles may be the product of mothers' (or other primary caregivers') strategic recruitment or arrangement of multiadult household members, or the result of primary caregivers joining households to produce this effect. We therefore did not see the reduction in household investment we predicted would drive 1BP juveniles to seek resources elsewhere. Juveniles themselves may have had a hand in choosing where to live, based on their assessment of which households could best support them. Indeed, five individuals appear to have done this, but the numbers are too small for us to conclude much from them.

The reason we see few differences in the work strategies of 1BP and 2BP juveniles could be that their work is essentially practice; hence, increasing time allocation to work does not increase juvenile fitness. This seems untenable given the amount of time juveniles spend working, the life-history pattern of this work, and the fact that adolescent fishing return rates are indistinguishable from adult rates. This raises the question of why juveniles forage, and whether differences in time allocated to fishing and hunting indicate that hunting requires more investment in skill and or knowledge than fishing.

Although Yora children had ample leisure time and relatively few household responsibilities, they nevertheless spent significant time foraging. As Konner (Chapter 2 in this volume) notes, reports of children's foraging suggest that there is much play involved, and Yora children's foraging conforms to this observation. However, watching children hungrily devour the proceeds of their foraging gave us the distinct impression that—as with the Mer, Hadza, and others—the goal of Yora children's foraging was, at least in part, production. Our data on fishing support this conclusion. Time allocated to fishing increases across the juvenile period until adolescents are spending more time fishing than adults, with equal hourly returns. As noted earlier, the knowledge and skill necessary for effective hook and line, net, and bow fishing seem to develop rapidly (albeit most Yora juvenile fishing was of the less skill-intensive hook and line or net varieties). One advantage that increases throughout the juvenile period is strength (e.g., Blurton Jones and Marlowe 2002; Walker et al. 2002). Older Yora children have the strength to pole a canoe greater distances upriver (which opens up a wider territory for exploitation) and to pull in bigger fish. Smaller children, in contrast, tended to request and use smaller hooks.

For adult males, hourly return rates are higher from hunting than fishing (Sugiyama and Chacon 2000), yet, as predicted, time allocated to hunting does not catch up with time allocated to fishing until well into adulthood. Of course, we would not expect neotropical hunting to completely replace fishing at any time during the lifespan, given that fishing and hunting are complementary strategies that have different payoffs depending on season, water levels, rain, and so on (e.g., Beckerman, 1994). Nevertheless, the trend line (Figure 11.4) regressing male time allocation to fishing on age has a strikingly similar shape and peak to the strength curves reported for Ache (Walker et al. 2002) and Hadza (Blurton Jones and Marlowe 2002) foragers, showing a relatively steep increase during the juvenile years that peaks around age 23. Conversely, the shape of the trend line for male time allocation to hunting is similar to the individual age related return rate curves for neotropical hunting among the Ache (Walker et al. 2002). It accelerates more slowly but continues until relatively late in the lifespan. Further, independent hunting by juveniles was almost exclusively for small prey (e.g., lizards, birds) around the village, or in the company of adult males. Strength does affect accuracy with a bow (Blurton Jones and Marlowe 2002; Walker et al. 2002), but if that is what delays juvenile entry into successful independent hunting, why does the hunting curve not mirror the strength or fishing curves?

Yora bow hunting with dogs requires speed and stamina to corner the animal, strength to jam poles into the ground to secure the prey where it has been cornered, animal knowledge to decide whether it is worth continuing a pursuit, tactical knowledge for extracting the animal, and territorial knowledge to find one's way home after chasing quarry erratically through the forest. Hunting this way entails much higher energy costs per unit time than fishing. When accompanying adults in the chase, older adolescents appear to be effective hunting partners, and younger adolescents and children provide assistance. However, adolescents rarely hunt alone, and children are not physically up to the task of independently cornering and dispatching larger prey without high risk (e.g., Hill and Hurtado 1996). Effective bow hunting by stalking requires extensive knowledge of animal behavior, signs, tracking, calls, strategic approach, and shot positioning. It also requires sufficient skill to handle the bow (something learned fairly early) and strength to shoot arrows high into the canopy (something that takes a period of growth to attain). Even so, the size and strength arguments do not explain the pattern of Yora results. And while speed, strength, and technical skill with a bow all feature in Yora hunting, all are in place before the hunting time overtakes fishing.

Studies across forager groups suggest that knowledge-based foraging skills may depend on experience, which in turn may be a function of ecology and foraging techniques. For instance, when foraging knowledge was assessed directly, Aka children had knowledge comparable to that of adults (Hewlett 1988). Aka hunt cooperatively in multiage groups using nets; from infancy, then, Aka children have recurrent experience with all aspects of the hunt. In contrast, Ache infants and small children are not normally present on Ache or Yora bow hunts, so opportunities for observational learning are more limited. The greater dangers associated with neotropical hunting may also act to limit Ache and Yora juvenile time allocated to hunting.

The age related tradeoff between time allocated to hunting and fishing superficially appear consistent with the idea that delayed maturity is an evolved life history strategy for reducing risks of entering adult competition before juveniles have a reasonable chance of success (Bogin 1999). On this view hunting is a part of adult male mating competition, but entering this competition before one has the requisite social skills to succeed may lead to irrevocable setbacks. So, juveniles do not enter the competition until nearly adult. On the other hand, Yora males allocate the most time to hunting in their late forties, when they are already adults with dependents. If hunting is primarily mating competition, then it should be most intense in early, rather than late adulthood.

One variable that may explain both the high levels of adolescent fishing and the slow increase in time allocation to hunting is number of dependents. When number of dependents is low, low but consistent fishing return rates may be preferable to higher but more variable hunting return rates. However, if increasing time allocated to fishing is not sufficient to support higher numbers of dependents, then a higher but more variable rate of return from hunting may be preferential. Increase of time allocation to hunting may be motivated by one's parental investment interests rather than constraints upon foraging ability per se (e.g., Bird and Bliege Bird 2002). This hypothesis is not supported by our data: number of household juveniles was negatively correlated with time spent hunting.

Of course, hunting may have fitness benefits beyond its dietary contribution to self and dependents. The view that provision of public goods via hunting is a costly signal of coalitional intent (e.g., Gurven et al. 2000; Hawkes and Bliege Bird 2002; Smith and Bliege Bird 2000; Smith et al. 2003; Sugiyama and Chacon 2000; Sugiyama and Scalise Sugiyama 2003) is more consistent with increased time allocation to hunting with age than is the hunting as (solely) mating competition explanation. If hunting and meat sharing is an honest signal of coalitional intent, then hunting should increase as reliance upon larger, extra-familial coalitions increases. And, because younger individuals may depend on parents for provisioning during illness and injury, and coalitional support networks in times of conflict, the need to generate and maintain adult alliances might be expected to increase, all else equal, with age (e.g., Sugiyama and Chacon 2000; Sugiyama and Scalise Sugiyama 2003).

Age is correlated with a number of life history variables such that correlation of age and behavior alone is unlikely to settle the question of why juveniles forage (e.g., Bird and Bliege Bird 2002). Behavioral data have been unable to settle the issue of why juveniles take a long time to reach adult levels of hunting efficiency. Experimental data, in contrast, have missed the knowledge hypothesized to be critical for efficient hunting of larger game. We know that not all foraging techniques take a long time to master (e.g., Bird and Bliege Bird 2002), and that different hunting technologies require different levels of knowledge. One possible prediction, then, is that in areas where a mix of hunting technologies is available, younger or more inexperienced hunters will, all else equal, devote more time to technologies that compensate for knowledge-based or other deficits in hunting skills. Among the Yora, for example, the one cast net available in the village was preferentially adopted over bow and arrow fishing by older adolescents, even though their return rates with the net were no different than those of adult males using bow and arrow.

Bock (2002a, Chapter 5 in this volume) presents a punctuated embodied capital model for explaining the life history of foraging competency, with which our Yora data fit fairly well. Less skill-intensive fishing shows age- and probably strength-based increase in time allocation. Very young children fish in the river in front of their homes; older children fish from all points in the village, or go fishing with adults, adolescents, or mixed-age groups. As they gain the strength to pole a canoe upriver, they can fish in pairs or mixed-age groups. Hunting competency, in contrast, is acquired sequentially over a longer period. First, juveniles accompany and assist adults, allowing observational learning of the strategies, animal behavior, and risks involved. Growth allows them to begin hunting independently and, perhaps, to further hone their knowledge and skills. Finally, dependence on adult social alliances may increase hunting because hunting allows one to provision others, thereby providing a costly signal of coalitional intent that may pay off in social support of various kinds (e.g., Gurven et al. 2000; Smith and Bliege Bird 2000; Sugiyama 2004; Sugiyama and Scalise Sugiyama 2003).

Three things seem clear from our analysis. First, Yora juveniles benefit from both biparental and alloparental investment, as predicted from the cooperative breeding hypothesis. Second, predicted patterns of facultative variation in juvenile behavior in response to different household parental ecologies were not observed. Less clear is why this is the case, but facultative cooperative breeding (alloparenting) alliances may buffer juveniles who have lost a parent, and probably invalidated our expectations about differences between 1BP and 2BP household ecologies. Further analysis of the patterns of adult behavior in relation to the number, age and type of their dependents is clearly called for. A fourth set of findings, addressing why juveniles forage and why they take a long time to reach adult hunting proficiency, suggests that (1) juveniles engage in significant work-related activities, (2) both practice and production are key incentives for Yora juvenile foraging, and (3) time allocated to less skill-intensive foraging (i.e., fishing) reaches adult levels before time allocated to skill-intensive foraging (i.e., hunting) does, in a manner consistent with a punctuated embodied capital model of development, and a social signaling model of hunting.

ACKNOWLEDGMENTS

We deeply appreciate funding from the Andrew Isbell Memorial Fund for Anthropological Research; University of California, Santa Barbara Social Sciences/Humanities Research Grants, Graduate Research Mentorship Program Grant, and Regents Fellowship; and University of Oregon TOFF Award. Barry Hewlett, Patricia Draper, and Michelle Scalise Sugiyama provided valuable comments and editorial advice. Katie Burns provided indispensable advice and data analysis. George Pryor assisted with data entry. Hillard Kaplan generously provided logistical information. Our interpreter Miguel Garcia and the cooperation of the Yora people of Putaya made the research possible.

12

The Growth and Kinship Resources of Ju/'hoansi Children

Patricia Draper and Nancy Howell

In 1967–69 the present authors took part in a multidisciplinary study of people we then usually called the !Kung Bushmen in Botswana.[1] The so-called Dobe !Kung are well known in the anthropological literature from the studies of a dozen or more investigators and are now known by several terms, such as Basarwa, San, or Ju/'hoansi. Howell and Draper were involved in different kinds of studies, though we worked among the same thousand or so people who shared an environment, a language, and a culture. Draper's focus was on child behavior (Draper 1985; Draper and Cashdan 1988). Howell studied the population structure and the reproductive histories of women (Howell 1976, 1986, 2000). Both of us were interested in how a simple technology, absence of schooling and Western medicine, varying reliance on hunting and gathering vs. cultivated food, and living in an extreme, desert environment might influence the behavior of our subjects, in comparison with similar kinds of data collected on people of other cultures in different parts of the world.

Ju/'hoansi have been known for their small stature, slender bodies, and low fertility. Since our original fieldwork, their social and economic lives have changed, particularly in terms of diet, access to Western medicine and the availability of schooling (Biesele 1993, 1995; Hitchcock et al. 1996; Hitchcock and Biesele 1997; Lee 1993). These factors undoubtedly have played a role in changing patterns of growth and demographic variables. Recent reports indicate that 20 and 30 years later people of the same ethnic group are a bit taller, heavier, and are showing somewhat higher fertility (summarized in Howell 2000:364).

In this chapter we return to data we collected on children in the late 1960s, when many of the changes now fully observable were much more weakly expressed. In particular we will look at indicators of growth and development on a sample of children and youths and consider the relationship these physical indicators may have with demographic variables, kinship networks, and behavioral profiles of individual children. The physical measurements were collected by Nancy Howell and Richard Lee in 1968 and 1969 (Howell 1979; Lee 1979). The behavioral data in the form of "scan samples" were collected by Draper in the same period (Draper 1973, 1975, 1976).[2] When we worked on the same project many years ago we did not anticipate writing the chapter we are now presenting. However, as the population of Ju/'hoansi was small and widely scattered, and we were committed to visiting many different communities on a repeated basis, we ended up with a subset of children on whom each of us have gathered considerable information at almost the same time, and we have now merged our data into a single framework.

THE RESEARCH PROBLEM

The topics we address in this chapter are the following: First, how small are the Ju/'hoansi children for their age, and how do their heights, weights, and body mass indexes express themselves across the period of childhood and adolescence? How do the children compare among themselves and how do they compare with other populations? What implication for well-being may be attached to their reduced size? Nutritional studies generally assume that bigger is better, associating small size with "stunted growth" and malnutrition. Small size may, however, be an advantage under circumstances of hunting and gathering in a hot, desertic climate.

Second, we ask, What role has kinship with its implications for economic reciprocity played in the growth of children? The Ju/'hoansi have been described as a quintessentially kin-based society; many investigators have reported a social norm for sharing as well as the actual practice of widespread sharing, particularly of meat but also of other goods, which were exchanged through *hxaro* or trade partnerships (Wiessner 1977, 1982). The continuous redistribution of goods has been shown to be a leveling mechanism that made it difficult for any one individual to dominate others or to accumulate significant wealth. On the other hand, even in an egalitarian, kin-based society people differ, not only in genetic makeup, but in access to kin. What role may the presence of numerous close kin have played in buffering children from food shortage? If children had relatively few key senior relatives (such as parents and grandparents), did this put them at risk? Alternatively, kin may be competitors. We reasoned that children who had numerous younger siblings might have been disadvantaged because of competition from brothers and sisters.[3]

Third, can we see any features in the behavioral profiles of children that may indicate the effects of reduced growth? If there was variability among children in their attainment of certain heights and weights for age, might not well-nourished children distinguish themselves from poorly nourished children by showing more vigorous physical activity, having greater spatial range, and/or choosing children rather than adults for close association?

METHODS

Draper, Howell, and Lee (and other researchers) collected genealogical information from virtually every permanent resident of the Dobe area of Ngamiland, Botswana, with the result that it has been possible to count, for each of our children, the number and status of each child's living lineal ascendants (parents and four grandparents) as well the number of living siblings for each child at the time of the study. Good estimates of absolute ages are available for children and adults from Howell (1979, 2000). The total number of children on whom we have both genealogical and height and weight data is 165.

Draper collected different types of behavior observations on Ju/'hoan children who were living in different camps or villages in the Xangwa district of Western Ngamiland, Botswana (which we often call, informally, the Dobe area). The total number of children on whom we have both behavioral and body size data is 51. About half of these children were living at the same village or within a few kilometers of the villages of Bantu pastoralists. For these people, the basic bush diet was supplemented to some degree by cow's milk and garden crops. The other half of the children lived in camps in which nearly all food was collected locally by hunting and gathering (described in detail in Lee 1979).

JU/'HOANSI CHILDREN'S GROWTH AND DEVELOPMENT

Ju/'hoansi people are known for being characteristically short and slender people at all ages, and it is not surprising to find that Ju/'hoan children generally fall below the standards of expected weight for age established and distributed by the U.S. National Center for Health Statistics and distributed by the Centers for Disease Control (http://www.cdc.gov/growthcharts). These charts have been found to describe the normal range of children from birth to age 20 in all industrialized societies. There are small average differences for regions (children who live at high altitudes are slightly lighter than others) and minor average ethnic group differences, but nevertheless these generalized charts provide a useful tool to reassure parents of the normal growth of their children, and to identify the occasional child who is not growing normally and who needs medical attention to identify the nutritional, infectious or parasitic, or genetic cause of the slow rate of growth. A recent trend in distributions of growth in industrialized societies is the so-called epidemic of obesity in children, which is pushing the top part of the range (over the 75th percentile of weight by age) higher and higher, a problem not seen in the Kalahari.

Figures 12.1 and 12.2 show the standard weight distribution for girls and boys 2–20 years of age with the observations for our 165 Ju/'hoan boys and girls plotted as individual points on the graph. We see that up to about age seven, the Ju/'hoan children fall into the lower half of the normal range on these charts, but after age seven only a very few children are as high as the 25th percentile, and the vast majority are "off the chart," weighing less than the fifth percentile of weight for age, often considerably less. Especially between the ages of ten and 15, all the children are below the fifth percentile, a level of weight that is associated in the medical and nutritional literature with sickness, "failure to thrive," lowered immune system functioning, and increased risk of death (Jenike 2001:224–225).

Are all the !Kung children unhealthy and malnourished? Weight alone does not provide the answers to these questions, as the children (and adults) are also short and small-boned.

Figures 12.3 and 12.4 show the height of Ju/'hoan girls and boys by age, also plotted over the Western standards of height for girls by age, and again we see the Ju/'hoan children clustered below the bottom of the normal range for Western children by age. Ju/'hoan children grow more slowly than Western children, and stop their growth in height at lower levels. As Lee has pointed out, the Ju/'hoansi may be showing a healthy adaptation to their special circumstances of life (Lee 1979:290–292). It may be advantageous to be short and light when your life consists of hunting and gathering in a hot environment. But the issue deserves more careful assessment.

The measure of weight controlled for height generally used is the Body Mass Index (BMI), which is calculated as weight (kilograms) divided by height (centimeters) squared, a measure that provides an index commonly seen in the range of 12 to 30 (or even higher in groups in which obesity is a common phenomenon). Generally speaking a BMI of 27 and over indicates obesity, and is associated with a high risk of diabetes and other serious health problems. BMI levels of 25–27 are considered to be "overweight"; 20–25 is called the desirable, "normal" range, and those below 20 are called "underweight" or "undernourished." Jenike (2001:225) states flatly that a BMI of 18.5 (or lower) is a recognized indicator of chronic energy deficiency (citing Ferro-Luzzi et al. 1992; James et al. 1988) and provides a figure (8.1) showing that the Dobe Ju/'hoansi have the lowest BMI (average less than 18.5 for females of all ages) among studied hunter-gatherer groups.

266

Patricia Draper and Nancy Howell

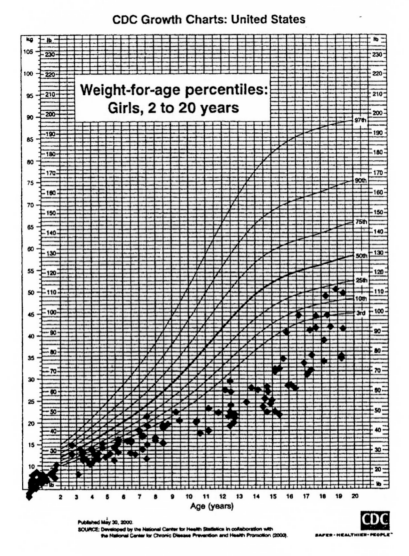

Figure 12.1. Weight-for-age percentiles: Girls, 2 to 20 years

Figures 12.5 and 12.6 show the BMIs for the 165 Ju/'hoan children who
are the basis for the height and weight analyses. All of the indices are
under 20, even those who are considered "chubby" Ju/'hoan children. Although there is no correlation between age and BMI overall for the
Ju/'hoansi, among the children there is a strong (quadratic) relationship

CDC Growth Charts: United States

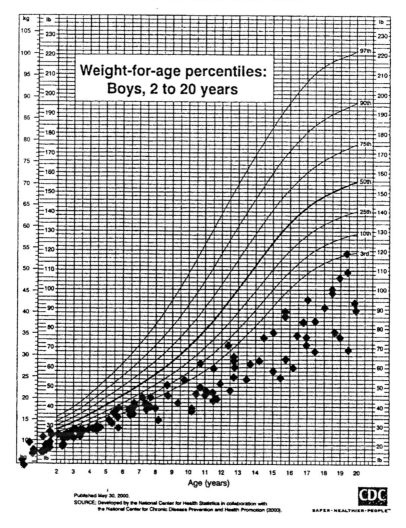

Figure 12.2. Weight-for-age percentiles: Boys, 2 to 20 years

between BMI and age, as can be seen in Figures 12.5 and 12.6. The correlation of age and BMI is $r = 0.65$ for girls and $r = 0.63$ for boys, accounting for about 40 percent of the variance in BMI by age, with high scores and high variance for the youngest and the oldest children, with low scores (and low variance) for the children 5–15. An "expected BMI" is calculated for each child from that quadratic equation, and subtracted from the BMI at

CDC Growth Charts: United States

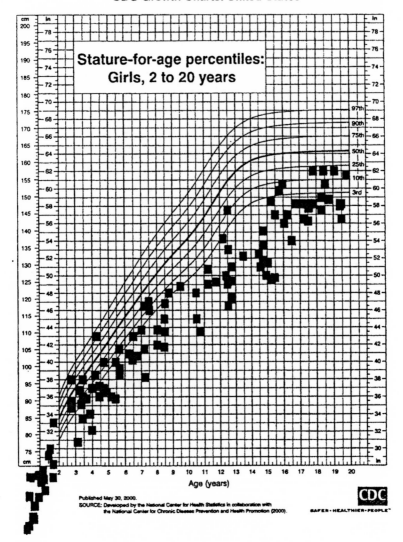

Figure 12.3. Stature-for-age percentiles: Girls, 2 to 20 years

the time of observation, providing a measure (BMIDiff) of body mass adjusted for age and sex of Ju/'hoan children (note that we are *not* adjusting here by the standards for industrialized societies), and normalized with a mean of zero and a standard deviation of one, showing how much above (fat) or below (skinny) the expected that particular child is at that time.

CDC Growth Charts: United States

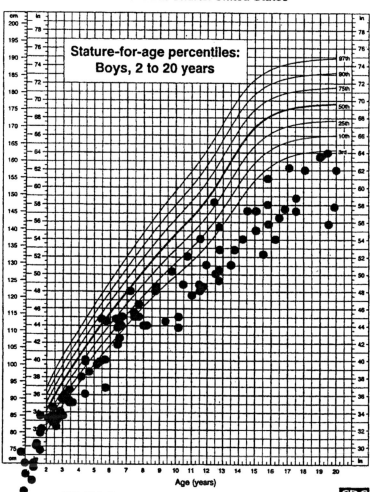

Figure 12.4. Stature-for-age percentiles: Boys, 2 to 20 years

The children show no over all difference in BMI by sex.[3] Their scores range from 3 to –3. This measure will be our primary indicator of the nutritional status of particular Ju/'hoan children to compare with their individual characteristics.

We acknowledge that we have not exhausted the possibilities of the relationships between BMIDiff and other variables. We are only looking at

CDC Growth Charts: United States

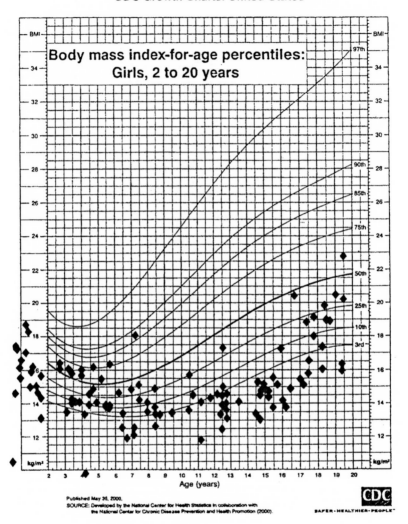

Figure 12.5. Body mass index-for-age percentiles: Girls, 2 to 20 years

the BMI adjusted for age and sex at one point of time, and it may be that we need to average a series of such measures. And it may be that the variables we explore here need to be combined in some way, or are only causal over part of the range of BMIDiff or at particular ages. We are continuing to explore these possibilities.

CDC Growth Charts: United States

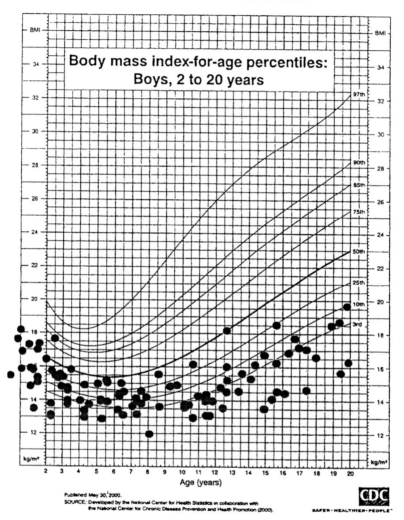

Figure 12.6. Body mass index-for-age percentiles: Boys, 2 to 20 years

KINSHIP VARIABLES AS CONTRIBUTORS TO CHILDREN'S NUTRITIONAL STATUS

We have 165 children on whom we have data regarding nutritional status and kinship connections. We asked two questions of our data. First: What benefit might children have received by having a full complement of living lineal ascendants as contrasted with having only a few? As extreme examples, we have children in our sample who possessed all six lineal ascendants (mother, father, and four grandparents; see Table 12.1). A few children were full orphans and lacked all four grandparents. However, the overwhelming majority of our children (93 percent) had at least two lineal ascendants (see Table 12.2).

Because we did not measure the direct contribution of the ascendants to the child, and because we did not know what duration of co residence our children had actually shared with each of these people over the course of their lives, we did not distinguish among adult ascendants who actually lived with the children versus those who did not. The hypothesis, simply expressed, was: Children who have more rather than fewer living lineal ascendants will have better outcomes as measured by BMIDiff and by improved survivorship among their sibs.

We reasoned, on the other hand, that siblings were competitors and would negatively impact BMIDiff, and that having more sibling competitors and having more siblings under 19 years would be especially harmful to children. The variables that concern sib survivorship are NkdAliv (number of a child's living siblings) and NkdUn19 (number of a child's

Table 12.1   Number of Children Who Have Different Numbers of Lineal Ascendants (*N* = 165 children)

N *children*	N *ascendants*
3	0
9	1
44	2
41	3
38	4
24	5
6	6

Table 12.2   Number of Children by Living Status of Mother and Father (*N* = 165 children)

	Mother	*Father*
Alive	154	121
Dead	11	40
Unknown	0	4

siblings who were under 19 years) We have already shown that the relationship between BMIDiff and age is curvilinear for our sample with high scores and high variance for the youngest and the oldest children and with low scores (and low variance) for the children 5–15 years. Therefore our analysis separates the children into different age groups. The youngest children are at the greatest risk of undernutrition because their growth trajectories are the steepest. We reasoned that all siblings might count as a drain on parents' resources but those under 19 years were particularly unlikely to be self-supporting in this society. Children who had several sibs under 19 were likely to face the most serious competition for resources.

Children Less Than Six Years

We consider children under six years separately because children in this age group had better BMIDiff scores and higher variance in comparison with older children. For children under six years of age our hypotheses about kinship factors that might influence MBIDiff were not supported. The total number of ascendants (TotAsc) did not improve a child's nutritional status. TotAsc was not significantly related to the child's number of siblings, or the number of siblings who were under 19 years, or their probability of surviving, after controlling for the mother's age. This step (controlling for mother's age) was necessary because we knew that as mothers aged their numbers of children, on the average, increased and the probability that the children's grandparents would die also increased (see Table 12.3). We suspect that children under six are so immediately dependent upon adequate nutrition that they either obtain the minimum or die, therefore, not a lot of children are found in various stages of undernutrition in the earliest age group.

Table 12.3   Children Six Years and Under

		r	p	n
TOTAsc	BMIDiff	−0.033	.796	63
BMIDiff	NkdAliv	−0.128	.318	63
BMIDiff	NkdUn19	−0.039	.764	63

Children 6-15 years

The children of the six- to 15-year age range were the thinnest children on the measure of BMIDiff. As we noted above, we looked at indicators of numbers of ascendants and numbers and types of sibling competitors as predictors of poor nutritional status. As can be seen below, we report no significant findings for the correlates of BMIDiff in this group of cases. Number of ascendants shows a strong negative correlation with sibling numbers, an effect that contradicts our hypothesis that lineal elders play a beneficial role (see Table 12.4). The likely explanation is that older mothers have more living children (siblings of the child) and that older mothers have fewer living ascendants (grandparents of the child). After controlling for mother's age we find no strong association between the total numbers of as ascendants and the sibling variables.

Again we find having more ascendants does not help the nutritional indicator and having more sibs and more younger sibs does not correlate with low BMIDiff. Somehow, families are managing to feed their children, adequately or inadequately, without being highly influenced by the family composition.

Table 12.4   Children over Six Years and under 15 Years

		r	p	n
TOTAsc	BMIDiff	−0.072	.567	66
BMIDiff	NkdAliv	−0.006	.962	66
BMIDiff	NkdUn19	−0.082	.521	66

THE BEHAVIORAL VARIABLES

We turn now to the behaviors of Ju/'hoan children and ask whether the differences among the children in their nutritional status as indicated by BMIDiff bears any relationship to indicators of their physical vigor. Our behavioral indicators are taken from observations conducted by Draper on a subsample of children also measured and weighed by Howell and Lee in the same time period. Given that all Ju/'hoan children show low BMIs in comparison with other populations, we expected that the behavioral profiles of the most poorly nourished children would show evidence of lowered physical activity. As stated previously, the children of approximately ages 6-15 are the thinnest. In the scan samples the following kind of information was noted: the child's whereabouts in terms of his or her household or home camp, the child's distance from the home base, all the names and kinship relationships of the people who were in the child's "immediate presence," and the total number of these people; the whereabouts of the child's mother or father; whether the child was in physical contact (touching) with another person. If the child was absent at the time of the observation, information was collected later for the child's location, associates, and reason for absence. At the conclusion of each scan sample, three or four sentences were written describing the child's apparent activity at the onset of the observation and what his or her physical posture was, whether sitting, standing, walking, running or otherwise engaged in vigorous activity.

Our findings are presented for children under six years and for children 6–15 years. There were 51 children, ranging in age from one to 15 years on whom we collected data on behavior, weight, and height. The sample of 51 children is composed of children on whom we have a minimum of three and maximum of ten observations each. The children's ages are shown in Table 12.5.

Table 12.5   Distribution of Children's Ages

Child age	Number in Category
<1 year	10
<2 years	3
<3 years	5
<4 years	4
<5 years	4
<6 years	0
<7 years	4
<8 years	6
<9 years	2
<10 years	0
<11 years	4
<12 years	4
<13 years	1
<14 years	2
<15 years	1
<16 years	1
	N = 51

The children observed in the study were not always available for observation due to the frequent mobility of some families. As a result, total number of observations per child was not the same. We converted raw "counts" of behaviors exhibited in each observation to proportion scores, achieved by dividing the number of times a particular behavior occurred by the number of ratable observations on that child. This meant that children with unusually high numbers of observations did not weigh disproportionately in the final analysis. We used the following variables from Draper's scan samples of children as predictors of BMIDiff:

- Percent Touch (PcTouch): child is in physical contact with another person)

- Percent in Close Presence of Mother (PMoClose): mother is in child's interactive group)
- Percent in Close Presence of Father (PFaClose): father is in child's interactive group
- Average Number of Children Present (AvKidPre): children in child's interactive group)
- Percent Low Activity (PLoAct): child is sleeping, resting, or sitting)
- Percent In or Near Home Village (PcClose)

Our reasoning was that in the face of nutritional scarcity children would have conserved energy and would have contrasted with better nourished children on these variables. In fact, the intercorrelations of these variables suggests that they cluster together. Below we list our hypotheses in which on various measures, we expect children with low scores on BMIDiff will have a more inactive behavioral profile.

- Children frequently in physical contact with another person would be quiescent.
- Children frequently in close physical proximity to the mother or the father were more quiet than children who were away from a parent.
- Children frequently observed sleeping, sitting, or lying down were expending less energy than children who were observed standing, running, or otherwise engaged in vigorous activity.
- Children in close physical proximity to fewer children were physically less active than children who typically associated with more children.
- Children most often observed close to the parents' hearth fires were expending less energy than children more often found at a distance from the village.

Our results are presented below in two tables for children less than six years (Table 12.6) and for children over six years and less than 16 years (Table 12.7). We combine the children into these rather large age categories for two reasons: the small sample size requires some collapsing of ages in order to achieve some statistical power and because the height and weight data indicate that the younger children showed different patterns of body mass index in comparison with the older children. We use "under six years of age" as the cutoff point for young children because Draper's behavioral sample happened to include no children who were age five.

Our prediction that the nutritional indicator BMIDiff would be associated with various behavioral indicators of low energy expenditure was confirmed only in the finding that showed low physical activity (PLoAct) was negatively correlated with BMIDiff (meaning that the thinner children

Table 12.6   Children Six Years and Under

Variable	Variable	R	p	n
BMIDiff	PcTouch	0.053	.844	16
BMIDiff	PLoAct	−0.524*	.037	16
PcTough	PLoAct	0.592**	.002	24
PcTouch	PMoClose	0.691**	.00	25
PMoClose	PLoAct	0.517**	.010	24

*Significant at the .05 level.
**Significant at the .01 level.

Table 12.7   Children Ages Six to 15 Years

Variable	Variable	R	P	n
BMIDiff	PcTouch	0.164	.491	20
BMIDiff	PLoAct	−0.031	.491	20
BMIDiff	PFaClose	−0.756**	.000	20

**Significant at the .01 level.

had an energy-conserving style). However, the variable that measures physical activity (PLoAct) is itself correlated with touching another person. Inactive children were high on physical contact. Inactive children were frequently in close association with the mother (PMoClose). A number of behavioral indicators that we predicted would *separately* be associated with low energy expenditure are in fact significantly associated with each other, but *not* with BMIDiff itself, as can be seen in Table 12.6.

We recognize that in Ju/'hoan society, nursing children, all those in their first three years, and some of the older children are closely associated with their mothers and that it was quite possible that the mothers of especially thin children might confine their activities and act in other protective manners that could impair the activity of the children. We therefore looked for behavior correlates of BMIDiff in the children four to six years who were of interest for two reasons: they were physically mature enough to exercise some independent action, even if their mothers wished to confine them, and they fell within the age range of children we knew to show the greatest variance in the BMI. Our sample size, already small, becomes smaller still with this age restriction. The only correlate of BMIDiff to reach significance for the four- to six-year-olds was PcLoAcT (percent low activity) ($r = -0.921$, $p = .026$, $n = 5$). This result is in line with our expectations: the thinnest children who were of an age to exercise some independent action were the most inactive.

For older children, ages six- to fifteen years old, BMIDiff is associated with only one of the behaviors and not one that we predicted would be a manifestation of an energy-conserving style. We found that older children who were low on the nutritional indicator were frequently in close association with their fathers (PFaClose) ($r = -0.756$, $p = .000$). We speculate that these thinner and older children gravitated to their fathers, perhaps because they were displaced by their younger sibs from their mothers. It is worth noting that there is no significant association between the variables that measure a child's close proximity to the mother and the child's close proximity to the father for children of either age group. In other words, the children who are often with their fathers are not also often with their mothers. Perhaps the most interesting finding among the behavioral indicators is that there is no association for older children between BMIDiff and percent low activity ($r = -0.031$, $p = .897$), nor an association between BMIDiff and the numbers of children in close association with the observed child. We predicted that children who were conserving energy would avoid clusters that included several children, thinking that a high concentration of children would call forth higher levels of activity.

CONCLUSION

In this chapter we addressed three topics: (1) We examined the pattern and variation in Ju/'hoan growth and development in childhood and adolescence and the comparison of the !Kung statistics with those from other populations. (2) We explored the possibility that factors of kinship and family composition might predict children's nutritional status. But we did not find empirical support for this possibility. (3) We looked at differences in the behaviors of children for an indication of low energy expenditure and found a modest correlation (though in the predicted direction) between the nutritional indicator and level of physical activity. Thin children aged six years and below engaged in low-activity behavior. However, this latter finding did not hold for the older children.

The findings about the absolute differences in stature and body mass index for !Kung in comparison with other groups did not surprise us, though we think many of our readers will (may) not have appreciated the extent of the contrast.

Our findings regarding the effect of such demographic variables as numbers of senior kin and sibling competition went contrary to our initial hypotheses. We expected children to benefit from having a full complement of parents and four grandparents, yet we found no such relationship. Further, the discovery that neither the number of a child's siblings nor the number of young siblings bore strong relationships to nutritional status ran contrary to our hypothesis that numerous siblings would be reflected in a poorer physical condition in the children. Children prospered or not, regardless of these particular features of family constellation. In a last effort to wring evidence that dissimilar family characteristics were contributing to nutritional inequality, we looked at the associations between BMIDiff vs. low activity, physical contact, and mother and father closeness to a child while controlling for maternal age. We found no support for the possibility that mothers' ages were affecting the interaction of their children's behaviors with nutritional status.

Our expectations that children with low BMIDiff would show an overall profile of reduced physical activity characterized by reduced spatial range, less time spent with children, and more time in physical contact and with their mothers were not strongly supported. Instead we found very few significant and direct associations between a poor BMIDiff score and behavioral variables we thought would be associated with an energy-conserving style. With the exceptions that children under six years of age showed a significant correlation between BMIDiff and percent low activity (Table 12.6) and children ages 6-15 years showed a significant negative correlation between BMIDiff and close presence of the father (Table 12.7), we have no other direct links between the measure of poor physical condition and indications of an energy-conserving behavioral profile.

Other explanations are possible. We reported earlier in this chapter that the mean BMIDiff and the variance for children ages 6–15 years were the lowest, in comparison with the younger children. It is possible that the variation in the nutritional indicator was too small to be tested against the behavioral variables we had to work with. It is also possible that the !Kung children were, relative to children elsewhere, more inactive because their physical reserves were less. We plan to explore these points in the future.

The !Kung children are small in stature and low in weight, a point abundantly illustrated in the first part of this chapter. However, our efforts to uncover antecedents that are intrinsic to the social system in which they lived have not been successful. The absence of a "kinship effect" may be a sign of another factor at work. Our results showing no relationship between children's nutritional status and certain kinship variables may be an indication of egalitarian treatment within the family and an indication of a degree of nutritional homogeneity across the population. Perhaps the small size of many of the settlements and their separation from each other by many kilometers meant that few grandparents lived in close proximity to their adult children and were therefore unable to help in ways that could have been reflected in children's nutritional standing. Ju/'hoansi children ate and grew, apparently oblivious to the potential impact of various advantageous and disadvantageous family situations.

We wish to stress the value of data analyses such as we have presented here in which there can be independent investigation of the impact of cultural patterns and practices. Researchers who reported from the 1950s and

1960s have characterized the !Kung as an egalitarian group, lacking incipient patterns of stratification based on gender and wealth (Lee 1968, 1982; Marshall 1957, 1961, 1976). On the basis of our reports of children's nutritional status, it appears that kin groups, some more powerful than others either in influence or in sheer numbers, were not able to gain superior access to resources and then divert them to their own children. The multiple cross linkages created by bilaterality, bilocal residence practices, name relationships, trading relationships, and the pervasive rule on sharing were apparently holding at the time of the study.

We hope that follow-up work will be done on the same population now living under very different conditions, particularly in terms of adopting settled village life, consuming agricultural crop foods, and attending Western-style medical clinics. Some work of this nature has been done in terms of collecting information of the physical status of !Kung (Hansen et al. 1993). As social scientists we particularly urge that data on physical indicators of health be investigated for their association with internal divisions within the society such those based on age, gender, household, kinship, and other contextual factors that can have crucial, albeit often invisible, significance for variation among individuals.

Our study reports on relationship of nutritional and other indicators for children at a particular time period. Forthcoming work by Howell will address nutritional differences among adults and children and effects of seasonal variation for the population at the same time period.

NOTES

1. National Institute of Health grant to Harvard University, 1967–69; principal investigators, Irven DeVore and Richard Lee.

2. Scan samples, sometimes called "spot observations" or "instantaneous observations" are brief observations conducted in very short intervals of time. This method typically has one individual as the focus of the observation. The observer records a small number of behavioral variables that are of theoretical interest to the investigator. Because the time devoted to any one sampling of behavior is small, repeated observations can be conducted on the same subject, or multiple subjects, thus building up a behavioral profile in which one can assess, for example, the effects that season, time of day, geographical location, or some other contextual factor may have on the behaviors of interest.

3. The analysis of Body Mass Index for !Kung children and adults proceeds in three stages. The first is merely calculating the standard index for each individual on the occasions during 1967–69 at which we have measures of height and weight (BMI = (wt(kgs)/ht (cms)squared)). In childhood, both sexes start life with a BMI around 16, which declines on average to a lifetime minimum in mid-childhood, around age 7–8. BMI typically increases in adolescence, at a somewhat younger

age for girls than for boys, but overall the differences between the sexes are small. After menarche the girl's increase in body weight takes the form of increases in fat deposits, as shown on their skin fold measures, while the boys' increases in weight are muscle-based, and their height goes on increasing to higher ages. Because BMI has characteristic changes with age, our analysis standardized for age and sex differences by calculating the "expected" BMI from the observed. The age pattern for the two sexes is similar, but we see that girls have somewhat lower expected BMI throughout childhood than boys, and we note that their expected BMI increases more quickly and sharply than that of boys during adolescence.

When we subtract Expected BMI from Observed BMI for individuals, to create a measure of "BMI Difference", we have a measure which allows a clearer view of the characteristics of those individuals who are "fatter" or "thinner" than average for their age-sex group. There are no significant differences between the sexes in childhood in BMI Difference.

4. See also Wiessner (1981) and Wilmsen (1982) for discussion of hxaro relationships and seasonality on nutritional variables on this same population, though for a later time period than the one that is the basis for the data reported in the current chapter.

IV

Social, Emotional, Cognitive, and Motor Development

Photo 4.   Aka infant plays with machete. Courtesy of B. Hewlett

Introduction

Michael E. Lamb

In the next four chapters, our focus shifts from patterns of childcare to child development. Of course, how children develop is, in part, a function of the ways in which they have been treated and so, not surprisingly, the older individuals (parents and alloparents) discussed in the preceding chapters reappear in the chapters that follow. In addition, aspects of development—especially motor and cognitive development—were discussed while pondering why humans have such a long period of childhood dependency. Hrdy (Chapter 3), too, addressed developmental issues in her analysis of the circumstances that potentiate cooperative breeding and childcare, while the development of attachment was discussed at length by Konner (Chapter 2).

Although the importance of social interactions and relationships is evident in each of the chapters that follow, the extent to which the other parties actively seek to influence the youngsters' behavior varies. Thus, for example, Takada (Chaper 13) describes in some detail how nursing !Xun mothers stimulate their young infants in ways that promote nursing, nutrition, and motoric development, whereas Fouts and Lamb (Chapter 14) underscore the extent to which Bofi mothers let their toddlers decide when to wean themselves and Kamei (Chapter 16) notes that adults avoid interfering with their children's play. Two of the chapters in this section address the affective quality of the relationships between children and others in their community (Fouts and Lamb, Chapter 14; Hewlett, Chapter 15), and similar issues were addressed earlier in the book, both by proponents of evolutionary theory (Konner, Chapter 2) and other researchers who focused on the quality of child-adult interactions (Ivey-Henry et al., Chapter 9). And both Takada (Chapter 13) and Kamei (Chapter 16) develop aspects of the cultural approach introduced by Bird David in Chapter 4.

Takada's account of nursing among the !Xun complements earlier reports of the ways in which nursing provides a context for socially important interactions. Whereas Kaye (1982) emphasized the ways in which Western mothers jiggled their babies and nipples in order to extend the duration of nursing bouts (and, concomitantly, increase the length of interbout intervals) and teach babies the rules of reciprocal social interaction, the !Xun mothers studied by Takada seemed less concerned about promoting social skills or maximizing the amount of milk consumed per nursing bout and, if anything, more interested in promoting motor and muscle development. Their behavior is consistent with reports that African infants are motorically advanced relative to infants in industrialized European and American cultures (Super 1981), as well as with reports that face-to-face social interaction with infants is much less common in African societies than it is in most of the Western industrial societies that have been studied (e.g., Hewlett et al., 1998). Vocal conversations with infants are simply not prominent in African societies [see Konner (1976, Chapter 2 in this volume), and LeVine et al. (1994) for exceptions], including hunter-gatherer societies, although infants in these cultures are held much more and are seldom if ever, alone, while the "gymnastic" behaviors described by Takada may represent salient social communications that have implications for social and emotional development. Such kinesthetic interactions are likely to be more salient when infants are almost always in skin-to-skin contact with others even when the parents and alloparents are not explicitly seeking to socialize their infants.

Cultural differences in explicit commitment to the exercise of social influence over young children are also apparent in the chapter by Fouts and Lamb. Indeed, the Bofi forager mothers described here characteristically allow their children to decide, not only when and how much to nurse, but also when to cease nursing altogether. Clearly, the behaviors of hunter-gatherer mothers do not reflect disinterest or lack of commitment: Their availability throughout the first years of life is near total. Instead, all they may lack is the contemporary Western belief in the superordinate importance of early experiences.

Kamei's discussion of play among the now relatively sedentary Baka also underscores the extent to which parents in such non-Western societies allow children a much more active role in shaping their own interactions and experiences and do not promote parental interference in the service of "socialization." The behavior of children is influenced by that of adults in either case, of course; the difference lies in the extent to which adults actively seek to shape children's development, as opposed to providing models that their children can imitate and emulate.

It is important not to misinterpret the passivity of the parents described in these chapters. As all the contributors to this volume make clear, forager parents are emotionally and physically committed to their children, well aware of the many threats to their very survival. One might argue, in fact, that the self-consciously active roles in socialization assumed by parents in industrial societies are designed not so much to maximize their impact but to buttress their own self-importance.

Whereas children in Western industrial societies are predominantly raised by parents (especially mothers) in isolated nuclear families, often supported by a changing array of paid assistants (babysitters, care providers, and nursery and elementary school teachers), children in hunter-gatherer societies grow up in small groups of individuals who typically know one another well and are all committed to the welfare of young group members. As a result, there is a much greater potential for meaningful and socially significant relationships in foraging societies than in industrial societies. Their subjective meaningfulness is well-illustrated here by Bonnie Hewlett's evocative description of Aka adolescents' wistful and emotion-laden reflections on those they have lost through death. Western children "lose" friends often too, of course, but these transitions due to migration and relocation appear to be shrugged off by American children, in particular, whereas Hewlett recounts more impressive levels of grief among Aka adolescents whose friends and relatives have died. It is also noteworthy that these adolescents mourned the social and emotional losses, whereas their peers among the neighboring agriculturalists emphasized their material losses. Such differences and observations again make clear that the diminished societal focus on explicit socialization should not be misinterpreted as disinterest in the welfare and well-being of others. Stated differently, hunter-gatherer and Western industrial societies may differ not with respect to the formative importance of social interaction and relationships, but only with respect to the adults' convictions regarding the salience of these experiences.

13

Mother-Infant Interactions among the !Xun

Analysis of Gymnastic and Breastfeeding Behaviors[1]

Akira Takada

The San are indigenous to southern Africa and have been the subject of extensive research. In the domain of caregiving behaviors and child development, researchers believe that the San can provide vital clues toward understanding the species-specific essence of caregiver-infant interactions in humans (cf. Blurton Jones 1972; Blurton Jones et al. 1996; Draper 1976; Konner 1972, 1973, 1976, 1981; Zelazo 1983).

This chapter aims to broaden this discussion and provide fruitful insights for future study. The chapter focuses, particularly, on two characteristic caregiving behaviors of the San: "gymnastic" behavior and frequent breastfeeding. Some researchers have assumed that features of these behaviors developed in association with a nomadic way of life that was based on hunting and gathering activities, as discussed in the following section.

"GYMNASTIC" BEHAVIOR

The San consist of several clusters of people. The Ju/'hoan,[2] who constitute one of these clusters, have been more studied than the other groups (Barnard 1992). In their traditional settings, Ju/'hoan caregivers frequently keep infants standing or jumping on their lap, beginning several weeks after birth (Konner 1973, 1976). This behavior is referred to as "gymnastic" behavior in this chapter. Other peoples in East and West Africa also practice gymnastic behavior. For instance, Super (1976) reported that mothers in a Kipsigis farming community in western Kenya started to make their infants jump (holding the infant under the arms and bouncing him or her on her lap) when the infant was about one month old. Later, mothers deliberately taught the infant to sit and walk in a standard way. A similar form of training has been recognized among 12 other groups in East Africa (Super 1976), as well as in the Bakongo of Kongo-Brazzaville (Bril et al. 1989). Additionally, it has been reported that Bambara women in Mali say that one should stretch, swing, and suspend the infant in order to develop the bone and muscle structure (Bril et al. 1989). LeVine et al. (1994) have reported that caregivers among the Gusii agriculturists in Kenya "shake" infants in response to crying.

Gymnastic behavior induces the stepping reflex in an infant. This reflex, also called the "U-shaped" primitive reflex, is present at birth but usually disappears within the first few months of life. Subsequently, the stepping response reappears when the infant begins to stand and walk (Bly 1994; Cole and Cole 1993). Researchers have suggested that the first stepping reflex completely disappears, and that the early presence of this reflex is irrelevant to subsequent mechanisms involved in later independent walking (Bruner and Bruner 1968). However, Zelazo and his colleagues found that when caregivers continue to engage infants in "gymnastic" exercises, infant stepping does not disappear. Additionally, such continuous exercises result in unaided walking at a younger age (Zelazo et al. 1972; Zelazo 1983).

Konner (1976) showed that neuromotor development, such as independent sitting and the most developed phase of independent walking, was more advanced in Ju/'hoan infants than in their American counterparts. He argued that such precocity results from the exceptional amount of time these infants have spent in the vertical position, through a training routine on the caregiver's lap as well as through continuous holding in the sling. Indeed, many works have confirmed the strong influence of such early experience on neuromotor development (e.g., Hopkins and Westra 1988; Super 1976, 1981).

Konner also emphasized the importance of parental attitude as a motivation for promoting such development. According to Konner (1976), the Ju/'hoan do not believe in the idea of motor milestones occurring through maturation. They insist that a child who is not taught to sit, crawl, stand, and walk will never perform these behaviors and that the bones of a child's back will remain "soft" unless this teaching occurs. Konner (1973, 1976) also suggested that early walking is adaptive to the arid savanna environment. Ju/'hoan mothers carry their infants constantly, both to breastfeed them and to ensure their security. In the traditional mobile subsistence pattern of the Ju/'hoan, caregivers must move over long distances, and children who cannot walk constitute major burdens the mothers must carry (Lee 1979). Therefore, the practice of deliberately accelerating infant motor development might be of considerable antiquity.

BREASTFEEDING

Ju/'hoan young children have an extremely close relationship with their mothers, a degree of mother-infant physical contact much greater than that between their American and English counterparts. Konner (1976) found that in the first months after the birth, infants stayed in physical contact with their mothers for about 70 percent of observational periods (all daylight hours). The rate declined gradually to about 30 percent in the middle of the child's second year (Konner 1976). Traditionally, children are not weaned until they are three or four years old, or until the mother becomes pregnant again (Konner 1976; Draper 1976). Moreover, according to Konner and Worthman (1980), the nursing of 12- to 139-week-old infants lasts only about two minutes at a time, about four times each hour. Infant age does not relate to the bout length or to nursing time. Konner and Worthman (1980) suggested that the constant physical contact sensitizes mothers to any change in their infants' state.[3] Close relationships like these, which provide infants with abundant food, security, and psychological support, have been recognized among other groups of San (Tanaka 1980, 1989).

The Ju/'hoan have a long interbirth interval. According to Lee (1979), the mean birth interval among nomadic Ju/'hoan between 1963 and 1973 was 44 months. This puzzled investigators, because, at that time, the Ju/'hoan did not practice contraception or refrain from sexual intercourse after childbirth (Howell 1979; Lee 1979). Konner and Worthman (1980) postulated that frequent breastfeeding constitutes the key variable in maternal gonadal suppression that could account for the long interbirth interval. Moreover, like the Ju/'hoan, humans have depended on foraging activities for survival throughout most of history. Therefore, Konner and his colleagues proposed that for most of human evolution, mothers carried their infants continuously and nursed them frequently, thus offering them selective advantages such as preventing infants from getting lost and reducing their risk of illness (Konner 1972, 1976, 1981; Konner and Worthman 1980; Barr 1990).[4]

THE PURPOSE OF THIS STUDY

As noted above, research on gymnastic and breastfeeding behavior among the Ju/'hoan has stimulated numerous discussions. However, two mutually related aspects of the study undertaken thus far must be questioned. First, virtually all research on the Ju/'hoan has been carried out in a few, similar locations (Barnard 1992). Although these studies have reconstructed human nature, through the hunter-gatherer childhood (HGC) model (Konner, Chapter 2 in this volume), there are insufficient data to make generalizations even about the San, much less about all human foragers. Accordingly, an empirical inquiry with a comparative perspective has recently commenced (e.g., Hewlett 1996; Konner, Chapter 2 in this volume). It should also be noted that recent research has indicated that marked cultural differences exist among various groups of San. These differences are found in subsistence strategies, residential patterns, politics and ideologies, and kinship systems, among other practices (e.g., Barnard 1992; Kent 1996), whereas in the domain of caregiving behaviors, cultural diversity has not yet been fully explored. This is not to say that previous studies neglected this issue. Draper, for example, noted,

> It is interesting to consider the factors I have described and to speculate how typical they may be of hunter-gatherers in general—how factors of small group size, mobility, and simple technology can affect the interaction of children with adults and the nature of their training in childhood. (1976:217)

To explore cultural diversity more deeply, the present study has focused on the !Xun (or !Xũ) San. This group is highly suitable for studying cultural diversity with respect to caregiving behavior among groups of San, since the !Xun are neighbors of the Ju/'hoan and have close associations with agropastoral peoples (see below).

Second, since the study of child development has emphasized "adaptationist" approaches (e.g., Lee and DeVore 1976; LeVine et al. 1994; Whiting 1963; Whiting and Whiting 1975), it has often been assumed that ecology and subsistence patterns have strongly influenced behavior and thought. Although this argument has acquired both academic and public attention, the assumption itself has not been fully examined. For example, it is highly plausible that not all nomadic foragers engage in gymnastic behavior and continuous maternal holding with frequent nursing and, at the same time, those who do engage in these behaviors are not always nomadic foragers (cf. Barry and Paxson 1971; Bril et al. 1989; Hewlett 1991b; LeVine et al. 1994; Murdock and Morrow 1970; Murdock and Wilson 1972; Super 1976).[5] Hence, further consideration is required as to the relationship between a mobile subsistence pattern and these behaviors.

To study socialization, a model of the cultural structure within which caregiving behaviors arise must be further developed. Super and Harkness (1986) advocated an interesting framework that should be examined in relation to this topic. In their model of a "developmental niche," they postulated that cultural practices, parental ideology, and physical and social setting constitute the most important components of cultural structure affecting child development. It is useful to examine the relationships between these components. A promising starting point is to observe and record people's daily activities in detail. In this respect, the daily context of gymnastic and breastfeeding behaviors has been described anecdotally for the most part (Hopkins and Westra 1988; Konner 1973, 1976, 1977; Super 1976). Quantitative materials are limited to the following works. Konner and Worthman (1980) provided quantitative data on the context in which Ju/'hoan breastfeeding occurs. They observed infants from dawn to dusk (13 hours) over four days, and recorded the behavioral sequence of fretting, crying, and sleeping by infants, as well as nursing and holding by the mother. Unfortunately, they did not analyze the sequence thoroughly. As for foragers of Central Africa, Hewlett and his colleagues examined parental care, including breastfeeding, with regard to this group (e.g., Fouts et al. 2001; Fouts and Lamb, Chapter 14 in this volume; Hewlett 1991b, 1996). Their focus of analysis, however, was on a comparison of the extent of caregiving behaviors in various cultural settings; they did not scrutinize the sequential organization of these behaviors. In other instances, previous studies have not collected quantitative data on gymnastic behavior. In sum, previous research projects have not examined in detail the daily context in which gymnastic and breastfeeding behaviors are practiced. Hence, this study investigated sequential features of these caregiving behaviors, as well as the parental ideology that prompts them. In addition, the research design provides for a "natural experiment," in which the effect of a mobile subsistence pattern on these behaviors is studied, since the !Xun are less nomadic than the Ju/'hoan (see below).

THE !XUN AND JU/'HOAN

The !Xun and Ju/'hoan exhibit several similarities; these similarities form the basis for a "regional structural comparison" (Barnard 1992; Kuper 1979) between the two societies. The two groups share moderately related languages. Since Bleek's (1929) description of the languages, San languages have traditionally been classified into northern, central, and southern language families (Traill and Vossen 1997). According to this classification, both the !Xun and Ju/'hoan languages belong to the northern family. Furthermore, the northern family is subdivided into three groups: NI, NII, and NIII. The !Xun belong to NIII, while the Ju/'hoan belong to NII. Recent works have detailed the similarities of these languages (Heikkinen 1986;

König and Heine 2001). The author's ongoing study has also elucidated
similarities, as well as considerable differences, between these two groups
with respect to kinship and naming systems (cf. Takada 2000, 2002a).

The two societies show clear divisions in terms of history. Researchers
have extensively documented the Ju/'hoan's Kalahari Desert lifestyle (Lee
and DeVore 1976; Lee 1979, 1993). It should be noted that the Ju/'hoan have
been *relatively* isolated from other peoples until recently, although the actual extent of their interaction has been the subject of much debate (Wilmsen 1989; Lee and Guenther 1991). In contrast, the !Xun of north-central
Namibia have had close associations with the neighboring Owambo, an
agropastoral people, for centuries. The !Xun have also undergone drastic
social changes throughout the 20th century. The transformation of their society can be divided into four critical periods (see Takada 2000 2002a):

(1) 1920s–1950s: South Africa started to dominate present-day north-
central Namibia through so-called indirect rule, exploiting the area's people as a cheap labor source. The need for cash pushed both the Owambo
and the San into the southern part of the colony.

(2) 1950s–1970s: After many years of working toward this end, missionaries won the confidence of local people. Most of the San, who had previously lived in small-scale camps, were concentrated in villages under the
control of a mission. These villages developed a flourishing agriculture.

(3) 1970s–1980s: The "liberation movement" became active in this period and an intensifying war interrupted missionary work. During this
period, the San who had remained in north-central Namibia had to rely increasingly on foraging.

(4) 1990s: After Namibian independence in 1990, fighters and refugees,
including San, returned to north-central Namibia. Several development
programs began that had high hopes of success. An important recent
study, however, has reported that the San status and situation has been little improved (Susman 2001).

METHODS

Field research was conducted for seven months (July–October 1998 and
October–December 1999) in Ekoka village, located in north-central Namibia. Missionaries founded the village in the 1950s as a station for their
San project. The leaders of these missionaries came from Finland and a
great number of San became involved in the project. Later, Owambo from
nearby villages gradually immigrated to Ekoka. Agriculture flourished in
Ekoka, partly because the missionaries promoted cultivation among the
San. In the late 1970s, however, the Namibian liberation movement became
active in this area, and most of the missionary activities declined. After

independence, the government and NGOs started several development projects in the area (Takada 2000).

During the study period, Ekoka had a population of 168 !Xun. Data were collected by the following methods. First, based on a list of residents, all houses with a two- to four-month-old infant were visited. The exact time of the visit was not controlled. The visits took place during the dry season, when agricultural activity is less intense, and mothers and infants spend much of the day in their own or in friends' huts or *shebeens*. A total of five infant subjects (two males and three females with a mean age of 2.8 months) were studied. All the subjects could be found on a regular basis in their own hut or in friends' huts inside the village. In every case, the mother was near the infant. Mother-infant interactions were recorded in a natural setting using a video camera. All infants were awake when the recording started. Although all mothers were occupied, mainly, in taking care of their infants, some also engaged in light housework (for example, basket weaving). Table 13.1 classifies the behaviors examined and analyzed in this study. Occurrences of these behaviors were checked every five seconds and behavioral correlations and sequences (i.e., temporal organization) were analyzed.

Second, to provide an example of daily life, a 16-week-old male infant was observed continuously from dawn to dusk over one day. Occurrences of the behaviors listed in Figure 13.1 were checked at one-minute intervals

Table 13.1 Classification of Behaviors

Infant Behaviors
    Moving: apparent movement of the extremities
    Stepping: rhythmical movement of the legs
    Crying: crying aloud or the appearance of crying
    Cooing: soft murmuring, such as "ah" or "coo"
    Smiling: giggling or appearing to smile
    Vocalizing: vocalization other than crying, cooing, or giggling
    Suckling: suckling on a breast
    Hand/finger sucking: sucking his/her hand(s) or finger(s)
    Sleeping: sleeping
Caregiver Behaviors
    Gymnastic behavior: keeping the infant standing or jumping
    Patting 1: holding one's hands under the infant's arms and tapping its body rhythmically
    Patting 2: holding the infant and tapping its body rhythmically (other than Patting 1)
    Jiggling: jiggling the mother's breast or the infant
    Grooming: cleaning or stroking the infant softly
    Verbal talking: talking to the infant
    Nonverbal talking: making nonverbal sounds for the infant
    Gazing: gazing at the infant
    Smiling: smiling at the infant

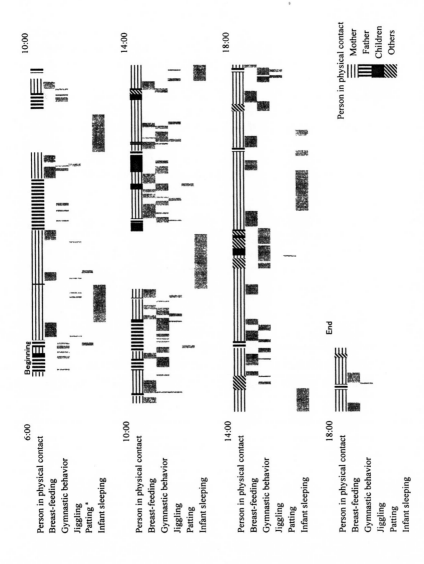

Figure 13.1. Dawn-to-dusk continuous caregiving observation of !Xun infant (16-week-old boy)
[a]Patting 1 or patting 2 (see Table 13.1)

on the recordings. Although such a small sample cannot statistically prove a trend, it does make it possible to draw a tangible image of !Xun infant daily life during the dry season.

Finally, sporadic interviews were conducted with caregivers about gymnastic and breastfeeding behaviors. A number of prepared questions (e.g., on the folk terms used to describe the relevant behaviors and the reasons for the behaviors) structured the interviews. Animated conversations often deviated from the questions and afforded glimpses into parental ideology.

RESULTS AND DISCUSSION

Gymnastic behavior

Figure 13.1 shows that gymnastic behavior occurred once every five minutes on average. The VTR analysis (Table 13.2) shows that gymnastic behavior occurred 6-20 times in approximately 45 minutes, and lasted from 20 seconds to one minute each time. Mothers practiced gymnastic behavior much more than did other youth or relatives (mostly female) of the infant.[6] These data illustrate that !Xun caregivers frequently engage infants in gymnastic exercises. Comparable data have not been published for the Ju/'hoan and other peoples. Thus further research is needed to fully assess the frequency of this behavior.

Table 13.3 shows that gymnastic behavior significantly correlated with stepping in all infants. This indicates that gymnastic behavior induced the stepping reflex and prevented its disappearance in infants over two months of age (Tl, Hl, At, and Dw). The finding supports the hypothesis that the stepping reflex is not innately programmed to disappear after a few months of life but is a flexible behavior that will occur in certain situations (Thelen 1986; Zelazo 1983).

The frequent occurrence of gymnastic behavior among the !Xun may stimulate further debate on this issue. Ju/'hoan caregivers appear to engage infants in gymnastic exercises to accelerate infant motor development, which could reduce caregiver burdens in a nomadic lifestyle (Konner 1976). However, it is difficult to apply this hypothesis directly to the !Xun, as they live in more permanent villages than the Ju/'hoan. The !Xun also make their living from a variety of activities including foraging, livestock herding, agriculture, and laboring for agropastoral groups (Takada 2002a). Therefore, we should tentatively suspend the "reducing-the-burden" hypothesis and inquire into the behavioral context of gymnastic behavior.

Table 13.3 shows a negative correlation between moving and gymnastic behavior in four pairs of subjects. Additionally, Table 13.4 illustrates

Table 13.2 Frequency and Duration of Gymnastic Behavior and Breastfeeding

Subject	Sex	Weeks of age	Length[a] (minutes)	Gymnastic behavior							Breastfeeding[c]		
				Frequency	Caregiver				Duration (minutes)	Frequency	Duration (minutes)	Pause (frequency)
					Mother	Father	Youth[b]	Other				
Nl	Female	6	50	15	15	0	0	0	0.8	13	0.7	0.5
Tl	Female	12	43	6	6	0	0	0	0.3	2	9.2	1.0
Hl	Female	12	45	14	3	0	0	11	0.9	3	0.9	0
At	Male	17	45	15	12	0	0	3	1.0	5	1.9	2.0
Dw	Male	17	44	20	4	0	4	12	0.5	2	1.5	1.0

[a] Length of videotape analyzed.
[b] Unmarried male or female.
[c] Pause: a break in suckling for less than 30 seconds; termination: a break in suckling for more than 30 seconds (cf. Barr and Elias 1988).

Table 13.3 Correlation of Gymnastic and Suckling Behaviors with Other Infant Behaviors

	Gymnastic behavior		Suckling behavior	
Correlation coefficient	+	−	+	−
Moving	1	4	1	3
Stepping	5	0	0	2
Crying	2	1	1	1
Cooing	1	0	0	1
Smiling	1	0	0	0
Vocalizing	1	2	1	1
Hand/finger sucking	0	2	0	1
Sleeping	0	2	1	1

Notes: Data represent the number of subjects who have a significant ($p < .05$; two-sided test) positive (+) and negative (−) Pearson's correlation coefficient between columns (i.e., gymnastic behavior and suckling behavior) and rows (i.e., moving, stepping, etc.).

Table 13.4 Correlation of Gymnastic and Suckling Behaviors with Other Caregiver Behaviors

	Gymnastic behavior		Suckling behavior	
Correlation	+	−	+	−
Gymnastic behavior	—	—	0	5
Patting 1	4	0	0	2
Patting 2	2	0	1	2
Jiggling	1	1	2	1
Grooming	0	2	2	1
Verbal talking	4	0	0	2
Nonverbal talking	4	0	0	1
Gazing	5	0	0	3
Smiling	4	0	0	2

Notes: —, correlation coefficient cannot be calculated because of autocorrelation.

that caregiver behaviors such as patting 1 behavior, verbal talking, nonverbal talking, gazing, and smiling tend to correlate positively with gymnastic behavior. These data suggest that gymnastic behavior occurs in a "cheerful" or "stimulating" atmosphere.

Moreover, Tables 13.5 and 13.6 show a number of interesting tendencies, although the small sample size precludes statistical significance. Table 13.5 shows that the infants were frequently moving, crying, and vocalizing before gymnastic behavior occurred. Table 13.6 shows that caregivers gazed at infants more often than the base rate before gymnastic

Table 13.5   Infant Behaviors before a "Gymnastic" Event and before the Onset of Suckling

Time period	Mean		
	BR	GM	NB
Moving	28.4	43	65.2
Stepping	5.2	5	8.8
Crying	4.6	9.6	27.8*
Cooing	2.2	2.4	6.2
Smiling	0.8	0.6	0
Vocalizing	6.8	16.8	23
Suckling	18.8	3.8	0*
Hand/finger sucking	2	2.8	0.6
Sleeping	8.4	1.4	6.2

Notes: Data denote the mean percentage of the observation time engaged in the given activity. BR, base rate; GM, 10 seconds before the onset of gymnastic behavior; NB, a pause of less than 10 seconds before the onset of suckling, or the 10 seconds before the onset of suckling when the break lasts for more than 10 seconds. Asterisks in the columns of GM and NB indicate that paired *t*-tests showed significant differences (*p* < .05) between BR and GM, and BR and NB, respectively.

Table 13.6   Caregivers' Behaviors before the "Gymnastic" Event and after Breaking Off Suckling

Time period	Mean		
	BR	GM	NA
Gymnastic	24.8	8.8*	6.8*
Patting 1	5	0*	0*
Patting 2	3	2.4	6.6
Jiggling	8	11.2	8.4
Grooming	3.8	1.8	3.2
Verbal talking	8.8	12.2	1.2*
Nonverbal talking	3.2	3	1.2
Gazing	49.8	62	48.2
Smiling	6.4	8.8	10

Notes: NA, pause of less than 10 seconds after breaking off suckling or the 10 seconds after breaking off suckling when the break lasted for more than 10 seconds.

behavior took place. According to the follow-up analysis, the mean rate of crying during gymnastic behavior was 5.8 percent. Three infants (Nl, Tl, and Dw) cried less during gymnastic behavior than the base rate, and the other two (Hl and At) cried at the same rate as the base rate. These data suggest that, in many cases, infants made a fuss just before the gymnastic behavior occurred and that the caregivers soothed the infants by engaging them in gymnastic activity. It is conjectured that frequent gymnastic activity and frequent nursing (see later section) constitute important infant-soothing techniques among the !Xun.

This conjecture is substantiated by the fact that gymnastic behavior brings pleasure to infants (Konner 1976; Korner and Thoman 1972; Zelazo 1976, 1983). Unfortunately, Konner (1973, 1976, 1977) did not report data on the behavioral sequence of the gymnastic exercise among the Ju/'hoan. Thus, we cannot conclude here whether the difference between the two societies in this respect is limited to caregivers' beliefs or whether it extends to their practices as well.

In connection with this, Barr et al. (1991) reported that the duration of crying and fretting behaviors among Ju/'hoan infants was shorter than that of their Western (Dutch) counterparts. They attributed the difference to culturally distinct caregiving behaviors, such as continuous holding and carrying, frequent feeding, keeping infants in an upright posture in a sling, and an infallible and immediate response to infant signals (Barr 1990; Barr et al. 1991). Although Barr et al. (1991) did not mention gymnastic behavior, gymnastic behavior certainly functions like these culturally distinct caregiving behaviors.

In addition to the behavioral sequence, folk accounts of gymnastic behavior support the hypothesis that !Xun caregivers practice gymnastic behavior to soothe infants. In the !Xun language, *!kain* typically means a series of behaviors in which the caregiver keeps his or her hands under the infant's arms and taps the infant rhythmically (i.e., patting 1 in Table 13.1). *!'ubu* is roughly equivalent to "jump" in English. *Khali ma* means to toss something up and catch it. People say that *!kain*, *!'ubu*, and *khali ma* are done to "make infants happy." It is plausible that their historical contact with the Owambo agropastoralists has had some impact on their folk accounts of gymnastic behavior, because *!kain*, *!'ubu*, and *khali ma* correspond to the Owambo-language (*Oshiwambo*) words *tembula*, *nuka*, and *yakela*, respectively. My qualitative observation shows that they do engage in these actions. The Owambo also claim that these actions are undertaken to "make infants happy."

Furthermore, as a probable consequence of historical contact with other peoples, the !Xun have developed several naming systems. Accordingly, each !Xun person has a number of names. *!Kain !xoa*[7] is one such naming system, although further study is needed before we can elucidate its diachronic formation. Most !Xun infants are given a *!kain !xoa* name, such as *Tuotoma, Gongo*, or *Tchatchawa* by their consanguineous kin (mostly their mother or grandmother). In many cases, caregivers repeat the *!kain !xoa* when they practice gymnastic behavior.[8] People stop using the *!kain !xoa* as infants grow. This custom does not seem to be as popular among the

Ju/'hoan (Miller-Ockuizen, personal communication, 2001). The !kain !xoa
utterances appear to exhibit several features of "motherese" or "infant-
directed speech" (hereafter referred to as IDS), such as a higher overall
pitch, preference for certain contours, simple phonation, and the predominance of reduplication. These features serve to create a cheerful atmosphere for gymnastic exercises.

It also should be mentioned that some features of !Xun utterance when
addressing infants may not be compatible with those of IDS that previous
studies have reported thus far. First, !Xun utterances for infants probably
maintain the tonal information of the language, while Grieser and Kuhl
(1988) have reported that IDS in Mandarin Chinese, which uses four distinct tones phonemically, loses some tonal information. Second, !Xun caregivers probably do not aim to facilitate infant language acquisition,
although several studies have argued that caregivers aim to make language easier to learn when addressing infants and young children (Ferguson 1964; Ninio and Bruner 1978). Third, the !Xun language itself has
features of IDS to some extent. For example, frequent use of clicks makes
the narrative rhythmical. These points suggest that the agenda behind
most psychological studies on IDS mediates the developmental theory or
pedagogy of industrialized populations; !Xun caregivers, however, oper-
ate with a different cultural model.[9]

In summary, local interpretations of gymnastic behavior differ between
the !Xun and Ju/'hoan. The !Xun predominantly regard gymnastic behavior as having an infant soothing function, while the Ju/'hoan lay more
stress on its promoting infant motor development. The !Xun have had
close associations with Owambo agropastoralists for centuries. In contrast,
the Ju/'hoan have depended more on a nomadic subsistence pattern until
recently. It is thus plausible that the !Xun came to emphasize "soothing" in
place of "training," due to the development of a sedentary lifestyle, accompanied by interaction with the Owambo.[10]

BREASTFEEDING

Figure 13.1 shows that the mother was in close contact with her infant for
most of the day. The mother was in touch with the infant for 62 percent of
the observation time. The infant stayed in his mother's hut, except for when
the mother took him to a shebeen from 13:52 to 18:44. There were 31 bouts of
nursing. The interval between nursing bouts averaged 17 minutes. Table
13.2 shows a similar tendency. There were from 2–13 bouts of nursing
within a period of approximately 45 minutes, and the mean nursing time
added up to a few minutes.[11] In all observed cases, mothers breastfed their
own infants. Overall, observations show that !Xun mothers nurse their in-

fants briefly and frequently, with short intervals between nursing periods. Interestingly, all these results are nearly identical to those for the Ju/'hoan (Konner and Worthman 1980), despite the fact that the !Xun have adapted to a sedentary lifestyle.

Here, it is important to ask what determines this pattern of breastfeeding. To answer this question satisfactorily, the daily context of breastfeeding among the !Xun was investigated, with the following results. First, observations indicated that !Xun mothers are free to nurse their infants at any time and in any location. In other words, nursing is regarded as the primary work of mothers, to be undertaken in any situation. For example, VTR observations showed that mothers breastfed infants while cooking, sewing, or smoking. Moreover, mothers do not hesitate to nurse their infants in the presence of others.

Second, Table 13.3 shows a negative correlation between suckling and moving in three out of five infants. In addition, Table 13.5 shows that infants cried significantly more than the base rate before suckling. Additionally, infants tended to move or vocalize before suckling took place, though statistically significant differences were not found. These data suggest that mothers nurse their infants to soothe them. This suggestion is consistent with the studies of Konner (1972, 1976) and Barr (1990).

These two findings afford a better understanding of the context of frequent nursing. However, the matter of how !Xun mothers end these brief bouts of nursing is also of interest. Infants will inevitably take a break after a burst of suckling. The clustering of sucks into bursts separated by pauses is unique to humans (Kaye 1977; Kaye and Wells 1980; Masataka 1993). For example, two-week-old infants suckle continuously for 25 seconds on average, followed by a pause (Masataka 1993). Therefore, it is reasonable to expect a few pauses even during a short nursing bout. As predicted, Table 13.2 shows that there were up to two pauses during nursing bouts. These pauses are the key to the short nursing duration.

Three out of five pairs showed a negative correlation between suckling and the caregivers' gaze (Table 13.4). Additionally, Table 13.6 shows that the rate of gazing after a break in suckling was almost the same as the base rate.[12] These results are interesting and the opposite of what might be expected if caregivers concentrate exclusively on breastfeeding. The context in which nursing occurs helps us understand the results. !Xun mothers certainly keep in close contact with their infants and are very sensitive to their needs. However, when infants suckle the mother's breast, infants are often quiet. Subsequently, during infant suckling, mothers seem more relaxed than usual.

In the videotapes, gymnastic behavior was observed seven times after an infant broke off from suckling. Interestingly, in six of the seven cases, breastfeeding terminated with the onset of gymnastic behavior.[13] (By

definition, in Table 13.2, the termination of breastfeeding is a break in suckling that lasts more than 30 seconds.) This is reasonable, because infants
are in a vertical position after the onset of gymnastic behavior, and they
probably stop paying attention to their mother's breast while in this posture. In addition, maternal activity tended to shift away from breastfeeding after the termination of gymnastic behavior. Hence, gymnastic
behavior serves to terminate breastfeeding. Moreover, Table 13.4 shows a
negative correlation between suckling and gymnastic behavior in all pairs.
This negative correlation[14] is a consequence of the fact that both suckling
and gymnastic behaviors occurred frequently and tended to be complementary (see Figure 13.1, too). These findings suggest that mothers frequently alternate between breastfeeding and gymnastic behavior while
their infants are awake.

Note that the rate of jiggling (i.e., jiggling the mother's breast or the infant; also see Table 13.1) after a break in suckling was almost the same as
the base rate (Table 13.6).[15] This result is interesting, as Kaye and Wells
(1980) have reported that mothers in the U.S. frequently jiggled their infants immediately after a pause in suckling. Masataka (1993) also indicated that mothers jiggled their eight-week-old infants for four seconds on
average within one or two seconds after a break in suckling. Kaye and
Wells (1980) additionally demonstrated that the cessation of jiggling
tended to elicit a new burst of suckling in an infant. Furthermore, during
several weeks after the birth of an infant, the duration of jiggling and the
duration of pauses became shorter. Based on these findings, it is thought
that there is a contingent, turn-taking relationship between suckling and
jiggling (Kaye 1977, 1982; Kaye and Wells 1980; Masataka 1993). It is highly
probable that this relationship enables prolonged breastfeeding in the
United States and Japan. In other words, mothers actively work to encourage longer nursing bouts. Conversely, !Xun mothers tend to ignore
their infants for a while after the onset of a break in suckling. That is, mothers do *not* react to the infant *until* the infant starts fretting or crying, though
they are quick responders to those behaviors once they occur (cf. Barr
1990; Konner 1972). The break in suckling thus tends to be longer than, for
example, what Masataka (1993) has reported. Accordingly, the number of
observed pauses, defined as a break in suckling for less than 30 seconds
(Table 13.2), was small and the duration of nursing bouts was short.

The !Xun have some concepts relevant to jiggling. /'a /'ani is an action
whereby someone gently strokes another's body with his or her hand,
while //'ou is a series of actions wherein an individual holds something
and moves it up and down. *Lolo*, a word borrowed from Oshiwambo,
means to hold an infant on one's back or chest and to rock him/her tenderly. Caregivers generally state that they use these behaviors to quiet infants or to make them fall asleep. By contrast, Kaye and Brazelton (1971)
found that mothers in the United States believe that jiggling during pauses

in suckling prompts further suckling. These findings suggest that the /'a /'ani, //'ou, and lolo behaviors in the !Xun differ from the jiggling activity during suckling pauses noted in the United States with regard to both function and folk explanation.

GENERAL DISCUSSION

This study had limitations in terms of its sample size, study area, and duration, making it difficult to generalize from its results. Nevertheless, it provides a number of insights into the study of caregiving behaviors and child development.

First, this study demonstrates the advantage of observing everyday practices in detail. Particularly, features that shape the !Xun breastfeeding pattern, in which mothers nurse their infants briefly and frequently at short intervals, emerged from such observation:

1. mothers could nurse infants at any time and in any location;
2. mothers nursed their infants to soothe them;
3. during suckling, mothers gazed at their infants less than usual;
4. gymnastic behavior sometimes interrupted breastfeeding; and
5. mothers seldom jiggled their infants after a break in suckling.

The last three of these findings have not been reported in previous studies (Konner 1973, 1976, 1977; Konner and Worthman 1980). Moreover, this study demonstrates that gymnastic and breastfeeding behaviors, both of which have been discussed separately, are closely linked. Note that if we had adopted a questionnaire or an experimental method, we might have lost sight of the inherent relevance of these activities; a detailed observational study not only reduces such risks, but also generates new hypotheses for future examination.

Second, this study points to the existence of cultural diversity in the incipiency of caregiver-infant interactions. Kaye and his followers asserted that turn-taking between suckling and jiggling is a fundamental, universal feature of mother-infant interaction (Kaye 1982; Masataka 1993). However, this was rarely observed among the !Xun. This finding implies that the jiggling after a break in suckling may be a culturally distinct caregiving behavior that occurs in countries such as the United States and Japan. It is likely that fretful infant behaviors trigger an interaction between infant and caregiver, and that this is a universal characteristic. However, it is also likely that the form this interaction takes is culturally based. Furthermore, interactions that affect the development of the infant evolve gradually after birth (e.g., the interaction between gymnastic behavior and the stepping response in the !Xun or between jiggling and suckling in the United

States and Japan). Therefore, the investigation of cultural diversity in the processes of early interaction is of great importance.

Finally the assumption that ecology and subsistence patterns essentially determine caregiving practices should be reconsidered. Evolutionary theories, particularly evolutionary ecology, have regarded ecology and subsistence patterns as the ultimate cause of behavior and have seen psychological and physiological factors as proximal causes (Hewlett and Lamb 2002; Blurton Jones et al., Chapter 10 in this volume). These causes are neither necessarily contradictory nor mutually exclusive and thus are assumed to constitute different kinds of explanation (Hewlett and Lamb 2002).

Evidently, it is insufficient to explain the pattern of caregiving behaviors among groups of San by ecology and subsistence patterns *alone*. As demonstrated above, caregivers engage in gymnastic behavior whether their lifestyle is sedentary or nomadic. The interpretation, however, emphasizes "soothing" in the sedentary lifestyle and "training" in the nomadic lifestyle. That is, the relationship between the practice of gymnastic behavior and ecology and subsistence patterns is indirect, and parental ideology seems to fill the gap. We need, therefore, further examination of the semantic organization of such parental ideology.[16] With regard to breastfeeding, the short bout length is probably the product of a behavioral sequence, namely, the infant's break in suckling and the caregiver's response to it, together with relevant parental ideology.

Thus, in order to explain the pattern of caregiving behaviors, we should discuss *relations* between ecology and subsistence patterns, parental ideology, and behavioral sequences, rather than segregating proximal causes from the ultimate cause. And then we should inquire into the processes of transmission of behavior and pattern modification, a perspective shared by evolutionary cultural anthropologists (Hewlett and Lamb 2002). At the very least, this approach would seem vital to the description of socialization in postforaging societies contending with rapid transformation.

ACKNOWLEDGMENTS

I would like to acknowledge the useful comments and suggestions made by Barry Hewlett, Bonnie Hewlett, Melvin Konner, and Michael Lamb on earlier drafts of this chapter.

NOTES

1. This chapter is a revised version of Takada (2002b).

2. Many publications have applied the term !Kung to this group. However, I use the term Ju/'hoan," which constitutes their self-designation, to distinguish them

from the !Xun (see below). Studies have increasingly adopted the term Ju/'hoan or its plural, Ju/'hoansi (cf. Lee 1993).

3. High responsiveness to infant requests was reported for Aka fathers, too (Hewlett 1991). Hewlett (1991) noted that Aka fathers do more caregiving than fathers in any other known society.

4. Konner (1976) pointed out that though the primacy of the mother-infant bond was exceptional, children two years old and younger also had a good deal of physical contact with others.

5. There is considerable discussion on this point; also see Konner's important argument in Chapter 2 in this volume.

6. In the VTR analysis, the father and other adult males did not engage infants in gymnastic behavior. However, such cases were recognized in the dawn-to-dusk observation (Figure 13.1). More data are necessary to discuss the extent of nonmaternal care or alloparenting.

7. *!kain* is defined above, *!xoa* means "name."

8. In the VTR analysis, most of the verbal talk contained *!kain !xoa* (40, 25, and 34 percent of all bouts for Nl, At, and Dw, respectively).

9. Also see Bril et al. (1989), LeVine et al. (1994), and Konner (Chapter 2 in this volume) for insightful discussions on this topic.

10. In this respect, it is worthwhile to describe the differences and similarities of parental ideology across cultures. Unfortunately, comparable materials are not known for the neighboring pastoralists of the Ju/'hoan (e.g., Herero, Tswana) (P. Draper, M. Konner, personal communications, 2003). Interestingly, in other cultures, several distinct views of infant motor development have been found (Hopkins and Westra 1988; Bril et al. 1989; LeVine et al. 1994). For example, according to LeVine et al. (1994), although Gusii caregivers occasionally encourage the infant to stand and walk, these actions were not regarded as necessary for normal motor development. Moreover, infant motor development is generally thought to bring the caregiver more workload. Mobile infants have to be watched, or they stumble into dangerous situations. We can assume the following reasons for this view. First, the sedentary lifestyle did not require Gusii caregivers to move long distances with the children. Thus, they have no strong motivation for promoting infant motor skills. Second, Gusii caregivers, particularly mothers, have much more domestic work, such as cultivation and food processing, than do their Ju/'hoan counterparts. Subsequently, it would be more burdensome for the former to watch a mobile infant.

11. In the VTR analysis, one infant (Tl) seemed to sleep lightly during breastfeeding. Consequently, she had a much longer mean nursing time (9.2 minutes) than the others (see Table 13.2). During that time the mother barely responded to her.

12. The base rate of gazing was 52, 18, 51, 70, and 58 percent of all bouts for Nl, Tl, Hl, At, and Dw, respectively. After suckling, the base rate of gazing was 39, 63, 33, 56, and 50 percent for Nl, Tl, Hl, At, and Dw, respectively. Thus, four mothers gazed at their infants less than the base rate after suckling.

13. Gymnastic behavior after a break in suckling was observed twice for Nl, four times for At, and once for Dw. Breastfeeding terminated twice for Nl, three times for At, and once for Dw.

14. Due to their definitions (suckling = sucking on a breast, gymnastic behavior = keeping the infant standing or jumping), it is unreasonable to expect a positive correlation between suckling and gymnastic behavior. However, suckling still need not correlate significantly with gymnastic behavior.

15. The base rate of jiggling was 10, 1, 28, 0, and 1 percent of all bouts for Nl, Tl, Hl, At, and Dw, respectively, while that after suckling was 9, 0, 33, 0, and 0 percent for Nl, Tl, Hl, At, and Dw, respectively.

16. In this respect, Takada (2004) analyzes the relationship of several interpretations, including "soothing" and "training," of the gymnastic behavior observed among groups of San. The analysis suggests that the concept of a sound body, which is inseparable from strong bones and good blood circulation, might form the basis of these interpretations.

14

Weanling Emotional Patterns among the Bofi Foragers of Central Africa

The Role of Maternal Availability and Sensitivity

Hillary N. Fouts and Michael E. Lamb

In this chapter, we attempt to understand variability in fussing and crying frequencies among Bofi forager children during the weaning process by examining the possible impact of demographic variables and individual differences in caregiver sensitivity. As shown earlier (Fouts 2002; Fouts et al. 2001), the ages and nursing statuses (stage of the weaning process) of the children were not associated with differences in the levels of fussing and crying. For example, children closest in age to weaning did not exhibit more distress then other children, as predicted by evolutionary theorists (Daly and Wilson 1988; Draper and Harpending 1987; Trivers 1974) and many other scholars (e.g., Ainsworth 1967; Albino and Thompson 1956). The goal of this chapter is to examine other factors that may influence levels of emotional distress.

CRYING AND WEANING

Weaning is often viewed as the classic example of parent-offspring conflict. Trivers (1974) predicted that offspring would resist any decrease in parental investment, using "psychological weapons" such as temper tantrums and crying to combat these decreases in investment. Because nursing involves a significant investment, providing nutritional and immunological benefits to offspring (Cunningham 1995), weaning has mostly been viewed as a decrease in investment and therefore as an event that should trigger parent-offspring conflict and elicit protest such as temper tantrums (for a more thorough review of weaning and parent-offspring conflict theory, see Fouts 2002). Since the publication of Trivers's parent-offspring conflict theory, other evolutionary theorists have also proposed that weaning is a "distressful" time for infants and that infants are not eager to be weaned (Daly and Wilson 1988; Draper and Harpending 1987).

In our previous study of weaning (Fouts 2002; Fouts et al. 2001) we found that weaning among the Bofi foragers did not conform to Western scholarly images of weaning. For example, Western scholars suggest that children inevitably resist weaning, and assume that mothers utilize specific techniques and weaning foods to end breastfeeding quickly. Among the Bofi foragers, by contrast, nursing declined gradually prior to its cessation. Bofi forager children stopped nursing of their own accord, and their parents did not employ any specific techniques (e.g., applying hot peppers to their nipples) to speed the process. Likewise, weaning distress or conflict was not observed among Bofi forager children. The weaning process among the Bofi foragers was embedded within a caregiving context; for example, maternal involvement decreased with weaning but weaned children were still cared for by adults rather than by juvenile alloparents. In fact, fathers, grandparents, and aunts provided substantial amounts of care directly before and after weaning.

CRYING IN CHILDHOOD

Most scholars have examined crying in infancy rather than childhood, but Lummaa et al. (1998) offered two hypotheses about intense crying by human infants, which are also relevant to crying in childhood. Specifically, Lummaa et al.'s "historical hypothesis" predicted that infants would cry more in the absence of their parents because infants were rarely left by their parents in evolutionary history. This hypothesis contradicts Bell and Ainsworth's (1972) report that crying occurred more frequently when an infant was within sight and earshot of his or her mother.

Lummaa et al. also predicted that the function of crying is to elicit more care—the "blackmailing hypothesis"—and emphasized that offspring continue to cry in order to elicit and maintain maternal care after weaning, because "the overall probability that the offspring will survive might depend not only on behavior such as nursing, but also on pre- and post-weaning maternal care" (Lummaa et al. 1998:197).

Lummaa et al.'s blackmailing hypothesis and Bowlby's (1958, 1969) attachment theory depict crying as a proximity-promoting behavior and assume that close mother-infant proximity promotes infant survival. Bowlby identified protection from predators as the selective force that promoted mother-infant proximity. By contrast, Trivers (1974) and Chisholm (1993, 1999) suggested that the denial of parental care threatens offspring survival more than predators do. As a result, offspring strive to elicit parental investment especially when parental investment decreases. Chisholm proposed that children adapt their behavior to the particular caregiving strategies that their parents employ. Likewise, Lamb et al. (1984, 1985) explained that infant attachment patterns reflect adaptations to the parents' caregiving styles. When their attachment figures attempt to leave, for example, some infants may be clingy and exhibit marked distress because they are trying to enhance investment by rejecting or unresponsive caregivers.

Contrasting the quality and function of crying among infants as opposed to children, Zeifman (2001) noted that "crying does not disappear during childhood, rather it is encompassed within and elaborated by other recently developed communication skills including, most notably, language" (2001:274). Bell and Ainsworth (1972) also suggested that verbal abilities come to supplement crying in the course of development, and that these abilities contribute to developmental decreases in the amount of crying. Zeifman noted that crying is essentially acoustic communication in infancy, but that it becomes much more visual in early childhood when children cannot only cry for assistance, but can also approach perhaps vocalizing to caregivers to show them how upset they are. Zeifman further explained:

> most children learn to direct crying toward individuals who are highly motivated to provide care for them and inhibit crying in the presence of those who may be disinclined to tolerate it. (2001:275)

If one assumes that mothers are the "highly motivated" individuals that Zeifman described, then her hypothesis contradicts Lummaa et al.'s historical hypothesis, which predicts that crying increases when mothers are absent.

CRYING AND MATERNAL SENSITIVITY

Many researchers have reported significant relationships between maternal sensitivity and infant security (see Ainsworth et al. 1978; Barnett et al. 1998; Bell and Ainsworth 1972; De Wolff and van IJzendoorn 1997; Goldsmith and Alansky 1987; Moran et al. 1992; NICHD 2001a; Vereijken et al. 1997). Bell and Ainsworth (1972) found a positive correlation, near the end of the first year, between crying episodes that were ignored and the frequency of crying. Likewise, infants whose mothers had been responsive cried less frequently than children with less responsive mothers. Bell and Ainsworth explained this pattern by suggesting that infants cry more insistently as a result of their "past history of mother's ignoring tactics" (1972:1180).

Maternal sensitivity is influenced by parents' personalities and developmental histories and should thus remain fairly stable (Belsky et al. 1991), although changes in maternal sensitivity are expected to occur in the context of "major life stress and/or changes in social support" (Vereijken et al. 1997:38). As a result, patterns of maternal sensitivity in early childhood (as described in this chapter) may be representative of maternal sensitivity in infancy. Vereijken et al. (1997) showed that infant security was similarly associated with maternal sensitivity at 14 and 24 months of age.

HYPOTHESES

The following hypotheses were derived from the literature summarized above:

1. Children will cry more frequently when their mothers are absent than when they are present (Lummaa et al. 1998).
2. Children are more likely to cry in the presence of caregivers who are "highly motivated to provide care," such as mothers (Zeifman 2001).
3. Children whose mothers have been less responsive will cry more frequently than children whose mothers have been more responsive.

METHODS

The data presented in this chapter were collected for a larger project concerned with the social and emotional contexts of weaning among the Bofi foragers and Bofi farmers of Central Africa (see Fouts 2002; Fouts et al. 2001). Twenty-two forager children were observed between 1998 and 2001. Bofi forager children were selected for observations if they were between the ages of 18 and 59 months old, and had two living parents. Because only children with two living parents were selected, all of the focal children were perceived (by parents and observer) as healthy at the start of observations. Because of our interest in fussing and crying as it is related to socio-emotional development rather than as it relates to health, observations were discontinued if parents reported that their child was ill.

Observations were made using an on-the-mark regimen. The observer wore a small cassette player and earpiece, which indicated when to record following a twenty-second observation period. Each child was observed for nine hours, distributed across twelve daylight hours with each observation session of 45 minutes followed by a 15-minute rest period. Two children were observed for only seven and a half and six hours due to scheduling conflicts and because one child became ill.

Behavioral Codes

Nursing Categories.   After data collection was completed, Bofi forager children were divided into three categories depending on their nursing status: high nursing ($n = 9$), low nursing ($n = 5$), and weaned children ($n = 8$). Low nursing children were closest to weaning, because the duration of nursing had declined to an average of 7.6 percent of the intervals, compared to an average of 22.4 percent for the high nursing children.

Fussing and Crying.   Although the theorists discussed earlier have addressed crying in general, our codes distinguished between two different kinds of distress vocalizations, fussing and crying, both of which are relevant to the hypotheses evaluated. Crying was coded whenever a focal child had tears coming out of his/her eyes, whereas whining and whimpering without tears were coded as fussing. In the following analyses, crying and fussing occurrences are considered together as "fuss-cry." Fussing and crying that continued through consecutive intervals were considered as bouts.

Maternal Sensitivity.   Physical soothing was coded any time a caregiver tried to quiet or calm a fussing or crying child physically by rocking, patting, and swaying. Nonphysical soothing was coded any time a caregiver tried to soothe a fussing or crying child verbally or visually, perhaps by trying to distract the child by pointing to objects or people, or by speaking or singing to the child. Maternal sensitivity was credited when mothers responded to fuss-cry bouts with physical or verbal soothing in the same observational unit and these frequencies were compared to the overall patterns of distress exhibited by the child.

Statistical Analyses.   Because of the high degree of variability, Welch's *t*-tests were used to compare means. This sample was small and thus both significant differences and nonsignificant differences with p values of .10 are discussed.

ETHNOGRAPHIC BACKGROUND

The Bofi foragers live in the northern regions of the Congo Basin rainforest in the southwest of the Central African Republic (CAR). Like other Central African foragers such as the Aka (see Bahuchet 1985; Hewlett

1991b), they live part of the year in settlements on the outskirts of farming villages and part of the year in camps in the forest.

The Bofi foragers subsist primarily through hunting and gathering; they obtain most carbohydrates by exchanging forest products (e.g., meat, caterpillars, mushrooms) with their neighbors (the Bofi farmers) for manioc. The Bofi foragers are primarily net-hunters, and like other net-hunting foragers, men, women, and children participate in the hunt. Men and women have traditional roles in the net-hunt: men are primarily responsible for scaring the animals, while women guard the nets and trap the animals. Bofi foragers also collect a variety of insects, snails, leaves, yams, mushrooms, and fruits.

The Bofi foragers are egalitarian, and do not designate chiefs or give special power to individuals because of age or gender. They are loosely patrilineal, recognize membership in patriclans, and generally live patrilocally after two to seven years of matrilocal residence right after marriage during which husbands perform bride-service for their wives' families. The majority (90 percent) of marriages are monogamous and a minority (10 percent) are polygynous. The Bofi foragers have a total fertility rate (TFR) of 5.54, with infant (birth to 12 months) and child mortality rates (birth to 15 years) around 20 and 40 percent, respectively.

Bofi forager parenting is characterized by close physical proximity in infancy and early childhood, with an emphasis on adult alloparenting rather than juvenile or sibling alloparenting. Bofi forager parenting is quite permissive and indulgent by Western standards. Children spend more time in close physical contact with parents, and are rarely directed or punished by parents. Children are allowed to play with knives, machetes, and campfires without the warnings or interventions of parents; this permissive parenting style has been described among other forager groups as well (see Hewlett 1991b; Marlowe, Chapter 8 in this volume). Prior to weaning, two- to three-year-old children are left in camp from time to time during the day when parents leave to hunt or gather in the forest; however like the Hadza (Marlowe, this volume), children who protest greatly are typically carried along instead. Children are usually left under the supervision of one or two adults during the day, and as Marlowe (this volume) also describes, the supervising adult is not necessarily the most qualified adult and is sometimes simply the most available. For example, an elderly blind women was often left in charge during the day in one of the focal camps, though in other camps one or two adults typically stayed in camp during the day. There is typically not one designated daytime alloparent, but adults (young and elderly) informally rotate through the position. This system is supported by extensive sharing patterns, because the adults who stay in camp are given food by individuals who went to the forest that day.

Bofi forager children generally nurse until they are three or four years of age, and likewise have an interbirth interval (IBI) of three to five years.

Bofi forager mothers reported that it was their children who decided when to stop nursing; mothers were never observed verbally or physically prohibiting children from nursing. Around the time of weaning, children were not given special "weaning foods," but instead ate an array of food similar to the diet of older children and adults.

PATTERNS OF FUSSING AND CRYING

Nursing Status and Age

As reported by Fouts (2002) and Fouts et al. (2001), nursing status did not predict frequencies of fussing and crying. Weaning distress or resistance, which are commonly predicted (see Albino and Thompson 1956; Daly and Wilson 1988; Trivers 1974), were not observed either. Three-year-olds who nursed infrequently did not fuss or cry more than three-year-olds who nursed frequently (see Fouts 2002), suggesting that nursing duration did not predict frequencies of crying among Bofi forager children as others have predicted (Daly and Wilson 1988; Trivers 1974).

There was no significant correlation between age and the frequency of fussing and crying, although younger children were expected to cry more frequently than older children (Zeifman 2001), suggesting that factors besides age influenced the fuss-cry patterns of Bofi forager children. Bout length was positively correlated with age (Pearson's $r = 0.50$; $p = .02$), however, indicating that older children had longer bouts of fussing and crying whereas younger children had more frequent but shorter bouts. This may be because three- and four-year-old children were regularly left in camp when their parents went to the forest, whereas one- and two-year-old children were carried along by their parents. This factor is noteworthy because parents are presumably more motivated than other adults (e.g., inclusive fitness benefits) to comfort young children (Zeifman 2001). Furthermore, if we assume that parental soothing is usually effective, then three- to four-year-old children may have had longer bouts than younger children because their crying did not elicit soothing responses from alloparents or because soothing by alloparents was ineffective. This hypothesis is examined later in the chapter.

EVALUATION OF HYPOTHESES

Do Children Cry More Frequently When Their Mothers Are Absent?

The average length of fuss-cry bouts was substantially longer when mothers were absent (4.76 intervals, SD 3.39) than when mothers were present (2.97 intervals, SD 1.30), though these differences were not statistically significant ($t(8) = 1.54$; $p = .16$, NS). Interestingly, although children had longer fuss-cry bouts in the absence of their mothers, most of their fussing and crying occurred in the presence of their mothers (3.79 percent of intervals) rather than when their mothers were absent (1.80 percent of intervals) [$t(29) = 2.33$; $p = .03$]. Lummaa et al.'s historical hypothesis was not confirmed, however, because Bofi forager children fussed and cried more frequently (overall percentage of intervals observed) when their mothers were present.

Do Children Cry More Frequently in the Presence of Individuals (Such as Mothers) Who Are "Highly Motivated to Provide Care" (Zeifman 2001)?

Children cried more often in the presence of their mothers but bouts of crying were also longer when their mothers were absent. Children were also more likely to receive "no response" to their fussing and crying when mothers were absent (62.18 percent of fuss-cry bouts) than when their mothers were present (34.51 percent of fuss-cry bouts) [$t(11) = 2.23$; $p < .05$]. Mothers were on average more likely (60.30 percent of fuss-cry bouts) than any other caregivers (25.20 percent of fuss-cry bouts, nonmaternal caregivers combined) to respond to the children.

This finding appears to be consistent with Zeifman's hypothesis, but it is unclear why children had longer bouts of fussing and crying when their mothers were absent. Two interpretations are possible: (a) children had longer fuss-cry bouts because they were signaling their mothers to return (i.e., missing their mothers) and therefore could not be soothed by nonmaternal caregivers or (b) children had longer bouts because they were infrequently soothed. These interpretations are evaluated next.

Do Children Who Cry More Frequently Have Mothers Who Are Less Responsive to Their Fussing and Crying?

Table 14.1 displays the frequencies of fussing and crying for individual children. Zie, Zonbo, and Kal fussed and cried more frequently than either their age mates or younger children. Although all the three and four-year-olds were healthy and were left in camp with allomothers when their mothers and/or fathers went to the forest, Zie, Zonbo, and Kal also had unique demographic characteristics determining which individuals took care of them (see Table 14.2). For example, Zie was most often cared for by his maternal grandmother, perhaps because his mother was expecting another child soon and his father was frequently absent on trips to his first wife's camp (approximately ten kilometers away). Furthermore, because

Table 14.1 Focal Child Characteristics

Child Pseudonym	Child's Age (months)	Age Category	Sex	Nursing Status (HN,[a] LN,[b] W[c])	Percentage of Intervals Spent Fussing and Crying
Bara	18.5	1	F	HN	5.67
Boko	18.5	1	F	HN	2.87
Gakodi	18.5	1	M	HN	3.89
Bolee	21	1	M	HN	4.35
Sombo	21	1	F	HN	3.15
Goti	24.5	2	F	HN	6.48
Yeko	25	2	M	LN	6.38
Nassa	26	2	M	HN	3.61
Dee	26	2	M	LN	5.83
Gaisi	27.5	2	M	HN	1.30
Zokon	36.5	3	F	LN	5.37
Yokopi	37	3	F	W	2.59
Yena	37	3	F	LN	1.11
Zie	39.5	3	M	W	8.98*
Zonbo	44	3	M	LN	14.07*
Kosi	45	3	F	W	6.48
Yala	49	4	F	HN	4.07
Lyn	49	4	F	W	0.37
Kanga	53.5	4	M	W	2.13
Kogu	53.5	4	M	W	5.37
Fetigo	57	4	F	W	1.30
Kal	58	4	M	W	11.02*

[a] HN: High nursing frequency (nursed for 16 percent or more of intervals).
[b] LN: Low nursing frequency (nursed for 12 percent or fewer intervals).
[c] W: Weaned (never observed nursing).
*High frequency of fussing and crying relative to peers.

Table 14.2 Child Characteristics

	Zie	Zonbo	Kal
Marriage type	Polygynous	Monogamous	Monogamous
Mother pregnant	3rd trimester	No	No
Younger sibling	No	No	No
Birth order	First	First	Second
Caregiver responsible when mothers were absent	Maternal grandmother	Father	Father's mother's sister

Zie was a first-born child, he did not have older siblings to help in his care. Zonbo was also a first-born child, and he was exclusively taken care of by his mother and father. Kal, on the other hand, had an adolescent sister, but was instead watched by his great-aunt (father's mother's sister) when his parents were absent. His great-aunt, however, was blind and often responsible for several children in camp because she rarely traveled to the forest.

Overall Fuss-Cry Patterns

Zie, Zonbo, and Kal cried more frequently than the other three- and four-year-old children, but their average bout lengths were similar to those of their age mates (Table 14.3). In order to explain why Zie, Zonbo and Kal cried more frequently, we examined the responsiveness of their caregivers (Table 14.4), as well as the children's fussing and crying patterns in the presence and absence of their mothers (Tables 14.6 and 14.8, respectively) and the responsiveness of their caregivers in these two contexts (Tables 14.5 and 14.7, respectively). These data show that Zie, Zonbo, and

Table 14.3 Fuss-Cry Patterns

	Zie	Zonbo	Kal	Averages for other 3- and 4-year-olds[a]
Intervals fussing and crying (percentage of total)	8.98	14.07	11.20	3.20, SD = 2.19
Number of fuss-cry bouts	36	29	27	9.44, SD = 6.88
Average length of fuss-cry bouts (minutes)	2.69	5.24	4.41	3.81, SD = 1.40

[a] Three- and four-year-old focal children, excluding Zie, Zonbo, and Kal.

Table 14.4 Responses to Fuss-Cry Bouts (%)

	Zie	Zonbo	Kal	Averages for other 3- and 4-year-olds[a]
Fuss-cry bouts ignored	72.22	48.28	70.37	35.36, SD = 25.80
Soothing responses to fuss-cry bouts	27.78	44.83	29.63	62.79, SD = 24.87
Scolding responses to fuss-cry bouts	0.00	6.90	0.00	1.85, SD = 5.56

[a] Three- and four-year old focal children, excluding Zie, Zonbo, and Kal.

Table 14.5 Fuss-Cry Patterns When Mothers Were Present

	Zie	Zonbo	Kal	Averages for other 3- and 4-year-olds[a]
Intervals spent fussing and crying (of total)	7.78	7.50	4.26	2.52, SD = 1.72
Average length of bout (minutes)	2.80	3.86	2.56	3.73, SD = 1.49

[a] Three- and four-year-old focal children, excluding Zie, Zonbo, and Kal.

Table 14.6   Responses to Fuss-Cry Bouts When Mothers Were Present

	Zie	Zonbo	Kal	Averages for other 3- and 4-year-olds[a]
Fuss-cry bouts ignored	66.67	52.38	61.11	32.84, SD = 26.70
Soothing responses to fuss-cry bouts	33.33	38.10	38.89	65.31, SD = 26.01
Scolding responses to fuss-cry bouts	0.00	9.52	0.00	1.85, SD = 5.56

[a] Three- and four-year-old focal children, excluding Zie, Zonbo, and Kal.

Table 14.7   Fuss-Cry Patterns When Mothers Were Absent

	Zie	Zonbo	Kal	Averages for other 3- and 4-year-olds[a]
Intervals spent fussing and crying (of total)	1.20	6.57	6.76	1.41, SD = 1.63
Average length of bout (minutes)	2.17	8.88	8.11	3.45, SD = 3.73

[a] Three- and four-year-old focal children, excluding Zie, Zonbo, and Kal.

Table 14.8   Responses to Fuss-Cry Bouts When Mothers Were Absent

	Zie	Zonbo	Kal	Averages for other 3- and 4-year-olds[a]
Fuss-cry bouts ignored	100	37.50	88.89	72.16, SD = 21.19
Soothing responses to fuss-cry bouts	0.00	62.50	11.11	27.84, SD = 21.19
Scolding responses to fuss-cry bouts	0.00	0.00	0.00	0.00

[a] Three- and four-year-old focal children, excluding Zie, Zonbo, and Kal.

Kal were less likely to receive responses from their caregivers than other three- and four-year-olds (Table 14.4).

The Presence and Absence of Mothers

Zonbo and Kal's bouts were much longer (Table 14.7) when their mothers were absent than when their mothers were present (Table 14.5). In addition, both Zie and Kal were typically left in the care of postmenopausal female relatives when their mothers were absent and these women seldom responded to their fusses or cries (Table 14.8). As a result, Zie and Kal were less likely to receive responses when their mothers were absent than other three- and four-year-old children were (Table 14.8). This pattern perhaps contributed to Zie and Kal's overall high levels of fussing and crying.

Furthermore, when Zie's mother was present, his grandmother soothed him more often than his mother did, yet when his mother was absent the grandmother was never observed soothing him. It is also important to note that Zie's mother was in her third trimester of pregnancy, and gave birth two weeks after the observations. This means that the observations may not have captured features of Zie's previous relationship with his mother, as she may have been decreasing investment as a result of fatigue and in preparation for the arrival of her next infant. Zie's strikingly high levels of fussing and crying may thus be symptomatic of parent-offspring conflict, although earlier observations would have been necessary to substantiate this hypothesis.

Zonbo, in contrast, was left in the care of a father who responded frequently but ineffectively to fussing and crying, as indicated by the long bouts. The most intense crying was observed at the end of a day that Zonbo's mother had spent in the forest collecting caterpillars with other women. During Zonbo's crying, his father turned to the observer and said, "Zonbo misses/longs-for his mother."

When Zonbo's mother was present she verbally scolded him several times for fussing or crying. Only one other mother (the mother of Yokopi) was observed speaking firmly to her child during a fuss-cry bout, and her reprimand lasted only one interval. By contrast, Zonbo's mother shouted at him to stop crying and moved him away from her during his fuss-cry bouts. Qualitative observations indicated that Zonbo seemed more "clingy" and "fussy" than other children. He often started to fuss-cry and cling to his mother when she began working in camp (e.g., pounding manioc), even though the initiation of her work did not move her away from Zonbo. Although attachment quality was not systematically studied, the descriptions of Zonbo make him appear insecurely resistant (Ainsworth et al. 1978). Zonbo's distinct patterns of fussing and crying may thus reflect the quality of his attachment to his mother, rather than the process of weaning or his age. Cassidy and Berlin (1994) proposed that insecure-resistant patterns of attachment behavior are adaptive for children who are attempting to attain more care, or to improve the quality of care that has been inconsistent.

DISCUSSION

Lummaa et al.'s (1998) prediction that children would cry more in the absence of their mothers was not supported by the data reported here, but the data were consistent with Bell and Ainsworth's (1972) and Zeifman's (2001) predictions that crying is more likely to occur in the presence of mothers. Perhaps this was because Bofi forager children fussed and cried to promote continued investment when their mothers were present, whereas fussing and crying had little apparent value when mothers were absent and could not hear the signals. We cannot assume that infants and young children understand the differential value of signaling in the presence as opposed to the absence of their mothers, but it does seem that higher levels of fussing and crying are responsive to specific circumstances that are contingent upon the presence of mothers. For example, fussing and crying may occur when a mother moves away from her child or pays attention to another offspring, and the child tries to regain proximity and attention. When the mother is absent, these situations are less likely to occur and fussing and crying are thus triggered less often.

The finding that longer fuss-cry bouts occurred when mothers were absent may reflect the unresponsiveness of nonmaternal alloparents as well as efforts to summon the mothers. We do not know which process was more important.

To examine the effect of maternal sensitivity on fussing and crying patterns, we looked closely at three children (Zie, Zonbo, Kal) who fussed and cried much more frequently than their age mates. No single factor explained the behavior of all three children, but their specific circumstances appeared influential. Four factors helped to explain Zie's high levels of fussing and crying: (1) when his mother was absent, his grandmother was never observed soothing him, (2) when his mother was present, the grandmother rather than the mother responded to his fussing and crying, (3) his mother was in the late stages of pregnancy when the observations took place, and (4) his father was often absent traveling between his two wives. Two factors seemed to explain Zonbo's fussing and crying patterns: (1) his mother infrequently responded by soothing and instead scolded him more often then any other caregivers, and (2) Zonbo was not easily soothed, perhaps because he was insecurely attached to his mother. When Kal's mother and father were absent, meanwhile, he was left in the care of his great-aunt, who was blind and responsible for other children as well. As a result, Kal's fussing and crying rarely elicited responses when his mother and father were absent. This examination of Zie, Zonbo, and Kal's circumstances, illustrates how important it is to consider demographic factors and children's caregiving histories when attempting to explain social and emotional patterns.

In sum, the Bofi forager patterns of fussing and crying were generally consistent with the predictions of attachment and evolutionary theorists, that fussing and crying are used by offspring to elicit more parental care. Individual circumstances also helped explain individual differences and deviations from normative developmental patterns.

15

Vulnerable Lives

The Experience of Death and Loss among the Aka and Ngandu Adolescents of the Central African Republic

Bonnie L. Hewlett

This chapter examines the context and nature of responses to loss among two culturally distinct adolescent groups in central Africa-Aka foragers and Ngandu farmers. Cross-cultural research on grief among adolescents has seldom been conducted (for exceptions, see Eisenbruch 1991; Oltjenbrun 1989; Bachar et al.1997). As far as I am aware, grief among adolescents in small-scale, relatively egalitarian cultures has never been systematically studied. When grief is examined cross-culturally, it is placed within a Euroamerican context, giving the impression that the experience of adolescent grief is similar across cultures.

The study of grief in small-scale cultures may be important for identifying potential human universals of loss and grief and how various demographic and cultural contexts contribute to diversity in how grief is experienced. Anthropologists working with small-scale cultures have documented the relatively high (by Western standards) mortality rates. Infant mortality is often 10-20 percent and juvenile mortality 25-60 percent (Hewlett 1991; Hewlett et al. 1996). Researchers have also demonstrated that many children in these cultures live with stepparents in late childhood and adolescence due to the loss of one or both parents (Chagnon 1997; Hewlett 1991). Life history theory indicates adult and child mortality rates predict a variety of behavioral and reproductive patterns later in life (Charnov 1993; Chisholm 1996). LeVine et al. (1992) note that infant mortality is the prime factor that explains differences in childcare patterns between industrialized and agricultural cultures (i.e., agricultural parents being more indulgent with children due to higher mortality rates). While these studies describe frequent death among foragers and farmers, and hypothesize a variety of consequences in adult life, few, if any, studies have examined how children or adolescent foragers or farmers view or deal with recurrent death. Some studies describe funeral rituals (emphasizing adult burials) but seldom do they try to understand how individuals view and feel about the deaths of family and friends, how death and loss impact their lives, how they deal with recurrent loss, or how age (e.g., the loss of children versus adults) or gender may influence one's feelings of loss and grief.

Woodburn (1982a) has conducted one of the only studies of death in hunting and gathering societies. He indicates that, by comparison to farmers and pastoralists, foragers have relatively temporary grief; social continuity is not stressed because of their immediate return system. By comparison, he hypothesizes that farmers and pastoralists, with delayed return systems, have more prolonged grief for particular kin (e.g., lineage-based kin).

Euroamerican research is of limited use for understanding loss and grief in small-scale cultures. Western research is based upon the adolescent's experiences of loss of one or two family members or friends, or adolescents who have not experienced loss but are given fictitious situations of death within the family. I call this hypothetical grief, because they have not actually experienced the loss of a loved one, and they then are asked how they would feel and respond to this hypothetical situation (Swain 1979; Orbach et al. 1994; Mitchell 1967).

Adolescents were selected for study because they can cognitively fully understand death, according to Piaget and others (Baker et al. 1996; Cook and Oljetenbruns 1998; Koocher 1973; Nagy 1989; Piaget 1963). Other developmentalists, such as Erickson (1963) and Bowlby (1972) suggest that adolescence is a particularly difficult time in terms of identity development, balancing attachment, and exploratory or autonomy-seeking behavioral systems. Presumably, a loss experienced at this point would be especially traumatic and would resonate throughout the life of the individual. Not all researchers agree on this (Hogan et al. 1984,1994; Pollock 1986; Mufson 1985; Walker 1993).

This chapter utilizes an integrated evolutionary approach (Hewlett and Lamb 2001) to interpret the data. An integrated approach predicates that it is essential to understand the ecology, psychology, and culture of grief. The potential adaptive design of grief is hypothesized, whereby grief is seen as a "cry for survival" and a time when corollary social networks of kin and other caregivers are established and a reorganization of attachment figures takes place.

METHODS

Three methods were utilized: informal interviews with individuals regarding their feelings and experiences with loss, free listing of all deaths remembered, and a ranking of the individuals who caused the greatest feelings of loss and grief. Twenty Aka and twenty Ngandu were asked to participate in the study. Demographically the sample consisted of 13 Aka males, seven Aka females; 12 Ngandu males, eight Ngandu females; nine younger (10–15) Aka adolescents and 11 older (16–20) adolescents; 11 younger Ngandu adolescents and nine older Ngandu adolescents. In order to check reliability and validity of the data and obtain some sense of changes over time, 15 [seven Ngandu (three females and four males) and eight Aka (two males and six females)] of the 40 adolescents were reinterviewed six months after the initial interviews and were asked to again list the two or three individuals who caused them the greatest feelings of loss and grief. Reproductive histories of the adolescent's parents were also obtained to understand the number, age, and gender of siblings as well as the mortality and morbidity experienced by the family.

Finally, I spent time living and traveling with the adolescents and talking to them about death and loss in a variety of subsistence and social contexts. The interviews were conducted via two research assistants, both from the village, who spoke DiAka and French.

Setting

This research was conducted in the rural southern region of the Central African Republic in and near the village of Bokoka, where the Aka foragers and Ngandu farmers make a living from the same dense tropical rainforest. The forest camps of the Aka are located throughout southwestern Central African Republic (CAR) and the northeastern part of the Republic of Congo (ROC), with an approximate population of 20,000 and population density of less than one person per square mile (Hewlett et al. 2001). About three hundred Aka live in association with approximately five hundred farmers in the village of Bokoka. Ngandu adolescents were interviewed in the village. The Aka were interviewed in both the forest and the village camps. Three Aka bands are associated with Bokoka and each band has a forest trail from the village to forest camps (Hewlett et al. 1988).

During the dry season, the Aka generally live in patriclan camps consisting of 25–35 individuals, subsisting in the forest by net hunting, with the entire family regularly participating, and for the remainder of the year living in the village camps. The Aka have lived in the forest for at least two thousand years and have a semisymbiotic relationship with the Congolese farmers, spending the wet season in the village working on the Ngandu farms. They have minimal political hierarchy, high gender and intergenerational egalitarianism, weak patriclans, and flexible resident patterns. The Aka share with many people on a daily basis, and to further promote egalitarianism, the Aka avoid drawing attention to themselves, avoid ranking each other, and have a great respect for autonomy and individuality (Hewlett et al. 1996:654).

The Ngandu farmers also live in patriclan-based villages where they practice subsistence farming of manioc, corn, plantains, peanuts, and a variety of other crops. The Ngandu have strong (relative to Aka) age and gender inequality. Men and elderly individuals often receive more than others. Violence against women is not unusual and deference and respect of older siblings, parents, and individuals is expected. Sharing with family members (especially patriclan members) is encouraged, as households that accumulate and do not share are targeted for sorcery (i.e., jealousy sorcery). The Ngandu promote social unity and conformity rather than autonomy and individuality (Hewlett et al. 1996:654).

The comparison between the Aka and Ngandu adolescents' views and feelings of grief are potentially interesting because they live in similar natural ecologies; hunt, trap, and gather in the same tropical forest; and have similar mortality (infant mortality is 15–20 percent, juvenile mortality is 30–40 percent), and fertility rates (TFR 5.6–6.2). It is an important point to note that the community of individuals the Aka and Ngandu encounter throughout their lifetimes are similar in number. The regional community or "exploration range" (Hewlett et al. 1988), that is, the geographical area individuals explore during their lifetime searching for a mate, visiting friends and family, hunting, and acquiring subsistence knowledge, is the final social unit. This exploration range for the Aka is approximately 50 kilometers, and includes an area where the Aka can meet and get to know about seven hundred individuals. About 2500 Aka live in the Bagandou region (which includes Bokoka). The Ngandu live in villages consisting of 50–500 related (including clan affiliation) individuals. Therefore, the number of individuals the Aka and Ngandu adolescents get to know throughout their lifetime is approximately the same.

The Aka and Ngandu, neighbors in this rural southern region, have frequent social, economic, and religious interactions, but have very distinct modes of production and social relationships. As a result, Aka-Ngandu comparisons may provide insights into how social structures and relationships influence the manifestation of individual patterns of grief, as the context of grief influences the experience of grief.

RESULTS

Informal Interviews

The following section tries to place Aka and Ngandu deaths into personal and cultural context. Emphasis is placed upon how individuals
viewed and coped with the deaths of particular family members. Beliefs
and practices regarding burial and the afterlife are also provided.

The Ngandu. The Ngandu were interviewed in the village, generally
one on one. The interviews in the village took on a particular note of
poignancy, as there was at least one death per week during the field study,
and several times two deaths in one week. Each night in the village one
could hear the "grief wailing" of the bereaved accompanied by drum-
ming, singing, and dancing. Women were frequently observed walking
alone down the main road of the village crying and loudly sobbing, "an-
nouncing," the death of a loved one. People would then follow behind the
women as they walked. Twice the body of the deceased, both times a child,
was carried by the mother as the procession made its way through the village.

For the Ngandu adolescents, the interviews seemed to echo the theme
that, as one 13-year-old female noted, "life became hard" after the death
(*kwa*) of a loved one (her father) because he had provided "many things
and he had loved me a lot and now [my] mother cannot give me these
things." Another 13-year-old female spoke about the grief she felt for an
Aka man who had died because he had "provided *koko* for the family and
now that he is gone I don't eat as well." A 17-year-old male mentioned his
grandfather's death as being particularly difficult as he "was nice and he
gave to everyone." After the death of a parent or grandparent, the adolescents all indicated that they had family to care for them, so no child was
left on his or her own. Life just became more difficult, as there was less
food, clothes, or medicine.

One 12-year-old boy had lost both his father and mother within one
week (four years prior to the interview). He said he was looked after by his
mother's younger brother, "He is like a father, he gives me food and I live
with him and we go fishing." I then asked if he had someone who was
"like a mother" and the young boy began to cry and said, "no one is like a
mother to me, I miss my mother and still feel very sad because my mother
and father are gone." Often their lives did seem to change after the death
of a loved one, for the reasons mentioned, but what seemed to console
these adolescents was that they were given "clothes, some money, and
some medicine" to help ease their grief. As one 13-year-old said, "I was
made happy again because after his death [older brother of her mother] I
was given clothes and money." Another 13-year-old female noted that her

grief was greatest after the death of her father's brother because "he had given me many things." Another 19-year-old said that her grief was "diminished because I got a lot of beautiful clothes [the deceased's clothes]." A 19-year-old male also noted that the death hardest for him was the death of his uncle, who had "been nice and gave to everyone." One young girl whose grandmother had died "because she was just tired of life" was given a pot to cook with, to earn money, which she noted had helped to diminish her feelings of grief, but changed her life as now she had to begin working. For the older adolescents it was when they were given "clothes and money," which then enabled them to "find a husband [or wife], get married and have a baby" that their grief was "forgotten."

Several expressed the feeling that it was family who consoled them, and many noted that it was "doing things [hunting, cooking etc.]" and mainly "getting clothes, food, medicine, and money" and "just living" that got them through the experience of loss. The grief felt over the loss of a loved one seemed to be tied into the grief over the loss of what that person had provided for the adolescent. Equally so, the diminishment of grief for the bereaved adolescents was often noted to be after they had received clothes, and so forth, the material possessions of the deceased, which were distributed after the funeral. The expression of grief was for the most part seemingly experienced during the grief gathering or funeral, the *matanga*.

The male adolescents said that men did not cry very often, that "crying was for women and children." They did note, however, that they grieved as deeply as the women, they just did not cry. They expressed the notion that it was not important for the adolescents to know the cause of death of their loved ones. They did, however, know exactly how each person listed had died, (i.e., whether from natural illness, *ekila* (breaking a taboo), or sorcery, *likundu*. They did not experience, or at least express, increased anger if the death occurred due to sorcery, *ekila*, or illness and noted the ones who died due to sorcery as being those who had "not given much" or had accumulated without sharing, as being the targets of what was described as "jealousy sorcery."

All the adolescents, the younger as well as older, were very much aware of what death "meant," that is, that death was final. As one 13-year-old noted, "When you die it is finished." However, there was a recurrent theme of the loved one returning as a spirit to watch over the family. This is consistent with a general cultural belief in ancestor spirits. Another 13-year-old male recounted that after his grandfather died,

> He came into my room at night and saw that I needed money so he left money for me. The spirit gives things after death, if someone you love dies and they see you suffer and have need they come at night and give what's needed.

If the deceased was a child under the age of ten, the child would "return," that is, be reincarnated and born again. The child would often return to the same family, but not always. The family would recognize their lost one by some physical or personality trait that they had had in their previous life (e.g., scratch or birthmark). Infants (less than one year old) were immediately wrapped in palm leaves and buried close to the outer wall of the house. The mother would then spread the earth from the grave on her abdomen to help insure the child's quick return.

A few of the adolescents expressed fear at the thought of their own, or a loved one's death, but the majority did not fear death. As one 16-year-old expressed, "Death is for all the world, young and old." A 19-year-old said that she had no fear of death because "there is a certain time for death for me and that is all." Many expressed this same sentiment, regardless of their age. A 12-year-old explained that she had no fear of death as "many people die and I see this, the body and lots of death and I know death so I do not fear." One 15-year-old however, was more emotional in his response, he was in fact afraid of death because "with death, it is finished and what happens to the people who die is a mystery, and for this I am afraid."

There was no sense of a timely or good death (i.e., only the old or "bad" should die) versus a bad (suicide, murder) death. However, most expressed that they felt "saddest" when an adult dies (regardless of age) because they cannot return, while a child up to the age of ten can come back. For the most part the *ame* or spirit that was good (shared with others, was "nice") "flew up to God," sometimes but not often described as "heaven," while the bad spirits (those who had been sorcerers and had eaten people) went "into the forest to cry." "Heaven" was described as being like a large village, exactly like the one they lived in, but without sickness, hunger, death, or sorcery. The bad spirits also included the children of sorcerers' as young as two or three, who are born with the "sorcerer's substance" (an extra organ that was described as initially pale, round, with mouths circling it, which would become redder, larger, and with more mouths, the more people the sorcerer ate) in them and who had begun to eat people with their father (or mother) sorcerer. They were "bad children" who did not return (become reincarnated) but rather flew up to God, who threw them back down to earth where they would "cry in the forest." No one mentioned that the bad spirits went to a hell, or purgatory but rather to the forest, where they cried at night because "they felt bad about not being with family and God." Many of the adolescents related that the bad spirits could continue to cause problems for the people, scaring them and causing sickness, especially at night when they would walk about. For the adolescents, the forest at night was a frightening place. In the words of one 13-year-old female, "the forest is good, but has bad spirits and I am afraid of the forest."

The influence of the church could be seen in the ceremonies surrounding death. If the family was heavily involved in their religion then there would be no ceremonial wailing, singing, or dancing, but rather a quiet church funeral. If, however, the family was only moderately involved (or not at all) in the church, they would set the body on a table in the yard of the family, mats would be laid about for people to sit upon, and family, friends, and acquaintances would come to view the deceased and grieve. The grief wailing would often begin in early evening and continue for much of the night. The men would drum and sing, with women joining in the singing. The men would also dance, the *mambo*, but the women generally would not. This would also continue late into the night. Food would be served or people would leave to eat and then return. Children would be present and families would come and go throughout the evening. The greater the prominence of the deceased, the longer the grief gathering would continue, with family and friends coming from some distance to participate. For deceased children, there would be no grief gathering as such, mainly immediate family and, depending on the age of the child, playmates or those children who had helped with the care of the younger child, would attend. The body, the *kwoui*, would be washed by a close female relation, laid out in nice clothes, wrapped in a clean sheet, placed in a wooden casket, and interred, *loungozo*, close to the house. Children are also washed, dressed in nice clothes, and then buried. For those who were not strongly affiliated with a religion, there would also be a one-year ceremony, the *salaka*, honoring the memory of the deceased, with singing, dancing, drinking, and eating. As a young adolescent noted, the one-year ceremony is to "see family and we dream of him [her deceased cousin] and we have a ceremony to remember and dream of him again." For those belonging to the church this would not take place, but occasionally a quieter Catholic mass would occur, one year later, to remember.

The Aka. The Aka were interviewed in both the village and forest camps. Often the entire camp would listen to and respond to the interview questions, but when possible the adolescents were asked the more personal questions privately. For the Aka adolescents the recurring themes that seemed to emerge were the sense of the finality of death, the sadness of loss experienced, and the thought that it was family who comforted the grieving adolescent, "My family consoled me and happiness came again." When in camp, the Aka are always in close physical contact, often sitting as close as space allows. This physical closeness was a source of comfort in grief also, as many adolescents noted that their mother, father, or other kin would "hold" them as they grieved. One young girl noted that she was sad when her mother's older brother died as he had loved her a lot and was "happy and good with all the children." After his death her life changed because she felt,

> sad and I had a feeling of love for the others and I was afraid that they would die too. I was sad for a long time and then I sang and danced again, but at first it was hard because my mother and father said that with death it is finished, it is goodbye for all my life.

She further explained, "I cried a lot and after the burial the people in camp listened to me and held me and after awhile the sadness lessened. I understand that death is for all the world, and with death it is all finished." One 12-year-old female expressed her feelings in the following way, "After the death, I was afraid for a long time. I did not eat well or sing and dance, and I cried for a long time, but then my mother held me and helped to find good food for me and amusing things to do, then the sadness diminished." Another young adolescent, a ten-year-old male, felt deep grief when the brother of his mother's father died, because,

> I loved him a lot and he went with me into the forest to hunt and walk and when a person dies, it is finished for their life, all is finished. The spirit, *yingo* soars to *Komba*. It does not matter if it is a baby or adult who dies, I feel the same sadness and my father consoles me. The person I love a lot I grieve for the most. When I am sad I keep crying, but the death is finished and the sadness decreases, but I still love the person.

He further commented that it was when he "played with my brothers and sisters, I felt happy again and the sadness diminished." Almost all Aka adolescents mentioned that it was family, a mother, father, older sibling, or other kin who consoled them during their time of grief and that it was in the interaction with family that their sadness diminished. When I asked how they dealt with so much recurrent loss in their life, they all responded that it was being close and interacting with family that helped them to cope.

A 12-year-old female explained that when her father died, "I was afraid for the others, that they would die too and I stayed close to the people I loved because I was afraid." Her grandmother also "told me to stop crying or I would get sick." She further commented that it was her grandmother and mother who comforted her and that she "speaks to my family to feel happy again." Another 11-year-old explained that she too stayed close to her family after a death in her family and that she had also been told that she "would get sick if I kept crying." A 14-year-old male related that for him the sadness "stays and comes again and again," and that "when others get sick, I am afraid and I guard my brothers and sisters well." It is interesting that in contrast to the Ngandu, none of the Aka stated that their lives became harder after the death of a loved one. They did, however, list the family members in camp who consoled them, gave them food to eat, and helped them to "be happy again."

For those who die, the spirit "soars" to *Komba*, God, if good, or gets thrown back to earth to cry in the forest if bad. For the Ngandu adolescents then, the forest at night became a frightful place, one filled with bad, wailing, revengeful spirits. However, for the Aka, the forest is seen at all times as "mother, father, provider, lover," in spite of the "bad" spirits who roam at night, and none of the adolescents expressed any fears regarding these spirits crying at night in the forest. A "bad" person then is one who does not share and who is often accused of being a sorcerer; conversely, a "good" person is one who "shares and is nice and happy to people." When people "soar to *Komba*," the place is described as being like a camp in the forest and, as with the Ngandu, without sickness, death, or sorcery: "All the camp is there, all the family is there." There is no Aka word for heaven or paradise, but rather, several of the Aka adolescents used the Sango word to describe their thoughts regarding an afterlife, (i.e., heaven). Of the 20 adolescents interviewed, approximately four seemed to have been influenced by the Christian notion of "paradise," God, and people being "punished" for their disbelief. All seemed to believe in the reincarnation of young children. As one 12-year-old male explained to me, "All the spirits are the same, the babies and the adults, but the ceremonies are for the adults because the babies return. They return to the same mother, but adults do not return." Regarding the funeral, another 12-year-old explained it this way,

> the (burial) ceremony, *edjengi* is to say goodbye, this is the last moment on earth. This is for the person who dies, to say goodbye, it is in their memory. The burial place, *mbindo*, is close to the house, but when we leave, the place stays in camp. We visit the place of burial to remember the person.

The death of a young child or baby is often thought of as a temporary "goodbye," until that child returns, either to the same mother, or another woman in the same camp. However, in the words of one adolescent, "The sadness is still the same."

Regarding the causes of death, like the Ngandu, none of the adolescents questioned seemed to feel that knowing the cause was important in helping to diminish their grief, but again all knew the cause of death of each person they listed. However, for one young adolescent couple who had lost their first baby, it was important for the father to know the cause of death. The young mother said:

> My baby was killed by a poison dart, *ndoki*, because of jealousy. The baby had a fever and did not nurse and then died. There was a small ceremony

and dance and after the dance we buried the baby. I cried a lot and my husband and mother consoled me. My husband cried also and did not eat. He wanted to find who had caused our baby to die. My parents came and helped me, I cried a lot, it was my first baby, but my parents said to not cry so much, it causes sickness to be so sad and cry.

This was the only person who said that it was important to know the cause of death, although, as noted, all adolescents interviewed knew the exact cause of death for each person listed.

As with the Ngandu, the causes were broadly listed as sorcery, *ekila* (of which there are many types), and accidents (e.g., falling from trees) (for a more complete study of causes of death see Hewlett et al. 1986). A 14-year-old explained what happens after a death in camp:

When a person dies, the men, women and children all cry. They all stay in a group and talk about the person and then begin the funeral and dance to *edjengj* (the forest spirit). The women wash the body and the men find the bark, *dikoko*, to bury the body in. The men arrange the burial place, *mbindo*, and put the body into to the ground and cover it with dirt. After the burial there is a little ceremony, they dance, they sing, they cry. This is on the same or the next day. It is short, they dance for two or three days and then it is finished.

Another 19-year-old described the burial in much the same way:

The person who died is arranged like a person who is asleep, on the bark. The parents, people of the camp, and patron of the Aka dance a long time, the *elimo* (the *makondi* and *edjengi* were also given as funeral dances). Before they bury the body they dance and after sleeping and eating they dance again. The dance is special for the person who died and the song is special, *bolingo baizela*, and after the funeral, the song and dance are different. You dance in memory of the person.

The ceremony is the same for younger people and adults, but not for babies because babies return. If it is a bad person (a sorcerer) then you cannot dance, *bajengi*, or you can dance a dance that is significant, "We are now free and peaceful and thank you for dying because now there is no fear." The name of this dance is the same but it is a dance of thankfulness from freedom from fear, it is a dance of liberty. The same day that the bad person dies they start to bother the camp and cry in the night.

As with the Ngandu, there was no sense of there being a "timely," "good," or "bad" death, justified by old age or accusations of murder. The one-year ceremony, the *peli*, is a "little ceremony of the time of their death and when the date arrives of their death, there is a lot of feeling, of emotion for that person. The people dance, eat, and sing together. It is for the memory of that person." It is also a time, as with the Ngandu, that signals the end of the grieving time for widows. Women who lose their mates, around the time of the one-year ceremony, shave their heads, wash, put on clean garments, and have a close female relative rub them with a special oil. They are then ready to marry again. During my first field study, in the rainy season, far in the forest, there was a large "memorial ceremony" in which many camps gathered to sing, dance, eat and drink, and remember their lost loved ones. This apparently occurs only when someone (or several) people of prominence have died.

An older Aka male ended the interview by saying, "Life is not always good with so much death, it is difficult sometimes, but it is good to be alive . . . but then there is death and life is finished." Another male Aka felt that "I can live in the forest, I eat well, I have family, life is good."

Free Listing

Twenty Aka and twenty Ngandu adolescents were asked to free list the names of adults and children, family, or friends who had died during their lifetime. Overall, the 40 adolescents remembered the loss of 953 individuals or an average of 24 individuals per adolescent. The adolescents were more likely to remember the loss of adults than they were children (an average of approximately 16 adult deaths versus 8 child deaths, $t = 5.4$, $p = .000$), and, not surprisingly, older adolescents remembered the loss of more individuals than younger adolescents (25 versus 20 individuals), but the differences were not statistically significant. Adolescent males remembered the loss of more individuals than did females (26 versus 20 individuals), but again the differences were not statistically significant. Figure 15.1 illustrates the intercultural variability in number of deaths remembered in the ethnic groups and the propensity of Ngandu adolescents to remember about 30 percent more individuals than do Aka adolescents. The X axis represents numbered individuals (1–20) and the Y axis represents the number of deaths each of these individuals remembered. (For example, Aka number 1 remembered five deaths, and Ngandu number 1 remembered 12 deaths.)

Ethnicity/mode of production and its interactions with gender helped to explain some of the variability. Figure 15.2 summarizes some of the differences between the two ethnic groups. Ngandu adolescents remembered more deaths overall than Aka adolescents (30 individuals versus 18.0 individuals; ($t = 3.82$, $p = .000$). Aka and Ngandu remembered the loss of a similar numbers of females (seven females for Aka and eight females for Ngandu), but significant differences existed in the number of male deaths they remembered. Ngandu adolescents remembered the loss of twice as many males by comparison to Aka adolescents (22 males remembered for

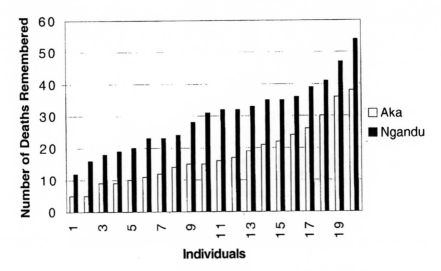

Figure 15.1.   Number of deaths remembered by Aka and Ngandu individuals.

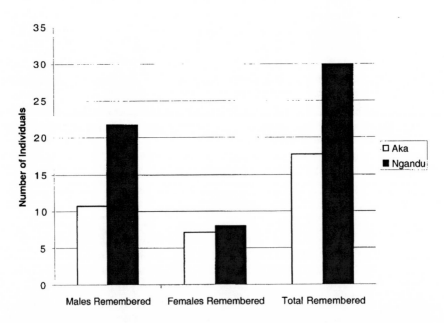

Figure 15.2.   Number of male and female deaths remembered by individuals.

Ngandu versus 11 for Aka ($t = 5.1$, $p = .000$). Both Aka and Ngandu adolescents remembered significantly more adult than child deaths, 12.5 adults versus 5.5 children for Aka ($t = 3.70$, $p = .000$); 19.6 adults to 10.3 children for Ngandu ($t = 4.8$, $p = .000$).

Table 15.1 examines the role of gender and ethnicity in remembering the death of someone of the same or opposite sex. Ngandu adolescent males and females remembered similar numbers of males and females, Aka males and females remembered a similar number of male deaths, but Aka adolescent males were more likely to list more female deaths than were Aka adolescent females ($t = 2.09$, $p = .05$).

Table 15.2 examines the impact of age for remembering a male or female death. As expected, older Aka and Ngandu adolescents recalled more deaths of both males and females than did younger adolescents. The Ngandu pattern of remembering more male than female deaths is also found in both younger and older adolescents.

Ranking

The 20 Ngandu and 20 Aka adolescents were asked to name the two or three deceased individuals who caused them the greatest sense of loss and grief. Aka adolescents named 39 individuals (mean of 2.1 individuals per adolescent) and Ngandu named 40 individuals (mean of 2.0 individuals

Table 15.1   Number of Female and Male Deaths Remembered by Gender and Ethnicity

	Number of Adolescents	Mean Number of Female Deaths Remembered	S.D.
Aka			
Males	13	8.1	4.2
Females	7	5.1	2.4
Ngandu			
Males	12	8.2	5.5
Females	8	8.0	3.7
	Number of Adolescents	Mean Number of Male Deaths Remembered	S.D.
Aka			
Males	13	11.8	7.1
Females	7	8.4	4.0
Ngandu			
Males	12	24.1	7.1
Females	8	18.2	4.2

Table 15.2 Females and Males Remembered by Age of Informant[a]

	Number of Adolescents	Mean Number of Female Deaths Remembered	S.D.
Aka			
Younger adolescents	9	6.2	3.8
Older adolescents	11	7.9	3.9
Ngandu			
Younger adolescents	11	7.2	5.1
Older adolescents	9	9.1	4.3
	Number of Adolescents	Mean Number of Male Deaths Remembered	S.D.
Aka			
Younger adolescents	9	10.1	6.5
Older adolescents	11	11.1	6.5
Ngandu			
Younger adolescents	11	20.2	7.9
Older adolescents	9	23.8	6.4

[a] Older adolescents ranged in age from 16 to 20, younger from 10 to 15.

per adolescent). Both Aka and Ngandu were most likely to mention biological kin (i.e., not kin by marriage or friends) as causing the greatest amount of grief. Ninety percent of the individuals listed by Aka and 85 percent of individuals listed by Ngandu were biological kin. Consistent with the patterns described in the free listing, Ngandu adolescents were much more likely than Aka adolescents to list males rather than females (41 percent by Ngandu versus 15 percent by Aka). Table 15.3 shows that the biological kin remembered among the Aka came from both sides of the family, whereas the biological kin remembered among the Ngandu were primarily patrilateral relatives.

It is also worth noting, in terms of attachment theory, that Aka and Ngandu may or may not have placed lost parents on this short list of individuals causing the most grief. One Aka adolescent's mother died when he was eight years of age; she was listed as second on the free list and not at all on the shorter list. A Ngandu adolescent male listed his father on the free list as fourth, and not at all on the ranked list. It was also clear that being first to be listed on the free list did not necessarily mean this death caused the greatest grief. An Aka male's father was listed as fourth on the free list and first on the short list. Another Aka listed his father second on the free list and first on the ranked list.

In order to try and check the reliability and validity of the short list, 15 adolescents were asked the same questions six months after the initial in-

Table 15.3   Types of Biological Kin (%) Remembered as Causing the Greatest
Amount of Grief

	Patrilateral	Matrilateral	Both (i.e., brothers and sisters)
Aka	31	33	36
Ngandu	63	34	03

terviews. Among Ngandu, the first person listed (save one adolescent) remained the same. Three Ngandu adolescents changed their lists to reflect
the deaths that had occurred in the past six months, where one woman had
lost her baby, another two a younger sibling. A similar pattern existed for
Aka. Four Aka adolescent lists remained exactly the same, while the other
four slightly altered their list to reflect deaths in past six months.

DISCUSSION AND CONCLUSIONS

Universalistic and particularistic points that emerge from the qualitative
(i.e., interviews) and quantitative (i.e., listing, ranking, and statistical
analysis) data are listed below.

Universal Themes

1. Both Aka and Ngandu adolescents experienced and remembered
   many deaths. Aka adolescents, on average, could easily list 18 deaths
   that occurred in their lifetime, while Ngandu remembered about 30.
   One adolescent listed 52 deaths in his relatively short life.
2. Both Aka and Ngandu remembered almost twice as many adult as
   child deaths. This was not because they had experienced more adult
   deaths, as Aka and Ngandu juvenile mortality is about 40 percent.
   Further, the camp composition of the Aka is about 25-35 individuals,
   with 40 percent of the camp being children, and demographically the
   same composition of individuals surrounding the Ngandu adolescent exists.
3. Younger (10–15 year-olds) remembered slightly, but not significantly,
   fewer deaths than older adolescents.
4. The majority of the individuals listed by Aka and Ngandu adolescents as causing the greatest feelings of loss and grief were biological
   kin. It was also biological kin who responded to the adolescents' expressions of grief.

Particularistic Themes

1. Aka and Ngandu remembered a similar number of female deaths (about eight), but Ngandu adolescents (both males and females) remembered significantly more males than Aka (22 male deaths, on average, for Ngandu, 11 male deaths, on average, for Aka).
2. Consistent with the patterns described in the free listing, Ngandu male and female adolescents were much more likely than Aka adolescents to list male deaths as causing more grief than female deaths.
3. The biological kin remembered among the Aka came from both sides of the family whereas the biological kin remembered among the Ngandu were primarily patrilateral relatives.
4. Aka male adolescents remembered more Aka female deaths than Aka female adolescents.
5. For the Ngandu, the grief felt over the loss of a loved one seemed to be tied to the grief over the loss of what that person had provided for the adolescent. Equally so, the diminishment of grief for bereaved Ngandu adolescents was often tied into their receiving the distributed articles of the deceased person. This was not the case for the Aka adolescents. It is interesting to note that in contrast to the Ngandu, none of the Aka stated that their lives became harder after the death of a loved one. They did, however, list the family members in camp who consoled them, gave them food to eat, and helped them to "be happy again." For the Aka, their grief seemed to be tied more directly to the relationship they had with the deceased, which was not expressed as a provisioning one. That is, they did not express grief over the loss of what that person had given them, as the Ngandu had, but rather over the loss of that person in their life. Also what consoled them after their loss was simply being with family.
6. Both Ngandu and Aka adolescents reported that extended family responded to their sadness and grief, but in quite different ways. Many Aka adolescents indicated that physical comforting took place (e.g., "my mother, father . . . held me when I cried") and others described how family talked to and consoled them. For the Ngandu, the family responded and sadness decreased with acts of provisioning. When they were given the deceased's material articles, they felt their "sadness diminish."

Woodburn's Model

I found general support for Woodburn's hypothesis regarding distinctions between immediate and delayed-return cultures' views of death. Death rituals were longer among the Ngandu farmers (delayed return) than for the Aka (immediate return). Among the Aka, the body is buried quickly, generally the same or next day, whereas among the Ngandu the body would be laid out for viewing for a few days and rituals existed to remember the individual (adults only) for several years. The physical burial of Aka also involved less physical time and effort. Also, the Ngandu (both males and females) remembered significantly more males, patrilateral males, in particular, than did the Aka. This is consistent with Woodburn's prediction that farmers' grief should be greater for particular individuals (e.g., lineage members).

While some of the data support Woodburn's model, other data question his propositions. First, his descriptions give the impression that hunter-gatherers experience less ("temporary") grief than farmers/pastoralists. While Aka buried their dead quickly and listed fewer individuals, they remembered many dead family members and there was no indication that their felt loss was more "temporary" than the Ngandu. Second, both Aka and Ngandu knew a cause of death for each individual. Woodburn suggests foragers are not as concerned with knowing the cause as are farmers. Aka may not act as concerned as Ngandu, in part, due to the fact that so many Ngandu deaths are attributed to sorcery.

Explaining Diversity and Unity

Some studies, such as Woodburn's, emphasize cultural diversity, while others emphasize universal patterns of grief (Archer 2001; Badcock 1990; Bowlby 1970-1980; Parkes 1972). Here I examine factors that influence diversity and uniformity in feelings of grief in the Aka and Ngandu communities.

Three cultural-ecological factors are important for understanding the particularistic responses to grief: the nature of patrilineal descent and social organization, the nature of social relations, and immediate versus delayed systems of thought.

Strong patriclan social organization among the Ngandu provides a mechanism to defend and protect material (e.g., land and crops) and reproductive (e.g., spouse) resources. Consequently, the number, age, and sex of geographically close kin, especially males, is important (e.g., male-male alliances). The Ngandu accumulate goods and property (e.g., planted crops) that must be guarded from mobile Aka and other farmers. Also intra- and intergroup hostilities over women are not uncommon—polygyny is about 40 percent (Hewlett 1991) and many men do not have spouses, which leads to conflict and violence.

By comparison, Aka are mobile and intra- and intergroup hostilities are infrequent. Consequently clan organization is weak. As Woodburn suggests (1982a) patriclan organization leads to remembering a greater

number of specific others. In this case, Ngandu remember more individuals overall, in particular males who are important for resource defense. Aka
on the other hand, remember both male and female deaths from both sides
of the family, because it is important for them to be flexible in response to
wild food resource availability. For the Aka, the number, age, and sex of geographically close biological kin, specifically male kin, are of less importance, as there is little need for resource defense (of accumulated goods,
property holdings) and male-male alliances. This strong ideology of the
Ngandu emphasizes deference and respect for elders, males, and ancestors.
Ancestor spirits are shown a continued respect and deference, and they
maintain an active place within the lives of the living. For the Ngandu,
social relations continue beyond the grave; the commitment of a delayed-
return system extends beyond death. The formal obligations and commitments extended to the living are equally important in being extended to the
dead. Economic activity, social continuity, delayed production and consumption, and long-term planning and concern are bound in the sense of
the patrilineal lineages, social commitments, and the importance of remembering those to whom you are bound and committed, even beyond the
grave.

The Aka have, as noted, "immediate return" values and social organization (Woodburn 1982a: 205). This means that their activities are orien-
tated directly to the present, in which they labor to obtain food and other
resources that are consumed or used that day or in the immediate days
that follow. There is a minimum of investment in accumulating, in long-
term debts or obligations, or in binding commitments to specific kin or to
other partners. Commitment, as Woodburn suggests, ends at the grave
(Woodburn 1982a).

Another cultural difference that exists between the two groups is the material versus emotional basis of social relations. Several have written about
the material basis of social relations in Bantu-speaking Central Africans
(e.g., Levine 1992). Social relations cannot continue without a material exchange. For the Ngandu, the grief felt over the loss of a loved one seemed
to be tied to the grief over the loss of what that person had provided for the
adolescent. Equally so, the diminishment of grief for bereaved Ngandu
adolescents was often tied to their receiving the distributed articles of the
deceased person. For the Aka, their grief seemed to be bound more directly
to the relationship they had with the deceased, which was not expressed as
a provisioning one. What consoled them after their loss was simply being
with family.

Diversity exists in the experiences and expression of grief, but as noted
there are also several commonalities. Evolutionary psychologists are interested in identifying genetic or biologically based universals of the

human mind that evolved during the environment of evolutionary adaptation (EEA, i.e., the long period of human hunting and gathering) in response to recurrent adaptive problems. One recurrent problem faced by humans was the regular death of individuals who had assisted them in many ways (e.g., subsistence, defense, childcare, physical and emotional health). What is the adaptive design of grief?

Several common patterns found in the data from the study of Aka and Nagandu adolescents are (1) grief is a response to loss (obviously this is seen in other cultures as well as in nonhumans primates); (2) the expression of grief tends to illicit a response from others; (3) those responding tend to be genetically related to the grieving adolescent; and (4) the "soothing" of the grief expression and the practices of response in provoking the diminishing of the grief emotion follow specific cultural patterns.

Given the adaptive problem of recurrent loss, the grief response to that loss and the cross-cultural commonalities existing between the Ngandu and Aka might suggest that humans have "grief" modules of the mind that are in part the flip side to the attachment or proximity module as described by John Bowlby (1969). Infants cannot care for or protect themselves, so they seek the proximity of others by crying and reaching for these individuals (Hewlett et al. 2001:25). Infants who sought proximity, in the EEA, survived. In much the same way, perhaps the crying, mourning, and grief expressions following loss might represent an evolved psychology for the communication of need following the loss of an individual who enhanced survival. Like crying and fussing, expressions of grief may be helpful in communicating the needs of one who has experienced loss.

When survival is threatened, following loss and the physiological responses to this psychological assault, grief becomes an important emotion that elicits a response from others who may benefit reproductively from the individual experiencing grief. For the grieving person, the soothing of grief, the social interaction of compassion, leads to closer bonds with both existing figures and the establishment of new corollary social networks—all of which serve to enhance the survival of the individual. Grief is a "cry for survival."

The EP approach helps to explain and understand the four common features of grief:

1. Both Ngandu and Aka adolescents remembered many deaths.
2. Both Aka and Ngandu were very clearly attached to those individuals who died, but cultural themes (e.g., level of patriarchy, immediate or delayed return systems) helped to explain the number and gender of those remembered.
3. Family responded to the adolescents' expressions of grief.

4. Both Aka and Ngandu experienced the greatest grief over the loss of biological (genetic) kin, but again cultural forces influenced whether they were patrilateral or matrilateral biological kin.

There is, I suggest, a developed adaptive design to grief that enabled our hunter-gatherer ancestors, and enables ourselves, to survive loss, through a "cry of survival"—the expression of grief.

This chapter examined the nature of and responses to loss among two culturally distinct adolescent groups in central Africa: Aka foragers and Ngandu farmers. The study of grief in small-scale cultures may be important for identifying potential human universals of loss and grief and how various demographic and cultural contexts contribute to diversity in how grief is experienced. An integrated biocultural approach emphasizes the interactions between culture, ecology, and biology, and provides an opportunity to examine adolescent grief from a holistic perspective. Aka and Ngandu comparisons provide insights into how ecological, psychological, and cultural structures and relationships influence the manifestation of individual patterns of grief—the context of grief influences the experience and expression of grief.

16

Play among Baka Children in Cameroon

Nobutaka Kamei

INTRODUCTION

Anthropology of Childhood

The "anthropology of childhood" is one of the most significant topics that anthropologists should conduct but one in which they have shown little interest (Hirschfeld 2002). Because children are adept in acquiring culture, because they are incontrovertibly members of the society, and because they constitute themselves into semiautonomous subcultures, they can be explored by anthropologists as well as other ethnic groups and cultural communities (Hirschfeld 2002).

However, issues of children have not been included in mainstream anthropology because of stereotypes of childhood that keep researchers away from child-focused research. One problem in anthropology is the "socialization model." In this model, children should be "adults-in-the-making" whose actualities are "way-stations on the pathways to adulthood," and the contributions that children make to their own development are often obscured (Hirschfeld 2002:613, 620). Since children are competent members of their own society (Harris 1998), their communities and their cultures should be focused upon and described by anthropologists taking appropriate viewpoints and using appropriate procedures.

Evidence of Children's Cultures

Some works have discussed children's cultures in modern and traditional societies (Fujimoto 1985; Iwata 1987; Opie and Opie 1959). These works, based on the authors' fieldwork, offer empirical evidence of the existence of children's cultures. Anthropologists need to extend these first

343

attempts with further cross-cultural investigations and to construct a general theory on the nature and role of children's cultures in human societies.

Play activities are especially proper materials for this because they are activities initiated by children themselves, frequent events in daily life, and universal phenomena found in every society. These activities can provide both opportunities to observe children's culture and useful data for future cross-cultural studies.

Characteristics of Hunting-Gathering Societies

In order to clarify the nature of children's cultures, obviously it is necessary to conduct investigations into various societies, including urban and traditional communities. Research into hunting-gathering societies is especially essential because it may tell us something about human nature, which we acquired during long period of hunting-gathering lives before the neolithic revolution, the beginning of agriculture.

Hunting-gathering societies very similar in many aspects of culture (Lee and Daly 1999). Subsistence activities, knowledge of edible wild resources, simple material culture, nomadic lifestyle, and egalitarianism in food sharing are some of the common characteristics of cultures adapted to natural and social environments.

A general lack of direct teaching and formal education are common features of hunter-gatherer life. Ethnographic works indicate that adults show little interest in educating their children and that children learn skills and knowledge by observing the activities of others (Hara 1979; Harako 1980; Yamamoto 1997). This is intimately connected to modes of cultural transmissions and is suggestive for anthropologists who are interested in children's culture (Hewlett and Cavalli Sforza 1986).

Descriptions of Hunter-Gatherer Children's Play

Some researchers have mentioned children's activities in hunter-gatherer societies, including play. Two of the pioneers are Turnbull (1962) and Harako (1980), who studied the Mbuti foragers in the Ituri Forest of the Democratic Republic of Congo. Their ethnographies include some descriptions and analyses of children playing in forest camps.

Turnbull described such children's play as swings, climbing trees, bows and arrows, and net hunting, which he considered "the beginning of their schooling" (Turnbull 1962: 114). He argued that children's life as a long frolic "is all part of their training" and "one day they find that the games they have been playing are not games any longer, but the real thing, for they have become adults" (Turnbull 1962:114). Harako also found mimicry play such as hunting with bows and arrows, spears, and net (Harako 1980). He

Figure 16.1. Play of ngbasa (safari). Four Baka boys walking around in the forest as hunters with spears. Ages 8-9, 6, 8, 13-14 (from left to right, estimated). In this hunting session, they succeeded in getting a papaya fruit, but they lost their dog.

argued that hunting play was a part of children's "unconsciously conducted" education (Harako 1980: 28).

There are some common findings and analyses in their works. Both of them found similarities between children's play and adult activities, especially hunting. Both of them also considered these similarities a mimicry of adult activities by children and considered these mimicry activities a part of education and training.

Other brief descriptions of children in ethnographies of hunting-gathering societies agree with these points (Aoyagi 1977; Sawada 1998; Takeuchi 1998; Yamamoto 1997).

Paradox in the Socialization Model

However, these claims, obviously based on the socialization model, obscure the actual experiences of playing children. Normally children play simply for the purpose of having fun with their peers and do not have any intention to teach or train themselves with a goal in mind. Why do

they devote themselves to their self-education through play? The socialization model cannot solve this paradox because it assumes that all activities are similar in that they are directed toward learning to be an adult in
the society.

Considering this paradox, we have several questions to be answered on
children's play. Is it true that children play in ways similar to adult activities? If so, why and how do they come to do that? Are they really enjoying
mimicking adults or is it something else? If play has educational effects,
what are the conditions for achieving "unforced initiative learning"? Are
there features of human nature involved in children's play processes?

I tried to address these issues by conducting and analyzing detailed
systematic fieldwork with hunter-gatherer children. I also utilize a "children's culture model," rather than a socialization model to interpret the
data.

METHODS

Introduction of the Baka Hunter-Gatherers

In this chapter, the play of children of the Baka hunter-gatherers in the
tropical forests of Africa is analyzed. The Baka, also called "Baka Pygmy,"
are an ethnic group who traditionally hunt and gather in the tropical
forests of the Congo Basin in Central Africa (Althabe 1965; Bahuchet 1992;
also see Chapter 17 by Hirasawa). During the dry season they live in simple huts in forest camps in order to hunt, gather, and fish. They have skills
and knowledge to get and use wild resources for their food and material
culture. The Baka people are famous for their traditional songs and dances
with ritual spirits that are imagined to live in the forests (Tsuru 1998). We
can observe the egalitarianism among them through the everyday food
sharing and noncompetitive social relationships. Division of adults' labor
by sex, such as hunting by men and gathering by women, is clearly observed. We seldom observe educational attitudes by adults toward children. Children more than four or five years old form groups with older
children and spend most of their daytime hours with peers. Children not
only stay in the settlements, but also go into the forest to conduct various
kinds of activities including play. Adults seldom interfere with these
activities.

Recently some signs of change have been found in the lifestyle of the
Baka (Altabe 1965; Kamei 2001). Most have adopted small-scale cultivation. Their settlements are located near roads where cars pass every day
and they remain there during the rainy season to lead a partially sedentary
life. Missionaries have set up schools for Baka children and some of them

have started to attend them. Despite these signs of changes in modernization and cultivation, they have continued to sustain their traditional
culture as hunter-gatherers in the forests (see Hirasawa, Chapter 17, for
a description of aspects of childcare that persist under conditions of
sedentarization).

Procedures

The investigation was conducted in a village in the East Province of the
Republic of Cameroon from August 1997 to March 1998. This village consists of around 600 habitants of three ethnic groups, one of which is Baka.
I lived in a Baka settlement with about 60 Baka. A Christian mission built
a small school tailored to Baka children in this settlement. I observed 34
Baka children (17 boys and 17 girls) aged 4-15 (estimated) who usually
spent daytime apart from their parents. This included 14 Baka children
from this settlement and 20 Baka children from neighboring settlements. I
described whatever play activities I observed.

In this study, "play" is a generic term for the activities that meet all of
the following conditions: (1) activities conducted by children without direction from adults; (2) continuous activities that appear to involve specific
tools, rules, or purposes; and (3) activities that are not primarily intended
to make a productive contribution. One session of play is defined as a continuous activity in which children do not change the nature of the play.

In all, 269 sessions of play were observed and described. These data
were analyzed with respect to subjects and means, materials, play areas,
spirits of play, and involvement and roles.

RESULTS

Subjects and Means

Considering the main subjects and means, the 269 sessions are classified
into 85 kinds of play, which can be grouped into seven categories: (I) play
related to foraging activities; (II) playing house; (III) songs, dances, and
music; (IV) play related to modern things; (V) competitive games; (VI)
play related to the body and physical exercise; and (VII) others (see Table
16.1).

Categories I (foraging) and III (songs, dances, and music) can be called
tradition-oriented play because these include play that is related to traditional activities such as hunting in the forest and dances with ritual spirits. On the other hand, IV (modern things) and V (competitive games) can
be called modernity-oriented play because of the existences of modern ac-

Table 16.1 Play of the Baka Children (85 Kinds)*

Category	Subgroup	Kinds of Play	Number of Sessions	Involvement Boys	Girls
(I) Play related to forageing activities (15 games)	Hunting	Making a trap	10	++	–
		Making a gun with a stem of a papaya	9	++	–
		Attacking animals with stones	7	++	–
		Lizard-hunting with bows and arrows	6	++	–
		Mouse-hunting with bows or spears	5	++	+
		Playing "*leka*", shooting a rolling papaya with spears	5	++	–
		Shooting plants and inanimate objects with bows and arrows	4	++	–
		Playing "*ngbasa*," going on a safari with a dog	2	++	–
		Shooting plants and inanimate objects with spears	1		
		Playing with a slingshot	1		
	Gathering	Termite gathering	1		
		Insect collecting	1		
	Fishing	Fishing with fishing rods	9	++	+
		Fish bailing	2	+	++
		Fishing with baskets	1		
(II) Playing house (20 games)	Hut	Making a hut	4	+	++
	Food and cooking	Play cooking with inedible materials	4	++	–
		Actual cooking using a can as a pot	3	++	–
		Miniature bunch of bananas	2	–	++
		Food-getting competition	1		
		Throwing and catching food with their mouths	1		
		Using chopsticks	1		
		Making and smoking paper cigarettes	1		
	Clothes	Making eyeglasses out of vines	3	++	++
		Making and wearing false breasts	2	++	++
		Wearing a sash	2	–	++
		Wearing a cap	2	++	–
		Using a hairdressing item	1		
		Item for wearing on torso	1		
		Wearing a blindfold	1		
	Housework and tools	Doll	2	–	++
		Playing with fire	2	++	++
		Humouring babies	1		
		Funnel	1		
		Umbrella	1		
(III) Songs, dances, and music (13 games)	Songs and dances	Playing "*be*", a traditional dance	23	++	++
		Group play with songs	10	+	++
		Singing songs	10	++	++
		Dancing	6	++	++
		Mimicking the forest spirits without songs	3	++	–
		Reciting the words of songs	1		
	Instruments	Playing "*aita*", a guitar with seven strings	2	–	++
		Grass flute	2	++	–
		Drum	2	++	–
		Bursting leaves	2	++	–
		Flute made of a stem of a papaya	2	++	–
		Sticks of a drum	1		
		Playing "*limbindi*", a handmade guitar with two strings	1		

Table 16.1   (Continued)

Category	Subgroup	Kinds of Play	Number of Sessions	Boys	Girls
				Involvement	
(IV) Play related to modern things (9 games)	Cars	Playing "*motuka*", sliding down a hill on a board	7	++	++
		Mimicking drivers while walking around	6	++	−
		Making and driving a pushcart	4	++	−
		Toy cars made of banana (smaller cars)	4	++	+
		Toy cars made of raffia palm (larger cars)	3	++	−
		Mimicking drivers using chairs	2	+	++
	Others	Mimicking a motorcycle rider using chairs	1		
		Miniature airplance made of a stem of a papaya	1		
		Toy radio made of a stem of a yautia	1		
(V) Competitive games (3 games)	Games	Playing "*masee*", a group game with paper-rock-scissors	11	−	++
		Playing "*songo*", an African board game with stones	10	++	++
		Soccer	5	++	−
(VI) Play related to the body and physical exercise (13 games)	Playing with their body	Wrestling	6	++	++
		Everting their eyelids	4	++	−
		Chasing each other	2	++	−
		Swordfight	2	++	−
		Playing tag	1		
		Frolicking	1		
		Spanking each other on the bottom	1		
		Filling their nostrils with beans	1		
		Counting their fingers with a song	1		
		Swimming	1		
	Fingering with objects	Playing catch	1		
		Throwing underpants	1		
		Playing with mud	1		
(VII) Others (12 games)	Play related to animals	Mimicking monkeys	5	++	−
		Fingering dead snakes	5	++	−
		Teasing a dog	2	++	++
		Mimicking birdsongs	1		
	Toys independent from other subjects	Playing on the swings of an oil palm tree	4	+	++
		Playing with a pendulum	2	++	−
		Playing with a balloon	2	−	++
		Balancing a broom in their hands	1		
		Doing magic with stones	1		
	Mimicking workers	Mimicking cake sellers	1		
		Mimicking teachers	1		
	Art	Drawing	1		

*The 269 sessions of play were classified into 85 games, which could be grouped into categories (I)–(VII) considering their main subjects. For each game observed more than twice, the level of the involvement by boys and girls is shown.

++: Main player / +: player with auxileary roles / −: Rare or no observation of playing.

tivities imported from outside Baka society. Category II (playing house) includes play of both types. Category VI (body/physical exercise) is difficult to distinguish in character because it often included improvisational play by children.

Table 16.2a summarizes the frequently observed play categories ($N = 269$ sessions). It shows that tradition-oriented play attracts children very much. However, it is not rare to observe modernity-oriented play. Table 16.2b shows the variations included in each play category ($N = 85$ kinds of play). We can notice wider variations of tradition-oriented play as compared with those of modernity-oriented play. Category II (Playing house) includes subjects and means involving household and foods, with which it seems to be easy for children to create various kinds of play. We also notice few variations of category V (competitive games).

More concrete comparison with a corresponding adult activity is possible for each kind of play (see Table 16.3).

Table 16.2a.   Frequency of Sessions within Each Play Category (N = 269 sessions)

Order	Categories	Number of Sessions	%	Note
1	(III) Songs/dances/music	65	24	Tradition-oriented
2	(I) Foraging	64	24	Tradition-oriented
3	(II) Playing house	36	13	Mixture
4	(IV) Modern things	29	11	Modernity-oriented
5	(V) Competitive games	26	10	Modernity-oriented
6	(VI) Body/physical exercise	23	9	Improvisational
	(VII) Others	26	10	
	Total	269	100	

Table 16.2b.   Frequency of Kinds of Play within Each Category
(N = 85 Kinds of Play)

Order	Categories	Number of Kinds	%	Note
1	(II) Playing house	20	24	Mixture
2	(I) Foraging	15	18	Tradition-oriented
3	(III) Songs/dances/music	13	15	Tradition-oriented
4	(VI) Body/physical exercise	13	15	Improvisational
5	(IV) Modern things	9	11	Modernity-oriented
6	(V) Competitive games	3	4	Modernity-oriented
	(VII) Others	12	14	
	Total	85	100	

Table 16.3　Favorite Types of Play of Baka Children and Their Relationships to Adult Activities

---

Play independent of current adult activities
Play without constructed objects
- SWING—Girls pull down leaves of oil palm tree and hang on them

Play with objects from outside of Baka culture
- MOTUKA—Boys and girls get on a board with rollers and slide down a hill as if they were riding a bus
- TOY CAR—Boys carve plantains with knives to make cars

Play in subsistence activities that occurred in the past
- MOUSE-HUNTING—Group of boys hunt with bows; girls sometimes act as beaters

Play with elements of adult activities
- TRAP—Primarily boys making and immediately breaking small animal traps
- GUN—Guns made from the papaya stem and bullets made of pith of cassava; used to shoot insects, chickens, and each other
- LEKA—Boys shoot a rolling papaya with spears
- NGBASA—Boys go on play hunt with spears and dog; attack and obtain fruits, but sometimes loose their dog
- MAKING A HUT—Girls build play hut with forest materials they collect; girls stay in hut and boys sometimes nap here in afternoon
- BE—Ritual spirit dances which include imitation of adults' traditional spirits and children's improvised spirits

Imitation of adult activities
Adult activities in miniature
- PLAY COOKING—Boys pull apart insects or leaves and sharing them equally among the child group
- MINIATURE BUNCH OF PLANTAINS—Girls make and carry around a miniature bunch of immature plantains (around 5 cm long)

Exact replication of adult activities
- FISHING—Boys fish with rods; group bail fishing by girls

Notes: Kinds of play are classified by the degree of similarity with corresponding adults' activities. Although fishing can be regarded as a foraging activity, it also can be included in the category of play because they often enjoy the activity itself without any games.

The children's favorite kinds of play were classified into three groups with respect to the similarity to adult activities: (1) play independent of adults' present activities; (2) play with elements extracted from adults' activities, in which children borrow some elements as means to create play; and (3) mimicry of adults' activities, in which children enjoy mimicking or doing exactly the same things adults do. Children often extract only part of adults' activities for their interests as in (2), and do not always make exact replicas or miniatures of adults' activities as in (3).

Materials

Table 16.4 lists materials that are collected by children and mainly used for purposes of play. As can be seen, their toys are mainly made of plants. Only 11% of the children's toy materials (8 out of 72 types) come from adult material culture. Most items are shared and transmitted only among children. Indeed, they have affluent toy culture.

However, they share common characteristics with the attitude toward material culture of adult forest foragers, i.e., things are made with available materials and thrown away immediately after use (Tanno 1984).

Play Areas

Play areas are analyzed and categorized into three groups: forest, settlement, and schoolyard. Each area corresponds to particular kinds of play.

In the forest, we can observe tradition-oriented play such as foraging and making huts. The forest is also a place where the little ritual spirits mimicked by the children appear. This "forest" does not always mean the real forest, but the forest in the minds of the children. Young children often shout, "We are going to the forest!" when they actually intend to play within three to five meters of their settlement. However, it is exciting enough for them because the forest is a mysterious, potentially dangerous but attractive space with creatures for hunting and ample materials for toys.

In the settlement, children play house, especially cooking; they sing and dance (i.e., tradition-oriented play); and they play with subjects involving modern things like cars (i.e., modern-oriented play). The schoolyard is for competitive games of soccer and "*masee*", a group game played by girls. These seem to have diffused recently from children of other ethnic groups.

Distinguishing between *bele* (forests) and *bala* (settlements) is one of the most important spatial differentiations of Baka adults. On the other hand, the distinction between settlements and the schoolyard is one made and frequently used by children. It can be said that children take over adults' recognition of forests, whereas they create their own spatial recognition of school as a symbol of their own outer world.

Spirits of Play

While each kind of play has its own particular rules, some of the rules have common tendencies that can be called "spirits of play." Three spirits of play are found among Baka children as follows.

Aggressiveness. Aggressiveness is commonly found in many kinds of play. However, it is always toward wild creatures or something similar

Table 16.4   Materials Used for Baka Children's Play*

Names of Materials	(Baka)	Parts	Uses
(1) Plants of the forest			
Raphia spp.	*(peke)*	Leaf	Sash, cap, hairdressing item
		Midrib	Fishing rod, (outer part) arrow, spear, (inner part) toy car
Landolphia spp.	*(ndembo)*	Sap	Ball, balloon
Megaphrynium spp.	*(ngongo)*	Leaf	*Roof of a hut*
Aframomum spp.	*(njii)*	Stem and leaves	Spear, frame of a hut, *costume of spirits*
Woods		Branch	*Sticks of a trap,* arc of a bow, *frame of a hut,* rollers of *"motuka",* pushcart
		Twig	Chopsticks, sticks of a drum, guitar
Grasses		Leaf (small)	Ingredient for playing cooking
		Leaf (large)	*Cover of a trap,* roof of a hut, pot for playing cooking, *funnel,* grass flute, bursting
Vines		Vine	String of a trap, bowstring, *rope for a hut constructing,* rope for a doll, eyeglasses, false breasts, item on torso, *costume of spirits,* string of a guitar, rope for a soccer ball, string of a pendulum
		Fruit	Filling nostrils
(2) Cultivated plants			
Papaya	*(papaye)*	Stem	Body of a gun, flute, miniature airplane
		Fruit	Target of shooting with spears
Cassava	*(boma)*	Stem (inner part)	Bullet of a gun
Sweet potato	*(petete)*	Vine and leaves	Costume of spirits
Yaoutia	*(langa)*	Leaf	Roof of a hut
		Stem	Toy radio
		Spadix	Toy fish
Plantain banana	*(ndo)*	Leaf	Roof of a hut, umbrella, costume of spirits, soccer ball, sword
		Finger	Toy car, (immature) miniature bunch
Grapefruit	*(mboke)*	Fruit	Ball for playing catch
Maize	*(mbombo)*	Cob	False breasts
		Husk	Playing with fire
(3) Animals			
Snake	*(kpolo)*	All the body	Fingering
Spider	*(kpakpapu)*	All the body	Sharing and playing cooking after hunting
Millipede	*(ngongolo)*	All the body	Weight of a pendulum
(4) Inanimate objects			
Can	*(ngongo)*	—	Pot
Paper	*(mbopi)*	—	Cigarette, drawing
Plastic bag	*(sase)*	—	Blindfold, resonator of a papaya flute
Stone	*(timi)*	—	Attacking animals, bullet of a slingshot, magic, cake for seller mimicking
Mud	*(tolo)*	—	Playing with mud

* This table lists materials that are (1) collected by children themselves and (2) mainly used for purposes of play. The table excludes (1) living animals (dogs for chasing, insects, lizards, birds, cocks, and mice for hunting, etc.); (2) living plants (leaves of oil palm trees as swings, stems of bananas as targets of bows and arrows, etc.); and (3) adult material culture (chairs and boards for car games, cloths to make bodies of dolls, etc.).

Terms in italics in the "Uses" column indicate material culture shared with adults (8 of 72 kinds of uses).

that fires children's imaginations as hunters. Animate creatures are victims, such as insects, lizards, birds, small mammals, and anything that crawls in the bush. Even inanimate objects like papayas rolling on the ground and dead snakes become their ready targets.

Noncompetitiveness. Most kinds of play do not include competitive rules, for the targets of aggressiveness are usually wild creatures and not their peers. Competitive rules are found in three kinds of games. *"Masee"* and soccer are played with children of other ethnic groups in the schoolyard. *"Songo"*, an African board game, was introduced by adults from outside Baka society and children often join this game. It seems that Baka children do not invent new competitive games themselves. However, it is also true that children do enjoy playing these competitive games repeatedly (Tables 16.1 and 16.2).

Egalitarianism. Baka children often share things equally that they have caught during play. In one episode of play cooking, for example, a eight-year-old boy shot a spider while hunting with a bow. He pulled apart his "game" and carefully shared the parts for three participants, including me, the researcher. He divided the eight legs into three groups and made up the difference with the cephalothorax, which he divided into two pieces. The abdomen was thrown away because it is "inedible" (see Figure 16.2). This episode makes clear that children exactly recognize adult food-sharing activities and mimic them in their play.

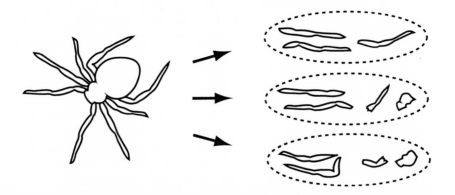

Figure 16.2. "Egalitarianism" in the play of spider sharing. An eight-year-old boy pulled apart his "game", a spider, and carefully shared the parts with three participants. He divided the eight legs into three groups and made up the difference with the cephalothorax, which was divided into two pieces. The abdomen was thrown away because it is "inedible."

I try to compare the spirit of this play to that of adult activities. Aggressive attitudes toward animals are similar to those of adult hunters. Lack of competitiveness is one of the characteristics of hunting-gathering societies. Egalitarianism, as typified by food sharing, is another. These similarities support the idea that the spirit of children's play is based on the traditional nature of hunting-gathering societies. However, it is also important to note that children also enjoyed competitive games.

It is interesting to notice the origin of these similarities, however. Egalitarianism is actualized by an exact mimicry of adult food sharing, whereas aggressiveness toward objects is derived from the elements extracted from attacking behaviors, for children are excited not as mimickers but as real attackers. Noncompetitiveness is linked to the relative lack of modes of and opportunities for competitive games.

Involvement and Roles

The last analysis is on gender differences in level of involvement and in the roles assumed. For each activity observed more than twice, the levels of involvement by boys and girls are shown in Table 16.1.

Some kinds of play are unisex. Hunting, fishing with rods, cooking, and most kinds of play involving cars are played mainly by boys, while fish bailing, and making huts, dolls, and miniature bunches of bananas is done mainly by girls.

Other kinds of joint play by both boys and girls include play with fixed gender roles and gender-free play. Examples of the former are mouse-hunting (boys are hunters; girls are the beaters who flush out the game), making a hut (girls construct; boys lie inside), and "*be*", traditional dances (boys drum; girls sing; infants dance as "forest spirits"). Other examples of gender-free play are some kinds of playing house, "*songo*", an African board game, and "*motuka*" , play involving cars.

With reference to adults, unisex kinds of play obviously reflect the division of labor by sex among Baka adults. Similar situations are found in play with fixed gender roles. We find that children use lots of elements of adult activities almost in the appropriate manner for each gender. It is interesting to note that some of the gender-free play does not have as background the activities of Baka adults, such as cars and board games.

Summary of the Results

All the kinds of play observed here were conducted, shared, transmitted, and acquired among children's groups without adult interference. Moreover, in subjects and means, materials, play areas, spirits of play, and involvement and roles, we can see characteristics that were not observed in adult culture. Some of them were children's inventions, some were introduced from the outer world, and others were partial modifications of adult activities.

On the other hand, we can see that every aspect of children's play shares some common characteristics with adult culture. Despite their autonomous activities, to some degree the culture of the Baka children can be regarded as "loosely based on the majority adults' culture" (Harris 1998: 199).

DISCUSSION

To resolve the paradox cited above, I try to restore the process of cultural diffusion from adults to children and argue the conditions for the "educational effects" of play, focusing on the autonomous aspects of children's culture.

Position of Children's Community

While children's community can be regarded as one of the cultural minorities in their society, they still have a given position that can be stated as follows: (1) everyday contact with the majority adults; (2) economic dependence on the majority; and (3) inevitable transition into the majority. These are the very conditions that lead most anthropologists to the socialization model of children. It is important also for us to take them into consideration when we attempt to construct an alternative heuristic model.

Adults as Resources

I posit three aspects of cultural diffusion: resources, channels and recreations.

Adult activities, such as subsistence activities and traditional rituals, provide the resources for elements of behaviors for children, because of two characteristics that make them constant models for children.

Patterns of Behavior.   Adult activities are conducted with particular repeated patterns, which are bound by economic, reproductive, and social needs.

Playful Elements in Activities.   Adult culture has attractive elements itself that children can easily borrow and apply. While some anthropologists have noted playfulness embedded in foraging activities (Blurton Jones,

Hawkes and O'Connell 1997; Huizinga 1955; Takeuchi 1995), none of them has focused on the essential functions for sustaining the culture. Rituals involving songs and dances also can be understood in a similar model.

Channels of Diffusion

Diffusion needs channels that connect resources and children, the receivers.

Everyday Contacts. Children have everyday contacts with adults. This close relationship provides frequent chances for children to observe them.

Mimicry and Extraction. Children borrow various parts of adults' activities mainly in two ways: mimicry and extraction. While children do play at mimicking adults, they often extract only elements of adults' activities that seem to be interesting and useful for them. Elements chosen in the latter way are especially useful for creating "chimera play," supplying the deficiencies with available subjects and materials around children. This process, probably conducted with the inherent ability of children, contributes to make children's culture richer than replicas.

Children as Re-Creators

On the supposition that mimicry and extraction constitute the creative side that Willis called "penetration," I should note the opposite side as "limitation" (Willis 1977). After penetrating and getting something from adult activities, children create their own activities using these elements and other available resources. In this process, both freedom and limitation are involved.

Freedom of Creation. Children are free to create their own play, especially since they are free from economic needs. Indeed, most of their foraginglike activities are not aimed at getting something edible, but simply at enjoying behaving in such ways.

It is also interesting to notice that children's personality is not overwhelmed by adult culture, as we saw in the cases of competitive or gender-free play, which indicate the existence of wide and unpredictable interests of children.

Limitation of Available Opportunities. However, adult culture is always present as the largest source of elements for children's behaviors. The frequently available examples make it easy for children to apply and follow them. More variation in tradition-oriented play and less in modernity-oriented play (see Table 16.2b) show the limitation of original inventions by children. These levels of opportunities for play can limit the actualization of certain kinds of play, such as competitve games.

Also a distinction by gender was clearly found among them. Children may have some sensitivity in distinguishing men and women and being involved positively in male/female gender roles.

Contribution to Reproduction of Culture?

I add here some reflections on the "educational effects" of play, which the "socializationists" claim. Does children's culture contribute to the reproduction of adult culture? Through these analyses, it is not easy to answer this question. Cultural diffusion depends on children's choices based on their interests. What we can say is that some adult elements can be applied as resources for children's activities. The similarities are not always guaranteed to achieve effective learning.

However, if some activities with playful elements satisfy the needs of the society at the same time, such as subsistence, they can be easily transmitted to the next generation and sustained without the intervention of education. Cultural forms are stable and widely distributed because children find them easy to think about and easy to learn (Hirschfeld 2002; Sperber 1996). Children may extract some elements of play to carry with them after the inevitable "graduation" from children's community and these may contribute to easy learning among the adult community. Hunting-gathering societies with few educational interventions offer an example of the continuous reproduction of culture with profound involvements of children's culture.

Future Issues

Two suppositions remain be resolved, both related to children's sensitivity that achieves nonrandom diffusions from adults to children: the sense of playfulness and the sense of distinction by gender.

Sense of Playfulness. Each child is sensitive enough to easily detect playfulness in certain adult activities and perform something similar. What are this sense and these behaviors derived from? I pose a hypothesis that all human beings including children have an inherent universal sensitivity that reacts to particular playful situations, which have been called the universal nature of play (Caillois 1967).

Sense of Distinction by Gender. Each child is also sensitive enough to distinguish men and women, as well as activities by men and those by women. Each child likes to follow the adult models of his/her gender and borrow elements of their activities. What are this sense of distinction and these behaviors derived from? A clue to solving this question may be found in humans' way of thinking based on "binary opposition" (Levi-Strauss 1962). Each society may have its own way of arbitrarily connecting gender opposition and the resulting division of activities in initiative learning of "appropriate manners" in each society. I pose a hypothesis that the achievements of play with gender roles are due to children's ability to recognize particular binary oppositions and follow them.

These two questions have profound relevance to both human nature and education embedded in each culture. Their answers will contribute to the clarification of the mechanisms of the construction and diffusion of human culture in general.

ACKNOWLEDGMENTS

This study was supported by financing from the Grant-In-Aid for International Scientific Research (No. 08041080) from the Ministry of Education, Science, Sports and Culture, Japan, and a research permit from the Ministry of Scientific and Technical Research of the Republic of Cameroon. Dr. Terashima (Kobe Gakuin University), Dr. Ichikawa, Dr. Nishida, Dr. Kimura (Kyoto University), Dr. Sato (Hamamatsu University of Medicine), and Dr. Nguima Mawoung (University of Yaounde I) helped my research. Discussions with my colleagues and partici-pants of the 9th International Conference on Hunting and Gathering Societies in Edinburgh were very useful for improving the manuscript. The Baka informants, especially the children in Nguilili Village, kindly helped my research. To these ministries and persons, I make grateful acknowledgment.

V

Culture Change and Future Research

Photo 5.   Ongee children in new school at Dugong Creek, Little Andaman Is-
    lands. Courtesy of V. Pandya

V

Introduction

Barry S. Hewlett

The chapters in the final section of the book examine the impact of culture change on hunter-gatherer children. As noted in the first chapter, all ethnic groups discussed in this volume are undergoing various forms of culture change. The Yora recently lost half of their population to diseases of contact (Chapter 11), Martu adults drive trucks to hunt (Chapter 6), and !Xun live in settled reserves (Chapter 13). The authors in each chapter describe the changes occurring in the ethnic groups being studied and incorporate the changes into their analyses and interpretation of their results, but the first two chapters in this section are different, in that culture change is the focus of the research. Hirasawa (Chapter 17) examines the impact of sedentarization on Baka infant care and Pandya (Chapter 18) examines the impact of history, colonialization, and political economies on the "schooling" of Ongee children. Studies of culture change among foragers are common (Biesele et al. 2000), but none explicitly address the impact of change on children.

Hirasawa's chapter contributes to the natural history of forager childhood as it is the only infant-focused study of the Baka, who are one of the largest remaining forager groups in the world, with an estimated population of 30,000 in three countries. Her study shows that some features of forager infancy (e.g., frequent close proximity and breastfeeding) common to other active foragers persist after the group becomes sedentary, but that other features change with changes in the economy, such as the importance of sibling care with increased farming and earlier and more abrupt weaning. Pandya's chapter is one of the few accounts of the impact of formal schooling on a foraging culture, but it is likely the only study to place the impact of schooling in historical perspective. It is also the only chapter in this book to use political economic analysis to explain forager childhood (for more studies from this perspective, see Scheper-Hughes and Sargent 1998). It is also interesting to contrast how quickly and easily forager children learn in the chapters in Part II with the long history of failures of the formal education systems described by Pandya.

The final chapter reflects on all the chapters in the book and provides concluding remarks and suggestions for future research.

17

Infant Care among the Sedentarized Baka Hunter-Gatherers in Southeastern Cameroon

Ayako Hirasawa

Studies of infancy in hunter-gatherer societies[1] were set in a fashion by Konner (1973, 1976) and his colleagues, who worked with the !Kung (Ju/'hoan) in the northern part of the Kalahari Desert in the late 1960s. Their work was conducted from an evolutionary framework where universal characterizations of infant development were investigated (see Konner, Chapter 2 in this volume). The number of studies of hunter-gatherer infants increased in the 1980s. Some researchers examined attachment theories in child development (e.g., Tronick et al. 1989; Hewlett 1991) while others examined how natural ecology influenced infant care (e.g., Blurton Jones et al. 1989). These studies questioned the universality of child development theories and pointed out how particular ecological and social settings contributed to diverse patterns of infant care. Issues of universal versus particularistic views of hunter-gatherer infancy persist (Konner, Chapter 2 in this volume). This chapter examines some of the universal versus particularistic questions discussed by Konner in Chapter 2 by providing a detailed ethnographic description of infant care among the Baka of southeastern Cameroon. In particular this chapter examines the impact of sedentarization and farming on infant care practices. The chapter takes a more "culturalist" approach, emphasizing social and cultural contexts (Harkness and Super 1980; Hatano and Takahashi 1997; Tanaka 1982; Yoshida 1984).

Many investigators have worked with the Baka since the 1940s. Baka are forest foragers and perform unique dances characterized by polyphonic song. In recent years, research on the Baka has focused on various topics, such as studies on their utilization of natural resources (Dounias 2001; Sato 1998, 2001), quantitative analysis of their dancing and singing

performances (Bundo 2001; Joiris 1996, 1997; Tsuru 1998), detailed description of children's play (Kamei, Chapter 16 in this volume), studies of social
interactions (Kimura 2001), and linguistic reconstruction of their historical
prehistory (Bahuchet 1993). Furthermore, recent studies have examined the
impact of culture change; Kamei (2001) has examined how Baka have responded to schooling and Hewlett (2000) has examined how governments
and nongovernmental organizations view and provide "development"
projects for Baka. Few descriptions of Baka infancy exist, systematic behavioral studies on Baka infants have never been undertaken, and no study
to date has examined the impact of sedentarization and farming on forager
infant care. This study is an ethnographic and theoretical contribution to
existing studies of forager infants. Ethnographically it describes the details
of Baka infant care. Observational methods were also similar to previous
forager infant studies so comparisons of infancy in other foragers are also
evaluated. Theoretically, the chapter addresses issues of universal versus
particularistic nature of forager infant care.

Childrearing serves the universal purpose of securing the survival and
growth of biologically and socially immature individuals, but childrearing
practices vary from society to society. This diversity in infant care practices
can be explained in terms of various factors, including the natural environment, subsistence activities, social structure, interpretation of the
world, and societal history. Infant care is one of the phenomena through
which the prominent features of a society emerge. This chapter attempts
to home in on the Baka society and its people through their infant care
practices.

SEDENTARIZED BAKA HUNTER-GATHERERS

I conducted field research in the subvillage of Mbeson, a part of Landjoué
village, Yokadouma District, Bumba-Ngoko Division, in East Province of
the Republic of Cameroon. I stayed there for about ten months, from September 2000 to June 2001.

Mbeson is located alongside the logging load penetrating the tropical
forest. The nearest town is Yokadouma, 17 kilometers east of Mbeson. People from Mbeson sometimes stay in Yokadouma for several days to buy
daily household staples or to go to the hospital. Mbeson is inhabited mostly
by the Baka and the Bombong. The Baka are one of the ethnic groups that
have been referred to as Pygmies. They speak an Oubanguian language,
and live in the tropical rain forests that extend from northwestern Congo to
southeastern Cameroon. The Baka population is estimated to be 33,000
(Cavalli-Sforza 1986). The Bombong are Bantu-speaking farmers who live
in southeastern Cameroon. In September 2000, the population of Mbeson
numbered 235 people, of which 153 (65.1 percent) were Baka.

According to Baka and Bombong elders, the first immigrants were a family of Bombong, who arrived in the late 1940s from Central Landjoué, 1 kilometer west of Mbeson, seeking a larger area to cultivate. At that time, the Baka led a foraging lifestyle in the forest, living in much smaller residential groups than now. In the process of interviewing women in Mbeson about their childbirth experiences, I found that until the 1950s their children had been born in various areas in East Province in abandoned camps, and some of them had been born in different places, which suggests that the Baka used to move around in the forest, changing residence frequently.

In the 1950s, some of the Baka near Mbeson started working for the Bombong in order to procure agricultural products. Soon after, they established semisedentary camps in the forest near Mbeson and commenced small-scale self-sufficient cultivation,[2] partly retaining their foraging life. From the late 1950s to the early 1960s, the colonial administration issued an order to the chiefs around Yokadouma, appealing to the Baka to settle along the road. As a result of the chiefs' efforts, two residential groups, familiar with the Bombong, settled down to live alongside the Bombong in the early 1960s. In the 1970s, after sedentarization, the Baka began growing cacao as a cash crop, as their neighbors did. They still continue many kinds of activities, such as hunting, gathering, and fish-bailing in the forest. They also move into forest camps for several weeks during the agricultural off-season.

However, the cultivation of subsistence and cash crops quantitatively provides the most important part of their livelihood and the major part of their diet. In addition to working in their own fields, the Baka often provide the Bombong with agricultural labor to procure cash. This helps the Bombong to maintain their cacao fields because of the labor shortage existing because many young Bombong leave the village for school and to work in towns or for logging companies. This relationship between the Baka and the Bombong partly promotes a sedentary life and a dependency on cultivation among the Baka.

Since their livelihood has shifted from hunting and gathering to agriculture, other social dimensions also seem to be changing. For instance fission and fusion of the residential groups, which is regarded as a regular feature of hunter-gatherer societies, does not happen frequently in Mbeson. The membership of Mbeson is fairly stable. Today, most of the Baka men possess cacao fields, which require substantial labor to maintain; therefore, they are somewhat reluctant to migrate to other villages. It is also noteworthy that I did not observe extensive daily food sharing and cooperation, which is said to enhance close relationships among the constant members of hunter-gatherer societies. Among the Baka in Mbeson, the basic unit of production and consumption is the household based on the nuclear family, although relatives who shared experiences before sedentarization are still very familiar to one another. I did not discern a sense of unity binding the entire village. It appeared to me that the Baka lifestyle in Mbeson is no longer identical to that of hunter-gatherers, but is quite similar to that of the neighboring Bombong. During the initial phases of my research, I expected that Baka infant care would be dramatically different from that described among other hunter-gatherers.

METHODS

I employed the following two observational methods to identify characteristics of infant care among the Baka. One was instantaneous sampling, in which each focal infant was followed and observed for three days. The three-day sampling series was conducted in the village and the forest camp, during the rainy and dry season, respectively, in four settings in all. Daytime (6:30–18:30) was divided into 12 one-hour time blocks, during which a 30-minute observation was conducted. The following parameters were recorded every 5 minutes during the 30-minute observation: (1) behaviors of the focal infant, (2) behaviors of the mother, (3) behaviors of the most proximal individual, (4) distance between the focal infant and his/her mother, and (5) distance between the focal infant and the most proximal individual. I followed a total of twenty-three Baka infants ranging in age from 1 to 13 months. For comparison, I used the same method to observe three Bombong infants in the village during the rainy season, when both the Baka and the Bombong were exclusively engaged in cultivation. Details on the focal infants' and mothers' activities in instantaneous sampling are summarized in Table 17.1.

The other method I employed was focal continuous sampling, which was conducted the day following instantaneous sampling. Focal infants, both the Baka and the Bombong, were traced continuously for 12 hours from 6:30 to 18:30, and the following parameters were recorded: (1) time of nursing, (2) context of nursing.

In the following sections, I describe Baka infant care, focusing on four issues, which are common to most studies of hunter-gatherer infants: (1) Who cares for infants? (2) How often do mothers nurse the infants? (3) How do caregivers stimulate the infants? (4) How proximal are infants to caregivers?

CHILDREN AS SECONDARY CAREGIVERS

As in many other societies, the primary caregivers of infants among the Baka are the mothers. The instantaneous sampling showed that infants' mothers are the most proximal individuals for 59.3 percent of the daytime

Table 17.1   Details on Instantaneous Sampling

Ethnic Group	Baka					Bombong
Season	Dry		Rainy			Rainy
Place	Village	Camp	Camp	Village	Total	Village
Number of infants						
Boy	7	2	1	2	13	1
Girl	5	1	2	3	10	2
Total	12	3	3	5	23	3
Average age in month of infants						
Mean	6.8	8.7	11.0	9.2	8.1	11.7
SD	2.6	3.3	2.8	3.1	3.2	3.8
Mothers' activities						
Gathering	25.7	66.7	33.3	0.0	24.0	0.0
Fishing	17.1	33.3	66.7	0.0	17.0	0.0
Farming	28.6	0.0	0.0	93.3	40.0	100.0
No activity	28.6	0.0	0.0	6.7	19.0	0.0
Total	100.0	100.0	100.0	100.0	100.0	100.0

1) the rate of mothers' activities means how many days the mothers are engaged in each activity during observational season.
2) The average rate of mothers' activities does not reflect the actual rate of subsistence activities through one year.
3) When the mother is engaged in more than two kinds of subsistence activities, the longest one is employed as the main activity on that day.

on average.[3] Other individuals cared for the infants for the remaining five daylight hours when the mothers were engaged in subsistence activities including food preparation and collecting water. On average, 5.3 people besides the mother were observed as caregivers of the infant during the day.

Hewlett pointed out that multiple or allomaternal caretaking is one of the common features of Pygmy societies (1996). The highest level of multiple caretaking is reported among the Efé. According to Tronick et al. (1987), Efé multiple caretaking is characterized as follows: (1) 14.2 different people on average had physical contact with the infant during their observation, (2) the infant was often nursed by individuals other than the mother, and (3) the infant was transferred from caregiver to caregiver about eight times per hour. Tronick et al. suggest that this parenting system helps Efé infants acquire culturally appropriate behaviors, such as cooperation, sharing, and group identification, by associating with many caregivers in the residential group. In regard to the high transfer rate, they maintain that it is adaptive for increasing infants' heat production in a cool forest environment.[4]

Among the Aka, paternal involvement in infant care is much higher than in any other known societies (Hewlett 1991b). Aka fathers show a strong intimacy and affection toward their infants. They are likely to hug and kiss them more frequently than the mothers. Hewlett identified their technique of net-hunting and the relationship between husbands and wives as some of the influential factors that have led to the evolution of this practice. Aka men and women cooperatively engage in net-hunting, and their relationships are very egalitarian in other social dimensions. In this society, infant care is also shared by both the father and the mother.

These two cases are different in respect to who act as secondary caregivers and what kind of ecological and social contexts involve them in infant care. However, they are consistent in the sense that infant care is assisted by available adults in the residential group. Hewlett says that older siblings may help periodically, but often it is because they want to care for the infants, not because they are given the infant to care for by the mother or are given responsibility (1991b). Children's contribution to infant care has seldom been addressed in the literature on hunter-gatherer societies (see Ivey Henry et al., Chapter 9 in this volume, for the only study to date).

However, I was impressed that Baka children, not only girls but also boys, played an essential role in infant care. Baka mothers rely more on their older children, who are six to ten years old, than on their husbands or other women who are not caring for children in the same residential group. I often observed mothers asking the older siblings of the infant to accompany her and look after the infant while she is working. These older children usually follow the mothers' request meekly. But sometimes they ignore the request, preferring instead to go on short excursions with their peers. It is likely that the Baka children are strongly expected to act as caregivers and are given responsibility for the care of infants, though they, of course, also enjoy being with the infants. In most cases, child caregivers are the infants' older sisters and brothers, but if the infant is the first child or older ones are still too young, it may be the mother's younger brother or sister, who is purposely brought into the residential group into which the mother married to help with infant care and other chores. These children were the proximal to the infants 19.1 percent of the observation time, which is second to mother and much higher than the time infants spent with their fathers (7.7 percent) or grandmothers (7.5 percent).

Why are the Baka children so involved in infant care as secondary caregivers, unlike the Efé and the Aka? The answer may lie in sedentarization and introduction of cultivation. The size of the unit for production and consumption has decreased in line with the progress in substantial cultivation. Furthermore, cultivation has reduced the number of social relationships, which might previously have been enhanced through daily cooperation and extensive food sharing among the Baka in Mbeson. As a result, it has become difficult for adults to provide infant care outside the family. Infant care by children as caregivers also may be enhanced by a dependence on cultivation in the subsistence activities of the Baka. Among the Aka and Mbuti, the secondary caregiver is the father (Hewlett 1996). In contrast, Baka fathers do not participate in infant care as much, particularly in the village. The Aka and Mbuti primarily engage in net-hunting, which requires a long time exploring in the forest. Other children may not be present to care for infants, and the father or other adults may have no choice but to help the mother with infant care. On the other hand, it is not difficult for Baka children to take care of infants while the mother is engaged in subsistence activities, as the Baka mothers mainly work in the fields near the village and the children do not have to move around a large area while holding the infants.

NURSING

Short Nursing Interval Continuing for One Year after Birth

According to childrearing guidebooks, babies settle down to a nursing pattern at the age of three months, which varies from baby to baby. However, most will want to be nursed about six times a day with the intervals varying from three to five hours (Minett 1994). Nursing infants is recommended at fixed intervals in order to make them learn regular habits, but it is also important to nurse them on demand. Furthermore, it is necessary to increase the amount of solid food and reduce the frequency of nursing to wean them about at the age of one (Imamura 1995, 1999).

The Baka nursing pattern is completely different from the regular and deliberate nursing recommended by Japanese and American child-rearing guidebooks. Figure 17.1 shows the change in average interval between nursing sessions[5] per day from the age from 1 to 13 months, which was obtained by continuous sampling. It is clear in this figure that the average Baka nursing interval ranges from 30 to 60 minutes throughout the first year after birth. This contrasts with the Japanese, where the nursing interval is gradually extended to complete weaning by approximately one year of age. Baka infants are nursed more frequently than the Japanese newborns at least for one year. This frequent nursing over a long period reflects the Baka's attitude toward infants.

Many investigators have pointed out that one of the striking features of hunter-gatherer infant care is "indulgence" or "nonrestriction." I witnessed how the Baka are tolerant of infants' demands in various situations. They affirmatively respond by nursing the infants when the infants

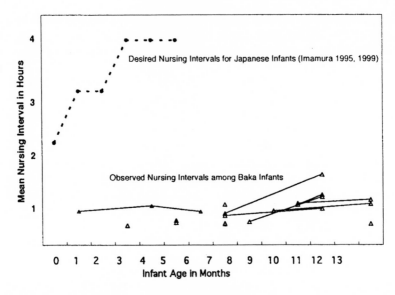

Figure 17.1. Comparisions of desired nursing intervals for Japanese infants and actual nursing intervals of Baka infants.

are fussing or crying. The infants are allowed to begin suckling at their discretion, reminding their mothers by touching or pulling out the mothers' breast. Baka mothers rarely ignore behaviors that are self-initiated by infants, and they do not distract the infants' attention from nursing. They are also very sensitive about infants' crying, which is the only way infants can express their discomfort. I occasionally observed old women reprimanding young mothers who left infants fussing and crying. One day, a Baka infant 13 months of age who was being cared for by her older sister while her mother was out for collecting firewood had been crying for a while. When the mother returned, the girl dressed down her mother severely: "She has been crying. Where have you been wandering for such a long time?" The mother took the baby up in her arms and looked very apologetic. I was surprised that even a seven- or eight-year-old child was accusing her mother of having left the infant crying. The Baka strongly believe that leaving infants frustrated is detrimental to them and that infants' discomfort should be diminished as soon as possible.

Baka infants are weaned all at once when the mother becomes aware of her next pregnancy because they believe that the infant will suffer serious sickness or emaciation if a pregnant mother nurses him/her. So, they refuse infants who want to nurse, no matter how eager the infants are for the milk. Weaning is completed forcibly, sometimes by spreading a red pepper paste or a bitter drink made from *guga* (*Alstonia boonei*) on their nipples. Another way they wean the infant is to forcibly separate the infant from the mother. Occasionally, the grandparents or other related adults take an infant whose mother is pregnant with them into a forest camp.

Interviews with 45 women who experienced childbirth more than once showed that the average childbirth interval in the 1990s was 35 months (41 cases) and that most of the infants weaned at about the age of two. On the other hand, the estimate for pre-1965 was 54 months (25 cases) and 45 months, respectively. This suggestion that the nursing period became shorter after sedentarization is consistent with the Baka's own recognition that weaning is becoming ever earlier. When I was interviewing, one explanation was repeated by elderly women: "Nowadays we have plantain, and we can give ripe plantain to infants. They are satisfied with sweet plantain even though they are not nursed frequently." This discourse by the Baka themselves may support Konner's (2003) prediction that weaning age depends in part on the availability of suitable weaning foods (but see Fouts and Lamb, Chapter 14 in this volume, for an alternative view)).

Until six months of age, Baka infants are fed by breast milk and water. After this stage, they start to eat semisolid food. The Baka do not prepare any special weaning food for infants but give them plantain or wild yam mashed by hand. If they have a dish cooked with hot pepper, the mother puts it in her mouth first, to remove the hot sauce for the infants. At the age of ten months, Baka infants are able to eat all the same foods as their parents, except for some kinds restricted in this period. However, frequent nursing continues and infants are still far from weaning.

Nursing Facilitated by the High Proximity between Infants and Mothers

Frequent nursing continues into late infancy and is partly facilitated by regular physical contact between infants and mothers. A mother begins nursing when her infant cries, regardless of physical contact before nursing (Figure 17.2). She will place her nipple in the infant's mouth if she is already holding the infant, or if she is not already holding the infant, she will quickly pick him/her up and begin nursing. When an infant is away from his/her mother, someone who is near the infant will bring him/her to the mother for nursing.

On the other hand, in 74.8 percent of nursing sessions that started in response to fussing by the infants, mother and infant had been touching prior to nursing. In 76.7 percent of nursing sessions that began with no articulation by the infants, physical contact between the mother and infant had been observed, as well. In short, physical contact between infants and mothers leads to nursing before infants begin crying very much. It is likely

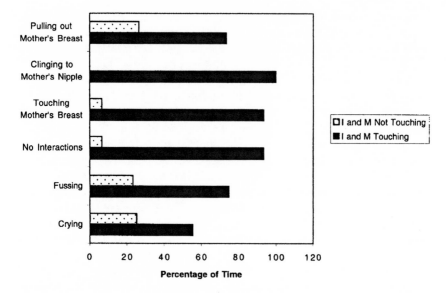

Figure 17.2.   Infant-mother behaviors while not nursing.

that by maintaining contact with their infants, mothers can initiate nursing based on the recognition of minute changes in behaviors that are not obvious to an observer.

Infants aged seven months or older, who are able to manipulate their hands at will, play an important role in initiating nursing. In more than 70 percent of nursing sessions initiated by infant behaviors, physical contact between infants and mothers was observed prior to nursing. In other words, it is due to physical contact that nursing can easily be initiated, by unconstrained behaviors such as clinging to the mother's nipple, pulling out the mother's breast to suck, or touching the mother's breast to provoke her into nursing.

In summary, characteristic nursing is facilitated by regular physical contact between infants and mothers, which occurs more than 50 percent of daylight hours as well as the Baka attitude that infants' demands should be met as soon as possible.

Frequent and Brief Nursing

Another characteristic of Baka nursing is that the duration of nursing bout is quite short. In some nonindustrial societies, a short nursing interval is not always remarkable. The actual difference in the average nursing interval between the Baka and the Bombong is not very great: 39 minutes and 26 seconds for the Baka (23 infants, 8.1 ± 3.8 months of age) and 42 minutes and 22 seconds for the Bombong (3 infants, 11.7 ± 3.8 months of age). Both the Baka and the Bombong are much more frequently nursed than the Japanese.

However, focusing on the pattern of each nursing bout, disparity between the Baka and the Bombong stands out. As I indicate in Table 17.2, duration per nursing bout of the Baka, which is only one to two minutes, is much shorter and frequency of nursing bouts per hour is much higher than that of the Bombong. Furthermore, the pattern of the Baka is somewhat similar to that of other hunter-gatherers in Africa.[6]

The data and contexts of the short duration of nursing bouts among the !Xun San is shown in more detail by Takada (Chapter 13 in this volume). He suggested that a lack of jiggling—a maternal behavior of gently jiggling the infant when the infant stops suckling, which is said to encourage the infant to restart sucking (Masataka, 1993)—as one of the reasons why !Xun nursing occurs frequently and has a much shorter duration than that of other societies such as Japanese and American.

I was under the impression that the maternal behavior he described for the !Xun corresponded in part to that of the Baka. The Baka mothers are highly responsive to infants' demand for nursing. As soon as the infant's suckling is initiated, however, they are no longer attentive to the suckling infant; rather, they converse, prepare food, and even walk through the forest while the infants are suckling. Jiggling is not observed in most nursing bouts among the Baka. The context of maternal behavior during nursing is said to be similar among the Aka (Hewlett, personal communication)

TACTILE STIMULATION

As I emphasized above, the nature of Baka infant care is "indulgence." Another reason why I see the Baka caregivers as abundantly generous with infants' demand is that I did not observe infants cry and fuss very frequently.

According to my instantaneous sampling, Baka infants showed crying for 2.9 percent and fussing for 1.8 percent on average of the daylight hours. In the case of Bombong infants, it was 4.6 and 6.5 percent, respectively. It is likely that Baka infants are left in physiological and psychological discomfort, which is acted out by crying and fussing less frequently than the Bombong.

Cole and Cole (1993) made an interesting proposal that may help to understand the difference of infants' expression between the Baka and the

Table 17.2   Comparison on Sucking Duration

Ethnic Group	Method	Age in Months	Sucking Time per Daytime (%)	Number of Sucking Bouts per Hour	Sucking Duration per Bout (min.)	Reference
Bombong	A	Avg. 11.7	10.2	2.9	2.1	—
Baka*	A	Avg. 8.1	14.9	4.8	1.3	—
Euro-American	B	3–4	12.5	1.6	4.7	Hewlett et al. 2000
Ngandu	B	3–4	12.6	2.2	3.4	Hewlett et al. 2000
Aka*	B	3–4	15.2	4.0	2.4	Hewlett et al. 2000
!Kung*	B	Avg. 13.8	—	4.1	1.9	Konner & Worthman 1980

A: Sucking time per daytime is based on the data from instantaneous sampling and the others are based on the data from continuous sampling.
B: Nursing is coded every thirty seconds and bouts are defined as sequences of intervals separated by at least one interval.
* Active or post forager society.

Bombong. They pointed out that the behaviors for soothing fussing and crying infants vary from society to society, such as patting, tenderly rocking, and swaddling. But the common feature of all these behaviors is to give continuous or rhythmic stimulation to the infants.

How do the Baka and the Bombong caregivers stimulate infants? According to my instantaneous sampling, Baka infants are stimulated both physically and vocally by caregivers more than is the case for the Bombong. In particular, Baka infants were physically stimulated for 12.0 percent of the daylight hours on average, twice as long as the Bombong. Baka caregivers often groom, soothe, kiss, and tenderly rock infants. Japanese caregivers provide strong stimulation such as throwing infants up in the air to please and excite them, but the Baka rarely do so.

In terms of how the Baka stimulate their infants, the following two observations are noteworthy. First, caregivers do not seem to seek to become more deeply involved with the infants. They do not gaze constantly at the infants, but are often absorbed in conversation with others while they physically stimulate the infants. Second, the Baka do not always use physical contact to soothe crying and fussing infants, nor to please and excite them. Rather, infants stay calm when they are physically stimulated. It seems to me that the Baka simply happen to touch their infants, who remain in close contact.

PROXIMITY

Holding Time Influenced by Mothers' Activities

Most researchers who have conducted research with forager infants describe a high level of skin-to-skin contact between infants and caregivers. From the initial stage of the observation, I was impressed how Baka infants are held for a longer time than the Japanese, but, at the same time, I wondered whether they are held for much longer than the Bombong.

Baka infants are held in a sling mostly on the left side of the caregiver. They are carried everywhere the mothers go including into the forest for subsistence activities. The mothers do not mind holding their infants even when they are preparing food.

Baka infants are held 85 percent of daylight hours on average until they are six months old. This continuous holding drastically decreases to an average of 46.9 percent after seven months of age, when most Baka infants are able to sit and adjust their position by themselves. It is also remarkable that holding time in late infancy can differ from day to day by as much as 10 to 80 percent of daylight hours. This fluctuation in holding time depends on the subsistence activities in which the mother is engaged that day. The time infants are held by caregivers increases when the mother moves around the forest for fish-bailing (average 61.9 percent) or gathering (average 51.7 percent), compared to when she is farming in fields near the village (average 36.4 percent). The Bombong infants were held 47.7 percent of daylight hours on average (interestingly they were held slightly longer than the sedentarized Baka hunter-gatherers). In the case of the Aka, who conduct net-hunting in the forest for six to seven hours a day, infants aged nine to ten months are held for 86.7 percent of daylight hours (Hewlett et al. 1998). They are probably held for much longer than Baka infants because of the higher mobility of their mothers' activities. The shorter holding time during late infancy among the Baka may be related to the decreased mobility of mothers' activities since the introduction of substantial cultivation.

Various predictions on continuous holding among hunter-gatherer societies have been proposed. For instance, Kaplan and Dove (1987) say that Ache mothers in eastern Paraguay continuously hold their infants to protect them from a hazardous environment. Tronick et al. (1987), who reported outstanding multiple caretaking among the Efé, suggest that continuous holding with high rate of transfer is adaptive in cool forests because the infants are always incorporated into another's temperature regulatory system. Hewlett et al. (1998) suggested another explanation, considering that the Aka change camps several times a year in a broad area of forest: the Aka continuously hold the infants to take into account potential hazards in a changing environment. In this way, continuous holding is said to enhance infants' fitness. Nevertheless, intracultural variability in holding time among the Baka shows that holding is strongly affected by the mobility of mothers' activities. The Baka, who adapted to lower mobile subsistence activity and sedentary lifestyle, no longer need to hold their infants as long as other active hunter-gatherers do.

High Proximity between Infants and Caregivers Compared with the Bombong

The difference between the Baka and the Bombong in regard to proximity between infants and caregivers emerges in time of physical contact. Baka infants are seldom left alone even after they are able to sit by themselves. They usually sit near the caregivers or within the caregivers' legs whose knees are drawn up.

As I mentioned above, holding time fluctuates with the mothers' activities during the day. However, the time of tactile contact, including holding, between infants and caregivers reached about 80 percent among the Baka regardless of the kinds of mothers' activities, compared to 62.2 percent among the Bombong. Bombong infants were left out of reach of caregivers twice as long as Baka infants were (Figure 17.3).

High proximity between infants and caregivers is said to be one of the features of high infant mortality societies (LeVine 1974). Compared to the Bombong, who are one of the ethnic groups of African farmers, the Baka caregivers are more proximal to the infants. While Baka caregivers are more proximal than Bombong caregivers, caregiver-infant interactions vary dramatically by context (see Table 17.3).

One day, I asked a Baka mother, who remained in the village during the season when most of the Baka were out plowing the fields, "Why aren't

Table 17.3 Behaviors of Most Proximal Individuals

Ethnic Group											Bombong	
Season	Dry				Rainy						Rainy	
Place	Village		Camp		Camp		Village		Total		Village	
	M	SD	M	SD	M	SD	M	SD	M	SD	M	SD
Behaviors with Infants												
Behaviors for infants' survival												
Nursing	16.1	5.5	13.7	6.2	14.4	3.5	12.5	4.6	14.9	5.5	10.2	5.7
Giving food or water	0.7	1.0	0.2	0.5	0.5	0.7	2.2	4.6	1.0	2.5	0.0	0.0
Bathing or dressing	0.3	0.6	0.2	0.5	0.0	0.0	0.8	1.5	0.4	0.9	0.0	0.0
Others	1.9	1.6	0.5	0.7	0.0	0.0	2.7	2.1	1.8	1.8	4.6	2.4
Physical stimulations of infant												
Grooming	1.9	1.9	3.0	1.5	3.7	1.7	4.7	3.0	2.8	2.5	0.9	0.7
Soothing	2.5	2.1	2.1	1.6	1.9	0.7	1.8	1.7	2.2	1.9	0.9	0.7
Swinging	1.7	1.9	0.8	1.1	1.0	0.8	1.9	2.1	1.6	1.8	0.3	0.5
Kissing	2.1	2.0	1.4	0.8	2.8	2.3	1.1	1.1	1.8	1.8	1.4	1.1
Patting	1.2	1.4	0.9	1.5	1.9	1.3	1.6	1.5	1.3	1.4	1.4	1.1
Others	1.5	1.5	1.4	1.1	1.9	1.3	2.2	4.7	1.7	2.6	0.9	0.7
Vocal stimulation of infants												
Talking	3.2	2.1	4.4	1.5	2.8	2.3	4.7	3.9	3.7	2.7	3.2	1.3
Nonverbal vocalizing	2.7	2.5	1.6	1.0	2.3	1.3	2.2	2.0	2.4	2.2	1.9	1.7
Singing	1.1	1.5	0.9	1.0	0.0	0.0	1.1	1.9	1.0	1.5	0.0	0.0
Others	1.0	2.6	1.4	1.6	0.0	0.0	1.3	1.8	1.0	2.3	0.0	0.0
Other involvement with infants												
Watching	0.5	1.2	0.0	0.0	0.0	0.0	0.0	0.0	0.3	1.0	0.0	0.0
Gazing	18.9	8.5	17.6	4.7	15.3	5.2	19.6	8.0	18.8	8.0	18.1	2.3
Others	1.2	1.3	1.6	1.0	1.4	1.1	1.6	1.8	1.3	1.4	3.7	1.3
Subsistence activities and work												
Cultivation	0.4	1.3	0.2	0.5	0.0	0.0	3.0	7.5	1.0	4.0	3.7	0.7
Fish-bailing	1.1	3.3	2.8	3.9	16.7	12.0	0.0	0.0	1.8	5.3	0.0	0.0
Hunting	0.1	0.5	0.0	0.0	0.0	0.0	0.0	0.0	0.1	0.4	0.0	0.0
Gathering	0.4	1.0	0.0	0.0	0.5	0.7	0.3	0.6	0.4	0.9	0.0	0.0
Walking outside	9.1	8.7	12.7	5.1	7.4	4.6	5.4	4.6	8.5	7.7	6.0	5.6
Other work	9.3	6.0	9.0	4.1	8.3	5.9	6.7	5.9	8.6	5.9	13.9	5.2
"Others (Sleeping, Eating, Leisure, etc.)"	80.0	22.0	82.3	12.6	69.9	15.5	86.2	12.9	81.3	19.3	74.1	1.3

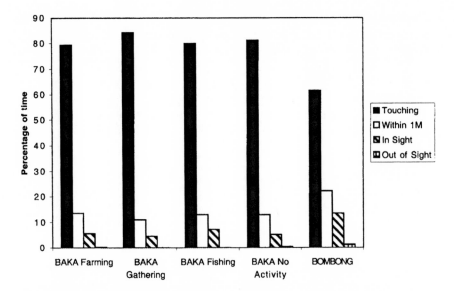

Figure 17.3.   Percentage of time Baka (in various contexts) and Bombong are proximal to another individual.

you going to work today?" She said, "My son doesn't want to go along with me. Who will look after my baby while I am working?" Her baby was nine months old at that time. Had she been a Bombong infant, she would have been left alone at a corner of the field while her mother was working. This infant's mother, however, chose to stay with her in the village, rather than leave her alone in the field. Baka caregivers seem to aspire to be with the infants or not leave them alone as much as possible.

High proximity between infants and caregivers is one of the most quintessential features of infant care among the Baka, considering that physical contact between infants and mothers enables a high frequency of nursing, and tactile stimulation to infants might provide psychological comfort to the infants and create a difference in infant expression between the Baka and the Bombong.

DISCUSSION

Two Facets of Infant Care among the Baka

This chapter has described infant care among the Baka, and has partly examined the impact of sedentarization and introduction of substantial cultivation on infant care practices. These results lead to the conclusion that two facets of infant care, which could be regarded as "possibly changed" and "unchanged," exist among the Baka.

The first facet pertains to infant care practices that are new or partly modified from previous ways. First, Baka children are given the responsibility of being secondary caregivers and therefore play an important role in infant care. Second, holding time during late infancy appears to have decreased because of the lower mobility associated with the mothers' subsistence activities. Third, Baka wean infants earlier than before, as ripe plantains are easily available.[7]

The second facet involves infant care patterns that differ from those of neighboring farmers, but that are similar to those of other hunter-gatherer societies in tropical and subtropical regions. Baka mothers frequently nurse in response to the demands of the infants, and their infants are often stimulated through tactile contact. There is also highly close proximity between infants and caregivers.

The two facets "possibly changed" and "changed" suggest that infant care practices have not changed uniformly, even though Baka society has experienced considerable ecological, social, and economic change following sedentarization and the introduction of farming. The contribution of children to infant care may have been necessitated to mitigate the weakening of mutual assistance among adults of the same residential group. Holding during late infancy may be directly related to mobility, so that the Baka caregivers no longer hold their infants as much as active Aka foragers do. Thus, infant care practices that are closely related to certain social conditions may be more likely to change when the social conditions change. On the other hand, the interaction between infants and caregivers, such as abundant tactile stimulation, frequent nursing, and high proximity, are so deeply ingrained in Baka society that they have not changed in the 40 years since sedentarization.

Infant Care as Embodied Interaction

In their comparative study of the Aka and the neighboring Ngandu farmers, Hewlett and his colleagues suggested the existence of a "forager-pattern of infant care" (Hewlett et al. 1998, 2000). This parenting pattern includes continuous holding, frequent nursing, and proximal interaction between infants and caregivers, and is generated by the unique niche of the Aka as foragers. The "forager pattern of infant care" is explained as follows. First, the Aka continuously hold their infants to mitigate potential hazards in the changing environment incidental to their high mobility. Second, a denser social context, such as remaining within the limited space of a camp and frequent cooperative activities, allows Aka parents to be more willing to hold and nurse infants, which may provide substantial stimulation for both mothers and infants. Third, mutual assistance through cooperative hunting and extensive food sharing may ensure that Aka mothers are less concerned about food supplies, which in turn may leave them free to invest in energetically costly infant care. Fourth, the Aka focus on immediate rather than delayed gratification; this encourages care providers to satisfy the demands of infants as soon as possible.

As I mentioned above, the forager pattern of infant care has been re-tained among the Baka without serious modifications, even though some aspects of infant care practices have changed. This characteristic infant care pattern among the Baka must have been established throughout genera-tions of foraging. However, considering that the sedentarized Baka still re-tain the forager pattern of infant care, it can be said that forager pattern of infant care does not contradict a sedentarized and agriculture-centered lifestyle. The direct causal relation between infant care practices and macro-social factors (i.e., ecological environment, subsistence activity, and social structure) should be reconsidered. This case study is too limited to deter-mine why the Baka have retained the forager pattern of infant care, or what its meaning is for the Baka people. To examine this gap between macroso-cial conditions and infant care patterns among the Baka, I would like to point out similarities between infant care behavior and the behavior pat-tern of the Baka in other situations.

Baka adults are often seen spatially very close to one another, as well as when they care for infants. When the Bombong sit in their houses, they leave some space between individuals, whereas aggregation of the Baka, especially females, is much denser, such that their bodies are often in con-tact. Furthermore, Baka females frequently groom one another and their infants. Grooming the Baka seems to be not only a sanitary affair but also a "friendly and sociable interaction," as Sugawara (1990) suggested in his study of the Bushmen. The size and type of housing in the Baka village dif-fers from that of the Bombong. Like the Bombong, the Baka now construct houses with mud walls and roofs made of raffia palm leaves. However, Baka houses are smaller and placed closer together. It is likely that the Baka adults are very proximal to each other and seem to depend on phys-ical communication more than their neighbors.

The style of interaction among the Baka is fundamentally congruous with the forager pattern of infant care. In other words, the style of embod-ied social interactions of each individual among the Baka emerges in their contact with infants, and generates the forager pattern of infant care. In-fant care practices among the Baka tell me that infant care should be examined as a microsocial interaction in addition to analysis from the per-spective of macrosocial conditions.

ACKNOWLEDGMENTS

This study was financially supported by Grant-in-Aid for International Scientific Research (No. 12371004) from the Ministry of Education, Science, Sports and Culture, Japan. The research authorization was obtained from the Ministry of Scientific and Technical Research of the Republic of Cameroon. Dr. Nguima-Mawong (University of Yaoundé) was gracious to offer me a research permit. Dr. Ichikawa (Kyoto University) and Dr. Kimura (Kyoto University) gave me the opportunity for research and instructive advice throughout my work. Dr. Hewlett and other participants of the Ninth International Conference on Hunting and Gathering Societies gave me productive suggestions to improve my manuscript. To these ministries and persons, I make grateful acknowledgment. Finally, I wish to express my hearty thanks and immense respects to the Baka and the Bombong in Mbeson for their generosity and patience.

NOTES

1. See Konner, Chapter 2 in this volume. He reviews some important studies and summarizes discussions on infancy among hunter-gatherer societies.

2. The Bombong report that the first Bombong immigrant in Mbeson introduced the Baka to cultivation by working together with them in his fields.

3. Maternal primacy varied from 39.8 percent in the forest camp during dry season to 80.6 percent in the forest camp during rainy season. This great fluctuation is attributable to the mothers' workload and camp composition. In the first case, the Baka wandered from place to place in the forest every two days for hunting and gathering wild yams. While they were moving to another camp, the infants were usually held by their fathers, because the mothers had to carry lots of baggage such as pots, sleeping mats, and bunches of plantains. Whenever they arrived at the camp, the mothers built new huts. The mothers in dry season camp were very busy, so that maternal primacy in infant care was quite low. On the other hand, they stayed at one campsite for a few weeks during the rainy season. On most days the men were out of camp for hunting during daylight hours. Though the mothers made a short trip for fish-bailing in the stream near the camp, they spent much time in relaxing at the campsite. This allows the mothers to concentrate on childcare for longer than in the dry season. In addition, in the rainy season camp, caregivers other than mothers were not available, since this camp had been set up by the young couples who did not have any older children.

4. Hewlett and Konner suggest a different version of the observed multiple caretaking among the Efé, focusing on their low fertility. Among the Efe, total fertility rate is 2.6 per woman, which is exceptionally lower than other societies. As a result, the number of potential women as caregiver is much larger and a high level of multiple caretaking takes place among the Efé (Hewlett 1989, 1991a; Konner 2003).

5. In this chapter, "nursing bout" and "nursing session" are operationally defined as follows: "nursing bout" means the situation when the mother's nipple is

in the infant's mouth, whereas "nursing session" involves more than one nursing bout and is considered over when the interval between bouts exceeds five minutes.

6. It is not appropriate to compare the numerical data shown here rigorously, because observational methods are different from one another. However, a certain tendency is clearly shown in this table.

7. Further research and comparison with another residential group of the Baka, who are still relying on hunting and gathering more than the Baka in Mbeson, are expected to examine the impact of sedentarization and introduction of substantial cultivation more carefully.

18

Deforesting among Andamanese Children

Political Economy and History of Schooling

Vishvajit Pandya

For Andaman Islanders (Andaman Island is located in the Bay of Bengal) in spite of the shrinking forest and the increasing numbers of outside settlers, being in the forest is still important. For Andamanese, being in the forest is much like belonging to a church as conceived by Durkheim (1915:59). In this conception, church is something that makes individuals adhere to practices connecting the group, uniting the individuals by the fact that they think in the same way about the "sacred" and its relation to the world of the "profane." Much like members of a church translate common ideas into common practices, Andaman Islanders also translate their ideas about the forest into various practices within the forest. Their practice of hunting and gathering in the forest shows the Andaman Islanders' shared fundamental cultural concern, particularly in responding to the world beyond the forest. Outsiders who invade the forest are seen in much the same way as are the "profane" with regard to the church. This chapter focuses on three Andamanese ethnic groups: (1) the Great Andamanese, who were resettled on Strait Island after India's independence, (2) the Ongees of Little Andaman, who in 1952 were provided with a settlement within the reserved forest, and (3) the Jarwas of Middle Andaman and South Andaman, who are confined to a tribal reserve forest (see Figure 18.1 for locations). The chapter emphasizes the Ongee situation as this is where I have conducted most of my ethnographic research.

Classical accounts of the Andaman Islands (Man 1883; Portman 1899; Radcliffe-Brown [1922] 1964) relate that twelve groups of hunting and gathering Negritos shared language and customs within the cluster of islands. Today about 450 hunting and gathering individuals survive. With

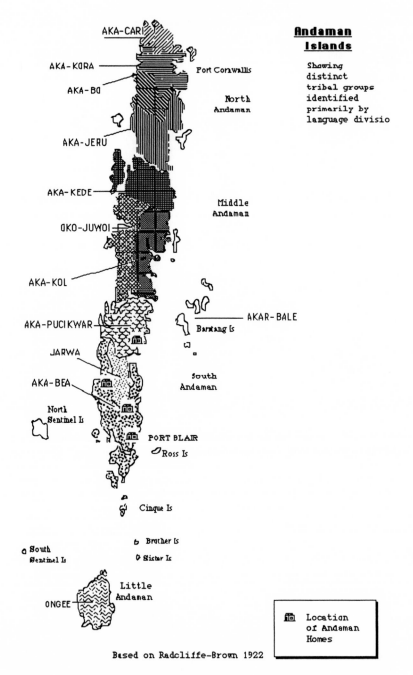

Figure 18.1.   Map of the Andaman Islands.

the exception of the Sentinels and the slowly changing position of the Jarwas, other groups of Andaman Islanders hardly practice hunting and gathering as a primary activity. All these groups make up less than 0.32 percent of the Andaman Islands' population, and are surrounded by an ever-increasing nontribal population known locally as settlers. The settlers began as small farmers and exploiters of the forest resources, but over a period of time they have become wage earners in the nearby towns. After India's independence in 1947, the Andaman Islands were incorporated as a union territory, which resulted in the formulation of a welfare policy to protect the declining tribal population. According to the 1956 Tribal Act, tribal territories were designated, and the presence of outsiders was controlled and minimized. However, the increasing number of settlers on the island has not curbed illegal encroachment involving collecting and poaching in the tribal reserved area.

Throughout the historical period of colonialism (1750–1940s), postindependence, and the contemporary situation on the islands, outsiders have figured prominently in the worldview of the Andaman Islanders living in different parts of the islands (Figure 18.1).

This chapter focuses on the role of schools brought into the forest by the outsiders, forms of schooling that evolved with the drive to exploit the forest resources in tribal areas, the functioning of schools, and the impact of school among the hunter-gatherers. I intend to analyze the extraneous ideas of schooling for the children of hunter-gatherers and how it creates a dissonance in the forest, which has been systematically destroyed, while attempting to transform the children in the forest into something that is not of the world of the forest.

The Great Andamanese, who were among the earliest to be settled, and the Jarwas, whose future is still in flux and whose circumstances are rapidly changing around them, form the two extremes of schooling and socialization. That is, for the Great Andamanese schools have been functioning for a long time, while among the Jarwas no schools have been formally introduced, but a process of Jarwas and non-Jarwas learning and socializing about each other's values has been going on since 1999. I use the observations from the community of Ongees whom I have known since the days when they had no children's school (1983) to the days when school for Ongee children started, around 1990. Like some of the contributions in this book that have directly or indirectly focused on the acquisition of skills by hunter-gatherer children (Chapters 5–7), my concern here is to outline what schools and schooling have accomplished in different communities of Andamanese hunter-gatherers. The socialization of children in the forest as "school" and the socialization of Andamanese children in a school within the forest have had a tremendous impact on the children of the hunter-gatherers of the Andaman Islands. This is an analysis that uses

ethnographic and historical accounts to understand the very idea of what
Andamanese socialize their children for and what the state-designed various educational institutions accomplish among the Andaman Islanders.
Politically and historically, in school children learn about society, but, in
the Andamans' case, schools are a place that socializes the children for the
state-conceived and -constructed society that exists outside the forest. It is
the aspiration of the government-funded and welfare agency-managed
schools that children of hunter-gatherers will become citizens, participating in a political economy in which individuals should be productive, and
gainfully employed.

As the extraneous idea of school has played an increasingly significant
role, outsiders have systematically and subtly insisted on denying Andamanese participation in their forest, which is the basis of their value system and practice for the parents of the children who continue to live in the
forest but go to schools that are appropriate neither for the world of forest
nor for the world outside. In Durkheim's perception, education is a social
reality, much like the forest or the church, "a collection of practices and institutions that have been organized slowly in the course of time, and are
integrated with all the other social institutions, and express them" (Durkheim 1956:65). As a result, the socialization of children becomes a means of
instilling in them the idea of society, and the pedagogical ideals, relative to
history, are explainable by social structure (Durkheim 1956:122). The function of education is thus to inculcate in the child a certain number of physical and mental attitudes that society considers should not be lacking in
any of its members and certain physical and mental attitudes that the particular social group considers, equally, ought to be found in all its members (Durkheim 1956:67–70). If education is the image and reflection of
"society" (Durkheim 1951:372) how do the Andamanese in the forest educate children in the practices idealized, both physically and morally by
Andamanese culture, and what impact do outsiders have on the Andamanese, who have their own notion of education and children of the
forest? The colonial administration and later the postindependence government of India both had a different notion of the society in which the
children of the forest had to live. This invariably implies three different
models of and for Andamanese children of the forest: (1) school, where
Andamanese learn about the forest, making the forest itself a school; (2)
the colonialists' presentation and imposition on the parents and children
of Andamans of a school that is "out of forest"; (3) the present-day school
structure "put in the forest" by the Indian government. All three are based
on the society or state idealizing what role an individual should have in
the political economy (cf. Bourdieu 1997; Illich 1971). All three forms of
"education" indicate historical shifts and become progressively collapsing
structures. In the process of pulling the children out of the forest, the con-

cern for controlling the Andamanese remains constant. Through schools, outsiders have organized the strategy and instruments to control the hunter-gatherers of Andaman forests. This is particularly evident in the ongoing production of Andamanese tribal language books that the children of forest can comprehend in order to become "productive citizens." This process outlines a progressive trajectory of the "administrators" gaining more control over the Andamanese to make them settle down. In spite of the presence of schools "outside the forest" and "within the forest," an idea of what children should become by going to school has failed to produce a productive citizen who can read, write, and count. Strangely enough, the schools have also failed to instill the socialized and idealized image of society that the forest used to instill as a school and church for the children of Andamanese hunter-gatherers.

CHILDREN IN THE FOREST AND THE FOREST AS SCHOOL

In the Andamanese culture children are highly valued (Pandya 1993:183–189, 242). They are not regarded as a product of a reproductive act between husband and wife; instead the man and woman become father and mother as the spirit enters the womb of a woman in the form of food consumed by the Andamanese (Radcliffe-Brown [1922] 1964:51, 76, 79–80, 89–90). It is common practice that even before the child is born the expectant parents appoint a couple to be responsible for raising the child as adopted parents. The children in the camp are always regarded as the collective responsibility of all the campmates, so much so that only the parents administer discipline but the whole camp very much indulges children and constantly looks after them. In 1983 when I first started my fieldwork among the Ongees of Little Andaman Island, for the first month the job I was given by the Ongees was to assist the elders in looking after the children in the campsite as the men and women went out to the forest or to the coast for their daily activities. Much of my understanding of children growing up in a so-called "traditional" pattern of socialization within the forest context is based on my fieldwork done in 1983–84.

Until the age of seven or eight the children stay back and spend time playing particularly games that develop their sense of interdependence and observation (Pandya 1992b). Children also make play out of trying to mimic adults, like playing with smaller versions of bows and arrows, tying knots, or making temporary shelters with materials on hand within the campground. After reaching the age of ten, children are encouraged to go with adults to various locations in the forest, in the creeks, and along the coast. However, this increases in duration and distance as the children grow up, and learn about the safety and dangers of being hunter-gatherers, particularly when they too might be hunted by the spirits all around them. The important value to be learned is that work is specific to place and is not decided by the amount of time it takes to finish it. As a result, if the young boys went out hunting pigs in the appropriate season they would try not to return till they had succeeded, even if it took two or three days. However, the boys accompany only men and the girls accompany only women. It is not that the children essentially contribute to the actual hunting and gathering but they are trained to remain quiet as they follow the elders, carrying baskets, digging sticks, nets, or smoldering branches of wood. With children remaining quiet, a virtue expected of a good child, the adults constantly talk and show the children what to look for in the forest around them. The Ongee term for this socialization and learning, or becoming educated, is *eneyebelabe*. This is the way all the indexes and signs of resources required and shared are imparted to the child. For instance, various birds are pointed out, which would indicate the presence of honeycombs or fruits. The presence of various types of wood needed for various forms of material culture is shown to the children. Young girls learn where to dig for tubers and where to look for crabs.

For children, going to the forest is not just to assist in production, but is a visit to the forest as a repository of knowledge and for learning practical techniques pertaining to the forest. In order to encourage the children to come along with adults, depending on gender and the division of labor, adults often cook part of the food gathered away from the camp and serve it to the accompanying child. They then let them take part of it back to the campground to share with their siblings and cousins and to give as small treats, like betel leaves for aged relatives confined to the campground. As the boys and girls grow up, they form groups of teenagers who can go out without any adults. Groups are encouraged to bring in all they can from the forests. Young boys often set up their own shelter adjacent to the main camp site and cook their own meals, but girls always return to their parents' home and contribute to the home kitchen or the communal cooking area within the middle of the campground. In this way the children are educated in the forest as school, so that they grow up as well-integrated individuals who are socialized into what Radcliffe-Brown ([1922] 1964) expressed as individuals having a sense of dependence on the collective or society. By the time teenagers are ready to perform these activities on their own, they have learn the important issue of getting resources without endangering themselves in the forest and bringing back resources to be shared within the campsite. The Andamanese forest represents society with all its articulation of relations and needs. Being in the forest is idealized for children growing up, as they learn about the forest. Life for the Ongees is so invariably and inexorably tied to the forest that it affects all social practices. It is not difficult to comprehend the paraphrase of Durkheim's notion of belonging to church for Andamanese as belonging to a forest. What was observed among the relatively unchanged life of the Ongees in 1983 perhaps was culturally true for various Andaman Islanders before they came in contact with the outside world and experienced different degrees of impact from the outside world. (Outsiders began arriving in Middle Andaman and South Andaman in 1789.)

HISTORY OF THE "HOSTILE SAVAGE" AND THE "UNDISCIPLINED CHILD"

Early attempts at creating a British settlement at Port Blair, by clearing the forest, were met with great hostility and resentment by Andamanese tribal groups. The isolated location of the island, inhabited only by a hostile tribal population, made the Andamans a perfect location for a prison. By 1858 the process of clearing the forest for a penal settlement was undertaken. Captain John Campbell wrote in favor of selecting the Andaman Islands as a penal settlement that while convicts could not be prevented from escaping when working on the mainland, on the Andamans they would only be able to escape to the jungles and could not get away from the Andamans, as the savages were far too hostile to allow one to escape (Portman 1899). In fact, within six to ten months after the first shipload of 733 convicts, 240 prisoners were found dead in the vicinity of the penal settlement killed by native arrows. Seventy prisoners were reported to have escaped and disappeared without trace (letter no. 1079, 12 July 1859, from J. P. Walker to C. Beadon, secretary to the Government of India). Early contact with the Andamanese was characterized by dealing with the extremely hostile and unreliable tribes in the forest. Alexander Hamilton, who navigated the Bay of Bengal between 1688 and 1723, asserted that the Andamanese were cannibals and extremely violent and used to take slaves from the neighboring islands of Nicobar (1930:36–38). Andaman Islanders had a reputation for killing any sailor who landed on the islands, either through shipwreck or while in search of fresh water. In fact, they would wait in armed groups of various sizes to ambush and kill anyone who landed on islands like the Little Andamans (Alexander 1827:8–12). Colebrooke (1795) confirmed the hostility of the natives of the Little Andamans. Records of the colonial administrator's trips within the Andamanese forests, published in early census reports (Temple 1903), show how British "punitive expeditions" sustained and perpetuated such violent images of the outsiders for the Andaman Islanders.

Attempts to make friendly contact with "the natives" were generally unsuccessful, and were soon replaced by a pattern of gift-giving and -receiving, which involved mostly food and implements. Over a period, this led to the Jarwas being brought aboard the ships. Lieutenant Colonel Albert Fytche (1861) notes that in order to make proper observations and learn about the Andamanese, the captured natives were taken to Rangoon, but this was not very successful. This lack of success was apparently mainly due to the fact that the captives mostly adopted the captors' language, but in order to learn the language of the tribals, it was important to observe them as a larger group interacting among themselves. On board, the Jarwas could observe the clothed British naval officers with the same curiosity as the nontribals observed their nakedness. This interaction was reportedly characterized by the outsiders trying not to laugh as they gave gifts to establish relations, while the Jarwas were childishly amused and ran around chaotically. Often Jarwas were thrown overboard to swim back to the coast.

In addition to being characterized as hostile, they were perceived to be childlike, impressionable, unpredictable, and undisciplined. Because of their short stature, the Negrito tribal populations in other parts of insular South East Asia also have been represented as children by ethnologists and missionaries (Schebesta 1929; Stewart 1975; Skeat and Blagden 1906). The work and influence of Father Willhiem Schmidt is particularly interesting for seeing how Negritos in Asia were represented as children in a vision that blends Christian missionary sensibility with ethnological pursuit. As the colonial authority established itself near the region of Port Blair, the Andamanese were no longer synonymous with hostile people, but "child" became the metaphor for the Andamanese in the forest.

OUT OF THE FOREST INTO THE SCHOOLS, THE COLONIAL SITUATION, AND ANDAMANESE "CHILDREN"

Taking a position against all previous conceptions and representations of the Andamanese, Portman, who was the officer in charge of the Andamanese in the 1890s, said

> Often one hears the English schoolboys described as savage and after sixteen years of experience of Andamanese, I find that in many ways they closely resemble the average lower class English country schoolboy. (Portman 1896: 362–371).

What led to this image of the Andamanese "schoolboy" was a new policy started in May 1861. All Andamanese were to be treated like children and schooling them was going to be a strategy for facilitating effective occupation of the Andamanese territory. Three young Andamanese boys were captured and sent to Burma for education. The object was that these Andamanese boys after receiving education and training in Burma would serve as a medium of intercourse with the tribes of the Andamans (NAI, Delhi Home Department, Judicial Branch, O.C. No 59, 18 March 1861). These boys, named Crouso, Jumbo, and Friday could not adjust to Burma and attempted to escape in a crude raft. The project of sending the boys to Burma for schooling failed and on 12 September 1861, without anything being learned, the Andamanese returned (Portman 1899:320–33). The only thing accomplished by this "schooling project" was that the returning two individuals narrated to their countrymen their newly gained experience, which started the process of the Andamanese extending friendly relations to the British authorities at Port Blair.

By 1863 Reverend Corbyn (Portman 1899:378–459) started his version of a boarding school, known as "Andaman Home," and took care of an increasing number of the islanders (Ball 1897). Andaman Homes were soon set up all around the cleared area of Port Blair and Reverend Corbyn was assisted by convicts in keeping up the growing institution of Andaman Homes. Soon these homes became a place to house various tribal captives who had broken some law, and individuals from different areas who were brought in by allurements of gifts.

At these homes there was a program of teaching English and some money was provided to the residents for clearing the forest. Corbyn's training at Andaman Home in fact created the first group of Andamanese interlocutors between Andamanese culture and colonial authorities (NAI, Delhi Home Department, Public Branch, O.C. Nos. 17–20, 31 July 1863, April 1864; O.C. Nos. 37–41, April 1864; O.C. Nos. 24–26, 28 July 1864). By 1865 about 150 Andamanese from different areas were regular residents of Andaman Home, a place that was part school and part prison outside the forest. What could not be achieved by sending the Andamanese to faraway places for education was now being achieved by bringing them out of the forest and training them to work in gardens, to help in the administration's negotiations with other Andamanese, and to track escaped convicts from the main prison. The appointment of a European family to provide full-time instruction to the Andamanese in "English ways" was even considered, but lack of funding made it difficult. J. N. Homfray succeeded Reverend Corbyn in 1866 and took some of the Andamanese, suitably transformed, out for enrollment in missionary schools in Calcutta, Pennang, and Rangoon. However, like the first batch of boys sent to Rangoon in 1861, it was realized that schooling of Andamanese far away was impossible. While away for schooling, many fell sick and died or acquired habits unacceptable to the authorities. By 1870 tribal boys and girls were being housed in a new home that was significantly represented as an orphanage/school and managed by the wife of E. H. Man.

Apart from English and arithmetic, Indian convicts taught Hindustani. It was reported that Andamanese children after learning some English were employed as domestic help but soon their learning skills would come to an abrupt end (Census Report of 1911). The orphanage had strict regulation of children being constantly fed and rules to keep boys separate from girls, but in the classes for handicraft needlework was taught to both sexes (annual reports cited in Portman 1899:849-51). By the end of 1871 a number of matrons and teachers had to be replaced because as orphanage/school staff they had resigned in order to go back to other colonial posts for marriage, but the institution had started making money from what the Andamanese children were producing. Success was also measured in terms of the dozen or so Andamanese boys and girls who had been baptized and regularly attended church services on Ross Island. According to R. C. Temple, Andamanese in childhood were bright and intelligent but soon reached a peak in development. An adult Andamanese was now comparable to "a civilized child of ten or twelve" (Temple 1903: 47–66). In spite of the schooling, disciplining them, and making them somewhat productive within the political economy of the colonial administration, Andamanese adults were considered nothing more then children of the "authority" (Nandy 1988:11–18).

During the year 1872–73 the increased participation of the Andamanese in church activities and their capacity to recite prayers opened a path for translating, transcribing, and producing texts in various dialects, including some aspects of grammar (see Figure 18.2). The language manuals pro-

Figure 18.2.   1874. Andamanese photographed in Port Blair Andaman Home. Note the Choir Boys of Andamanese descent in church uniform. Source: Anthropological Survey of India.

duced contained various commands and orders, which the colonial officer could give to the islanders in categories like hunting, camping, and cleaning as well as a section on photography commands for the natives to sit in different ways and not move. Projects were undertaken to compile dictionaries (Man 1923; Portman 1887; Temple 1899, 1908) so that the natives could be communicated with and administered. It was in this period that the Lord's Prayer translation into Northern Andamanese dialect was completed (Man and Temple 1877) so that the residents of the Andaman Home could pray with the local chaplain. Andamanese who had practically become inmates of the so-called Homes were now fluent in conversational Hindustani and English.

This also opened up the situation for Andamanese young boys and girls to be abused in all possible ways by the convict population on the island. In 1867 a large number of the "home" residents were found to be suffering from syphilis. This was mainly because the convicts could tempt Andamanese for sexual favors by gifts of tobacco, opium, and liquor. Authorities now realized that the morality and chastity of Andamanese girls, married or unmarried, was not protected even by being in Andaman Homes (Portman 1899: 605-606, NAI, Delhi Home Department, Port Blair Branch, B progs. No. 30, July 1876). In addition to these efforts to know and communicate with the islanders and civilize them, 1877 was marked by a peak in the number of deaths, due to an outbreak of measles in the Andaman Home, which spread beyond into the forest. In 1892, the chaplain of Port Blair wrote: "Andamanese islanders are like British schoolboys who love freedom but hate discipline, which we have instilled up to a degree through prayers!" (Annual Report, Andamans of 1892).

By 1892 the islanders, now characterized as British schoolboys, had become a twofold management problem: how to manage a hostile and fierce savage and how to deal with the native who, under British influence, had become timid and childlike. The problem of management was complicated by the rapid decline in the tribal population. Preserving the rapidly dying population was seen as the responsibility of the administration. However, change and transformation could not be denied, since the total population of the Andamanese in 1901 had declined to 1,895, implying a loss of nearly 47 percent of the people in a span of only about a hundred years. The attempt to put the Andamanese into schools made in the image of the colonial authorities to produce productive and obedient Andamanese subjects had succeeded. The British acquired the language and got reliable support from the Great Andamanese to deal with the Jarwas and the Ongees. Trained Andamanese would track escaped convicts from prison and help conduct punitive expeditions. At a very high cost, the school created a small class of native orderlies. The Andamanese Home that had functioned as a school and orphanage under the colonial power became a place for the Andamanese to lose their dignity and identity. Above all, the school outside the forest also became a source for the spread of various diseases, causing a large number of deaths in the forest.

POSTINDEPENDENT INDIA AND SCHOOLS AMONG THE ANDAMANESE

In 1914 the government of India framed a new policy toward the remaining Andamanese. One of the principles to be followed was that "the attempts to educate should be of simplest and natural character" (NAI, Delhi Home Department, Port Blair Branch, A Progs., No. 32, October 1914). In pursuance of the above policy, all Andaman Homes were closed except the one at Dundas Point, which was converted into a Great Andamanese troop of bush police to specially deal with the Jarwas in Middle and South Andaman. After the independence of India, by 1968 all the remaining 15 families of Great Andamanese of mixed decent from nontribal parentage were settled on Strait Island. They were provided with all the free rations and clothing they would need to live a settled life. Government reports (ASI 1952; Department of Social Welfare 1969) asserted that to keep the Great Andamanese alive was its most important priority. The welfare agency responsible for all the tribes on the island, AAJVS, in 1976 set up a nonformal education center on Strait Island for the Great Andamanese. Daily about three to five children come there to learn languages spoken in the mainland communities because they want to interact with their extended family members who do not understand Hindustani. The social workers' main concern is to keep their mental and physical health at a satisfactory level, for the survival of the so-called tribe. So nonformal education for the children as well as adults is fulfilled by three hours of daily television viewing in the afternoon (soap operas or cricket matches) and two hours at night (news, songs, and dance shows). The welfare agency's noble goal is to instill among the Great Andamanese a sense of pride in self-identity. However, in 1998 Lichu from Strait Island told me in a long interview:

> In our community young boys want to become dancer like Michel Jaykson or play cricket all day and make money! Can the government do it for us! If I become the prime minister or make it to capital I would do it, for sure. But the problem is I have a Muslim lover and nobody likes it.

In contrast to the Great Andamanese, one finds a very different stance toward the Jarwas, who continued to resent the outsiders even in postindependence India. The attitude toward Jarwa after independence was no different from that of colonial authorities who wanted to learn some of the Jarwa language so that they could train a Jarwa in the authority's own language. The welfare agency and the Anthropological Department of India replicated the same colonial attitude of capture and educate to produce "messengers and interlocutors" between the Jarwas and the government. In June 1968 during a Jarwa raid on a village near Kadamtalla three young Jarwa boys were captured. They were taken into custody by the villagers out of revenge but the administration brought them to Port Blair jail to look after them and after a month to take them, having learned something about the world outside the forest, to their place of capture, bearing gifts. The Anthropological Survey of India studied the three Jarwa boys and found them "intelligent enough to prefer cooked food as opposed to raw fish" (Sarkar 1990). The study team (Department of Social Welfare 1969: 4–5) observed that because of inadequate preplanning, the rare opportunity to establish communication with Jarwas could not be adequately utilized. It suggested that plans should be drawn up to lodge such captives in a quiet spot away from Port Blair. Arrangements should be made to conceal microphones and tape-recorders, and to work out a system for helping the captives comprehend simple Hindi words. It added that a panel of linguists should be appointed whose services could be drawn on to study the Jarwa dialect.

There was a historical basis to this policy to "capture and school" the Andamanese outside the forest. Historical records indicate that since 1827, Ongees, like other Andamanese, resisted the presence of outsiders in their forest. In January 1885, under M. V. Portman's supervision, about 11 Ongees were taken captive for what could be regarded as "deforesting" and "schooling" and brought to Port Blair. By November 1885 some degree of mutual understanding was established and the Ongees were taken back to Little Andaman Island with loads of gifts. The schooling experiment of 1885 had succeeded in establishing "friendly relations" with Ongees. By 1966 a permanent settlement at Dugong Creek was set up for the Ongees. Residential structures, storerooms, a wireless station, a power generator, and medical outposts were added and workers from the welfare agency of AAJVS were appointed. The concern was to check the declining Ongee population trend and establish some basis for the Ongees to become self-sufficient as a settled group within the forest. As a result a coconut plantation was created for the Ongee hunter-gatherers to regularly tend. They could work for money generated from the plantation and they could hunt and gather in the forest and coastal area whenever they had time. The success of this school within the forest itself was essential, as policymakers had learned that bringing the people out for any kind of "schooling" had historically been disastrous.

SCHOOLS IN THE FOREST FOR ONGEE CHILDREN

For the Ongee children at Dugong Creek, in 1981 a wooden schoolhouse was made operational (see Figure 18.3). There was a single classroom with charts and a transistor radio, and a teacher was appointed. The school-room, called *baal wadi* (children's yard) was to attract and serve about 18 children from 5 to 13. The plan was that the mothers would bring the children, and while they wove baskets and bags their children would form a group to learn and play under the supervision of the teacher. In the last 17 years I have followed the progress of this school and seen groups of children come and go through it. None of the Ongee children have really gone through the complete school system. The first problem was one of a language with which the teacher could impart effectively any instructions to a mixed-gender and -age group of Ongee children. Then there was the problem of how to get seven- to nine-year-olds to play together with younger children and to get boys and girls to play volleyball together and recite poetry acting out the lines in front of each other. Ongee children as well as adults never sing or dance together. It is strictly an activity divided along gender lines. In fact, men are not supposed to sing in a chorus and should be seen only with women of their own family. As a result of this cultural phenomenon, even the children from as early as age six are encouraged to participate in activities among members of their own gender

Figure 18.3.   Ongee children at Dugong Creek (1983), before the school was operational.

and age group. Ongee mothers thought that going to school with their children took them away from gathering activities and wondered why they all had to be under the tin roof when one or two elder Ongee elders could look after the children in the camp ground equally well.

Soon the women gave up visiting the school, in spite of the promise that at the end of the month they would be paid for the baskets they had make in the schoolyard. The women felt that they should all be paid as soon as they finished a basket before they started on the next one. For Ongees, work is not divided into units to be done over time; they believe that work started must be finished before they start on the next task. Failure to realize this has affected also the coconut plantation provided by the administration where the Ongees can collect a monthly salary for 30 days of work. The Ongees would report for long enough to finish the month's work assigned by the plantation supervisor and expected to be paid even if it was not the end of the month. Similar ramifications are evident in the operation of a school among the Ongees. As the teachers' competency in the Ongee language developed enough for them to give basic commands, the children refused and showed complete apathy in repeating the Hindi words they had been told to memorize in previous weeks.

The early establishment of a settlement for the Ongees led to the compilation of an Ongee vocabulary, especially by the medical assistant (Janardan Shukla 1970). This led to the compilation of a Hindi-Ongee list of body parts and questions about general well-being. The AAJVS added more command sentences, directly substituting Hindi word for word with Ongee terms. This limited the orientation of the Ongees toward learning Hindi. Only in 1982 (Dasgupta and Sharma 1982) was a systematic syntax of Ongee language produced. Strangely this fine work of the Anthropological Survey of India has had no impact on the practice of the Ongee language by outsiders nor has it been considered in the later production of textbooks for the Ongee school. The reason for this seems to be that the necessity of learning the language of the Ongees is to only to give orders to them and govern them, not to communicate with them. As a field worker among the Ongees, I have marveled at the fact that more Ongees understand Hindustani than the other way around. If language is politics, then among Ongees learning and teaching of language has become a political practice. Soon fresh appointments from Port Blair frequently replaced the teachers, drawing a hardship salary, in the posts among the Ongees. There were long spells with no teacher in the school, but a list of commands in the Ongee language was handed down from teacher to teacher. Teachers inherited the Ongee translations of phrases like "Go collect fire wood," "Clean the place," "Do you have any fresh meat or fish in your house?" "Give this to me!" "Do not be so quiet—Speak up loud and clear." Moreover the terms selected for the Ongee children to learn were from the world of children being raised in mainland India, such as "steam engine." For Ongee children there were no steam engines or railroad tracks in the forests of the Little Andamans. So frequently children in the seven to nine age group would never report to school. When the teacher visited the camp and asked about their absence, the Ongees would gather around and express their resentment:

> Yesterday we took all the children to the forest, for seeing and listening! It is more worthy! After all even if they end up taking care of the coconut plantation and get lot of money for it they will not get paid for a long time. In the forest they learn to get things we need every day and are of use to all of us. Coconut is for you and the school is yours, not ours.

By the 1990s five boys who had been in the school off and on for about eight years had learned conversational Hindustani, as spoken on the island. They could not read or write but could draw the characters, which they had memorized, for their names. This created a gradual increase in Ongee interpreters for the administration. The Ongees also benefited from the school culturally since there are now more of them who can mediate between the Ongee community and the administration. So the boys chosen from the "school in the forest" were given a salary to assist the welfare agency (AAJVS) staff in managing the storeroom, power generator, wireless station, and plantation around the Ongee settlement.

The Ongees understood that the only function of the school was to teach boys to "cut patterns on paper" as opposed to putting their thumb impression whenever they received payment for their work. At the end of the month each Ongee is paid about the equivalent of five U.S. dollars by the government. Some individuals make more for working in the plantation or assisting the welfare agency in various operations. For the sake of record keeping, Ongees are expected to put their thumbprint on a paper as an acknowledgment of receiving the cash. This *angotha chaap* (thumb imprint) degree of consciousness is pretty common in mainland Indian villages where illiterate and uneducated villagers who cannot sign their name are regarded as *kala akshar bhens brabar* (dumb and dark as the water buffalo).

Autographical statements of two Ongee boys are very revealing as far as the impact of the school in the forest is concerned. In June 2001, Ramu was found dead in the forest of Little Andamans. Ramu was in fact the first to have been taken under the wing of the welfare agency and was practically raised in the house of a local social worker in the late 1970s. He was supposedly quite well versed in moving within the world outside the forest. The administration vaunted Ramu as the ideal "product of the school." The administration gave him a job with the island shipping authority and a place to stay in Port Blair. Here he picked up the habit of spending his wages and time drinking, and become a target of criticism by society at large. His alienation caused him to return to the Ongee community in the forest. He gave up his khaki uniform to fit into the Ongee community but none of the Ongees really accepted him, particularly when it came to his demand for a bride. Ramu's cause of death in the forest was the timber industry's mad elephant stampede. (Elephants were used for timber operations in the forest. Timber operations have stopped but some elephants have gone feral and roam around the forest, posing a problem.) About Ramu's unfortunate death, his stepbrother said:

> See this is what happens! Spending too much time with outsiders and authority—what good did it do Ramu! Just a uniform and some money. One forgets the ways of the forest, you know the streets and ships but not the forest, you even miss a big elephant, it is all a nightmare with these outsiders occupying place around and among us.

Mohan, who lives outside the Dugong Creek camp, had attended the school for a fairly long time, but while he learned practically nothing in the way of reading and writing he did learn how to understand commands and follow verbal instructions. As a result, about six years back he was appointed as a police guard for the Dugong Creek Region. He was entitled to a regular paycheck and a khaki uniform. His parents and in-laws were keen that he should not accept any posting away from Ongee settlement. Now he just gets his paycheck delivered and does none of the duties he is expected to. The authorities cannot take him off the payroll, and he has really no job to do but gets one of the highest payments of all the Ongees. However, he is sort of ostracized. In November 2000, Mohan said:

> What good has happened to me! I had a uniform to wear and be in the world outside the forest. But can the world outside take me, as I am an Ongee policeman and not a policeman? For my people I am neither a policeman nor an Ongee. I make enough money to get all my requirements from the nearby market, why should I bother with working in the forest? No wonder many Ongees resent me!

Money earned in the form of wages, a uniform, and the loss of the ability to exist within the forest are common themes in the case of both Ramu and Mohan.

The school in the forest has attempted to reproduce wage earners for the distinct political economy that is outside the forest. Ongee children who have gone through the Dugong Creek school find themselves in a world that is neither theirs nor the outsiders'. The school for the Ongee hunter-gatherers is only a model for the society that is outside the forest. By around 1998, the administration and policymakers had begun to realize the problem. Teachers had learned enough of the Ongee language to make them comfortable in their jobs, but Ongee children had not evolved beyond just repeating Hindi words. To attract Ongee children to school and retain them, daily biscuits were distributed, but the parents argued that children should be given enough so that they could bring a portion home for sharing within the community. By 1999, Ongee children had memorized the Hindi national song and learned to stand around a flag-pole singing:

Sarey Jahan se acca Hindustan hamara, Hindi hey ham watan hai Hindustan hamara [In the whole world the best is our country of India. We are Indians and India is our country].

But when school is over, the same Ongee children run back to their shelters singing different words to the same tune:

Eneyekulla injubey ethee kuta gacheengy megeyabarotta, vuey Ongeevueye gayebarrota [Of all the places the best is our forest, the forest is ours, and we are the Ongees of the forest].

Clearly Ongee children have learned to translate and articulate their feelings into song structures memorized by them in school. A text of the outsiders' school is translated for a different church, the forest. In spite of this the state has continued to train Ongee children, in the hope that they will become citizens of India and some day fully participate in the political economy as productive citizens. But how will this happen? An expensive government project commissioned linguists from the Central Institute of Indian Languages at Mysore to produce books that would assist the teachers as well as the Ongees at school (CIIL 1993a, 1993b). Textbook pages they produced are full of single Ongee verbs that are given as the equivalent of full sentences, failing to teach the basic concept of constructing a sentence. The *Bilingual Primer* (CIIL 1993b) outlines the intent to train the "monolingual" community in ideas about production and wages, and not to depend on the government dole. Interestingly it also attempts to teach Ongees to become fishermen and stop depending on the forest as hunters. Apparently this idea of what education should be and how fishing is important for the Andamanese community has traditionally undermined the Andamanese dependence on hunting in the forest. The intent behind this is to get Andamanese hunter-gatherers to depend less on the forest and more on a settled life, with a cash economy that is seen as beneficial to the nontribals on the islands (Awradi 1990:183). There is a question as to whether this will ever succeed, as the Ongees have never been provided with rights to their forestland but have come to depend only on social welfare in a steadily shrinking forest. Moreover, beyond the number three, the concept of numbers for most Andamanese is just "many."

There is a serious conceptual problem to be resolved in order for the schoolgoing Ongees to become productive in a political economy based on cash. Nothing is done to orient them to the process of making money—for them money is basically something to be collected at the welfare agent's outpost. Meanwhile, the school has trained Ongee children to be uncomfortable in both worlds, within the forest and beyond the forest. What has been insured definitely for the Ongee children is to become more obedient and willingly subservient to the authorities.

SCHOOLING: A TOOL FOR TRANSFORMING HUNTER-GATHERERS

From the days of colonial control of the island, when Andamanese tribal children were taken out of the forest and sent away to schools, to the establishment of schools among the Ongees in postindependent India, outsiders and the administration have learned something about the instrumentality of schooling. Historically the purpose of school was to socialize the Andamanese children in the image of the non-hunter-gatherers' idea of what a person in society is: disciplined, obedient, capable of following orders, and productive in a settled cash-based economy. However, in interacting with the Andamanese, the authorities' failure to use the group's language as the language of instruction for school and their failure to comprehend the forest itself as a school has led to a breakdown of how schools were idealized for the Great Andamanese and Ongee children.

The notion of work and learning is not something time bound and simply acquired by sitting in a mixed-gender and -age classroom. Learning for Andamanese children is based on constantly "hearing" and "observing" within the forests facts that are directly based on how to live in a forest. Qualities of hearing and seeing are much exalted among the Andamanese. Ongees in fact have two basic identities for each individual. One either belongs to a clan of *eahansakwe*, those who hear well (pig hunters), and *eahambelakwe*, those who see well (turtle hunters). Each individual is prescribed a marriage rule of exogamy making the two identities interdependent (Pandya 1993:8, 20, 23). Traditionally interdependence is fostered between the two groups by their acting as both hosts and guests (*Eramtaga* and *ar-yoto*) (Radcliffe-Brown [1922] 1964:26–27).

Children have failed to be socialized within the imposed school structure. But for the outside authorities school has generated an awareness of the Andamanese language as a political tool to control the Andamanese in relation to the forest. The effectiveness of this realization particularly among the Ongees had conditioned the authorities' recent contact with the Jarwas, who resented contact with the outsiders as late as 1995. The British first contacted the Jarwas in 1790, but in the following years with assistance from the Great Andamanese of the Andaman Homes a schism was created between the Jarwas and the other Andamanese as well as the non-tribals. The 1931 Census of India documents one of the earliest compilations of the Jarwa language, done in the early phase of colonial contact with the Jarwas. In this account, Bonnington reports that captured Jarwa boys were sent to a Catholic boarding school in Ranchi (Bihar) so that they would come back educated and able to assist the colonial administration. A similar report of a captured Jarwa girl who learned English appears in the 1951 Census reports. Unfortunately there are no records on what happened in later years to these individual captives who were on their way to becoming educated.

Since 1997, in postindependent India there has been no change in the intensity of the old colonial practice of distributing gifts during expeditions among the Jarwas (Pandya 1999a). This continuity of the colonial practice was seen as a way to overcome ongoing hostility from the Jarwas and the violence and resentment they had experienced at the hands of those outside the forest (Pandya 2000). With the increasing use of the road cutting through the reserved Jarwa territory, interactions between the outsiders and the Jarwas became intense and much more magnified. In spite of the outbreak of measles in late 1999, Jarwa children and youth interact with bus passengers and tourists near the side of the road. Jarwa children and occasionally adult Jarwa men and women have been successfully learning to interact with the outside world: in order to collect money from passersby they block the traffic, and they are quickly acquiring the language skills to ask outsiders for what they wanted. For the Jarwa children the roadside was just a place in the forest to observe and exploit what resources they could gain from it (Pandya 2002). But the problems of the clash between the two worlds posed a major problem for the administration. Exotic, primitive, naked savages could not themselves be placed in a tourist market as a commodity. Jarwas were becoming more and more dependent on whatever the outsider would charitably and senselessly hand them. In order to control the situation controlled by the Jarwa children, the administration's action plan included a group of linguists, anthropologists (from ASI, the Anthropological Survey of India), and welfare workers to be stationed near Kadamtalla. A school was set up for the administrators to learn the Jarwa language (CIIL 2000:vii–viii). As the Jarwa boys could be relied upon to come and collect gift items, the appointed group could make use of what Hindi the Jarwa knew to learn more of the Jarwa language. Contact with outsiders had caused a breakdown of the monolingual Jarwa community situation. The groups of linguists who had worked on the Ongee textbook (CIIL 1993a, 1993b) were commissioned by the administration to create a textbook whereby the authorities could acquire simple sentences like, "You should not come out of the forest. Stay and gather things from the forest. If you want something from outside world tell me and I will bring it to you!" (CIIL 2000:76, 80, 82). These simple instructions obviously enable the authorities to control the Jarwas. Unlike the agenda of turning the Ongees into productive cash-based individuals, with this new approach the Jarwas need to be identified and controlled from becoming dependent on the outside world. This orientation of the administration has resulted in about a dozen of its workers being stationed along the roadside to see that the Jarwa children do not come out of the forest to beg from the outsiders. Interestingly the workers along with the ASI anthropologists continue to control the Jarwas like some sort of herd of cattle, shouting the phrases from the book. The book has sections to be memorized, like how to interact with Jarwas, how to ask their name and where they are from, but to this day the administration does not know what Jarwas call themselves. "Jarwa" is a name given to the group by the historical conglomerate of what was called the Great Andamanese. Regular refresher classes are held for the welfare agencies to update their training in the Jarwa language, a version of the language not representative of the culture itself but one that is used to control individuals within Jarwa culture. The prevalent idea is to complement the achievements of seeing the Jarwas and not to really know how the Jarwas organize their world, how to communicate it to others, or how to understand the nature of the Jarwas' own learning process. The ASI recently published two books on Jarwa languages that prove my point (Senkuttuvan 2000; Sreenathan 2001). Sreenathan's work (2001) at least reveals how his contact situation limited his collection of vocabulary, but the other two works (CIIL 2000; Senkuttuvan 2000) pretend to be about the Jarwa language and culture but fall short and only demonstrate what the authorities are capable of learning and eager to learn from Jarwas. Senkuttuvan's compilation of 480 Jarwa words and their analysis (2000:2) is deplorable. Without any evidence he reduces Jarwa phonology to that of proto-Dravidian.

Much like the colonial administrators contacting the Andamanese in the early 1800s (Clark 1874; Man 1901) these linguistic anthropologists, in their effort to write about the Jarwa language and culture, have the same vocabulary as early Jarwa language publications. Treating Jarwas as childlike in their contacts with them, the linguists, anthropologists, and administrators have really no difficulty in asking the names of parts of bodies, cloth and paper, bus and trucks, and trees and fish without placing them in any kind of context and indicating their use within Jarwa culture. In fact these recent language compilations tell us more about how the authorities

view the Jarwas as children. Perhaps these are the first steps of administration's schooling so that some day even the Jarwa forests would have a
school to train them to move out of the forest. Administrators are learning
the Jarwa language so that like the Ongee situation, the Jarwas can be dis-
connected from the forest life by putting the forest completely under the
administration's control

CONCLUSION

The presence of Andamanese hunter-gatherers in the forest has always
been a problem for outsiders trying to access the resources of the island. In
different historical periods school was regarded as a way to turn the Andamanese adults and children, metaphorically and physically, into disciplined, productive, obedient subjects. Schools were seen first to be best if
set up outside the world of the forest or outside the forest area, as in the
colonial period. In the postindependence phase schools were set up within
the forest. But in their unstated agenda of "deforesting," the authorities are
imposing a constructed, synthetic process of socialization and education,
not realizing that the product of this schooling is not compatible with the
"church" to which the Andamanese belong. I wonder if ever any authority would, like our schoolteachers, ask:

> Hey, Andamanese child, what do you want to be when you grow up? Be-
> cause it is possible that your forest world will not be around much longer.

Perhaps by not posing this question to Andamanese children the authorities, as in the contemporary Jarwa situation, are educating themselves to deconstruct the forest world more effectively. The language
books produced among the Ongees and Jarwas are a case in point. For the
Andamanese, work and acquiring knowledge are not durational con-
structs. The Andamanese way of work and teaching children indicates that
the process of acquiring skill and knowledge has immediate and direct effects. Something remains to be learned about how hunter-gatherer children undergo schooling in the forest.

19

Reflections on
Hunter-Gatherer Childhoods

Michael E. Lamb and Barry S. Hewlett

At a time when the foraging lifestyle has never been more threatened by farmers, miners, foresters, and politicians, the chapters in this volume illustrate how much we continue to learn about hunting and gathering cultures and how much these studies enrich our understanding of humanity. Although the contributors adopt many different perspectives and address a diverse array of questions, each has enriched our understanding of the foraging lifestyle in general and, more particularly, of childhood in hunting and gathering societies. In addition, the contributors have all used their data to address broader and more fundamental questions about human behavior and its origins. In this concluding chapter, we briefly revisit some of the major overarching issues raised earlier in the book.

WHY STUDY HUNTERS AND GATHERERS?

Anthropologists have described and studied a diverse array of small scale (i.e., "traditional" nonindustrial) cultures throughout the 20th century, but widespread interest in childrearing and childhood in hunting and gathering cultures emerged in the last half of the century, stimulated in large part by the near-simultaneous emergence and popular acceptance of attachment theory (Bowlby, 1958, 1969) and the first in-depth reports from studies of hunter-gatherers. In his efforts to explain why children appeared to be so badly damaged psychologically by separation from their parents, Bowlby proposed that human infants had an innate tendency to form emotional relationships with those responsible for their early care. He proposed that, in the environment of evolutionary adaptedness (EEA), infants needed to seek protective proximity to these adults, first by signaling (crying, smiling) and later through active locomotion and clinging. Repeated associations between the child's signals and the adult's timely and appropriate responses, he suggested, permitted the development of an affectional relationship in which the child came to count on, or trust, the adult's availability and commitment. Of course, the EEA had long since disappeared, but Bowlby adduced support for his theory from studies of nonhuman primates illustrating both the importance of proximity-promoting signals and behavior as well as the high levels of distress manifested by infants who were separated from their established sources of protection and care. Robert Hinde, a renowned animal behaviorist at Cambridge, played a crucial role in helping Bowlby to draw appropriate and useful inferences from the research on other species, and his integrative treatise, *Animal Behaviour* (1966), became Bowlby's touchstone reference. Bowlby also argued that much could be learned about the evolution and meaning of human infant behavior by studying early childhood and patterns of childcare in contemporary hunting and gathering societies because their ways of life more closely resembled the presumed human EEA than did the lifestyles that characterized Western industrial cultures. More ominously, Bowlby emphasized the risks inherent in modern childrearing practices that deviated dramatically from those for which humans were evolutionarily adapted.

Konner's extraordinarily detailed descriptions of childcare among the !Kung hunter-gatherers were just becoming known in 1969, and they substantiated many of Bowlby's presumptions and predictions about the evolutionary origins of human behavior. In particular, Konner showed that !Kung infants were held nearly continuously and nursed frequently around the clock while enjoying frequent opportunities for social interaction with all the individuals living in their social groups. In this book (Chapter 2), Konner reviews and summarizes his observations and their implications, strikingly underscoring Bowlby's prescience as well as the extraordinary heuristic and integrative importance of attachment theory. Further careful observations of the !Kung by researchers such as Takada (Chapter 13) confirm Konner's detailed reports that !Kung infants are nursed frequently, and also illustrate intimate patterns of interaction that may play a role in fostering motor development on the part of young infants.

DIFFERENCES AMONG HUNTER-GATHERER GROUPS

Of course, Bowlby emphasized the importance of research on the !Kung not only because more was known about them than about any other foraging culture at the time, but also because their habitat most closely resembled the savannah grasslands in which humans were believed to have emerged as a species. As the chapters in this book make clear, however, hunters and gatherers inhabit and exploit many other habitats and ecologies, and it is clear that the social ecology dramatically shapes the lifestyles, including the patterns of childcare, in different hunting and gathering societies. Thus, for example, some (but not all) forest-dwelling hunting and gathering groups benefit from an ecology in which adequate nutrition can be obtained by gathering fruit or honey and trapping small game, whereas hunting and gathering groups living in more arid conditions have to travel much farther to locate tubers that are worth digging up or to locate small animals or reptiles to pursue and hunt. Some environments (like the West Australian desert environment described by Bird and Bliege Bird in Chapter 6 and the Mikea forest described by Tucker and Young in Chapter 7) permit children to forage or hunt quite effectively and productively, while others (such as the Ituri forest described by Ivey Henry and her colleagues in Chapter 9) are perceived as dangerous because the Efe fear marauding men from the neighboring social groups. Several chapters in this volume document the ways in which these differences in the social ecology shape the ways in which children are reared.

These differences notwithstanding, striking similarities among hunting and gathering groups are also noteworthy. Regardless of ecology, for example, hunting and gathering groups are characterized by frequent and extended breastfeeding and extraordinarily high levels of parent-child physical contact and proximity, especially in comparison with the practices not only of parents in industrial societies, but also in contrast with the practices of neighboring groups of farmers exploiting very similar social ecologies. These characteristic patterns of forager childcare may in part account for the relatively long interbirth intervals that characterize hunting and gathering societies.

Interestingly, Hirasawa's (Chapter 17) data suggest that many of these characteristic features change when foragers settle down. After becoming increasingly reliant on farming, for example, the Baka that Hirasawa studied began to draw siblings into childcare roles and to accelerate weaning on the mothers' initiative. In these regards, their patterns of childcare became similar to those of traditional simple farmers although some characteristic features of forager childcare (e.g., frequent holding and nursing when mothers and infants are together) appear to persist.

Whereas sedentary groups tend to live in larger, more stable villages, hunting and gathering societies are typically characterized by residence in small groups or camps. Group membership is somewhat fluid, with individuals moving from group to group quite frequently, although the core membership of the groups tends to remain stable for years at a time. The camps also tend to be physically small and the members frequently visit relatives. As a result, children grow up in fairly intimate social groups instead of in the isolated nuclear families or households experienced by children in industrial societies. From early infancy, children in foraging so-cieties are frequently held by adults other than their mothers, siblings, and other children and their early experiences are characterized by frequent opportunities to observe and interact with a tight and intimate group of individuals.

As Bird-David points out in Chapter 4, anthropologists and cross-cultural psychologists have long paid surprisingly little systematic at-tention to childhood and childrearing patterns. Nevertheless, whereas scholars like Bowlby and Konner emphasized the intensity and exclusive-ness of mother-infant interactions and relationships, many anthropolo-gists have begun to examine the roles played by other individuals—adults and children, related and unrelated—in the social experiences and care of young children in hunting and gathering societies. In this book, for exam-ple, Draper and Howell (Chapter 12) suggest that many individuals be-sides lineal relatives (i.e., mother, father, grandparents) contribute to the general health of forager children.

PARENTING AND ALLOPARENTING

As illustrated in Chapter 3, Hrdy has played a particularly important role in drawing attention to the roles played by "alloparents" and explaining the evolutionary basis for such patterns of shared care. She argues persua-sively that extensive allocare is a consistent feature of hunter-gatherer childhood and that its prominence is linked to the extensive sharing of food. Hrdy's analysis is well complemented by detailed observations of early childcare among the Efe of the Ituri Forest by Ivey Henry and her colleagues (Chapter 9). Among the Efe, these scholars note, young and old individuals play a prominent role in childcare even while the young chil-dren remain exclusively dependent on feeding by their mothers. The fact that alloparenting, especially by children who cannot themselves forage or hunt, allows parents, especially mothers, to obtain food more efficiently underscores the importance of activities in which resources, like responsi-bilities, are shared among group members rather than only within nuclear households. As Hrdy predicted, furthermore, increased participation in agricultural work, rather than hunting and gathering, by Baka mothers was associated with increased reliance on sibling care providers (Hira-sawa, Chapter 17).

Similarly, Blurton Jones, Hawkes, and O'Connell (Chapter 10) have fo-cused particular attention on the ways in which postmenopausal women, especially grandmothers, promote the survival and well-being of young children by providing food, childcare, and support for their parents. Par-allel observations by Marlowe (Chapter 8) among the same Hadza people studied by Blurton Jones and his colleagues show that the social worlds of Hadza infants quickly broaden as they become emotionally competent. By the age of three years, most Hadza children are spending more time with other individuals—principally, other children—and by the age of five they are, on average, spending as much time with their fathers as with their mothers. Sugiyama and Chacon (Chapter 11) similarly show that Yora juveniles tend to live in households with more rather than fewer individuals who could provide alloparental care. These observations clearly support Hrdy's emphasis on the extensiveness and importance of alloparental behavior among hunter-gatherer groups, especially in comparison with farming and industrial societies.

Other contributors, such as Ivey Henry et al.(Chapter 9), Kamei (Chapter 16), and Bird and Bliege Bird (Chapter 6), focus not on the ways in which other adults help parents provide food for their children but on the ways in which other children provide custodial care, companionship, socializing experiences, and the contexts in which children seek food both for themselves and for the group as a whole while perhaps acquiring life-enhancing expertise in hunting and foraging strategies. These observations all contribute to a growing understanding of the diverse ways in which multiple adults and children shape children's early experiences and promote their survival.

Bonnie Hewlett's (see Chapter 15) interviews of adolescents among the Aka hunter-gatherers and their Ngandu neighbors revealed that the extensive social relationships enjoyed by hunting-gatherer children have emotional significance, as reflected in accounts of profound grief over the death of those with whom they had relationships. Interestingly, furthermore, the Aka were much more likely to mourn the emotional loss and less likely to mourn the loss of a deceased individual's concrete contributions than were the Ngandu youth.

The observations and reports compiled in this volume reflect the broadening and maturation of scholarship on childhood in hunting and gathering cultures. They reflect the shift from an exclusive focus on infant care to a realization that humans are dependent on adults far longer than the young of any other species. Although children remain dependent on adults for many years, of course, their capacities and abilities to contribute increase as they grow older, thereby changing the patterns and purposes of childcare and making it important to examine different phases of the lifespan closely. In addition, scholars like those contributing to this book have shifted from an exclusive focus on mothers to recognition of the array of figures who contribute in diverse ways to child survival and socialization. This has permitted a broader range of hypotheses to be examined, and has contributed to a richer understanding of human culture, behavior, and its evolution.

Consider, for example, Fouts and Lamb's discussion in Chapter 14 of weaning among the Bofi foragers of the Ngotto rain forest (Central African Republic). Although studied surprisingly little, weaning has traditionally been viewed as a process involving efforts by mothers to change the ways in which they nourish their children. Theorists such as Trivers (1974), meanwhile, have portrayed weaning as a classic source of conflict as children try to take more and mothers strive to offer less because each is pursuing his or her individual fitness interests. As Fouts and Lamb show, however, weaning among the Bofi foragers not only appears to be driven by the children rather than by the mothers, but is also characterized by very little overt conflict. In most cases, furthermore, the child care and provisioning responsibilities of these mothers are shared with other group members and the weanlings have long since abandoned exclusive reliance on breast milk to satisfy their nutritional needs. By contrast, weaning among the now relatively sedentary Baka has become earlier and more adult-driven, Hirasawa (Chapter 17) reports, indicating that the hunter-gatherer patterns of nursing and infant care may be threatened when foraging gives way to agricultural production.

WHY ARE HUMAN CHILDREN SO DEPENDENT?

Interestingly, although human offspring are more dependent on adult conspecifics than the young of other species, children in hunter-gatherer societies are clearly much more independent than are children in industrial societies like our own, and they also contribute to the welfare and provisioning of the groups in which they live much more extensively than one might expect (see Sugiyama and Chacon, Chapter 11, for example). Many of the contributors to this book describe a gradual transition from being a dependent recipient of care and provisions to being a participant in the care and provisioning of others-a transition that facilitates the transfer of social and survival skills more seamlessly than the typical patterns of socialization in Western industrial cultures. Interestingly, Kamei (Chapter 16) describes foraging as one of the most common play themes observed among the Baka, whereas contributors such as Bird and Bliege Bird (Chapter 6) and Tucker and Young (Chapter 7) describe children's involvement in actual hunting and foraging, respectively. Comparisons among these chapters underscore the permeability of boundaries between play and work, as well as the gradual nature of the transitions between childhood and adulthood.

Taking a different approach, Bird-David argues in Chapter 4 that children other than infants and toddlers are central and active participants in and contributors to the social groups in which they live. As a result, she wisely cautions against implicit assumptions that childhood in hunting and gathering societies is helpfully understood by assuming that adults play explicit roles socializing children in order to integrate them into the society. Indeed, Bird-David argues, children are viewed as contributing members of the group and the need for explicit "socialization" is not recognized. From this perspective, it is easier to understand frequent ethnographic descriptions of surprisingly lax efforts made by hunters and gatherers to protect children from such dangers as fires and sharp tools than it is from a Western perspective in which adults' protective and socializing responsibilities are emphasized.

Bird-David's reasoning is consistent with that offered by Bird and Bliege Bird (Chapter 6), who show that age and physical stamina, rather than the lack of expertise or adult guidance, determine the hunting strategies of Martu children in the Western Desert of Australia. At least in this group, apprenticeship is not sought, offered, or necessary and this raises further questions about the value and importance of the lengthy periods of dependency that characterize the human species. Kamei (Chapter 16) similarly describes how children "play" at activities they have observed adults performing, thereby acquiring and honing skills necessary for adult life without coaching or adult guidance. Western societies have developed elaborate structures and institutions to educate and socialize children and adolescents but it is abundantly clear that such institutions are not necessary in most societies, and that many cultures do not afford children the same kinds of explicit education or instruction. In most hunter-gatherer societies, the contributors to this book suggest, adult responsibilities are assumed at reproductive maturity or marriage, not when youngsters complete an apprenticeship or educational program.

Like the Baka children studied by Kamei (Chapter 16), children among the Mikea in southwestern Madagascar (see Tucker and Young, Chapter 7) are collectors rather than hunters, spending long hours digging for tubers. As Tucker and Young point out, this foraging is as much to kill time and dispel boredom as it is to produce food, thereby underscoring the differing decisions, constraints, and responsibilities faced by adults and children. Again, however, Mikea adults do not make active efforts to improve the efficiency and productivity of young foragers, although children do seem to focus their efforts on patches that have previously been prepared and partially exploited by adults.

Offering another perspective on developmental changes in the extent to which children come to contribute provisions to the group, Bock (Chapter 5) shows that both strength (essentially a product of maturation) and skills (the product of experience) affected performance, with their relative importance differing depending on the specific activity concerned. Mongongo nut processing, for example, requires skill rather than strength, whereas canoe fishing requires strength as well. One implication of these findings is that children's contributions to the diet should increase slowly as they become stronger and acquire skills through practice and play. Interestingly, in none of the groups studied by contributors to this volume did adults either explicitly coach children to accelerate the acquisition of skills or direct them to perform activities for which they had sufficient skills or strength to be productive members of the society.

QUESTIONS FOR FUTURE RESEARCH

Even as scholars ponder questions about the meaning and function of childhood in our species, research on childhood in hunting and gathering cultures is more important than ever today, in part because the hunting and gathering lifestyle has never been more threatened by encroachment. Each of the societies described in this book is at least under threat. In at least four cases—the !Kung, the Ongee, the Martu and the Baka—reliance on hunting and gathering has declined dramatically, while all other groups increasingly count on trade with neighboring groups, occasional or seasonal farming, nonindigenous tools and weapons, sporadic schooling, and increased, if partial, access to Western medicine. Many of these changes may be welcomed by at least some of the hunters and gatherers themselves, but they promise to eliminate, surprisingly soon, the opportunities for scholars and scientists to understand humanity better by studying the behavior of individuals and groups whose modes of subsistence and ecologies perhaps resemble the environment in which we evolved. For that reason, the ethnographic descriptions provided and the hypotheses tested by the contributors to this book are of considerable importance to anthropologists, psychologists, and population biologists.

To the extent that hunter-gatherer groups have ecologies that resemble the environment in which we evolved, research on these groups might fruitfully focus on a number of questions implicitly or explicitly addressed in the preceding chapters. First, why do humans have such a long period of dependency? Other primates are able to fend for themselves, nutritionally speaking, from the time of weaning, whereas human children remain dependent on adult providers for years. Even when the environment is sufficiently rich and accessible that children could generate at least a significant portion of their nutritional needs, they are not expected to do so, and thus contribute only when so motivated. This tolerance on the part of adults reflects a common hunter-gatherer propensity to share, but the absence of explicit cultural beliefs about the incompetence, innocence, or weakness of children that justify the tolerance for extended dependency in industrial societies is perhaps surprising. Regardless of cultural beliefs, why has an extended period of filial dependence become characteristic of our species?

Second, why do hunter-gatherers appear so unmotivated and uninterested in facilitating or speeding up children's acquisition of either the social or provisioning skills needed for success in their environment or culture? The lack of commitment to "socialization" is particularly noteworthy because parents in Western industrial countries consider this to be so important and because children in most hunter-gatherer societies could indeed make substantial contributions to their groups much earlier if they were encouraged to do so.

Third, although they are not unique to hunter-gatherer groups, the high rates of infant and juvenile mortality, primarily as a result of infections and parasites over which parents have no control, should encourage hunter-gatherer parents to strive for high fertility levels and to limit investment in individual offspring. Instead, however, we find very high levels of investment in individual offspring, with more holding, carrying, and nursing than in any other groups. Does the quality of hunter-gatherer parenting vary depending on the availability of alternative ways of promoting inclusive fitness and, if so, how are these differences manifested?

Finally, to what extent does the apparent lack of interest in communicating skills and speeding up the assignment of responsibility to children and adolescents reflect the hunter-gatherers' disinterest in social comparison and competition ("Who cares if he is the best hunter? Is he good enough?")? Would an explicit focus on socialization threaten these fundamental beliefs and the hunter-gatherer way of life in such profound ways that the potential costs outweighed the potential benefits? If so, a careful analysis of the origins and benefits of the commitment to noncompetitive egalitarianism may be in order.

References

Ahnert, L. and M. E. Lamb (2003). Shared care: Establishing a balance between home and child care settings. *Child Development 74:1044–1049*

Aiello, L. and J. Wells (2002). Energetics and the evolution of genus Homo. *Annual Reviews of Anthropology* 31:323–338.

Ainsworth, M. D. S. (1967). *Infancy in Uganda: Infant care and the growth of attachment.* Baltimore, MD: Johns Hopkins University Press.

Ainsworth, M. D. S., S. Bell, and D. F. Stayton (1974). Infant-mother attachment and social development: Socialisation as a product of reciprocal responsiveness to signals. In M. P. M. Richards (Ed.), *The integration of the child into a social world.* Cambridge: Cambridge University Press.

Ainsworth, M. D. S., M. C. Blehar, E. Waters, and S. Wall (1978). *Patterns of attachment: A psychological study of the strange situation.* Hillsdale, NJ: Lawrence Erlbaum Associates.

Ainsworth, M. D. and B. A. Wittig (1969). Attachment and exploratory behavior of one-year-olds in a strange situation. In B. M. Foss (Ed.), *Determinants of infant behavior,* vol. 4, London: Methuen.

Akiyama, H. (2001). The influence of schooling and relocation on the G/wi pupil companionship. *African Study Monographs Supplementary Issue (African hunter-gatherers: persisting cultures and contemporary problems)* 26:197–208.

Albino, R. and V. J. Thompson (1956). The effects of sudden weaning on Zulu Children. *Medical Psychology* 3–4:178–207.

Alcorta, C. (1982). Paternal behavior and group competition. *Behavior Science Research* 17:3–23.

Aldrich, C. A., & Hewitt, E. S. (1947). A self-regulating feeding program for infants. *Journal of the American Medical Association 135*: 340–342.

Alexander, J. E. (1827). *Travels from India to England.* London: Parbury, Allen.

Alexander, R. D. (1974). The evolution of social behavior. *Annual Review of Ecology and Systematics* 5:325–383.

Alexander, R. D. (1979). *Darwinism and human affairs.* Seattle: Washington University Press.

Alley, T. (1983). Growth-produced changes in body shape and size as determinants of perceived age and adult caregiving. *Child Development* 54:241–248.

Altmann, J. (1974). Observational study of behavior: Sampling methods. *Behaviour* 49:227–267.

Altmann, J. A. (1980). *Baboon mothers and infants.* Cambridge, MA: Harvard University Press.

Alvarez, H. (2000). Grandmother hypothesis and primate life histories. *American Journal of Physical Anthropology* 113:435–450.

Alvarez, H. P. (2004). Residence groups among hunter-gatherers: A view of the claims and evidence for patrilocal bands. In B. Chapais and C. M. Berman (Eds.), *Kinship and behavior in primates*. Oxford, UK: Oxford University Press: pp. 420–42.

American Academy of Pediatrics. (1997). Breastfeeding and the use of human milk. *Pediatrics* 100(6):1035–1039.

Aoyagi, M. (1977). *Cultural anthropology of play* (in Japanese). Tokyo: Kodansha.

Archer, J. (2001). Grief from an evolutionary perspective. In M. S. Stroebe, R. O. Hannson, W. Stroebe, and H. Schut (Eds.), *Handbook of bereavement research*. Washington, DC: American Psychological Association.

Asa, C. S. (1997). Hormonal and experiential factors in the expression of social and parental behavior in canids. In N. G. Solomon and J. A. French (Eds.), *Cooperative breeding in mammals* (pp. 129–149). Cambridge: Cambridge University Press.

ASI (1952). Report of the survey of the inhabitants of the Andaman and Nicobar Islands (1948–49), edited by B. S. Guha. *Bulletin of the Department of Anthropology, Calcutta* 1(1).

Althabe, G. (1965). Changements sociaux chez les Pygmées Baka de l'est-Cameroun. *Cahiers d'Etudes Africaines* 5 (20): 561–92.

Awradi, S. A. (1990). *Master Plan 1991–2021, for welfare of primitive tribes of Andaman and Nicobar Islands*. Port Blair: Andaman and Nicobar Administration.

Ayres, B. (1954). *A cross-cultural study of factors relating to pregnancy taboos*: Unpublished doctoral dissertation, Radcliffe College/Harvard University.

Babchuk, W. A., R. B. Hames, and R. A. Thompson (1985). Sex differences in the recognition of infant facial expressions of emotion: The primary caretaker hypothesis. *Ethology and Sociobiology* 6:89–101.

Bachar, E., L. Caneti, O. Bonne, A. Denour, and A. Y. Shalev (1997). Psychological well-being and ratings of psychiatric symptoms in bereaved Israeli adolescents: Differential effect of war versus accident-related bereavement. *Journal of Nervous and Mental Disease* 185:402–406.

Badcock, C. 1990. *Oedipus in evolution: A new theory of sex*. Oxford: Blackwell.

Bahuchet, S. (1985). *Pygmées Aka et la Forêt Centrafricaine: Ethnologie écologique*. Paris: Selaf.

Bahuchet, S. (1992). *Dans la forêt d'Afrique Centrale: Les Pygmées Aka et Baka*. Paris: Selaf.

Bahuchet, S. (1993). History of the inhabitants of the Central African Rain Forest: Perspectives from comparative linguistics. In C. M. Hladik, A. Hladik, O. F. Linares, H. Pagezy, A. Semple, and M. Hadle (Eds.), *Tropical forest, people and food* (pp. 37–54). Paris: UNESCO, New York: Parthenon.

Bahuchet, S. (1999). Aka Pygmies. In R. B. Lee and R. Daly (Eds.), *The Cambridge encyclopedia of hunters and gatherers* (p. 190). Cambridge: Cambridge University Press.

Bailey, R. (1991a). *The behavioral ecology of Efe Pygmy men in the Ituri Forest, Zaïre*. Anthropological Papers 86, Museum of Anthropology, University of Michigan.

Bailey, R. (1991b). The comparative growth of Efe Pygmies and African farmers from birth to age five years. *Annals of Human Biology* 19:113–120.

Bailey, R. C. (1988). The significance of hypoergyny for understanding the subsistence behavior of contemporary hunters and gatherers. In B. V. Kennedy and G. M. LeMoine (Eds.), *Diet and subsistence: Current archaeological perspectives.* Calgary: University of Calgary Press.

Bailey, R. C. and R. Aunger, Jr. (1989). Significance of the social relationships of Efe pygmy men in the Ituri forest, Zaire. *American Journal of Physical Anthropology* 78:495–508.

Bailey, R. C. and I. DeVore (1989). Research on the Efe and Lese populations of the Ituri Forest, Zaire. *American Journal of Physical Anthropology* 78:495–508.

Bailey, R. C. and N. R. Peacock (1988). Efe Pygmies of Northeast Zaïre: Subsistence strategies in the Ituri Forest. In I. De Garine and G. Harrison (Eds.), *Uncertainty in the food supply.* Cambridge: Cambridge University Press.

Baker, J. E., M. A. Sedney, and E. Gross (1996). Psychological tasks for bereaved children. *American Journal of Orthopsychiatry* 62:105–116.

Bales, K., J. A. French, and J. M. Dietz (2002). Explaining variation in maternal care in a cooperatively breeding mammal. *Animal Behavior* 63:453–461.

Ball, V. A. (1897). Visit to the Andaman home. *Antiquary* 26:170–174.

Bard, Kim. In press. Emotions in chimpanzee infants: The value of A comparative developmental approach to understand the evolutionary bases of emotion. In: J. Nadel and D. Muir (Eds.), *Emotional development: Recent research advances.* Oxford: Oxford University

Bardi, M., A. Petto, and D. E. Lee-Parritz (2001). Parental failure in captive cottontop tamarins (*Saquinus oedipus*). *American Journal of Primatology* 54:159–169.

Barnard, A. (1992). *Hunters and herders of Southern Africa: A comparative ethnography of the Khoisan peoples.* Cambridge: Cambridge University Press.

Barnard, A. (2002). Foraging: Mode of production or mode of thought. Paper presented at International Conference on Hunting and Gathering Societies, Edinburgh, Scotland.

Barnett, D., S. L. Kidwell, and K. H. Leung (1998). Parenting and preschooler attachment among low-income urban African American families. *Child Development* 6:1657–1671.

Baron-Cohen, S. ([1995] 2001). *Mind-blindness: An essay on autism and theory of mind.* Cambridge, MA: MIT Press.

Barr, R. G. (1990). The early crying paradox: A modest proposal. *Human Nature* 1:355–389.

Barr, R. G. and M. F. Elias (1988). Nursing interval and maternal responsivity: Effect on early infant crying. *Pediatrics* 81:529–536.

Barr, R. G., M. Konner, R. Bakeman, and L. Adamson (1991). Crying in !Kung San infants: A test of the cultural specificity hypothesis. *Developmental Medicine and Child Neurology* 33:601–610.

Barry, H., M. K. Bacon, and I. L. Child (1957). A cross-cultural survey of some sex differences in socialization. *Journal of Abnormal Social Psychology* 55:327–332.

Barry, H., III, Bacon, M. K., & Child, I. L. (1967). Definitions, ratings and bibliographic sources for child training practices of 110 cultures. In C. S. Ford (Ed.), *Cross cultural approaches.* New Haven: HRAF Press.

Barry, H. I. and L. Paxson (1971). Infancy and early childhood: cross-cultural codes 2. *Ethnology* 10:466–508.

Bartels, A. and S. Zeki (2000). The neural basis of romantic love. *Neuroreport* 11(17, November). US http://www.vislab.ucl.ac.uk

Bateman, P. (1948). Intra-sexual selection in Drosophila. *Heredity* 2:349–368.

Baumann, O. ([1894] 1968). *Durch Massailand zur Nilquelle.* New York: Johnson Reprint.

Beckerman, S. (1994). Hunting and fishing in Amazonian: Hold the answers, what are the questions? In A. Roosevelt (Ed.), *Amazonian Indians from prehistory to the present.* (pp. 177–200). Tucson: University of Arizona Press.

Beckerman, S. (1994). Hunting and fishing in Amazonia: Hold the answers, what are the questions? In A. Roosevelt (Ed.), *Amazonian Indians from prehistory to the present* (pp. 177–202). Tucson: University of Arizona.

Beckerman, S., R. Lizarralde, C. Ballew, S. Schroeder, C. Fingelton, A. Garrison, and H. Smith (1998). The Barí partible paternity project: Preliminary results. *Current Anthropology* 39(1):164–167.

Beckerman, S. and P. Valentine (2002). *Cultures of multiple fathers: The theory and practice of partible paternity in lowland South America.* Gainesville: University of Florida Press.

Beise, J. and E. Voland (2002). A multilevel event history analysis of the effects of grandmothers on child mortality in a historical German population (Krummhorn, Ostfriesland, 1720–1874). *Demographic Research* 7: article 13. http://www.demographic-research.org./.

Bell, S. M. and M. D. S. Ainsworth (1972). Infant crying and maternal responsiveness. *Child Development* 43:1171–1190.

Belsky, J. (1997). Attachment, mating, and parenting: An evolutionary interpretation. *Human Nature* 8(4):361–381.

Belsky, J. (1999). Infant-parent attachment. In L. T.-L. C. S. Balter (Ed.), *Child psychology: A handbook of contemporary issues* (pp. 45–63). Philadelphia: Psychology Press/Taylor and Francis.

Belsky, J., L. Steinberg, and P. Draper (1991). Childhood experience, interpersonal development, and reproductive strategy: An evolutionary theory of socialization. *Child Development* 62(4):647–670.

Ben Shaul, D. M. (1962). The composition of the milk of wild animals. *International Zoological Year Book* 4:333–342.

Bender, B. (1975). *Farming in prehistory: From hunter-gatherer to food producer.* London: John Baker.

Benthall, J. (1992). A late developer? The ethnography of children. *Anthropology Today* 8:1.

Bernal, J. (1973). Night waking in infants during the first fourteen months. *Developmental Medicine and Child Neurology* 20:760.

Betzig, L., M. Borgerhoff Mulder, and P. Turke (Eds.) (1988). *Human reproductive behavior: A Darwinian perspective.* Cambridge: Cambridge University Press.

Biesele, M. (1993). The Ju/'hoan Bushmen: Indigenous rights in a new country. In M. S. Miller and Cultural Survival (Eds.), *The state of the peoples: A global human rights report on societies in danger* (pp. 33–39). Boston: Beacon.

Biesele, M. (1995). Human rights and democratization in Namibia: Some grass-roots political perspectives. *African Rural and Urban Studies* 1(2):49–72.

Biesele, M., R. K. Hitchcock, and P. P. Schweitzer (Eds.) (2000). *Hunters and gatherers in the modern world*. New York: Berghahn.

Binford, L. R. (1968). Post-pleistocene adaptations. In S. Binford and L. Binford (Eds.), *New perspectives in archaeology* (pp. 313–341). Chicago: Aldine.

Binford, L. R. (1980). Willow smoke and dogs' tails: Hunter-gatherer settlement systems and archaeological site formation. *American Antiquity* 45:4–20.

Binford, L. (1983). *In pursuit of the past*. New York: Thames and Hudson.

Bird, D. W. and R. Bliege Bird (2000). The ethnoarchaeology of juvenile foragers. *Journal of Anthropological Archaeology* 19:461–467.

Bird, D. W. and R. Bliege Bird (2002). Children on the reef: Slow learning or strategic foraging? *Human Nature* 13:269–298.

Bird, D.W., R. Bliege Bird, C.H. Parker (2003). Women who hunt with fire: Aboriginal resource use and fire regimes in Australia's Western Desert. *Arid Lands Newsletter*, 54(1): ISSN 1092–5481.

Bird, D. W., R. Bliege Bird, C. H. Parker, and B. Bass (submitted). Aboriginal burning regimes and hunting strategies in Australia's Western Desert. *Human Ecology*.

Bird-David, N. (1983). *Conjugal families and single persons: An analysis of the Naiken social system*. Cambridge: Cambridge University Press.

Bird-David, N. (1987). Single persons and social cohesion in a hunter-gatherer society. In P. Hockings (Ed.), *Dimensions of social life: Essays in honour of David G. Mandelbaum* (pp. 151–165). Berlin: Mouton.

Bird-David (1992) Beyond the "Original Affluent Society," A culturalist reformulation. Current Anthropology 31: 183–196.

Bird-David, N. (1999). "Animism" revisited: Personhood, environment, and relational epistemology. *Current Anthropology* 40(Supplement):S67–S91.

Bird-David, N. (in press). *The property of relations: Modern notions, Nayaka contexts*. In T. Widlok, (Ed.), Property and Equality, New York: Berghahn.

Black, J. M. (1996). *Partnerships in birds*. Oxford: Oxford University Press.

Bleek, D. F. (1929). *Comparative vocabularies of Bushman languages*. Cambridge: Cambridge University Press.

Bliege Bird, R. (1999). Cooperation and conflict: The behavioral ecology of the sexual division of labor. *Evolutionary Anthropology* 8:65–75.

Bliege Bird, R. and D. W. Bird (1997). Delayed reciprocity and tolerated theft: The behavioral ecology of food sharing strategies. *Current Anthropology* 38:49–78.

Bliege Bird, R. and D. W. Bird (2002). Constraints of knowing or constraints of growing? Fishing and collecting among the children of Mer. *Human Nature* 13:239–268.

Bliege Bird, R. and D. W. Bird (in press). Human hunting seasonality in savanna grasslands: A case from Australia. In D. Brockman and C. van Shaik (Eds.), *Primate Seasonality*. Cambridge: Cambridge University Press.

Bliege Bird, R., D. W. Bird, and J. M. Beaton (1995). Children and tradition subsistence on Mer (Murray Island), Torres Strait, Australia. *Australian Aboriginal Studies* 1995:2–17.

Bliege Bird, R., D. W. Bird, and E. A. Smith (2001). The hunting handicap: Costly signaling in human male foraging strategies. *Behavioral Ecology and Sociobiology* 50:9–19.

Bliege Bird R., D. W. Bird, E. A. Smith, and G. C. Kushnick (2002). Risk and reciprocity in Meriam food sharing. *Evolution and Human Behavior* 23:297–321.

Bloch, M. and J. Parry (1982). *Death and the regeneration of life*. Cambridge: Cambridge University Press.

Blurton Jones, N. G. (1972). Comparative aspects of mother-child contact. In N. G. B. Jones (Ed.), *Ethological studies of child behaviour*. Cambridge: Cambridge University Press.

Blurton Jones, N. G. (1990). The costs of children and the adaptive scheduling of births: Towards a sociobiological perspective of demography. In A. E. Rasa, C. Vogel, and E. Voland (Eds.), *The sociobiology of sexual and reproductive strategies*. London: Chapman and Hall.

Blurton Jones, N. (1993). The lives of hunter-gatherer children: effects of parental behavior and parental reproductive strategy. In M. E. Pereira and L. A. Fairbanks (Eds.), *Juvenile primates: Life history, development, and behavior* (pp. 309–326). New York: Oxford.

Blurton Jones, N., K. Hawkes, and P. Draper (1994a). Differences between Hadza and !Kung Children's work: Original affluence or practical reason? In E. S. Burch (Ed.), *Issues in hunter-gatherer research* (pp. 189–215). Oxford: Berg.

Blurton Jones, N., K. Hawkes, and P. Draper (1994b). Foraging patterns of !Kung adults and children: Why didn't !Kung children forage? *Journal of Anthropological Research* 50:217–248.

Blurton Jones, N. G., K. Hawkes, and J. F. O'Connell (1989). Modelling and measuring costs of children in two foraging societies. in V. Standen and R. A. Foley (Eds.), *Comparative socioecology: The behavioural ecology of humans and other mammals* (pp. 367–390). Oxford: Blackwell Scientific.

Blurton Jones, N. G., K. Hawkes, and J. F. O'Connell (1996). The global process, and local ecology: How should we explain differences between the Hadza and the !Kung? In S. Kent (Ed.), *Cultural diversity in twentieth century foragers* (pp. 159–187). Cambridge: Cambridge University Press.

Blurton Jones, N. G., K. Hawkes, and J. F. O'Connell (1997). Why do Hadza children forage? In N. L. Segal, G. E. Weisfeld, and C. C. Weisfeld (Eds.), *Uniting psychology and biology: integrative perspectives on human development* (pp. 279–313). Washington DC: American Psychological Association.

Blurton Jones, N. G., K. Hawkes, and J. F. O'Connell (1999). Some current ideas about the evolution of human life history. In P. C. Lee (Ed.), *Comparative Primate Socioecology* (pp. 140–166). Cambridge: Cambridge University Press.

Blurton Jones, N. G., K. Hawkes, and J. F. O'Connell (2002a). Antiquity of postreproductive life: Are there modern impacts on hunter-gatherer postreproductive lifespans? *American Journal of Human Biology* 14:184–205.

Blurton Jones, N. G., and M. J. Konner (1973). Sex differences in behavior of two-to-five-year-olds in London and amongst the Kalahari Desert Bushmen. In R. P. Michael and J. H. Crook (Eds.), *Comparative ecology and behavior of primates*. London: Academic Press.

Blurton Jones, N. G. and F. Marlowe (2002). Selection for delayed maturity: Does it take 20 years to learn to hunt and gather? *Human Nature* 13:199–238.

Blurton Jones, N. G., F. W. Marlowe, K. Hawkes, and J. O'Connell (2000). Paternal investment and hunter-gatherer divorce rates, In by L. Cronk, N. Chagnon, and W. Irons (Eds.), *Adaptation and human behavior: An anthropological perspective* (pp. 69–90). New York: Elsevier.

Blurton Jones, N. G., J. F. O'Connell, K. Hawkes, C. L. Kamuzora, and L. C. Smith (1992a). Demography of the Hadza, an increasing and high density population of savanna foragers. *American Journal of Physical Anthropology* 89:159–181.

Blurton Jones, N. G. and R. M. Sibly (1978). Testing adaptiveness of culturally determined behavior: Do Bushman women maximize their reproductive success by spacing births widely and foraging seldom? In *Human Behavior and Adaptation*. S.S.H.B. Symposium 18. London: Taylor and Francis.

Blurton Jones, N. G., L. C. Smith, J. F. O'Connell, K. Hawkes, and C. L. Kamuzora (1992b). Demography of the Hadza, an increasing and high density population of savanna foragers. *American Journal of Physical Anthropology* 89:159–181.

Bly, L. (1994). *Motor skills acquisition in the first year: An illustrated guide to normal development.* Tucson, AZ: Therapy Skill Builders.

Bock, J. (1995). *The determinants of variation in children's activities in a Southern African community.* Ph.D. dissertation, University of New Mexico.

Bock, J. (1998). Economic development and cultural change among the Okavango Delta peoples of Botswana. *Botswana Notes and Records* 30:27–44.

Bock, J. (1999). Evolutionary approaches to population: Implications for research and policy. *Population and Environment* 21:193–222.

Bock, J. (2002a). Learning, life history, and productivity: Children's lives in the Okavango Delta of Botswana. *Human Nature* 13(2):161–198.

Bock, J. (2002b). Evolutionary demography and intrahousehold time allocation: Schooling and children's labor among the Okavango Delta Peoples of Botswana. *American Journal of Human Biology* 14(2):206–221.

Bock, J. and K. Braun (1999). Filial imprinting in domestic chicks is associated with spine pruning in the associative area, dorsocaudal neostriatum. *European Journal of Neuroscience* 11(7):2566–2570.

Bock, J. and S. E. Johnson (2002a). The Okavango Delta peoples of Botswana. In R. K. Hitchcock and A. J. Osborne (Eds.), *Endangered peoples of Africa and the Middle East* (pp. 151–169). New York: Greenwood.

Bock, J. and S. E. Johnson (2002b). Male migration, remittances, and child outcome among the Okavango Delta peoples of Botswana. In C. S. Tamis-LeMonda and N. Cabrera (Eds.), *Handbook of father involvement: Multidisciplinary perspectives* (pp. 308–335). Mahwah, NJ: Lawrence Erlbaum Associates.

Bock, J. and D. W. Sellen (2002a). Introduction to special issue on childhood and the evolution of the human life course. *Human Nature* 13(2):153–161.

Bock, J. and D. W. Sellen (Eds.) (2002b). Special issue on childhood and the evolution of the human life course. *Human Nature* 13(2):153–329.

Boesch, C. and H. Boesch-Achermann (2000). *The chimpanzees of the Tai Forest: Behavioural ecology and evolution.* Oxford: Oxford University Press.

Bogin, B. (1988). The evolution of human childhood. *Bioscience* 40:1624.

Bogin, B. (1996). Human growth and development from an evolutionary perspective. In D. J. K. Henry and S. J. Ulijaszek (Eds.), *Long-term consequences of early environments: Growth, development and the lifespan developmental perspective* (pp. 7–24). Cambridge: Cambridge University Press.

Bogin, B. (1998). Evolutionary and biological aspects of childhood. In C. Panter-Brick (Ed.), *Biosocial perspectives on children* (Biosocial Society Symposium Series 10). Cambridge: Cambridge University Press.

Bogin, B. (1999). *Patterns of human growth*. Cambridge: Cambridge University Press.

Borgerhoff Mulder, M. and T. M. Caro (1985). The use of quantitative observational techniques in anthropology. *Current Anthropology* 26:323–335.

Bourdieu, P. (1997). *Reproduction in education, society and culture*. Beverly Hills, CA: Sage.

Bowlby, J. (1958). The nature of the child's tie to his mother. *International Journal of Psychoanalysis* 39:350–373.

Bowlby, J. (1969). *Attachment*. New York: Basic Books.

Bowlby, J. ([1969] 1972). *Attachment*, vol. 1. Middlesex: Penquin.

Bowlby, J. (1970–1980). *Attachment and loss* (3 vols.). New York: Basic Books.

Brand Miller, J., K. James, and P. Maggiore (1993) *Tables of Composition of Australian Aboriginal Foods*. Canberra: Aboriginal Studies Press.

Brazelton, T. B. (1990). Commentary: Parent-infant co-sleeping revisited. *Ab Initio*, 2(1):1–7.

Bretherton, I. (1992). The origins of attachment theory: John Bowlby and Mary Ainsworth. *Developmental Psychology* 28(5):759–775.

Briggs, J. L. (1998). *Inuit morality play: The emotional education of a three-year old*. New Haven, CT: Yale University Press.

Bril, B., M. Zack, and E. Nkounkou-Hombessa (1989). Ethnotheories of development and education: A view from different cultures. *European Journal of Psychology of Education* 4:307–318.

Brisson, R. (1984). *Lexique: Français-Baka*. Douala: College Libermann.

Brisson, R. and D. Boursier (1979). *Petit Dictionnair Baka-Français*. Douala.

Brown, J. K. (1963). A cross-cultural study of female initiation rites. *American Anthropologist* 65:837–853.

Bruner, J. S. and B. M. Bruner (1968). On voluntary action and its hierarchical structure. *International Journal of Psychology*, 3:239–255.

Buchan, J. C., S. A. Alberts, J. B. Silk, J. Altmann (2003). True paternal care in a multi-male primate society. *Nature* 425:179–181.

Bugos, P. E. and L. M. McCarthy (1984). Ayoreo infanticide: A case study. In G. Hausfater and S. B. Hrdy (Eds.), *Infanticide: Comparative and evolutionary perspectives* (pp. 503–520). Hawthorne, NY: Aldine de Gruyter.

Bundo, D. (2001). Social relationship embodied in singing and dancing performances among the Baka. *African Study Monographs Supplementary Issue* 26: 85–101.

Burbank, V. K. (1989). *Aboriginal adolescence: Maidenhood in an Australian community*. Newark, NJ: Rutgers University Press.

Byrne, R. W. and A. Whitten (1985). *Machiavellian intelligence: Social expertise and the evolution of intellect in monkeys, apes and humans*. Oxford: Clarendon.

Caillois, R. (1967). *Les jeux et les hommes,* édition revue et augmentée. Paris: Gallimard.

Caldwell, B. M., C. Wright, A. Honig, and J. Tannenbaum (1970). Infant day-care and attachment. *American Journal of Orthopsychiatry* 40:397–412.

Cassidy, J. (1999). The nature of the child's ties. In J. S. P. R. Cassidy (Ed.), *Handbook of attachment: Theory, research, and clinical applications* (pp. 3–20). New York, NY, USA: The Guilford Press

Cassidy, J. and L. Berlin. 1994. The insecure/ambivalent pattern of attachment: Theory and research. *Child Development* 65:971–991.

Cassidy, J. and P. R. Shaver (1999). *Handbook of attachment, theory, research and clinical applications.* New York: Guilford.

Cavalli-Sforza, L. L. (Ed.) (1986). *African Pygmies,* Orlando, FL: Academic Press.

Chagnon, N. A. (1997). *Yanomamö.* New York: Harcourt Brace.

Chappell, J. and A. Kacelnik (2002). Selectivity of tool length by New Caledonian crows. *Animal Cognition* 5:71–78.

Charnov, E. L. (1976). Optimal foraging, the marginal value theorem. *Theoretical Population Biology* 9(2):129–136.

Charnov, E. L. (1993). *Life history invariants: Some explorations of symmetry in evolutionary ecology.* New York: Oxford University Press.

Charnov, E. (2001). Evolution of mammal life histories. *Evolutionary Ecology Research* 3:521–535.

Charnov, E. L. and D. Berrigan (1993). Why do female primates have such long lifespans and so few babies? *Evolutionary Anthropology* 1:191–194.

Chayanov, A. V. ([1925] 1986). In D. Thorner, B. Kerblay, and R. E. F. Smith (Eds., Trans.), *The theory of peasant economy.* Homewood, IL: Irwin.

Chisholm, J. S. (1983). *Navajo infancy: An ethological study of child development.* Hawthorne, NY: Aldine de Gruyter.

Chisholm, J. S. (1988). Toward a theory of developmental evolutionary ecology of humans. In K. B. MacDonald (Ed.), *Sociobiological perspectives on human development.* London: Springer Verlag.

Chisholm, J. S. (1993). Death, hope, and sex: life-history theory and the development of reproductive strategies. *Current Anthropology,* 34(1, February):1–24.

Chisholm, J. S. (1996). The evolutionary ecology of attachment organization. *Human Nature* 7(1):1–37.

Chisholm, J. S. (1999). *Death, hope and sex: Steps to an evolutionary ecology of mind and morality.* New York: Cambridge University Press.

Chisholm, J. (2003). Uncertainty, contingency and attachment: A life history theory of mind. In K. Sterelny and J. Fitness (Eds.), *From mating to mentality: Evaluating evolutionary psychology.* Hove: Psychology.

CIIL (1993a). *Ongee-Hindi-English pictorial glossary.* Rajsingh, V., Raganatha, M. (Eds.). Mysore: Central Institute of Indian Languages.

CIIL (1993b). *Ongee-Hindi bilingual primer.* Rajsingh, V., Raganatha, M. (Eds.). Mysore: Central Institute of Indian Languages.

CIIL (2000). *A handbook on Jarwa language.* Rajsingh, V., Raganatha, M. (Eds.). Mysore: Central Institute of Indian Languages.

Clark, H. (1874). Notes on the languages of Andaman Islands. *Journal of the Royal Anthropological Institute* 3:467–469.

Clark, C. B. (1977). A preliminary report on weaning among chimpanzees of the Gombe National Park, Tanzania. In S. Chevalier-Skolnikoff & F. E. Poirier (Eds.), *Primate bio-social development: biological, social and ecological determinants.* New York: Garland Publishing.

Clutton-Brock, T. H. (1982). *Red deer: Behaviour and ecology of two sexes.* Chicago: Chicago University Press.

Clutton-Brock, T. H. (1991). *The evolution of parental care.* Princeton, NJ: Princeton University Press.

Cockburn, A. (1998). Evolution of helping behavior in cooperatively breeding birds. *Annual Review of Ecology and Systematics* 29:141–177.

Cole, M. and S. R. Cole (1993). *The development of children* (2nd ed.). New York: Scientific American Books.

Colebrooke, Lt. R. H. (1795). On the Andaman Islands. *Asiatic Researches* 4:385–394.

Condon, R.G. (1987) Inuit youth. Piscataway, NJ: Rutgers University Press.

Cook, A. S. and K. A. Oljetenbruns (1998). *Dying and grieving: Lifespan and family perspectives.* Fort Worth, TX: Harcourt and Brace.

Corbett, K. S. (2000). Explaining infant feeding style of low-income black women. *Journal of Pediatric Nursing* 15(2):73–81.

Crawford, C. B., B. E. Salter, and K. L. Jang (1987). Human grief: Is its intensity related to the reproductive value of the deceased? *Ethology and Sociobiology* 10:297–307.

Creel, S. and N. M. Creel (1991). Energetics, reproductive suppression and obligate communal breeding in carnivores. *Behavioral Ecology and Sociobiology* 28: 273–270.

Creel, S. and N. M. Creel (2002). *The African wild dog: Behavior, ecology and conservation.* Princeton, NJ: Princeton University Press.

Cunningham, A. S. (1995). Breast-feeding: Adaptive behavior for child health and longevity. In P. Stuart-Macadam and K. A. Dettwyler (Eds.), *Breast-feeding biocultural perspectives* (pp. 243–264). Hawthorne, NY: Aldine de Gruyter.

Daly, M. and M. Wilson (1984). A sociobiological analysis of human infanticide. In G. Hausfater and S. B. Hrdy (Eds.), *Infanticide: Comparative and evolutionary perspectives* (pp. 487–502). Hawthorne, NY: Aldine de Gruyter.

Daly, M. and M. Wilson (1985). Child abuse and other risks of not living with both parents. *Ethology and Sociobiology* 6(4):59–73.

Daly, M. and M. Wilson (1987). *Sex evolution and behavior.* Hawthorne, NY: Aldine de Gruyter.

Daly, M. and M. Wilson (1988). *Homicide.* Hawthorne, New York: Aldine de Gruyter.

Dasgupta, D. and S. R. Sharma (1982). *A handbook of Ongee language.* Calcutta: Anthropological Survey of India.

Davies, N. (1992). *Dunnock behaviour and social evolution.* Oxford:: Oxford University Press.

de Flacourt, E. ([1660] 1908). Histoire de la Grande âle de Madagascar, 1642–1660. In A. Grandidier, H. Froidevaux, and G. Grandidier (Eds.), *Collection des ouvrages anciens concernant Madagascar.* Paris: Union Coloniale.

De Wolff, M. S. and M. H. van IJzendoorn (1997). Sensitivity and attachment: A meta-analysis on parental antecedents of infant attachment. *Child Development* 68(4):571–591.

Dempwolff, O. (1916–1917). Beitrage zur Kenntnis der Sprachen in Deutsch-Ostafrika. 12. *Worter der Hatzasprache. Zeitschrift für Kolonialsprachen* 7:319–325.

Department of Social Welfare (1969). *Report of the Study Team on the Negrito tribes of Andaman Islands.* Government of India, New Delhi.

Dietz, W. H., B. Marino, N. R. Peacock, and R. C. Bailey (1989). Nutritional status of Efe pygmies and Lese horticulturalists. *American Journal of Physical Anthropology* 78:495–509.

Dixson, A. and L. George (1982). Prolactin and parental behavior in a male New World primate. *Nature* 299:551–553.

Douglass, W. A. (1969). *Death in Murelaga: Funerary rituals in a Spanish Basque village.* Seattle: University of Washington Press.

Dounias, E. (2001) The management of wild yam tubers by the Baka Pygmies in Southeastern Cameroon., *African Study Monographs Supplementary Issue* 26: 135–156.

Draper, P. (1972). *!Kung bushman childhood.* Unpublished Ph.D. dissertation, Harvard University.

Draper, P. (1973). Crowding among hunter gatherers: The !Kung Bushmen. *Science* 182(9109):301–303.

Draper, P. (1975). Cultural pressure on sex differences. *American Ethnologist* 2:602–616.

Draper, P. (1976). Social and economic constraints on child life among the !Kung. In R. B. Lee and I. Devore (Eds.), *Kalahari hunter-gatherers* (pp. 199–217). Cambridge, MA: Harvard University Press.

Draper, P. (1985). Two views of sex differences in socialization. In R. Hall (Ed.), *Male-female differences: A biocultural perspective* (pp. 5–25). New York: Praeger.

Draper, P. and A. Buchanan (1992). If you have a child you have a life: Demographic and cultural perspectives on fathering in old age in !Kung society. In B. S. Hewlett (Ed.), *Father-child relations: Cultural and biosocial contexts* (pp. 131–152). Hawthorne, NY: Aldine de Gruyter.

Draper, P. and E. Cashdan (1988). Technological change and child behavior among the !Kung. *Ethnology* 27:339–365.

Draper, P. and R. Hames (2000). Birth order, sibling investment, and fertility among Ju/'Hoansi (!Kung). *Human Nature* 11:117–156.

Draper, P. and H. Harpending (1982). Father absence and reproductive strategy: An evolutionary perspective. *Journal of Anthropological Research* 38:255–273.

Draper, P. and H. Harpending (1987). Parental investment and the child's environment. In J. Lancaster, J. Altmann, A. Rossi, and L. Sherrod (Eds.), *Parenting across the lifespan: Biosocial dimensions* (pp. 207–235). Hawthorne, NY: Aldine de Gruyter.

Drury, R. ([1729] 1826). *The pleasant and surprising adventures of Robert Drury during his fifteen years' captivity on the Island of Madagascar.* London: Hunt and Clarke. (Reprinted: Oxford University Press.)

Durkheim, E. (1915). *The elementary forms of the religious life.* New York: Allen and Unwin.

Durkheim, E. (1951). *Suicide: A study in sociology.* Glencoe IL: Free Press.

Durkheim, E. (1956). *Education and sociology.* Glencoe IL: Free Press.

Durnin, J. V. G. A. and R. Passmore (1967). *Energy, work and leisure.* London: Heinemann Educational Books.

Early, J. D. (1985). Low forager fertility: Demographic characteristic or method-
ological artifact? *Human Biology* 57:387–399.

Eibl-Eibesfeldt, I. (1983). Patterns of parent-child interaction in a cross-cultural perspective. In A. Oliverio and M. Zappella (Eds.), *The behavior of human infants.*
New York: Plenum.

Eibl-Eibesfeldt, I. (1988). *Human ethology.* Hawthorne, NY: Aldine de Gruyter.

Eisenbruch, M. (1991). From post-traumatic stress disorder to cultural bereavement: Diagnosis of Southeast Refugees. *Social Science and Medicine* 33:673–680.

El Hassan Al Awad, A. M. and E. J. S. Sonuga-Barke (1992). Childhood problems in
a Sudanese city: A comparison of extended and nuclear families. *Child Development* 63:906–914.

Elias, M. F., N. A. Nicholson, and M. J. Konner (1986). Two sub-cultures of maternal care in the United States. In D. M. Taub and F. A. King (Eds.), *Current perspectives in primate social dynamics.* New York: Van Nostrand Reinhold.

Elias, M., J. Teas, J. Johnston, and C. Bora (1986). Nursing practices and lactation
amenorrhoea. *Journal of Biosocial Science* 18:1–10.

Ellison, P. T. (2001). *On fertile ground: A natural history of human reproduction.* Cambridge, MA: Harvard University Press.

Ellison, P. T., N. R., Peacock and C. Lager (1986). Salivary progesterone and luteal
function in two low-fertility populations of northeast Zaire. *Human Biology*
58:473–483.

Elowson, A. M., C. Snowdon, and C. Lazaro-Perea (1998). "Babbling" and social
context in infant monkeys: Parallels to human infants. *Trends in Cognitive Sciences* 2(1):31–37.

Ember, C. R. (1975). Residential variation among hunter-gatherers. *Behavior Science
Research* 13:199–227.

Emlen, S. T. (1984). Cooperative breeding in birds and mammals. In D. L. Krebs
and N. B. Davies (Eds.), *Behavioural ecology: An evolutionary approach* (pp.
305–339). Oxford: Blackwell.

Emlen, Stephen T. (1991). Evolution of cooperative breeding in birds and mammals. In J. R. Krebs and N. B. Davies (Eds.), *Behavioral ecology* (3rd ed.). Oxford:
Blackwell Scientific.

Emlen, Stephen T. (1995). An evolutionary theory of the family *Proceedings of the
National Academy of Sciences* 92:8092–8099.

Engle, P. L. and C. Breaux (1998). Fathers' involvement with children: Perspectives
from developing countries. *Social Policy Report, Society for Research in Child Development* 12(1):1–23.

Erickson, E. (1963). *Childhood and society* (2nd ed.). New York: Norton.

Essock-Vitale, S. M. and M. T. McGuire (1980). Predictions derived from the theories of kin selection and reciprocation assessed by anthropological data. *Ethology and Sociobiology* 1:233–243.

Estioko-Griffin, A. (1985). Women as hunters: The case of an eastern Cagayan Agta
group. In P. B. Griffin and A. Estioko-Griffin (Eds.), *The Agta of Northeastern
Luzon: Recent studies* (pp. 18–32). Cebu City, Philippines: San Carlos.

Estioko-Griffin, A. and P. B. Griffin (1981). Woman the hunter: The Agta. In F.
Dahlberg (Ed.), *Woman the gatherer* (pp. 121–151). New Haven, CT: Yale University Press.

Ewer, R. F. (1968). *Ethology of mammals*. London: Elek.

Fagereng, M. E. (1950). Dynastie Andrevola. *Bulletin de l'Academie Malgache* 28: 136–159.

Farroni, T., G. Csibra, F. Simion, and M. Johnson (2002). Eye contact detection in humans from birth. *Proceedings of the National Academy of Sciences* 99(14): 9602–9605.

Fehr, Ernst and Urs Fischbacher (2003).The nature of human altruism: Proximate patterns and evolutionary origins.*Nature* 425:785–791.

Ferguson, C. A. (1964). Baby talk in six languages. *American Anthropologist* 66(6), Part 2, Special publication: *The ethnography of communication*, 103–114.

Ferro-Luzzi, A., M. Franklin, and W. P. T. James (1992). A simplified approach of assessing adult chronic energy deficiency. *European Journal of Clinical Nutrition* 46:173–186.

Fleming, A., C. Corter, J. Stallings, and M. Steiner (2002). Testosterone and prolactin are associated with emotional responses to infant cries in new fathers. Hormones & behavior, 42, 399–413.

Flinn, M. V. (1988). Step- and genetic parent/offspring relationships in a Caribbean village. *Ethology and Sociobiology* 9(6):335–369.

Flinn, M. V. (1989). Household composition and female reproductive strategies in a Trinidadian village. In A. E. Rasa, C. Vogel, and E. Voland (Eds.), *The sociobiology of sexual and reproductive strategies*. London: Chapman and Hall.

Flinn, M. V. (1992). Paternal care in a Caribbean village. In B. S. Hewlett (Ed.), *Father-child relations: Cultural and biosocial contexts*. Hawthorne, NY: Aldine de Gruyter.

Flinn, M. V. (1999). Family environment, stress, and health during childhood. In C. Panter-Brick and C. M. Worthman (Eds.), *Hormones, health, and behavior: A socioecological and lifespan perspective* (pp. 105–138). Cambridge: Cambridge University Press.

Fomon, S. J. (1974). *Infant nutrition* (2nd ed.). Philadelphia: W.B. Saunders.

Fouts, H. N. (2002). *The social and emotional contexts of weaning among the Bofi farmers and foragers of Central Africa*. Dissertation thesis, Washington State University.

Fouts, H. N., B. S. Hewlett, and M. E. Lamb (2001). Weaning and the nature of early childhood interactions among Bofi foragers in Central Africa. *Human Nature* 12(1):27–46.

Fouts, R. (1997). *Next of kin*. New York: Morrow.

French, J. A. (1997). Proximate regulation of singular breeding in Callitrichid primates. In N. G. Solomon and J. A. French (Eds.), *Cooperative breeding in mammals* (pp. 34–75). Cambridge: Cambridge University Press.

Freud, S. ([1916] 1967). Mourning and melancholia. In J. Strachey (Ed. and Transl.), *The standard edition of the complete works of Sigmund Freud*, vol. 14 (pp. 243–258). London: Hogarth.

Fujimoto, K. (1985). Toward a theory of child culture (in Japanese). *Kyoto University Research Studies in Education* 36(March):1–31.

Furstenberg, F. (1976). *Unplanned parenthood: The social consequences of unplanned parenthood*. New York: Free Press.

Fytche, A. (1861). A note on certain aborigines of the Andaman Islands. *Journal of Asiatic Society* 30:263–267.

Garber, P. A. (1997). One for all and breeding for one: Cooperation and competition as a Tamarin reproductive strategy. *Evolutionary Anthropology* 5:187–199.

Goldsmith, H. H. and J. A. Alansky (1987). Maternal and infant temperamental predictors of attachment: A meta-analytic review. *Journal of Consulting and Clinical Psychology* 55(6):805–816.

Golombok, S., F. Tasker, and C. Murray (1997). Children raised in fatherless families from infancy: Family relationships and the socioemotional development of children of lesbian and single heterosexual mothers. *Journal of Child Psychology and Psychiatry* 38:783–791.

Goodall, J. (1986). *The chimpanzees of Gombe*. Cambridge, MA: Harvard University Press.

Goodlin-Jones, B. L., M. M. Burnham, E. E. and Gaylor, T. F. Anders (2001). Night waking, sleep-wake organization, and self-soothing in the first year of life. *Journal of Developmental and Behavioral Pediatrics* 22(4):226–233.

Goodman, M. J., A. Estioko-Griffin, P. B. Griffin, and J. S. Grove (1985). Menarche, pregnancy, birth spacing and menopause among the Agta women foragers of Cagayan province, Luzon, the Philippines. *Annals of Human Biology* 12(2): 169–177.

Goss, R. E. and D. Klass (1997). Tibetan Buddhism and the resolutions of grief, the Bardo-Thodol for the dying and the grieving. *Death Studies* 21:377–395.

Grey, P. B., S. M. Kahlenberg, E. S. D. Barrett, S. F. Lipson, and P. Ellison (2002). Marriage and fatherhood are associated with lower testosterone in males. *Evolution and Human Behavior* 23(3):193–201.

Grieser, D. L. and P. K. Kuhl (1988). Maternal speech to infants in a tonal language: Support for universal prosodic features in motherese. *Developmental Psychology* 24:14–20.

Griffin, P. B. and A. Estioko-Griffin (Eds.) (1985). *The Agta of Northeastern Luzon: Recent studies*. Cebu City, Philippines: San Carlos.

Griffin, P. B., M. Goodman, A. A. Estioko-Griffin, and J. Grove (1992). Agta women hunters: Subsistence, child care and reproduction. In P. Bellwood (Ed.), *Man and his culture: A resurgence* (pp. 173–179). New Delhi: Vedams.

Griffin, P. B. and M. B. Griffin (1992). Fathers and childcare among the Cagayan Agta. In B. S. Hewlett (Ed.), *Father-child relations: Cultural and biosocial contexts* (pp. 297–320). Hawthorne, NY: Aldine de Gruyter.

Griffin, P. B. and M. B. Griffin (1999). The Agta of eastern Luzon, Phillipines. In R. B. Lee and R. Daly (Eds.), *The Cambridge encyclopedia of hunters and gatherers* (p. 289). Cambridge: Cambridge University Press.

Gubernick, D. J., C. M. Worthman, and J. F. Stallings (no date). Hormonal correlates of fatherhood in men. Unpublished ms.

Gurven, M., W. Allen-Arave, K. Hill, and A. M. Hurtado (2000). It's a wonderful life: Signaling generosity among the Ache of Paraguay. *Evolution and Human Behavior* 21(4):263–282.

Guttman, N. and D. R. Zimmerman (2000). Low-income mothers' views on breastfeeding. *Social Science and Medicine* 50(10):1457–1473.

Guyer, J. (1994). Lineal identities and lateral networks: The logic of polyandrous motherhood. In C. Bledsoe and G. Pison (Eds.), *Nuptiality in sub-Saharan Africa: Contemporary anthropological and demographic perspectives*. Oxford: Oxford University Press.

Hagen, E. (1999). The functions of postpartum depression. *Evolution and Human Behavior* 20:325–359.

Hagen, E., R. Hames, N. M. Craig, M. T. Lauer, and M. E. Price (2001). Parental investment and child health in a Yanomamö village suffering short-term food stress. *Journal of Biosocial Science* 33:503–528.

Hames, R. B. (1988). The allocation of parental care among the Ye'kwana. In L. Betzig, Monique Borgerhoff Mulder, and Paul Turke. *Human reproductive behaviour: A Darwinian perspective* (pp. 237–251). Cambridge: Cambridge University Press.

Hames, R. (1992a). Variation in paternal care among the Yanomamo. In B. S. Hewlett (Ed.), *Father-child relations: Cultural and biosocial contexts* (pp. 85–110). Hawthorne, NY: Aldine de Gruyter.

Hames, R. (1992b). Time allocation. In E. A. Smith and B. Winterhalder (Eds.), *Evolutionary ecology and human behavior* (pp. 203–235). Hawthorne, NY: Aldine de Gruyter.

Hames, R. B. and P. Draper (2001). Parental investment and sex ratio. Paper presented to Human Behavior and Evolution Society, University College London.

Hames, R. and P. Draper (in press). Women's work, child care and helpers at the nest in a hunter-gatherer society, *Human Nature*.

Hamilton, A. (1930). *A new account of the East Indies*. London: Argonaut.

Hamilton, W. D. (1964). The genetical evolution of social behaviour, 1. *Journal of Theoretical Biology* 7:1–16.

Hamilton, W. D. (1966). The moulding of senescence by natural selection. *Journal of Theoretical Biology* 12:12–14.

Hanks, C. and F. Rebelsky (1977). Mommy and the midnight visitor: A study of occasional co-sleeping. *Psychiatry* 40:277–280.

Hansen, J. D. L., et al. (1993). Hunter-gatherer to pastoral way of life: Effects of the transition on health, growth, and nutritional status. *Southern African Journal of Science* 89:559–564.

Hara, H. (1979). *Cultural anthropology of children* (in Japanese). Tokyo: Shobunsha.

Harako, R. (1980). Growth and play in a hunter-gatherer society (in Japanese). *Collection of papers of collage of liberal arts, Meiji University* 137:1–44.

Hare, B., M. Brown, C. Williamson, and M. Tomasello (2003). The domestication of social cognition in dogs. *Science* 298:1634–1636.

Harkness, S. and C. M. Super (1980). Child development theory in anthropological perspective. In C. M. Super and S. Harkness (Eds.), *Anthropological perspective on child development* (pp. 1–13). San Francisco: Jossey-Bass.

Harley, J. K. (1963). *Adolescent youths in peer groups: a cross-cultural study*: Department of Anthropology, Harvard University.

Harris, J. R. (1998). *The nurture assumption: Why children turn out the way they do*. New York: Free Press.

Harris, P. (2000). *The work of the imagination*. Oxford: Blackwell.

Harvey, P., R. D. Martin, and T. H. Clutton-Brock (1987). Life histories in comparative perspective. In B. B. Smuts et al. (Eds.), *Primate societies*. Chicago: University of Chicago Press.

Hatano, G. and K. Takahashi (1997). *Cultural psychology: Children and education* (in Japanese). Tokyo: Iwanamisyotenn.

Haughton, J. C. (1861). Papers relating to the aborigines of the Andaman Islands. *Journal of the Asiatick Society of Bengal (Calcutta)* 30:251–267.

Hauser, M. D., M. K. Chen, and E. Chuang (in press). Give unto others: Genetically unrelated cotton-top tamarin monkeys preferentially give food to those who give food back. *Proceedings of the Royal Society, Biological Processes.*

Hausfater, G. and S. B. Hrdy (1992). *Infanticide: Comparative and evolutionary perspectives.* Hawthorne, NY: Aldine de Gruyter.

Hawkes, K. (1983). Kin selection and culture. *American Ethnologist* 10:345–363.

Hawkes, K. (1987). Limited needs and hunter-gatherer time allocation. *Ethology and Sociobiology* 8:87–91.

Hawkes, K. (1990). Why do men hunt? Benefits for risky choices. In E. Cashdan (Ed.), *Risk and uncertainty in tribal and peasant economies* (pp. 145–166). Boulder, CO: Westview.

Hawkes, K. (1991). Showing off: Tests of an hypothesis about men's foraging goals. *Ethology and Sociobiology* 12:29–54.

Hawkes, K. (1993). Why hunter-gatherers work: An ancient version of the problem of public goods. *Current Anthropology* 34:341–361.

Hawkes, K. (1996). Foraging differences between men and women: Behavioral ecology of the sexual division of labor. In *Power, Sex and Tradition: The Archaeology of Human Ancestry* , S. Shennan and J. Steele, eds., 283–305. London: Routledge

Hawkes, K. (2001). Is meat the hunter's property?: Big game, ownership, and explanations of hunting and sharing. In C. B. Stanford and H. T. Bunn (Eds.), *Meat eating and human evolution* (pp. 219–236). Oxford: Oxford University Press.

Hawkes, K. (2004). Mating, parenting, and the evolution of human pair bonds. In B. Chapais and C. Berman (Eds.), *Kinship and behavior in primates.* Oxford: Oxford University Press. Pp. 443–473

Hawkes, K. and R. Bliege Bird (2002). Showing off, handicap signaling, and the evolution of men's work. *Evolutionary Anthropology* 11:58–67.

Hawkes, K., J. F. O'Connell, and N. G. Blurton Jones (1989). Hardworking Hadza grandmothers. In V. Standen and R. Foley (Eds.), *Comparative socioecology* (pp. 341–366). Oxford: Blackwell.

Hawkes, K., J. F. O'Connell, and N. G. Blurton Jones (1991). Hunting income patterns among the Hadza: big game, common goods, foraging goals and the evolution of the human diet. *Philosophical Transactions of the Royal Society of London* B 334:243–251.

Hawkes, K., J. F. O'Connell, and N. Blurton Jones (1995a). Hadza children's foraging: Juvenile dependency, social arrangements and mobility among hunter-gatherers. *Current Anthropology* 36:688–700.

Hawkes, K., J. F. O'Connell, and N. G. Blurton Jones (1997). Hadza women's time allocation, offspring provisioning, and the evolution of long postmenopausal life spans. *Current Anthropology* 38:551–577.

Hawkes, K., J. F. O'Connell, and N. G. Blurton Jones (2001a). Hadza meat sharing. *Evolution and Human Behavior* 22:113–142.

Hawkes, K., J. F. O'Connell, and N. G. Blurton Jones (2001b). Hunting and nuclear families: Some lessons from the Hadza about men's work. *Current Anthropology* 42(5):681–709.

Hawkes, K., J. F. O'Connell, N. G. Blurton Jones, H. Alvarez, and E. L. Charnov (1998). Grandmothering, menopause, and the evolution of human life histories. *Proceedings of the National Academy of Sciences, USA* 95:1336–1339.

Hawkes, K., J. F. O'Connell, N. G. Blurton Jones, H. Alvarez, and E. L. Charnov (2000). The grandmother hypothesis and human evolution. In L. Cronk, N. A. Chagnon, and W. Irons Eds.), *Human behavior and adaptation: An anthropological perspective* (pp. 371–395). Hawthorne, NY: Aldine de Gruyter.

Hawkes, K., J. F. O'Connell, K. Hill, and E. L. Charnov (1985). How much is enough? Hunters and limited needs. *Ethology and Sociobiology* 6:3–15.

Hawkes, K., A. R. Rogers, and E. L. Charnov (1995b). The male's dilemma: Increased offspring production is more paternity to steal. *Evolutionary Ecology* 9:662–677.

Headland, T. N. (1989). Population decline in a Philippine Negrito hunter-gatherer society. *American Journal of Human Biology* 1:59–72.

Heikkinen, T. (1986). Phonology of the !Xu dialect spoken in Ovamboland and western Kavango. *South African Journal of African Language* 6(1):18–28.

Heinsohn, R. and M. C. Double (2004). Cooperate or speciate: New theory for the distribution of passerine birds. *Trends in Ecology and Evolution* 19(2):55–60.

Henrich, J., et al. (2001). In search of homo economicus: Behavioral experiments in 15 small-scale societies. *American Economic Review* 91:73–78.

Hertz, R. I. (1960). A contribution to the study of the collective representation of death. In *Death and the right hand* (R. and C. Needham, trans.). London: Cohen and West.

Herzfeld, M. (2001). *Anthropology: Theoretical practice in culture and society.* Oxford: Blackwell.

Hewlett, B. (1988). Sexual selection and paternal investment among Aka Pygmies. In L. Betzig, M. B. Mulder, and P. Turke (Eds.), *Human reproductive behavior: A Darwinian perspective.* Cambridge: Cambridge University Press.

Hewlett, B. S. (1989). Multiple caretaking among African Pygmies. *American Anthropologist* 91(1):186–191.

Hewlett, B. S. (1991a). Demography and childcare in preindustrial societies. *Journal of Anthropological Research* 47(1):1–37.

Hewlett, B. S. (1991b). *Intimate fathers: The nature and context of Aka Pygmy paternal infant care.* Ann Arbor, MI: University of Michigan Press.

Hewlett, B. S. (Ed.) (1992a). *Father-child relations: Cultural and biosocial contexts.* Hawthorne, NY: Aldine de Gruyter.

Hewlett, B. S. (1992b). Husband-wife reciprocity and the husband-wife relationship among Aka pygmies. In B. S. Hewlett (Ed.), *Father-child relationships: Cultural and biosocial contexts* (pp. 153–176). Hawthorne, NY: Aldine de Gruyter.

Hewlett, B. S. (1996). Cultural diversity among African Pygmies. In S. Kent (Ed.), *Cultural diversity among the twentieth century foragers* (pp. 215–244). Cambridge: Cambridge University Press.

Hewlett, B. S. (2000). Central African government's and international NGO's perceptions of Baka Pygmy development. In P. P. Shweitzer, B. Megan, and R. K. Hichcock (Eds.), *Hunters and gatherers in the modern world* (pp. 380–390). New York: Berghan.

Hewlett, B. S. (2001). The cultural nexus of Aka father-infant bonding. In C. B. Brettell and C. F. Sargent (Eds.), *Gender in cross-cultural perspective* (3rd ed., pp. 45–56). Saddle River, NJ: Prentice Hall.

Hewlett, B. S. and D. Alster (no date). Prolactin and infant holding among American fathers. Unpublished ms.

Hewlett, B. S. and L. L. Cavalli-Sforza (1986). Cultural transmission among the Aka Pygmies. *American Anthropologist* 88:922–934.

Hewlett, B. S. and M. E. Lamb (2002). Integrating evolution, culture and developmental psychology: Explaining caregiver-infant proximity and responsiveness in central Africa and the USA. In H. Keller, Y. H. Poortinga, and A. Schölmerich (Eds.), *Between culture and biology: Perspectives on ontogenetic development* (pp. 241–269). Cambridge: Cambridge University Press.

Hewlett, B. S., M. E. Lamb, D. Shannon., B. Leyendecker, and A. Scholmerich (1998). Culture and early infancy among Central African foragers and farmers. *Developmental Psychology* 34:653–661.

Hewlett, B. S., M. E. LAMB, D. Shannon., B. Leyendecker, and A. Scholmerich (2000). Internal working models, trust, and sharing among foragers. *Current Anthropology* 41:287–297.

Hewlett, B. S., J. M. H. van de Koppel, and M. van de Koppel (1986). Causes of death among Aka pygmies of the Central African Republic. In L. L. Cavalli-Sforza (Ed.), *African Pygmies*. New York: Academic Press.

Hill, K. and A. M. Hurtado (1991). The evolution of reproductive senescence and menopause in human females. *Human Nature* 2:315–350.

Hill, K. and A. M. Hurtado (1996). *Ache life history: The ecology and demography of a foraging people*. Hawthorne, NY: Aldine de Gruyter.

Hill, K. and M. Hurtado (1999). The Aché of Paraguay. In R. B. Lee and R. Daly (Eds.), *The Cambridge encyclopedia of hunters and gatherers* (p. 92). Cambridge: Cambridge University Press.

Hill, K. and H. Kaplan (1989). Population description and dry-season subsistence strategies of the recently contacted Yora (Yaminahua) of Manu National Park, Peru. *National Geographic Research* 5:317-334.

Hill, K. and H. Kaplan (1999). Life history traits in humans: Theory and empirical studies. *Annual Review of Anthropology* 28:397–430.

Hill, K., H. Kaplan, K. Hawkes, and A. M. Hurtado (1985). Men's time allocation to subsistence work among the Ache of Eastern Paraguay. *Human Ecology* 13: 29–47.

Hill, K., J. Padwe, C. Bejyvagi, A. Bepurangi, F. Jakugi, R. Tykuarangi, and T. Tykuarangi (1997). Monitoring hunting impact on large vertebrates in the Mbaracayu Reserve, Paraguay, using native research assistants. *Conservation Biology* 11:1339–1353.

Hinde, R. A. (1966). *Animal behaviour: A synthesis of ethology and comparative psychology*. New York: McGraw Hill.

Hinde, R. (1984). Biological bases of the mother-child relationship. In J. D. Call, E. Galenson, and R. L. Tyson (Eds.), *Frontiers of infant psychiatry*. New York: Basic Books.

Hirschfeld, L. A. (2002). Why don't anthropologists like children? *American Anthropologist* 104:611–627.

Hitchcock, R. K., et al. (1996). Subsistence hunting and resource management among the Ju/'hoansi of northwestern Botswana. *African Study Monographs* 17(4):153–220.

Hitchcock, R. K. and M. Biesele (1997). *Twenty-five years of indigenous political development among the Ju/'hoansi San of Southern Africa*. Austin, TX: Kalahari Peoples Fund.

Hogan, N. S. (1988). The effects of time on adolescent bereavement. *Pediatric nursing* 14:333–335.

Hogan, N. S. and L. DeSantis (1994). Things that hinder adolescent sibling bereavement: An ongoing attachment. *Qualitative Health Research* 2:159–177.

Holmberg, A. (1950). *Nomads of the long bow*. Washington DC: Smithsonian Institution Press.

Hopkins, B. and T. Westra (1988). Maternal handling and motor development: An intracultural study. *Genetic, Social, and General Psychology Monographs* 114: 377–420.

Horn, G. (1991). Cerebral function and behaviour investigated through a study of filial imprinting. In P. Bateson (Ed.), *The development and integration of behaviour: Essays in honor of Robert Hinde* (pp. 121–148). Cambridge: Cambridge University Press.

Horwich, R. H. (1974). Regressive periods in primate behavioral development with reference to other mammals. *Primates* 15, 141–149.

Howell, N. (1976). The population of the Dobe area !Kung. In R. B. Lee and I. DeVore (Eds.), *Kalahari hunter-gatherers* (pp. 137–151). Cambridge, MA: Harvard University Press.

Howell, N. (1979). *The demography of the Dobe !Kung*. New York: Academic Press.

Howell, N. (1986). Feedbacks and buffers in relation to scarcity and abundance: Studies of hunter-gatherer populations. In D. Coleman and R. Schofield (Eds.), *The state of population theory: Forward from Malthus*. Oxford: Basil Blackwell.

Howell, N. (2000). *Demography of the Dobe !Kung* (2nd ed.). Hawthorne, NY: Aldine de Gruyter.

Hrdy, S. B. (1976). Care and exploitation of nonhuman primate infants by conspecifics other than the mother. *Advances in the Study of Behavior* 6:101–158.

Hrdy, S. B. (1977). The puzzle of langur infant sharing, chapter 7 of *Langurs of Abu: Female and male strategies of reproduction* (pp. 198–241). Cambridge, MA: Harvard University Press.

Hrdy, S. B. (1977). The puzzle of langur infant sharing. In *Langurs of Abu: Female and male strategies of reproduction* (pp. 198–241). Cambridge, MA: Harvard University Press.

Hrdy, S. B. (1981). *The woman that never evolved*. Cambridge, MA: Harvard University Pres.

Hrdy, S. B. (1992). Fitness tradeoffs in the history and evolution of delegated mothering with special reference to wet-nursing, abandonment, and infanticide. *Ethology and Sociobiology* 13(5–6):409–442.

Hrdy, S. B. (1997). Fitness tradeoffs in the history and evolution of delegated mothering with special reference to wet-nursing, abandonment, and infanticide. In L. Betzig (Ed.), *Human nature: A critical reader* (pp. 402–422). New York: Oxford University Press.

Hrdy, S. B. (1999). *Mother Nature: A history of mothers, infants and natural selection*. New York: Pantheon.

Hrdy, S. B. (2001a). Infanticide as a primate reproductive strategy. In P. W. Sherman and J. Alcock (Eds.), *Exploring animal behavior: Readings from American Scientist* (3rd ed., pp. 31–40). Sunderland, Mass.: Sinauer.

Hrdy, S. B. (2001b). Mothers and others. *Natural History* 110(4):50–62.

Hrdy, S. B. (2001c). The optimal number of fathers. *Annals of the New York Academy of Sciences* 907:75–96.

Hrdy, S. B. (2002). On why it takes a village: Cooperative breeders, infant needs and the future. Part II of The past, present and future of the human family. In G. Peterson (Ed.), *The Tanner Lectures on Human Values* 23 (pp. 86–110). Salt Lake City: University of UtahPress*www.tannerlectures.utah.edu/lectures/Hrdy_02.pdf*

Hrdy, S. B. and D. B. Hrdy (1976). Hierarchical relations among female hanuman langurs. *Science* 193:913–915.

Huizinga, J. (1955). *Homo ludens: A study of the play-element in culture.* Boston: Beacon.

Huntington, R. and P. Metcalf (1979). *Celebrations of death.* Cambridge: Cambridge University Press.

Hurtado, A. M., K. Hawkes, K. Hill, and H. Kaplan (1985). Female subsistence strategies among Ache hunter-gatherers of Eastern Paraguay. *Human Ecology* 13:1–27.

Hurtado, A. M. and K. Hill (1987). Early dry season subsistence ecology of Cuiva (Hiwi) foragers of Venezuela. *Human Ecology* 15(2):163–187.

Hurtado, A. M. and Hill, K. (1992). Paternal effect on offspring survivorship among Ache and Hiwi hunter-gatherers: Implications for modeling pair bond stability. In B. S. Hewlett (Ed.), *Father-child relations: Cultural and biosocial contexts* (pp. 31–56). Hawthorne, NY: Aldine de Gruyter.

Hurtado, A. M., K. Hill, H. Kaplan, and I. Hurtado (1992). Tradeoffs between female food acquisition and childcare among Hiwi and Ache foragers. *Human Nature* 3(8):185–216.

Illich, E. (1971). *Deschooling society.* London: Calders and Boyers.

Imamura, E. (1995). *Basics of weaning* (in Japanese). Tokyo: Ishiyakusyuppann.

Imamura, E. (1999). *Contemporary child rearing* (in Japanese). Tokyo: Ishiyakusyuppann.

Ingold, T. (1994). Introduction to social life. *Companion encyclopedia of anthropology: Humanity, culture and social life* T. Ingold (Ed.). London and New York: Routledge.

Ingold, T. (2000). *The perception of the environment: Essays in livelihood, dwelling and skill.* London and New York: Routledge.

Insel, T. R. (1997). A neurobiological basis of social attachment. *American Journal of Psychiatry* 154(6):726–735.

Insel, T. R. (2000). Toward a neurobiology of attachment. *Review of General Psychology* 4(2):176–185.

Isaac, G. L. (1978). Food sharing in human evolution: Archaeological evidence from the Plio-Pleistocene of East Africa. *Journal of Anthropological Research* 34:311–325.

Ivey, P. K. (1993). *Life-history theory perspectives on allocaretaking strategies among Efé foragers of the Ituri Forest of Zaire.* Ph.D. dissertation, University of New Mexico, Alburquerque.

Ivey, P. K. (2000). Cooperative reproduction in Ituri forest hunter-gatherers: Who cares for Efe infants? *Current Anthropology* 41(5):856–866.

Iwata, K. (Ed.) (1987). *Children's cultures in the world* (in Japanese). Osaka: Sogensha.

James, W. P. T., A. Ferro-Luzzi, and J. C. Waterlow (1988). Definition of chronic energy deficiency in adults. *European Journal of Clinical Nutrition* 42:969–981.

Jamison, C., L. L. Sorenson, P. L. Cornell, and H. Nakazato (2002). Are all grandmothers equal? A review and a preliminary test of the "grandmother hypothesis" in Tokugawa, Japan. *American Journal of Physical Anthropology* 119: 67–76.

Janson, C. H. and C. P. van Schaik (1993). Ecological risk aversion in juvenile primates: Slow and steady wins the race. In M. E. Pereira and L. A. Fairbanks (Eds.), *Juvenile primates* (pp. 57–74). New York: Oxford University Press.

Jenike, M. (2001). Nutritional ecology: Diet, physical activity, and body size. In C. Panter-Brick, R. Layton, and P. Rowley-Conwy (Eds.), *Hunter-gatherers: An interdisciplinary perspective* (pp. 205–238). Cambridge University Press.

Johnson, A. (1975). Time allocation in a Machiguenga community. *Ethnology* 14:301–310.

Johnson, A. W. and T. Earle (1987). *The evolution of human societies: From foraging group to agrarian state.* Stanford, CA: Stanford University Press.

Johnson, L., J. Petto, and P. Sehgal (1991). Factors in the rejection and survival of captive cottontop tamarins (Saquinus oedipus). *American Journal of Primatology* 25:95–102.

Joiris, V. D. (1996). A comparative approach to hunting rituals among Baka Pygmies (Southeastern Cameroon). In S. Kent (Ed.), *Cultural diversity among the twentieth-century foragers* (pp. 245–275). Cambridge University Press.

Joiris, V. D. (1997). *La chass, la chance, le chant: Aspects du systeme rituel des Baka du Cameroun.* Thèse présentée pour l'obtation du grade de Docteur en Sciences Sociales, 1997–1998.

Kaare, B. and J. Woodburn (1999). The Hadza of Tanzania. In R. B. Lee and R. Daly (Eds.), *The Cambridge encyclopedia of hunters and gatherers* (pp. 200). Cambridge: Cambridge University Press.

Kagan, J., R. B. Kearsley, and P. R. Zelazo (Eds.) (1978). *Infancy: Its place in human development.* Cambridge, MA: Harvard University Press.

Kamei, N. (2001). An educational project in the forest: Schooling for the Baka children in Cameroon. *African Study Monographs Supplementary Issue (African Hunter-Gatherers: Persisting Cultures and Contemporary Problems)* 26:185–195.

Kaplan, H. (1994). Evolutionary and wealth flows theories of fertility: Empirical tests and new models. *Population and Development Review* 20(4):753–791.

Kaplan, H. S. (1996). A theory of fertility and parental investment in traditional and modern human societies. *Yearbook of Physical Anthropology* 39:91–135.

Kaplan, H. (1997). The evolution of the human life course. In K. W. Wachter and C. E. Finch (Eds.), *Between Zeus and the salmon: The biodemography of longevity* (pp. 175–211). Washington: National Academy Press.

Kaplan, H. S. and J. Bock (2001). Fertility theory: The embodied capital theory of human life history evolution. In N. J. Smelser and P. B. Baltes (Eds.), *The international encyclopedia of the social and behavioral sciences* (pp. 5561–5568). Oxford: Elsevier Science.

Kaplan, H. and H. Dove (1987). Infant development among the Ache of Eastern Paraguay. *Developmental Psychology* 23(2):190–198.

Kaplan, H. and K. Hill (1985). Food sharing among Ache foragers: Tests of explanatory hypotheses. *Current Anthropology* 26:223–246.

Kaplan, H., K. Hill, and A. M. Hurtado (1990). Risk, foraging and food sharing among the Ache. In E. Cashdan (Ed.), *Risk and uncertainty in tribal and peasant economies* (pp. 107–144). San Francisco, CA: Westview.

Kaplan, H., K. Hill, A. M. Hurtado, and J. B. Lancaster (2001). The embodied capital theory of human evolution. In P. T. Ellison (Ed.), *Reproductive ecology and human evolution*. Hawthorne, NY: Aldine de Gruyter.

Kaplan, H., K. Hill, J. Lancaster, and A. M. Hurtado (2000a). A theory of human life history evolution: diet, intelligence, and longevity. *Evolutionary Anthropology* 9:149–186.

Kaplan, H., J. Lancaster, and A. Robson (2003). Embodied capital and the evolutionary ecomics of the human life span. *Population and Development Review*.

Kaplan, H. S., J. B. Lancaster, J. A. Bock, and S. E. Johnson (1995). Does observed fertility maximize fitness among new mexican men? A test of an optimality model and a new theory of parental investment in the embodied capital of offspring. *Human Nature* 6(4):325–360.

Kaplan, H. S., J. B. Lancaster, K. Hill, and A. M. Hurtado (2000b). A theory of human life history evolution: Diet, intelligence, and longevity. *Evolutionary Anthropology* 9:156–183.

Kaplan, H. and A. Robson (2002). The emergence of humans: The coevolution of intelligence and longevity with intergenerational transfers. *Proceedings of the National Academy of Sciences* 99:10221–10226.

Katz, M. M. and M. J. Konner (1981). The role of the father: An anthropological perspective. In M. E. Lamb (Ed.), *The role of the father in child development* (2nd ed., pp. 155–186). New York: Wiley.

Kaye, K. (1977). Toward the origin of dialogue. In H. R. Schaffer (Ed.), *Studies in mother-infant interaction* (pp. 89–117). New York: Academic Press.

Kaye, K. (1982). *The mental and social life of babies: How parents create persons.* Chicago: University of Chicago Press.

Kaye, K. and T. B. Brazelton (1971). Mother-infant interaction in the organization of sucking. Paper presented to the Society for Research in Child Development, Minneapolis.

Kaye, K. and A. Wells (1980). Mothers' jiggling and the burst-pause pattern in neonatal feeding. *Infant Behavior and Development* 3:29–46.

Keller, L. and M. Genoud (1997). Extraordinary lifespans in ants: A test of evolutionary theories of aging. *Nature* 389:958–960.

Kelly, R. L. (1995). *The foraging spectrum: Diversity in hunter-gatherers' lifeways.* Washington: Smithsonian Institution Press.

Kelly, R. L. and L. Poyer (1997). The Mikea of Madagascar: Report of activities 1993–1995. Unpublished report.

Kent, S. (Ed.) (1996). *Cultural diversity among twentieth-century foragers: An African perspective.* Cambridge: Cambridge University Press.

Kimura, D. (2001). Utterance overlap and long silence among the Baka Pygmies. *African Study Monographs Supplementary Issue* 26:103–121.

Kitanishi, K. (1998). Food sharing among the Aka hunter-gatherers in northeastern Congo. *African Studies Monographs* 25:3–32.

Kleiman, D. G. and J. R. Malcolm (1981). The evolution of male parental investment in mammals. In D. J. Gubernick and P. H. Klopfer (Eds.), *Parental care in mammals* (pp. 347–387). New York: Plenum.

Kloss, B. C. ([1903] 1971). *The Andaman and Nicobar Islands.* Delhi: Vikas.

Kohl-Larsen, L. (1958). *Wildbeuter in Ostafrika: Die Tindiga, ein Jager und Sammlervolk.* Berlin: Dietrich Reimer Verlag.

König, C. and B. Heine (2001). *Khoisan forum, working paper.* Vol. 17: *The !Xun of Ekoka: A demographic and linguistic report.* Cologne: University of Cologne.

Konner, M. J. (1972). Aspects of the developmental ethology of a foraging people. In N. G. B. Jones (Ed.), *Ethological studies of child behavior.* Cambridge: Cambridge University Press.

Konner, M. J. (1973). Newborn walking: Additional data. *Science* 179:307.

Konner, M. J. (1976). Maternal care, infant behavior and development among the !Kung. In R. B. Lee and I. DeVore (Eds.), *Kalahari hunter-gatherers: Studies of the !Kung San and their neighbors* (pp. 218–245). Cambridge, MA: Harvard University Press.

Konner, M. J. (1976a). Maternal care, infant behavior and development among the !Kung. In R. B. Lee and I. DeVore (Eds.), *Kalahari hunter-gatherers* (pp. 218–245). Cambridge, MA: Harvard University Press.

Konner, M. J. (1976b). Relations among infants and juveniles in comparative perspective. In M. Lewis and L. Rosenblum (Eds.), *Friendship and peer relations* (pp. 99–129). New York: John Wiley and Sons.

Konner, M. J. (1977). Infancy among the Kalahari Desert San. In P. H. Leiderman, S. R. Tulkin, and A. Rosenfeld (Eds.), *Culture and infancy.* New York: Academic Press.

Konner, M. J. (1981). Evolution of human behavior development. In R. H. Munroe, R. L. Munroe, and B. B. Whiting (Eds.), *Handbook of cross-cultural human development* (pp. 3–51). New York: Garland STPM.

Konner, M. J. and M. J. Shostak (1986). Adolescent pregnancy and childbearing: An anthropological perspective. In J. B. Lancaster and B. A. Hamburg (Eds.), *School-age pregnancy and childbearing: Biosocial dimensions.* Hawthorne, NY: Aldine de Gruyter.

Konner, M. J. and C. M. Super (1987). Sudden infant death syndrome: An anthropological hypothesis. In C. M. Super (Ed.), *The role of culture in developmental disorder* (pp. 95–108). New York: Academic Press.

Konner, M. J. and C. Worthman (1980). Nursing frequency, gonadal function, and birth spacing among !Kung hunter-gatherers. *Science* 207:788–791.

Koocher, G. P. (1973). Childhood, death and cognitive development. *Developmental Psychology* 9:369- 375.

Korner, A. F. and E. B. Thoman (1972). The relative efficacy of contact and vestibular-proprioceptive stimulation in soothing neonates. *Child Development* 43:443–453.

Kramer, K. L. (2002). Variation in juvenile dependence: Helping behavior among Maya children. *Human Nature* 13:299–325.

Kramer, K. and J. L. Boone (2002). Why intensive agriculturalists have higher fertility: A household labor budget approach to subsistence intensification and fertility rates. *Current Anthropology* 43:511–517.

Krebs, J. R. and N. B. Davies (1981). *An introduction to behavioural ecology.* Sunderland, MA: Sinauer.

Krebs, J. R. and N. B. Davies (1993). *An introduction to behavioural ecology.* Oxford: Blackwell.

Kruger, A. C. and M. Konner (2002). The social context of maternal responsiveness to infant crying among the San (Bushmen) of Botswana. Paper presented to the 8th International Workshop on Infant Cry Research, Padova, Italy.

Kuper, A. (1979). Regional comparison in African anthropology. *African Affairs* 78:103–113.

Lamb, M. E., R. A. Thompson, W. P. Gardner, E. L. Charnov, and D. Estes (1984). Security of infantile attachment as assessed in the "strange situation": Its study and biological interpretation. *Behavioral and Brain Sciences* 7:127–171.

Lamb, M. E., R. A. Thompson, W. P. Gardner, and E. L. Charnov (1985). *Infant-mother attachment: The origins and developmental significance of individual differences in strange situation behavior.* Hillsdale, New Jersey: Lawrence Erlbaum.

Lancaster, J. B. (1986). Human adolescence and reproduction: An evolutionary perspective. In J. B. Lancaster and B. A. Hamburg (Eds.), *School-age pregnancy and parenthood* (pp. 17–38). Hawthorne, NY: Aldine de Gruyter.

Lancaster, J. B. (1994). Human sexuality, life histories, and evolutionary biology. In A. Rossi (Ed.), *Sexuality across the life course.* Chicago: University of Chicago Press.

Lancaster, J. B. and R. Gelles (1987). *Offspring abuse and neglect biosocial dimensions.* Hawthorne, New York: Aldine de Gruyter.

Lancaster, J. B. and H. Kaplan (2000). Parenting other men's children: Costs, benefits, and consequences. In L. Cronk, N. A. Chagnon, and W. Irons (Eds.), *Adaptation and human behavior: An anthropological perspective* (pp. 179–201). Hawthorne, NY: Aldine de Gruyter.

Lancaster, J. B. and C. S. Lancaster (1983). Parental investment: The hominid adaptation. In D. Ortner (Ed.), *How humans adapt* (pp. 35–56). Washington, DC: Smithsonian Institution Press.

Lancaster, J. B. and C. S. Lancaster (1987). The watershed: Change in parental-investment and family-formation strategies in the course of human evolution. In J. B. Lancaster, J. Altmann, A. S. Rossi, and L. R. Sherrod (Eds.), *Parenting across the life-span. Biosocial dimensions* (Pp. 187–205). Hawthorne, NY: Aldine de Gruyter.

Langen, T. A. (2000). Prolonged offspring dependence and cooperative breeding in birds. *Behavioral Ecology* 11(4):367–377.

Langen, T. A. and S. L. Vehrencamp (1999). How white-throated magpie-jay helpers contribute during breeding. *Auk* 116(1):131–140.

Larson, T. J. (1970). The Hambukushu of Ngamiland. *Botswana notes and records* 2:29–44.

Latz, P. (1996). *Bushfires and Bushtucker: Aboriginal plant use in Central Australia.* Alice Springs, Australia: IAD Press.

Lawrence, P. R. and N. Nohria (2002). *Driven: How human nature shapes our choices.* San Francisco: Jossey Bass.

Lee, R. B. (1968). What hunters do for a living, or how to make out on scarce resources. In R. B. Lee and I. DeVore (Eds.), *Man the hunter* (pp. 30–48). Chicago: Aldine.

Lee, R. B. (1979). *The !Kung San: Men, women and work.* Cambridge: Cambridge University Press.

Lee, R. B. (1982). Politics, sexual and non-sexual in egalitarian societies. In E. Leacock and R. B. Lee (Eds.), *Politics and history in band societies.* New York: Cambridge University Press.

Lee, R. B. (1993). *The Dobe Ju/'hoansi.* Fort Worth: Harcourt Brace College Publishers.

Lee, R. B. and R. Daly (1999). *The Cambridge encyclopedia of hunters and gatherers.* Cambridge: Cambridge University Press.

Lee, R. B. and I. DeVore (1976). *Kalahari hunter-gatherers.* Cambridge, MA: Harvard University Press.

Le, R. B. and I. DeVore (Eds.) (1968). *Man the hunter.* Chicago, Aldine.

Lee, R. B. and M. Guenther (1991). Oxen or onions: The search for trade (and truth) in the Kalahari. *Current Anthropology* 32:592–601.

Lee, R. D. and K. L. Kramer (2002). Children's economic roles in the Maya family life cycle: Cain, Caldwell, and Chayanov revisited. *Population Development and Review* 28(3):475–499.

Leiderman, P. H. and G. F. Leiderman (1977). Economic change and infant care in an East African agricultural community. In P. H. Leiderman, S. R. Tulkin, and A. Rosenfeld (Eds.), *Culture and infancy.* New York: Academic Press.

Leigh, S. R. (2001). The evolution of human growth. *Evolutionary Anthropology* 10:223–236.

Leonetti, D., D. C. Nath, N. S. Hemam, and D. B. Neill (2002). Cooperative breeding effects among the matrilineal Khasi of N.E. India. Paper presented at Human Behavior and Evolution Society Meetings, Rutgers University, Newark, New Jersey.

Lessells, C. M. (1991). The evolution of life histories. In R. J. Krebs and N. B. Davies (Eds.), *Behavioral Ecology.* Oxford: Blackwell.

Letouzey, R. (1976). *Contribution de la botanique au probléme d'une eventuelle langue Pygmée.* SELAF, Paris.

Levi-Bruhl, L. (1979). *How natives think.* New York: Arno.

Levi-Strauss, C. (1962). *Le totemisme aujourd'hui.* Paris: Presses universitaires de France.

LeVine, R. A. (1974). Parental goals: A cross-cultural view. *Teachers College Record* 76.

LeVine, R. A. (1980). Anthropology and child development. In M. C. Super and S. Harkness (Eds.), *Anthropological perspective on child development* (pp. 71–86). San Francisco: Jossey-Bass.

LeVine, R. A., S. Dixon, S. LeVine, A. Richman, P. H. Leiderman, C. Keefer, and T. B. Brazelton (1994). *Child care and culture: Lessons from Africa.* Cambridge: Cambridge University Press.

Liebenberg, L. (1990). *The Art of tracking: The origin of science.* Capetown: David Philip.

Linton, R. (1939). Marquesan culture. In A. Kardiner (Ed.), *The individual and his society, the psychodynamics of primitive social organization*. New York: Columbia University Press.

Lovejoy, O. (1981). The origin of man. *Science* 211:341–350.

Low, B. S. (1989). Cross-cultural patterns in the training of children. *Journal of Comparative Psychology* 103:311–319.

Lozoff, B. and G. Brittenham (1978). Infant care: Cache or carry, *Meeting of the Society for Pediatric Research*. New York: Society for Pediatric Research.

Lummaa, V., T. Vuorisalo, R. G. Barr, and L. Lehtonen (1998). Why cry? Adaptive significance of intensive crying in human infants. *Evolution and Human Behavior* 19:193–202.

Lutz, C. and G. M. White (1989). The anthropology of emotions. *Annual Review of Anthropology* 15:405–436.

MacArthur, R. H. and E. R. Pianka (1966). On optimal use of a patchy environment. *American Naturalist* 100:603–609.

MacDonald, D. H. and B. S. Hewlett (1999). Reproductive interests and forager mobility. *Current Anthropology* 40:501–523.

Maddieson I., B. Sands, and P. Ladefoged (1992). East African click languages. Paper presented at Annual Conference on African Linguistics 23, East Lansing, MI.

Maestripieri, D. (2001). Is there mother-infant bonding in primates? *Developmental Review* 21(1, March). US http://www.primate.uchicago.edu

Malcolm, J. and K. Marten (1982). Natural selection and the communal rearing of pups in wild dogs (*Lycaon pictus*). *Behavioral Ecology and Sociobiology* 10:1–13.

Malinowski, B.. (1959). *Magic, science and religion*. Garden City, NY: Doubleday.

Man, E. H. (1878). *A grammar of Boijingyida, South Andamanese language*. Calcutta: British Printing Press.

Man, E. H. (1883). On the aboriginal inhabitants of the Andamans. *Journal of the Royal Anthropological Institute*. 12:69–116.

Man, E. H. (1901). Account of the Andamanese languages. *Census reports of India. Calcutta.*

Man, E. H. (1923). *Dictionary of the South Andamanese languages*. Bombay: British India Press.

Man, E. H. ([1882] 1932). *On the aboriginal inhabitants of the Andaman Islands*. London: Royal Anthropological Institute.

Man, E. H. and R. C. Temple (1877). *The Lord's Prayer in Boijingyida language*. Calcutta: Thacker and Spink.

Mann, G. V., O. A. Roels, D. J. Price, and J. M. Merrill (1962). Cardiovascular disease in African Pygmies: A survey of the health status, serum lipids and diet of Pygmies in Congo. *Journal of Chronic Diseases* 15:341–371.

Marazziti, D., H. S. Akiskal, A. Rossi, and G. B. Cassano (1999). Alteration of the platelet serotonin transporter in romantic love [comment]. *Psychological Medicine* 29(3):741–745.

Marlowe, F. W. (1998). Paternal investment and mating effort: Paternal care among Hadza foragers of Tanzania. Ph.D. thesis, University of California, Los Angeles.

Marlowe, F. W. (1999a). Male care and mating effort among Hadza foragers. *Behavioral Ecology and Sociobiology* 46:57–64.

Marlowe, F. W. (1999b). Showoffs or providers? The parenting effort of Hadza men. *Evolution and Human Behavior* 20:391–404.

Marlowe, F.W. (2000a). The patriarch hypothesis. *Human Nature* 11:27–42.

Marlowe, F.W. (2000b). Paternal investment and the human mating system. *Behavioural Processes* 51:45–61.

Marlowe, F.W. (2001). Male contribution to diet and female reproductive success among foragers. *Current Anthropology* 42(5):755–760.

Marlowe, F.W. (2003). A critical period for provisioning by Hadza men: Implications for pair bonding. *Evolution and Human Behavior* 24(3):217–229.

Marlowe, F. W. (2004). Marital residence among foragers. *Current Anthropology* 45:277–284.

Marlowe, F. W. (in press a). What explains Hadza food sharing? *Research in Economic Anthropology*

Marshall, L. (1957). The kin terminology system of the !Kung Bushmen. *Africa* 27:1–25.

Marshall, L. (1961). Sharing, talking, and giving: Relief of social tensions among the !Kung bushmen. *Africa* 31(3):231–249.

Marshall, L. (1976). *The !Kung of Nyae Nyae*. Cambridge, MA: Harvard University Press.

Martin, P., and P. Bateson (1986) *Measuring behaviour*. Cambridge: Cambridge University Press.

Martin, R. D. (1990). *Primate origins and evolution: A phylogenetic reconstruction*. Princeton, NJ: Princeton University Press.

Martin, R. D. (1995). Phylogenetic aspects of primate reproduction: The context of advanced maternal care. In C. R. Pryce and D. Skuse (Ed.), *Motherhood in human and nonhuman primates. Biosocial determinants* (pp. 16–26). Basel: Karger.

Masataka, N. (1993). *Infant acquisition of language: The ethological approach* (in Japanese). Tokyo: Chuokoronsya.

Maynard Smith, J., R. Burian, S. Kauffman, P. Alberch, J. Campbell, B. Goodwin, R. Lande, D. Raup, and L. Wolpert (1985). Developmental constraints and evolution. *Quarterly Review of Biology* 60(3):265–287.

McKenna, J. J. (1981). Primate infant caregiving behavior: Origins, consequences, and variability with emphasis on the common Indian Langur monkey. In D. J. Gubernick (Ed.), *Parental care in mammals* (pp. 389–416). New York: Plenum.

McKenna, J. J. (1987). Parental supplements and surrogates among primates: Cross-species and cross-cultural comparisons. In J. Lancaster, J. Altmann, A. Rossi, and L. R. Sherrod (Eds.), *Parenting across the lifespan: Biosocial dimensions* (pp. 143–184). Hawthorne, NY: Aldine de Gruyter.

McKenna, J., S. Mosko, and C. Richard (1999). Breastfeeding and mother-infant cosleeping in relation to SIDS prevention. In W. R. Trevathan, E. O. Smith, and J. J. McKenna (Eds.), *Evolutionary medicine* (p. 53). New York: Oxford University Press.

McKenna, J. J., E. B. Thoman, T. F. Anders, A. Sadeh, V. L. Schectman, and S. F. Glotzbach (1993). Infant-parent co-sleeping in an evolutionary perspective:

implication for understanding infant sleep development in the Sudden Infant Death Syndrome. *Sleep* 16(3):23–282.

McKim, M. K., K. M. Cramer, B. Stuart, and D. L. O'Connor (1999). Infant care decisions and attachment security: The Canadian Transition to Child Care Study. *Canadian Journal of Behavioural Science* 31(2):92–106.

Mead, M. (1930). *Growing up in New Guinea*. New York: Blue Ribbon.

Mead, M. (1932). An investigation of the thought of primitive children with special reference to animism. *Journal of the Royal Anthropological Institute* 62:173–290.

Mead, M. (1933). *Coming of age in Samoa: A psychological study of primitive youth for Western civilization*. New York: Blue Ribbon.

Meltzoff, A. N. and W. Prinz (2002). *The imitative mind: Development, evolution, and brain bases*. Cambridge: Cambridge University Press.

Metcalf, P. (1982). *A Borneo journey into death*. Philadelphia: University of Pennsylvania Press.

Minett, P. (1994). *Child care and development* (3rd ed.). London: John Murray.

Mitani, J. C. and D. Watts (1997). The evolution of non-maternal caretaking among anthropoid primates: Do helpers help? *Behavioral Ecology and Scociobiology* 40:213–240.

Mitchell, G. and E. Brandt (1972). Paternal behavior in primates. In F. E. Poirier (Ed.), *Primate socialization*. New York: Random House.

Mitchell, M. E. (1967). *The child's attitude toward death*. New York: Schocken.

Moran, G., D. R. Pederson, P. Pettit, and A. Krupka (1992). Maternal sensitivity and infant-mother attachment in a developmentally delayed sample. *Infant Behavior and Development* 15:427–442.

Morelli, G. A. (1987). A comparative study of Efe (Pygmy) and Lese one-, two-, and three-year-olds of the Ituri Forest of northeastern Zaïre: The influence of subsistence-related variables, children's age, and gender on socio-emotional development. *Dissertation Abstracts International* 48:02b.

Morelli, G. A. (1997). Growing up female in a foraging and farming community. In M. E. Morbeck and A. L. Zihlman (Eds.), *Female biology, life history, and evolution*. Princeton, NJ: Princeton University Press.

Morelli, G. A., B. Rogoff, and C. Angelillo (2003). Cultural variation in children's access to work or involvement in specialized child-focused activities. *International Journal of Behavioral Development* 23(3):264–274.

Morelli, G. A. and E. Z. Tronick (1991). Efe multiple caretaking and attachment. In J. L. Gewirtz and W. M. Kurtines (Eds.), *Intersections with attachment* (pp. 41–51). Hillsdale, NJ: Lawrence Erlbaum.

Morelli, G. A. and E. Z. Tronick (1992). Efe fathers: One among many? A comparison of forager children's involvement with fathers and other males. *Social Development* 1(1):36–54.

Morelli, G. A., E. Tronick, P. Ivey, and M. Beeghley (1999). Is there security in numbers? Child care in a hunting and gathering community and infants' attachment relationships. Poster submitted to the Society for Research on Child Development, Albuquerque, New Mexico.

Morley, D. (1973). *Pediatric priorities in the developing world*. London: Butterworths.

Mouat, F. J. (1862). Narrative of an expedition to the Islands of Andamans in 1857. *Journal of the Royal Geographical Society* 32:109–126.

Mouat, F. J. (1863). *Adventures and researches among the Andaman Islanders*. London: Hurst and Blackett.

Mufson, T. (1985). Issues surrounding sibling death during adolescence. *Child and Adolescent Social Work Journal* 2:204–218.

Murdock, G. P. and D. O. Morrow (1970). Subsistence economy and supportive practices: Cross-cultural codes 1. *Ethnology* 9:302–330.

Murdock, G. P. and S. F. Wilson (1972). Settlement patterns and community organization: Cross-cultural codes 3. *Ethnology* 11:254–295.

Myers, F. (1986). *Pintupi country, Pintupi self: Sentiment, place, and politics among Western Desert Aborigine*. Washington, DC: Smithsonian Institution Press and Australian Institute of Aboriginal Studies.

Nag, M., B. N. F. White, and R. C. Peet (1978). An anthropological approach to the study of the economic value of children in Java and Nepal. *Current Anthropology* 19:293–306.

Nagy, M. (1989). The child's theories concerning death. *Journal of Genetic Psychology* 73:3–27.

Nandy, A. (1988). *The intimate enemy: Loss and recovery of self under colonialism*. New Delhi: Oxford University Press.

Napanangka, Y. (1995). Kid left behind in camp. In J. Crugnale (Ed.), *Footprints across our land* (pp. 143–144). Broome, Western Australia: Magabala.

Nath, D. C. and D. L. Leonetti (2001). Work activities of grandmothers and reproductive success: Evidence from traditional Indian women. Paper presented at Human Behavior and Evolution Society Meetings, University College, London, June 17.

Nerlove, S. B. (1974). Women's workload and infant feeding practices: a relationship with demographic implications. *Ethnology* 13: 207–214.

NICHD Early Child Care Research Network (1997). The effects of infant child care on infant-mother attachment security: Results of the NICHD study of early child care. *Child Development* 68(5):860–879.

NICHD Early Child Care Research Network (2001a). Child-care and family predictors of preschool attachment and stability from infancy. *Developmental Psychology* 37(6):847–862.

NICHD Early Child Care Research Network (2001b). Nonmaternal care and family factors in early development: An overview of the NICHD study of early child care. *Applied Developmental Psychology* 22:457–492.

Ninio, A. and J. Bruner (1978). The achievement and antecedents of labelling. *Journal of Child Language* 5:1–15.

Noppe, I. (2000). Beyond broken bonds and broken hearts: The bonding of theories of attachment and grief. *Developmental Review* 20:514–538.

Noss, A. J. and B. S. Hewlett (2000). The contexts of female hunting in central Africa. *American Anthropologist* 103:1024–1040.

O'Connell, J. F. and K. Hawkes (1981). Alyawarra plant use and optimal foraging theory. In B. Winterhalder and E. A. Smith (Eds.), *Hunter gather foraging stragies* (pp. 99–125). Chicago: University of Chicago Press..

O'Connell, J. F., K. Hawkes, and N. Blurton Jones (1999). Grandmothering and the evolution of *Homo erectus. Journal of Human Evolution* 26:461–485.

O'Connell, J. F., K. Hawkes, K. D. Lupo, and N. G. Blurton Jones (2002). Male strategies and Plio-Pleistocene archaeology. *Journal of Human Evolution* 43:831–872.

Obst, E. (1912). Von Mkalama ins land der Wakindiga. *Mitteilungen der Geographischen Gesellschaft in Hamburg* 26:2–27.

Ohtsuka, R. (1989). Hunting activity and aging among the Gidra Papuans: A biobehavioral analysis. *American Journal of Physical Anthropology* 80:31–39.

Olds, D., C. R. Henderson, R. Chaberlin, and R. Tatelbaum (1986). Preventing child abuse and neglect: A randomized trial of nurse home visitation. *Pediatrics* 78:65–78.

Olds, D., J. Robinson, R. O'Brien, D. Luckey, L. Pettitt, C. Henderson Jr., R. Ng, K. Sheff, J. Korfmacher, S. Hiatt, X. Talmi (2002). Home visiting by paraprofessionals and by nurses. A randomized controlled trial. *Pediatrics* 110(3):486–496.

Oltjenbrun, K. A. (1989). Ethnicity and grief response: Mexican-American and Anglo college students. Unpublished doctoral dissertation, University of Colorado at Boulder.

Opie, I. and P. Opie (1959). *The lore and language of schoolchildren.* Oxford; New York: Oxford University Press.

Orbach, I., M. Weiner, and D. Har-even (1994). Children's perception of death and interpersonal closeness to the dead person. *OMEGA* 30(1):1–12.

Osorio-Beristain, M. and H. Drummond (2001). Male boobies expel eggs when paternity is in doubt. *Behavioral Ecology* 12:16–21.

Pagel, M. D. and P. H. Harvey (1993). Evolution of the juvenile period in mammals. In M. E. Pereira and L. A. Fairbanks (Eds.), *Juvenile primates: Life history, development, and behavior,* New York: Oxford University Press.

Paine, R. H. and H. Kristen (Eds.) (in preparation). Santa Fe, NM: School of American Studies Press.

Palombit, Ryne (1999). Infanticide and the evolution of pair bonds in nonhuman primates. *Evolutionary Anthropology* 7:117–129.

Pandya, V. (1992a). *Above the forest. A study of Andamanese ethnoanemology, cosmology and the power of ritual.* New Delhi: Oxford University Press.

Pandya, V. (1992b). Gukwelonone: The game of hiding fathers and seeking sons. In B. Hewlett (Ed.), *The father-child relationship: Cultural and biosocial perspectives* (pp. 263–279). New York: Walter de Gruyter.

Pandya, V. (1993). *Above the forest: A study of Andamanese ethnoanemology, cosmology and the power of ritual.* New Delhi: Oxford University Press.

Pandya, V. (1997). Sacrifice and escape as counter-hegemonic rituals: A structural essay on an aspect of Andamanese history. *Journal of Social Analysis* 41(2, July):66–98.

Pandya, V. (1999a). Contact or not to contact: Questions about Jarwas of Andaman Islands. *Cultural Survival Quarterly* (Winter):59–65.

Pandya, V. (1999b). Making of the other: Vignettes of violence in Andamanese Culture. *Critique of Anthropology* 20(4):359–391.

Pandya, V. (2000). Making of the other: Vignettes of violence in Andamanese culture. *Critique of anthropology* 20(4):359–391.

Pandya, V. (2002). Contact, images and imagination: The impact of roads in Jarwa Reserve Forest of Andaman Islands. In *Bijdragen tot de Taal-, Land-en Vokenkunde* (pp. 799–820). 158.4. Leiden. KITLV.

Papouk, H., M. Papouk, S. Suomi, and C. W. Rahn (1991). Preverbal communication and attachment: Comparative views. In J. L. Gewirtz and W. M. Kurtines (Eds.), *Intersections with attachment* (pp. 97–122). Hillsdale, NJ: Lawrence Erlbaum.

Parish, A. (1998). Reciprocity and other forms of food sharing among foragers. Paper presented at Symposium on Cooperation, Reciprocity and food Sharing in Human Groups, at 18th Annual Meeting of Politics and Life Sciences Association, Boston Sept. 3–6, 1998.

Parker Pearson, M. (1997). Close encounters of the worst kind: Malagasy resistance and colonial disasters in southern Madagascar. *World Archaeology* 28(3): 393–417.

Parkes, C. M. (1972). *Bereavement: Studies of grief in adult life.* London: Tavistock.

Passmore, R. and J. V. G. A. Durnin (1955). Human energy expenditure. *Physiological Review* 35:801–840.

Peacock, N. R. (1985). *Time allocation, work and fertility among Efe Pygmy women of northeast Zaire.* Unpublished doctoral thesis. Harvard University, Cambridge, Massachusetts.

Peacock, N. R. (1991). Rethinking the sexual division of labor: Reproduction and women's work among the Efe. In M. di Leonardo (Ed.), *Gender at the crossroads of knowledge: Feminist anthropology in the postmodern era* (pp. 339–360). Berkeley: University of California Press.

Pen, I. and F. J. Weissing (2000). Towards a unified theory of cooperative breeding: The role of ecology and life history re-examined. *Proceedings of the Royal Society London* B. 267:2411–2418.

Pereira, M. E. and L. A. Fairbanks (Eds.) (1993). *Juvenile primates. Life history: development, and behavior.* New York: Oxford University Press.

Perner, J., T. Rufman, and S. R. Leekam (1994). Theory of mind is contagious: You catch it from your sibs. *Child Development* 65:1228–1238.

Peterson, J. T. (1978). *The ecology of social boundaries: Agta foragers of the Philippines.* Urbana: University of Illinois Press.

Peterson, N. (1993). Demand sharing: Reciprocity and the pressure for generosity among foragers. *American Anthropologist* 95:860–874.

Piaget, J. (1963). *The origins of intelligence in children.* New York: International Universities Press.

Pianka, E. R. (1970). On "r" and "K" selection. *American Naturalist* 104:453–464.

Pianka, E. (1988). *Evolutionary ecology.* New York: Harper and Row.

Pollitt, E. and R. Leibel (1980). Biological and social correlates of failure to thrive. In L. Greene and F. Johnston (Eds.), *Social and biological predictors of nutritional status, physical growth and neurological development* (pp. 173–200). New York: Academic Press.

Pollock, G. H. (1986). Childhood sibling loss: A family tragedy. *Pediatric Annals* 15:851–855.

Poole, F. J. P. (1994). Socialization, enculturation and the development of personal identity. In T. Ingold (Ed.), *Companion encyclopedia of anthropology: Humanity, culture, and social life.* London, Routledge.

Portman, M. V. (1887). *Manual of the Andamanese language*. London: W. H. Allen.

Portman, M. V. (1889). *Notes on the languages of Andamans*. Calcutta: India Press.

Portman, M. V. (1896). Notes on the Andamanese. In *Journal of the Anthropological Institute* 25:362–371.

Portman, M. V. (1899). *A history of our relations with Andamanese*. Calcutta: Superintendent of Government Printing Press.

Poyer, L. and R. L. Kelly (2000). Mystification of the Mikea: Constructions of foraging identity in southwest Madagascar. *Journal of Anthropological Research* 56:163–185.

Preston-Mafham, K. (1991). *Madagascar: A natural history*. New York: Facts on File.

Quiatt, D. and J. Kelso (1985). Household economics and hominid origins. *Current Anthropology* 26(2):207–222.

Radcliffe-Brown, A. R. ([1922] 1964). *The Andaman Islanders*. Illinois: Free Press.

Rebelsky, F. and S. Hanks (1971). Fathers' verbal interaction with infants in the first three months of life. *Child Development* 42:63–68.

Reidman, M. L. (1982). The evolution of alloparental care and adoption in mammals and birds. *Quarterly Review of Biology* 57:405–435.

Ricklefs, R. E. (1984). The optimization of birth rates in altricial birds. *Ecology* 65:1602–1616.

Rilling, J. K., D. Gutman, T. Zeh, G. Pagnoni, G. S. Berns, and C. D. Kilts (2002). A neural basis for social cooperation. *Neuron* 35:395–405.

Rogoff, B. (1978). Spot observation: An introduction and examination. *Quarterly Newsletter of the Institute for Comparative Human Development* 2:21–26.

Rogoff, B. and G. A. Morelli (1989). Perspectives on children's development from cultural psychology. *American Psychologist* 44(2):343–348.

Rogoff, B., M. J. Seller, S. Pirrotta, N. Fox, and S. H. White (1975). Age assignment of roles and responsibilities of children: A cross cultural survey. *Human Development* 18:353–369.

Rosenfeld, A. A., A. O. R. Wenegrat, D. K. Haavik, B. G. Wenegrat, and C. R. Smith (1982). Sleeping patterns in upper-middle-class families when the child awakens ill or frightened. *Archives of General Psychiatry* 39(August):943–947.

Ross, C. and A. MacLarnon (2000). The evolution of non-maternal care in anthropoid primates: A test of the hypotheses. *Folia Primatologica* 71(1–2, Jan–Apr). Switzerland http://www.roehampton.ac.uk

Rossi, A. and L. R. Sherrod (Eds.) (1987). *Parenting across the life span: Biosocial dimensions* (pp. 143–184). Hawthorne, NY: Aldine de Gruyter.

Rowley, I. and E. Russell (1990). Splendid fairy-wrens: Demonstrating the importance of longevity. In P. Stacey and W. Koenig (Eds.), *Cooperative breeding in birds*. Cambridge: Cambridge University Press.

Rubin, S. S. (1999). The two-track model of bereavement: Overview, retrospect and prospect. *Death Studies* 23:681–714.

Ruffman, T., J. Perner, M. Naito, L. Parkin, and W. Clements (1998). Older (but not younger) siblings facilitate false believe understanding. *Developmental Psychology* 34(1):161–174.

Russell, A. F., L. L. Sharpe, P. N. M. Brotherton, and T. H. Clutton-Brock. (2003). Cost minimization by helpers in cooperative vertebrates. *Proceedings of National Academy of Sciences*, 100:3333–3338.

Russell, C. M. (1999). *A meta-analysis of published research on the effects of nonmaternal care on child development*. Calgary: University of Calgary Press.

Sagi, A., M. H. van IJzendoorn, O. Aviezer, F. Donell, N. Koren-Karie, T. Joels, and Y. Harel (1995). Attachments in a multiple-caregiver and multiple-infant environment: The case of the Israeli kibbutzim. *Monographs of the Society for Research in Child Development*, No. 244, 60(2–3):71–91.

Sagi, A., M. H. van IJzendoorn, O. Aviezer, F. Donnell, and O. Mayseless (1994). Sleeping out of home in a kibbutz communal arrangement: It makes a difference for infant-mother attachment. *Child Development* 65:992–1004.

Sands, B. (1998). The linguistic relationship between Hadza and Khoisan. In M. Schladt (Ed.), *Language, identity, and conceptualization*. Koln: Rudiger koppe.

Sarkar, R. (1990). *The Jarwa*. Calcutta: Seagull Books and Anthropological Survey of India.

Sato, H. (1998). Folk etiology among the Baka, a group of hunter-gatherers in the African rainforest. *African Study Monographs Supplementary Issue* 25:33–46.

Sato, H. (2001). The potential of edible wild yams and yam-like plants as a staple food resource in the African tropical forest. *Africa Study Monographs Supplementary Issue* 26:123–134.

Sawada, M. (1998). Democratic Republic of Congo (in Japanese). In *Encyclopedia of ethnic play and games*. Tokyo: Taishukan Shoten.

Schacter, F. F., M. L. Fuchs, P. E. Bijur, and R. Stone (1989). Co-sleeping and sleep problems in Hispanic-American urban young children. *Pediatrics* 84:522–530.

Schebesta, P. (1929). *Among the forest dwarfs of Malaya*. London; Hutchinson.

Scheper-Hughes, N. (1987). Culture, scarcity, and maternal thinking: Mother love and child death in northeastern Brazil. In N. Scheper-Hughes (Ed.), *Child survival*. Boston: D. Reidel.

Scheper-Hughes, N. and C. Sargent (Eds.) (1998). *Small wars: The cultural politics of childhood*. Berkeley: University of California Press.

Schiefflein, B. B. 1990. *The give and take of everyday life*. Cambridge, MA: Cambridge University Press.

Schlegel, A. and H. Barry III (Eds.) (1991). *Adolescence: An anthropological inquiry*. New York: Free Press.

Schoener, T. W. (1971). Theory of feeding strategies. *Annual Review of Ecology* 2:369–404.

Schoesch, S. J. (1998). Physiology of helping in Florida scrub jays. *American Scientist* 86:7–77.

Schradin, C. and G. Anzenberger (1999). Prolactin, the hormone of paternity. *News in Physiological Science* 14:221–331.

Schultz, A. H. (1963). Age changes, sex differences, and variability as factors in the classification of primates. In S. L. Washburn (Ed.), *Classification and human evolution*. Chicago: Aldine.

Schultz, A. H. (1969). *The life of primates*. London: Weidenfield and Nicolson.

Sear, R., R. Mace, and I. A. McGregor (2000). Maternal grandmothers improve nutritional status and survival of children in rural Gambia. *Proceedings of the Royal Society London* B 267:1641–1647.

Sear, R., F. Steel, I. McGregor, and R. Mace (2002). The effects of kin on child mortality in rural Gambia. *Demography* 39(1):43–63.

Sears, W. and M. White (1999). *Nighttime parenting: A La Leche League International book* (rev. ed.). New York: Penguin Putnam/Plume.

Sellen, D. W. (1998). Infant and young child feeding practices among African pastoralists: The Datoga of Tanzania. *Journal of Biosocial Science* 30(4):481–499.

Sellen, D. (1999). Polygyny and child growth in a traditional pastoral society. *Human Nature* 10:329–371.

Senkuttuvan, V. (2000) *The language of the Jarwa*. Calcutta: Anthropological Survey of India.

Service. E. R. (1966). *The hunters*. Englewood Cliffs, NJ: Prentice-Hall.

Shennan, S. J. and J. Steele (1999). Cultural learning in hominids: A behavioural ecological approach. In H. Box and K. Gibson (Eds.), *Mammalian social learning*. Symposia of the Zoological Society of London 70 (pp. 367–388). London: Cambridge University Press.

Sherman, P. W., J. U. Jarvis, and R. D. Alexander (Eds.) (1991). *The biology of the naked mole rat*. Princeton, NJ: Princeton University Press.

Sherman, P. W., E. A. Lacey, H. K. Reeve, and L. Keller (1995). The eusociality continuum. *Behavioral Ecology* 6:102–108.

Shostak, M. (1981). *Nisa: The life and words of a !Kung woman*. Cambridge, MA: Harvard University Press.

Silk, J. 2002. Females, food, family and friendship. *Evolutionary Anthropology* 11:85–87.

Silverman, P. R. S. L. Nickman, and D. Klass (Eds.) (1999). *Continuing bonds: New understandings of grief* (pp. 3–27). Washington, DC: Taylor and Francis.

Silverman, P. R. (1999). *Never too young to know: Death in children's lives*. New York: Oxford University Press.

Skeat, W. and C. Blagden (1906). *Pagan races of the Malay Peninsula*. London: MacMillan.

Small, M. (1999). *Our babies, ourselves: How biology and culture shape the way we parent*. New York: Dell.

Smith, E. A. (1987). On fitness maximization, limited needs, and hunter-gatherer time allocation. *Ethology and Sociobiology* 8:73–85.

Smith, E. A. (1991). *Inujumiut foraging strategies: Evolutionary ecology of an Arctic hunting economy*. Hawthorne, NY: Aldine de Gruyter.

Smith, E. A. and R. Bliege Bird (2000). Turtle hunting and tombstone opening: Public generosity as costly signaling. *Evolution and Human Behavior* 21:245–261.

Smith, E. A., R. Bliege Bird, and D. W. Bird (2003). The benefits of costly signaling: Meriam turtle hunters and spearfishers. *Behavioral Ecology* 14:116–126.

Snowdon, C. (1984). Social development during the first twenty weeks in the cotton-top tamrain (*Saguinus o. oedipus*). *Animal Behavior* 32:432–444.

Snowdon, C. (1996). Infant care in cooperatively breeding species. *Advances in the Study of Behavior* 25:643–689.

Solomon, N. and J. French (Eds.) (1997a). *Cooperative breeding in mammals*. Cambridge: Cambridge University Press.

Solomon, N. and J. French (1997b). The study of mammalian cooperative breeding. In N. Solomon and J. French (Eds.), *Cooperative breeding in mammals* (pp. 1–10). Cambridge: Cambridge University Press.

Sperber, D. (1996). *Explaining culture: A naturalistic approach*. Oxford: Blackwell.

Spieker, S. J. and L. Bensley (1994). The roles of living arrangements and grandmother social support in adolescent mothering and infant attachment. *Developmental Psychology* 30:102–111.

Spock, B. (1976). *Baby and child care*. New York: Pocket Books

Spock, B. and S. J. Parker (1998). *Dr. Spock's baby and child care* (7th ed.). New York: Pocket Books/Simon and Schuster.

Sreenathan, M. (2001). *The Jarwas language and culture*. Calcutta: Anthropological Survey of India.

Sroufe, L. A., E. A. Carlson, A. K. Levy, and B. Egeland (1999). Implications of attachment theory for developmental psychopathology. *Development and Psychopathology* 11(1):1–13.

Sroufe, L. A. and E. Waters (1977). Attachment as an organizational construct. *Child Development* 48:1184–1199.

Stacey, P. and W. D. Koenig (1990). *Cooperative breeding in birds: Longterm studies in ecology and behavior*. Cambridge: Cambridge University Press.

Stack, C. (1974). *All our kin: Strategies for survival in a black community*. New York: Harper and Row.

Stander, P E, //Ghau, D. Tsisaba, //#oma, and |Ui (1997). Tracking and the interpretation of spoor: A scientifically sound method in ecology. *Journal of Zoology London* 242:329–341.

Stearns, S. C. (1992). *The evolution of life histories*. Oxford: Oxford University Press.

Stephens, D. W. and J. R. Krebs (1986). *Foraging theory*. Princeton, NJ: Princeton University Press.

Stern, J. M. (1986). Licking, touching, and suckling: contact stimulation and maternal psychobiology in rats and women. *Annals of the New York Academy of Sciences* 474:95–107.

Stern, J. M., M. Konner, T. N. Herman, and S. Reichlin (1986). Nursing behavior, prolactin and postpartum amenorrhoea during prolonged lactation in American and !Kung mothers. *Clinical Endocrinology* 25:247–258.

Stewart, K. (1975). *Pygmies and dream giants*. New York: Harper Row

Storey, A., C. J. Walsh, R. L. Quinton, and K. E. Wynne-Edwards (2000). Hormonal correlates of paternal responsiveness in new and expectant fathers. *Evolution and Human Behavior* 21(2):79–95.

Strassman, B. I. (1997). Polygyny as a risk factor for child mortality among the Dogon. *Current Anthropology* 38:688–695.

Stroebe, M., M. M. Gergen, K. J. Gergen, and W. Stroebe (1992). Broken hearts or broken bonds: Love and death in historical perspective. *American Psychologist* 48:991–992.

Sugawara, K. (1990). Interactional aspects of the body in co-presence: Observations on the Central Kalahari San. In M. Moerman and M. Nomura (Eds.), *Culture embodied*. Osaka: National Museum of Ethnology.

Sugiyama, L. S. (1996). *In search of the adapted mind: A study of human cognitive adaptations among the Shiwiar of Ecuador and the Yora of Peru*. Ph.D. dissertation. University of California, Santa Barbara.

Sugiyama, L. S. (2004). Illness, injury, and disability among Shiwiar forager-horticulturalists: Implications of health risk buffering for the evolution of human life history. *American Journal of Physical Anthropology* 123:371–389.

Sugiyama, L. S. and R. Chacon (2000). Effects of illness and injury on foraging among the Yora and Shiwiar: Pathology risk as adaptive problem. In L. Cronk, N. A. Chagnon, and W. Irons (Eds.), *Human behavior and adaptation: An anthropological perspective* (pp. 371–395). Hawthorne, NY: Aldine de Gruyter.

Sugiyama, L. S. and M. Scalise Sugiyama (2003). Social roles, prestige, and health risk: Social niche specialization as a risk-buffering strategy. *Human Nature* 14:165–190.

Sulloway, F. (1996). *Born to rebel: Birth order, family dynamics, and creative lives.* New York: Vintage.

Sunderland, T. C. H., L. E. Clark, and P. Vantomme (1999). *Non-wood forest products of Central Africa: Current research issues and prospects for conservation and development.* Rome: Food and Agriculture Organization.

Super, C. M. (1976). Environmental effects on motor development: The case of African infant precocity. *Developmental Medicine and Child Neurology* 18: 561–567.

Super, C. M. (1981). Behavioral development in infancy. In R. H. Munroe, R. L. Munroe, and B. B. Whiting (Eds.), *Handbook of cross-cultural human development* (pp. 181–270). New York: Garland STPM.

Super, C. M. and S. A. Harkness (1982). The infant's niche in rural Kenya and metropolitan America. In L. L. Adler (Ed.), *Cross-cultural research at issue* (pp. 247–255). New York: Academic Press.

Super, C. M. and S. Harkness (1986). The developmental niche: A conceptualization at the interface of child and culture. *International Journal of Behavioral Development* 9:545–569.

Super, C. S. (1981). Cross-cultural research on infancy. In H. C. Triandis and A. Heron (Eds.), *Handbook of cross-cultural psychology: Developmental psychology*, vol. 4. Boston: Allyn and Bacon.

Susman, J. (2001). *Regional assessment of the status of the San in Southern Africa*, No. 4: *An assessment of the status of the San in Namibia.* Windhoek: Legal Assistance Centre.

Swain, H. L. (1979). *Childhood views of death.* Milwaukee: Hemisphere.

Takada, A. (2000). *"The San" in Ohangwena, Namibia: Lifestyles of the !Xu and Hai//om.* Report presented to UNESCO, Windhoek.

Takada, A. (2002a). The !Xu San: Poverty and tension. *Cultural Survival Quarterly* 26(1):18–19.

Takada, A. (2002b). Caregiving behaviors among the San and the meaning for child development. *Japanese Journal of Developmental Psychology* (in Japanese) 13(1): 63–77.

Takada, A. (2004). Nomadic lifestyle and childrearing: Analysis of gymnastic behavior among the Central Kalahari San. In J. Tanaka, S. Sato, K. Sugawara, and I. Ohta (Eds.), *Nomad: Life in the wilderness of Africa* (in Japanese). Kyoto: Showado.

Takeuchi, K. (1995). Ritual aspects and pleasure in hunting activity: Cooperation and distribution in the net-hunting activity of Aka hunter-gatherers in northeastern Congo (in Japanese). *Journal of African Studies (Afurika kenkyu)*:57–76.

Takeuchi, K. (1998). Republic of Congo (in Japanese). In *Encyclopedia of ethnic play and games.* Tokyo: Taishukan Shoten.

Tanaka, J. (1980). *The San: Hunter-gatherers of the Kalahari, a study in ecological anthropology.* Tokyo: University of Tokyo Press.

Tanaka, K. (1982). *Methodology of psychology* (in Japanese). Tokyo: Keisosyobo.

Tanaka, J. (1989). Social integration of the San society from the viewpoint of sexual relationships. *African Study Monographs* 9(3):153–165.

Tanner, A. (1979). *Bringing home animals: Religious ideology and mode of production of the Mistassini Cree hunters.* London: E. Hurst.

Tanner, J. M. (1962). *Growth at adolescence* (Second ed.). Oxford: Blackwell Scientific Publications.

Tanno, T. (1984). Life and material culture of Mbuti Pygmy. In J. Itani and J. Tanaka (Eds.), *Anthropology of societies in nature* (n Japanese) (pp. 71–109). Kyoto: Academia Shuppankai.

Tardieu, C. (1998). Short adolescence in early hominids: Infantile and adolescent growth of the human femur. *American Journal of Physical Anthropology* 107: 163–178.

Taub, D. and P. Mehlman (1991). Primate paternalistic investment: A cross-species view. In J. D. Loy and C. B. Peters (Eds.), *Understanding behavior: What primate studies tell us about human behavior* (pp. 51–89). New York: Oxford University Press.

Temple, R. C. (1899). Theory of universal grammar as applied to group of savage languages: Andamanese. *Journal of the Royal Anthropological Society* 29:565–604.

Temple, R. C. (1903). *Census of India* 13(3). Calcutta: Government of India Publications.

Temple, R. C. (1908). *Plan for a uniform scientific records of the languages of savages as applied to Andamanese and Nicobarese.* Bombay: Educational Society Press.

Temple, R. C. (1909). *Imperial Gazetteer of India, Andaman and Nicobar.* Calcutta: Government Press.

Temple, R. C. (1930). *Remarks on the Andamanese and their country.* Bombay: British India Press. (Originally printed in Indian Antiquary from 1923 to 1930.)

Temrin, H., S. Burchmayer, and M. Enquist (2000). Step-parents and infanticide: New data contradict evolutionary predictions. *Proceedings of the Royal Society B* 267:943–945.

Textor, R. B. (1967). *A cross-cultural summary.* New Haven, CT: HRAF.

Thelen, E. (1986). Treadmill-elicited stepping in seven-month-old infants. *Child Development* 57:1498–1506.

Tinbergen, N. (1963). On aims and methods of ethology. *Zeitschrift fur Tierpsychologie* 20:410–433.

Tomasello, M. (1999). *The cultural origins of human cognition.* Cambridge, MA: Harvard University Press.

Tonkinson, R. (1974). *The Jigalong mob: Aboriginal victors of the desert crusade.* Menlo Park, CA: Cummings.

Tonkinson, R. (1991). *The Mardu Aborigines: Living the dream in Australia's desert* (2nd ed).. Fort Worth: Holt, Rinehart and Winston.

Tooby, J. and L. Cosmides (1992). The psychological foundations of culture. In J. H. Barkow, L. Cosmides, and J. Tooby (Eds.), *The adapted mind* (pp. 19–136). New York: Oxford University.

Tooby, J. and I. DeVore (1987). The reconstruction of hominid behavioral evolution through strategic modeling. In W. Kinzey (Ed.), *The evolution of human behavior: Primate models* (pp. 183–237). Albany: SUNY Press.

Toren, C. (1993). Making history: The significance of childhood cognition for a comparative anthropology of mind. *Man* 28:461–478.

Toren, C. (1996). Childhood. *Encyclopedia of social and cultural anthropology* (pp. 92–94). A. Barnard and J. Spencer (Eds.). London and New York: Routledge.

Traill, A. and R. Vossen (1997). Sound change in the Khoisan languages: New data on click loss and click replacement. *Journal of African Languages and Linguistics* 18:21–56.

Triver, R.L. (1972a). Parental investment and sexual selection. *Nature* 112:164–190.

Trivers, R. L. (1972b). Parental investment and sexual selection. In B. Cambell (Ed.), *Sexual selection and the descent of man* (pp. 1871–1971). Chicago: Aldine.

Trivers, R. L. (1974). Parent offspring conflict. *American Zoologist* 14:249–263.

Trivers, R. L. (1985). *Social evolution*. Menlo Park, CA: Benjamin/Cummings.

Trivers, R. L. and D. E. Willard (1973). Natural selection of parental ability to vary the sex ratio of offspring. *Science* 179:90–92.

Tronick, E. Z., G. A. Morelli, and P. K. Ivey (1992). The Efe forager infant and toddler's pattern of social relationships: Multiple and simultaneous. *Developmental Psychology* 28(4):568–577.

Tronick, E. Z., G. A. Morelli, and S. Winn (1987). Multiple caretaking of Efe (Pygmy) infants. *American Anthropologist* 89:96–106.

Tronick, E. Z. and S. A. Winn (1992). The neurobehavioral organization of Efe (pygmy) infants: *Journal of Developmental and Behavioral Pediatrics* 13:421–424.

Tsuru, D. (1998). Diversity of ritual spirits performances among the Baka Pygmies in southeastern Cameroon. *African Study Monographs, Supplementary Issue* 25:47–84.

Tucker, B. (2001). *The behavioral ecology and economics of variation, risk, and diversification among Mikea forager-farmers of Madagascar*. Ph.D. dissertation, University of North Carolina at Chapel Hill.

Tucker, B. (2003). Mikea origins: Relicts or refugees? *Michigan Discussions in Anthropology* 14:193–214.

Tulkin, S. R. (1977). Social class differences in maternal and infant behavior. In P. H. Leiderman, S. R. Tulkin, and A. Rosenfeld (Eds.), *Culture and infancy*. New York: Academic Press.

Tulkin, S. and J. Kagan (1972). Mother-child interaction in the first year of life. *Child Development* 43:31–41.

Turke, P. (1988). "Helpers at the nest": Childcare networks on Ifaluk. In L. Betzig, M. Borgherhoff Mulder, and P. Turke (Eds.), *Human reproductive behaviour: A Darwinian perspective* (pp. 173–188). Cambridge: Cambridge University Press.

Turnbull, C. M. (1962). *The forest people: A study of the Pygmies of the Congo*. New York: Simon and Schuster.

Turnbull, C. M. (1965). *Wayward servants: The two worlds of the African Pygmies*. Garden City, NY: Natural History Press.

Tylor, E. B. ([1871] 1958). *Primitive culture*. New York, Harper and Row.

UNICEF. *We the Children: Meeting the Promises of the World Summit for Children*, 2000, section on breastfeeding. Available at http://www.unicef.org/specialsession/about/sgreport-pdf/14_Breastfeeding_D7341Insert_English.pdf van Gennep, A. ([1908] 1960). In M. B. Vizedom and G. L. Caffee (Eds.). *The rite of passage*. Chicago: University of Chicago Press.

van IJzendoorn, M. H. and A. Sagi (1999). Cross-cultural patterns of attachment: Universal and contextual dimensions. In J. S. P. R. Cassidy (Ed.), *Handbook of attachment: Theory, research, and clinical applications* (pp. 713–734). New York: Guilford.

Veth, P. M. and F. J. Walsh (1988). The concept of "staple" plant foods in the western desert of Western Australia. *Australian Aboriginal Studies* 2:19–25.

Vereijken, C. M. L. J., J. M. Riksen-Walraven, and K. Kondo-Ikemura (1997). Maternal sensitivity and infant attachment security in Japan: A longitudinal study. *International Journal of Behavioral Development* 21(1):35–49.

Voland, E. and J. Beise (2002). Opposite effects of maternal and paternal grandmothers on infant survival in historical Krummhorn. *Behavioral ecology and sociobiology.* 52:435–443.

Volk, A. and V. L. Quinsey (2002). The influence of facial cues on adoption preferences. *Human Nature* 13(4):437–55.

Walker, C. L. (1993). Sibling bereavement and grief responses. *Journal of Pediatric Nursing* 23:587–593.

Walker, P. L., L. S. Sugiyama, and R. Chacon (1998). Diet, dental health, and cultural change among recently contacted South American Indian hunter-horticulturalists. In J. Lukacs and B. E. Hemphill (Eds.), *Human dental development, morphology and pathology: Essays in honor of Albert Dahlberg*. University of Oregon Anthropological Papers.

Walker, R., K. Hill, H. Kaplan, and G. McMillan (2002). Age-dependency in hunting ability among the Ache of Eastern Paraguay. *Journal of Human Evolution* 42:639–657.

Walsh, F. J. (1990). An ecological study of traditional Aboriginal use of "country": Martu in the Great and Little Sandy deserts, Western Australia. *Proceedings of the Ecological Society of Australia* 16:23–37.

Walters, T. (1996). A new model of grief: Bereavement and biography. *Mortality* 1:7–25.

Washburn, S. and C. Lancaster (1968). The evolution of hunting. In R. Lee and I. Devore (Eds.), *Man the hunter* (pp. 293–303). Hawthorne, NY: Aldine de Gruyter.

Weddell, N. (1993). Mating effort or paternal investment? Incorporation rate and cost of male donations in the wartbiter. *Behavioral Ecology and Sociobiology* 32:239–246.

Weisner, T. S. (1987). Socialization and parenthood in sibling caretaker societies. In J. B. Lancaster, J. Altmann, A. S. Rossi, and L. R. Sherrod (Eds.), *Parenting across the life span* (pp. 237–270). Hawthorne, NY: Aldine de Gruyter.

Weisner, T. S. (1996). The 5–7 transition as an ecocultural project. In A. Samaroff and M. Haith (Eds.), *Reason and responsibility: The passage through childhood* (pp. 295–326). Chicago: University of Chicago Press.

Weisner, T. and R. Gallimore (1977). My brother's keeper: Child and sibling caretaking. *Current Anthropology* 18:169–170.

Weitoft, G. R., A. Hern, B. Haglund, and M. Rosén (2003). Mortality, severe morbidity, and injury in children living with single parents in Sweden: A population-based study. *Lancet* 361:289–295.

Werner, E. E. 1984. *Child care: Kith, kin and hired hands*. Baltimore, MD: University Park Press.

Werner, E. E. and R. S. Smith (1992). *Overcoming the odds*. Ithaca: Cornell University Press.

West, M. M. and M. Konner (1976). The role of the father in ?cross-cultural perspective. In M. E. Lamb (Ed.), *The role of the father in child development*. New York: John Wiley.

West-Eberhard, M. J. (2003). *Developmental plasticity and evolution*. Oxford: Oxford University Press.

Westneat, D. F. and R. C. Sargent (1996). Sex and parenting: The effects of sexual conflict and parentage on parental strategies. *Trends in Ecology and Evolution* 11:87–91.

Westbrook, J. T. (1967). Unpublished codings. Published in modified form: Murdock, G.P. Ethnographic Atlas: a summary. *Ethnology* 6, 109–236.

Whiting, B. B. (Ed.) (1963). *Six cultures: Studies of child rearing*. New York: Wiley.

Whiting, B. B. (1972). Work and the family: cross-cultural perspectives, *Women: resource for a changing world*. Radcliffe Institute, Cambridge, MA.

Whiting, B. B. and C. P. Edwards (1988). *Children of different worlds: The formation of social behavior*. Cambridge, MA: Harvard University Press.

Whiting, B. and J. Whiting (1975). *Children of six cultures: A psycho-cultural analysis*. Cambridge, MA: Harvard University Press.

Whiting, J. W. M. (1941). *Becoming a Kwoma: Teaching and learning in a New Guinea tribe*. London: Oxford University Press.

Whiting, J. W. M. (1971). Causes and consequences of the amount of body contact between mother and infant. Paper presented at 70th Annual Meeting of the American Anthropological Association, New York

Whiting, J. W. M. and I. L. Child (1953). *Child training and personality: A cross-cultural study*. New Haven, CT: Yale University Press.

Whitten, A., V. Horner, and S. Marshall-Pescini (2003). Cultural anthropology. *Evolutionary Anthropology* 12:92–105.

Widdowson, E. M. (1951). Mental contentment and physical growth. *Lancet* 260: 1316–1318.

Wiessner, P. (1977). *Hxaro: A regional system of reducing risk among the !Kung San*. Ph.D. thesis, University of Michigan.

Wiessner, P. (1981). Measuring the impact of social ties on nutritional status among the !Kung San. *Social Science Information* 20(4/5):641–678.

Wiessner, P. (1982). Risk, reciprocity and social influences on !Kung San economics. In E. Leacock and R. Lee (Eds.), *Politics and history in band societies* (pp. 61–84). Cambridge: Cambridge University Press.

Wiessner, P. (2002). Hunting, healing and hxaro exchange: A long-term perspective on !Kung (Ju/'hoansi) large-game hunting. *Evolution and Human Behavior* 23:407–436.

Wilkie, D. S. (1988). Hunters and farmers of the African forest. In J. S. Denslow and C. Padoch (Eds.), *People of the tropical rain forest* (pp. 111–26). Berkeley and Los Angeles: University of California Press.

Wilkie, D. S. (1989). Impact of roadside agriculture on subsistence hunting in the Ituri Forest of northeastern Zäire. *American Journal of Physical Anthropology* 78:485–494.

Wilkie, D. S. and B. K. Curran (1993). Historical trends in forager and farmer exchange in the Ituri rain forest of northeastern Zaire. *Human Ecology* 2:389–417.

Willis, P. E. (1977). *Learning to labour: How working class kids get working class jobs.* Farnborough, England: Saxon House

Wilmsen, E. N. (1982). Studies in diet, nutrition, and fertility among a group of Kalahari Bushmen in Botswana. *Social Science Information* 21(1):95–125.

Wilmsen, E. N. (1989). [[must be the same person as above—which are the correct initials?]] *Land filled with flies: A political economy of the Kalahari.* Chicago: University of Chicago Press.

Wilson, E. O. (1975). *Sociobiology: A new synthesis.* Cambridge, MA: Harvard University Press.

Winterhalder, B. (1996). Social foraging and the behavioral ecology of intragroup resource transfers. *Evolutionary Anthropology* 5:46–57.

Woodburn, J.C. (1964). *The social organization of the Hadza of North Tanganyika.* Ph.D. thesis, Cambridge.

Woodburn, J.C. (1968a). An introduction to Hazda ecology. In R. B. Lee and I. DeVore (Eds.), *Man the hunter* (pp. 49–55). Chicago: Aldine.

Woodburn, J. C. (1968b). Stability and flexibility in Hadza residential groupings. In R. B. Lee and I. DeVore (Eds.), *Man the hunter.* Chicago: Aldine.

Woodburn, J. C. (1970). *Hunters and gatherers. The material culture of the nomadic Hadza.* London: British Museum.

Woodburn, J. C. (1982a). Social dimensions of death in four African hunting and gathering societies. In M. Bloch and J. Parry (Eds.), *Death and the regeneration of life.* Cambridge, Cambridge University Press.

Woodburn, J. C. (1982b). Egalitarian societies. *Man* 17:431–451.

Woodburn, J. C. (1998). "Sharing is not a form of exchange": An analysis of property-sharing in immediate-return hunter-gatherer societies. In C. M. Hann (Ed.), *Property relations: Renewing the anthropological tradition* (pp. 48–63). Cambridge, Cambridge University Press.

Wolff, P. H. (1968). Sucking patterns of infant mammals. *Brain, Behavior and Evolution, 1,* 354–367

Worden, J. W. (1991). *Grief counseling and grief therapy: A handbook for the mental health practitioner* (2nd ed.). New York: Springer.

Worthman, C. M. (1999). Evolutionary perspectives on the onset of puberty. In W. R. Trevathan, E. O. Smith, and J. J. Kenna (Eds.), *Evolutionary medicine (pp. 135–163).* Oxford: Oxford University Press.

Wright, P. C. (1990). Patterns of paternal care in primates. *International Journal of Primatology* 11:89–102.

Wynne-Edwards, K. E. and C. J. Reburn (2000). Behavioral endocrinology of mammalian fatherhood. *Trends in Ecology and Evolution* 15(11):464–468.

Yamamoto, M. (1997). Children of the Baka hunter-gatherers in southeast Cameroon: Subsistence activities, housework, leisure and gathering. In H. Terashima (Ed.), *A report on the project: "A Study of Multi-Ethnic Societies in the African Evergreen Forest."* Faculty of Humanities and Sciences, Kobe Gakuin University.

Yoshida, A. (1984). Developmental Theories. In H. Katori (Ed.), *Contemporary psychology,* vol. 10, *Development* (pp. 253–276) (in Japanese). Tokyo: Tokyo-daigakusyuppannkai.

Yount, J. W., Tsiazonera, and B. T. Tucker (2001). Constructing Mikea identity: Past or present links to forest and foraging. *Ethnohistory* 48:257–291.

Zeifman, D. M. (2001). An ethological analysis of human infant crying: Answering Tinbergen's four questions. *Developmental Psychobiology* 39(4):265–285.

Zelazo, P. R. (1976). Comments on genetic determinants of infant development: An overstated case. In L. Lipsitt (Ed.), *Developmental psychobiology: The significance of infancy.* Hillsdale, NJ: Lawrence Erlbaum Associates.

Zelazo, P. R. (1983). The development of walking: New findings and old assumptions. *Journal of Motor Behavior* 15:99–137.

Zelazo, P. R., N. A. Zelazo, and S. Kolb (1972). "Walking" in the newborn. *Science* 176:314–315.

Index